DISCARDED

ENGLISH AS A WORLD LANGUAGE

ENGLISH AS A WORLD LANGUAGE

Edited by
Richard W. Bailey
and Manfred Görlach

Ann Arbor   The University of Michigan Press

Copyright © by The University of Michigan 1982
All rights reserved
Published in the United States of America by
The University of Michigan Press and simultaneously
in Rexdale, Canada, by John Wiley & Sons Canada, Limited
Manufactured in the United States of America

1985 1984 1983 1982   4 3 2 1

Library of Congress Cataloging in Publication Data

Main entry under title:

English as a world language.

Bibliography: p.
Includes index.
1. English language—Variation. 2. English language—Dialects. 3. English language in foreign countries. 4. Communication, International.
I. Bailey, Richard W. II. Görlach, Manfred.
PE1700.E5   420'.9   81-21904
ISBN 0-472-10016-5   AACR2

Acknowledgments

Grateful acknowledgment is made to the following publishers and authors for permission to reprint copyrighted materials:

Miguel Algarín, for lines 1–18 from his poem, "San Juan/an areest/Maguayo/a vision of Malo dancing." Copyright 1975 by Miguel Algarín.

Edward Arnold Ltd., for table 1 and an example from "Variation and Consistency in Glaswegian English," by R. K. S. Macaulay. Reprinted by permission from *Sociolinguistic Patterns in British English*, edited by Peter Trudgill, 1978.

Cambridge University Press, for figures 12, 13, and 14 from *The Pronunciation of English* by Daniel Jones, 1956.

Center for Applied Linguistics, for table 9 and selected examples from *Appalachian Speech* by Walt Wolfram and Donna Christian, 1976.

Harcourt Brace Jovanovich, for figure 4.2 from *A Course in Phonetics* by Peter Ladefoged. © 1975 by Harcourt Brace Jovanovich, Inc. Reproduced by permission of the publisher.

Linguistic Society of America, for examples 1–12, 29–45, and 47–52 from "Contraction and Variability of the English Copula," by William Labov. Reprinted by permission from *Language* 45, no. 4 (December, 1969).

Minister of Supply and Services Canada, for the map "English in Canada," redrawn from *Talking about Canadian English . . . and Canadian French as Well*, by Cornelius von Baeyer. © Minister of Supply and Services Canada, 1976.

Orient Longman Ltd. and Kamala Das, for lines 4–20 from her poem "An Introduction." Reprinted by permission from *The Old Playhouse and Other Poems* by Kamala Das, 1973.

Oxford University Press, Kuala Lumpur, for extracts from "A Tiger Is Loose in Our Community," by Edward Dorall. Reprinted by permission from *New Drama One*, edited by Lloyd Fernando, 1972.

Oxford University Press, Oxford, for a portion of section 6.1.1 of the Introduction to *Krio-English Dictionary* by C. H. Fyle and Eldred Jones, 1980.

3M Corporation, for the map "English as a World Language," adapted from "World Population Projection Map." Copyright 1973 by 3M Corporation. Reprinted by permission of and copyrighted by 3M Corporation.

Woodrose Publications Pte. Ltd., Singapore, for a selection from *Eden 22* by Mervin G. Mirapuri, 1974.

Yorkshire Dialect Society and Michael Park, for his poem "Three Seaside Views." Reprinted by permission from *Transactions of the Yorkshire Dialect Society* 75 (1975).

In memory of
Eleanor Bowman Bailey,
1961–80

And who in time knowes wither we may bent
　The treasure of our tongue, to what strange shores
　This gaine of our best glorie shal be sent,
　T'inrich vnknowing Nations with our stores?
　What worlds in th'yet vnformed Occident
　May come refin'd with th'accents that are ours?
　　　　　　　　　　　　Samuel Daniel, *Musophilus*, 1599

Preface

Since English began to spread around the world in the great age of exploration five hundred years ago, all its varieties have taken on an independent history, some of them much influenced by local circumstances, others responding to changes in the prestige dialects of Great Britain and the United States, and all of them affected by the inexorable trends in language change that affect every community from one generation to the next. By 1975, English was the sole official language of twenty-one nations, and in sixteen more it is the co-official language of government, education, broadcasting, and publication. According to the best estimates, English is the first language of some 300 million people around the world; nearly an equal number claim some proficiency—from full fluency to limited speaking ability—in English as an additional language.

While the essays assembled in this volume reflect the diverse circumstances in which English is used, we cannot claim that our contributors have exhausted the complexity of the separate histories and present varieties of English. Some places where English is commonly used are not discussed (for example, the Philippines), and even within the regions analyzed here, only representative varieties or those that account for the greatest numbers of speakers are given detailed treatment. Nonetheless, we feel confident that the essays open a broad perspective on the diversity of English considered from a global viewpoint. Readers should gain a lively sense of the consistent structures and patterns that join English speakers into a community of one language; at the same time, they will recognize that English is a diverse language, enriched by varying national standards and reflecting the complexity of the communities in which it is used.

Each contributor to this volume was invited to prepare a survey that would give the whole collection a degree of uniformity of scope and style. Our intended audience includes persons with some prior training in linguistics or English language studies, but we believe that people who have personal or professional interests in the varied uses of English will find much to attract their attention here. In all cases, our authors provide a brief historical sketch and an overview of the present-day functions of English (particularly when it competes with other languages or other standards). All of them give detailed illustration of the features of pronunciation, vocabulary, and the processes of word formation and syntax that characterize each national or regional variety, and all of them suggest the diversity of English within the communities they discuss.

We are grateful to the staff at the University of Michigan Press and to Robin Melanie Fosheim who helped to prepare the manuscript for publication and assisted us in verifying quotations, reconciling inconsistencies, and refining the varied styles of our authors and ourselves. Our greatest debt, of course, is to our contributors. All of them have shown great patience in response to our importunings, and all have willingly made changes in their essays to respond to our sense of the need for consistency and completeness. The great value of each contribution, we believe, is enhanced by comparison with its neighbors, and we hope that the entire collection will be stimulating to travelers (whether they be readers or tourists) and provocative to those who will engage in future studies of this exciting subject.

Richard W. Bailey
Manfred Görlach

Contents

Introduction	1
Richard W. Bailey and Manfred Görlach	
The Phonetic Alphabet	7
The Geographical and Social Variation of English in England and Wales	11
Charles V. J. Russ, University of York	
The English Language in Scotland	56
Suzanne Romaine, University of Birmingham	
The English Language in Ireland	84
Michael V. Barry, Queen's University, Belfast	
The English Language in Canada	134
Richard W. Bailey, University of Michigan	
Geographical Variation of English in the United States	177
Frederic G. Cassidy, University of Wisconsin	
Variation in Contemporary American English	210
Thomas E. Toon, University of Michigan	
English in the Caribbean	251
David L. Lawton, Central Michigan University	
The English Language in West Africa	281
Loreto Todd, University of Leeds	
English in East Africa	306
Ian F. Hancock and Rachel Angogo, University of Texas	
English in South Africa	324
L. W. Lanham, Rhodes University	
South Asian English	353
Braj B. Kachru, University of Illinois	
English in Singapore, Malaysia, and Hong Kong	384
John T. Platt, Monash University	
English in Australia and New Zealand	415
Robert D. Eagleson, University of Sydney	
Tok Pisin in Papua New Guinea	439
Peter Mühlhäusler, Technical University of Berlin	
Suggested Readings	467
Index	481

Introduction

Richard W. Bailey and Manfred Görlach

Only in the last decade has the study of the forms and functions of English around the world begun to take shape as an academic discipline. In earlier scholarship, the most detailed studies were those of the English of Great Britain and the United States, and within those two countries the historical orientation of dialectology drew attention to the obsolescent words and pronunciations of elderly rural people of English-speaking descent. Urban speech was neglected since it was often regarded as corrupted by innovations arising from modern life or through the influence of other language groups. Hence published information reflected a distorted and incomplete image of the variety and vitality of the English language. Today, that image is presented in sharper focus through intensive studies of representative groups of speakers—their differences and similarities that correlate with age, sex, occupation, social class, ethnic descent, and place of residence. Linguists have come to recognize not only the diversity of English according to various demographic factors but also the range of each individual's repertoire of English. Naturally enough, the expanded scope of descriptive studies has considerably complicated the task of research, but scholars now recognize that they must acknowledge the complexity of the diverse language communities that make up the English-speaking world.

Studies of English outside Britain and North America have had, until recently, a strong prescriptivist bias, and observers within communities where English was long spoken have often urged their compatriots to follow the linguistic direction of the prestige dialect of the "mother country." Writing for a South African audience in 1913, Charles Pettman articulated a view that was not then new nor obsolete now: "It gives an Englishman, who loves the sentence that is lucid and logical, a shock to hear his native tongue maltreated by those who are just as English in blood as himself" (1913, p. 16). Before such shock can give way to dispassionate analysis, a variety of changes in outlook appear to be required: the recognition of political and cultural independence, a stronger interest in the social sciences, and the training of scholars who can describe the English of their own language communities as participant-observers.[1] As these changes have taken place around the world, it has become possible for a book like *English as a World Language* to be compiled and published.

The geographical dissemination of the English language is a unique case of language spread and language imposition. As late as the seventeenth century, expectations remained rather modest as to the possible expansion of English as compared with French, Spanish, or even German. Its low status as a vehicle for important compositions and its variability and apparent impermanence made it appear weak in comparison to Latin. When Milton contemplated writing a national epic, he rejected the idea of writing in Latin, though he might easily have done so. In selecting his native English, he believed that he must be "content with these British Ilands as my world" (1641, p. 39) and not expect recognition abroad nor the enduring reputation of classical authors.

At the same time that Milton wrote, however, other English speakers began to make their language a vehicle for exporting religion, education, and culture to the uncivilized in North America, Africa, the Caribbean, and even in the remote north of Britain itself. The *Statutes of Iona* (1609) convey the rationale that led "the vulgar Inglische tounge" to grow in importance not only in Scotland but also around the world:

> Forsamekle as the Kingis Majestie haveing a speciall care and regaird that the new religion be advanceit and establisheit in all pairts of this Kingdome, and that all his Majesties subjectis, especially the youth, be exercised and trayned up in civilitie, godlines, knawledge and learning, that the vulgar Inglische tounge be universallie plantit, and the Irische language, which is one of the chief and principal cases of the continewance of barbaritie and incivilitie amongis the inhabitants of the Iles and Heylandis, may be abolisheit and removit. . . . [Quoted from Withers 1979, p. 44]

What is perhaps remarkable is that there have been few losses to other international languages in the countries where English was implanted.[2] This worldwide spread has not only resulted in a greater number of native speakers—about 300 million (see Fishman, Cooper, and Conrad 1977)—than any other language except Chinese, but has also made English the most common additional language, one supported in school programs in virtually every nation. Even in sub-Saharan Africa, where only about 1 percent of the population learns English as a first language, the use of English as a lingua franca helps to maintain national unity and serves more than 160 million people as a vehicle for international commerce and diplomacy.

No other language has undergone a similar expansion since Greek and Roman times. Perhaps the only similar case in modern history is that of another language of a sustained colonial empire, French. In the eighteenth century, French was probably of greater international importance than English, but its functions declined in the nineteenth, through losses to other languages in continental Europe and through the surrender of colonies in America and India. Although this decline was partly counterbalanced by the acquisition of new colonies in Africa and expanding French influence in the Middle East, the use of French has diminished in the twentieth century, especially outside the francophone countries. The teaching of impeccable French to those born without that grace has long been the explicit policy of French governments, while the British

Introduction 3

have made little attempt to do the same for English. The concept of *la mission civilatrice*—an idea "related to a subconscious faith that France is a bearer of the universal idea that human nature is everywhere the same and . . . that its laws have been most fully realized by France" (Gordon 1978, p. 6)—was bound to suffer setbacks when the objectives of foreign language learners veered towards command of an international language to serve a more instrumental function.

The social meanings attached to French and to English in the colonies where they were used differed markedly. Ali A. Mazrui, a Ugandan scholar, has summarized this difference by pointing to the "militant linguistic cosmopolitanism among French-speaking African leaders," a factor that inhibited national liberation movements in countries where French served as the sole common national language. "The English language, by the very fact of being emotionally more neutral than French," he writes, "was less of a hindrance to the emergence of national consciousness in British Africa" (1973, p. 67). This view is confirmed by President Leopold S. Senghor of Senegal, himself a noted poet who writes in French. English, in Senghor's opinion, provides "an instrument which, with its plasticity, its rhythm and its melody, corresponds to the profound, volcanic affectivity of the Black peoples" (1975, p. 97); writers and speakers of English are less inclined to let respect for the language interfere with their desire to use it. One consequence of this difference in attitudes is that French is generally more uniform across the world (see Valdman 1979), while English has developed a series of distinct national standards.

The history of English around the world, its various functions, and its means of dissemination have given rise to innumerable forms of the language, some stable and others ephemeral. Indeed, whether a variety can be said to be English at all is sometimes open to debate. Historical derivation, structural similarity, intelligibility, and even the opinions of speakers about whether or not their language is "English" have all been adduced in support of claims about the essential unity of the language. The following examples, however, suggest some of the complexities that enter the debate; all represent varieties current today, yet it is unlikely that persons who regard one of them as "English" will accept the other two as equally "English":

1. One day Jesus jelled into a boat with his mushes, and rokkered to them, "Let's jell over the pani."
2. And it cam, that on ane o' the days, he gaed intil a boat, he and his disciples, and he said till them, "Lat us gang ower till the other side o' the Loch!"
3. Long wanpela de Jisas i goap long wanpela bot wantaim ol disaipel bilong en. Na em i tokim ol, "Yumi go long hapsait bilong raunwara."

These examples, all of them versions of Luke 8:22, are admittedly extreme. The first is from Anglo-Romani as spoken by Travellers in Britain; the second from

Lowland Scots; the third from the Tok Pisin of Papua New Guinea. They would not easily qualify as English if submitted to a general test of reading comprehension, and habitual users of any one of them would not necessarily claim to be speaking English. Yet both historical and structural reasons argue that these examples are all closely related to the English of the wider international community in both vocabulary and syntactic patterns.

The three examples just quoted suggest how greatly varieties of English may differ from each other, and even the types discussed by scholars contain within them further dimensions of systematic variation. As Braj B. Kachru explains in his contribution to this volume, there is certainly a "South Asian English," but there is also "Indian English" and within Indian English a distinct variety typical of speakers whose first language is Tamil. The "cline of bilingualism" of which Kachru speaks suggests further dimensions of variety arising from the diverse degrees of perfection in the acquisition of English in communities where some other language is in widespread use. Fluent command of English in one domain may not imply mastery of English in another. Local norms arise in speech and then in writing when the forces of standardization are weakened, and when a more localized English becomes the birthright of those who use it. These developments give rise to what has been called the "indigenization" of English as norms develop within communities without reference to the prestige varieties of Britain or the United States. The rise of local varieties (now described by some linguists as *lects*) or the generalization of imperfectly learned English, however, pours innovation back into the international mainstream of English, a fact recognized by the policy of the *Supplement to the Oxford English Dictionary* now being edited. While the initial editors of the *OED* virtually excluded words not in general use in Great Britain and the United States, their successors have recognized the international dimension of English by what the editor calls "bold forays into the written English of regions outside the British Isles, particularly that of North America, Australia, New Zealand, South Africa, India, and Pakistan" (Burchfield 1972, p. xiv).

The development of new varieties of English is intimately bound up with historical and social factors. In the history of West Africa, as Loreto Todd shows in her contribution to this volume, these factors include the slave trade, economic exploitation, missionary activities, repatriation of freed slaves from Britain and North America, arbitrary imposition of political boundaries by the colonial regimes, and, eventually, independent self-government with a residue of European customs and language. The very different histories of South Africa and Australia have produced distinct local standards of English in those two countries, even though the language and social origins of the settlers of the Cape Colony in Africa and of Botany Bay in Australia were virtually identical. In North America, the English-speaking settlers of Canada and the United States were alike in origin, but even two hundred years of intimate contact between these two neighbors have not prevented the rise of distinct and distinctive national differences in English.

Introduction

Linguistic developments in the various countries where English is now in use have not arisen solely from the inexorable forces of history. Governments and the schools they support have overtly shaped language policies, and the impact of official language planning is well illustrated in Malaysia, where the growth of a local standard of English has been curtailed by the decision of the government to promote Bahasa Malaysia in official functions. Some governments respond enthusiastically to assertions of linguistic independence in English, a trend begun in the United States by Noah Webster in his *American Dictionary* (1828) and in Australia by Sidney J. Baker's *The Australian Language* (1945). Others maintain the official authority of the Queen's English despite the flourishing local standards of their citizens. Language policies and the linguistic attitudes they promote thus act as an additional factor in the complex pattern of forces that shape the development of varieties of English around the world.

The articles included in this volume have been selected to represent societies in which English is the dominant language (for instance, Britain, Ireland, and the United States); in which it coexists with other languages (as in Canada); in which it is the language of a substantial minority (as in South Africa); and in which it plays a significant role in national affairs (as in India and the countries of East and West Africa). In some areas discussed here, English coexists with an English-based pidgin or creole, as it does in Jamaica and Nigeria. In still others, English has a distinct local flavor that may be regarded as evidence of an emerging national standard within the world community of English users. We have not, however, attempted to account for English in European or Latin American countries, for instance, where it exists mainly as a foreign language, even though large numbers of speakers may make regular use of it in science and technology, trade, tourism, aviation, or diplomacy. Such an inquiry would be the subject for yet another book, one that needs the informed attention of linguists who wish to complete the picture of English as a world language.

We regard this volume as much more than a collection of linguistic data woven into a narrative involving history, local circumstances, social and political institutions, and patterns in the use of English. Thanks to the splendid cooperation of our contributors in writing to a common set of themes, it is possible for readers to see comparisons and to recognize trends. The study of language in its social and historical context is by no means confined merely to the collection of facts. The essays here presented allow for the formulation of hypotheses about the consequences of languages in contact and about the general patterns of change apparent in English throughout the world—for instance, the variant restructurings of the English verb phrase or the continued influence of the change in English pronunciation begun in the Great Vowel Shift of the Early Modern English period. Matters of interest to those concerned with the sociology of language also become apparent in comparisons of demographic factors, education, the media that disseminate English in both spoken and written forms, and the consequences of overt and covert programs that implement national language policies.

We believe that our contributors have made the facts of variation in English apparent to our readers; it is the task of those readers to interpret the facts in light of their own experience of the range of English.

NOTES

1. While we were eager to have each region represented by scholars native to their area, it was unfortunately not always possible to do so. We are certain, however, that the growing number of trained investigators will complete the process by which participant-observers provide insights into every English-speaking community.
2. One exception is the resurgence of Gaelic in English-speaking areas of eastern Ireland in the sixteenth century, a case discussed in the essay by Michael V. Barry in this volume.

REFERENCES

Burchfield, R. W. Introduction to *A Supplement to the Oxford English Dictionary*, vol. 1, pp. xii–xvii. Oxford: Clarendon Press, 1972–

Fishman, Joshua A.; Cooper, Robert L.; and Conrad, Andrew W., eds. *The Spread of English: The Sociology of English as an Additional Language*. Rowley, Mass.: Newbury House, 1977.

Gordon, David C. *The French Language and National Identity (1920–1975)*. Contributions to the Sociology of Language, no. 22. The Hague: Mouton, 1978.

Labov, William. *The Social Stratification of English in New York City*. Washington, D.C.: Center for Applied Linguistics, 1966.

Mazrui, Ali A. "The English Language and the Origins of African Nationalism." In *Varieties of Present-Day English*, edited by Richard W. Bailey and Jay L. Robinson, pp. 56–70. New York: Macmillan Co., 1973.

Milton, John. *The Reason of Church-government Urg'd against Prelaty*. London: Edward Griffin, 1641.

Pettman, Charles. *Africanderisms: A Glossary of South African Words and Phrases and of Place and Other Names*. London: Longman, Green and Co., 1913.

Senghor, Leopold S. "The Essence of Language: English and French." *Culture* 2, no. 2 (1975):75–98.

Valdman, Albert, ed. *Le français hors de France*. Paris: Champion, 1979.

Withers, C. W. J. "The Language Geography of Scottish Gaelic." *Scottish Literary Journal*, supp. no. 9 (1979):41–54.

The Phonetic Alphabet

Representations of pronunciation employed in this book follow the conventions of the International Phonetic Alphabet. Most transcriptions should be readily transparent to those who consult the accompanying chart of consonants and the two vowel diagrams. Reference to these displays should help readers grasp unfamiliar sounds that have developed in separate varieties of English—for instance, differing articulations of historic *r*—or that have entered English through the influence of other languages. For more detailed narrative explanations, see Catford 1977, Jones 1962, and Ladefoged 1975.

The consonant chart found on p. 8 categorizes phonetic symbols in columns based on the place of articulation (from the front to the back of the articulation zone) and in rows by the manner of articulation. When pairs of symbols appear within a single box in the matrix, the one on the left is voiceless (i.e., is produced without vibration of the vocal chords) and the one on the right is voiced (i.e., is produced with such vibration).

In a book devoted to the exploration of the distinct and independent varieties of world English, it would be a contradiction to presume that a list of key words could illustrate more than a limited subset of pronunciations likely to be used by readers of this volume. Nonetheless, most varieties of English share the following consonants which, in transcriptions, normally have the values associated with their corresponding letters in the spelling system: p, b, t, d, k, m, n, l, r, f, v, s, z, h, and w. Other commonly occurring phonetic symbols represent the sounds found in the italicized positions of the following words:

[g] *g*ive   [ʒ] plea*s*ure
[ŋ] so*ng*   [j] *y*et
[θ] *th*in   [tʃ] *ch*op
[ð] *th*en   [ʤ] *j*udge
[ʃ] *sh*op

The additional consonant symbols found in the chart are usually explained as they occur in the articles in this book. In cases where the explanation lacks sufficient detail, readers may approximate the sounds by comparing the unfamiliar symbols with adjacent familiar sounds that share the same manner or place of articulation.

The vowel diagrams found on p. 8 show the schematic values—based on the idea of phonetic reference points or cardinal vowels—of the English monophthongs. Multiple vowel sequences involve a movement of the tongue from the

Rounded Vowels

	Front	Central	Back	
High	y	ʉ		u
Half-close	ø	Y U		o
		ɵ		
Half-open	œ			ɔ
Low				
	Œ			ɒ

Unrounded Vowels

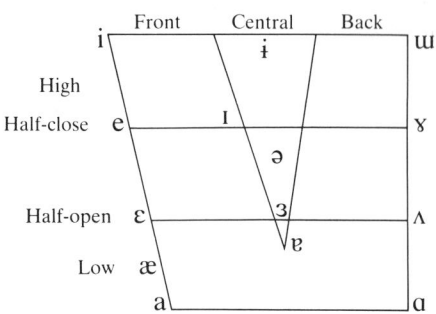

	Front	Central	Back	
High	i	ɨ		ɯ
Half-close	e	I		ɤ
		ə		
Half-open	ɛ	ɜ		ʌ
		ɐ		
Low	æ			
	a			ɑ

Diacritics: ¨ centralized vowel, ˜ nazalization, · half-long, : full-long, . half-close, ˛ half-open, | half pause, || full pause, ⊤ lowered, ⊥ raised, ⊣ fronted, ⊢ backed, ' primary stress, ˌ secondary stress, superscripts indicate partial articulation

Consonants

Manner of Articulation	Bilabial	Labio-Dental	Dental	Alveolar	Retroflex	Palato-Alveolar	Palatal	Velar	Uvular	Pharyngeal	Glottal
Plosive	p b			t d	ʈ ɖ		c ɟ	k g			ʔ
Nasal	m			n	ɳ		ɲ	ŋ			
Lateral fricative				ɬ ɮ							
Lateral nonfricative				l				ʎ			
Rolled				r					R		
Flapped				ɾ	ɽ				ʀ		
Fricative	ɸ β	f v	θ ð	s z ɹ		ʃ ʒ	ç j	x ɣ	ʁ		h ɦ
Frictionless continuents and semivowels	ʍ w	ʋ					j	w	ʁ		

Diacritics: ₀ devoiced, ˌ syllabic, ˻ dental articulation, ' aspiration, ₊ tongue advanced from normal position

The Phonetic Alphabet

position of the initial vowel toward or through additional vowel positions. The pronunciation values for such sequences can easily be determined by reference to these two charts. In virtually all varieties of English, vowels formed at the back of the vowel space are rounded (i.e., involve rounding of the lips) and those at the front of the space are unrounded. Hence the most commonly encountered symbols are found at the left of the unrounded vowels chart and at the right of the rounded vowels chart.

Since varieties of English differ greatly in the inventory and incidence of vowels, a list of key words must be treated with great caution as a guide to pronunciation. In the list that follows, broad transcriptions indicate the phonetic values of vowels in two varieties, one *rhotic* (characterized by consonantal *r* after vowels in final or preconsonantal position) and the other *nonrhotic*. The nonrhotic variety is RP, the prestige dialect of southeastern England and a model for many international varieties. The rhotic variety is the Inland Northern subvariety of American English.

	American English	RP		American English	RP
bead	[i]	[i]	booed	[u]	[u]
bid	[ɪ]	[ɪ]	bird	[ɚr]	[ə]
bayed	[eɪ]	[eɪ]	bud	[ʌ]	[ʌ]
bed	[ɛ]	[ɛ]	bide	[aɪ]	[aɪ]
bad	[æ]	[æ]	bowed	[aʊ]	[aʊ]
bard	[ɑr]	[ɑ]	Boyd	[ɔɪ]	[ɔɪ]
bod	[ɑ]	[ɒ]	beard	[ir]	[ɪə]
bawd	[ɔ]	[ɔ]	bared	[er]	[ɛə]
good	[ʊ]	[ʊ]	fired	[aɪr]	[aə]
bode	[oʊ]	[oʊ]	feud	[ju]	[ju]

The positions of the vowels shown in the diagrams are a standard in reference to which individual speech sounds can be positioned. Though RP and American English generally resemble each other in the quite broad transcriptions provided for the vowels of the key words given above, the actual positions of vowels within the vowel space differ quite considerably, a fact that will emerge only when narrower transcriptions with more detailed information are provided (e.g., the use of [æ˔] to represent a vowel higher than cardinal [æ]). In the following diagram (from Ladefoged 1975, p. 68), the vowels in Inland Northern American English are indicated in relation to the background of the "vowel triangle" used in the schematic representations. Monophthongs are indicated by dots, and diphthongs by lines showing the direction of movement from one vowel to the next:

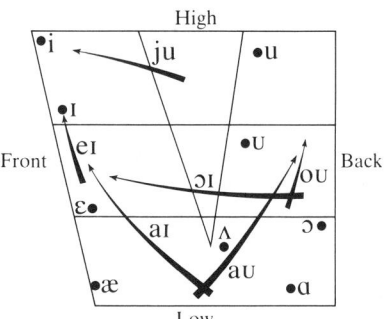

The impressionistic judgments usual in phonetics are here supported by instrumental measurement of actual vowels. Comparisons of the sound systems of the various kinds of English described in this book can usefully be made on the basis of such diagrams as these. In particular, readers should examine the discussion of RP by C. V. J. Russ (pp. 28–29), of the English of Belfast and Dublin by Michael V. Barry (pp. 123, 125), and of East and West African English by Loreto Todd (p. 287) and by Ian F. Hancock and Rachel Angogo (p. 314).

REFERENCES

Catford, J. C. *Fundamental Problems in Phonetics*. Bloomington: Indiana University Press, 1977.
Jones, Daniel. *Outline of English Phonetics*. 9th ed. Cambridge: Heffer, 1962.
Ladefoged, Peter. *A Course in Phonetics*. New York: Harcourt Brace Jovanovich, 1975.

The Geographical and Social Variation of English in England and Wales

Charles V. J. Russ

England and Wales are by no means large in comparison to other communities where English is spoken. In the 1971 census, 46 million people were counted in England and 2.8 million in Wales, and they occupied just under 60,000 square miles (or 150,000 square kilometers) of territory. But both areas show a great diversity of regional and social variation in the use of English.

In present-day England, the use of the prestige dialect is closely connected with social and economic standing. While a few national leaders retain features of a regional or class dialect, most persons in government, the professions, and positions of economic power use or approximate Received Pronunciation (RP). These speakers are often heard in broadcasting both at home and abroad, and it is their usage that is commonly used as the basis for teaching English as a foreign language. Nonetheless, it is important to note the estimate that "only about three percent of the English population speak RP" (Hughes and Trudgill 1979, p. 3).

In Wales, variation in English follows generally the same pattern of diversity and prestige, but the situation is complicated there because Welsh, a Celtic language, is known by 542,425 people (or 20 percent of the population), though a smaller number speak it at home and in their communities. Most Welsh speakers live in the center and in the north of Wales. In Glamorgan in the south (with the cities of Swansea, Cardiff, and Newport), English predominates and is normally used by the majority of the population.

"English" emerged from a variety of mutually intelligible Germanic dialects spoken in what is now northern Germany. Early in the fifth century A.D., tribes from this region invaded England and forced most of the Celtic-speaking inhabitants into the west and north. During the next five hundred years, the newcomers established separate spheres of influence, and their common language underwent the natural process of language change toward separate regional varieties. The island itself continued to be known as *Britannia*, or Britain, but the people, despite their diverse origins, eventually took the name derived from that of one of the invading Germanic tribes and called themselves *Angelcynn* 'the English nation'.

With the Norman Conquest of 1066, speakers of Norman French displaced the English ruling class and fostered the use of Latin and French as the languages of government and religion. Vernacular varieties of English emerged with a greatly simplified inflectional system and the admixture of borrowed words from

French and, to a lesser degree, Latin. With the rise of London as the national capital, the variety of English spoken there became the prestige norm, and it was used as a guide for fixing some of the varied spelling conventions after the introduction of printing in England by William Caxton in 1475. Evidence for the emergence of prestige norms is provided by Sir Thomas Elyot's warning in 1531 that noble families should select servants to raise their children who "speke none englisshe but that which is cleane, polite, perfectly and articulately pronounced, omittinge no lettre and sillable, as folisshe women oftentimes do of a wantonnesse, whereby diuers noble men and gentilmennes chyldren (as I do at this daye knowe) have attained corrupte and foule pronuntiation."[1] Such concern for correctness and a prestige norm continues to occupy the minds of English people to this day, especially those who hope that they or their children will assume the positions of power and authority that demand the use of the standard dialect and an RP accent.

Before the upheavals connected with the Industrial Revolution of the late eighteenth century, most English people spoke one or another of the well-defined regional dialects. Standard English was associated with the court and the area immediately surrounding London, but most colonists who emigrated to North America and later to Africa, India, Australia, and New Zealand established in the new territories varieties of English that derived from areas outside the London metropolis or from the lower-class speech of London itself. Nonetheless, changes in the prestige norm of London continued to affect the English of the colonies, particularly that of the port cities and other settlements where travel from and to London was common. Despite the emergence of national varieties of English elsewhere in the world, influence of this kind continues today, aided by the formal efforts of the British Council and by the tendency of the children of elites throughout the Commonwealth to migrate to England for education.

With the Industrial Revolution, rural villagers were forced from the land and into the cities, where established urban dialects were modified by the admixture of variously labeled rural dialects under new conditions of manufacturing and city life. Expansion of the national elite in the nineteenth century was accompanied by an extension of the standard English of upper-class London through the boarding schools, the universities, the Church of England, the command ranks of the military, and the growing civil service. These trends were reinforced in the twentieth century by the selection and training of broadcasters for the British Broadcasting Corporation (BBC) and the increasing acceptance of the idea that use of a particular variety of English was a requisite for participation in national leadership.

A variety of economic, social, and political factors have thus shaped the choice of forms by speakers of English throughout its history. After a brief sketch of the earlier stages of English, I will identify some of the linguistic varieties used today in England and Wales.

Map 1. England and Wales

Old English (750–1150)

Germanic tribes from the European continent began to invade Britain early in the fifth century, and by the middle of the sixth century they had driven most of the native British into Wales and Cornwall in the west and Cumberland in the north. Following the tradition established by Bede, historians have recognized three main tribes and assigned their influence to distinct regions: the Jutes in Kent, the Angles in East Anglia and the Midlands and north, and the Saxons in the south and west. Recent scholarship, however, suggests that the traditional "three-fold division reflects the orderliness of [Bede's] mind rather than the realities of the settlements" (Blair 1956, p. 11), and evidence from place-names suggests that the language of the tribes was relatively uniform. It is the language of all three groups, then, that is described as Old English or Anglo-Saxon.

While regional differences developed within Old English, particularly in pronunciation, none of the dialects enjoyed national prestige because until quite late there was no dominant court or city that fostered a "standard" variety. In the ninth century, Alfred the Great, king of Wessex, encouraged the translation of works from Latin into English, among them Bede's *Ecclesiastical History of the English People*, Pope Gregory's *Pastoral Care*, Orosius's *History of the World*, and Boethius's *Consolation of Philosophy*. The Old English of the translations is generally the regional variety used by the translators; hence, Werferth, the bishop of Worcester, translated Gregory's *Dialogues* into the Mercian dialect of Old English, while the king himself translated Orosius into his native West Saxon. When a single work was transcribed at widely separated scriptoria, the scribes introduced variant spellings (reflecting their local pronunciations) and even employed local vocabulary where Alfred's terms were unfamiliar. Thus, as Gneuss (1970, p. 68) points out, there is little reason to believe that King Alfred was "the founder or [even] the harbinger of standard Old English." Not until the mid-tenth and the eleventh centuries were there conscious attempts to standardize one of the dialects for literary purposes. Such efforts as there were apparently spread during the middle of the tenth century from the monastery at Winchester where, under the direction of Bishop Æthelwold, English texts were produced that were relatively uniform in spelling and vocabulary. The influence of the authors, translators, and scribes of Winchester was widespread and in the century before the Norman invasion produced a written variety of West Saxon that may reasonably be called "standard Old English."

Old English was an inflected language and hence very different from Modern English. Nouns, for instance, had up to six different forms, depending on case, number (singular or plural), and the declension to which they belonged. Adjectives and verbs were similarly varied in their forms. With so much grammatical information realized in the inflectional system, word order in Old English was more varied and flexible than in modern varieties. Nonetheless, many patterns found in Modern English were in common use: demonstratives and adjectives usually preceded nouns; adverbs appeared in various places but most commonly before the words they modified; in prose, subjects-verbs-complements generally occurred in that order; questions and imperatives were usually formed with verbs placed before their subjects and complements.

While the vowels of Old English were subsequently transformed through the sound changes of the Middle and Early Modern periods, certain effects of the Old English sound system are still apparent in present-day usage. By the process known as *i*-mutation, for instance, the back vowels [u], [o], and [a] were fronted in northern Germanic dialects in nouns forming plurals with *-i*; these mutation plurals in Old English still remain in Modern English: *goose/geese*, *mouse/mice*, *louse/lice*, *man/men*.

Other sound changes that took place in the Old English period help account for some of the dialect difference still current in England. In early Old English, Germanic [a] was fronted and raised to [æ] except when the following syllable contained a back vowel; hence Old English *dæg* 'day' retained its original vowel in the plural form—*dagas* 'days'. Not long after 1200, the plural form began to be assimilated to the singular, but the Midlands and north of England still show evidences of [a] in this word. Likewise, during Old English times there was a general lengthening of short vowels before consonant clusters combining a liquid or nasal with a voiced stop, leading through subsequent changes to the diphthongs in modern *child* and *blind*. With clusters involving nasals, however, lengthening was not as common as with liquids, and the northern dialects retain the short vowels in such words as *blind*, *find*, and *pound*.

Old English had two forms of the verb *to be*—*wesan* and *bēon*—each with a different paradigm. In the Old English period, *bēon* had no preterite inflections and meant 'become, come to be', thus serving as a marker for futurity or intention. While the two verbs have collapsed into one paradigm in standard English, their difference underlies the distinction found in present dialects between, for example, *Are they married?* in the east, Midlands, and north and *Be they married?* in the south and southwest.

Middle English (1150–1500)

The assignment of precise dates to linguistic periods is usually a scholarly convenience rather than a record of sudden discontinuity. Abrupt political and social changes have an impact on language, however, and both factors are apparent in the transformation from Old to Middle English. From the eighth century onward, the Vikings—most of them Danes and Norwegians—raided England, and by the eleventh century they were firmly established in the Danelaw, a territory stretching from the river Tees in the north to the Welland in Northamptonshire. By the Middle English period, Scandinavian loans were becoming current all over the country (e.g., *egg*, *sky*, *take*, and *raise*), though the greatest concentration of them survives in the Danelaw. Scandinavian influence is also apparent in the system of personal pronouns universally used in modern standard English (*they*, *their*, and *them*).

The most important changes from Old to Middle English can be attributed to the influence of the French invaders from Normandy. After the Battle of Hastings in 1066, the use of English as a language of literature, religion, and administration declined drastically. As the Normans replaced English people in positions of authority in the government and church, English was modified by the introduction of loanwords, gradually at first but more rapidly after the separation of French and English courts in 1204. Words for some titles of nobility continued from Old English (*king, queen, earl, lord, lady*), but others were introduced from French (*prince, duke, marquess, viscount, baron*). Farm animals were known by their English names (*cow, pig, calf, sheep*), but the meat served for human consumption acquired French terms (*beef, pork, veal,* and *mutton*) (see Pyles 1964, p. 335). Some French loans from the Middle English period are retained in regional dialects and have spread from them to varieties of English around the world, though they are not found in the modern prestige dialect of England (e.g., *round* 'rung of a ladder', *poke* 'bag', and *scallions* 'spring onions').

With the social transformation brought about by the Conquest, developments toward a standard language were curtailed and the regional dialects continued their separate existence. John Gower (1330–1408) and Geoffrey Chaucer (1340–1400) wrote in an East Midland variety that shows the influence of southern forms. Other writers produced literary works in their own regional dialects: the *Cursor Mundi* (ante 1325) in the northern dialect; *Sir Gawain and the Green Knight* and *Pearl* (ca. 1400) in the West Midland dialect; the *Ormulum* (ca. 1200) and *Havelok the Dane* (ante 1325) in the East Midland dialect; *Ayenbyte of Inwyt* (ca. 1340) in the southeastern dialect; and *The Owl and the Nightingale* (ca. 1250) in the southwestern dialect. With the rise of London as the source of national norms, the English spoken there gradually became the prestige variety. Though the dialects of the west and north were allowed to have some standing well into the English Renaissance, those who took it upon themselves to recommend proper speech commended the dialect that was "the vsual speech of the Court, and that of London and the shires lying about London within lx. myles, and not much above."[2]

A variety of the features that distinguished Middle English dialects persist in the rural varieties heard today. In the south, [f] and [s] were voiced in most positions to [v] and [z], and it is likely that *th* was pronounced as [ð]. Verbs that formed their participles in Old English with *ge-* and in Middle English with *y-* or *i-* continue in the same region with the prefix *a-* (as in the standard *ago*). In the north, Middle English *sall* 'shall' is still heard in central and east Yorkshire. While *she* is the universal form in the modern written language, Middle English displayed a variety of forms: *sche* in the East Midlands, *heo* in the southern dialects, and *scho* in the northern ones. In modern rural dialects, *she* is regular as a nominative pronoun in the east, *her* in the Southwest, and *shoo* in the north.[3]

English in England and Wales

Similarly, short vowels were lengthened in open syllables (ones where the vowel was followed by a single consonant and unstressed [ə]) in all the Middle English dialects except that of the north.

Inflectional suffixes also varied from one region to another in the Middle English period. Present participles were formed with *-and(e)* in the north, *-ende, -ing(e)* in the Midlands, and *-inde, ing(e)* in the south. In modern written English, of course, *-ing* is universally used, and most varieties use *-in* as a stylistic alternative in speech. Some rural dialects of the north, however, preserve the relic form [-ɑn] (from *-ande*) in such words as *cursing, doing, writing,* and *laughing*. The northern and Midland dialects of Middle English formed third-person present singular verbs with *-(e)s* and the East Midland and southern with *-eth*; in Modern English *-(e)s* prevailed except in the restricted domain of liturgical English and consciously archaic literary styles. The pronoun forms borrowed from Scandinavian sources in the Danelaw—*they, them,* and *their*—supplanted the corresponding forms in other dialects: *hi, hem,* and *hir*. But *hem* remained as an alternative to *them* in unstressed positions and underlies the modern usage in, for instance, *we beat 'em*.

The Development of a Standard English

While the earliest public document written in English after the Conquest is a proclamation of Henry III written in 1258, state papers were normally prepared in French or Latin until 1430. From these two languages come many of the words now adopted in legal English: *state, judge, jury,* and *royal* from French and *client, subpoena,* and *conviction* from Latin. Even though literary works were produced in English throughout the Middle English period, only a few readers had access to scarce manuscripts. With the development of printed books and increased opportunities for schooling in the early sixteenth century, more and more people in England became aware of the diversity of their language, and authors were obliged to select a standard from among the varying regional dialects. In a famous passage, William Caxton expressed his difficulties in finding the right kind of English for his translation of a French prose *Aeneid*:

> An certaynly our langage now vsed varyeth ferre from that whiche was vsed and spoken whan I was borne / For we englysshe men / ben borne vnder the domynacyon of the mone whiche is neuer stedfaste / but euer waueryinge / wexynge one season / and waneth & dyscreaseth another season / And that comyn englysshe that is spoken in one shyre varyeth from another In so moche that in my dayes happened that certayn marchauntes were in a shippe in tamyse for to haue sayled ouer the see into zelande / and for lacke of wynde thei taryed atte forlond and wente to lande for to refreshe them And one of theym named sheffelde a mercer cam in to an hows and axed for mete and specyally he axed after eggys

> And the good wyf answered that she coude speke no frenshe And the marchaunt was angry for he also coude speke no frenshe but wold haue hadde eggys / And she vnderstode hym not / And thenne at laste a nother sayd that he wolde haue eyren / then the good wyf sayd that she vnderstod hym wel / Loo what sholde a man in thyse dayes now write egges or eyren / certanyly it is harde to playse euery man / by cause of dyuersite & chaunge of langage. For in these dayes euery man that is in ony reputacyon in his countre wyll vtter his commynycacyon and maters in suche maners & termes that fewe men shall vnderstonde theym /

Egges, though etymologically related to *eyren*, comes into English through Scandinavian sources in the Danelaw, and it was natural enough that the southern "good wyf" should understand only the southern form derived from Old English. For Caxton, who could not foresee which of the competing terms would prevail, the choice of a written form was perplexing.

Modern varieties of the standard dialect have not emerged from a consistently evolving dialect but have developed from a mixture of pronunciations and forms from various regional sources. As London grew in importance as the national capital, English from various places and social classes joined with the southern dialect in the growth of a national language. In the English used in the Royal Chancery for government records, Midland forms (probably influenced by migrants from Leicestershire, Northamptonshire, and Bedfordshire) were mixed with the London dialect: *they* and *them* from the north and *-eth* and *be(n)* from the south. Chancery English then provided the model used by Caxton and others who began to print and distribute books from London that influenced the norms for written English (see Fisher 1977).

Early Modern English (1500–1700)

The Early Modern English period is correctly recognized as the great era of the consolidation and dispersion of English. With the growth of printing and the extension of English into all domains of use, vocabulary increased through borrowing and new formations; syntax and spelling were gradually regularized through the influence of the printed book; and the language spread from Britain to lands around the earth. Nonetheless, it is important to emphasize that the basic core of English was well established before the period opened. Using the two thousand most frequent words in 5 million words of modern English text, Finkenstaedt and Wolff have demonstrated that 70 percent of them were established by 1450; "the 'great age of vocabulary growth' (1520–1620) added another 15 percent and three more centuries have contributed the remaining 8%" (1973, p. 72). The introduction of new vocabulary in the Early Modern period added words from Latin and Greek, from all of the European languages, and from the languages of remote parts of the world visited by English explorers and colonists.

During the fifteenth and sixteenth centuries, there remained a strong undercurrent of resistance to the use of English for the most serious purposes of life. English, many felt, was subject to rapid change and decay; it lacked sufficiently "copious" vocabulary; it did not allow the principles of classical quantitative meter to be applied in the composition of "lofty" verse and had few of the figures and ornaments available to writers in Latin and Greek. Many of these complaints were summed up by John Skelton in his poem "Philip Sparrow" (written about 1510):

> Our natural tongue is rude,
> And hard to be enneude
> With polished terms lusty;
> Our language is so rusty,
> So cankered and so full
> Of frowards, and so dull,
> That if I would apply
> To write ordinately,
> I wot not where to find
> Terms to serve my mind.[4]

Such complaints continued well into the seventeenth century; because he doubted the expressive power of English (and was not sure that it would endure), Sir Francis Bacon composed his scientific works in both English and Latin to ensure that one version or the other would survive.

One stabilizing influence on the use of English was the translation of the Bible by Wycliffe and his followers at the end of the fourteenth century, but not until the establishment of the Church of England under Henry VIII and the translations by William Tyndale and Miles Coverdale was an English Bible used in services and for widespread private reading. The Authorized or King James Version was published in 1611 and continued as an influence on English style and usage until modern English was fully established. Likewise, the *Book of Common Prayer* (1549, 1552, 1662) provided a liturgy for the English church that demonstrated the potential of English for serious uses. In addition, literary works of great popularity were written during the period by such authors as Marlowe (1564–93), Shakespeare (1564–1616), Milton (1608–74), and Dryden (1631–1700), and these helped to settle the doubts of the learned that the "rude" and "rusty" English language could be the vehicle for eloquence.

As the literate public increased in numbers, English was used more and more for public and private letters, business documents, and legal proceedings as well as for literary and scholarly writings. Spelling was still unstable and tended to reflect the spoken language of the writer, but by the end of the Early Modern period, spelling conventions were relatively settled along the lines now used throughout the world. While spoken varieties continued to differ by region and class, the prosperous and powerful moved gradually toward uniformity. Sir Walter Raleigh (ca. 1552–1618) was remembered as distinctive by his speech in Queen Elizabeth's court; "notwithstanding his so great Mastership in Style and his conversation with the learnedest and politest persons, yet he spake broad Devonshire to his dying day" (Aubrey 1962, p. 255). That Raleigh's southwestern dialect was regarded as rustic is made plain in Shakespeare's *King Lear*, where Edgar contrives to disguise himself from the blind King by affecting southwestern speech:

> *Edgar:* Chill not let go Zir, Without vurther [cagion].
> *Steward:* Let go Slaue, or thou dy'st.
> *Edgar:* Good Gentleman goe your gate, and let poore volke passe: and 'chud ha'bin zwaggered out of my life, 'twould not ha'bin zo long as 'tis, by a vortnight. Nay, come not neere th'old man: keepe out che vor' ye or ice try whither your Costard, or my Ballow be the harder; chill be plaine with you. [*King Lear* 4.6.235–42]

As Dobson points out, the use of this dialect "would be pointless . . . if the upper classes generally had used dialect" (1969, p. 423).

A variety of regional and social dialects were described or censured by writers of the Early Modern period. With fair accuracy, Richard Verstegan noted in 1605:

> we see that in some seueral partes of *England* it self, both the names of things, and pronountiations of woords are somwhat different. . . . and of this different pronountiation one example in steed of many shal suffise, as this: for pronouncing according as one would say at *London*, *I would eat more cheese yf I had it* / the northern man saith, *Ay sud eat mare cheese gin ay hadet* / and the westerne man saith: *Chud eat more cheese an chad it*. Lo heer three different pronountiations in our owne countrey in one thing and heerof many the lyke examples might be alleaged. [Quoted by Barber 1976, p. 25]

In addition to questioning the status of regional dialects, observers were also inclined to mock the affected language of the rising middle class and to attack the Puritans for their distinctive speaking styles. All such comments reflect a growing consensus in favor of a single national standard.

The Early Modern period, then, marks a time when the social meanings attached to varieties of English begin to take on a recognizably modern form. Literary uses establish the scope of the written language; spoken varieties tend toward uniformity among the elite; departures from educated norms are treated as aberrant. During the period, the first monolingual English dictionaries appear to instruct people in the use of their language (Robert Cawdrey's *Table Alphabeti-*

call [1604]), and grammars and usage manuals are compiled in response to a desire to regulate the language, ensure the permanence of English writings, and make command of one dialect a requirement for positions of power and authority.

Many of the conventions of Modern English spelling create difficulty today for children learning to read since they reflect pronunciations current five hundred years ago rather than modern usage. At least some of the modern "silent letters" were formerly pronounced; for instance the *g* of *sing* reflected the pronunciation [sɪŋg], the *gh* of *thought* [θɔuxt], and the initial consonants of *write*, *knee*, and *gnat* [wr], [kn], and [gn]. For nearly all consonants and short vowels, however, the values current today are those used at the end of the Middle English period with just a few differences to be discussed later. In the long vowels, the Middle English system underwent a systematic change during the Early Modern period, a restructuring known as the Great Vowel Shift.

While the Great Vowel Shift operated systematically on the prestige dialect of southern England, it did not proceed at the same rate in all regions or influence all social classes in the same way. For those dialects in which the change was systematic and complete, we can begin with the seven Middle English long vowels and trace their changes.

Middle English	Modern Spellings	Examples
ī	i, y, iCe, ie	*child, fly, tide, pie*
ẹ̄	ee, ie	*seed, field*
ẹ̈	ea, ei, eCe	*heath, conceit, complete*
ā	aCe	*make, dame*
ọ	oa, oCe	*boat, hope*
ọ̈	oo	*food, goose*
ū	ou, ow	*house, how*

Source: Barber 1976, p. 290.
Note: The symbol C stands for any single consonant.

The first stage of the shift involved the diphthongization of ī and ū so that Middle English *tide* [tiːd] and *house* [huːs] became [təɪd] and [həus]; the change in these two high vowels made way for a chain-shift in which the mid and low long vowels were elevated to their modern positions.

Middle English ī and ū were first diphthongized in the fifteenth century, but the onset position of the new diphthongs remained varied over the next two hundred years. Innovative speakers of the standard dialect began to use [aɪ] and [au] during the seventeenth century, but more conservative ones continued to use a centralized vowel (either [əɪ] or [əu]) until the eighteenth century. Modern regional dialects show a great variety of sounds in the reflexes of Middle English ī and ū, ranging among [æɪ, aɪ, ɑɪ, ɔɪ, ʌɪ] in words like *white, time,* and *sky* and among [əu, æu, ʌu, ɛu] in words like *house, shout,* and *clouds*. Insofar as any generalization can be made about present-day regional dialects, the region of least change in *house* is the north (where [hus] is still current); centralized onsets predominate in the east (where [həʊs] is common); the lowest onsets are found in the south central region (where [haʊs] and [hɑʊs] occur). The modern reflexes of *ī* in *white* are less subject to easy generalization since [i] nowhere occurs, but the highest onsets for the diphthongs tend to be in the north and the lowest in the southwest.

Words with Middle English *oi* were pronounced then, as now, with [ɔɪ] (as in *noise*, *royal*, and *boy*). Other words with *oi* spellings (such as *boil*, *coin*, *join*, *moist*, *point*, *poison*, *soil*, *spoil*, *turmoil*, and *voice*) derive from Middle English *ui*, and these came to be pronounced with [əɪ] in the seventeenth century or earlier, thus providing a case of apparent merger with the reflexes of Middle English *ī*. As a result, Shakespeare could rhyme *die* with *joy*, and other poets paired *join* and *line*, *child* and *spoiled*, and *toils* and *smiles*. The merger of these sounds was evidently not complete, for during the eighteenth century the diphthongs from *ī* and *ui* were separated along the lines apparent in RP today (see Labov and Nunberg 1972). Four words deriving from Middle English *ī* were grouped with the *ui* reflexes: *boil* 'inflammation', *joist*, *hoist*, and *groin*.

The long mid-front vowels in Middle English were divided between "half-close" $\bar{e}$ and "half-open" $\bar{ę}$, and the distinction was retained for much of the Early Modern period. Shakespeare apparently distinguished *meat* [mɛːt] from *meet* [miːt] since *meet* (from Middle English $\bar{e}$) had been raised to high front positions while *meat* (from Middle English $\bar{ę}$) remained as a mid-front vowel. Subsequently, in the standard dialect, the reflexes of $\bar{ę}$ were raised to [e] and then, in response to a change in nonstandard London speech, to a merger of both Middle English $\bar{e}$ and $\bar{ę}$ in the modern [i] with only a few exceptions (e.g., *break*, *drain*, *great*, *steak*, and *yea*). Some of the modern dialects, however, show varying treatments of these sounds. In *deaf*, for instance, the raised form of Middle English $\bar{ę}$ produces [dif] in the north and southwest, but in the central and southern part of the country, folk speech and the prestige dialect share [dɛf]. Variation in the vowel height and in the extent to which $\bar{e}$ and $\bar{ę}$ were merged help account for some of the variation in the distribution of the modern varieties of English spoken abroad.

Just as Middle English distinguished between front $\bar{e}$ and $\bar{ę}$, so too it contained a contrast between long "half-close" $\bar{o}$ and "half-open" $\bar{ǫ}$. Reflexes of Middle English $\bar{o}$—invariably spelled with *oo* as in *goose*, *moon*, and *school*—were raised in southern dialects to [u]. Some of them retain [u] in modern English; others underwent shortening at an early period and lead to the *oo* words now pronounced [ʌ] (e.g., *flood* and *blood*); still others were shortened in the seventeenth century and are now pronounced with [ʊ] (e.g., *good* and *hood*). There is no systematic approach to distinguishing the words that changed in one of these three ways, and doubtless there was considerable variation from word to word and from region to region. Within standard English today, [u] and [ʊ] continue to alternate in such words as *room*, *broom*, and *soot*; RP has [ʊ] in *roof* and *hoof* but the regional dialects of the West Midlands and East Anglia have [u] in these words. In dialects where the initial diphthongization of Middle English *ū* did not take place, the reflexes of Middle English *ǭ* were raised and fronted, probably to the rounded vowel [y], a change that underlies the modern northern variants of the reflexes of this vowel.

The half-open mid-back long vowel, Middle English *ǭ*, was raised to the position of [o:]; hence [bɔ:t] became [bo:t] 'boat'. At the end of the eighteenth century, the reflexes of Middle English *ǭ* were diphthongized to [ou] as in modern *go*, *loaf*, *spokes*, and *toad*, though the modern English of Scotland and the north of England tends to show [o] without diphthongization.

Middle English long *ā*, a low-front vowel, was [a:] in Middle English, but by 1500 it had come to be pronounced [æ:]. In the course of the Early Modern period, reflexes of Middle English *ā* became progressively raised, and in the sixteenth century it is possible to find evidence of [mæ:k], [mɛ:k], and [me:k] for the pronunciation of *make*. Apparently there was some stylistic variation in these words; the lower variants were regarded as conservative and the higher ones as innovative. The raising of the reflexes of *ā* did not cause a merger with Middle English *ẹ̄* since the reflexes of that vowel were correspondingly raised; conservative speakers distinguished [mæ:t] *mate* (Middle English *ā*) from [mɛ:t] *meat* (Middle English *ę̄*), and innovative ones formed the contrast as [mɛ:t] *mate* and [me:t] *meat*. Eventually, words from both sources seem to have merged as [e:], and *mate* and *meat* became homophones. As Barber (1976, p. 293) notes, eighteenth-century poets could rhyme *make/speak*, *shame/dream*, *case/peace*, *nature/creature*, and *shade/mead*. Nonetheless, it is obvious that this merger was more apparent than real, since most reflexes of Middle English *ę̄* merged with those of Middle English *ẹ̄* as [i] while the reflexes of Middle English *ā* are now generally pronounced [e] (see Labov and Nunberg 1972).

In summary, then, the seven long vowels of Middle English were affected by the Great Vowel Shift as follows: the two high vowels [i] and [u] became diphthongs; the half-close front vowel [e] rose to occupy the [i] position; and, eventually, the half-open front vowel [ɛ:] merged with it as [i] or with the reflexes of Middle English *ā* as [e]. The half-close back vowel [o] rose to assume the position of [u] (with subsequent developments establishing the contrast of [u], [ʊ], and [ʌ]). The half-open back vowel [ɔ:] was raised to occupy the [o] position.

Other sound changes in the Early Modern period were neither so systematic nor so sweeping, but they nevertheless help explain some of the variation in modern dialects and in international varieties of English. Middle English short *ŏ*, for instance, was unrounded and produced such variant spellings as *stap/stop* and *Gad/God*. A few of these were functionally differentiated: for example, *strap* and *strop* 'a strap of leather used for sharpening razors'. Modern English generally shows [ɒ] in the reflexes of Middle English *ŏ*, but some varieties of American English (as Frederic G. Cassidy shows elsewhere in this volume) retain [a] in such words as *bonnet*, *holly*, *fox*, and *cot*. Middle English short *ă* remains [a] in northern dialects (in *bat*, *man*, and *hand*), but in RP it developed as [æ] during the first half of the seventeenth century. Middle English short *ŭ* split into two variants: [ʊ] and [ʌ]. The reflexes of *ŭ* were lowered and unrounded to [ʌ] except with adjacent labial consonants; hence, *cut* and *hut* gained [ʌ] but *bull*, *bush*, and *wolf* retained [ʊ].[5] When the reflexes of Middle English *ǭ* were shortened from [u] to [ʊ], a merger took place between reflexes of *ǭ* and *ŭ* in many dialects and established a contrast between *look* and *luck*, *book* and *buck*. As in other cases, however, not all dialects took part in the change, and northern dialects retain [ʊ] in reflexes of *ŭ* (such as *butter* and *thunder*).

Consonant changes in the Early Modern period include the beginning of the shift from rhotic to nonrhotic pronunciations in standard English, though this change did not substantially affect prestige varieties until late in the eighteenth century. However, the presence of final and preconsonantal *r* had an effect on preceding vowels and fostered the centralizing of short vowels kept distinct in Middle English (e.g., *herb*, *birth*, and *curse*); intervocalic *r* had no such effect, and thus the vowels of *merry* and *stirrup* were not centralized. Postvocalic *r* also inhibited the raising of long vowels and was thus a countervailing tendency to the Great Vowel Shift; hence words with the same Middle English vowel now are differentiated (e.g., *meat* and *bear*). Other consonant changes in Early Modern English include the introduction of [ʒ] in French loans such as *rouge* and *beige*; the voiceless counterpart of this sound, [ʃ], already existed in English. The new consonant also took the place of the [zj] sequence in *occasion*, *division*, and *measure*. While [ŋ] had previously occurred before [g] and [k]—in [sɪŋg] *sing* and [θaŋk] *thank*—it now appeared in other contexts as well; most dialects simplified the final [ŋg] cluster of *sing* to [ŋ] and thus established a contrast between *sing* and *sin*. Standard varieties in the Early Modern period lost the [ç] and [x] consonants of Middle English—in [liçt] *light* and [θɔxt] *thought*—which had disappeared in eastern dialects in late Middle English.

Grammatical and morphological changes generally continued the pattern of standardization in which one variant came to be the dominant type. Present tense *-(e)s* replaced *-eth*; *you*, earlier the second person plural pronoun, took the place of *thee* and *thou*; some verbs that formed the past tense by a vowel change were adapted to the *-ed* pattern, though not all of the innovations persisted in standard English (e.g., *clomb/climbed*, *dolve/delved*, *run/runned*). In the formation of relative clauses, *which* could be used with a personal antecedent (*Our father, which art in Heaven*) but was eventually supplanted by *who*. Many adverbs had the same form as their corresponding adjectives, and the pattern of adding *-ly* to adverbs was greatly extended in the period (but " 'Tis noble spoken" in Shakespeare's *Antony and Cleopatra*, 2.2.98).

Late Modern English (1700–Present)

Standard English, as we have seen, arose in the area around London from a mixture of southern and Midland dialect features. If a modern speaker of standard

English were to meet an educated Londoner of 1700, he or she would find little difficulty in communicating. Pronunciation differences would not constitute a significant barrier. Both would regard the speech of the other as markedly provincial or blemished by low-status usages, but both would generally agree in their attitudes toward standardization even while differing in their judgment of specific features. In vocabulary, the modern speaker would be at a considerable advantage, since he or she would recognize most vocabulary in use in 1700 even though some confusion might arise over words whose senses have changed since that time. The eighteenth-century speaker, on the other hand, would find much of the modern speaker's vocabulary bewildering, not only because words for modern inventions would be unfamiliar but also because the vocabulary of English has greatly increased in the last three hundred years through borrowing and word creation from the stock of English roots and affixes. In the domain of syntax, a few grammatical changes might cause confusion, but the general patterns of word order and the formation of questions, negations, and subordinate clauses resemble each other sufficiently to cause little difficulty. In conversation, the eighteenth-century speaker would probably be surprised to find that his modern counterpart did not sprinkle the conversation with titles and surnames (or with *Sir* and *Madam*) in exchanges between intimate friends, while the modern speaker would impute coldness and distance even to the friendliest talk of the eighteenth century.

Since 1700, several changes have taken place in the phonological system of standard English—some of them in phonetic realization and others by addition or deletion of segments. The long mid-vowels [e] and [o] became diphthongized to [eɪ] and [oʊ] respectively. While selection of [ɑː] as the vowel of *chaff* and *last* was regarded as a vulgar alternative to [æː] in the eighteenth century, during the nineteenth century it came to be regarded as a prestige feature in England; [æ] remains the norm in some dialects and in the English of Canada, the United States, Australia, and New Zealand. The [ʌ] vowel in *love* and *come* continued the downward drift from a position near [ʊ] that it had previously occupied in London speech and that it retains in the modern dialects of the north and west.

In the Early Modern period, the vocalization of preconsonantal and final [r] was regarded as a rustic feature, and only at the end of the eighteenth century do nonrhotic pronunciations begin to appear in prestige varieties. Nonrhotic styles established themselves in standard speech, though the Victorian prime minister W. E. Gladstone (1809–98) persisted in pronouncing postvocalic [r] despite the change that took place around him. Loss of [r] through vocalization had a significant effect on the vowel system. One such effect was to lengthen vowels in, for example, *card* and *horse*; another was the merger of [ɪr], [ɛr], and [ʌr] (in *perfect*, *turn*, and *first*) to [ɜː]. When [r] was lost after vowels that were already long, [ə] was generally inserted in its place; thus, the earlier pronunciations of [ɛː] and [ɔː] (in *bear* and *board*) gave way to [ɛə] and [ɔə] (the latter, having subsequently lost its centering vowel, is now pronounced [ɔː]).

A variety of other sound changes can be traced to the influence of spelling and the growing sense that spelled forms provide a useful guide to pronunciation. In French loan words, for example, the *h* of *herb* or *hotel* was not originally pronounced, but the general stigmatization of the loss of [h] in native words influenced the modern pronunciations of these loans in which [h] now appears. Similarly, the final *-ing* of present participles and verbal nouns was generally pronounced [ɪn] through the eighteenth century, but an increased emphasis on correctness early in the nineteenth century fostered the change to [ɪŋ], an innovation supported by spelling and the supposed example of earlier varieties of English (see Wyld 1936, p. 289). The same "authority" of spelling led to the restoration of [w] in such words as *woman*, *swollen*, and *Ipswich*, and today the pronunciation of [w] in *toward* is spreading in response to the same impulse. Other consonants that were "restored" in prestige varieties during this period include the [d] in *London*, the [l] in *soldier*, the [v] in *pavement*, and the final consonant [t] of *respect* and *strict* (see Strang 1970, p. 82). The final syllables of such words as *fertile* and *missile* came to be pronounced [aɪl] in the nineteenth century, supplanting the earlier [əl] that underlies the syllabic [l̩] of American pronunciations of these words.

In the domain of vocabulary, English since 1700 has continued the earlier pattern of borrowing. Many French loans came into use following the Napoleonic Wars. These words are likely to be recognized as from French sources today and hence sometimes retain some trace of their original pronunciations (e.g., *coup* and *corps*—the latter having first been borrowed early in the eighteenth century and pronounced with [p] but later joining the other French loans and acquiring its modern pronunciation). Most borrowings from all sources during the period were nouns, and, though some new vocabulary from the far reaches of exploration and colonization are first attested before 1700, most of them were borrowed or entered general use after that time.

Technical vocabulary arising in the sciences and as a consequence of the industrial revolution generally draws on elements from Greek or Latin, though purists often objected when words were formed according to English rather than classical principles. The prefix *hyper-*, for instance, occurs with words of Greek origin (e.g., *hypertrophy*), with learned words generally (e.g., *hypercritical*), and more recently with English words of considerable variety (e.g., *hyperconservative* and *hyperactive*). Many other prefixes from classical sources have become productive since 1700—for instance, *micro-*, *mono-*, *neo-*, and *ultra-*. Derivational suffixes are now widely used, particularly to form nouns or verbs from other word classes. The suffix *-ize*, for example, was first used to form verbs from roots of Greek or Latin origin (e.g., *baptize*, *harmonize*, and *tyrannize*), then in the Early Modern period with words well established in English (e.g., *criticize*, *fertilize*, and *sterilize*). Nineteenth-century science promoted additional words with *-ize*, though most *-ize* formations affected words derived from classical sources (e.g., *immunize* and *visualize*). In the twentieth century, words of nearly all sources and types

English in England and Wales

can now be converted to verbs by means of the suffix (e.g., *winterize*, *weatherize*, and *tenderize*) (see Marchand 1969, pp. 255–59).

Grammatical changes that have developed since 1700 are not numerous and generally extend patterns that were already current before that time. The tendency for declarative sentences to follow the pattern subject-verb-complement has continued, and sentences not following that order tend to be regarded as nonstandard (*a good doctor is he*) or as poetic (*fair was she*). The prop-word *one* is now more generally used (e.g., *five yellow coats and a red one*); passive constructions are now possible with all verb phrases (sentences like *the lift has been being repaired for more than six months* begin to appear only in the nineteenth century); *that* formerly introduced both nonrestrictive and restrictive clauses but is now used almost exclusively in restrictive clauses in standard English.

Social forces that have supported the development and dispersion of standard English became particularly strong after 1700. Dictionaries compiled in the eighteenth century by Nathaniel Bailey in 1721 and by Samuel Johnson in 1755 came to be regarded as arbiters of good usage and were followed by a plethora of grammars and handbooks designed to promote a uniform standard. In the nineteenth century, the ancient public schools drew more and more of the children of the elite, and with the imposition of universal primary education late in the century, the schools became an important vehicle by which the standard was promoted. When the BBC was established in the 1920s, it too became an influence in the dissemination of one particular variety of English as the mark of education and cultivation. Throughout the period, standard English continued to be one of several dialects spoken by educated persons, but more and more it came to be the variety used by the upper and upper-middle classes and was imitated by those who aspired to membership in those classes.

The growth in the perceived prestige of standard English (particularly with the pronunciation style associated with RP) has caused a consequent lowering of the status of regional varieties of English. In an experiment conducted in 1970, Giles presented thirteen taped specimens of various accents and dialects to schoolchildren in South Wales and Somerset. The children believed that they were listening to different speakers, though in fact a single male speaker read the same prose passage using different guises. The rank order of these varieties according to the perceived status of the speaker was as follows:

1. RP	8. Italian
2. Affected RP	9. Northern English
3–4. North American and French	10. Somerset
5. German	11–12. Cockney and Indian
6. South Welsh	13. Birmingham
7. Irish	

It is noteworthy that older children gave relatively low rankings to the variety of English that they and their parents used and that they were able to identify the accents and dialects quite accurately and to discuss their supposed virtues and defects (see Giles and Powesland 1975, pp. 28–31).

English in Wales followed the general pattern of development found in England. Universal primary education was introduced in 1870 under the same legislation that applied in England, and English was the medium of teaching even in areas where children commonly learned Welsh as their first language. English immigration, particularly into the South Wales industrial area, supported the extension of English and the RP prestige form. Though Welsh English has its own characteristics (as will be described later), it never gained the prestige that was achieved by Scottish or Irish English.

Standard English in England Today

RP is generally regarded as the standard of pronunciation among modern prestige accents in Britain, and, like other varieties, it participates in regional and stylistic variation. Most descriptions of the individual sounds of RP begin with the detailed account provided by Daniel Jones (1909 and subsequently revised and reprinted). The following chart, slightly adapted, shows the simple vowels of RP as displayed by Jones (1956, p. 23).

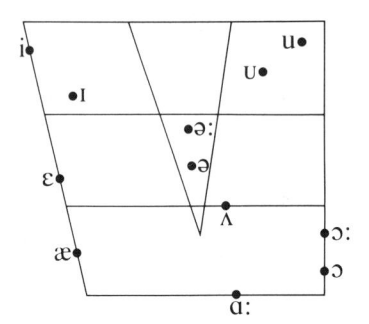

These vowels appear in the following words: [i] *meet*, [ɪ] *bit*, [ɛ] *head*, [æ] *man*, [ɑ:] *star*, [ɔ] *hot*, [ɔ:] *saw*, [ʊ] *good*, [u] *moon*, [ʌ] *cup*, [ə:] *fur*, and [ə] in the unstressed syllables of *attack* and *method*. In recent years, some of these vowels have commonly been shifted to positions different from those shown in the chart: [ʌ] is now lower and pronounced further to the front; [ɔ:] is raised; and all of the short vowels have been centered (see Barber 1964, pp. 41–42).

Five "closing diphthongs"—i.e., ones in which the off-glide involves raising of the tongue—are charted by Jones in the following diagram.

English in England and Wales

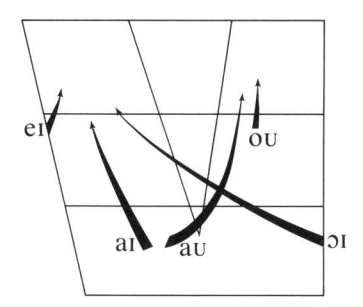

As will be explained in greater detail later, these diphthongs have many variants in present-day urban and rural dialects. These sounds occur in the following words: [eɪ] *day*, [oʊ] *go*, [aɪ] *time*, [aʊ] *how*, [ɔɪ] *boy*. In educated southeastern speech, the onset of [aɪ] appears to have been retracted in recent years (Barber 1964, p. 42).

Four centering diphthongs occur in environments where rhotic dialects have [r].

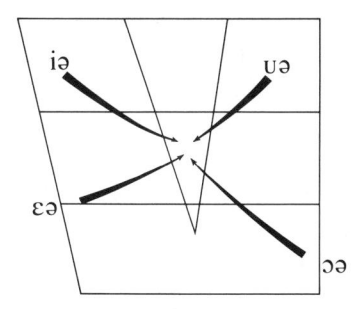

Words in which these diphthongs appear in RP are: [ɪə] *here*; [ɛə] *there*; [ɔə] *more*; and [ʊə] *tour*.

RP is not entirely uniform and shows variation according to age, region, and style. Generational differences can be found in such features as the following variants within RP:

	home	*white*	*poor*
Old-fashioned	ou	ʍ	ʊə
Neutral	əu	w	ʊə
Innovative	ɜːʊ	w	ɔː

In *home*, the onset of the diphthong is becoming centralized, lowered, and lengthened. Preaspirated initial [ʍ] in such words as *white* and *which* is giving way to unaspirated [w]. The vowel of *poor* is being monophthongized and lowered so that *poor* and *pour*, *sure* and *shore*, tend to become homophones.

Regional variation within RP tends to follow some of the tendencies of regional dialects. Northern RP tends to have lower vowels in *bed* and *man* than southern RP; southern RP has a lower vowel in *but* while northern RP may have a higher one.

	RP	Southern	Northern
bed	[ɜ]	[ɜ]	[ɛ]
bat	[æ]	[æ]	[a]
but	[ʌ]	[a]	[ʊ]

Most southern varieties of RP maintain the contrast between [ə] and [ʌ], and while the former occurs mainly in unstressed and the latter in stressed syllables, there are instances of opposition between [ə] and [ʌ] in both stressed and unstressed environments (Wells 1970, p. 234). Midland and northern regional dialects lack [ʌ]—[ʊ] is the normal alternative to RP [ʌ]—and RP speakers from these regions are likely to lack the [ə]/[ʌ] contrast. Within RP, there are also contrasts in addition to those specified in the charts above; in Wales, for instance, RP speakers are likely to contrast [θrɪu] *threw* and [θru] *through*.

Stylistic variation involves the incidence of vowels in unstressed syllables and serves to distinguish careful, formal styles from rapid, informal ones. Variation between [ɪ] and [ə] is common in the unstressed syllables of such words as *system*, *exact*, *ability*, *become*, *horrible*, *waitress*, and *corporate*, particularly in fast speech (Barber 1964, p. 49). In general, RP has not extended the preference for [ə] in unstressed syllables as have American and Australian English, and [ə] for [ɪ] in plural *-es* and past tense *-ed* is uncommon. Other stylistic variants involve the smoothing of diphthongs or a shift in the position of articulation: in slow speech, *I'm going* is likely to be [aɪmgəʊɪŋ], but in rapid speech [amgoɪŋ] is regarded as normal.

Other types of variation occur within RP. Speakers differ in the selection of [æ] or [ɑ:] in *photograph* and *transport* (see Fudge 1977), and the contrast between [i] and [ɛ] as the initial vowel of *economics* is not obviously predictable from region, age, sex, or style. Individual sounds may also vary greatly in articulation within RP; intervocalic *r* in *very* and *sorry* ranges from an alveolar tap to a lingual roll to a retroflex flap. The consonant in such words as *Asia*, *transition*, and *version* may be [ʃ] or [ʒ], though the former is regarded as slightly old-fashioned. Word stress may also vary in RP; in the following words, second-syllable stress tends to be old-fashioned and first-syllable stress innovative, though both older and younger speakers may employ either: *garage*, *adult*, *allow*, and *ally* (noun).

Vocabulary differences within standard English tend to be a function of occupation and education, though there may be individual prejudices against "jargon" and "Americanisms" (a term broad enough to cover any supposed innovation of which the speaker disapproves). In the twentieth century, borrowing has diminished and the existing word stock provides material for the creation of new senses and new vocabulary. In the 1950s, Alan S. C. Ross, Nancy Mitford, and other writers discussed vocabulary within the standard that supposedly distinguished upper-class (designated *U*) from other usage (*non-U*). Nearly all of these distinctions involve words generally employed in the standard, and the claimed difference in social value was based more upon prejudice than upon observation: *rich* (U)/*wealthy* (non-U); *bus/coach*; *sick/ill*; *looking glass/mirror*; *table napkin/serviette* (see Ross et al. 1956).

Grammatical variation also occurs within standard English, and some alternatives are not immediately connected with style, age, or region. The verbs *need*, *dare*, and *have* may occur with or without a form of *do* in questions and negations: *he does not need to come/he need not come*. Alternatives with *have* do have some regional pattern, and northern speakers and more old-fashioned persons are less likely to employ the alternative with *do*: *have you any money?/do you have any money?* Questions formed with *have* and *got* are apparently being supplanted by structures with *do* or *have* alone; *have you got any money?* is now thought to be less common than formerly (Strevens 1972, p. 48).

Variety within standard English syntax may also be traced to regional differences. Both *I want it washed* and *it needs washing* occur in the south; in the Midlands and north, only the latter typically occurs. Similarly, contracted negatives with *will* and *have* in the south involve the use of *n't*: *I won't do it* and *I haven't done it*; in the north, the auxiliary verbs undergo contraction: *I'll not do it* and *I've not done it*. In the south and, particularly, the southwest, sentences with ditransitive verbs are likely to be formed with *to* before the indirect object (*give it to me*; *he gave it to him*); in the East Midlands and north, the alternative without *to* is generally preferred (*give me it*; *he gave him it*); in the West Midlands, the indirect object is likely to occur first (*give it me*; *he gave it me*).

English in Wales[6]

Through the Acts of Union of 1536 and 1542, English was established in Wales as the official language of trade, law, and education. Welsh continued to be used among the people, however, and for many centuries a diglossic situation obtained in which English was the high-level language and Welsh the low-level language. During the nineteenth century the use of English spread through education and the industrialization of the southeast, leading inexorably to the decline of Welsh in that region. In 1911, 35 percent of the total population were bilingual in Welsh and English, but the proportion had fallen to 19.6 percent by 1971. Welsh speakers are not distributed evenly throughout the country but live mostly in the northwest and center. The areas with the fewest Welsh speakers are those counties nearest to England. About half the total population—just under 3 million persons were counted in the 1971 census—lives in the county of Glamorgan with its three industrial centers—Swansea, Cardiff, and Newport. Only 11 percent of the population in that region speak Welsh.[7]

Welsh English differs in several ways from RP and standard English, varying both in the number of phonemes and their phonetic realization; it is especially likely to be used in casual speech and among lower social classes. Welsh English lacks some of the phonemes of RP: e.g., the glottal fricative [h] and the aspirated bilabial frictionless continuant [ʍ]. On the other hand, Welsh English has some sounds not used in RP: for instance, the voiceless lateral [ɬ] (spelled *ll*) which appears in such place-names as *Llanelli*, and the voiceless velar fricative [x] which appears in a few Welsh loanwords (e.g., [baːx]). Other differences between RP and Welsh English consist in the different realization of various sounds. For instance, the low front [a] is always substituted for RP [æ] as in most Midland and northern dialects in England, and RP [ʌ] is [ə]: *cup* [kəp]. The RP diphthongs [eɪ] and [ou] are generally realized as the monophthongs [eː] and [oː], especially when they are spelled *a* and *ea* (*late, great*) or *o, oor,* and *ou* (*so, door, pour*). However, they are distinguished from the diphthongs [ɛɪ]—spelled *ai, ay, ei,* and *ey* (*sail, pay, eight, they*)—and [ou]—spelled *ow, ou,* and *ol* (*blow, soul, old*). In northern Welsh English, however, these latter diphthongs have merged with the monophthongs [eː] and [oː]. The RP diphthongs [aɪ] and [ɑu] are pronounced [əɪ] and [əu]: *might* [məɪt], *loud* [ləud]. The RP centering diphthong [ɛə] (in *bear*) becomes the monophthong [ɛː], but the other centering diphthongs remain the same. In the case of the centering triphthongs [aɪə], [auə], [eɪə], [əuə], [ɔɪə], a homorganic semivowel develops after the vowels [ɪ] and [u]: *fire* is pronounced [faɪjə]; *shower* as [ʃəuwə]. This pattern is due to the unstressed syllable not being as "weak" as in RP, and in general in Welsh English, an unstressed syllable has nearly equal prominence with a stressed one that precedes it. This trait has two phonetic consequences. First, unstressed vowels resist deletion: *separate* is [sɛpərɛt] and not [sɛprɪt]; *disastrous* is [dɪzastərəs] and not [dɪzaːstrəs]. Second, medial consonants after a short vowel tend to be lengthened: *supper* is [səpːə], *dinner* is [dɪnːə]. The *l* in Welsh English does not have the "dark" velar [ɫ] allophone which exists in RP. Final [ʒ] in words such as *prestige* and *beige* becomes [dʒ] in Welsh English. The semivowels [j] and [w] are lost in word initial position before [i] and [u] respectively; thus, the following words are homophonous: *east, yeast*; *hood* (h is lost), *wood*.

Welsh English varies regionally, although only to a small extent. In Cardiff, for instance, long [aː] in *cart* and *Cardiff* becomes [æː]. In the southwest of Wales postvocalic *r* is retained, and RP [h] and [ʍ] occur as in northern Welsh English. In the north, [dʒ] and [z] are lacking and speakers use [tʃ] and [s] instead. These last three features—retention of postvocalic *r*, presence of [h] and [ʍ], and

English in England and Wales

lack of [ʤ] and [z]—are due to the influence of the Welsh sound system. In Breconshire and Radnorshire along the English border, Welsh English [a] is realized as RP [æ] and the vowels have *r* coloring probably as a result of the influence of the neighboring English dialects.

Many of the features of grammatical variation in Welsh English are those widespread in most English dialects: e.g., the use of the past tense of strong verbs as the past participle form, *the window was broke*; multiple negation, *I 'aven't done nothin'*; extension of the third person singular *-s* to other persons. In the south of Wales the indefinite article only has one form, *a*, even before a vowel: *a apple, a orange*. Welsh may influence or support the use of definite articles before diseases—*the measles, the toothache*—though this feature also occurs in other varieties of English. In rural areas, the tag *isn't it?* is generalized after any question no matter what subject pronoun or noun is used: *you're going home now, isn't it?*; *she came to see me yesterday, isn't it?* Also very common is sentence-initial placement of those items that the speaker considers important (topicalization), a frequent device in Welsh: *coming home tomorrow he is*; *loud he was singing*; *sad she looked*. Very few Welsh words have been borrowed into Welsh English. Some examples are *tollut* (< *taflod*) 'hay-loft', *llymru* 'a porridgelike dish' (first attested in 1623), and *del, bach* [ba:x], both terms of endearment. Some expressions used in distinctive ways in southern Welsh English are: *he's got a delight* ('interest') *in football*; *he was off* ('angry'); and the repetition of an adjective to show intensification, *it was long, long* (i.e., 'very long'). Southern Welsh English employs a discontinuous adverb of place *where...to*: *where's the train to?* 'where is the train?'

The distinctive English of Welsh speakers has long been recognized through certain salient features. In Shakespeare's *Henry V*, for instance, several of the linguistic variables already mentioned appear in the speeches of the Welshman, Captain Fluellen (e.g., loss of initial [w] in *world*); other features are the substitution of [p] for [b]—a misunderstanding by an outsider of the process of consonant mutation in Welsh—and the pervasive *look you* that is a hallmark of the Welsh speaker in English literary works:

> I think it is in Macedon where Alexander is porn. I tell you, captain, if you look in the maps of the orld, I warrant you sall find, in the comparisons between Macedon and Monmouth, that the situations, look you, is both alike. There is a river in Macedon, and there is also moreover a river at Monmouth. It is call'd Wye at Monmouth; but it is out of my prains what is the name of the other river; but 'tis all one, 'tis alike as my fingers is to my fingers, and there is salmons in both. [*Henry V*, 4.7.22–31]

Other English writers have evoked the same stereotype in representing Welsh English; in the twentieth century, Evelyn Waugh provides a typical example in which topicalization is a prominent feature:

"Well, my good man?" said the Doctor.
"The young lady I have been telling that no other tunes can we play whatever with the lady smoking at her cigarette look you."
"God bless my soul! Why not?"
"The other tunes are all holy tunes look you. Blasphemy it would be to play the songs of Sion while the lady at a cigarette smokes whatever. *Men of Harlech* is good music look you." [Waugh 1959, p. 295]

Using a matched guise technique in an effort to elicit opinions about Welsh, Welsh English, and RP, Giles found that the degree to which the respondents used Welsh themselves was hardly a factor. All respondents judged the Welsh speaker to be trustworthy, friendly, and sociable, and of the three varieties, the Welsh speaker was supposed to be the most patriotic and nationalistic. Welsh English immediately followed Welsh on the positive traits of the evaluation scale, while the RP-accented Welshman was given high ratings only on such dubiously valued traits as conservatism, snobbishness, and arrogance (Giles and Powesland 1975, p. 76). From these results, it would appear that Welsh English constitutes a variety with positive traits for its speakers and thus is likely to continue to be fostered within the community.

English Rural Dialects

The first systematic attempt to classify rural dialect pronunciations was carried out in the mid-nineteenth century by A. J. Ellis, who distinguished six major dialect areas (including Lowland Scots); in 1905 Joseph Wright completed a description of English dialects which generally agrees with Ellis's. No further large scale studies of the dialects of England were made until the Survey of English Dialects (SED) between 1948–61 under the leadership of Eugen Dieth (1893–1956) and Harold Orton (1898–1975). The SED material was derived from answers to a carefully designed questionnaire, and interviews were carried out by eleven fieldworkers; informants were mostly men over sixty who had lived in their locality most, if not all, of their lives, and nearly all the localities were villages or small towns. The SED is the most thorough survey of English rural dialects, and by the choice of localities and informants gives a picture of archaic and rustic dialects. The answers to the SED questionnaires were tabulated and published (Orton and Dieth 1962–71) and subsequently plotted on maps in *Word Geography of England* (Orton and Wright 1974) and *The Linguistic Atlas of England* (Orton, Sanderson, and Widdowson 1978). The results confirm the division of dialects made by Ellis and Wright but give much more detailed and reliable information. An introduction to English dialects using the material from the SED is provided by Wakelin (1977).

There are four main dialect areas in England: the North, Midland, Southwest, and Southeast, each of which contains subareas. The Midland and northern

Map 2. Main dialect areas in England

dialects have [a] for both RP [æ] (in words like *apple* and *cat*) and RP [ɑː] (in words like *chaff* and *last*). These dialects also lack the RP phoneme [ʌ] in words such as *butter* or *thunder* and use [ʊ] instead. The northern dialects are distinguished by different reflexes of the Middle English long vowels, including retention of the Middle English *ū* as [u] in words like *house* and *cow*. The Midland dialects show a bewildering array of different forms and can best be characterized negatively as being non-northern and non-southern.[8] They do not contain [u] for [aʊ] of the northern dialects, but they do have [a] for RP [æ] and [ɑː] and [ʊ] for RP [ʌ]. The southwestern dialects are rhotic dialects (that is, they retain preconsonantal and postvocalic [r] in words like *hard, bar,* and *butter*), and they are characterized by voiced initial fricatives in words like *five, seven, thimble,* and *sure*. The southeastern dialects in the area around London show fewer developments that diverge from the standard, and only East Anglia exists as a separate dialect subarea. The SED material is listed according to the counties as they existed before the local government reorganization of 1974, and those designations will be kept in the following description. A summary of these main dialect areas is found in map 2.

The Southern Dialects

Southern dialects stand in contrast to northern ones in the following features: northern [ʊ] versus southern [ʌ] in words like *butter* and *thunder*; northern [a] versus southern [æ] in words like *apples* and *carrots*; and northern [a] versus Midlands [aː] versus southern [ɑː] in words like *chaff* and *last*. The isoglosses—lines representing the geographical extent of a dialect feature—form a broad belt rather than being compressed together, and the separation of northern from southern dialects is somewhat sharper in the east (see Viereck 1980). The front [a] in words like *apple* also extends into the southwestern counties. The main vowel in *chaff* in the south and South Midlands is [aː]. The back or retracted [ɑː] is concentrated in the counties to the south and west of London. Retracted [ɑː] is probably of recent origin and possibly arose in the nineteenth century. In *butter*, [ʌ] appears in a small area of Shropshire and Herefordshire north of the main course of the [ʊ]/[ʌ] line. The sounds used in the southeast—[ʌ], [æ], and [ɑː]—all agree with RP. In such words as *uncle*, an isogloss separates northern clear [l] from southern dark [ɫ]. In some dialects around London and southward into Sussex, *l* has been vocalized.

Southwestern Dialects

Within the southern area marked off by the [ʊ]/[ʌ] distinction in words like *butter* and *thunder*, an important boundary is defined by the treatment of preconsonantal and postvocalic *r*. In words like *farm, forks, third, worms, butter,* and *farmer*, rural speakers in the west have [r] or *r*-colored vowels; dialects with this feature are classified as rhotic. In the east, rural speakers generally conform to the non-

English in England and Wales

rhotic pronunciations found in RP and supported by such institutions as schools and broadcasting. In the south the nonrhotic area has expanded westward, and in the north (especially in Lancashire and Northumberland), rhotic pronunciations also occur.

A very noticeable innovation of the consonant system of southwestern dialects is the voicing of the Middle English initial voiceless fricatives—[f], [θ], [s], and [ʃ] in words like *finger, thimble, seven,* and *sure*—which have been retained as voiceless sounds in RP. The extent of the voicing varies slightly from fricative to fricative, with the voicing of [ʃ] covering the smallest area and that of [f] the largest. Voicing of [f] occurs in initial consonant clusters in words like *floor* and *Friday*. With initial [s]—in words like *snow, swearing,* and *sweat*—voicing occurs in an area smaller than that for *fr-, fl-*, comprising chiefly Devon, eastern Cornwall, and parts of Hampshire and Dorset. The dental fricative [θ] which forms an initial consonant cluster with *r*—*three* and *thread*—has developed into the plosive [d]; this feature occurs in the same area as the initial fricative voicing. Another innovation which characterizes southwestern dialects is the pronunciation of initial *r*—*rat* and *red*—as a retroflex frictionless continuant. Most of the southwest retains [a] for RP [æ] in words such as *apples*, except for Somerset, where [a] has become [æ] as in RP.

The southwestern dialects are also characterized by the retention of morphological forms which have died out in the standard and in most other dialects. As noted above, in Old English two main stems were used for the singular present of the verb *to be*, one with the series *eom, eart, is* and the other with *be*. The southwestern dialects have retained many of the forms with *be*, as can be seen from the following paradigm for the present tense:

	Singular	Plural
First person	*I be*	*we be*
Second person	*thee art, you be, thee bist*	
Third person	*she is (be)*	*they be*

The forms for the second person—*thee art, you be,* and *thee bist*—are distributed throughout the southwestern region. *Thee art* occurs in a broad belt from Cornwall to Dorset, while *you be* occurs in two small separate areas (southern Devon and Somerset) and also in a thin belt stretching from Sussex to Herefordshire. Between Somerset and the thin belt of *you be* is the area containing *thee bist*, comprising Gloucestershire, Wiltshire, and West Hampshire. These are, of course, archaic forms, since the separate singular pronouns *thou* and *thee* died out in the standard in the eighteenth century, although retained in the *Book of Common Prayer* and the Authorized or King James Version of the Bible. In the third person, *be* occurs in a central area, comprising central Wiltshire, central Gloucester, central Oxfordshire, and western and central Berkshire.

Another southwestern characteristic is the use of the prefix *a-* with the past participle. For the past participle *done*, a prefixed form *a-done*—in central Devon *a-doed*—is widespread, though *done* occurs in Cornwall, western Somerset, and areas outside the Southwest. For the past participle *put*, the SED records three occurrences of *a-put*: one in Herefordshire, two in Berkshire, and one in Devon. For the past participle *taken*, there are four occurrences of *a-took(ed)*. This use of *a-* is apparently dying out. More widespread is the form *en* for *him*, possibly from Old English *hine* (accusative) which occurs throughout the Southwest except for three localities in northern Somerset. (*En* is also quite often used for *it*.) Although there is no material in the SED to plot its extent accurately, the dummy auxiliary *do* is widely used in the Southwest in affirmative nonemphatic sentences: e.g., *I do go* for *I go* (see Wright 1905, p. 297).

There are also some lexical items which are restricted to the southwestern dialects: *aftergrass* for 'aftermath' (second mowing of the grass); *(a)thwart* 'diagonally' (a Scandinavian loan word, cf. Old Norse *þvert*); *grandfer* 'granddad'; *pin-(bone)* 'hipbone' (of cattle); and *chibboles* 'spring onions' (a Romance loan word, cf. Old French *cibole*). Fischer (1976) discusses the lexical material in detail. The southwestern dialects are typically conservative, maintaining older forms and innovations—such as the voicing of fricatives—which were not taken into the standard except for isolated items such as *vat* (cf. German *Fass* 'barrel') and *vixen* (cf. *fox*).

The southwestern dialects can be divided into three subgroups: western Cornwall; eastern Cornwall, Devon, and western Somerset; and the rest of the southwestern region. In western Cornwall, Cornish, a Celtic language, was used until the end of the eighteenth century, and the English that replaced it reflects the standard more than the other southwestern dialects do. The influence of Cornish can be chiefly seen in some lexical borrowings peculiar to this area, although not occurring throughout it: *pig's crow* 'pigsty', *bucca* 'scarecrow', *cram* 'swath', *(piggy-)whidden* 'weakling'. Other words which are limited to western Cornwall include *riggers* 'cart-ladders' and *claw* 'prong' (see Fischer 1976).

The second area—eastern Cornwall, Devon, and western Somerset—is characterized by two phonological innovations. It has a front high rounded vowel [y:] where RP has [u:]. Historically this [y:] has developed from several sounds: Middle English *ǭ* (*boots*, *moon*, and *school*); Middle English *ŭ* (*bull* and *wool*); Middle English *eu* (*blue*, *dew*, and *few*); and Middle English *iu* (*new*). The development of Middle English *ī* and *ū* shows some peculiarities in this area. Middle English *ī*, in words like *time*, is represented by [æ:] in northern and southern Devon and [a:] in central Devon—both probably further developments from [aɪ] which is found in Cornwall. Western Somerset has [æɪ], and the rest of Somerset has [ɔɪ] which, together with [əɪ], is widespread in the rest of the South and West Midlands. In this latter area the [ɔɪ] from Middle English *ī* has merged with

Middle English *oi*. There are a few lexical items restricted to this second area: *saving* 'carting' (from Old French *salver*), *tamelamb* 'pet lamb', *is the daps of* 'resembles', and *swar* 'swath'.

There are also some dialect features which are shared by both of the two areas just described. The distinction between Middle English ẹ̄ and ę̄ has mostly been retained, although each map gives a slightly different picture. The latter has become [i] in *geese* and *green*, but the former—in *beans*, *peas*, *speaks*, *eat*, and *meat*—is either [ɛɪ] (in northern Devon and eastern Cornwall) or else [e:]. The words *east* and *team*, however, show [i] throughout the area, even though they are historically derived from Middle English ę̄. Middle English *ai* in words like *daisy* and *faint* merges with these reflexes of Middle English ę̄ as [ɛɪ].

The third subarea comprises the rest of the southwestern dialects and is characterized by nonoccurrence of the features of western Somerset, Devon, and Cornwall, although it retains preconsonantal and postvocalic [r] and participates in the voicing of initial fricatives.

In the space available here, it is not possible to present specimens from each of the three southwestern subregions, but the following passage shows some of the typical features characteristic of the whole area—*a*-prefixing and voicing of initial voiceless [f] and [s]:

> You're a-coming round to vind out something now as far as the old dialect is concerned, but you're really, what, fifty years or more too late. You zee, as far as that's concerned, the like o' me's spoilt. I'm spoilt as far as that's concerned.... The people has left here and that contact's gone, and you're contacting other people that have come in here (Smith 1973, p. 8).

Like many of the SED informants, this speaker believes that regional dialects have declined or are on the verge of disappearing, and while it is undoubtedly true that the southwestern dialects have changed in response to pressures of standardization, the passage shows some of the features long established in the English of this region.

Southeastern Dialects
The southeastern dialect area is much closer to the standard and RP, since its dialects—with strong influence from the central Midlands—provided the source for the standard. Many of the criteria that Ellis (1889, p. 131) used to characterize his southeastern area—comprising Kent and eastern Sussex—can no longer be found or occur sporadically and infrequently: [d] for [ð] in *that*, *there*, and *these*; or [w] for [v] in *vinegar* and *victuals*. The comparative particle is always *than*, there being no trace of *nor* which Ellis cites for this area. Two features that are still found, albeit receding, are [ɛ] for *a*, in words like *apples*, which occurs in central and northeastern Kent and in one locality each in Surrey and Sussex, and [i] for southeastern Middle English ę̄ (in words like *mice* and *lice*), which occurs in

southwestern Kent and in a larger area in southeastern Sussex (see Kurath and Lowman 1970, pp. 35-38).

Trudgill (1974) discusses several East Anglian features which are obviously recessive and gradually being replaced by RP or approximate RP forms. In many words, Middle English ǭ (RP [əu]) is shortened to [u] in northern and central Suffolk (in *both*, *comb*, and *food*). In *home*, [u] and [ʌ] extend westward into Cambridgeshire and Northamptonshire. The vowels in *hear* and *hare* merge in eastern Norfolk in [ɛ:ə], whereas in RP they are kept apart. Several lexical items are only to be found in all or parts of East Anglia: *dicky* 'donkey' in most of Norfolk and Suffolk; *dug* 'udder' in northern and central Norfolk; *pightle* 'paddock' in most of Norfolk and Suffolk and further west in Bedfordshire and Cambridgeshire; *hale* '(potato-)clamp' in northern and central Norfolk; *pushes* 'boils' and *ranny* 'shrew-mouse' in Cambridgeshire, parts of Essex, and one locality in Hertfordshire; *petman* 'weakling' in Norfolk and northern Suffolk; *broaches* 'pegs' (for thatch) in Norfolk, Suffolk and one locality in Essex. East Anglia is a relic area which retains many individual forms and yet, being so near London, its dialect is being continually influenced by the standard.

Aside from the material collected for this region by the SED, various studies have explored the dialects of rural people. The following specimen, though written by a person with no formal linguistic training, gives some sense of what outsiders view as the salient features of the southeastern rural dialects:

> They tell yow about th' owd dows [doves] in Trafalgar Square bein' so tame that fooks feed 'em out o' their hands. Somehow Oi fancy they sometime wish they could be a-layin' up in a dyke under an owd ellum tree wi' a double-barrelled gun a-waitin' t' git a shot at the dows comin' arter Farmer Giles' pays [peas] in the fild alongside the copse. [Claxton 1954, p. 116]

In addition to the features already mentioned, the epenthetic vowel in *ellum* 'elm' is typical of the region; the first *r* in *arter* is merely a convention to indicate vowel length in this nonrhotic area where the pronunciation [a:tə] *after* is widespread; and *Oi* 'I' indicates the centralized onset of the reflexes of Middle English ī in the Southeast (see Kurath and Lowman 1970, pp. 4-5). Vocalization of [l] is apparent in *owd* 'old' and *fooks* 'folks'; [e] in words spelled *ea* (e.g., *pays* 'peas') is apparently disappearing in the Southeast (see Orton, Sanderson, and Widdowson 1978, Ph76 and Kökeritz 1932, p. 18) though still found in the south central region and in Devon; [ɪ] in *git* 'get' is "extremely common in the Suffolk dialect" (Kökeritz 1932, p. 13) and likewise occurs in other regions.

The Midland Dialects

The Midland dialects are characterized by having [u] in words like *butter* and *thunder* and [a] in words like *chaff* and *last* where the southern dialects have [ʌ]

English in England and Wales

and [a:] or [ɑ:]. These dialects extend further to the north than the usual geographical concept of the Midlands and take in Cheshire, southern and central Lancashire, and the West Riding of Yorkshire. In the north they are separated from the northern dialects by a number of important distinctions shown by isoglosses stretching from the Humber estuary northwest to the Lune, the Humber-Lune Belt (see Kolb 1965). The Midland dialects are not uniform, and several Midland forms correspond to one northern form as can be seen from the following list:

1. Northern [u] (Middle English ū) versus a variety of diphthongs in the Midlands: [aʊ], [ɛʊ], [aɪ] in *house*, *snout*, and *cow*.
2. Northern [i] and [u] before *-nd* versus the Midland diphthongs [aɪ] and [aʊ] in *blind* and *pound*.
3. Northern [iə] (Middle English ǭ) versus Midland [u] and [ʊɪ] *boots*, *goose*, and *moon*.
4. Northern [iə] (Middle English ā, ǭ) versus Midland [ɛʊ]/[ʊə] in *spade*, *naked*, *both*, and *loaf*.
5. Northern [ʊə] (Middle English ǭ in open syllables) versus Midland [ɔɪ] in *coal*, *foal*, and *coat*.
6. Northern [i] and [iə] versus Midland [ɛɪ] and [e:] in *eat* and *speak*.

The Midland dialect region contains the large industrial conurbations of Merseyside, Manchester, West Yorkshire, and the West Midlands; these areas seem to be centers of linguistic development. It is almost impossible to find distinctive characteristics of the Midland dialects. Even internal divisions, although present, are extremely difficult to delimit accurately. On many SED maps there is a bewildering patchwork of different realizations of one sound—for example, the vowel in *house* occurs as [aʊ], [a:], [ɛə], [ɛʊ], [aɪ], [æ:], [ɛ:], and [æʊ]—and this gives the impression of complete randomness. However, on closer inspection, several areas emerge which show a consistent variety of different innovations or retentions. The East Midland counties—Nottinghamshire, Leicestershire, Rutland, Northamptonshire, and Bedfordshire—show mostly the forms of the standard language and thus will not be treated separately.

The West Midland dialect area—comprising southern Lancashire, Cheshire, Derbyshire, Staffordshire, northeastern Shropshire, and northern Warwickshire—is characterized by the retention of [g] in the word final cluster [ŋg] (in words like *tongue* and *tongs*) and the use of [ɔ] for RP [æ] before *n* (in *man*), although this latter feature extends further than *ng*, covering the whole of Lancashire in the north and extending as far as Herefordshire and Worcestershire in the south. The form *no* appears for *not* and *n't* in expressions like *(I) can no, (he) dare no* in the West Midlands. The southern part of this area—Staffordshire, Herefordshire, Worcestershire, and Gloucestershire—also shows the retention of preconsonantal and postvocalic [r] in words like *birds, forks, hare, hear, floor, flower*, and *farmer*, and a lengthened vowel, [æ:] or [a:], before *f* or *s* in *chaff* and *last*. These last two features are also found in southwestern dialects. In Shropshire there are relics of verb forms with the ending *-n*: *I bin* 'I am', *he bin* 'he is', *I han* 'I have', and *he han* 'he has'. The RP diphthong [ɔɪ] has three reflexes, all with unrounded first components, in the northern part of this area: [ɛɪ] in southeastern Lancashire, Cheshire, and northern Staffordshire, [ɑɪ] in southwestern Lancashire and western Derbyshire, and [aɪ] in northern and eastern Shropshire. In the case of the latter two—[ɑɪ] and [aɪ]—there is a merger of RP [ɔɪ] and [aɪ] (in *boy* and *by*, *voice* and *vice*). In Worcestershire and Gloucestershire, there are some occurrences of [əɪ] and [æɪ] in words like *boiling* and *oil*; the vowel in *voice* shows the unrounded forms only in Cheshire, northern Shropshire, northern Staffordshire, and western Derbyshire.

A second area among the Midland dialects comprises southern Lancashire, Cheshire, and western Yorkshire. Southern Lancashire and Cheshire show the development of a high front round [y:] from Middle English ǭ (RP [u]) in words like *goose* and *school*. This subarea shows [ɛə] for Middle English ǭl/ + *d* (RP [əu]) in *cold* and *old*, which extends into central and southern Derbyshire, northern Shropshire, and northern Staffordshire. The retention of preconsonantal and postvocalic *r* in words like *third*, *four*, and *butter* is also found in the north of Cheshire and southern and central Lancashire; *r* is pronounced as a dental fricative [ɹ] or frictionless continuant. Within this rhotic area, Middle English *ār* (in words like *hare*) and Middle English *ēr* (in words like *mare* and *pears*) merges as [ɜ:ʴ], but Middle English *air* (in *chair*) remains distinct and becomes [ɪəʴ]. A feature which characterizes this area is the form *hoo* for *she*, which occurs in southern and central Lancashire, Cheshire, northern and central Derbyshire, and the extreme west of Yorkshire, exactly parallel to the distribution of *hoo* in Middle English. Central and southern Lancashire, and on many maps most of western Yorkshire and northern Derbyshire, show [ɛɪ] for the lengthened vowel from Middle English ĕ in words like *speaks* and *meal*. In these areas, the reflexes of Middle English ĕ are distinguished from those of Middle English ę̄ (words like *beans* and *team* are pronounced with [ɪə]) and from those of Middle English ē̦ (words like *geese* and *green* are pronounced with [i]).

A third area is represented by Lincolnshire and shows some independent developments, in many cases with northern forms: [ɪə] for Middle English ę̄ (RP [i]) in words like *beans*; and [uə] for Middle English short ŏ when lengthened in words like *coal*. Middle English *ur* and *ir* in words like *cursing* and *birds* have become [ɔ] in Lincolnshire, northern and central Nottinghamshire, and southern Derbyshire, but in eastern Yorkshire they have become [ɒ]. The pronunciation [ɛə] occurs in Lincolnshire and occasionally in Yorkshire for Middle English ā (RP [eɪ]) in words like *spade*, whereas [e:] occurs in central and southern Lancashire, southern Yorkshire, Nottinghamshire, and northern Derbyshire.

A fourth and much smaller area is represented by the West Riding of Yorkshire or *Elmet* (the name of an ancient British Kingdom) (see Kolb 1973;

Petyt 1978). The form *shoo*, a blend of *hoo* and *she* occurs for 'she', a form which was also current in this area in Middle English. Verbs such as *speak* and *eat* have [e:] as their stem vowel in the past tense. *Mistall* 'cow-house', *(h)ime* 'hoarfrost', and *ranty-pole* 'seesaw' are lexical items which characterize this area. Phonological characteristics include the development of [uɪ] for Middle English ǭ (RP [u]) in words like *boots* and *goose*. Middle English short ŏ when lengthened (RP [əu]) has become [ɔɪ] in words like *coal*, *foal*, and *coat*.

With an area so diverse as the Midlands, it is difficult to illustrate the variety of its features in a brief passage. Tennyson's poems in Lincolnshire dialect are well-known but not entirely accurate representations of rural Midland dialect (see Tilling 1972); D. H. Lawrence has also used Midland features to distinguish cultivated and rustic characters in his fiction and drama. Nonetheless, the Midland region (outside of its urban centers) lacks a clear and uniform stereotype of the kind associated with the Southwest, East Anglia, or the northern region.

Northern Dialects

Northern dialects are separated from the Midland dialects by the differences reflected in the isoglosses of the Humber-Lune Belt. The vowel systems represented by the phonological isoglosses show that the northern dialects have very different reflexes of the Middle English long vowels which were transformed by the Great Vowel Shift in both the standard language and the dialects of the Midlands and the south. In northern dialects, Middle English ū (RP [au]) is retained as a monophthong; Middle English ǭ (RP [u]), ā (RP [eɪ]), and ǭ (RP [əu]) have merged in the diphthong [ɪə]; and Middle English short ŏ when lengthened has become [uə]. A morphological form which coincides with the Humber-Lune Belt is the distinction between northern *(I) is* and Midland *(I) am* (although eastern Yorkshire has both *am* and the contracted form *'s*). Northern *is* is attributed to Scandinavian influence, and a number of Scandinavian words have a southern boundary that coincides with the Humber-Lune Belt (the northern form is given first): *efter/after*, *stee/ladder*, *shoop/hip* 'fruit of the rose', *slaip/slippy*, *beck/brook*, *laik/play*. Another isogloss paralleling the Humber-Lune Belt is northern [n] versus Midland [ŋg] in words like *finger* and *hungry*.

The northern area is primarily rural apart from the conurbations of Tyneside and Cleveland (Middlesbrough). Like the Southwest, it is a relic area showing archaic forms as well as innovations which have not been accepted into the standard language. To the north, these dialects are separated from the dialects of Lowland Scots by the Scots [ʌ] versus northern [u] and the lack of palatal and velar fricatives [ç] and [x] which occur in Scots. The Scottish-English border is also marked by lexical items (see Glauser 1974).

Within the northern dialects, Northumberland has many features which set it off. RP *r* is pronounced as a uvular fricative—the Northumbrian burr—in words like *rat* and *red*, though [ɹ] does not occur in urban Tyneside (see Påhlsson 1972). RP initial *h* is retained in northern Durham, in eastern Cumberland, and in Northumberland in words like *hand* and *hearse*. In the same area, RP /ʍ/ is pronounced [hw]: *wheel* and *white*. Many characteristic forms in Northumberland are due to the development of unstressed vowels. RP [ə]—spelled *-er* in *butter* and *farmer*—occurs as [ɔʁ] in Northumberland and [əʁ] in northern Durham and the southern Northumberland coast. All the centering RP diphthongs end in [ɔʁ] in Northumberland in words like *fire, chair, flowers, hear, pears,* and *hare*. The unstressed vowel in the ending *-ing* (RP [ɪ]) in words like *shilling* and *morning* occurs as [ə] in Northumberland and northern Durham. A small area in southeastern Northumberland and northeastern Durham has [ə] as the vowel in plural ending *-es* in words like *bushes* and *(boot)laces*; a much larger area—comprising Northumberland, Durham, Cumberland, Westmoreland, and northern and central Lancashire—has [ə] for Middle English unstressed *-et* (RP [ɪt]) in words like *pocket* and *suet*.

Other features occur in smaller areas in the northeast. Middle English *ir* and *ur* (RP [ə:]) became [ɔʁ:] in central and southern Northumberland and northern Durham in words like *third, birds, words,* and *cursing*. In the eastern part of this area Middle English *ur* merges with Middle English *or* and *ōr* as [ɔʁ:] in words like *corn, ford, floor,* and *door*. Middle English *ŏ* has become [œ] in eastern Northumberland and northern Durham in *fox* and *dog*, but not in *bonnet* and *holly*. In Northumberland, eastern Cumberland, and northern Durham, Middle English *ī* (RP [aɪ]) in words like *ice, knife, white,* and *time* is diphthongized, but the resultant sound is [ɛɪ], which, in word final position, is restricted to northern Northumberland. The form *sall* for 'shall' occurs in central and eastern Yorkshire. A few lexical items are restricted to Northumberland and northern Durham: *sark* 'shirt' and 'vest', *wersh* 'insipid'. In Northumberland and nearly all of Durham, *netty* occurs for 'earth-closet', whereas *nessy* occurs in Cumberland, eastern Westmoreland, and northwestern Yorkshire.

Although many Scandinavian words have spread throughout England and into the standard, some are limited to the northern dialects: *whin* 'gorse', *laik* 'play', *lea* 'scythe', *lait* 'look for (it)', *blae-(berries)* 'bilberries', and *gaumless* 'silly'. Words not of Scandinavian origin found only in northern dialects include: *cuddy* 'donkey' in Durham, Cumberland, and Westmoreland; *bargham* 'collar' (for horses); and *fog* 'aftermath' and *cades* 'ticks' in Yorkshire, Westmoreland, Cumberland, Northumberland, and Durham.

A morphological feature of many northern dialects is *t'* as the definite article; it occurs in most northern counties except Lancashire and Northumberland. *T'* may occur before a vowel (e.g., *in t'oven*), but it is slightly more widespread before a consonant, *till t'sun*.[9] It is usually regarded as a feature of Yorkshire dialect but is in fact much more widespread.

Literary representations of northern dialects are relatively common and perhaps best known through Emily Brontë's *Wuthering Heights* (1847). Annual competitions of the Yorkshire Dialect Society continue to encourage both poetry and prose in the northern dialect; in the following stanza, Michael Park presents the views of a local resident of a seaside resort at the beginning of summer:

> Noo Summer's here, oor peace hes gone,
> Oor toon is oors noa mooar,
> Yon streets'll thrang wi rowdy fooak,
> An cars'll mek theer rooar;
> Thoo'll finnd noa space ti sit on t'sand,
> Thoo'll queue fer ivverythin,
> Soa lock up t'hoose, we'll stay i dooars
> Till Autumn cums agin!
>
> [Park 1975, p. 17]

Among the features represented here are: retention of [u] in *now*, *town*, *our*, *house*, and *comes*; [uə] in *no*, *more*, *folk*, *roar*, *so*, and *doors*; the definite article *t'* before consonants in *t'sand* and *t'hoose*; *thou* used here as it is found in rural dialects of the North Midland and northern regions (though *ye* is found in east central Northumberland); and [ɛ] in *make*—implied by the spelling *mek*—also a northern feature, though [a] also occurs in the region. Northern and nonnorthern dialects are sharply distinguished by the northern short [ɪ] in *find*.

English Urban Dialects

When serious interest in dialectal variation in English began in the nineteenth century, such investigators as A. J. Ellis and Joseph Wright devoted their attention to rural speech on the assumption that those varieties were relatively stable and hence could offer insights into earlier states of the language. Urban dialects were seldom described except for Cockney, the speech of people in the East End of London. Unlike other urban dialects, Cockney was regarded as the dialect of a coherent group of urban folk and thus worthy of study (though aspiring Londoners invested some effort in avoiding "Cockneyisms"). Recent field work from a sociolinguistic viewpoint, however, has provided more information about urban English, and it is largely from such sources that much of the following sketch has been drawn.[10]

Liverpool is part of the Merseyside conurbation (1971 population: 1,266,725), and its dialect—mainly used by working class speakers—is called *Scouse* (from *lobscouse* 'a stew made from leftover meat'). It contains elements from nearby rural dialects and is also influenced phonetically by Anglo-Irish since in the nineteenth century many Irish immigrants settled in Liverpool. Like northern speech varieties, it lacks RP [ʌ], replacing it by [ʊ]: [mʊd] 'mud'. Some speakers trying to avoid [ʊ] do not manage to arrive at [ʌ] but substitute [ə] for it: [məd]. Hypercorrections occur when [ʊ] is substituted in words that historically contain [ʌ]: [hʊd] for *hood*. RP [ɛə] *fare* and [ɔ:] *fur* merge in Scouse, but the resultant vowel varies from [ëə] to [ɛ:]: e.g., [bɛ:d] for *bird*. This merger is one of the most characteristic features of Liverpool speech. As in other West Midland dialects, the sequence *ng* in, for instance, *sing*, is pronounced [ŋg]. The consonant system shows some marked differences in phonetic realization from RP. The stops /p/, /t/, and /k/ may be realized as the corresponding fricatives [ɸ], [s], and [x] in word final position, and the stop /t/ is usually realized as a flap [ɾ] medially between vowels. The Anglo-Irish influence shows itself in the frequent substitution of [d] for [ð]: [də] 'the', [brid] 'breathe'. The glottal stop does not occur. The general articulatory setting is in the back of the mouth, making all consonants velarized. In intonation there is a threefold distinction between simple, intermediate, and complex tones, whereas RP has only simple and complex tones. The intermediate tones skip suddenly from one pitch level to another, whereas simple tones (i.e., fall or rise) and complex tones (i.e., fall-rise and rise-fall) glide smoothly up or down.

Like many other varieties of English that are readily identified by outsiders, Scouse has been provided with a humorous "phrase book" with sample texts (Shaw, Spiegl, and Kelly 1966). In addition to phrases with their "English" equivalents, this work contains a Scouse "translation" of portions of *The Rubáiyát of Omar Khayyám* of which the following is a sample (*moggies* 'cats', *jigger* 'back alley, passageway'):

> Gerrup dere La! De knocker-up sleeps light;
> Dawn taps yer winder, ends anudder night;
> And Lo! de dog-eared moggies from next-door
> Tear up de jigger fer an early fight.
>
> [P. 76]

The nineteenth-century translation of the *Rubáiyát* by Edward Fitzgerald provides the background for the Scouse version:

> Wake! For the Sun, who scattered into flight
> The Stars before him from the Field of Night,
> Drives Night along with them from Heav'n and strikes
> The Sultan's Turret with a Shaft of light.

The West Yorkshire conurbation (1971 population: 1,728,250) includes the cities of Leeds and Bradford. The variety described here is the model for the Yorkshire dialect as viewed by the average southerner. Many of its features are drawn from the surrounding rural dialects. The use of *t'* for the definite article is widespread in casual speech: *on t' road*. RP [ʌ] is pronounced as [ʊ]. The voiced stops /b/, /d/, and /g/ become devoiced before voiceless sounds: *Bradford* is [braḓfəd]; *good time* is [gʊḓ taim]. One semantic peculiarity is the use of *while* with the meaning 'until' which occurs in a large area of the north. (One widely known but unverified tale reports that British Rail supplied level crossings with signs saying "Stop while red light flashes"; according to the story, one literal-minded person waited patiently *while* 'until' the light began to flash and then stepped in front of the oncoming train!) Throughout West Yorkshire, negatives occur with secondary contractions (Petyt 1978). In RP the negative adverb *not* is contracted to *n't* after verbs: *is not* becomes *isn't* [ɪznt], *did not*, *didn't* [dɪdnt], and so on. In West Yorkshire speech, the last consonant of the verb is deleted—[ɪznt] becomes [ɪnt]; [dɪdnt] becomes [dɪnt]—a process that affects all the modals and auxiliary verbs. The forms *hasn't* and *hadn't* merge in [ant].

Many recent plays and films have been set in northern cities, and their authors sometimes draw on a repertoire of generally recognized features of northern urban varieties to establish the local identity of the characters. John Arden's *The Workhouse Donkey*, first produced in 1963, provides a typical example of what one might expect to hear in a "Yorkshire industrial town somewhere between Sheffield and Leeds":

> They'd take fright in this town if a centipede ran ower t'road. Get their names i' t'papers! They think it's worse nor doing murder! Ah well, we won't worry. We're getting some o' what we paid for. We can allus come again. [Arden 1964, p. 58]

The speaker of these lines, Labour Alderman Butterthwaite, is thus identified regionally, socially, and politically by his speech. Butterthwaite's Conservative counterpart in the play, Alderman Sir Harold Sweetman, is given no such distinguishing features of regional speech.

One identifying feature of the speech of the Bristol-Severnside conurbation (1971 population: 928,520) is the use of linking *l* after words ending in a vowel, (e.g., [əˈmɛrəkəl] 'America'); thus *Eva* and *evil* are both pronounced as [ivəl]. This "Bristol *l*" is a widespread but highly stigmatized feature and may result from the vocalization of final [l] in *bill*, *tool*, *nibble*, and *single* (see Wright 1905, p. 217; Hughes and Trudgill 1979, p. 47). Other features of this variety include the lack of contrast between [æ] and [ɑː], the presence of postvocalic [r], a general lengthening of short vowels, and a feature shared with London speech—a final [k] in words like *anything* and *something*.

The West Midlands conurbation (1971 population: 2,371,565) contains the cities of Wolverhampton, Birmingham, and Coventry. The speech of this area shows some similarities with that of Liverpool: *ng* is pronounced as [ŋg], and RP [ɛə] and [ɜː] merge as [œː]. There is no distinction between [ʊ] and [ʌ], and [a] occurs in *path* and *glass*. RP [i] and [u] are realized as [ɜɪ] and [ɜʊ] respectively, and [aɪ] is realized as [ɔɪ].[11]

The Tyneside Linguistic Survey, covering the Tyne and Wear conurbations (1971 population: 1,211,694), has produced several methodological papers, but there are few reports where data is discussed in detail. (There is, however, one case of a study of variation in intonation: Pellowe and Jones 1978.) Tyneside urban speech lacks the uvular [ʀ] or [ʁ] which occurs in rural Northumberland and Durham, but it shares other features with the surrounding rural dialects. RP [ɜ:] does not occur in broad Tyneside; instead, [ɔ:] is used and [fɔ:st] *first* is thus homophonous with *forced*. Tyneside has two long *a* phonemes, a back [ɑ:] in words spelled with *ar* (e.g., *farm*), and a front [a:] in words with *al* (e.g., *walk*). Final RP [ə] and the centering diphthongs [ɪə] and [ʊə] are pronounced [ɒ], [ɪɒ], [ʊɒ]. Intervocalic consonants are glottalized: e.g., [sɪtʔi] *city*, [hapʔi] *happy*. For the verb *to go* the form *gan* is used: *I gan* 'I go'.

The speech of Norwich (1971 population: 122,083) has been examined in detail by Trudgill (1974). Many of its features reflect the situation in the surrounding rural dialects, but one which does not is the loss of initial *h*, which is normally retained in the rural dialects. In the city, hypercorrection in an interview style is reflected in the above average number of *h*'s used by Trudgill's informants. The loss of [j] after initial consonants in *new*, *suit*, and *tune* is further advanced among working-class speakers than middle-class speakers. The use of [u] or [ʊ] for RP [əʊ] in words such as *road* is restricted to working-class speakers, whereas middle-class speakers have high scores for [əʊ] in all styles. RP [əʊ], from Middle English ǭ, is still kept separate from the reflexes of Middle English *ou* in Norwich (in, for example, [mʊun] *moan* and [mʌun] *mown*). The merger has taken place in the standard language and has been spreading through East Anglia from the southwest to the northeast and from middle-class speakers to working-class speakers. This tendency can be seen in Norwich, where the phonetic values for the reflexes of Middle English ǭ and *ou* are closer together for middle-class than working-class speakers (see Trudgill and Foxcroft 1978). A morphological feature that is differentiated by social class is the absence of the *-s* ending of the third person present in verbs. Middle-class speakers showed markedly fewer occurrences of no ending (e.g., *he go*) in both formal and casual style than working-class speakers.

One attempt to represent the speech of Norwich is found in Arnold Wesker's play *Roots* (first presented in 1959):

Beatie: What won't he give you now?
Jenny: 'Tent nothing wi' me gal. Nothing he do don't affect me. It's Mother I'm referring to.
Beatie: Don't he still give her much money?
Jenny: Money? She hev to struggle and skint all the time—*all* the time. Well it ent never bin no different from when we was kids hev it? [From Popkin 1964, p. 221]

Such dialogue, supplemented by a "Note on Pronunciation" supplied by the author, captures some of the attributes of Norwich speech described by Trudgill:

loss of present tense marker (*he do*), fronted [æ] in *hev* 'have', and shortened [e] in *ent* 'aint'. Multiple negation follows, in general, the patterns found in English throughout the world, and if Wesker can be regarded as accurate, this feature is well established in Norwich speech (e.g., *nothing he do don't affect me*).

The best-known of the London dialects is Cockney (the name is derived from *coken-ey* 'cock's egg', a contemptuous name for a town-dweller). It has always been regarded as nonprestigious but continues to thrive. The vowel system differs from RP in its phonetic realizations. RP [ʌ] is pronounced as [æ], and RP [æ] to avoid merging becomes [ɛ] or [ɛɪ]. Among the RP diphthongs [eɪ] becomes [æɪ], [əʊ] becomes [æʉ], [aɪ] becomes [ɒɪ], and [aʊ] becomes [æə]. These changes do not affect the number of distinctive units. However, Cockney has a contrast between [ɔ:] *paws* and [o:] *pause* which is absent in RP. Postvocalic *l*—either at the end of a word (e.g., *mill*) or before a consonant (e.g., *milk*)—is vocalized. The initial voiceless stops /p/, /t/, and /k/ are heavily aspirated before vowels, and the consonant *h* is invariably dropped. The distinction in RP between /θ/ and /f/—*thread* and *Fred*—or medially, between /ð/ and /v/—*slither* and *sliver*—does not exist in Cockney, where only the labiodental is present. A favorite example to show the incidence of /f/ and /v/ is: *How many feathers on a thrush's throat? Answer: Five thousand five hundred and thirty three.*

The Music Hall tradition of the comic Cockney has made available some of the stereotypes of the variety to persons who would not otherwise have direct exposure to it, and recently televised variety programs have extended the audience for this kind of entertainment. The adaptation of Shaw's *Pygmalion* in the musical *My Fair Lady* has given worldwide exposure to Cockney speech, and Shaw's representation of Eliza's speech when she first appears on stage gives a fair sample of Cockney style:

The Flower Girl: Nah then, Freddy; look wh' y' gowin, deah.
Freddy: Sorry.
The Flower Girl: Theres menners f' yer. Tə-oo banches o voylets trod into the mad.
The Mother: How do you know that my son's name is Freddy, pray?
The Flower Girl: Ow, eez yə-ooa san, is e? Wal, fewd dan y' də-ooty bawmz a mather should, eed now bettern to spawl a pore gel's flahrzn than ran awy athaht pyin. Will ye-oo py me f'them? [Here, with apologies, this desperate attempt to represent her dialect without a phonetic alphabet must be abandoned as unintelligible outside London.] [Shaw 1972, 4.671]

[Oh, he's your son, is he? Well, if you'd done your duty by him as a mother should, he'd know better than to spoil a poor girl's flowers and then run away without paying. Will you pay me for them?—Eds.]

Shaw's literal representation of Cockney, though quickly abandoned as his textual note shows, encompasses a remarkable number of features: loss of initial [h] in *eez* 'he's'; [ɛ] for [æ] in *menners* 'manners'; [æ] for [ʌ] in *banches* 'bunches', *mad* 'mud', and *mather* 'mother'; [æə] for [aʊ] in *flahrz* 'flowers' and *nah* 'now'; [aə] for [eɪ] in *pyin* 'paying'; [ɒɪ] for [aɪ] in *voylets* 'violets'; diphthongized [u] in *two* and *duty*. Though the accuracy of Shaw's Cockney dialogue has sometimes been questioned, the most careful examination of the subject concludes that "Shaw is a rather better observer than most other literary men" (Sivertsen 1960, p. 164).

Since 1945 there has been a widespread immigration into England from the West Indies and the Indian subcontinent. In 1971 the estimated population from the West Indies was 302,900, and the estimated population from the Indian subcontinent was 462,000, but these figures do not include children born in England and Wales of West Indian or Asian parents. The main reasons for this immigration were pressure of population in the homeland, the wish for economic prosperity, and political uncertainty or turmoil. Although the number of immigrants is small, they have tended to settle in urban centers and hence form significant communities in the major cities. As a minority with little political power, these immigrants have had virtually no effect on the established varieties of English except in the domain of loan words for types of food: *callaloo, cassareep, poppadom, birayani, korma*.

The younger generation of both groups has assimilated linguistically to the local urban speech variety. A recent study of the assimilation of Sikh children in Leeds (Agnihotri 1979) shows that after a stay of ten years or more, Sikh children used the following features almost as frequently as local nonimmigrant children: the glottal stop for [t]; [a] for RP [æ] (in words like *man* and *at*) and for RP [ɑː] (e.g., in *past*); [ʊ] in words like *bus* and *cup*; dropping of initial [h] in words like *half* and *home*; and [tˢ] for [tʰ] in words like *time*. They also lost typically Indian features, substituting RP nonretroflex alveolar stops for [ṭ] and [ḍ], losing any *r*-coloration of vowels, and lastly acquiring [θ] and [ð], for which they had previously substituted [d]. Girls assimilated slightly more quickly than boys and lost the Indian features more rapidly.

Language choice among immigrant groups presents a complex problem for the young. On the one hand, they wish to communicate with parents and other adults who are dominant in another language; on the other, they wish to participate in the full range of opportunities offered by British life. Recent studies illustrate just what competing loyalties influence immigrant communities; a study of language attitudes in Leicester, for instance, elicited the following two views:

> If I didn't speak Gujarati, I would feel drowned in a bucket of water. I would suffocate if I didn't speak Gujarati. If an Indian tries to speak to me in English I always ask "Can't you speak Gujarati?" If he can't, I feel distant from him.

I was at a polytechnic in London and a year passed before I spoke any Gujarati. Even when I met a Gujarati from Leicester we got to know each other in English and wouldn't dream of speaking anything else. [Mercer, Mercer, and Mears 1979, p. 23]

Both social and linguistic forces will shape the future of these two viewpoints and influence the maintenance of Gujarati, the acquisition of local norms of English, or the development of some variety of language mixture.

A study of young adult West Indians in London showed that they had adapted their speech more in the direction of RP than toward the local urban variety (see Wells 1973). When the adaptation was a phonetic one—using [ð] instead of [d] or [eː], or [oː] instead of [iɛ] or [uɔ]—most speakers were quite successful. However, in some cases one Jamaican Creole phoneme corresponded to two in RP and presented difficulties in the acquisition of RP; in Jamaican Creole [i] + [r] corresponds to both RP [iə] and [eə] (*fear* and *fare* being pronounced the same). There seems to be no sign, as yet, of any substantial impact of West Indian Creole and Indian English on English urban dialects, but it may be that there is some West Indian influence among younger English speakers, as intimated by the following quotation:

The endlessly stretched vowels of Alf Garnett, the absolute epitome of working-class narrowness and racial bigotry, were further inflected (and *undercut*) by the smattering of patois (ya raas!) picked up by every self-respecting skinhead from reggae records and from West Indian colleagues at school and work. [Hebdige 1979, p. 57]

Such observations suggest a complex set of interactions between urban working-class English people and immigrants from both the West Indies and the Asian subcontinent. While English will certainly come to dominate the immigrant communities, aspects of immigrant speech may continue to influence urban norms, particularly in domains like popular music, where—as in the case of reggae—the immigrant culture presents an appealing image to urban youth. Within the educational system, special attention is now being given to the varieties of English used by immigrant groups based on the growing awareness that "we are not meeting the legitimate needs of children from ethnic minorities" (Edwards 1979, p. 145; see also Miller 1980).

Conclusion

Linguistic variation in England and Wales has changed in character and extent over the centuries. In early times a mainly rural, nonmobile population maintained many rural dialects. In medieval and early modern times, as the city of London grew in importance and became the source and focal point of the standard language, the rural dialects became more restricted in use. As the written standard was diffused among educated speakers, the oral use of rural dialects subsequently became nonprestigious, and they came to typify rustic and lower-class speakers. With the rapid urbanization consequent on the industrial revolution, rural dialects declined even further. The influx of people to the towns and cities created new urban dialects, especially among lower-class speakers. We can trace linguistic variation on a social basis in London back to the sixteenth century, although it was in the nineteenth century that most urban dialects became fully established.

In linguistic variation in England and Wales, two opposing tendencies can be seen at work. The first leads toward uniformity through such channels as broadcasting and education and through the upward mobility of speakers who feel that they must refine their speech. The second tendency works toward the retention and acceptance of linguistic variation, often through appeals to regional or class loyalty. Responding to such loyalties, working-class men generally have more nonstandard features than working-class women, since the men feel more secure in their linguistic environment. The increasing prominence of successful people in business, sport, and entertainment who do not shed their regional or class accent shows that it is not necessary to drop one's local accent if one is to succeed. Of these two tendencies, it is probably the second which is in the ascendent, exemplified by the increasing use of [a] in words like *hat* instead of [æ] (in RP [hæt]). Today, then, there is a more tolerant attitude toward linguistic variation than was true a generation ago. Speakers are perhaps beginning to be judged more by what they are saying and less by whether they conform to the norms of a prestige dialect.

NOTES

I am deeply grateful to colleagues at York University for comments and assistance and to Richard W. Bailey, Manfred Görlach, and James Sledd for help in preparing this essay.

1. From *The Boke Named the Governour*, quoted in Dobson 1969, p. 420.
2. George Puttenham, *The Arte of English Poesy* (1589), quoted by Dobson 1969, p. 420.
3. This and similar information is published in Orton, Sanderson, and Widdowson 1978, maps M68–69.
4. Lines 621–30. *Enneude* 'restored', *frowards* 'perverse or ungovernable things', *ordinately* 'in due order', *wot* 'know'. Quoted from Rollins and Baker 1954, p. 77.
5. Some adjacent labials did not hinder the lowering of Middle English *u*: *pulse*, *bud*, and *butter*.
6. I am indebted to Dr. A. R. Thomas of the Department of Linguistics, University College of North Wales, Bangor, who generously made available to me his manuscript, "The English Language in Wales." Virtually all the data contained in this section stem from his detailed study.

7. While the use of Welsh has declined, its maintenance as a language through education and broadcasting remains focal for nationalist groups. For an analysis of this situation and a map showing the *increase* in Welsh in the northwest and center of the country, see Williams 1979.
8. The intermediate status of Midland dialects between North and South is very ancient. Writing in 1387, John Trevisa observed that "men of myddel Engelond, as it were parteners of þe endes, vnderstondeþ bettre þe side languages, norþerne and souþerne, þan norþerne and souþerne vnderstondeþ eiþer oþer" (quoted by Wakelin 1977, p. 34).
9. See Wright 1892, pp. 111–12; Kolb 1966, maps 12 and 13; and Barry 1972.
10. Unless otherwise noted, the following discussion is indebted to essays in Trudgill 1978, to Hughes and Trudgill 1979, and to Wells 1970.
11. A description of the urban dialect of Birmingham, though based on a series of comic "monologues," is to be found in Wilde 1938.

REFERENCES

Agnihotri, Rama Kant. *Processes of Assimilation: A Sociolinguistic Study of Sikh Children in Leeds*. Ph.D. dissertation, University of York, 1979.

Arden, John. *The Workhouse Donkey*. New York: Grove Press, 1964.

Aubrey, John (1626?–97). *Brief Lives*. Edited by Oliver Lawson Dick. Ann Arbor: University of Michigan Press, 1962.

Barber, Charles. *Linguistic Change in Present-Day English*. Edinburgh: Oliver and Boyd, 1964.

———. *Early Modern English*. London: Deutsch, 1976.

Barry, Michael V. "The Morphemic Distribution of the Definite Article in Contemporary Regional English." In *Patterns in the Folk Speech of the British Isles*, edited by Martyn F. Wakelin, pp. 164–81. London: Athlone Press, 1972.

Blair, Peter Hunter. *An Introduction to Anglo-Saxon England*. Cambridge: At the University Press, 1956.

Claxton, A. O. D. *The Suffolk Dialect of the Twentieth Century*. Ipswich: Boydell Press, 1954.

Dobson, E. J. "Early Modern Standard English." In *Approaches to English Historical Linguistics*, edited by Roger Lass, pp. 419–39. New York: Holt, Rinehart and Winston, 1969.

Edwards, V. K. *The West Indian Language Issue in British Schools: Challenges and Responses*. London: Routledge and Kegan Paul, 1979.

Ellis, A. J. *Early English Pronunciation*. Pt. 5, *The Existing Phonology of English Dialects*. London: Trübner and Co., 1889.

Finkenstaedt, Thomas, and Wolff, Dieter. *Ordered Profusion: Studies in Dictionaries and the English Lexicon*. Heidelberg: Carl Winter, 1973.

Fischer, Andreas. *Dialects in the South-West of England: A Lexical Investigation*. Cooper Monographs, no. 25. Berne: Francke, 1976.

Fisher, John H. "Chancery and the Emergence of Standard English." *Speculum* 52 (1977):870–99.

Fudge, Erik. "Long and Short [æ] in One Southern British Speaker's English." *Journal of the International Phonetic Association* 7 (1977):55–65.

Giles, Howard, and Powesland, Peter F. *Speech Style and Social Evaluation*. London: Academic Press, 1975.

Glauser, Beat. *The Scottish-English Linguistic Border: Lexical Aspects*. Cooper Monographs, no. 20. Berne: Francke, 1974.

Gneuss, Helmut. "The Origin of Standard Old English and Æthelwold's School at Winchester." *Anglo-Saxon England* 1 (1970):63–83.

Hebdige, Dick. *Subculture: The Meaning of Style*. London: Methuen, 1979.

Hughes, Arthur, and Trudgill, Peter. *English Accents and Dialects: An Introduction to Social and Regional Varieties of British English*. London: Edward Arnold, 1979.

Jones, Daniel. *The Pronunciation of English*. 4th ed. Cambridge: At the University Press, 1956.

Kökeritz, Helge. *The Phonology of the Suffolk Dialect*. Uppsala: Uppsala Universitets Årsskrift, 1932.

Kolb, Eduard. "Skandinavisches in den nordenglischen Dialekten." *Anglia* 83 (1965), maps 14 and 15.

———. *Phonological Atlas of the Northern Region*. Berne: Francke, 1966.

———. " 'Elmet': A Dialect Region in Northern England." *Anglia* 91 (1973):285–313.

Kurath, Hans, and Lowman, Guy S., Jr. *The Dialectal Structure of Southern England: Phonological Evidence*. Publications of the American Dialect Society, no. 54. University, Ala: University of Alabama Press, 1970.

Labov, William, and Nunberg, Geoffrey. "Two Problematic Mergers in the History of English." In *A Quantitative Study of Sound Change in Progress*, edited by William Labov, Malcah Yaeger, and Richard Steiner, pp. 276–97. Philadelphia: U.S. Regional Survey, 1972.

Marchand, Hans. *The Categories and Types of Present-Day English Word-Formation*. 2d ed. Munich: Beck, 1969.

Mercer, Neil; Mercer, Elizabeth; and Mears, Robert. "Linguistic and Cultural Affiliation amongst Young Asian People in Leicester." In *Language and Ethnic Relations*, edited by Howard Giles and Bernard Saint-Jacques, pp. 15–26. Oxford: Pergamon Press, 1979.

Miller, Jane. "How Do You Spell *Gujarati*, Sir?" In *The State of the Language*, edited by Leonard Michaels and Christopher Ricks, pp. 140–51. Berkeley: University of California Press, 1980.

Orton, Harold, and Dieth, Eugen. *Survey of English Dialects*. Introduction and 4 vols. Leeds: Edward Arnold, 1962–71.

Orton, Harold, and Wright, Nathalia. *A Word Geography of England*. London, New York, and San Francisco: Seminar Press, 1974.

Orton, Harold; Sanderson, Stewart; and Widdowson, John. *The Linguistic Atlas of England*. London: Croom Helm; New York: Humanities Press, 1978.

Påhlsson, Christer. *The Northumbrian Burr: A Sociolinguistic Study*. Lund: Gleerup, 1972.

Park, Michael. "Three Seaside Views." *Transactions of the Yorkshire Dialect Society* 75 (1975):17.

Pellowe, John, and Jones, Val. "On Intonational Variability in Tyneside Speech." In

Sociolinguistic Patterns in British English, edited by Peter Trudgill, pp. 101–21. London: Edward Arnold, 1978.

Petyt, Malcolm. "Secondary Contractions in West Yorkshire Negatives." In *Sociolinguistic Patterns in British English*, edited by Peter Trudgill, pp. 91–100. London: Edward Arnold, 1978.

Popkin, Henry, ed. *The New British Drama*. New York: Grove Press, 1964.

Pyles, Thomas. *The Origins and Development of the English Language*. New York: Harcourt, Brace and World, 1964.

Rollins, Hyder E., and Baker, Herschel, eds. *The Renaissance in England*. Boston: D. C. Heath, 1954.

Ross, Alan S. C., et al. *Noblesse Oblige*. London: Hamish Hamilton, 1956.

Shaw, Frank; Spiegl, Fritz; and Kelly, Stan [Stan Bootle]. *Lern Yerself Scouse*. Liverpool: Scouse Press, 1966.

Shaw, George Bernard. *The Bodley Head Bernard Shaw*. London: Bodley Head, 1972.

Sivertsen, Eva. *Cockney Phonology*. Oslo Studies in English, no. 8. Oslo: Publications of the British Institute in the University of Oslo, 1960.

Smith, J. B. "Oral Tradition in the South-West of England." *Transactions of the Yorkshire Dialect Society* 73 (1973):8–15.

Strang, Barbara M. H. *A History of English*. London: Methuen and Co., 1970.

Strevens, Peter. *British and American English*. London: Collier-Macmillan, 1972.

Tilling, Philip M. "Local Dialect and the Poet." In *Patterns in the Folk Speech of the British Isles*, edited by Martyn F. Wakelin, pp. 88–108. London: Athlone Press, 1972.

Trudgill, Peter. *The Social Differentiation of English in Norwich*. Cambridge: At the University Press, 1974.

Trudgill, Peter, ed. *Sociolinguistic Patterns in British English*. London: Edward Arnold, 1978.

Trudgill, Peter, and Foxcroft, Tina. "On the Sociolinguistics of Vocalic Mergers: Transfer and Approximation in East Anglia." In *Sociolinguistic Patterns in British English*, edited by Peter Trudgill, pp. 69–79. London: Edward Arnold, 1978.

Viereck, Wolfgang. "The Dialectal Structure of British English: Lowman's Evidence." *English World-Wide* 1 (1980):25–44.

Wakelin, Martyn F. *English Dialects: An Introduction*. 2d ed. London: Athlone Press, 1977.

Waugh, Evelyn. *Decline and Fall*. New York: Dell, 1959.

Wells, J. C. "Local Accents in England and Wales." *Journal of Linguistics* 6 (1970):231–52.

———. *Jamaican Pronunciation in London*. Publications of the Philological Society, no. 25. Oxford: Blackwell, 1973.

Wilde, Hans-Oskar. *Der Industrie-Dialekt von Birmingham*. Halle: Max Niemeyer, 1938.

Williams, Colin H. "An Ecological and Behavioural Analysis of Ethnolinguistic Change in Wales." In *Language and Ethnic Relations*, edited by Howard Giles and Bernard Saint-Jacques, pp. 27–55. Oxford: Pergamon Press, 1979.

Wright, Joseph. *A Grammar of the Dialect of Windhill in the West Riding of Yorkshire*. London: English Dialect Society, 1892.

———. *English Dialect Grammar*. Oxford: Oxford University Press, 1905.

Wyld, H. C. *A History of Modern Colloquial English*. Oxford: Blackwell, 1936.

The English Language in Scotland
Suzanne Romaine

The geographical area which is called Scotland today has long been the scene of great linguistic diversity.[1] By the ninth century A.D., there were four distinct groups of people who inhabited Scotland: (1) the Picts, a native group about whose origins and language little is known and who occupied the interior and the eastern coasts north of the Firth of Forth; (2) the Gaelic-speaking Scots, who were Irish in origin and who occupied the western coasts and islands from Kintyre north; (3) the Britons, who spoke a variety of early Welsh and who occupied the central valley and southern Scotland; and (4) the Angles, who settled in various parts of what is now southern Scotland but most numerously in the southeast. The northern islands, Orkney and Shetland, and the adjoining mainland of Caithness were ruled by peoples whose language, Norn, was akin to Old Norse.

Today, this linguistic diversity is still reflected in place names, distinctive elements of vocabulary, and certain substratum effects that can be identified in some varieties of Scots and Scottish English, but the long history of influence from the English of England has affected every native language and forced all of them toward functional restriction or extinction.

The profound changes in English that took place as a consequence of the Norman invasion of England in 1066 soon affected southern and central Scotland. During the long reign of Malcolm Canmore (1058 to 1093), English refugees fled northward and Malcolm married Margaret, sister of the claimant to the English throne. During Malcolm's reign, southern Scotland began to experience the first stages of anglicization, and his successors—Alexander I (d. 1124) and David I (d. 1153)—completed the process by which the church abandoned the Celtic calendar and practices in favor of those current in England and by which traditional patterns of land tenure were replaced by the Anglo-Norman feudal system. Political power was held by native Scots and by newcomers from England who eventually made Norman French the spoken language of the court. Written records, however, were kept in Latin, which also served as the spoken language of church services. All the languages of Scotland were doubtless stratified by region and social class. Peasants in rural areas were probably not much disturbed in their linguistic preferences, though the followers of the English and Norman lords included overseers who introduced languages new to the countryside. Scots who lived in or near the cities established by royal charter—the *burghs*—had more contact with English and French, while those in regular residence with the nobility were likely to have acquired the language that finally prevailed, "the new, highly-Frenchified English" (Murison 1979, p. 5).

As the numbers of Normans and English increased, Gaelic was forced into the hinterlands—into Galloway (where it eventually died out in the seventeenth century) and into the Highlands. Gaelic persisted as the primary language of the Highlands until the Jacobite risings of 1715 and 1745 opened the region to military occupation and English influence. Today, Gaelic is mainly restricted to the Outer Hebrides, the islands along the northwest coast of Scotland, where more than half the population make regular use of Gaelic and where the language is supported in school programs. According to the 1971 census, there are about 89,000 Gaelic speakers in Scotland, more than half of them resident in the Highlands and Western Isles. As a result of urbanization, more than 12,000 live in Glasgow (see Thomson 1979).

The medieval period in Scotland was marked by continued linguistic diversity and by a series of wars against English attempts to annex Scottish territory. Strong and effective nationalism helped to consolidate the distinctive English of Scotland into a national language enriched by foreign borrowings that came as a result of trade by Scottish merchants in northern Europe.[2] In Scotland, English began to supersede French at an early date. Literary works in English, most notably Barbour's *The Brus* (1375), began to appear, and from 1424, statutes adopted by the Scottish Parliament began to be written in English. By 1450, the northern dialect of English ceased to be used for official or literary purposes in England, but the northern English of Scotland flourished. By the end of the fifteenth century, Scots was a fully elaborated standard and used in all spheres of both public and private life.

A natural consequence of Scotland's political hostility to England was a growing sense of separate linguistic development. In the earliest records, the English of Scotland is referred to by Scottish writers as "Inglis," but by 1494, Adam Loutfut referred to his language variously as "Inglis" and "Scottis." A Spanish diplomat who visited the court of James IV in Edinburgh in 1498 compared the difference between Scots and English to that distinguishing Aragonese from Castilian Spanish. Some writers perceived Scots to be inadequate for literary purposes, and, though the same complaint was made against English throughout the sixteenth century, it is significant that Gavin Douglas justified his borrowings from Latin, French, and English in his translation of the *Aeneid* (1513) by saying that he had chosen borrowed words "quhar scant was Scottis." Though Scots continued its development as a fully elaborated standard, it reached its high-water mark as a literary language in the sixteenth century and was subsequently "improved" by imitation and borrowing from the English of England.

Throughout the period of the growth of Scots, the language remained closely affiliated with northern varieties of English, and regular contact between Edinburgh and London made Scottish merchants and diplomats aware of linguistic developments and fashions in the English capital. A large common core of shared features between Scots and English made the two varieties generally intelligible, and many borrowings and innovations in English eventually reached and were incorporated into Scots. English literature became popular in Scotland and shaped both the styles and language of native writers. Increasing numbers of face-to-face contacts and intermarriage across the border led by the seventeenth century to a situation in which Scots manifested the influence of dialect interference and change in the direction of English.

While sporadic anglicisms had been common under the influence of Chaucer and his successors, the practice of anglicizing texts apparently began as early as the fifteenth century in the adoption of English rhyme words in poetry. These words came to be regarded as stylistic options, and eventually it became fashionable for certain anglicisms and the corresponding Scots forms to occur side by side in some varieties of verse. After the Scottish Reformation in the sixteenth century, almost everything printed in England became available in Scotland, and publications in English greatly outnumbered those in Scots. English spellings and vocabulary became familiar to Scottish readers, and anglicisms began to appear more and more in the writings of Scots authors. This familiarity with English created a vicious circle and drew Scotland into a spiral of anglicization. The more Scots read, the more familiar and easier English became, and Scottish literature no longer held to an autonomous tradition.

Perhaps the greatest single influence in the anglicizing trend was the use in Scotland of an English translation of the Bible. Every householder worth 300 *merkis* 'marks' was obliged to possess a Bible according to a Scottish law of 1579. Virtually everyone had some exposure to this form of English either at home in the written form or at church in spoken form. Scottish children learned to read from an English Bible. At the same time, the Scottish gentry were becoming increasingly more anglicized. After the mid-seventeenth century, nearly all titled Scots spent some time in southern England, and nearly all eminent Scots had visited London. Eventually, in the late eighteenth century, it became common practice to send sons of upper-class families to English schools. There was more intermarriage between the Scots and English gentry, and the upper class increasingly became a hybrid group of Anglo-Scots. Thus, the use of Scots and English became polarized so that the most fully Scottish styles of writing and speaking were associated with less serious styles of writing, with a colloquial register, and with the lower classes; dignified writing and the spoken language of the Scottish gentry were associated with English.

Another factor with far-reaching implications was the practice of Scottish printers in the sixteenth century. Not only did they publish a large number of English works, but they were also responsible for the anglicization of Scottish ones. Anglicization depended on some linguistic sophistication and required an awareness of linguistic differences between Scots and English. The anglicization of Scots texts reveals that printers and the literate public were growing conscious of such differences. The *Basilicon Doron* of King James VI (James I of England after 1603) provides a revealing instance of the process. As composed in 1598, the text is in the normal Scots of the day, but when it was printed for private circulation in 1599, many changes were made in the direction of English: *ken* is replaced by *know*, *thir* by *these* and *mekill* by *much*. Enlarged and revised for a larger audience—apparently by the king himself with the assistance of an English printer—the published text of 1603 is almost entirely English, with Scots idioms replaced by English ones in addition to changes in spelling and vocabulary (see Templeton 1973, p. 8).

Scotticisms exist at all linguistic levels. Some variation in pronunciation is clearly reflected in the spelling system (e.g., *ony* and *mony* for English *any* and *many*); a few Scots spellings reflect only different spelling conventions (e.g., Scots *punischment* for English *punishment*; Scots *quhan* alternates with English *when*). Many Scots words, however, have no direct equivalents in English (e.g., *ashet* 'platter', *bairn*, *wean* 'child', *burn* 'stream', *ilk* 'each', *syne* 'since, ago'). Scots idioms and syntax, as I will show later in this essay, have gradually been anglicized, but often in a distinctively Scottish way. For instance, Scots followed the development of English periphrastic negative and interrogative constructions in the sixteenth century so that *he cums nocht* becomes *he's no cumin* and *he cam nocht* becomes *he didna cum* (Aitken 1979, p. 88).

An extract from the *Memoirs* of Sir James Melville, written late in the sixteenth century, shows the characteristic blend of Scots and English features that was typical of Scottish practices in his day:

> Then sche entrit to dicern what kynd of coulour of hair was reputed best; and inquyred whither the Quenis or hirs was best, and quhilk of them twa was fairest. I said, the fairnes of them baith was not ther worst faltes. Bot sche was ernest with me to declaire quhilk of them I thoucht fairest. I said, sche was the fairest Quen in England, and ours the fairest Quen in Scotland. Yet sche was ernest. I said, they wer baith the fairest ladyes of ther courtes, and that the Quen of England was whytter, bot our Quen was very lusome. Sche inquyred quhilk of them was of hyest stature. I said, our Quen. Then sche said, the Quen was ouer heych, and that hir self was nother ouer hich nor ouer laich. [Quoted by Templeton 1973, p. 18]

English spellings alternate with Scots ones (e.g., English *what* and *whither* with Scots *quhilk* 'which'), and the influence of Scots pronunciations is also present (e.g., *twa* 'two', *thoucht* 'thought', *baith* 'both', and *hich/heych* 'high, tall'). Scots cognate forms are also apparent—*laich* 'small' (cf. English *low*) and *lusome* 'lovely' (cf. English *lovesome*). Syntactic patterns generally agree with the ones current in the English of Melville's day.

As anglicization took place, the grammatical system was first to conform to English patterns in the written language, and by 1700, only a few distinctive points of Scots grammar remained. In earlier Scots, the present tense of the verb ends in *-is* or *-s* throughout the paradigm except when the subject is the first person singular or plural personal pronoun directly adjacent to the verb (e.g., from William Dunbar's "The Merchants of Edinburgh": "Your foirstairis makis your housis merk [Your stairs make your houses dark]"), a trait that disappeared from the written language in the eighteenth century.[3] The distinction in Middle English between present participle (formed with *-and/-end*) and verbal noun (formed with *-ing*) survived in Scots. These two endings make possible the contrast between *the kyng is cumand* 'the king is coming (tomorrow)' and *the kingis cuming* 'the king's coming (was soon expected)'. In some modern dialects the vowel quality of the final syllable preserves the distinction (e.g., [kʌmən] *coming* [participle] and [kʌmin] *coming* [verbal noun]). As Sir James A. H. Murray wrote a century ago, "It is as absurd to a Southern Scot to hear *eating* used for both his *eiting* and *eitand*, as it is to an Englishman to hear *will* used for both his *will* and *shall*. When he is told that 'John was *eating*', he is strongly tempted to ask what kind of *eating* he proved to be" (1873, p. 211). Yet another distinction in verb morphology separated Scots and English. In Scots, the past tense and past participle of weak verbs end in *-it* (e.g., *he callyt on hym* 'he called on him') rather than the *-d* used in English.

Anglicization followed a pattern in which a Scots element gave way to an English one through a period of alternation or variation where the options coexisted. There is good evidence to suggest that the relative marker, for example, varied in response to both stylistic and linguistic factors. The frequency with which noun phrases in certain syntactic positions are relativized is a sensitive indicator of stylistic level as well as of syntactic complexity in Middle Scots texts from the first half of the sixteenth century. As demonstrated more fully elsewhere (see Romaine 1980*a* and 1981), we can view the process by which WH-forms (e.g., *which*, *who*, etc.) and WH-relativizing strategies worked their way into the native Scots system as one of "syntactic diffusion." Consider, for example, the following, both from the sixteenth century:

> This Frenche man *that* is to cum . . . (epistolary prose).
> Eftir this counsale he slew all the friendis pertenyng to Durstis *quhilkis* wer convenit at his request (narrative prose).

It appears that WH-marked relative clauses entered the language and spread from more formal to less formal styles and from less frequently relativized syntactic positions (e.g., genitive) to more frequently relativized ones (e.g., subject), gradually displacing *that* as a relative clause marker. While the modern written language shows WH-forms in nearly all styles and all syntactic positions, there remains a significant residue of *that* forms in the spoken language:

> That's the man 'at's hoose was brunt.
> [That's the man whose house was burned.]

> The woman that's sister mairriet the postie.
> [The woman whose sister married the postman.]

The kye that's caur were born aa about the same time.
[The cattle whose calves were all born about the same time.]

Such examples—these are from the *Scottish National Dictionary*—illustrate that stylistically stratified variability can persist over long periods of time.[4] The absence of WH-relative markers in restrictive clauses is one of the striking features of modern spoken Scots.

By the beginning of the eighteenth century, there was little opposition to the anglicizing trend. Though Allan Ramsay (1684/5–1758) revived Scots poetry, his lyrics and short poems were explicitly colloquial and informal. In the following typical stanza, Ramsay dramatizes the reluctance of a young girl to be wooed by a *carle* 'old man':

> The carle has nae fault but ane,
>   For he has land and dollars plenty;
> But waes me for him! skin and bane
>   Is no for a plump lass of twenty.
> Howt awa! I winna hae him,
>   Na forsooth I winna hae him;
> What signifies his dirty riggs
>   And cash without a man with them?
>   [MacQueen and Scott 1966, pp. 323–24]

Scots vocabulary appears, but it is mostly transparent to English readers: *ane* 'one', *waes me* 'woe is me', *bane* 'bone', *hoot awa!* 'nonsense!', and *riggs* 'arable lands'. Scots patterns of negation—*nae fault* 'no fault', *is no* 'is not', and *winna* 'will not'—give a distinctive flavor to the text, but none of these features prevents the enjoyment of readers whose knowledge of spoken Scots is quite limited.

The Union of Parliaments in 1707 completed the process begun with the Union of Crowns in 1603. The first of these events removed the court and its patronage from Scotland; the second ended the long history of an independent parliament in Edinburgh. Together, these two political developments reduced the status of Scottish English from a national to a regional variety. By the mid-eighteenth century, systematic attempts to eradicate Scots usages became common, and the spoken language came under vigorous attack. In 1761, Thomas Sheridan arrived in Edinburgh to offer lectures on English usage, especially "those points with regard to which Scotsmen are most ignorant, and the dialect of this country most imperfect" (*Scot's Magazine* 23 [1761]:389). In the wake of his visit, Edinburgh literati established the Select Society for Promoting the Reading and Speaking of the English Language in Scotland, and schoolmasters began to advertise that "no Scotch" would be spoken in their classrooms.

To some extent, Scottish travellers were stigmatized by their speech, and

James Boswell (writing in 1764) observed the imbalance of prestige of the two varieties of English:

> I do not know the reason for it, but it is a matter of observation that although an Englishman often does not understand a Scot, it is rare that a Scot has trouble in understanding what an Englishman says: and certainly *Sawney* [i.e., the Scot] has an advantage in that. It is ridiculous to give as the reason for it that a Scot is quicker than an Englishman and consequently cleverer in understanding everything. It is equally ridiculous to say that English is so musical that it charms the ears and lures men to understand it, while Scots shocks and disgusts by its harshness. I agree that English is much more agreeable than Scots, but I do not find that an acceptable solution for what we are trying to expound. The true reason for it is that books and public discourse in Scotland are in the English tongue. [Boswell 1952, p. 159–60]

In interpreting such observations, it is important to note that Boswell represents Scots anglophiles. He was ashamed that his father, a judge in Scotland's principal court, used Scots, and, on hearing a sermon by Hugh Blair (one of the leading intellectuals of the day), he censured Blair's "burring pronunciation and drawling manner with the Lothian tone" (Boswell 1977, p. 31).

Scotland thus took part in the cultural climate of correctness and propriety that pervaded eighteenth-century Britain. Polite literature and social behavior, including speech, were prescribed according to literate London standards; virtually anything which deviated too far from this norm was likely to be considered vulgar and provincial. These polite ideals were taken up by educated Scots and the upper classes, and there came to be an increasing self-consciousness about the supposed inferiority of Scots speech.

At the same time, however, there occurred a renaissance in the use of Scots for literary purposes. Robert Fergusson (1750–74), Robert Burns (1759–96), and Sir Walter Scott (1771–1832) all exploited the rich colloquial resources of Scots, both for a native audience and for readers abroad who perhaps had little direct experience with Scots speech. In part, their choice of Scots reflected an interest in ordinary people and the drama of their lives (in contrast to the highly elaborated "decorous" literary tradition of the time); in part, Scots was a natural vehicle for literature with local settings and characters. Though Burns was regarded as something of a rustic prodigy by the Edinburgh literati—and his impoverished youth in rural Ayrshire had immersed him in spoken Scots—even while he was reviving the Scots tradition, Burns himself took care to command a southern English speaking style. According to one testimony, "as he aimed at purity in his turn of expression, [he] avoided, more successfully than most Scotchmen, the peculiarities of Scottish phraseology" (quoted by Craig 1961, pp. 248–49). Similarly, Sir Walter Scott extended his range of speech from Scots to a purified version of English, but like many of his contemporaries he felt that his command of English was uncertain and sometimes flawed by Scotticisms.

It may seem unfortunate for the revival of Scots as a literary language that it was virtually confined to a popular tradition. Given the severe functional restriction of Scots, however, it is perhaps remarkable that anyone should have bothered to write in Scots at all (see Robinson 1973). Of course, the literary revival was strongly tied to Romanticism on the one hand and nationalistic sentiment on the other.

In prose, writers like Scott, Robert Louis Stevenson (1850–94), and many others adopted the strategy of writing dialogue in Scots, wherever appropriate, and narrative in English. John Galt (1779–1839) and Lewis Grassic Gibbon (1901–35), however, experimented with a kind of Scotticized narrative that extended Scots-influenced English to a wider domain. Galt's *Annals of the Parish* (1821), purportedly a chronicle kept by the Reverend Micah Balwhidder, provides an example of this literary Scots:

> Nevertheless, I walked about from door to door, like a dejected beggar, till I got the almous deed of a civil reception, and who would have thought it, from no less a person that the same Thomas Thorl that was so bitter against me in the kirk on the foregoing day.
>
> Thomas was standing at the door with his green duffle apron and his red Kilmarnock nightcap—I mind him as well as if it was but yesterday—and he had seen me going from house to house, and in what manner I was rejected, and his bowels were moved, and he said to me in a kind manner, "Come in, sir, and ease yoursel'; this will never do, the clergy are God's gorbies, and for their Master's sake it behoves us to respect them. There was no ane in the whole parish mair against you than mysel', but this early visitation is a symptom of grace that I couldna have expectit from a bird out the nest of patronage." [Galt 1895, pp. 7–8]

Galt clearly distinguishes the clergyman from the folk of the parish by the density of Scots features, but there are evident Scots traits in Balwhidder's *almous* (a Scots form of *alms*), *that* as a relative, and *mind* 'remember'. Thorl's dialogue, like that of Balwhidder's other parishioners, contains much more Scots: *yoursel'* and *mysel'* as reflexive pronouns, *gorbies* 'unfledged birds', *ane* 'one', *mair* 'more', and the past tense formed with *-it* in *expectit*.

In the course of the nineteenth century, the literary tradition established by Burns and Scott made Scots widely known to a literate public outside Scotland but did little to enhance its prestige as a spoken language within the country. Among a variety of texts prepared to serve a romanticized vision of Scotland is *The New Testament in Braid Scots*, a rendering unlikely to have found much liturgical use. The author of this text recognized that native Scots speakers might enjoy such a translation, but he also had in mind the "hantle o' folk wha dinna speak Scots theirsels, but are keen to hear it, and like to read it" (Smith 1901, Preface). A brief specimen, parallel to a text quoted by Thomas E. Toon elsewhere in this volume (p. 239), gives some flavor of the literary tradition that emerged in the nineteenth century for representing Scots:

> Thar was ane o' the Pharisees, by name Nicodemus; and in authoritie amang the Jews. And he cam i' the mirk o' the nicht till Jesus, and quo' he, "Maister! we a' ken ye are a Teacher frae God; for nane could do sic wunner-warks as ye do, gin God warna wi' him!" Jesus said till him, "Truly say I t'ye, gin a man be-na born again, his een sal never see God's Kingdom!" Quo' Nicodemus, "But hoo's a man to be born in eild? Maun he return to his mither's womb, and be born ower again?" But Jesus spak; "Truly, truly say I t'ye, Gin a man be-na watir-born and Spirit-born, he'se no come intil God's Kingdom!"

In the twentieth century, Scots formed the basis of a literary renaissance in the work of Hugh MacDiarmid (1892–1978), Sydney Goodsir Smith (a New Zealander, 1915–75), Robert Garioch (1910–81), and other writers who created a composite of Scots features—called Lallans—as vehicle for a full range of literary effects. MacDiarmid led the way by borrowing vocabulary from Gavin Douglas and the other medieval "makars" that had long been obsolete, as well as drawing on personal observation of current Scots usage and even extracting words from John Jamieson's nineteenth-century *Etymological Dictionary of the Scottish Language* (see MacDiarmid 1967).

In general, Lallans writers renovated obsolete Scots vocabulary or drew on rural dialects for their sources. As a result, the language of some contemporary poetry is synthetic and far removed from virtually all readers. Writing of Alastair Mackie's volume, *Clytach* ['barbarous speech'] (1972), for instance, Robin Fulton notes that about 640 lines of verse are amplified in a glossary of more than 600 entries (Fulton 1974, p. 179). A few poets—and prose writers in the *Toonheid* tradition—have, however, used some of the distinctive features of urban speech for literary purposes.[5] Tom Leonard, for instance, draws on features of Glasgow speech:

> yonwuz sum night
> thi Leeds gemmit Hamdin
> a hunnirn thurty four thousan
> aw singin
> yilnivir wok alone
> [From Murray and Smyth 1977, p. 22]

Mixed with authentic traits of urban Scots English—e.g., *aw* 'all', *gemmit* 'game at'—are quasi-phonetic spellings that reflect merely eye dialect (e.g., *sum* 'some'). Similarly urban in language are some of the poems of Robert Garioch—for instance, "Nemo Canem Impune Lacessit" (its title an amplification of the motto of Scotland):

> I kicked an Edinbro dug-luver's dug,
> leastways, I tried: my timing wes owre late.
> It stopped whit it wes daein on my gate
> and skelpit aff to find some ither mug
> [From Lindsay 1976, p. 84]

These experiments in the use of Scots and Scots English are relatively unusual in modern communities abroad where English in all of its varieties is the dominant language.

As Duncan Glen (1964, p. 216) points out, "at the turn of the century the poet writing in Scots would have felt, and indeed have thought it quite natural to be treated as a poor and humble relation of the poet writing in English, in the fifties we had Anglo-Scottish poets claiming that they were being ostracised by a coterie movement led by MacDiarmid." Prose writers have not been much drawn to the Lallans movement, but a fair body of nondialogue prose in Lallans now exists and there continue to be stories and novels in which characters are represented as speaking Scots (see McClure 1979). But as Murison (1977, pp. 56–62) explains, the language of present-day Scotland is an amalgam of traditional Scots, standard and nonstandard English, Anglo-Irish, and even East Indian elements. Its considerable variety and restriction to *belles lettres* present difficulties to Scots writers who would extend and explore its creative potential.[6]

* * *

In examining the spoken English of Scotland today, I will consider five major dimensions of variation that have recently been investigated: region, social class, style, sex, and age.

The accompanying map shows the distribution of the four main regional dialects of Scotland. Like other dialect maps, this one suggests stability and sharp boundaries where in fact change and overlapping waves of features reflect the actual linguistic situation. In general, urban areas provide the source of innovation, and their influence spreads outward in varying degrees to the surrounding rural areas. Edinburgh, Glasgow, and Aberdeen serve as such focal areas. Along the border between Scotland and England, Scots features generally stop at or near the political boundary. In the border regions, a strong linguistic loyalty to Scots and Scots English helps to maintain more conservative Scots usages while innovations in the cities show developments not always parallel to the changes that have taken place in England.

Detailed information about the distribution of Scots dialects is now becoming available through the work of the Linguistic Survey of Scotland at the

Scotland

University of Edinburgh. Two volumes of lexical data have been published that summarize the results of a postal questionnaire first circulated in the 1950s (see Mather and Speitel 1975–77). The *Scottish National Dictionary* combines information from another questionnaire with the full resources of a dictionary on historical principles and is another major resource in the study of the geography of English in Scotland.

Highland English arose as Gaelic declined in the middle of the eighteenth century, and it apparently was more influenced by the standard varieties of Scottish English through books and imported schoolteachers than by the Scots and Scots English of the neighboring territory. Today, the vowel of *round* is [əu] rather than the [u] of Lowland varieties; *stool* has [u] rather than the [i] of the northeast or the [ɪ] of the central region; *porridge* ends with [ʤ] as in southern English rather than the [tʃ] of Central Scots; *pane* is pronounced with [e] as it is in Central Scots and not with the [i] of the northeast. In vocabulary, Highland English shows some borrowings from Gaelic (for instance, *bodach-rocais* 'scarecrow'), and speakers of this variety may make use of the Gaelic diminutive *-ag* (as in *bairnag*) rather than the *-ie* of *bairnie* (see Murison 1977, p. 33). In pronouncing *r*, users of Highland English employ the retroflex variety—rather than the trilled *r* of Scots and Scots English—a feature that "is spreading in the more fashionable parts of Edinburgh and Glasgow as an alternative to the ordinary trilled *r* of Scots and Scottish English" (Murison 1977, p. 33; see Romaine 1978*a*).

Insular Scots of Orkney and Shetland reveals something of the Norse substratum. The most general characteristic of pronunciation is the tendency of stressed monosyllables to display short vowels and lengthened consonants (e.g., in *met*, *fat*, *bad*, *hen*, and *pot*) or lengthened vowels and shortened consonants (e.g., *fault* and *fraud*). The consonants [d], [l], and [n] are often palatalized, and where they are not palatalized, the preceding vowel is often diphthongized (e.g., [bɛid] 'bed' and [mɛin] 'men'). Other effects of Norn include the lack of [ʤ] and a consequent change of the affricates so that *shop* and *chop* are homophones with [ʃ] and *John* is pronounced [tʃ]; [θ] and [ð] rarely occur and are replaced by [d] (e.g., in *then*, *that*, and *breathe*) and by [t] (e.g., in *three* and *north*); the initial clusters *kw-* and *hw-* are not contrastive (e.g., in *queer* and *where*) and the choice of one cluster or the other is regionally distributed in the area (see Catford 1957*a*, pp. 72–73). Even with Scots vocabulary, local terms have developed or been preserved in a way that makes Insular Scots distinctive: *mullders* 'crumbs', *ammer* 'glowing coal', *peedie finger* 'little finger', and *peerie bird* 'nestling'. Among the Norse vocabulary still current in Shetland are *haaf* 'deep sea', *noost* 'boat dock', and *voar* 'spring season'; in Orkney, *ayre* 'beach', *skaav* 'scrape', and *trowie* 'sickly' show similar evidences of this region's Scandinavian past (see Catford 1957*a* and Murison 1977, p. 36).

Northeast Scots has as its main feature of pronunciation the merger of Middle Scots ø̄ and of Middle Scots ā before *n* to [i]; this merger yields [gwid] *good*, [blid] *blood*, [in] for Scots *ane* 'one' from ø̄, and [stin] for *stane* 'stone' and [bin] for *bane* 'bone' from ā. In addition, [f] is often used for words spelled with *wh-*: *fat* 'what', *far* 'where', *fan* 'when', *fa* 'who', *fite* 'white', *fussle* 'whistle', and *furl* 'whirl', but *wheel* retains Scots [ʍ]. A representation of this dialect in William Alexander's (1826–94) *Johnnie Gibb of Gushetneuk* reveals several of these features:

> "Weel, I'se pit it to you, Hairry," says she. "Fan Samie an' me wus marriet there was a byowtifu' brakfist set doon—sax-an'-therty blue-lippet plates (as mony plates as mony fowk) naetly full't o' milk pottage wi' a braw dossie o' gweed broon sugar i' the middle o' ilka dish, an' as protty horn speens as ever Caird Young turn't oot o' 's caums lyin' aside the plates, ready for the fowk to fa' tee." [Quoted by Grant and Dixon 1921, p. 324]

> ["Well, I'll put it to you, Harry," says she. "When Sammy and me was married there was a beautiful breakfast set down—six-and-thirty blue-rimmed plates (as many plates as there were folk) brim full with milk porridge with a handsome little portion of good brown sugar in the middle of each dish, and as pretty horn spoons as ever Caird Young turned out of his moulds lying beside the plates, ready for the folk to fall to."]

Specific features of Northeast Scots illustrated in this passage include: *fan* 'when' and [i] in *gweed* 'good', *speens* 'spoons', and *tee* 'to'. As Murison (1977, p. 33) notes, Northeast Scots has also preserved many words that have become obsolete elsewhere in Scotland and is characterized by frequent use of the diminutive (as in *dossie* 'little portion', cognate with English *dose*, in the passage above).[7]

Southern Scots is the dialect of the southwest and the English border and shows some influence of the cities of Glasgow and Edinburgh on the north[8] and the northern dialect of English spoken in Cumberland and Northumberland to the south. Distinctively Scots features tend to form a sharp boundary along the political border, particularly when they are perceived as Scots. In response to Glauser's questioning, for instance, one border informant said, "*Thole* is right Scotch, and there is no English word to beat it" (1974, p. 98). Competing English words—*bear*, *stand*, and *bide*—were all reported in completing the sentence "Sometimes toothache may get so bad that you think you can hardly _____ (it)." Though *thole* formerly was used throughout England, it is now virtually restricted to Scotland. Perceived as a Scotticism, it helps define the linguistic boundary. Other such Scots words are similarly distributed along the English border. *He's aye busy* is clearly Scots; *he's always busy* English. From a historical point of view, isoglosses that formerly extended well into England have receded northward as Southern Scots and northern English have become more sharply defined.

In Southern Scots, the vowel of *cow* and *now* and other words with Scots word-final [u] has developed in parallel to the northern English values—[kəʊ] and [nəʊ] (Vaiana 1972, p. 76–77); *he*, *me*, *see*, and *tree* are all pronounced with [ʌi] in contrast to the word-final [i] of Scots (Murison 1977, p. 33). A century ago,

English in Scotland

Murray reported a "test sentence" that still generally distinguishes Southern from Central Scots: "You and I will go over the wall and pull a pea." In Central Scots, in Murray's phonetic spelling, the sentence is rendered as "Yoo an' mee 'll gyang uwr the duyke an' poo a pee"; in Southern Scots as "Yuw an' mey 'll gan owre the deyke an' puw a pey" (1873, p. 82).[9]

Of the major dialects of Scotland, Central Scots is the best known and most thoroughly documented. Its territory includes the cities of Edinburgh and Glasgow, and of the five major dialect regions it is the most varied and has the greatest numbers of speakers. Since examples of variation by social class, style, sex, and age will be drawn from this region, I will begin by sketching the features of the prestige dialect of the central region, Scottish Standard English.

In general, Scottish English draws on the same inventory of consonants found in varieties of English around the world. One exception is the use of [x] in Gaelic loans (e.g., *loch* 'lake, bay, or arm of the sea', *clachan* 'village'), and the same consonant may appear in *thought*. The distribution of consonants in Scottish English is in some ways distinctive. In *house* and *housing*, the intervocalic consonant is [s], while in *December*, [z] often occurs. In earlier Scots, [v] was often deleted after a vowel or liquid, producing such pronunciations as [ˈsɪlər] *silver* and [he] *have*; these forms have become conventionalized as archaisms or as conscious Scotticisms. Scottish English retains the contrast between *whales* and *Wales*, and reveals the heritage of Scandinavian influence in such pairs as *kirk* and *church*, *beseek* and *beseech*.

The best contrastive account of the vowels of the prestige dialects of Scotland and England is that compiled by Abercrombie (1979) and from which the following brief summary is drawn. In general, the inventory is quite similar in the two varieties, and the distinctions between them are found in the distribution of vowels. Since Scottish English retains postvocalic [r]—that is, it is a rhotic variety of English—it has not participated in the changes consequent on the development of nonrhotic prestige varieties in England. Hence, Scottish English retains a distinction among three vowels in *first* [ɪ], *word* [ʌ], and *heard* [ɛ] where RP has only [ɜ] and between two vowels in *forty* [ɔ] and *four* [o] where RP has [ʊə]. The realization of unstressed syllables makes for differences between the two varieties. In RP and other varieties of English, the selection of weak forms (e.g., [əv] for *have*) is syntactically determined. In Scottish English, Abercrombie reports, "weak forms are stylistically determined" (1979, p. 83). In formal styles, weak forms seldom occur; in informal ones, Scottish English makes use of the weak forms found in RP and adds to them weak forms for function words that do not appear with reduced vowels or consonant deletion elsewhere (e.g., *of* and *on*).

The system of vowel contrasts reveals, in general, the more conservative pronunciations of Scottish English in comparison to present-day "Anglo-English." *Pool* and *pull*, for instance, are both pronounced with [u] rather than being differentiated as in RP. Similarly, *not* and *nought* are realized with [ɔ] rather than with [ɒ] and [ɔ] as in Anglo-English. As Scottish English responds to the pressures of anglicization, the inventory of such contrasts is likely to change in the direction of RP, but the resulting variety may well remain distinctively Scottish in distribution. As nonrhotic varieties spread through imitation of RP, the contrasts before [r] may disappear. This change, Abercrombie reports, "is commonly heard from members of the professional classes in Edinburgh, Glasgow, and other towns, and it appears to be on the increase" (1979, p. 80). Even so, these varieties generally show "*r*-coloration" of preceding vowels and thus retain a distinctively Scottish character.

Any review of the regional dialects of Scotland should not obscure the many features that are found throughout the country. One of the principal phonological characteristics is the "Scottish vowel-length rule," a trait that was already established in medieval times and persists in virtually all varieties of Scots and Scottish Standard English today. In other types of English, stressed monophthongs are long in final position and before voiced consonants and shorter before voiceless consonants (in Anglo-English, for instance, in *bee*, *bead*, and *beat*). In Scotland, however, vowel length is both phonetically and morphemically conditioned. Long vowels occur before [v], [ð], [z], [ʒ], and [r] in morpheme final position; in other environments, short vowels occur.[10] Thus, by the vowel-length rule, the following words have short vowels in Scotland: *moon*, *part*, and *water*. When the final consonant represents the addition of a morpheme, the combination results in the selection of the long vowel. Hence Scottish English shows vowel-length contrasts in the following pairs that are homophonous in other varieties:

Monomorpheme	Bimorpheme
heed [hid]	*he'd* [hi:d]
brood [brüd]	*brewed* [brü:d]
road [rod]	*rowed* [ro:d]

In modern Scotland, the residue of the length rule also explains the selection of vowels in a variety of contexts. In the reflexes of Middle English and Early Scots [i], for instance, Anglo-English and most varieties of American English have [aɪ] (in, for instance, *night*, *high*, and *light*). In Scotland, there are two vowels in these words: [aˑe] in "long" environments and [əi] in "short" environments. Thus the single morpheme *tide* is pronounced [təid]; the bimorpheme *tied* is [taˑed]. *Fife* with its voiceless consonant is [fəif]; *five* with its voiced consonant is [faˑev].[11] In addition, a variety of pan-Scottish features produce characteristic rhythms, intonation, and voice quality that have resisted the forces of anglicization and are distinctive, just as the vowel-length rule has generally preserved a Scottish character even in the most anglicized varieties.

Variation in English according to social class has only recently been given detailed attention in Scotland, though there is a long history of informal comment on language and class distinctions. Following the precedents of Labov (1966) in New York City and Trudgill (1974) in Norwich, Macaulay (1977) examined five phonological variables in the speech of Glasgow. Though there have been other

English in Scotland

studies, Macaulay's work will be summarized as indicating some of the linguistic correlates of social stratification in Scotland.[12]

Macaulay investigated sixteen adults, sixteen fifteen-year-olds, and sixteen ten-year-olds chosen to represent an equal number of males and females and four social classes (as measured by the occupation of the principal wage earner in the family):

Class I: Professional and managerial occupations
Class II: White-collar workers
Class III: Skilled manual workers
Class IV: Semiskilled and unskilled manual workers

Five phonological variables were selected for study, and each one was graded on a continuum depending on the phonetic realization of the variable. The variables were:

(i): the vowel in *hit, kill, risk*, etc.
(u): the vowel in *school, book, fool, full*, etc.[13]
(a): the vowel in *cap, bag, hand*, etc.
(au): the diphthong in *now, down, house*, etc.[14]
(gs): the use of a glottal stop instead of [t] in *butter, get*, etc.

Macaulay constructed a scale for each of the variants of the variables and calculated an average score for each individual. The variable (i), for instance, proved to have five possible realizations:

(i 1) [ɪ]
(i 2) [ɛ˖] and [ɪ˞]
(i 3) [ɛ˖] and [ï˞]
(i 4) [ə˖]
(i 5) [ʌ˖]

[Macaulay 1977, p. 31]

A speaker who uses [ɪ] consistently in words of the *hit* class would be assigned a score of 100; a speaker consistently using [ʌ] would have a score of 500.

When Macaulay computed the incidence of the (i) variable for sex and social class, he found the following classic sociolinguistic pattern:

	Scores			
	Class I	Class II	Class III	Class IV
All respondents	202	247	284	294
Males	224	279	287	300
Females	180	215	280	288

Source: Macaulay 1978, p. 135.

In general, the highest social class uses the high and frontmost vowel [ɪ]; the lowest, the most retracted and lowest vowel. Classes III and IV (skilled and unskilled manual workers) are most like each other. In every class, women use a vowel that has higher prestige. Women in white-collar families imitate the class above; men in the same families resemble the classes below. Such patterns reflect the kind of "structured heterogeneity" found in other parts of the English-speaking world.

All five of Macaulay's variables reflect essentially the same pattern:[15]

Variable	Class I	Class II	Class III	Class IV
(i)	202	247	284	294
(u)	178	234	295	312
(a)	158	190	242	253
(au)	212	268	335	348
(gs)%	48.4%	72.9%	84.3%	91.7%

Each of these variables shows clear stratification, particularly between Class I and Class II, and between Class II and Classes III and IV. "On the whole," Macaulay concluded, "the most remarkable aspect of the Glasgow survey is the great consistency of the results and the impression they give of a relatively stable, socially stratified speech community" (1978, p. 139). He asserts that all classes participate in the same speech community; the variants show degrees of Glasgow speech with little effective influence from RP or other kinds of Scottish Standard English.

Stylistic variation in Scotland is often quite extreme and the conditions that produce it complex. Both my own work (Romaine 1975a) and Reid's (1978) suggest that young children acquire the adult norms of style shifting at an early age. Reid found that many eleven-year-old informants could begin to explain the functions of social and stylistic variation, and my work reveals that six-, eight-, and ten-year-old children begin to participate in style shifting in varying contexts much earlier than has been claimed.

Two features illustrate the degree of style shifting among young children:

Variable	Reading Passage	Interview	Peer Group	Playground
(ng)	14	45	54	59
(gs)	25	71	84	79

Source: Reid 1978, p. 163.

As in Macaulay's study, Reid's investigation of the speech of sixteen Edinburgh eleven-year-olds summarized in the preceding table scores linguistic variables according to the phonetic realization of their variants. Variable (ng) assigns a value of 0 to [ŋ] and a value of 1 to [n] in *-ing* suffixes; variable (gs) assigns 0 to [t] or [t'] and 1 to [ʔ] or [ʔt] in word-medial or word-final position.[16] In both cases, the children Reid studied used the least formal style in the least formal setting (and conversely).[17]

Such results make it clear that the essential facts of social and stylistic variation are communicated to children at a young age and that the children respond by patterning their usage more closely to adult norms. Each of Macaulay's phonological variables was differentiated by the sex of the speaker across all social classes, and other features follow the same patterns. Scots negative particles, for instance, include [ne], [nə], and [nɪ]—spelled in dialect literature as *nae*, *na*, or *ny*. Formerly, these particles could be used with such verbs as *ken*, *need*, and *care*, but they appear to be limited today to forms of *be*, *do*, *have*, and the modals *can/could*, *will/would*, and *should*. In my study (Romaine 1975a), I found that boys used Scots negatives in 41 percent of possible occurrences while girls used them only 23 percent of the time. Negation, like the other variables, is likewise age-graded; both boys and girls use the more Scots forms at age six, but by age ten they show the pattern of adult norms. (In my study, I found Scots negation decreased from 38 percent to 22 percent from age six to ten.) Likewise, the (au) variable shows a movement away from the [u] realizations toward the less Scots forms as children grow older; in this case the separate development of boys and girls is quite clear.

Six-year-olds		Eight-year-olds		Ten-year-olds	
Boys	Girls	Boys	Girls	Boys	Girls
53	10	31	6	11	2

Note: Figures show the percentage of /u/ realized as [u] in *about, house, down, mouth,* etc.

Such clear and separate development reflects the importance of both age and sex as factors in the acquisition of adult norms.

The following selection from my interview with a ten-year-old Edinburgh girl (Romaine 1975a, pp. 94–95) shows both the incidence of some of the salient variables in Edinburgh speech and the relative sophistication that quite young children have achieved in their awareness of them:

> *Interviewer:* Does your Mum ever tell you to speak polite?
> *Informant:* If [ɛf] there's somebody polite [ʔ] in. Like, see, some people come in [ɛn]. There's new people in the stair we've moved up to [te] and they come in and I'm always sayin' "Down" [dun] Shep, cause it's my wee dog, so I say "Down" [dun]. My Mum says: "That's not what [ʔ] you say." She says, "It's, sit down [dəun]." Ken, cause she doesn't like me speakin' rough.

Interviewer: Why do you think she doesn't like it?
Informant: Well, if I speak rough, she doesn't like it when other people are in because they'll think that we're rough tatties [?] in the stair.
Interviewer: Does your Mum ever speak polite?
Informant: She doesnae really speak polite but she corrects all her words.
Interviewer: How about your teachers, do they ever say anything to you about the way you speak?
Informant: I've never actually said "Down" [dun] to the teacher.

As this selection reveals, mothers and schools clearly play a large part in making children aware of salient stylistic and social differences in language.

Nearly all Scots have learned as children to identify the many competing options available to them as belonging specifically to "Scots" or "English," so that when a speaker uses a large proportion of those items which are "labeled" Scots, he will say that he is speaking Scots. Most Scots-marked items signal some degree of intimacy, familiarity, informality, or local identity, and these domains of usage may be thought of as constituting "the social meaning of speaking Scots." The use of English, on the other hand, may be selected to indicate distance, alienation, formality, politeness, or nonlocal identity (see Romaine 1980*b*).

Despite the recognition that speaking English—which may be variously referred to as speaking "properly," "politely," or "correctly"—is necessary to get on in the world (especially in school and on the job), a person whose speech is too "proper" in situations where it is not appropriate will quite often be ridiculed. There are a variety of terms for this type of speech: *pan-loaf* (which refers to the higher price of pan-loaf bread as opposed to ordinary bread), *Kelvinside,* or *Morningside*. These last two are names of residential areas in Glasgow and Edinburgh, respectively, with a high proportion of middle and professional classes, though the accents associated with them are socially rather than regionally distributed. The existence of the *pan-loaf* stereotype illustrates another social meaning which is signaled by the use of English: social distance, snobbery, or alienation.[18]

From the alternate positive and negative prestige which may attach to the speaking of English, we might expect to find a corresponding positive and negative evaluation of speaking Scots. It is certainly true that one can easily elicit negative reactions to Scots; however, if there is an equal and opposing positive prestige to speaking Scots, it is often covert or expressed in an ambiguous way.

Present-day attitudes toward varieties of speech in Scotland are highly complex and have been scarcely investigated systematically. Informal observation makes clear a bipolarization of attitudes toward urban and rural speech. The reaction to rural speech is likely to be positive, and the middle class readily reveals a slightly patronizing approval of "rich, old Scots speech." On the other hand, urban working-class speech, typical of the industrial areas in central Scotland and obviously sharing many characteristics not only with rural dialects but

English in Scotland

also with Scottish Standard English, arouses great disapproval and is often branded "slovenly" or "degenerate."

Macaulay's survey of attitudes toward Glasgow speech contains examples of this attitude (see 1977, p. 90). One Glaswegian, for example, said:

> Oh, it's the slovenly speech in the industrial areas I don't care for. No, it's like the Belfast accent, you probably heard that on the television—I detest that accent, and these industrial cities, I don't like the accents they have.

Another Glaswegian's comment reveals the widespread preference among many Scots for Highland English:

> There's no doubt either the Inverness or the Highland people or the English really have us beaten here. Their speech is much preferable to ours.

Trudgill (1974, p. 20) maintains that this attitude is characteristic of heavily urbanized Britain in general, so that rural accents such as those of Devonshire or the Scottish Highlands are considered pleasant, charming, quaint, or amusing, while urban accents such as those of Birmingham are thought to be ugly, careless, or unpleasant. In mentioning that this attitude is not so widespread in the United States, Trudgill suggests that this difference may well reflect the different way in which rural life is evaluated in Britain and the United States.

Attitudes towards rural and urban Scots also figure in the reports from school inspectors and certain publications of the Scottish Education Department. One of these reports from the north contained the following recommendation (see Withrington 1974, p. 14):

> It is a pity that the influence of the well-educated and well-cultivated teacher does not extend beyond this—namely to the scotching and eradicating of the horrible accent and vernacular in some parts of the North. If the accent were pleasing like the melodious intonation of the Highlands, I should be sorry to recommend any such course, and I allow that to reduce pronunciation to a dead level uniformity would be a most undesirable consummation, yet a number of excrescent branches might usefully be lopped off. The tree would be none the worse for the operation.

This report appeared at the turn of the century, but as late as 1946 the Advisory Council's Report on Primary Education in Scotland contained the following comment (see Low 1975, p. 24):

> It [Scots] remains the homely, natural and pithy speech of country and small town folk in Aberdeenshire and adjacent counties; and to a lesser extent in other parts outside the great industrial areas. But it is not the

language of "educated" people anywhere and could not be described as a suitable medium of education or culture.... Elsewhere, because of extraneous influences, it has sadly degenerated and become a worthless jumble of slipshod, ungrammatical and vulgar forms, still further debased by the intrusion of the less desirable Americanisms of Hollywood.

In the present hotbed of controversy over social dialect differences and alleged language deprivation, overt condemnations of "slovenly" speech no longer appear in such publications. However, these attitudes have by no means disappeared, as is apparent from Macaulay's survey of the attitudes of teachers and employers in Glasgow.

A great deal of prejudice often hides behind the seemingly liberal acceptance of "accent" in general (in a popular and loose sense), while a condemnation of certain arbitrarily selected features as "slovenly" and "unintelligible" continues. The following comment from an employer in Glasgow illustrates this attitude:

For instance, if a man came in and you couldn't understand his accent for glottal stops and things like that, you couldn't understand what he was saying then we would conclude that however brilliant he was he couldn't communicate. Unless he had a job where communication wasn't important, we wouldn't consider him for it. [Macaulay 1977, p. 117]

An unfortunate result of this attitude, among other things, has been the confusion of speech training and speech therapy in some schools in Scotland. Such attitudes are present, for example, in McAllister's book, *A Year's Course in Speech Training* (1963), which appears to have dominated instruction in the spoken language in the teacher training colleges of central Scotland for some time. It is clear from the features which McAllister accepts and condemns that she operates with a bipolar attitude toward different social varieties of Scots.

The relegation of Scots to homely and casual domains of use is reflected in the teacher's belief that there is little good spoken Scots which has a place in the classroom:

Scots does not have social status, and until it regains social status very little can be done in schools. Parents from all walks of life are essentially middle-class in their attitude towards Scots; and even people who pride themselves on being democratic in other fields—political, economic, literary—just do not believe that it has been the linguistic medium of great poetry, great stories and great novels, and has been used in everyday life by ordinary Scots folk for centuries. [Low 1975, p. 25]

Thus, the unofficial policy of the schools has been aimed at the eradication of Scots. In the classroom, the school teacher was expected to enforce the norms of so-called polite speech, and no doubt, in many cases, teachers were promoting the use of forms they themselves did not use. But the influence of the teacher did not extend far from the classroom, and many children continued to speak Scots on the playground and at home. This compartmentalization of domains of usage of two coexistent varieties into public and private is of course a familiar characteristic of diglossic situations. Diglossic behavior on the part of pupils reinforces a common belief among teachers that their students are "bilingual."

From a historical perspective, Scots has been dying out for centuries, but anglicization still has a long way to go. As far as accent is concerned it may never be completed. Nevertheless, virtually everyone who has written about Scots since 1768 has suggested that Scots will soon die out completely. It is a recurrent belief in each generation that it is the last to be able to read Burns without a glossary, though this was being said while Burns was still alive!

The alleged decline of Scots proceeded unhindered by any strong feelings of linguistic loyalty for so long because most Scots were uncertain of their own speech. Eventually, when the midle class became more confident in its linguistic usage, certain types of more fully Scots speech, particularly urban working-class speech, were condemned as markers of a generally stigmatized identity. People were "glad" Scots was dying out because it was a symbol of that stigmatized identity.

The situation today has its roots in the linguistic insecurity of the eighteenth century. Anglicization is transmitted by social class and is working its way down from the top of the social scale. There can be no doubt that this anglicizing influence has manifested itself in real attrition in a number of areas. For example, there are certainly fewer Scottish items today, and many of these appear in much more restricted contexts, both linguistically and socially. Some items have been lost altogether, and fewer new Scottish words are being coined. Most of the options for middle-class speakers are restricted to lexis, and yet there are a number of Scotticisms and dialect words which may be selected for special emphasis on certain occasions. These words might be thought of as constituting a middle-class notion about what counts as acceptable Scots speech. Such words—for instance, *laird* and *kirk-session*—are for the most part cultural Scotticisms in that they refer to peculiarly Scottish aspects of life and have characterized Scots speech and writing since the Middle Ages. Among them are a number of what Aitken (1979) calls marked or overt Scotticisms such as the expressions *that'll not set the heather on fire* and *come into the body of the kirk* which are well established in middle-class usage. There is also a large number of less overtly marked or unmarked Scotticisms which speakers may not recognize as being Scottish since they are generally undifferentiated from standard English items: *outwith* 'outside, beyond', *to go (for the) messages* 'to do the shopping', *to chum someone to the bus stop* 'to accompany someone to the bus stop'.[19] Many of these seem to have a narrow range of social acceptability and vary with age, sex, and social class in a way similar to other phonological and grammatical variables.

For more than two centuries, at least some varieties of Scots have aroused feelings of strong positive emotion through romantic and nationalistic impulses; contrary trends away from "local" circumstances and "provincial" dialects have, as I have shown, had profound effects on English in Scotland. The trend toward anglicization has continued, but it has not triumphed.[20]

NOTES

I would like to acknowledge both personal and financial sources of support to which my work on Scots at various stages owes a great deal. During the period in which my earlier investigations were carried out, it is my special pleasure to mention in particular the assistance of A. J. Aitken. The research reported on in the later sections of this article was sponsored by a grant from the Social Science Research Council for a sociolinguistic investigation of Edinburgh speech. I am also grateful for the careful reading of an earlier draft of this essay by A. J. Aitken, Richard W. Bailey, J. C. Catford, and Manfred Görlach.

1. The brief history of Scots that follows was derived from a number of different sources, especially Murison 1977, Templeton 1973, Craigie 1924, Bald 1926, 1927, and 1928, and Aitken 1979.
2. Murison (1971) lists vocabulary that has entered Scottish English from Dutch as a result of this trade (e.g., *golf*, *croon*, and *scow*).
3. In this feature, Older Scots differed from South Midland and southern Middle English. In Scots, all narrative and habitual present tenses of regular verbs were marked with *-is*, as were the indicatives except those immediately following *I* or *we*. Subjunctives were not marked. In southern Middle English, the singular inflections were *-e*, *-est*, and *-eth*; the plural *-e(n)* or *-eth*; the subjunctive *-e* (from a lecture given by A. J. Aitken in 1978).
4. A variety of factors condition the choice of relative. In both literary and nonliterary prose, *that* tends to occur in restrictive and *quhilk(is)* in nonrestrictive relative clauses; in verse, however, *that* is the most frequent relative in both functions. Late in the Middle Scots period, *quha* and *quho* came to replace both *that* and *quhilk(is)* with personal subjects. The examples in the paragraph above show the continued use of *that* as a restrictive relative in modern Scots. See Caldwell 1974.
5. Both fiction and the drama make use of Scots elements, though the main line of experimentation has been developed in poetry. For instance, in Roddy McMillan's *The Bevellers*, a play first produced in 1972, some of the distinctive features of modern Glasgow speech are used with great effect:

    Bob: Dae ye know whit bevellin is, young Norrie?
    Norrie: Naw.
    Bob: It's a' ower the bliddy place, though no wan in a million wid recognise it. No so much o it nooadays, right enough. Time wis there wisnae a boozer or a half-decent shitehouse in the country withoot a sample o the bevellers' craft screwed tae the wa'. Can ye no guess?
    Norrie: Tae dae wi gless, int it? [McMillan 1974, p. 9]

English in Scotland

Another play that makes use of Glasgow working-class speech is *Willie Rough* (Bryden 1972) whose characters and setting reflect the Clyde shipyards at the time of the First World War.

6. A detailed survey of recent uses of written Scots is found in McClure 1979. It is worth recalling the remarks of Sir William A. Craigie—editor of the *Oxford English Dictionary*, the *Dictionary of American English*, and the *Dictionary of the Older Scottish Tongue*—on the Lallans movement and the possibility of using "good Scottish prose" for serious subjects:

> I am still of opinion, . . . that the Scottish enthusiasts are working on lines which can lead nowhere. Any dying or dead language can receive only a spurious vitality if it is used only for poetry, in which rare or obsolete words are introduced at random. Whether it is now possible to write on serious subjects in good Scottish prose may be doubtful, but the attempt must be made if there is to be a real revival as in other countries. Otherwise the writing of Scots will remain merely a dilettante amusement. [From a letter written in 1950; quoted by Meier 1977, p. 209]

7. For additional details, see Dieth 1932.
8. One well-known feature that delimits the spheres of influence of Glasgow and Edinburgh is the distribution of the Scots and Scots English word for *child*. In the east, *bairn* is in common use, particularly in the Lothians and the border areas; in the west, *wean* is the more usual word (see Catford 1957b, p. 117).
9. The normal process of linguistic change has, of course, affected both Central and Southern Scots since Murray wrote; a detailed study of Southern Scots can be found in Vaiana 1972.
10. The vowel-length rule applies to many but not all vowels; [ɪ] and [ʌ], for instance, are always short. In some dialects, following [rd], [g], and [dʒ] also trigger the rule. For a detailed historical treatment of the vowel-length rule, see Aitken (1981).
11. For additional details see Aitken 1977 and 1979 and Lass 1974.
12. Apart from the useful information it contains, Macaulay's work was also responsible to some extent for stimulating interest in investigating the social aspect of linguistic variation in Scotland, with the result that two small-scale studies on variation in the language of schoolchildren (Romaine 1975a and 1975b; Reid 1976) followed shortly after; in 1977 a major research project, sponsored by the Social Science Research Council, was undertaken to conduct a large-scale sociolinguistic investigation of Edinburgh speech.
13. After completing his study, Macaulay recognized that the words selected for this variable did not all have the same distribution in Scots and Scots English as they have in RP. *Boot* and *school* have unrounded front variants close to [ɪ]; other words (e.g., *pull* and *push*) may have unrounded centralized variants; still others (e.g., *shoe* and *lose*) occur only as rounded vowels. In his published data, Macaulay did not reanalyze his sample to distinguish these classes (see Macaulay 1977, p. 30).
14. The use of [u] in these words may reflect the use of Scots and thus show a different correlation with social class than do the other variants.
15. The (u) variable ranges from a slightly fronted high back unrounded vowel [u˙] (scored 100) to a high front unrounded vowel [ɪ˙] (scored 400); intermediate vowels along the

front-back continuum receive intermediate scores. Variable (a) ranges from [æ] (scored 100) to [a] (scored 200) to a back vowel [ɑ] or [ɒ] (scored 300); because of varying influences from Scots and Scots English, only words with [ɑ:] in RP were included in measuring this variable. The (au) variable includes four variants: [ɑ˙ʊ] (100), [ʌu] (200), [əu] (300) and [u˙], [ü], or [ʉ] (400). Variable (gs) is measured on a percentage scale that shows the proportion of posttonic [t]'s realized as glottal stops. The number of glottal stops was averaged and multiplied by 100 to obtain the value shown in the table (Macaulay 1977, p. 45). In each case, low indices are closest to the prestige norms in Glasgow. In particular, the glottal stop is often singled out by teachers as a characteristic of Glasgow speech, though it certainly occurs elsewhere in Scotland. According to Hughes and Trudgill (1979, p. 34), "it is most common in the speech of younger urban working-class speakers, and is found in most regions [of Britain], with the particular exception of many parts of Wales."

16. Individual indices are averaged and multiplied by 100 to produce the figures shown in the table. Selection of [t] or glottal stop is phonetically conditioned. Word-medial position (e.g., *water*) least favors glottal stop; word-final position before a following consonant (e.g., *that would* or *quite soon*) most favors its selection. As noted above, some varieties of Scots and Scottish English show devoicing of final stops, thus increasing the number of potential environments for glottal stop. Macaulay's findings (1977, pp. 47–48) confirm my own (Romaine 1975*a*) that word-medial glottal stops are more highly stigmatized than ones in word-final position. Among Class I adults, there were no instances of word-medial glottal stops, but glottal stops appeared for 25 percent of potential [t] in word-final position.

17. I share the view held by Macaulay and the Milroys (Milroy 1980) that speaking and reading are distinct kinds of linguistic behavior and not in the same linear continuum for many speakers. The sharp discontinuity between the reading and interview styles for both Reid's (ng) and (gs) variables tends to support this opinion. See Romaine 1980*b*.

18. As Aitken (1979, p. 113) notes, the hallmarks of this variety include "the vowel-qualities roughly indicated in such spellings as *ectually Egnes*—[ɛ] in place of the more usual [a]; *naise* (=nice) and *faine* (=fine)—[ei] in place of more usual [əɪ] or [ʌɪ]; often along with special features of vowel-length, rhythm and voice-quality." For a discussion of speakers' attitudes toward Morningside speech, see Romaine 1978*b* and 1980*b*.

19. See Aitken 1979, pp. 108–9, for a more complete list.

20. David Murison (1977, p. 62) hopes that Scots will be "restored" by being "given an assured and permanent place in our schools and colleges." In considering "Language and Nationhood" in a Scottish setting, on the other hand, Randolph Quirk (1979, p. 69) urges respect for "every man's mother tongue" but points to the need for "a language of wider communication beyond whatever limits are set by his mother tongue—and especially beyond the limits set by his nation." Quirk commends "the major language of daily currency"—English, French, Spanish, and Arabic—and says that nations "would in my view be doing a disservice to their own people in attempting to replace [one of the major languages] by a language more private and specific to themselves."

REFERENCES

Abercrombie, David. "The Accents of Standard English in Scotland." In *Languages of Scotland*, edited by A. J. Aitken and Tom McArthur, pp. 68–84. Association for Scottish Literary Studies, Occasional Papers, no. 4. Edinburgh: W. and R. Chambers, 1979.

Aitken, A. J. "How To Pronounce Older Scots." In *Bards and Makars*, edited by A. J. Aitken, Matthew P. McDiarmid, and Derick S. Thomson, pp. 1–21. Glasgow: University of Glasgow Press, 1977.

———. "Scottish Speech: A Historical View With Special Reference to the Standard English of Scotland." In *Languages of Scotland*, edited by A. J. Aitken and Tom McArthur, pp. 85–118. Association for Scottish Literary Studies, Occasional Papers, no. 4. Edinburgh: W. and R. Chambers, 1979.

———. "The Scottish Vowel-Length Rule." In *So Meny People Longages and Tonges: Philological Essays in Scots and Mediaeval English Presented to Angus McIntosh*, edited by Michael Benskin and M. L. Samuels, pp. 131–57. Edinburgh: Middle English Dialect Project, 1981.

Bald, M. A. "The Anglicisation of Scottish Printing." *Scottish Historical Review* 23 (1926):107–15.

———. "The Pioneers of Anglicised Speech in Scotland." *Scottish Historical Review* 24 (1927):179–93.

———. "Contemporary References to the Scottish Speech of the Sixteenth Century." *Scottish Historical Review* 25 (1928):163–79.

Boswell, James. *Boswell in Holland, 1763–1764*. Edited by Frederick A. Pottle. London: William Heinemann, 1952.

———. *Boswell: Laird of Auchinleck, 1778–1782*. Edited by Joseph W. Reed and Frederick A. Pottle. New York: McGraw-Hill, 1977.

Bryden, Bill. *Willie Rough*. Edinburgh: Southside, 1972.

Caldwell, Sarah J. G. *The Relative Pronoun in Early Scots*. Memoires de la Société Néophilologique, no. 42. Helsinki: Société Néophilologique, 1974.

Catford, J. C. "Shetland Dialect." *Shetland Folk Book* 3 (1957a):71–75.

———. "The Linguistic Survey of Scotland." *Orbis* 6 (1957b):105–21.

Craig, David. *Scottish Literature and the Scottish People, 1680–1830*. London: Chatto and Windus, 1961.

Craigie, W. A. "The Present State of the Scottish Tongue." In *The Scottish Tongue*, edited by W. A. Craigie, John Buchan, Peter Giles, and J. M. Bulloch, pp. 1–47. London: Cassell and Co., 1924.

Dieth, Eugen. *A Grammar of the Buchan Dialect (Aberdeenshire)*. Cambridge: W. Heffer and Sons, 1932.

Fulton, Robin. *Contemporary Scottish Poetry: Individuals and Contexts*. Loanhead: MacDonald, 1974.

Galt, John. *Annals of the Parish and The Ayrshire Legatees*. London: Macmillan and Co., 1895.

Glauser, Beat. *The Scottish-English Linguistic Border: Lexical Aspects*. Cooper Monographs, no. 20. Berne: Francke, 1974.

Glen, Duncan. *Hugh MacDiarmid and the Scottish Renaissance*. Edinburgh: W. and R. Chambers, 1964.

Grant, William, and Dixon, James Main. *Manual of Modern Scots*. Cambridge: At the University Press, 1921.

Hughes, Arthur, and Trudgill, Peter. *English Accents and Dialects*. London: Edward Arnold, 1979.

Labov, William. *The Social Stratification of English in New York City*. Washington, D.C.: Center for Applied Linguistics, 1966.

Lass, Roger. "Linguistic Orthogenesis: Scots Vowel Quantity and the English Length Conspiracy." In *Historical Linguistics: Proceedings of the First International Conference on Historical Linguistics*, vol. 2, edited by John Anderson and Charles Jones, pp. 311–52. 2 vols. Amsterdam: North Holland Publishing Co., 1974.

Lindsay, Maurice. *Modern Scottish Poetry: An Anthology of the Scottish Renaissance, 1925–1975*. Manchester: Carcanet Press, 1976.

Low, J. T. "Scots in Education: The Contemporary Situation." In *The Scots Language in Education*, pp. 17–28. Association for Scottish Literary Studies, Occasional Papers, no. 3. Edinburgh: Association for Scottish Literary Studies, 1975.

McAllister, Anne H. *A Year's Course in Speech Training*. 9th ed. London: University of London Press, 1963.

Macaulay, R. K. S. *Language, Social Class, and Education: A Glasgow Study*. Edinburgh: University of Edinburgh Press, 1977.

———. "Variation and Consistency in Glaswegian English." In *Sociolinguistic Patterns in British English*, edited by Peter Trudgill, pp. 132–43. London: Edward Arnold, 1978.

Macaulay, R. K. S., and Trevelyan, G. D. *Language, Education and Employment in Glasgow*. Edinburgh: Scottish Council for Research in Education, 1973.

McClure, J. Derrick. "Scots: Its Range of Uses." In *Languages of Scotland*, edited by A. J. Aitken and Tom McArthur. Association for Scottish Literary Studies, Occasional Papers, no. 4, pp. 26–48. Edinburgh: W. and R. Chambers, 1979.

MacDiarmid, Hugh. *Collected Poems*. London: Collier-Macmillan, 1967.

McMillan, Roddy. *The Bevellers*. Edinburgh: Southside, 1974.

MacQueen, John, and Scott, Tom. *The Oxford Book of Scottish Verse*. Oxford: Clarendon Press, 1966.

Mather, J. Y., and Speitel, H. H. *The Linguistic Atlas of Scotland*. 2 vols. London: Croom Helm; Hamden, Conn.: Shoe String, 1975–77.

Meier, Hans H. "Scots Is Not Alone: The Swiss and Low German Analogues." In *Bards and Makars*, edited by A. J. Aitken, Matthew P. MacDairmid, and Derick S. Thomson, pp. 201–13. Glasgow: University of Glasgow Press, 1977.

Milroy, Lesley. *Language and Social Networks*. Oxford: Basil Blackwell, 1980.

Murison, David. "The Dutch Element in the Vocabulary of Scots." In *Edinburgh Studies in English and Scots*, edited by A. J. Aitken, Angus McIntosh, and Hermann Pálsson, pp. 159–76. London: Longman, 1971.

———. *The Guid Scots Tongue*. Edinburgh: William Blackwood, 1977.

———. "The Historical Background." In *Languages of Scotland*, edited by A. J. Aitken and Tom McArthur, pp. 2–13. Association for Scottish Literary Studies, Occasional Papers, no. 4. Edinburgh: W. and R. Chambers, 1979.

Murray, Brian, and Smyth, Sydney. *A Sense of Belonging: Six Scottish Poets of the Seventies*. Glasgow: Blackie, 1977.

Murray, James A. H. *The Dialect of the Southern Counties of Scotland*. London: Asher, 1873.

Quirk, Randolph. "Language and Nationhood." In *The Crown and the Thistle: The Nature of Nationhood*, edited by Colin MacLean, pp. 57–70. Edinburgh: Scottish Academic Press, 1979.

Reid, Euan C. "Social and Stylistic Variation in the Speech of Some Edinburgh Schoolchildren." M.Litt. thesis, University of Edinburgh, 1976.

———. "Social and Stylistic Variation in the Speech of Children: Some Evidence from Edinburgh." In *Sociolinguistic Patterns in British English*, edited by Peter Trudgill, pp. 158–71. London: Edward Arnold, 1978.

Robinson, Mairi. "Modern Literary Scots: Fergusson and After." In *Lowland Scots*, edited by A. J. Aitken. Association for Scottish Literary Studies, Occasional Papers, no. 2, pp. 38–55. Edinburgh: Association for Scottish Literary Studies, 1973.

Romaine, Suzanne. "Linguistic Variability in the Speech of Some Edinburgh Schoolchildren." M.Litt. thesis, University of Edinburgh, 1975*a*.

———. "Approaches to the Description of Scots English." *Work in Progress* (Department of Linguistics, University of Edinburgh), no. 8 (1975*b*):121–24.

———. "Post-Vocalic [r] in Scottish English: Sound Change in Progress?" In *Sociolinguistic Patterns in British English*, edited by Peter Trudgill, pp. 144–57. London: Edward Arnold, 1978*a*.

———. "Problems in the Investigation of Linguistic Attitudes in Scotland." *Work in Progress* (Department of Linguistics, University of Edinburgh), no. 11 (1978*b*):11–29.

———. "Syntactic Complexity and Diffusion: Some Historical and Social Dimensions of Syntactic Change." *Language in Society* 9 (1980*a*):221–47.

———. "The Relative Clause Marker in Scots English: Diffusion, Complexity, and Style as Dimensions of Syntactic Change." *Language and Speech* 23 (1980*b*):213–32.

———. "Syntactic Complexity, Relativization and Stylistic Levels in Middle Scots." *Folia Linguistica Historica* 2 (1981):56–77.

Smith, William Wye. *The New Testament in Braid Scots*. Paisley: Alexander Gardner, 1901.

Templeton, Janet M. "Scots: An Outline History." In *Lowland Scots*, edited by A. J. Aitken. Association for Scottish Literary Studies, Occasional Papers, no. 2, pp. 4–19. Edinburgh: Association for Scottish Literary Studies, 1973.

Thomson, Derick S. "Gaelic: Its Range of Uses." In *Languages of Scotland*, edited by A. J. Aitken and Tom McArthur, pp. 14–25. Association for Scottish Literary Studies, Occasional Papers, no. 4. Edinburgh: W. and R. Chambers, 1979.

Trudgill, Peter. *The Social Differentiation of English in Norwich*. Cambridge: At the University Press, 1974.

Vaiana, Mary Estelle. "A Study in the Dialect of the Southern Counties of Scotland." Ph.D. dissertation, Indiana University, 1972.

Withrington, Donald J. "Scots in Education: A Historical Retrospect." In *The Scots Language in Education*, edited by J. Derrick McClure. Association for Scottish Literary Studies, Occasional Papers, no. 3, pp. 9–16. Aberdeen: Association for Scottish Literary Studies, 1974.

The English Language in Ireland
Michael V. Barry

The establishment of English in Ireland was facilitated by earlier Norse settlements, especially on the east coast, since Norse was a language closely related to early English and the first Germanic language to be spoken in Ireland. The Norse established towns which were later taken over by the Anglo-Normans and their English-speaking followers on their arrival from 1164 onward, and these towns have continued to be bases from which new cultural influences have entered and spread throughout Ireland. They include Dublin, Wexford, and Waterford in the east and Cork and Limerick in the south and west. The Norse eventually intermingled with the Irish in rural areas after the Anglo-Norman invasion, but their direct influence upon the English language in Ireland was inconsequential. It is most noticeable in a few place names such as *Skerries* 'rocks' and *Strangford* 'ford' (< *fjord* 'inlet of the sea').

English itself was first introduced by the soldiers and retainers of the Anglo-Norman nobility (or Cumbro-Normans, as P. L. Henry calls them, since they crossed to Ireland from Pembroke in southern Wales).[1] After the conquest of England in 1066, the Normans spread southwest into Dorset and Somerset, and across the Bristol Channel into southern Wales, especially Gower and Pembroke. The Anglo-Norman aristocracy were of Norman stock, though by the twelfth century they had interbred with the Anglo-Saxons, and their contact with the English language was with the West Saxon variety, a dialect also used in Gower and Pembroke. When they invaded Ireland, the Anglo-Norman aristocrats, though they knew the English language of the southwest, still preferred to use French, but their soldiers and retainers spoke the southwestern dialect of English.

The Anglo-Normans continued to use French after their settlement in Ireland, but French gradually gave way among the aristocracy to Irish rather than to English, since they came eventually, along with the native Irish, to regard the mainland English as a common threat. Thus laws were promulgated in French in the major cities in the twelfth century, indicating the survival of French in the towns if not in the rural areas. The library of the ninth earl of Kildare in 1500 has a predominance of French and Latin works, with rather fewer in English or Irish. After the Anglo-Norman settlement in Ireland was secured, it is likely that increasing numbers of English people came to Ireland, but some at least returned to the mainland feeling that they were not well treated by the Anglo-Norman aristocracy.

French had probably a very limited effect upon the English of Ireland (apart, of course, from the influence it had already had upon the language in England itself). There has been much debate, still unresolved, about the shift of stress in the south of Ireland from the first to the second syllable in disyllabic words in both Irish and early Hiberno-English (compare the pronunciation of the name *Michael* as [miˈxɔːl] in the south and as [ˈmixɔl] in the north). Some scholars have argued that this shift is evidence of the influence of the French stress-pattern, but others have doubted that Anglo-Norman francophones were numerous enough to have effected such a basic change. There were many borrowings of French words into Irish, but very few into early Hiberno-English. French influence chiefly survives in personal names like that of the present writer (*Barry*).

The Anglo-Normans never effectively dominated the remoter mountainous regions to the west (for example, in western Cork and Kerry), and they never penetrated Connemara nor settled further north than Sligo in the west and Carrickfergus in the east. The influence of French was therefore not felt equally all over the land, as it was in eleventh-century England. Leinster, the south and east coasts, and the fertile midland plain, as well as Lecale and south Ards in eastern Ulster, are the main areas where castles and walled towns testify to a strong Anglo-Norman presence. The evidence suggests that the Anglo-Normans and their English followers were absorbed by the Irish in rural areas and only remained as a distinctive group in the fortified towns. Thus both English and French at first were town or garrison languages.

Two notable exceptions to this pattern existed. In Wexford and in north county Dublin, both English and Anglo-Norman settlers mixed with a concentration of Norse settlers and formed the only two significant rural areas where English was preferred to Irish before the seventeenth century. In Wexford, the Anglo-Normans had assigned lands to English settlers and the Irish had fled the area. However, these were isolated strongholds of English and did not contribute significantly to the eventual main thrust of English into Ireland in the seventeenth century and after.

English in this early period had little social prestige. Some poetry was composed in English in the early thirteenth century, but French and Latin were the languages of culture. The poetry that survives reflects "a milieu open to English, Irish, and French cultural and linguistic influence" (Henry 1958, p. 64; for a sample of this poetry, see Furnival 1862, pp. 21–22). A growing political tension between both the Anglo-Normans and the English in Ireland and the mainland government, especially during bad economic conditions in the early fourteenth century, caused a revival of Irish. There were fears about the ability of English to survive, and laws were passed in an attempt to strengthen its position, such as the well-known Statutes of Kilkenny (1366) which insisted upon the use of English forms of surnames and the use of English in speech.

There were no universities or other centers of "English" cultural influence, and during the fourteenth and fifteenth centuries, the language went into decline in most rural areas. Politically, by the fourteenth century, the Irish had effectively regained control of almost the entire country outside the town walls, and at times they even tended to move into the towns, thus spreading the use of their language. By 1500, many of the towns were in decay. Laws against the use of Irish, notably in Waterford, are a clear indication that it was widely spoken.

At the opening of the sixteenth century, English was almost a dead language except in the two rural areas of northern county Dublin and southeastern Wexford. As the Tudor and Stuart monarchs endeavored to gain control of Ireland, many of the old Anglo-Norman towns declined, and the remaining Anglo-Norman and English population associated more and more with the Irish in opposing the English attacks. By 1600, Irish was probably the normal language even of most of the eastern coastal region (the Pale). The fact that the Reformation virtually bypassed Ireland meant that the Anglo-Normans who were Roman Catholics, and the native Irish who were also Catholics, were in a position where language and religion united them against the Protestant English and their language. An interesting contrast existed between Ireland and the Isle of Man at this period. Both were Gaelic-speaking, but in Man, the Bible and the *Book of Common Prayer* were circulated in the vernacular, thus helping to establish the Protestant Reformation, whereas this did not happen to nearly the same extent in Ireland. Thus Irish came to be associated with the native religion—Roman Catholicism—and English with "foreign" Protestant settlers. The use of Irish is still today almost synonymous with being a Roman Catholic, and graffiti in Irish are common on walls in Catholic-Republican strongholds in modern Belfast, a city which has been totally English-speaking for more than a century.

After the Tudor-Stuart period, the towns which survived began to use a new form of English, but the older form of English lingered in an almost fossilized state in southeastern Wexford and northern county Dublin. The older English of these districts has from time to time aroused the interest of linguists since it preserved a very archaic form of the language; its latest form—the nineteenth-century dialect of the Forth and Bargy area of county Wexford—provides useful evidence concerning the nature of both medieval Hiberno-English and early medieval southwestern English dialects.

The older Hiberno-English lingered until about 1800 in Fingal, north county Dublin. In the 1670s, William Petty found that this dialect was similar to but not identical with the dialect of south Wexford. Arthur Young, in 1776, said that the Fingal dialect was more "intermixed with Irish" (1925, p. 33) than the (presumably) new Hiberno-English of the rest of Ireland. The common use of Irish in Dublin city at the time would probably explain this mixing. There is apparently almost no documentary evidence of the character of the Fingal dialect.

Some evidence for the character of the old Hiberno-English of the Anglo-Norman towns has been gathered by Bliss (1977) from Elizabethan and Restoration drama, in which it is likely that most Hiberno-English was represented in a stylized manner. An exception, however, is in *Captain Thomas Stukeley* (1605), a biographical play about an actual soldier and buccaneer involved in several Spanish attempts to wrest Ireland from English control including the siege of Dundalk in 1566. In this play, the prose in Hiberno-English shows a form of the language

English in Ireland 87

much influenced by Irish in both vocabulary and idiom and rendered far more correctly than was common in drama at that time. It is presented in sufficient detail so that the Irish influence is clearly shown to be that of the Gaelic of Oriel (south Armagh), a district close to Dundalk. The English itself is of a conservative type with some features still found in the nineteenth-century Forth and Bargy data but sharply different from modern Dundalk English.

Bliss (1977, p. 11) has suggested that the English dialects of the modern towns of Ireland (even including cities as far apart as Cork and Belfast) all have some features in common which are not found in rural Hiberno-English and that these features might be very old.

While relatively little is known of the old Hiberno-English of northern county Dublin, the dialect of Forth and Bargy is well documented, since it was still alive during the period of intense interest in philology in the nineteenth century. The main data consist of songs and poems, the oldest of which are from the early eighteenth century, and fragments of "conversations" collected by William O'Neill in the late nineteenth century (Ó'Muirithe 1977, p. 40). There is also a nineteenth-century version of the Lord's Prayer and a glossary, collected by Jacob Poole in the early nineteenth century and published in 1867 by the Anglo-Saxon purist and Dorset poet William Barnes and extensively edited by him.[2] A. J. Ellis used Barnes's material as a basis for an analysis of the Forth and Bargy dialect in *Early English Pronunciation* (1889, pt. 5, pp 25–31) along with two other papers published on the southeast Wexford dialect, one by Charles Vallancey (1773) and the other by Sir James A. Picton (1866). Ellis used additional information from correspondence with Edmund Hore, but he made no field inquiries himself, believing in the 1870s that the dialect was extinct.

Stanihurst (1577) felt that the Forth and Bargy dialect had diverged from mainland English and become much mixed with Irish.[3] The English element was archaic and reminiscent of Chaucer, and it showed the shift of stress to the second syllable in disyllables. Writing in 1672, Sir William Petty called the Forth and Bargy dialect a form of "old Saxon." Apparently the inhabitants of the region where the dialect was spoken traveled little, and there was much inbreeding. By the nineteenth century the region was regarded as very parochial. Thus the dialect remained little affected by the new forms of English introduced from the seventeenth century.

The area in which the dialect lingered last was the very tip of Carne—the extreme southeastern corner of Ireland, just south of the modern harbor of Rosslare. Decline began earlier in the Bargy barony, which was settled or "planted" by Cromwell after the massacre of Wexford town. In the 1642 Act of Settlement, the people of Bargy never recovered their lands, which remained in the ownership of Cromwellian soldiers. The more standard form of English of the Church of Ireland clergy and other establishment figures must have encouraged a decline of the older dialect.

Hore, Ellis's correspondent of 1873, knew some of the last surviving speakers of the older Hiberno-English and felt that they had been much influenced by the newer Hiberno-English forms. In 1834, a clergyman in Forth claimed that he could detect Chaucerian forms in the dialect and that when he read Chaucer to the locals, they understood his English. Such apparently far-fetched claims may at least be evidence of the archaic nature of the dialect. In 1857, the younger generation are reported as being ashamed of the older dialect.

Ellis attributed the late survival of the old Hiberno-English in the southeast to the geographical isolation of the area. The dialect came to be a manifestation in miniature of a characteristic of Hiberno-English in Ireland as a whole—the preservation of archaisms because of isolation from innovations in English.

Ellis placed the dialect of Forth and Bargy south of his dialect boundary lines 1 and 2 (i.e., those distinguishing north English [sʊm] *some* from south English [sʌm]), south of line 3 (i.e., it had *r*-coloring of vowels), and within the "Celtic Border." He describes the area of survival as the southeastern tip of Ireland. The dialect had a southern form of English of West Saxon origin but with Irish influence. He felt that by 1825 it was almost extinct as a vernacular and had been dying rapidly at the close of the eighteenth century.

A specimen of the Hiberno-English collected by Poole in the Forth and Bargy area is the following poem, "About an Old Sow Going to Be Killed" (Poole 1867, pp. 106–7):

"Murreen leam, kish am." Ich aam goan maake mee will.
At skelpearès an slaugheardhès mye leeigh aar oer vill.
Mot earch oan to aar die. Ich mosth kotch a bat.
A skudhelès, lhaung roosta, wull glaude leth aam what.

Ich aam a vat hog it's drue. Aar is ken apan aam.
Gooude var nat oan dhing, neither treesh ar thraame;
Na speen to be multh, nar flaase to be shaure.
Vear'd nodhing mot Portheare. Na skeine e'er ee-waare.

Eee crappès o' a shearde ich had a cousaane.
Ich woode be pitcht ee kurkeen, ar zippeen, to a coolaan.
A plaauge apan Portheare! Hea'de luther me waal,
Beteesh a kraaneberry-bushe an a ellena-ghou.

[To my grief, I am a big old sow. I am going to make my will,
That piglings and pigs may laugh their overfill.
But every one to his day. I must catch the bat ('take my turn').
The knives that long were rusty, well-pleased let them whet.

I am a fat hog, 'tis true. There is knowledge among them.
(While alive, I am) good for not one thing; neither for the trace nor the car.

(I have) no teat to be milked, nor fleece to be shorn.
I feared nothing but Porter (the dog). No skein (of wool) I ever wore.

In the bushes of the gap, I had a hole to go through.
I would be poked into the mow or the stack up to the back of my head.
A plague upon Porter, he'd hide me well,
Between the gooseberry bush and the elder tree.]

In the spelling of this poem, Poole and his editor Barnes intended to give some impression of the sounds of the dialect. A detailed interpretation of its features can be gained by consulting the inventory of features of the Forth and Bargy dialect given later in this article.

English began to be reintroduced into Ireland by an entirely fresh wave of settlement in the sixteenth and seventeenth centuries. This "new" Hiberno-English disturbed the remaining older Hiberno-English and established itself both where it had died out and in regions where it had never before existed as a vernacular. There is no real continuity between this new or modern Hiberno-English and the older Hiberno-English.

Once again English first took root in the major seaport towns around the coast—for example, Dublin, Drogheda, Wexford, Waterford, Cork, Limerick, and Galway, and also at Newry and Carrickfergus on Belfast Lough. It was further strengthened by "plantations" or settlements of English Protestants on land in rural districts—the answer of the English government to insurrection and Catholic influence. These settlements were strongest in parts of Leinster (sixteenth and seventeenth centuries), south Munster (by 1586), county Waterford, and parts of county Kerry. Plantation had also occurred in central and western Ulster by 1611 (in Donegal, Londonderry, Tyrone, Armagh, Fermanagh, and Cavan, and in the Lagan Valley area of counties Antrim and Down—now the hinterland of Belfast).

Cromwell established a policy of settlement that placed his favored retainers on Irish land. The former Irish or Anglo-Norman landowners (usually of royalist persuasion) were displaced onto poor land in southeastern Connaught by the plantations in Munster and Leinster. The period around 1650 marked the high point of English settlement.

The source of the new Hiberno-English was a form of seventeenth-century English. Hiberno-English was rapidly and increasingly cut off from mainland England, and this isolation persisted at least until the Act of Union in 1800 because of poor sea transport. The English language in Ireland once again became archaic or at least very conservative and also heavily gaelicized. When Irish speakers wished to learn English, as increasingly they did, they learned an archaic and nonstandard form of the language. Teachers were usually native Irish, and as the English language was taught by one generation to another, it became even more gaelicized. Not only was the English of Ireland archaic and gaelicized, but when first introduced, it was a regional rather than a standard variety. The majority of the settlers were from the west or northwest Midlands of England. Even if a few of the landowners used a "refined" form of the language, their many servants and retainers certainly did not, and it was they with whom the native Irish chiefly had dealings. The planters, though predominately from the west and northwest Midlands, were not exclusively from that area, and an unpublished map by G. B. Adams in the archives of the Ulster Folk and Transport Museum shows a complex pattern of source areas of planters in the north.

The fullest studies to date of early modern Hiberno-English have been made by Bliss (1972; 1975; 1977). Bliss (1975, p. 5) distinguishes three main varieties of Hiberno-English (apart from the complex group of dialects in Ulster): rural Hiberno-English, the most conservative and gaelicized form; urban Hiberno-English, influenced by contact with the outside world and possibly preserving some features of the old Hiberno-English of the Anglo-Norman period; and educated Hiberno-English, more influenced by standard English, perhaps because many wealthy landowners sent their children to English public schools during the nineteenth century. Educated speech retains a few characteristics of rural Hiberno-English and so sounds "Irish" to outsiders. Today in the Republic of Ireland, a more modern form of educated Hiberno-English is gaining currency; it is based on the speech of Radio Telefís Éireann (RTE) national news readers, national leaders, and school teachers trained in colleges in the Dublin area.

Geographically, P. L. Henry (1958, pp. 53 and 147) distinguishes two main dialect divisions in Hiberno-English. The first is Southern Hiberno-English, spoken south of a line which he does not pinpoint exactly, but which can now be shown to run from Bundoran on the west coast to Carlingford Lough on the east. This dialect is very homogeneous with few significant subdialects. The second is Northern Hiberno-English, which is subdivided into Ulster Scots (spoken in northeastern Ulster and heavily influenced by Lowland Scots English) and Mid-Ulster, the speech of the Lagan Valley, southern Tyrone, northern Monaghan, and northern Fermanagh—the parts of Ulster chiefly settled by the English but showing some Scots influence nonetheless.

Between 1700 and 1800, English and Irish existed in a state of equilibrium. The extent of the use of English did not differ greatly in 1800 from what it had been in 1700. During the eighteenth century, English was used in counties Dublin, Wicklow, central and northern Wexford, Kildare, and Carlow—roughly the area often referred to as the Pale. In the center of the country, the situation was more mixed, while the west remained solidly Irish-speaking.

The Act of Union and improved sea transport after 1800 increased the prestige and desirability of English. The language began to spread beyond those few who had dealings with the landowners and their stewards, and its growth became increasingly rapid during the nineteenth century. By 1850, in eastern Leinster, English was the first language of most people living within a thirty-mile radius of Dublin, while either Scottish English or Anglo-English[4] was firmly estab-

Map 1. Ireland

lished as the first language of the majority of people living in eastern and central Ulster, except in the Sperrin Mountains of county Tyrone. Whereas in 1800 less than 50 percent of the population used English as their first language, by 1851 the census figures on language show that only 23 percent spoke Irish as their first language, though it is widely believed that this figure is too low since many were unwilling to admit to being Irish speakers because of the low prestige of that language.

By 1861, only 2 percent of children under eleven were monoglot Irish speakers, according to de Fréine (1977). A variety of factors encouraged the rapid decline of Irish and the spread of English: the growth of the railway network radiating from Dublin and Belfast and linking the major (English-speaking) towns with all parts of the country; the establishment of unofficial hedge schools and from 1831 the national schools, in both of which the use of Irish was actively discouraged; and the famines and the resultant high death toll and emigration in which two million people either died or left the country between 1830 and 1850 (of whom the greater part came from the main Irish-speaking area of the west and southwest). It has been estimated that the number of Irish speakers was probably halved by the famine alone.

During the second half of the nineteenth century, it became increasingly desirable in the minds of country people to know English, since it was helpful to potential emigrants and to those travelling to England or Scotland or to non-Irish-speaking parts of Ireland for seasonal employment undertaken to eke out a barely adequate living gained from subsistence farming in the west. To learn English seemed to be a way to avoid a recurrence of the consequences of the famines. Even nationalist politicians like Daniel O'Connell believed that Irish was a hindrance to their cause and that the use of English would aid their fight for recognition and influence. It seemed that both individually and collectively, the people saw English as an easy road to progress and Irish as the chief stumbling block. There was an almost hysterical swing to English. A reaction toward Irish is not discernible until after the Easter Rising of 1916. From that time the use of Irish has been seen as part of the search for national identity and has continued to this day to be a token of Republican aspirations in Belfast and Londonderry, paralleled by political activists' painting the red letter boxes of Ulster in the green of the Irish Republic.

The use of Hiberno-English dialect by writers in the Anglo-Irish literary movement of the late nineteenth and early twentieth centuries (Synge, O'Casey, Yeats, and others) gave educated Hiberno-English and even rural Hiberno-English a higher standing culturally and indicated a sense of identity or linguistic independence even in the use of the "new" language.

Before the nineteenth century, Hiberno-English in literature was usually restricted to a "stage Irish" used to denote Irish characters who were often the butt of humor. In that tradition, Jonathan Swift (1667–1745) satirized the dialect in his *Irish Eloquence* and *Dialogue in the Hibernian Style*. Early in the nineteenth century, however, writers began to take a more serious attitude toward Hiberno-English. Maria Edgeworth (1767–1849), William Carleton (1794–1869), Gerald Griffin (1803–40), and Michael (1796–1874) and John (1798–1842) Banim attempted to write in an Irish manner for a world readership unfamiliar with Irish life. These writers and their contemporaries realized that they must use English rather than Gaelic to reach and influence a wide audience. Yet they wished to give an Irish flavor to their writing and so experimented with uses of Hiberno-English. One of the most important, though unintended, contributions to the development of this new style was the translation into Hiberno-English of Gaelic verses by Douglas Hyde (1860–1949), founder of the Gaelic League in 1893 and subsequently president of the Republic of Ireland. His translations were so attractive that they proved the potential of Hiberno-English for serious literary work of the kind later written by W. B. Yeats (1865–1939), Lady Augusta Gregory (1859–1932), and particularly J. M. Synge (1871–1909).

The essence of the style used by Hyde and in the plays by Synge was not realism but a heightened form of peasant speech in which a careful selection was made from both Standard English and dialect sources. They did not wish to claim that actual peasants used this form of English; their objective was to suggest the Irish national character by use of dialect vocabulary, idiom, syntax, and rhythm. Hence it is impossible to link this literary Hiberno-English with any particular region of Ireland—though it is definitely not Northern. Like other writers who employ dialect, they solved the problem of intelligibility by mixing dialect forms with Standard English so they might reach both an audience at the National Theatre in Dublin and, at the same time, a world-wide readership. Synge attempted to write as "Irish" a form of English as possible and often employed literal translations of Gaelic syntactic structures, selected loanwords, and even contrived "dialect" forms that together constituted what he called "the bilingual style."

In the half century after the work of Hyde and Synge, a more realistic use has been made of dialect for suitable characters in plays and novels. Sean O'Casey (1880–1964) tended to mix Dublin and rural forms of speech, perhaps because the Dublin urban dialect was beginning to have a widespread impact on adjacent rural dialects and because people were increasingly migrating into Dublin from rural areas and bringing their own forms of speech with them. James Joyce (1882–1941) carefully collected dialect phrases in a notebook and used them and other aspects of Hiberno-English in *Ulysses* and *Finnegans Wake*. More recently, Brendan Behan (1923–64) has employed the Hiberno-English of Dublin in plays, particularly in *The Hostage* (1958).

By 1900, the census showed that 85 percent of the population now spoke only English; 10 percent were bilinguals; just 5 percent (21,000), mainly in the extreme west, indicated that they were monoglot Irish speakers. Today it may safely be said that there are virtually no monoglot Irish speakers, and very many who know Irish have no social network in which to use the language and so grow "rusty" in it. Probably less than 100,000 survive who speak Irish from their mothers' laps, though many more use the language with varying degrees of fluency through the influence of the schools in the Republic since partition and of Catholic schools in Northern Ireland, and from various political or revivalist motives.

The complex pattern of Northern Hiberno-English dialects and their distinctive character stems from their largely independent history. There is evidence for some sort of boundary between the northern third and the southern two-thirds of Ireland from the earliest times. A series of earthworks analogous to Offa's Dike in the Marches of Wales runs from just south of Bundoran on the west coast in a southeasterly direction, reaching almost to the east coast near Newry. This was probably a dike to prevent cattle stealing, and it dates from at least 250 A.D. It approximately coincides with the southern edge of the ancient kingdom of Ulster. With the exception of parts of Down and Carrickfergus on Belfast Lough, the dikes also coincide with the most northerly penetration of the Anglo-Normans.

The Irish language had distinctive northern and southern forms, according to O'Rahilly (1932) and others. The position of word stress in disyllables referred to above is one of the most important distinctions between the two dialects. The northern dialect of Irish extended approximately to the line of the dikes and was characterized by an increasing influence of Scots Gaelic as one proceeded north and east. From the thirteenth century onward, the Irish of the north had been under increasing Scottish influence. The chief point of contact was between northeastern Antrim and Kintyre, Galloway, and the Isles.

While O'Rahilly traces Scottish features in the Gaelic as far south as Ballyshannon on the west coast and Drogheda on the east, he indicates that the Irish of the Antrim Glens, Rathlin Island, and the Inishowen peninsula in Donegal is the most Scots in flavor. In the boundary region indicated by the dikes, he shows that the Irish of Leitrim was almost completely southern in character, as that of Sligo probably was also, but the Irish of north Meath and northwestern Cavan seems to be of a more Northern type. O'Rahilly finds the first explicit reference to the north-south distinction in Irish dialects in 1577 but believes they emerged as early as the thirteenth or fourteenth centuries. Clearly the distinction existed before the arrival of Modern English in the seventeenth century. The importance of this distinction in Irish dialects is that when English arrived, it appears to have taken over the distribution patterns of the Irish dialects (see Henry 1958, p. 147), apparently because separate networks of communication supported distinct varieties of English just as they had maintained differences between north and south Gaelic.

The Irish language survived latterly in such a way as to form, for nearly three hundred years, a barrier between the English introduced in the south and that introduced in the north. This barrier was only finally eliminated by the spread of English southeast from Fermanagh and northward from county Louth in the early nineteenth century.[5] The barrier between the northern and the southern

English formed by the belt of Irish stretching across the area of the dikes was first breached near Clones and Granard in the north midlands, where an important road crosses the boundary region.

The English of the north is most influenced by Scottish or Anglo-English to the north and east of Ulster and by Irish to the west, especially in the Sperrin Mountains of Tyrone and in western Donegal, where Irish lingered late and still survives in some parts. The 1851 census map shows English much more widely established in the eastern half of Ulster.

Since English was rapidly accepted in the eastern coastal region of Ireland (the Pale), it was very little influenced by Irish. From that area, English spread to adjacent areas of southeast Ulster. However, a slow drift of people speaking Scottish English moved southwest from east Ulster, and there was probably a long period of bilingualism in west and southwest Ulster with much interlingual influence.

As has been indicated above, the Northern dialects can be divided into two main types: (1) the northeast—north Down, east Antrim, north Derry, and parts in east Donegal, all areas having dialects with a strong Scots flavor and often labeled Ulster Scots (Henry 1958, p. 53) or Scotch-Irish (Gregg 1972, p. 109); and (2) the Mid-Ulster (Henry 1958, p. 53) or Ulster Anglo-Irish (Gregg 1972, p. 109) based on Anglo-English. This second area had its origins chiefly in the west and northwest Midlands of England but shows some Scots influence.

Braidwood (1964) has thoroughly documented the cause of the distinctiveness of Northern Hiberno-English speech. He gives a detailed account of the Scots settlements and plantations from 1609 onward. It is impossible to separate English and Scots elements, since the two groups quite quickly blended both by a migration of the Scots into English-planted regions and from a mutual desire for security against the native Irish. The Ulster Scots area is merely one in which the Scots predominated, not one where they were found exclusively. Because the Scots were apparently better settlers than the English, their influence spread, and the result was that in addition to developing a distinct area of Scots dominance, they moved into other parts and influenced the speech of all nine northern counties. Even in the hub of the English settlement in the Lagan Valley, southwest of Belfast, and in the city itself, the influence of Scots is heard, and indeed few traces of the original English dialect remain because of the great mixing with the Scots (see Adams 1977).

The Scots settlers brought with them a form of English different from that of the English settlers and made little or no attempt to modify their speech. They developed links during the nineteenth century with the Scots literary tradition, which may have consolidated them somewhat as a linguistic community. During the late eighteenth and early nineteenth centuries, some members of the community followed with interest the developing literary tradition of Lowland Scotland. While the poetry written elsewhere in Ulster was composed in Standard English, a great deal of poetry was written in the Ulster Scots dialect in mid and southern Antrim and in north and east county Down. The principal writers of this poetry were James Orr (1770–1816) of Ballycarry, county Antrim; Samuel Thomson (1766–1816) and Samuel Walker (1803–85), both of Templepatrick, county Antrim; and Thomas Given (1850–1917) of Cullybackey, county Down. Much of their poetry shows the influence of the themes and language of Robert Burns of Scotland (1759–96), but some Ulster dialect poetry was being written at the middle of the eighteenth century (most notably that of Francis Boyle [1730–ca. 1810] of Gransha, county Down). The later poets were much influenced by Burns's example, but their best work sometimes equalled or surpassed the model he provided—particularly James Orr's "The Irish Cottier's Death and Burial." These Ulster poets were well educated through Sabbath and day schools, were active members of local book clubs, and sometimes accumulated large personal libraries. Most of them were farmers or involved in the weaving trade, but their reading included Shakespeare, Pope, Goldsmith, Gray, and, especially, the Bible. Many of them were United Irishmen as a consequence of their sympathy for the ideals of the French revolution; they were radical and liberal in politics and some participated in the rebellion of 1798 that attempted to expel English troops from Ulster. Their sense of Ulster national identity was one important factor in their decision to write poetry in the Ulster Scots dialect.

An idea of the kind of poetry written in Ulster Scots can be gained through the following selection of three stanzas from Samuel Thomson's "Lilting to Tobacco" (1799, p. 75):

> Some like to snuff thee, some to chow
> While frae their jaws the slavers flow
> Till it wad sconner my sow
>   an' poison pigs
> To see their beards a laggart grow
>   Like sooty wigs.
>
> An' wives forsooth wi' nebs like snipes' noses
> Stan' out frae cheeks like scrapit tripes
> Snievel an' dreep, but onie wipes
>   Save on their cuff
> Might gie a Highlandman the gripes
>   Ar takin' snuff.
>
> How hae I leugh a meikle deal
> At thoughtless gowks frae cutty stale
> Puff out great mouthfu's—syne grow pale
>   As onie hawkey
> Swear, shake an' bokin lose his meal
>   Then damn tobacco.

[Some like to sniff thee, some to chew
While from their jaws the saliva flows
Until it would sicken my sow and poison pigs
To see their beards grow contaminated like sooty wigs.

And wives indeed with noses like snipes
Standing out from cheeks like scraped tripe
Snivel and drip, but any wipes, save on their cuffs,
Might give a Highlandman nausea at the thought of taking snuff.

How have I laughed a great deal
At thoughtless fools from stale tobacco
Puffing out great mouthfuls—soon grow pale as a white faced cow
Swear, shake and vomiting lose his meal, then damn tobacco.]

These stanzas, with their distinctive English and strong moralistic flavor, are typical of the work of these poets.

Though the sense of Ulster national identity that motivated the Ulster dialect poets waned through the nineteenth century, the Ulster Scots continued to regard themselves as a distinct community. Contacts with Scotland and its centers of learning such as Edinburgh and St. Andrews were maintained notably through the Presbyterian church and the medical schools. The Test Acts prevented Presbyterians from being educated at Trinity College in Dublin, as many Anglicans were, and higher education was usually sought in Scotland. To a limited extent this pattern still survives. Today, many Ulster Scots speakers seem to be bidialectal and, regarding the Ulster Anglo-Irish as more prestigious, tend to modify their speech toward it in more formal situations. Recent findings from the Tape-recorded Survey of Hiberno-English Speech (see Barry 1981) seem tentatively to indicate that Ulster Scots is probably in decline; it is certainly often the object of humor.

One can perhaps speculate that the modern political frontier may have had some influence in maintaining distinctions along the line of the dikes (from Bundoran to Newry), though the line passes to the north of Monaghan and cuts off Donegal in the northwest. Certainly there are many people on both sides of the border who are reluctant to cross it, and indeed some have never done so, but it is difficult to quantify the impact of the situation since 1922 in linguistic terms. One of the most significant factors may be the reception of RTE broadcasts and the employment of Dublin-trained teachers in schools on the Republic side of the border. It may eventually be possible to demonstrate this influence in the speech of children.

The Characteristics of English in Ireland

The English language introduced by the followers of the Anglo-Normans in the early Middle English period included the following characteristics in the fourteenth and fifteenth centuries (according to Henry 1958, pp. 62–75).

Vowels

[i], [i:] derived from Middle English ī or ĭ—*silver, sin, hear; bride, fire, sky*
[e:] derived from Middle English ẹ̄ or ī—*week, high*
[ɛ] derived from Middle English ĭ—*fist, kiss, pity*
[ɛ], [ɛ:] derived from Middle English ẹ̄ or ĕ—*priest, star*
[æ], [a] derived from Middle English ĕ—*pence, rest, well* (although *pepper* had [ɪ])
[a], [ɒ] derived from Middle English ă + nasal—*land* ([ɒ] is a feature of West Midland Middle English)
[u] derived from Middle English ŭ remained as in *judge, gun* (although *dung* had [ɪ])
[ɛu] derived from Middle English ū—*town, house*
[u] derived from Middle English eu and y—*truth, due*

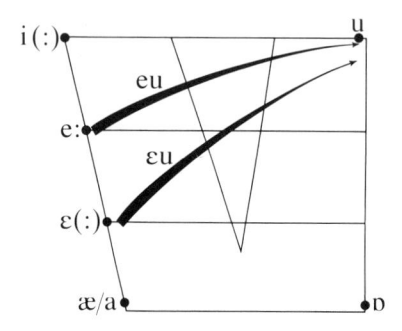

```
    i(:)●─────────────●u
          eu
       e:●
              ɛu
     ɛ(:)●
      æ/a●─────────────●ɒ
```

Final *-e* had been lost, as in *grace* and *come*, as it had in late Middle English in England, but the loss here was early according to the evidence of the Kildare Book (ca. 1300). Short vowels, evidenced by following double consonants, were retained in some words like *ette* 'eat' and *collis* 'coals'.

Consonants

There were occasional losses of *h-* (e.g., in *had*) and occurrences of hypercorrect *h-* (in *(h)all*) (*h-* is normally retained in Modern Hiberno-English).
ng was pronounced [n] in *hearing, being, length* (as in Modern Hiberno-English).
thr- remained [θr] ([t̠'r] in Modern Hiberno-English).
wh- remained [ʍ] (as in Modern Hiberno-English).
[w] and [v] were leveled under Irish [β] (but retained in the spelling)—*wiser, fire* (voiced to *vire* in southwest English). This tendency is present in Modern Hiberno-English.

English in Ireland

Final [d] was devoiced in *made* and *forehead*. This tendency is present in Modern Hiberno-English.

Homorganic final consonants were assimilated: *-n(d)* as in *spend*, *-l(d)* as in *hold*, and *-m(b)* as in *chamber* (as in Modern Scots-Irish).

[s] and [z] became [ʃ] in *trespass*, *grace* (a tendency present in Modern Hiberno-English).

[ʤ] became [tʃ] in *damage* (a tendency present in Modern Hiberno-English).

Some consonant changes took place under the influence of the initial consonant mutation known as *lenisation* in Irish:

tr > [d̥r] *true*
th [θ] > [d] *thing*, [t] *thumb*
k > [g] *market*
t > [d] *twenty* (as in Modern Scots-Irish)
p > [b] *poor*
t > [t̬] *sight*
st- > [st̬] *stand*
d > [d̥] *dirt*

The older English of Forth and Bargy, descended from that introduced by the followers of the Anglo-Normans, showed the following characteristics[6]:

Long Vowels

[i:]—*been* 'bees' (n. pl.), *een* 'eyes', *three, hearing, spend, send, dead, lead* (n.), *die* 'a weight', *Friday, might, kind; nose* [sic]

[ɛ:]—*wheat, beasts, meal* 'flour', *heart, earth,* and the second syllable (stressed) in *pipér*

[a:]—*take, make, ache, father, far, there, small, caul*

[ɔ:]—*hand, land, cold, old, store, who,* also the second syllable (stressed) in *erránd*

[u:]—*true, crow, dough,* and the second syllable (stressed) in *bacón, reasón*

[ə:]—*milk* (with dark [ɫ])

Short Vowels

[ɪ]—*hill, chimney, ich* 'I', *slip, son, sun, some, cover, bramble, nose* [sic]
[ɛ]—*very, feather, end, against, thatch, (h)im, hill*
[a]—*any, well* (adv.), *water, what, from, among, barm*
[ɒ]—*body, black*
[u]—*us, out, cock, body*
[ə (+ ɾ)]—*church, dirt, first, door*

Diphthongs

[ai]—*grain, prey, hail, may, neighbors, reason, cream, meal, quay, joint, voice, boil, comb*
[aʊ]—*daughter*
[əʊ]—*down, cow, house*
[ɪu]—*enough* (second syllable)
[ɪə]—*gate*
[eə]—*mate, leave, gate*
[ɛə]—*went, eager*
[aə]—*daughter* (perhaps with long first element)
[oə]—*oats, going, one*
[ʊə]—*good, blood, soot*

Triphthongs

[ɛəʊ], [ɛɒʊ]—*down, house, ground, mouth, cows, about*

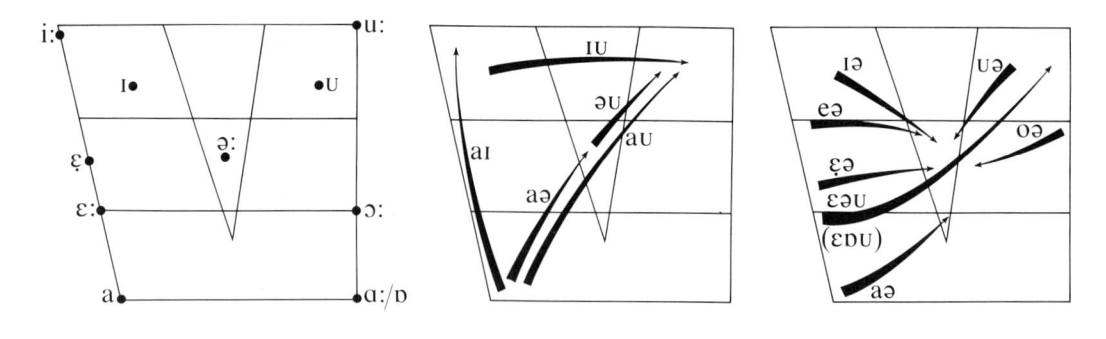

Consonants

Vowels followed by *r* or *r* plus a consonant retained *r*-coloring.
[l] was occasionally dark [ɫ]—*milk*.
[dɹ] appeared in *throw, three*, and *threshel* 'flail' (a southwest English feature).
[s], [f], [ʃ], and [θ] were often voiced (as in southwest English)—*send, side, fuller, first, sheep, ship*, and *thing* (also with [d̪ʰ]).
[gj] occurs in *gate, against*, and *give*; [j] is added to *old* [jɒlə].
-*ng* is represented by [in] and [ɪn] as in most modern Hiberno-English dialects.
[h] is usually preserved as in most modern Hiberno-English dialects.
[w] > [v] occasionally—*wiser*.

-th was lost (as in Irish)—*another*. This is a feature of modern Northern Hiberno-English.

[θ]/[ð] contrast was usually preserved but occasionally became [t̺ʰ]/[d̺ʰ] (as in most Southern Hiberno-English dialects).

wh- [ʍ] was spelled and probably pronounced as [f]—*what* (as in modern northwest Donegal English).

-ld lost the *d*—*old, cold* (as in modern Scots-Irish dialects).

Metathesis of *r* occurred in *thirst* and *bridge*.

the was *th'* or *ee*—[iː]—and these forms occur in *the ball, (th)e parish, (th)e boys*.

-ed was devoiced—*parted, hallowed*.

Morphology

thick 'this' was heard, as in southwest English dialects.

ich, 'ch were used for 'I'. This is represented by *utch(y)* in the old Somerset dialect.

-is was preserved occasionally in plurals—*neighbors, dogs, cats*.

-n plurals were occasionally retained as in some archaic English dialects—*shoon* 'shoes', *een* 'eyes', *been* 'bees', *peasen* 'peas', *ashen* 'ashes'.

-th was occasionally preserved—*knoweth*.

Old English *ge-* > Middle English *y-* [iː] (spelled *ee*) was used—*ee-loved, ee-sewed, ee-go* 'gone'.

Vocabulary

Some Old French, Old Norse, Irish, and English regional dialect words occurred in the dialect.

Stress was sometimes on the second syllable of disyllables—*castéale, bodý, daughtér, towér, markét*.

Modern Southern Hiberno-English

While the character of the new Southern Hiberno-English introduced in the seventeenth century is not thoroughly documented, it is likely that the West Midland dialect predominated.[7] But since the exact nature of West Midland English of that time is not known, Bliss and others have been compelled to take "standard," educated London English as if it were the form introduced and to use as a basis of comparison the variety described by Dobson (1968) and others. Some West Midland features can readily be identified, since the available evidence for Middle English and contemporary English in the West Midlands shows these features to have existed, though they neither spread into nor survived in educated London English: retroflexion of *r* after vowels; the close similarity of the realizations of modern RP /æ/ and /ɑ/ as /aʳ/ or /aːʳ/; rounding of *a* before nasals (e.g., *land*, *hand*); and the morphological and lexical items *childer* 'children' and *tundish* 'funnel'.[8] Southern Hiberno-English may be therefore described as dialectal and as an archaic and gaelicized form of English.

Archaism, the result of isolation from the source area of the English introduced, can be seen in the retention of monophthongal forms such as [eː] in *late* and [oː] in *load* (probably reinforced by the continued use of these sounds in the West Midland source area and by their existence in Irish); [əɪ] in *light* and *blind*; [əu] in *ground* and *house*; and [e] or [eɪ] in *reason* and *measles*. The distribution of the vowels and their treatment before *r* indicates that the English containing these features was introduced in Ireland not much later than 1650 (Bliss 1975, p. 6).

Gaelicization can be seen chiefly in the consonant system and in some characteristics of the vowels which will be discussed fully below.

Vowels

Since the English introduced in the seventeenth century probably had six long and six short stressed monophthongal and three diphthongal vowel sounds, there was a problem for Irish speakers who at that time had only five long and five short monophthongal phonemes. This deficiency was met by raising the main allophones of the Irish /a/ and /aː/—namely, [a], [ɑ], and [aː], [ɑː]—to phonemic status in order to represent the distinction in seventeenth-century English between the phonemes /a/, /ɒ/, /aː/, and /ɔː/. This development resulted in the following situation:

English long vowels:	iː	eː	aː (ɑː)	ɔː	oː	uː
Southern Hiberno-English:	i	eː	aː	ɑː	oː	uː
English short vowels:	ɪ	e(ɛ)	a(æ)	ɒ	ʌ	u(ʊ)
Southern Hiberno-English:	i	e	a	ɑ	o	u

The [ɑ(ː)] was generally more front (narrowly [aʳ(ː)]) than modern Anglo-English /ɑː/ and even more front in Northern Hiberno-English. This phonetic similarity could have been reinforced by the similarity in the realizations of modern Anglo-English /æ/ and /ɑː/ in the West Midland dialects. In west Cork, according to Lunny (1981), there is a tendency for distinctions between /æ/ and /ɑː/ to disappear under a single phoneme /a/ with or without length, probably because the functional load of the /æ/-/ɑː/ contrast is very low with probably only the three minimal pairs: *palm/Pam*, *psalm/Sam*, and *aunt/ant* (the majority of these words being rare anyway, since *Pam* and *Sam* are personal names not commonly found in the area).

A significant contrast exists between Northern and Southern Hiberno-

English in Ireland

English in the treatment of Anglo-English /ʌ/ and /ʊ/. This contrast was new in Anglo-English at the time of its introduction to Ireland and still does not occur in many of the northern districts of England. The contrast in development of /ʌ/ and /ʊ/ in Northern Hiberno-English and Southern Hiberno-English may best be seen alongside their treatment of /o:/ and /u:/.

Anglo-English phonemes:	/o:/	/u:/	/ʌ/	/ʊ/
Northern Hiberno-English:	[o:]	[ʉ(:)]	[ɔ̈]	[ʉ(:)]
Southern Hiberno-English:	[ǫ:]	[u:]	[ö]	[ö]

In other words, Northern Hiberno-English dialects often tend to merge /u:/ and /ʊ/ under /ʉ/, which phonetically can be either short or long—length has no phonemic significance. Southern Hiberno-English has kept the two phonemes apart, but merges /ʌ/ and /ʊ/ under /ö/ (often realized as close [ü] in the Dublin area, but as a more open [ɔ̈:] in other dialects); /ʌ/ and /ʊ/ are usually maintained as distinct phonemes in Northern Hiberno-English (see map 2).

In Irish, the distinction between long and short vowels is more important than vowel quality; on the other hand, vowel quality is more important than length in English. Thus Irish /o:/ is distinguished from /o/. In English, /o:/ is distinguished from /ʌ/ by quality as well as length, as are English /ɔ:/ and /ɒ/. A qualitative distinction is maintained in Southern Hiberno-English: /o:/ and /ʌ/ are represented by [ǫ:] and [ö] respectively—*coat, cut*; Northern Hiberno-English has [o:]-[ɒ].

The rounding of the English phonemes /ɔ:/ and /ɒ/ is not usually maintained in Southern Hiberno-English, though it is more commonly maintained in Northern Hiberno-English (see map 3). The reason for the weakening or complete disappearance of rounding is probably, first of all, because of the basic long-short nature of the vowel contrast in Irish, and second, because the Irish had no rounded open back phonemes, only /a/ and /a:/ with their front and back allophones [a(:)] and [ɑ(:)]. Thus *sad*, *sod*, and *sawed* can often appear as a homophone [sad] or on occasion with [ɑ] having length in *sawed* only.

The diphthongal phonemes introduced in the seventeenth century were probably /əɪ/, /əu/, and /ɔɪ/. The /əɪ/ and /əu/ were readily maintained, since Irish had similar sounds. They commonly remain today, though phonetically the first element of /əɪ/ is rather unstable, varying from [ɛɪ] to [əɪ], [ɑɪ], or [ɒɪ]. Lunny (1981) shows [əɪ] to be by far the most common form in west Cork, with [ɑɪ] and [ɒɪ] quite common and [ɛɪ] types rare. In Northern Hiberno-English, [ɛɪ] is more common.

There is a tendency for a phonemic clash to develop between /əɪ/ and /ɔɪ/ in some Southern Hiberno-English dialects. Irish had no diphthong with a back rounded first element, and early speakers of English seem to have tended to use the /əɪ/ phoneme for words like *boy* and *joint*. However, in west Cork, Lunny

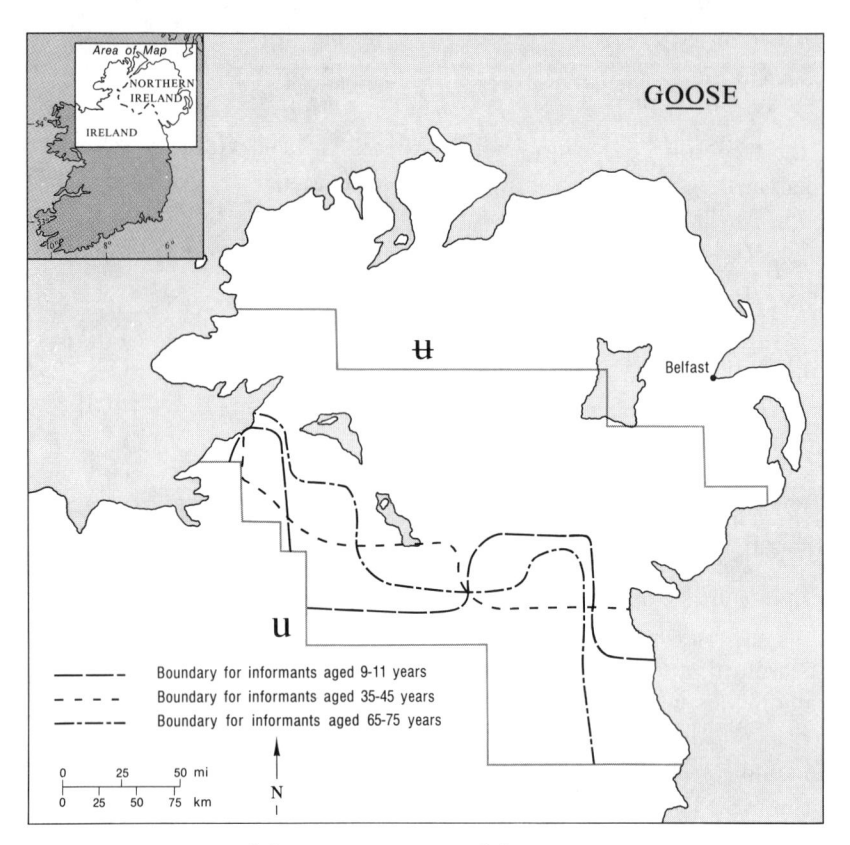

Map 2. Northern [ʉ] versus Southern [u]

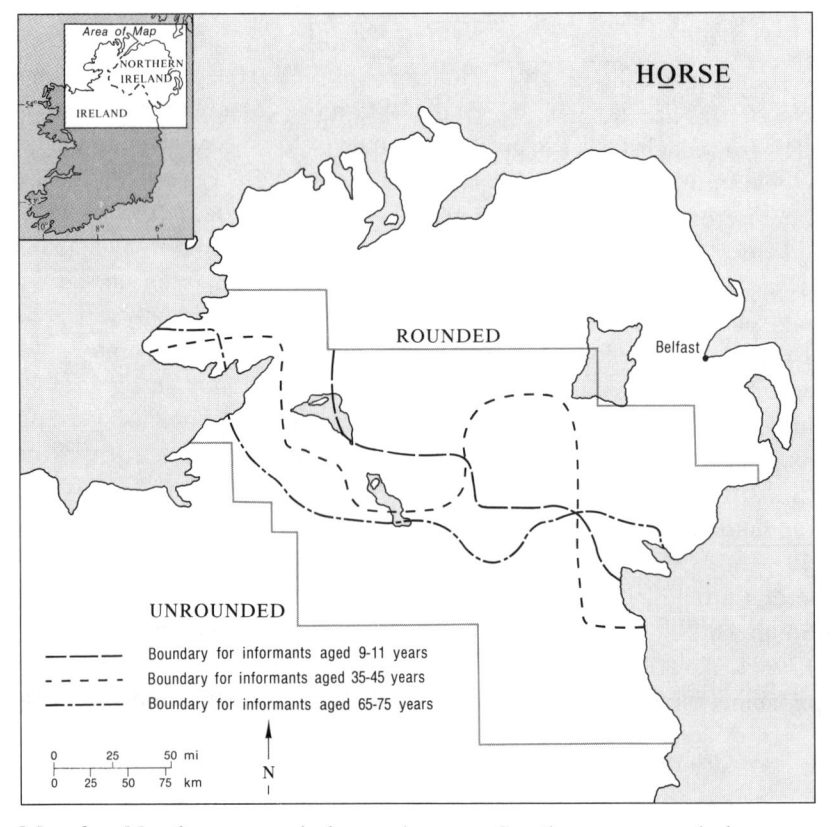

Map 3. Northern rounded vowel versus Southern unrounded

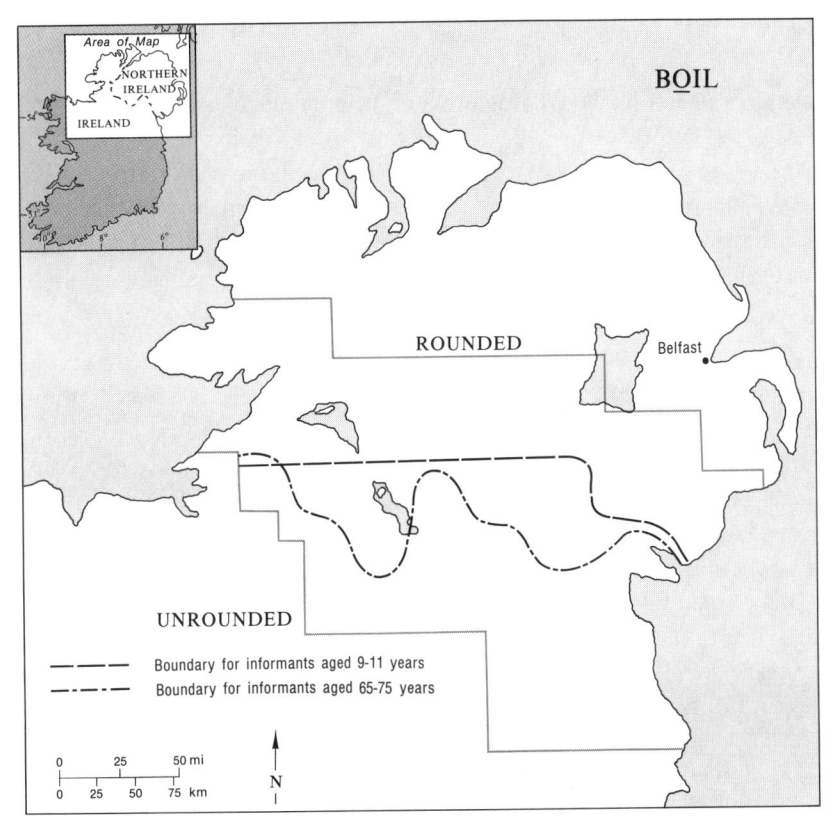

Map 4. Northern rounded first element of diphthong versus Southern unrounded

reports that the /ɔɪ/ phoneme shows a majority of realizations with [ɑɪ] (or occasionally [ɒɪ]), with rather fewer of the [əɪ] type and rare occurrences of [ɛɪ], so backness rather than centrality of the first element seems to be the chief means of phonemic distinction. In Northern Hiberno-English, slight or full rounding of a back first element is common (see map 4).

In Northern Hiberno-English the /əu/ often appears as [aʊ], [ɑʊ], or [ɛʊ], but in Southern Hiberno-English, especially in the south and southwest, [oʊ] is common: [ˈkounti ˈkɑrk] *county Cork* and [gɹound] *ground* (n.).

A further significant characteristic feature of Hiberno-English is the treatment of vowels followed by *r* or by *r* plus a consonant. Loss of this *r* in Anglo-English in the seventeenth and eighteenth centuries did not occur in the English of Ireland: [kɑːr] *car* and [kɑːrt] *cart*. R after vowels is usually retracted or retroflex (most notably so in Northern Hiberno-English), as in the West Midland and southwest Anglo-English dialects, but it may be slightly velarized after /ə/ (narrowly [ɤ̃r]) where *-er* endings occur—[wɑːtɤ̃r] *water*. This velarization has been recorded by the Tape-recorded Survey of Hiberno-English Speech in the north Pale, but its exact distribution has not yet been established. In Hiberno-English dialects where [a] and [aː] are always much fronted, *r*-coloring in words where Anglo-English has /ɑ:/ helps prevent a phonemic clash between words like *cat* and *cart*.

The exact realizations of each of the vowel phonemes of Hiberno-English vary somewhat around the country, but many realizational differences exist between Northern Hiberno-English and Southern Hiberno-English on either side of the Bundoran-Carlingford boundary.[9]

Consonants

When Irish speakers began to adopt English for everyday speech, they were obliged to increase their vowel inventories (as described above) but to decrease the number of their consonants. English at the time had twenty-five consonant phonemes, but Irish, depending on the dialect, had between thirty and forty. English speakers with an Irish background made a selection from the wider range of Irish phonemes to obtain suitable near equivalents for English sounds.

The phonemic system in Irish is one in which many of the consonant phonemes are found in pairs, one usually called "palatal" or "slender" and the other "velar" or "broad," though these labels should be seen as convenient *phonological* distinctions and not as representing strict phonetic reality. For instance, /ḱ/-/k/ and /ǵ/-/g/ indicate a more front or "palatal" and a more back or "velar" phoneme respectively. The distribution of these pairs is partly conditioned by following front or back vowels and by association with other front or back consonants in certain positions in the word. However, the pairs /ṕ/-/p/ and /b́/-/b/, though they too are called "palatal" and "velar," have a quite different phonetic quality. "Palatal" /ṕ/ and /b́/ in fact consist of a bilabial consonant in which the lips are rather spread and the front of the tongue raised toward the front of the palate (not lying neutral in the bottom of the mouth as in English); the "velar" /p/ and /b/ are formed as a bilabial consonant in which there is slight protrusion of the lips as well as a raising of the back of the tongue.[10]

In Hiberno-English, sometimes two Irish phonemes were used to distinguish two English phonemes.

Irish /f/ and /f́/ were used for English /ʍ/ and /f/ in Hiberno-English—*white*, *fish*.

Irish /v/ and /v́/ were used for English /w/ and /v/ in Hiberno-English—*well*, *very*.

Irish /t̪/ and /t́/ were used for English /θ/ and /tj/ in Hiberno-English—*thin*, *tube*.[11]

Irish /d̪/ and /d́/ were used for English /ð/ and /dj/ in Hiberno-English—*this*, *dew*.

Irish /s/ and /ś/ were used for English /s/ and /ʃ/ in Hiberno-English—*so*, *shoe*.

English in Ireland

In some urban dialects, the alveolar realizations [t] and [d] are replacing dental [t̪] and [d̪] realizations, and true homophones are appearing such as *true/threw* and *tree/three* (Bliss 1975).

English /ʍ/ and /w/ are often represented in Hiberno-English by [ɸ] and [β]. The result of the occurrence of [β] is that in Hiberno-English /v/ has come to sound like [w] (as in *invited* and *divided*) to English ears.

Sometimes distinct phonemes of Irish are used to represent distinctions which were merely allophonic in Anglo-English. In west Cork, *cat* and *coal* have [k̟] and [k] from Irish /k̟/ and /k/. In Northern Hiberno-English and some other areas, /k̟/ and /g̟/ are realized as a sequence of two full segments—initial [kj] and [gj]—especially south of Loch Neagh and in northwest Ulster (including county Donegal). These realizations may be partly the result of reinforcement from West Midland dialects in Britain, where initial [kj] and [gj] also occur: *cart* and *gape* (Orton and Barry 1969, p. 124; 1970, p. 601).

The English phonemic contrast between /z/ and /ʒ/ was not paralleled in Irish. Consequently, the English sounds were both accepted, perhaps by analogy with the Irish /s/-/ʃ/ distinction. /ʒ/ occurs in *dazzle* and *business*; /ʃ/ in *snow*, *listen*, *stick*, and *stuff*. [ʃ] occurs as a result of a rule in Irish: in certain consonant clusters, if one segment is palatal, the other must be palatal too. Since English /ʃ/ is used in Hiberno-English to represent Irish palatal /ś/, it appears in contexts where /ś/ would be expected if the words were Irish.

In some cases, only one of a pair of Irish phonemes was used in Hiberno-English. Irish has /l/-/ĺ/, but only the clear /ĺ/ was used in Hiberno-English. The lack of a dark [ɫ] is a feature of all Hiberno-English dialects, and even in the Scots-Irish regions of the north, the Scots dark [ɫ] has made little impact, though the very clear [l] is more noticeable in Southern Hiberno-English speech.

Similarly, of Irish /n/ and /ń/ (phonetically [n] and [ɲ]), only the /ń/ is used in Hiberno-English; *h-* is sounded in initial positions in Irish and consequently in Hiberno-English dialects also, and indeed this seems to be a feature of all Celtic areas of the British Isles.

The Irish *r* was usually a nonpalatal fricative, but a flap occurred after a vowel, after a vowel and before a consonant, and after a consonant and before a vowel. In west Cork, both forms are used in Hiberno-English. The flap is used for intervocalic *r* and the fricative usually occurs initially. In Northern Hiberno-English, the English alveolar frictionless continuant [ɹ] is common initially, but a rather fronted flap often occurs in clusters: *strip*, *three*, and *drew*.

Bliss indicates that "compromise" consonant sounds—neither completely Irish nor completely English in phonetic form—often occur in Hiberno-English. He gives /p/, /b/, /m/, and /ŋ/ as examples but does not describe them phonetically.

Syntax

Hiberno-English, throughout Ireland but more especially in areas where Irish died late, has structures which are literal translations from the Irish. In the following examples, the forms also found in Northern Hiberno-English are marked by an asterisk.[12]

Since perfect and pluperfect tenses do not occur in Irish, these tenses are represented in Southern Hiberno-English by the Irish structure which uses the adverb *after* + *to be*:

> *he was after getting up** 'he had (just) got up'
> *a fairy used to be after coming in the window* 'a fairy would (frequently) come in at the window'

Widespread use of rhetorical questions was common in Irish, though comparatively rare in English:

> *whatever way I turned my head, didn't I see him after coming into the field* 'wherever I looked, I saw that he had come into the field'
> *who was there but a woman and she milking the cow* 'there was a woman there milking the cow'

In sentences like these, the speaker implies a note of slight amazement or that what is being said is in some way rather remarkable.

English indirect questions preceded by *whether* or *if* have to be represented in Irish by a direct question.

> *I don't know is that right or not** 'I don't know whether or not that is right'
> *he wanted to see would he get something to eat** 'he wanted to see whether/ if he would get something to eat'

The use of *and* as almost the only conjunction and the use of *and* followed by a coordinate clause where English would normally use a subordinate clause is normal in Irish and therefore common in Southern Hiberno-English:

> *they were all there and they having great conversations in Irish* 'when they were all there, they were having great conversations in Irish'
> *he waved to me and he/him coming down the road* 'as he came down the road, he waved to me'

Possession is expressed in Irish by *to be* + one of the prepositions *at*, *near*, or *by*. This is literally translated in Southern Hiberno-English.

> *there weren't any candles by this man* 'this man hadn't any candles'
> *it was a custom by them to go out on Christmas Eve* 'it was their custom to go out on Christmas Eve'

English in Ireland

In Irish a distinction is made between a "punctual" present tense and a "consuetudinal" or customary present tense. This structure is rendered in Hiberno-English by the use of *be* or *does (be)* often followed by a present participle.[13]

> *it does stop and it does rain on* 'it keeps stopping and starting to rain'
> *he bees writing**
> *he does write*
> *he does be writing* } 'he is/they are in the habit of writing'
> *they be writing**

Irish does not use a relative pronoun, and relatives are often omitted in Hiberno-English.

> *it was Michael John saw yesterday* 'it was Michael (that/who) John saw yesterday'

There is a tendency to follow the Irish usage in placing the most important word or phrase forward in the sentence preceded by the copula.

> *is it/'tis out of your mind you are* 'are you/you are out of your mind (crazy)'

Idiom

Literal renderings of Irish expressions are quite common in Hiberno-English.

The compass points are often rendered in Irish by *above* 'north', *below* 'south', *over* 'east', and *back* 'west', respectively.

> *we see a crowd away from you, back straight from where you are* 'we see a crowd a little distance from you, to the west of where you are'

The use of *anyone* and a negated verb to mean *no one* is similarly influenced by Irish (which has no word for *no one*).

> *anyone doesn't go to mass here* 'no one goes to mass here'

The idea of oratorical speech is expressed by the phrase *putting from him*—a literal translation of the Irish *ag cur de* (cf. English *holding forth*).

> *he was there putting from him* 'he was there holding forth'

Vocabulary

There is some borrowing of Irish words, especially for concepts or objects, some of which may never have had an English name, but such borrowings tend to be falling out of use. English words borrowed into Irish at an early date and given an Irish pronunciation may be borrowed back in the Irish form:

cruiceog [krɪk'jog] 'heap of peat'
sceallan [skə'lɑ:n] 'small potato'
slean [ʃla:n] 'spade for cutting peat'
cliotar ['klɪtər] 'noise'
fiteog ['ɸɪtʃak] 'marsh grass'
bagun [ba'gu:n] 'bacon'

Borrowing of English words into Irish is much more common than the reverse, especially where the language is in serious decline. Words and phrases such as *well* (exclamation), *but, you know*, and "modern" terms such as *minibus, factory*, and *tape recorder* are reported by Gallagher (1981) as common in the Donegal Gaeltacht. English words may also be borrowed and given an Irish ending: *d'applyáil mé* 'I applied', *happyáilte* 'happy', and *houseen* 'small house'.

Intonation

The intonation patterns of Hiberno-English have not yet been extensively studied (Henry 1958, pp. 174–94). They suggest, as in other Celtic areas of the British Isles, strong influence from the Celtic and are most noticeable where the native vernacular survived late. In west Donegal, for instance, one hears what sounds like Northern Hiberno-English phonology, with a Southern Hiberno-English intonation. In south county Cork, especially around Cork city, there is an area not yet properly defined in which is heard an intonation pattern strikingly different from that of other parts of Ireland. It has often been described as being reminiscent of Anglo-Welsh intonation, though there is no convincing evidence of contact with Welsh or Wales. The matter deserves thorough investigation.

Modern Northern Hiberno-English

The character of Northern Hiberno-English is much more varied than that of Southern Hiberno-English. This is chiefly because of the mixture of Scots as well as Anglo-English in the dialects. Adams (1977) indicates that Northern Hiberno-English was also of West Midland or northwest Midland English origin, like Southern Hiberno-English, but it has developed separately, perhaps because of the barrier of Irish between the two. The admixture of some Scots in all northern regions gradually accentuated this difference. A narrow boundary of mixed Northern Hiberno-English and Southern Hiberno-English exists in south Fermanagh, north and central Monaghan, and south Armagh (see map 5). North of this area, three main dialect areas emerge: Scots-Irish (or Ulster Scots) in the northeast; Mid-Ulster English (or Ulster Anglo-Irish) in south Antrim, north Armagh, west Down, east Tyrone, and north Fermanagh; and Gaelic-influenced speech of

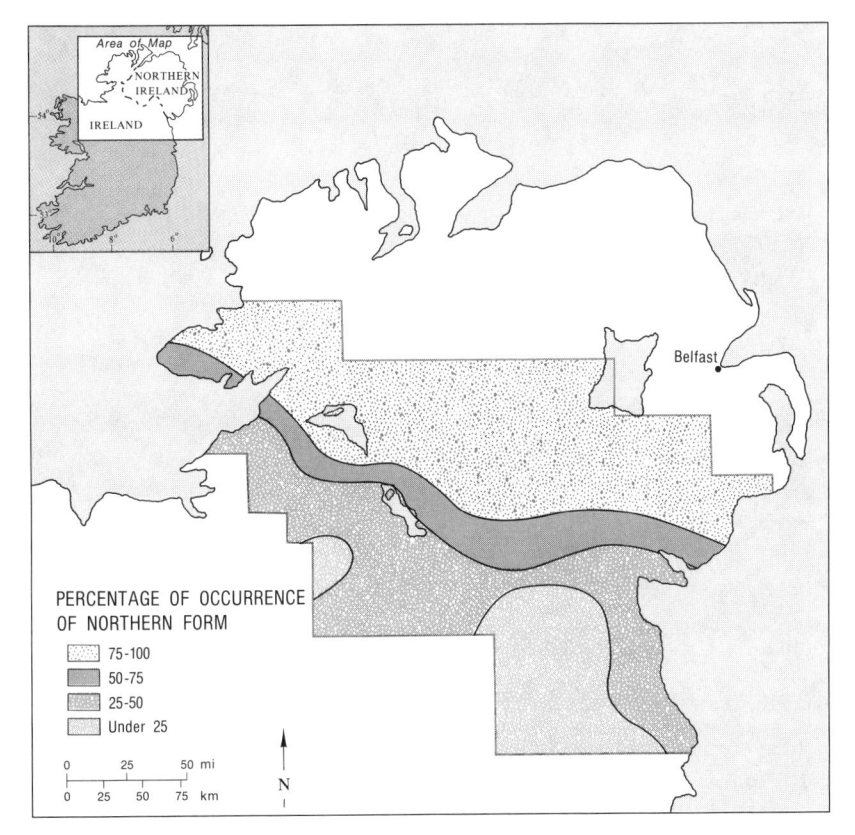

Map 5. Northern-Southern boundary region

the northwest, including much of Donegal and west Tyrone. Scots-Irish has been most studied. Little has been published on the northwest dialects, though the Tape-recorded Survey material and the work of Gallagher (whose Ph.D. dissertation is now in progress at the Queen's University of Belfast) should increase our knowledge of them.

Scots-Irish

The character of the Scots-Irish dialect has been described by Gregg (1964, 1972) and by Adams (1964). The principal features are as follows:

Vowels
The vowel system is complex and is based on that of Lowland Scots.

RP English /ɪ/ is represented by Scots-Irish:

    [æ̈], [ë]—*bit, brig* 'bridge'
    [ɛ:]—*dinner, kindling*
    [ʌ] (after *w-*)—*quilt, will, twist, wind*
    [i:]—*drip, live, swim*

RP English /ɛ/ is represented by Scots-Irish:

[ɛ(:)]—*bet*
[æ]—*red, kest* 'chest, trunk'
[ɑ:] (after *w*-)—*twelve, swell, wren, well* (n.)
[i(:)]—*breast, head, well* (adv.), *deaf*
[e:]—*seven, eleven, shed*
[ʌ]—*many, steady*

RP English /æ/ is represented by Scots-Irish:

[a]—*bat* (Donegal)
[ɛ:]—*apple, flat, hammer, gander*
[ɑ]—*bat* (south Antrim and Down), *narrow, married* (north Antrim)
[ɒ]—*barrow, tassel*

RP English /ɒ/ is represented by Scots-Irish:

[ɔ]—*pot*
[ɑ:] (before or after labials or before final [ŋ])—*porridge, drop, bottle, loft, long*
[o:], [əʉ], [ʌ]—*dog*
[o:]—*rock*

RP English /ʌ/ is represented by Scots-Irish:

[ʌ]—*but* (north and south Antrim, Derry, Down)
[ɑ:]—*mun* 'must'
[æ]—*nut, sun, son, one* ([jæn])
[ö] (Donegal)—*but*
[ɨ] (south Antrim, Down) ⎫
[e:] (north Antrim, Derry) ⎬ —*done, above*
[i] (Donegal) ⎭
[ü]—*plum, such, thumb, rust*
[ɪ]—*nothing*

RP English /ʊ/ is represented by Scots-Irish:

[æ]—*bull*
[ɨ] (south Antrim, Down) ⎫
[e:] (north Antrim, Derry) ⎬ —*good*
[i] (Donegal) ⎭
[ʉ:]—*full, pull* (+ loss of *l*)
[ʌ]—*butcher*

RP English /i/ is represented by Scots-Irish:

    [e:]—*beak, Easter, creature, tea*
    [i]—*beet*

RP English /ɑ:/ is represented by Scots-Irish:

    [ɛ:]—*grass, after, father, arm*

RP English /ɔ:/ is represented by Scots-Irish:

    [ɔ:], [ɑ:], [a:] (unrounded forms favored in Donegal)—*all, salt, wall, draw, hawk*
    [e:]—*straw, broad*
    [ɛ:]—*haunch*
    [əʉ]—*thaw*

RP English /u:/ is represented by Scots-Irish:

    [ɨ] (south Antrim, Down)
    [e:] (north Antrim, Derry) } —*school, shoon* 'shoes'
    [i] (Donegal)
    [əʉ]—*ewe, loose*
    [ɔ:], [ɑ:], [a:]—*two*
    [e:]—*do*

RP English /ə:/ often occurs as:

    [ɤ̈:r]—*heard, third*

RP English /aɪ/ is represented by Scots-Irish:

    [i:]—*die, lie* (n.), *eye*
    [əɪ]—*mine* (n.)
    [ae]
    [aɪ] (Donegal) } —*buy, dye, lie* 'recline', *mine* (poss.), *prize*
    [æ]—*climb, blind*
    [ɛ:]—*either*

RP English /eɪ/ is represented by Scots-Irish:

    [e:]—*bait*
    [ɛ:]—*eight, blade*
    [əɪ]—*clay, way, weigh, May*
    [ɑ:]—*wade*
    [ɔ:]—*away*

RP English /au/ is represented by Scots-Irish:

[ʉ]—*cow, thousand*
[ü]—*about, round, house*
[ʌ]—*found, ground, pound*

RP English /əu/ is represented by Scots-Irish:

[o:] *boat* (over-rounded, sounds like [u:] to English ears)
[ü]—*shoulder, coulter*
[ɔ:], [ɑ:], [a:], [ɑʷ]—*blow, crow* (unrounded forms common in Donegal)
[e:]—*bone, home, most, no, alone, stone*
[əʉ]—*cold, hold, bowl, pole, soul, grow*
[ɑ:]—*open*

Vowels + *r* have retracted *r*-coloring as in other Hiberno-English dialects. The following are reported by Gregg:

RP /ɑ:/ + *r* is represented by [ɛ:r]—*arm*.
RP /i:/ + *r* is represented by [ɛ:r]—*rear* (v.).
RP /ɔ:/ + *r* is represented by [əʉər]—*four*; [ɛ:r]—*more, sore*; and [o:r]—*cord, morning*.
RP /ɛ:/ + *r* is represented by [i:r]—*mare, pear*.
RP /aɪ/ + *r* is represented by [i:ər]—*briar*; [əɪər]—*wire, choir*.
RP /au/ + *r* is represented by [ʉ:ər]—*flower, hour, sour*; cf. [e:r] *flour*; and [ö:r]—*our* (also *moor, poor* in urban Larne Scots-Irish).

The development in Scots-Irish of the RP /ɔɪ/ is not discussed by Gregg (1972) and Adams (1964), but the recordings of the Tape-recorded Survey show that an [ɔɪ] or [ɔe] diphthong with occasional very slight unrounding of the first element is usual in *boil, boy, poison,* and *voice*. Gregg (1964) reports [ɔə] in the place name *Moyne*.

The following charts display the vowel system of the Scots-Irish dialect:

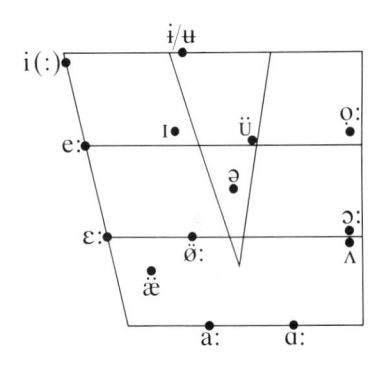

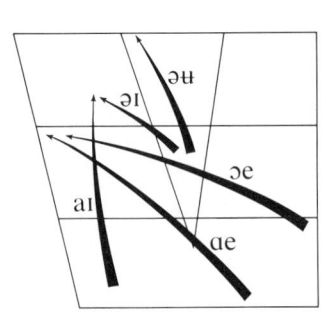

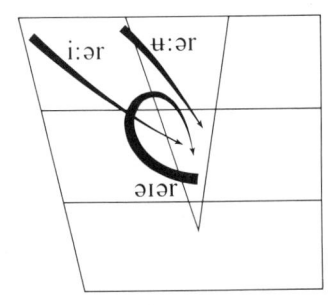

English in Ireland 115

Fronted [uː] is found in Scots English and in Ulster Gaelic (Gregg 1964, p. 187). The *Survey of English Dialects* recorded fronted forms of [uː] in north and northwest England,[14] and reinforcement from these sources, according to Adams, probably explains its presence in Scots-Irish and in all other dialects of the Northern Hiberno-English and its absence in Southern Hiberno-English.

Consonants

Intervocalic [ð] replaces [d] in *ladder* and *bladder*.

/x/ is more widely preserved in Scots-Irish than in other dialects of Northern Hiberno-English. It is recorded in *enough*, *fight*, and *bought*, and occurs commonly in *lough*, *sheugh* 'ditch', and *trough*. It is very common in place-names and dialect words: [əˈhɒxəl] *Ahoghill* and *laughter* 'brood of chickens'.

[h] is preferred to [x] in Donegal Scots-Irish perhaps because of a tendency for [x] > [h] or [ɦ] in Donegal Irish; [h] may be a halfway stage to a standard English form. One informant, when asked by Adams what he called a lake, said [lɒk], [lɒh], and [lɒx] in one breath!

A palatal allophone [ç] occurs in words with [hj]—*huge*.

Scots-Irish has the Irish clear [l] and not the dark [ɫ] of Scots English.

Scots-Irish has the West Midland retroflex or retracted *r*-coloring of vowels before *r* both finally and before a consonant, which is typical of all Hiberno-English dialects. It does not show the Scots English rolled *r*.

Dental allophones of /t/, /d/, /n/, and /l/ occur before [θ] and [ð]: *width* and *filth*. The use of glottal stop realizations of /t/ is common: *Latin* and *better*.

[b], [d], and [g] are frequently lost in *thimble*, *handle*, and *single*.

[d] is lost after [n] and [l] in *hand* and *cold*.

[l] is lost in *wall* and *all*.

A /w/-/ʍ/ contrast exists in *witch* and *which*.

Morphology

In Scots-Irish, according to Gregg (1972), there are a number of negative forms of the auxiliary verbs which are nonstandard and derive from Scots English, northern English, or both: [dɪne] *don't*; [hɪne] *haven't*; [kɑːne] *can't*; [dɪzne] *doesn't*; [hɪzne] *hasn't*; [mɑːne] *mustn't*. Other nonstandard verb forms are [gɪn] *gave, given* and [hədəˈbɪn] *had had*.

Elision is common: [dɪt] *do it*; [fɪt] *from it*; [wɪt] *with it*, cf. [weː] *with*; [heː] *have*; [hɪte] *have to*; [giː] *give*; [noː] *not*.

An [n] plural appears in *shoon* 'shoes' and *een* 'eyes'.

The plural of *cow* is *kye* [kɑe].

Above appears as *aboon* [əˈbin] in the Scots-Irish dialects.

Mid-Ulster

The Mid-Ulster English dialect is much closer to RP in its phonological structure than to Scots-Irish, which has its roots in a form of seventeenth-century Scots

English. The vowel system of Mid-Ulster English is much simpler and has fewer subgroups and isolated variants. The major characteristics of the Mid-Ulster English are as follows:

Vowels

RP English /ɪ/ is represented by Mid-Ulster English:

[ï]—*bridge, build, dinner, kindling, quilt, will, cinders, drip, king, live*

RP English /ɛ/ is represented by Mid-Ulster English:

[ɛ:], usually long (except in south Ulster) except before voiceless plosives and [n] or [l]—*chest, red, many, breast, devil, friend, thread, west*
[ɛˑ]—*seven, eleven*

RP English /æ/ is represented by Mid-Ulster English:

[aˑ]—*apple, flat, hammer*

RP English /ɒ/ is represented by Mid-Ulster English:

[ɒ]—*halter, crop, drop, hob, bottle, long, song, from, nothing, not, rock*
[ɒ:]—*dog*[15]

RP English /ʌ/ is represented by Mid-Ulster English:

[ö] (narrowly [ɔ:], [ɔ̜:])—*must, above, plum, such, thumb, done, dozen, nut, son*
[ɑ:], [ʊ]—*one*

RP English /ʊ/ is represented by Mid-Ulster English:

[ʉ:]—*good*
[ʉ(:)], [ö], [ÿ]—*pull, full, bull*

RP English /ə/ is represented by Mid-Ulster English:

[ə] (narrowly [ë])—*water, about*

RP English /i/ is represented by Mid-Ulster English:

[e:] (as in Scots-Irish)—*beak, creature, Easter, tea*
[i(:)] is the more common form—long only before voiced fricatives in north and northeast Ulster; elsewhere usually short—*beat, weed*

English in Ireland

RP English /ɑ:/ is represented by Mid-Ulster English:

[a(:)]—*after, father, grass*

RP English /ɔ:/ is represented by Mid-Ulster English:

[ɒ(:)]—*straw, haunch, all, walk, talk, scald*
[ɔ]—*salt*

RP English /u:/ is represented by Mid-Ulster English:

[ʉ(:)]—*school, shoes, loose, blue*
[o:]—*ewe*

RP English /ə:/ is represented by Mid-Ulster English:

[ö̞ɾ], [œ̈ɾ]—*bird*
[ɛəɾ]—*heard*

RP English /aɪ/ is represented by Mid-Ulster English:

[əɪ]—*blind, climb, bright, fight, height, die, eye, fly, lie* 'untruth' (n. and v.), *by, buy, lie* 'recline', *prize, tie, pie, mine* (poss.)

RP English /eɪ/ is represented by Mid-Ulster English:

[e:]—*blade, wade, May, pay, stay, clay, way, weigh, neighbor*

RP English /aʊ/ is represented by Mid-Ulster English:

[əʉ]—*allow, about, doubt, house, brown, plow, drought, pound, ground*

RP English /əʊ/ is represented by Mid-Ulster English:

[o:]—*coulter, poll, roll, grow, bone, clothes, home, no*
[oʉ:], [əʉ]—*solder*
[əʉ]—*cold, hold, old, bowl, soul* (as in Scots-Irish)
[aʉ]—*old, cold, bold* (according to Adams 1964)

Vowels + r have retracted *r*-coloring. The following are reported by Gregg (1972) or Adams (1964).

RP /ɑː/ + r represented by [ɑːr]—*arm, cart*
RP /ɔː/ + r represented by [oːr]—*more, sore, four*; [ɔːr]—*cord, morning*; and [ʉər]—*door, poor, course, coarse*
RP /aɪ/ + r represented by [əɪər], [əijər]—*wire, choir, briar*
RP /ɛ/ + r represented by [əːr]—*fair, mare*
RP /i/ + r represented by [ɛ(ə)ːr]—*beard*
RP /əʉ/ + r represented by [əʉər]—*hour*—[əʉwər]; [aːr] is generally found in the Lagan Valley region.
RP /uɪ/ represented by [øː]—*ruin*

The following charts show the vowel system of the Mid-Ulster dialect:

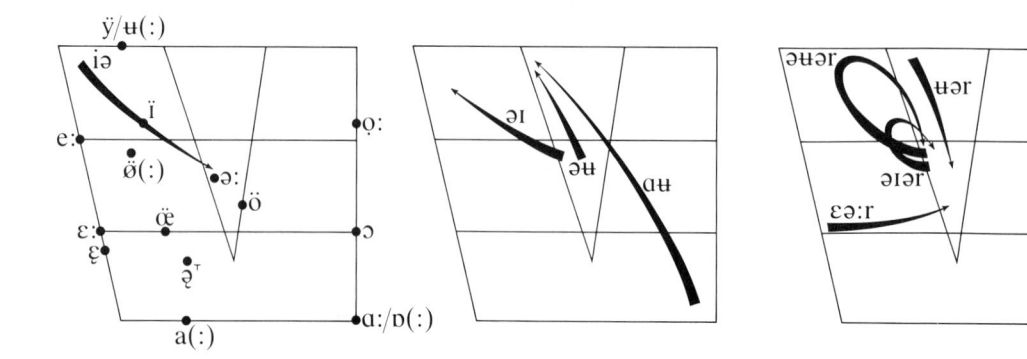

Consonants

/d/ and /t/ before r become [d̪r] and [t̪r] in *drum* and *country*.
/p/, /t/, and /k/ become somewhat voiced in *pepper, butter*, and *jacket*.
/k/ and /g/ frequently become [kj] and [gj] before front vowels—*cat, garden*.
r-coloring of vowels is very much retracted or even retroflex.
/x/ is lost or becomes [f]—*eight, enough*.

Mid-Ulster English is regarded as more prestigious than Scots-Irish, and Scots-Irish speakers in formal situations tend to move in the direction of Mid-Ulster English, presumably because of its greater similarity to Anglo-English (see Gregg 1972 and Adams 1964). Educated Ulster English is based on Mid-Ulster English, especially the Lagan Valley variety, but its sounds tend to conform even more to RP at least in distribution; for example, the archaic English /oː/ is found in *old, cold*, and *hold* (not [ɑu]), and in *code, coal*, and *robe*. Diphthongal forms of /oː/ are moving from RP into the educated speech, so that [oʉ] or [əʉ] occur for older [oː]; [eɪ] is also appearing for older [eː]. R-coloring is weakened or lost in the speech of educated persons, and the vowel qualities in *ant* and *aunt* are kept distinct as in RP ([a] and [ɑː]), as are the vowels in *food* and *good*, /ʉ/ and

/ʊ/. (Often *food* and *good* both have [ʉ(:)] in Northern Hiberno-English.) The centralized quality of /ʉ(:)/ is maintained. This sound is one of the most notable features in Northern Hiberno-English.

Gaelic-Influenced Speech of the Northwest

The character of the speech in the northwest (Donegal and west Tyrone) where Gaelic either survives or survived until recently has not yet been fully described but includes the following features according to Adams (1964) and Gallagher (1981):

Irish Sounds Used when Speaking English

>[ɸ] and [β] are used by older speakers of both languages.
>RP /ʍ/ > [ɸ]—*white, while, what's.*
>RP /v/ and /w/ > [β]—*river, caraway seed.*
>RP /v/ > /w/—*voice.*
>/ʍ/ > [f]—*when, what, why* in the speech of the young.[16]
>/t/, /d/, /n/, and /l/ are dental: [də n̪ɔrt̪ʰ ə sk̪ɔt̪lən] *the north of Scotland.*
>Initial /k/ and /g/ have very strong palatalization before front vowels, usually producing a clear semivowel—[kj] and [gj].
>R-coloring of vowels is usual, though it is rather less retracted and less strong than in other parts of the North.
>Consonant gemination occurs occasionally in intervocalic positions or finally—[wed:in] *wading* and [lïd:] *lid.*
>There is a tendency for a [ə] to occur between the consonants in certain clusters, especially after *l* or *r*—*film* and *farm*—perhaps because such clusters would be impossible in Irish.
>A Scots-sounding [ɔ:] occurs in *cot* and *pot.*

Syntax

The influence of Irish upon syntax in Donegal English is similar to that found in Southern Hiberno-English. Some examples follow.

An attempt is made to distinguish the "punctual" present and the "consuetudinal" present tenses as in Irish: *they be watching the pigs* and *they be clipping them* (i.e., the sheep), where the sense is that the watching and clipping are regular daily or annual tasks. Irish makes this distinction by the forms *bíonn siad ag* . . . (consuetudinal) and *tá siad ag* . . . (punctual).

The English verb *to be* is used to mean 'exist', as in the standard English sentence *there were a lot of hens on his farm*. This notion is rendered in Irish by the verb *bí* followed by *ann* 'in it'. Thus sentences appear in Hiberno-English in Donegal such as *is there rain in it again?* and *what day was in it?*

The notion of location in Irish is conveyed by an adverb *istigh* 'in, into' and the preposition *i* 'in'. When this structure is translated rather literally into English, a double preposition is the result: *she's in in the house*; *he was in in Letterkenny*.

The tendency present in many Anglo-English dialects to use a singular form of a noun, especially where measurements are concerned, is reinforced in Donegal Hiberno-English by the tendency in the Irish not to mark the number of a noun: *I give him four pound*; *I was three and a half year in New Zealand*.

Urban Hiberno-English

Studies have been made of three urban dialects in Ireland: Belfast, by the Milroys (1976); Larne, by Gregg (1964); and Dublin, by Bertz (1975).

Larne

The dialect of Larne is regarded by Gregg as typical of other urban districts within the Scots-Irish region. The townspeople tend to adjust their speech toward Mid-Ulster English in more formal situations, believing it to be closer to a "standard" form of the language (Gregg 1972, p. 113). "Broad" Larne town speech retains many of the Scots-Irish features but is different in some respects.

The consonant system is identical to that of rural Scots-Irish, but the vowel system differs in the following ways:

>   RP /ɪ/ is represented by [i̞], not [ë]—*bit, sit*.
>   RP /u:/ and /ʊ/ are represented by [ʉ(:)] and not [i̞], [ë] in *boot* and *put*.
>   RP /æ/ and /ɑ:/ are both represented by [a:] in *ant* and *aunt*.
>   Unrounded [a(:)] is retained in *warm* as in rural Scots-Irish.
>   Vowel length is unsystematic, but shorter forms of vowels are preferred
>   before laterals, nasals, and voiceless consonants.
>   Final unstressed -*y* is usually [e]—*quickly*.
>   Final unstressed -*ed* and -*es* are [əd] and [əz]—*wanted, glasses*.
>   Final unstressed -*ing* is usually [ən]—*walking, running*.
>   Vowels followed by *r* have developed as follows:
>   [ɛ] + *r* and [i] + *r* to [ɛ:r]—*early, berth, circuit, firm*
>   [o] + *r* and [ɔ] + *r* not merged as in RP but remaining distinct: [o:r] in
>   *hoarse, mourning* and [ɔ:r] in *horse, morning*

Belfast

The dialect of Belfast has features from both Scots-Irish and Mid-Ulster English which have become so merged that it is no longer possible to separate them. Other influences from Glasgow, Liverpool, and the Isle of Man may well have made themselves felt. A full description of the dialect has not yet been attempted but a great deal of valuable research has been done by the Milroys and their associates (1976). Much social variation is evidently present. The dialect has closely resembles that of the Lagan Valley to the southwest, and its influence is felt particularly in that direction.

The principal features of the sound system of Belfast, according to Milroy (1976, pp. 111–16) and others, are as follows.

Long Vowels

Vowel length is not phonemic, but more sensitive to phonetic context than in RP especially to following voiced-voiceless consonants.

Belfast [i] is slightly lowered from cardinal 1 [i] in *feet* and *see* and is long before [v] and [r] or in final position. A glide [ɪi] may occur. Archaic [e:]—always half-close and long—occurs in informal speech in *-ea* words: *meat, reason, tea*. The sound is kept separate from the more open [ɛ:(ə)] in *mate* and *place*.

The /a/ of Belfast speech is not differentiated into two separate phonemes as in the RP /æ/ and /ɑ:/. Belfast /a/, narrowly [ä] or [a], is usually long except before voiceless stops, nasals, liquids, and the voiceless obstruents [nt], [ls], and [lp]. Backing and rounding before nasals as in West Midland and Scots is recorded in the city where [ɔ] or [ɒ(:)] occur in any nasal or labial environment—*hand, man, bad*, and *Barry*. Backing and rounding is significantly more common among men than among women in protestant areas of east Belfast. Before or after velar consonants, the sound is raised to [æ:ə] or [ɛ]—*pack* (homophonous with *peck*), *bag, fang*, and (rarely) in *cab* and *gas*. Some instability exists, especially after [k]. Thus *cat* is recorded with [ɛ], [æ], and [ä]. A glide to [ⁱ] may occur before final velars: [bɛːⁱg] *bag*.

Belfast /ɔ/ is realized as [ɔ̈] or [ʌ̈]: RP *pot, doll, pod, saw,* and *bought*. Before voiceless stops, the contrast is one of length, not of quality: *caught/cot* and *stalk/stock*. Thus, before voiced plosives, homophones may result: *pod/pawed*. [ɑ] can occur before voiceless plosives: *cot* and *stock*. *Halt, haunt, watch, wasp, saw*, and *Paul* tend to have unrounded [aˑ:] and fall under /a/. The tendency to unrounding is not as great as in Southern Hiberno-English but is certainly present in the dialect, mainly before voiceless stops as in *pot* and *cot*.

In Belfast, words with RP /u:/ and RP /ʊ/ both have [ʉ(:)], often very much fronted, but always with some lip rounding, unlike Scots-Irish. Narrowly, it is often [ÿ], especially before alveolar and dental consonants—*boot, too*. Some speakers, perhaps the more socially conscious, attempt to parallel the distinction of /u:/ and /ʊ/ in RP by using [ʉ] and [ÿ]: *boot* and *pull*. A more remarkable development is the use by many speakers, especially young males, of [ʌ] for RP /ʊ/ in *pull, took*, and *would*, but this use is regarded as a "broad" pronunciation and is perhaps stigmatized. Those speakers using [ʉ:] and [y:] sometimes develop a glide—[ᵊʉ:] or [ᵊy:] before [z] or in final positions: *booze* and *too*. [ʉ] occurs before *-r* in *poor* [pʉːr].

Short Vowels

Belfast /ɪ/ (narrowly [ï]) is very much lower and more central than in RP [ɪ] in *city* and *bit*. Before [n] or [l], the sound is very much lowered to [æ̈] as in Scots-Irish: *thing*.

In Belfast, /ɛ/ is short before [t] and short or long before [s], but long in all other positions. The longer form is closer and may develop a glide [ẹ:] or [ẹ:ᵊ] in *well* and *bed*. The short form tends to be very open, almost [æ], in *set* and *less*; this lowering is most common among males. Before [ʃ] and [g] the glide form moves toward [ɪ] rather than [ə] because of the rather fronted quality of velar stops: [lɛ:ɪg] *leg*. [ɛ] + r falls together with RP [ə] so that *there* rhymes with *were* under [ë:r]. *Fair* tends to fall together with *fur* and *fir* under [ə:r].

Belfast /ʌ/ realized as [ʌ]—or [ɔ]—is always short. The degree of rounding is highly variable: *cut*, *up*.

Unstressed /ə/ occurs as [ə] in Belfast speech. Unstressed /ɪ/ tends to become [ə]: *Latin* and *running*.

Belfast has a variety of diphthongs between [æɪ] and [eɪ] in *light* and *time* which reflect social and stylistic registers very closely. The sound may be nasalized with nearby nasal consonants: [mẽis] *mice*. Diphthongs with a relatively close, front first element are not uncommon in all forms of Hiberno-English but are more common in Northern Hiberno-English than in Southern Hiberno-English. In Belfast, closer first elements are considered less socially acceptable; they seem to be preferred by male speakers in Belfast. The close first element—[eɪ] or [ɛɪ]—is recorded by Milroy before [t], [s], [d], [z], and [n] but a more open [ɛɪ] before [l], and an [æ:ˡ] in final position. Before r, the sound tends to be monophthongized to [ɑ:r], [a:r], or [æ:r] in the Belfast and Lagan Valley region—*fire*, *wire*. The contrast of [ɑe] and [ai] in Scots-Irish *tied/tide* and *die/dye* does not seem to occur in Belfast speech.

Belfast usually has [ɛ:ə] or [i:ə] for RP /eɪ/ in most contexts—for example, *face*, *mate*, and *save*—though [ẹ] before *t* and *s* may occur among the elderly. Plurals or possessives of *day* and *ray* tend to have [ɛ:] contrasting with [e:] in *daze* and *raise*. Thus some speakers have [de:] *day* and [dɛ:(ᵊ)z] *days*.

Belfast usually shows [ëʉ] for RP /aʊ/, but there are a number of variants according to social and other contexts in *louse*, *cow*, and *loud*. The first element of the diphthong is very weak before [t] and [s], almost becoming an [ʉ] monophthong. Whether this reflects an older [ʉ] form of a northern English or Scots type is difficult to say, though the same development occurs in the Isle of Man, where northern English and Scots influence is certainly perceptible. A variant [ɑ:ʉ] apparently appears more frequently before [n] and [l], often with an extremely front second element, which may be unrounded to [ɑy] or [ɑɨ] in *gown*, *growl*, and *now*. There is a tendency toward homophones in *how/high*, *now/nigh*, and *dawn/dine*, though distinctions between them may be made through a closer front first element of the [ɛɪ] for RP /ai/. This form may be accompanied by some nasalization when near a nasal consonant. Remarkably, [ɑ:ʉ] is sometimes changed to [a:r] in final position in [na:r] *now* and [ka:r] *cow*, a variant thought by Milroy to be a middle-class feature. Before *r*, a monophthong [ɑ:r] frequently occurs in Lagan Valley and Belfast speech in *hour* and *our*. Because [aɪ] diphthongs are also monophthongized before *r*, there is a tendency to a homophonic clash between *tyre/tower* as [ɑ:r].

Belfast /ɔɪ/ usually shows [ɔɨ], with the first element having almost the same rounding as in RP: *boy* and *voice*.

In words with RP /əʊ/, Belfast has [o(:)], longer before *v* and finally—*loaves* and *no*—but short in *loaf* and *boat*. [o] + *r* and [ɔ] + *r* seem (unlike the Scots-Irish forms) to have merged for some speakers; *four/for* and *hoarse/horse* are thus sometimes homophones.

The following figures display the vowels of Belfast speech:

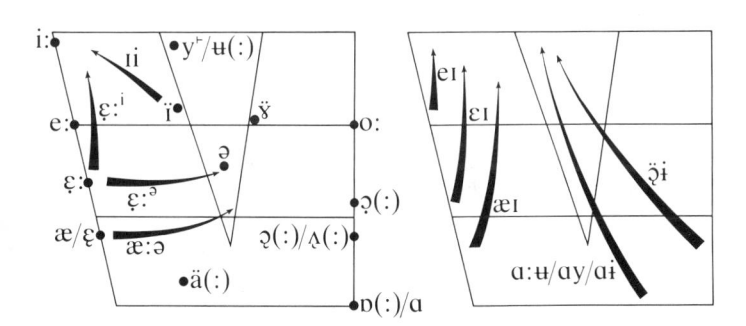

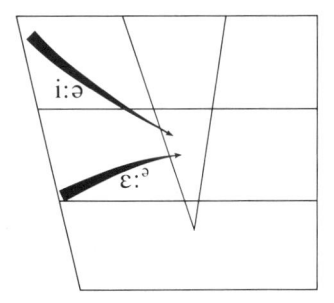

Consonants

The usual Hiberno-English *wh/w* contrast often disappears in Belfast, with *which/witch* tending to become homophones.

Initial [h] is usually preserved.

There is retracted *r*-coloring of vowels intervocalically and in word-final position.

-*ing* becomes [ən]—*running*.

[k] and [g] followed by a front vowel only rarely become [kj] and [gj] but perhaps do so more frequently in west Belfast speech, which may have a more western or rural flavor. This feature is regarded as comical and is heavily stigmatized.

-*th*- is lost between vowels, but the loss is compensated for by additional vowel length: [mɔ:r] *mother*, [ɔ:ər] *other*, and [bɹa:ən] *brethren*.

r may be lost occasionally in initial consonant clusters—[θi:] *three*, [sti:t] *street*.

New may be pronounced [nʉ:].

There is a tendency to have a darker, more English allophone of /l/ finally after vowels except after high vowels in Belfast speech: *fell*.

Dublin

Bertz (1975) has described the phonology of the Dublin dialect. He has attempted to distinguish variations between social classes in the city, though the basis on which the informants representative of the classes were selected does not seem very clearly defined. The Dublin urban dialect affects the speech of a wide area around the city, southwest along the main Naas Road into county Kildare, north along the Belfast Road at least as far as Drogheda, and south toward Dun Laoghaire.

Long Vowels

Overlengthening is a notable feature of Dublin speech. It is most remarkable before voiceless consonants where shorter allophones might be expected: [fi::t] *feet*, [ti::θ] *teeth*, [bu::k] *book*. This feature has so far not been adequately investigated.

Dublin /i/, narrowly [i:], has become [eɪ] in -*ea*- words which have the archaic [e:] in rural Southern Hiberno-English—*sea, tea,* and *please. Sea* and *please* are thus homophones with *say* and *plays* among conservative vernacular speakers. (Many of these speakers also produce an [ei] in such words as *see, me,* and *sneeze.* Thus, occasionally *see, sea,* and *say* appear to be homophones.) There is a tendency toward slight diphthongization of /i:/ to [ɪi].

Dublin /a:/ (in *path, blast, glass, father,* and a few other words) has developed a curious [ɔ:] which is rather stigmatized. In Northern Hiberno-English, the naming of the consonant *r* as [ɔ:ɾ] is regarded as something of a shibboleth identifying southern speakers, though its exact geographical distribution has not yet been determined.

Dublin usually has /ɔ:/, narrowly [ǫ:], for RP /ɔ:/ in educated and other forms of speech, but [ɑ:] forms occur occasionally, though not as commonly as in rural Southern Hiberno-English—*saw* and *pause*.

Dublin [u:] is rather more open than cardinal 8. To English ears the sound resembles an [o:]. An [ʊu] glide is not uncommon in *boots* and *smooth*. In broad Dublin vernacular, the diphthong [ɛʊ] has been recorded in a few words such as *school*.

Short Vowels

Dublin /ɪ/ resembles RP [ɪ] in educated speech, but in more vernacular talk it is realized as a closer [i˙]—*bit, hid,* and *it*.

In educated speech, /ɛ/ is realized as a sound very like the /ǫ/ of RP but is closer to cardinal 3 [ɛ] in vernacular talk: *bet* and *red*.

Dublin shows /æ/ in educated speech, but cardinal 4—[a]—in vernacular speech. The RP contrast between /æ/ and /ɑ:/ is maintained in *ant/aunt* and *Pam/palm* in educated speech, but some lengthening of /æ/ occurs and the sound is also sometimes lowered to [a:] even in educated speech. The phonemic contrast is apparently not secure in the dialect.

English in Ireland

Dublin /ɒ/ is usually realized as [ɑ˙] in vernacular speech but closer, more rounded forms occur in educated speech in *odd, not,* and *dog*. A contrast between /ɒ/ and /ɔ:/ is maintained in *cot/caught, stock/stalk,* and *body/bawdy*. The distribution of /ɒ/ and /ɔ:/ varies from that in RP in some speakers, notably in such derivatives as *bog* [ɒ] and *boggy* [ɔ:]. Stressed *was* frequently has [ɔ:].

Dublin usually has [ü] for /ʌ/ in vernacular speech, but [ʌ] occurs among the better-educated in *cut, bud,* and *dull*. The /ʌ/-/ʊ/ contrast of RP, absent in rural Southern Hiberno-English, is also absent in Dublin vernacular, but among educated speakers, this absence of contrast is somewhat stigmatized. The status of the contrast now seems to be unstable in the speech of the city.

Diphthongs
Dublin usually has [ɑɪ] for /aɪ/ in educated speech—*tide* and *sight*. The sound tends at times to fall together with the representatives of RP /ɔɪ/ in casual vernacular so that *tie/toy* and *buy/boy* become homophones; [eɪ] and [ö̞ɪ] also occur in vernacular speech.

Dublin has a diphthongal form [eɪ] for /eɪ/, not the archaic [e:] often found in rural Southern Hiberno-English, though diphthongal forms are spreading in the rural dialects—*say, hate, lane*.

Dublin usually has [æʊ] or [ɑ˙ʊ] for /aʊ/, but [ɛʊ] occurs in conservative vernacular speech in *house, cow,* and *loud*.

Dublin usually has a diphthong /oʊ/, not the archaic [o:] commonly found in rural Southern Hiberno-English in *go, note,* and *load*.

Dublin has /ɔɪ/, but the sound tends to fall together with the representatives of /aɪ/ in [ɑ˙ɪ] *boy* and *noise*. /ʊɪ/ is occasionally heard.

The following charts display the vowel system of Dublin English:

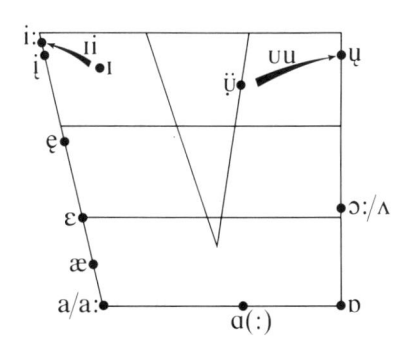

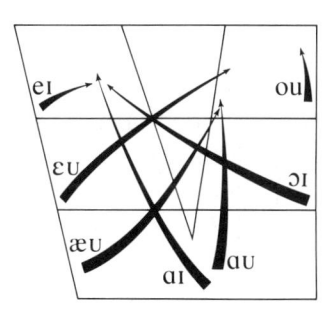

Vowels + *r*
R-coloring is preserved and is usually retracted but may in some cases be slightly velarized, a feature shared with some east coast dialects. Thus final *-er* in *water* and *daughter* may become [ɔ̈r] with velarized *r*. [ɔ] + [r] (*short* and *horse*) and [o]

+ [r] (*sport* and *hoarse*) are kept apart in the dialect. [a] + [r] occurs in *aren't* and *arse*; [e] + [r] occurs in *pear* and *mare* and in *heard* and *earn*.

Some contrasts occur between words which would all have [ə:] in RP, for example:

[e] + [r]	[ə:r]
earn	*urn*
fair, fare	*fur*
heard	*word*

Educated speakers sometimes substitute [ə:r] for [e:r], and the latter may be somewhat stigmatized. The following occur with [r]:

[u] + [r]—*poor, tour*
[aɪ] + [r]—*buyer, liar*
[eɪ] + [r]—*payer*
[ou] + [r]—*mower*
[au] + [r]—*power*
[ɔɪ] + [r]—*Boyer* (personal name)

Consonants

Final [d] may be lost, sometimes producing homophonic clashes: *fines/finds* and *mines/minds*.

Medial and final /θ/ and /ð/ are [t] and [d] in *breathes* (homophonous with *breeds*), *eighths* (homophonous with *eights*), and *both* (homophonous with *boat*). *Bath* and *bat* are contrasted only by vowel length ([ba:t] *bath* and [bat] *bat*). [t] may be voiced or glottalized between vowels: *getting, bottle,* and *better*. Initial and final [t] may be affricated and even become almost totally fricative [tˢ] and [ˈs]—*tax, bat*. The same less frequently happens to *d*—[dᶻ] initially in *did* and *day*. This feature of Dublin speech has spread widely among the young, perhaps through local broadcasting or through Dublin-trained teachers, and can be heard as far away as south Donegal among children. The sound also occurs widely in Liverpool speech, which may exert some influence on that of Dublin and vice versa.

R is preserved as *r*-coloring after vowels and may be slightly velarized.
Initial [h] is preserved as in all Hiberno-English dialects.
As in all Southern Hiberno-English dialects, /l/ is usually thin in quality, though a somewhat darker [lˠ] does occur in Dublin speech after vowels.

Conclusion

The future of the English language in Ireland may be predicted with some confidence in certain respects, but with less confidence in others. A continuing decline in the use of Irish Gaelic as a vernacular seems likely, especially if certain government policies in the Gaeltacht areas persist. Gallagher (1981) points out the disastrous effect of the closure of small local primary schools in Gweedore, Donegal, forcing the children to leave the close-knit Irish-speaking community in which they live to attend school in a larger township nearby which is predominantly English-speaking. More extensive broadcasting in Irish and other expedients can hardly counter the effects of such a policy. There seem to be almost no true monoglot Irish speakers, and unless a sudden change in present trends takes place, Irish may not survive as a true vernacular for much more than fifty years. While nationalist movements no longer regard the Irish language as a disadvantage, and it has come to be associated with the Republican cause, interest in the language might well decline if aspirations toward national unity are achieved. In the North, Irish is usually only taught in Roman Catholic schools—reflecting their political stance—and children almost everywhere, North and South, frequently find it hard to see value in the time they are forced to spend studying the language; they often resent its inclusion in the syllabus.

Unselfconscious dialect literature as an expression of regional identity has declined too and, except when used as a character marker, is rarely employed in serious literature today. The emotional drive for a form of expression that is truly "Irish" but not incomprehensible to readers outside Ireland, as Irish would be, seems to be spent, and most today either write in Irish and accept a limited audience or use Standard English. However, the Anglo-Irish tradition of the turn of the century did produce writers of international standing, and other Irish writers using much less dialect material have established similar reputations since.

The main north-south division of the modern Hiberno-English dialects seems likely to persist, and there is no tendency toward an overall standard of pronunciation. Links between the Protestants in the North and Scotland continue through the Presbyterian Church, old family ties, study in the Scottish Universities, and family holidays in the southeastern Scottish coastal resorts. Roman Catholics in the North tend to look toward Dublin and the Republic, listen to RTE broadcasts, and send their children to schools where a significant number of staff originate from the South. Northern Roman Catholics tend to take their holidays in Donegal or farther south and to cross the border more frequently. Family ties are maintained across the border, thus introducing or maintaining distinctive features from the Republic.

The preliminary findings of the Tape-recorded Survey of Hiberno-English Speech suggest that, at least among children, Southern Hiberno-English speech forms may be pushing into Donegal, while Northern Hiberno-English forms may be pushing south along the eastern coast routes toward Dublin, perhaps as far as the River Boyne at Drogheda. The main north-south dialect boundary may therefore in the future skew more sharply northwest to southeast. Some general changes are perceptible in the Northern Hiberno-English area. Probably the extreme form of the Scots-Irish dialect described by Gregg (1972) is in decline, and the area in which it is used will shrink more and more into the northeastern corner of Ulster. The speech of educated people in Belfast and the Lagan Valley area may continue its tendency to become a regional standard in the North and spread even further into rural areas around Belfast and south toward Newry and among educated people everywhere in Ulster.

Southern Hiberno-English is probably moving away from the heavily gaelicized English of the older generations as described by Henry (1957) in his account of Roscommon. Lunny's recent work in west Cork (1981) indicates that educated Dublin and even occasional RP influence can be detected in the speech of children. BBC radio and television are widely listened to along the east coast of the Republic, and RP may by this means be exerting an influence upon Southern Hiberno-English.

Educated Dublin urban speech seems to be exerting a widespread influence among children—presumably through Dublin-trained school teachers and RTE broadcasts—and is spreading geographically in a wide arc around the city. There is also a significant population shift toward the greater Dublin area, and many young people who come to find work in the city take the influence of its speech patterns back with them when they visit their often distant homes. Educated Dublin urban speech as used by RTE newsreaders seems to have ousted the old "ascendency accent"—the form of speech used by Anglican clergy trained at Trinity College in Dublin and by the old landed gentry—as the most desirable form of speech, much as BBC newsreaders' English ousted "Oxbridge" or "public school" accents as the most acceptable form of Anglo-English in postwar years.

The east coast, especially from Dundalk southward (the historical Pale), will probably continue to be an area of introduction of new and standard forms as suggested by Henry's lexical maps (1958) and the preliminary findings of the Tape-recorded Survey of Hiberno-English Speech. BBC broadcasts are most easily received in this region, and the majority of cross-channel ferries berth along this coast. The two largest cities, Belfast and Dublin, are located on the east coast. The east is the most developed part of the country from the point of view of industry and communication, and there is considerable migration into the area from rural districts to the west.

The great improvement in the quality of life in the Republic since the mid-1950s, with better roads and foreign investment in new industries, and more recently, Common Market investment and support, has opened up the whole country and modernized most of the formerly old fashioned rural areas. Occasionally, significant industrial growth is noticeable even in the west as at Shannon. Nevertheless both the north and the Republic are still basically rural, with only two cities of over half a million inhabitants and a pattern of scattered farms. There are few village nuclei, and the occasional country market towns often are the only centers of population of over 10,000 inhabitants. The pattern of villages and small towns produces a much more conservative linguistic situation than in England, and urban and regional standard dialects have as yet failed to make the impact they have made in England. Even those people who are well placed socially are inclined to be more at ease using dialect speech than is commonly the case in England. One would expect, therefore, a less rapid erosion of traditional rural speech forms than has been the case in most parts of these isles.

APPENDIX: *Specimens of the Hiberno-English Dialects*

Southern Hiberno-English, West Cork (recorded by A. Lunny)

d̯ə piːpl wər sə badlı 'af d̯ət d̯ə 'lanlard pət ə 'ʃkiːm ə 'wɔrk goːɪn | sɪtʃ əz d̯ə 'meːkɪn əɸ roːdz ən paːrts əv ɪz 'ɛʃtets ‖ ɸar dɪs pərˈtɪklər wɔn | d̯ət kem ˈt̯ruː d̯ə tʊonˈland ə ʃliːv riːɔx | d̯ə had ə hʊos ən koˈleː ɸɛr d̯ə juʃt meːk 'soːp ən brɪŋ ət ɒot ɪn ə 'wagɪn | ɪn 'drɔmz | tə ɸɛr d̯ə 'mɪn wər 'wɔrkɪn | ən 'skraps ə 'brɛd n oːtˈmiːl əz 'wɪl ‖ d̯e wər 'oːnlɪ gɪtɪn 'foːr 'pɪns ə 'deː | əˈkaːrdɪn tə d̯ə 'oːld 'piːpl ‖ maɪ 'faːd̯ər toːl mə d̯ət tri mɪn dəɪd ən d̯ə wɔrkɪn ə d̯ət 'roːd | wɪt̯ wiːknəs ‖ ən ɸɪn d̯ə 'roːd wəz kəmˈpliːtɪd d̯ɪn | d̯ə 'lanlard kem ɒot tə 'ʃuːt d̯ə 'geːm al 'oːvər hɪz 'ɛʃtets ‖

[The people were so badly off that the landlord put a scheme of work going, such as the making of roads in parts of his estates. For this particular one that came through the townland of Sliabh Riabhach, they had a house in Coolea where they used to make soup and bring it out in a wagon, in drums, to where the men were working, and scraps of bread and oatmeal as well. They were only getting four pence a day, according to the old people. My father told me that three men died on the working of that road, with weakness. And when the road was completed then, the landlord came out to shoot the game all over his estates.]

Southern Hiberno-English, North County Dublin (recorded by Máire Ní Rónain)

'aˑː nɔo | ɒni ə 'kɔ̆pl ə 'piːːpl ɔ̆p d̥ᵒɛər | d̥ᵒə 'mitərz wɛr raˑːbt | an n 'ɔol 'maˑn ə 'kɔ̆pl ə wiː—| ai 'dɔon 'nɔo ‖ i 'laˑːst ɛː | sɔ̆mwən tɔ̆k 't̥ʰri 'hɔ̆nd̥rəd 'paon an əm ‖ hi 'sɛd ɪt wəz d̯i 'iːntrənts | jə nɔo 'd̥o̝ːz | 'əi kaːl d̥ᵒəm d̥ᵒi 'ɪntrən? piːːpl | d̯ə 'tɪŋkɔ̆ʀs ‖ bət 'hɛo dɪd ʃi get 'ɪːˀn ‖ i sɛd ɪ had ɪt 'ɔ̆ndər ə 'ho̝ːli 'pɪtʃər | ə 'ho̝li 'pɪtʃɐ | 'ʍɛ d̯ə 'hɛl dɪd ɪ 'gɛd ɪtˢ ‖ ɪ wɔ̆dn 'go̝ n bəi ə 'baˑdl ə 'gaˑːs ər ə 'kɪʔl ə 'baˑil ɪz 'teːⁱ ‖ bɔ̆d i 'laːːst ɪtˢ ‖ ɪ 'sɛᵊd ‖ hiː sɛd ði aiˈtɪnərəns | 'ðat ʍət jə kaˑːl ɔ̆m | 'hi sɛd ðe | ðe kɔm ɪn n 'aˑːst ɪm t mek ə 'kɔ̆p? ə 'ti | bət 'riːli a 'kaˑːnt bəˈliːv ət bəkaːs 'ɔːl d̥ᵒə 'mɛn wɛr 'duən d̯ə 'rɔodz d̥ᵒə taˑɪm | 'duən d̥ᵒə geːt n d̥ᵒɪs 'rɔod an 'wʊdn ðe 'si ɛm ‖ 'siː d̥ᵒm ‖

[Ah, no. Only a couple of people up there, their meters were robbed, and an old man a couple of weeks—I don't know. He lost er—someone took three hundred pounds on (= off) him. He said it was the itinerants. You know, those—I call them the itinerant people—the tinkers. But how did she get in? He said he had it under a holy picture. A holy picture. Where the Hell did he get it? He wouldn't go and buy a bottle of gas or a kettle to boil his tea. But he lost it, he said. He said the itinerants—that what you call them?—he said they . . . they came in and asked him to make a cup of tea, but really I can't believe it because all the men were doing the roads (at) the time, doing the gate and this road—and wouldn't they see 'em? See them?]

Northern Hiberno-English: Mid-Ulster English in Belfast hinterland, South Antrim (recorded by Judith Riches)

ˈðaˈːts raet ǁ ˈaːe ˈsɛl ðm̩ː | wi: ˈsɛl ðm̩ | ɒz wi ˈkɔl ˈslɪŋks naː" | ˈdrɒp kɒːvz ˈæktʃəle | ðats ˈseː wɛn ðər əbæʉt ə wik oːlt ǁ m̩ˈmiːdɪətle ǁ ˈsɛl ðə ˈbʉːls | ðə ˈbuːls | ˈkɑˑld ˈbʉːlz ðæˀn | aːn ˈjʉːʒəli kip ðiː | ði ˈhæfəɾs fəɾ | brɪŋɪn ˈfɑrwərd fəɾ ˈkæʉz jə siː ǁ wæl əː | sumbdiː | ˈðaˑtsː əː | hɛz ə ˈsʌ̈klɪn hɛərd | nəʉ ˈðe bae ðm jə siː n ðe pət ðəm təɫ kæʉz | ðe ˈrɛər ðm ɪntəː | ˈbəlɪks n ði gu fər ˈbif ðæn ǁ ˈðaˈdɫ gu tə ɪz sɒ̈nz | əˈnɒ̈ðər ˈfaˈːrmər | əˈnɒ̈ðər ˈkaˈːˀ | ðats raˈːᵉt ǁ ʍɑˈt hɒpnz təɫ ðə ˈkæʉː ǁ ˈhɑ̈ːɾ | ʃi ˈhɛznt ə ˈkaˈːf leɪk ǁ ʃi | ˈhi baez wɒn tə pʏt təɫ ðə ˈkæʉ ǁ

[That's right. I—sell them, we sell them as we call slinks now, drop calves actually. That's (to) say when they are about a week old. Immediately. Sell the bulls, the bulls. (They're) called bulls then, and usually keep the . . . the heifers for bringing forward for cows you see. Well er, somebody, that's er—has a suckling herd, now they buy them you see and put them till (= to) cows. They rear them into bullocks and they go for beef then. That'll go to his son's—another farmer, another cow, that's right. What happens till (= to) the cow, her—she hasn't a calf like, she . . . he buys one to put till (= to) the cow.]

Northern Hiberno-English: Scots-Irish, North Antrim (recorded by Ellen Douglas-Cowie)

ðəːr ˈpiʔpl | kəs məbɛ ˈkaslroks ˈbrev ˈbɛg | ˈirɪɛ ɛs ɪʔ ǁ ðer ˈpiʔpl dʉn ðɛər | dji ˈnʉ ðm bɪ ðə ˈnem ə ˈkölans ǁ djə ˈnʉ ʍɛnævər jʉs wənʔ dʉn ðaʔ de ᵊʔ ˈtʃaʔəm | jə ˈkrost ʉvər ðɛər ǁ ɸər ðə njʉˑ ˈhəʉzəz æz | jᵊˈkroːst ʉvər ˈðaːʔ ˈkroːsn | n jə ˈwɛnʔ ˈstreʔ ˈoːn oʔp ðen ə ˈvɛrɪ streːʔ ˈrʉd | tə ðə ˈneks ˈkroːs | ðɛn jə ˈtərnʔd ən ˈreit | dʉn ʔə ɸər ˈai aːm ǁ wəl də jə si əˈwi ˈhys | n ðə ˈkɔrnər ˈjɔːnðər ǁ ˈwɛl ðəs ˈpiːpl feː ˈkaslroːk ˈʉːns ðaʔ pleːs | nem ə məˈkölans ǁ

[There are people—course maybe Castlerock's a brave (= very) big area isn't it? There are people down there, do you know them, by the name of Cullens. Do you know whenever (= when) yous (= you—plural) went down that day to Chatham, you crossed over there, where the new houses is, you crossed over that crossing and you went straight on up then a very straight road to the next cross, then you turned down right, down to where I am. Well, did you see a wee house on the corner yonder? Well, there's people fae (= from) Castlerock owns that place, name of McCullens.]

NOTES

1. South Pembroke was hardly "Cumbrian," as it was settled by Saxons and Normans, and was known as "Little England" since it was anglicized culturally.
2. Barnes also wrote a *Grammar of the Dorsetshire Dialect* (1867).
3. Ó'Muirithe (1977, pp. 41–42) quotes Stanihurst's colorful account of English-Irish language mixture: "But in our daies they haue so acquainted themselues with the Irish, as they haue made a mingle mangle, or gallimaufreie of both the languages, and haue in such medleie or checkerwise so crabbedlie iumbled them both togither, as commonlie the inhabitants of the meaner sort speake neither good English nor good Irish" (1577, p. 4).
4. David Abercrombie (1979, p. 73) has recently introduced this term into scholarly discussion to designate the English of England.
5. See the discussion of the language data from the censuses for 1851, 1891, and 1911 in O'Cuiv 1971 and Adams 1964, 1973, and 1974.
6. This account is compiled from the work of A. J. Ellis (1889, pp. 25–31), Henry (1958, pp. 75–93), and Ó'Muirithe (1977, pp. 37–55), who derive their data from Poole, Barnes, and others.
7. The following discussion relies on Bliss 1972 and Lunny 1981.
8. In *A Portrait of the Artist as a Young Man*, James Joyce describes the youth of his character Stephen Daedelus. In a conversation with the dean of his college, Stephen learns that what he calls a *tundish*, the dean (an English convert) calls a *funnel*. Proudly, Stephen explains that "it is called a tundish in Lower Drumcondra . . . where they speak the best English," but he feels frustrated that "the language in which we are speaking is his before it is mine." Stephen eventually finds out that *tundish* is "English and good old blunt English too."
9. These vowels are treated more fully by the present author elsewhere (Barry 1981).
10. See le Muire and Ó'Huallacháin 1966 for a detailed account of the nature of these sounds.
11. The dental /t̪/ and /d̪/ were used for English /θ/ and /ð/ because these are the only English dental sounds, and the distinguishing feature seemed to Irish speakers to be dentality versus nondentality rather than plosion versus friction. The distinction between plosion and friction is blurred for Irish speakers, since dental /t̪/ and /d̪/ are usually heavily aspirated.
12. These examples were noted by Bliss 1972 and 1975, Henry 1958, and Lunny 1981. Additional examples from west Donegal are noted later in this article.
13. A full discussion of this and other unusual verbal features of Southern Hiberno-English is given by Bliss 1972, pp. 72–78; 1975, pp. 15–18.
14. Orton and Halliday 1963, p. 726; Orton and Barry 1970, p. 714.
15. Adams reports slight loss of rounding of the [ɒ].

16. The use of [f] was also recorded in Scotland by Wright 1905 in the northeast Lowlands from the Firth of Forth to Wick.

REFERENCES

Abercrombie, David. "The Accents of Standard English in Scotland." In *Languages of Scotland*, edited by A. J. Aitken and Tom McArthur, pp. 68–84. Edinburgh: W. and R. Chambers, 1979.

Adams, G. Brendan. "Language in Ulster, 1820–1850." *Ulster Folk Life* 19 (1973):50–55.

———. "The 1851 Language Census in the North of Ireland." *Ulster Folk Life* 20 (1974):65–70.

———. "The Dialects of Ulster." In *The English Language in Ireland*, edited by Diarmaid Ó'Muirithe, pp. 56–69. Dublin: Mercier Press, 1977.

———, ed. *Ulster Dialects: An Introductory Symposium*. Holywood: Ulster Folk Museum, 1964.

Barry, Michael V. "The Southern Boundaries of Northern Hiberno-English Speech." In *Aspects of English Dialects in Ireland*, edited by Michael V. Barry, pp. 52–75. Belfast: Institute of Irish Studies, The Queen's University of Belfast, 1981.

Bertz, Siegfried. *Der Dubliner Stadtdialekt*. Freiburg: Albert Ludwigs Universität, 1975.

Bliss, Alan J. "Language in Contact: Some Problems of Hiberno English." *Proceedings of the Royal Irish Academy* 72, ser. C (1972): 63–82.

———. "The English Language in Ireland." MS, 1975.

———. "The Emergence of Modern English Dialects in Ireland." In *The English Language in Ireland*, edited by Diarmaid Ó'Muirithe, pp. 7–19. Dublin: Mercier Press, 1977.

Braidwood, John. "Ulster and Elizabethan English." In *Ulster Dialect Symposium*, edited by G. Brendan Adams, pp. 5–109. Holywood: Ulster Folk Museum, 1964.

de Fréine, Séan. "The Dominance of the English Language in the Nineteenth Century." In *The English Language in Ireland*, edited by Diarmaid Ó'Muirithe, pp. 71–87. Dublin: Mercier Press, 1977.

Dobson, E. J. *English Pronunciation, 1500–1700*. 2 vols. Oxford: Clarendon, 1968.

Ellis, Alexander J. *On Early English Pronunciation*. Pt. 5. London: Trübner and Co., 1889.

Furnivall, Frederick J., ed. *Early English Poems and Lives of Saints*. Berlin: Published for the Philological Society by A. Asher and Co., 1862.

Gallagher, Catherine. "Aspects of Bilingualism in North West Donegal." In *Aspects of English Dialects in Ireland*, edited by Michael V. Barry, pp. 142–70. Belfast: Institute of Irish Studies, The Queen's University of Belfast, 1981.

Gregg, Robert J. "Scotch-Irish Urban Speech in Ulster." In *Ulster Dialect Symposium*, edited by G. Brendan Adams, pp. 163–92. Holywood: Ulster Folk Museum, 1964.

———. "The Scotch Irish Dialect Boundaries in Ulster." In *Patterns in the Folk Speech of the British Isles*, edited by Martyn F. Wakelin, pp. 109–39. London: Athlone Press, 1972.

Henry, P. L. *An Anglo-Irish Dialect of North Roscommon*. Dublin: University College, Department of English, 1957.

———. "A Linguistic Survey of Ireland: Preliminary Report." *Lochlann: A Review of Celtic Studies* 1 (1958):49–208.
le Muire, An tSiúr Annuntiata, and Ó'Huallacháin, An tAthair Colmán. *Bunchúrsa Foghraíochta*. Dublin: Oifig an tSoláthair, 1966.
Lunny A. "Linguistic Interaction: English and Irish in Ballyvourney, West Cork." In *Aspects of English Dialects in Ireland*, edited by Michael V. Barry, pp. 118–41. Belfast: Institute of Irish Studies, The Queen's University of Belfast, 1981.
Milroy, James. "Synopsis of Belfast Vowels." *Belfast Working Papers in Language and Linguistics* 1 (1976):111–16.
O'Cuiv, Brian. *Irish Dialects and Irish-Speaking Districts*. Dublin: Dublin Institute for Advanced Studies, 1951. Reprint 1971.
Ó'Muirithe, Diarmaid, ed. *The English Language in Ireland*. Dublin: Mercier Press, 1977.
O'Rahilly, Thomas F. *Irish Dialects Past and Present*. Dublin: Browne and Nolan, 1932.
Orton, Harold, and Barry, Michael V. *Survey of English Dialects*. Vol. 2, *The West Midland Counties*, pt. 1. Leeds: E. J. Arnold, 1969; pt. 2, 1970.
Orton, Harold, and Halliday, Wilfrid J. *Survey of English Dialects*. Vol. 1, *The Six Northern Counties and the Isle of Man*, pt. 2. Leeds: E. J. Arnold, 1963.
Petty, William. *The Political Anatomy of Ireland*. London: D. Brown and W. Rogers, 1691.
Picton, James A. *Baronies of Forth and Bargey, County Wexford, Ireland*. Liverpool: D. Marples, 1866.
Poole, Jacob. *A Glossary of the Old Dialect of the English Colony in the Baronies of Forth and Bargy*, edited by William Barnes. London: J. R. Smith, 1867.
Stanihurst, Richard. *The Description of Irelande*. London: George Bishop, 1577.
Thomson, Samuel. *New Poems on a Variety of Different Subjects*. Belfast: Published by the author, 1799.
Vallancey, Charles. *A Grammar of the Iberno-Celtic, or Irish Language*. Dublin: G. Faulkner, 1773.
Wright, Joseph. *English Dialect Grammar*. Oxford: Henry Frowde, 1905.
Young, Arthur. *A Tour in Ireland* (1780). Edited by Constantia Maxwell. Cambridge: At the University Press, 1925.

The English Language in Canada
Richard W. Bailey

From the earliest times, the English language in Canada has taken a distinctively Canadian form, a combination of mutually intelligible but differing regional and social dialects. Some of these varieties were influenced by French, German, Gaelic, and other European languages, while others reflect the English brought by settlers from England, Scotland, Ireland, and what is now the United States. Until the confederation of the provinces in 1867, each region in Canada maintained something of its own linguistic autonomy, but each was subject to the influence of new immigrants, the special demands of the landscape and natural resources, and the speech of those who were encountered in the course of trade and transportation. Today, regional differences still exist in the English of Canadians, but they have become more alike in their speech and, at the same time, more and more distinct from the other Englishes of Great Britain and North America.

No generalization about so large and varied a country can properly reflect the diversity that characterizes each of its subdivisions. It is fair to say that both geography and history have conspired to place obstacles in the way of evolving Canadian national unity, and it is not surprising that the natural and social boundaries that divide Canada are reflected in its linguistic varieties—most of all in the variations in English that a traveler hears in moving from east to west across the continent. On the east, the Atlantic Provinces (Newfoundland, Labrador, Prince Edward Island, Nova Scotia, and New Brunswick) contain less than 10 percent of the 22,992,600 people counted in the census of 1976. Within this region, the Maritimes (Prince Edward Island, Nova Scotia, and New Brunswick) constitute the oldest settled area in which English speakers have predominated, and they enjoy a sense of cohesiveness and national importance both within their region and across the country. To the west of the Maritimes, Quebec maintains French traditions of culture and language that antedate the establishment of English-speaking Canada. Resistance to settlement by anglophones, whether native Canadians or immigrants from Britain or the United States, continues today with renewed vigor as separatists challenge the principles of confederation that join the individual provinces into a nation. Of the 6,235,000 people in Quebec in 1976, 80 percent reported French as their mother tongue. Only 12.8 percent learned English as children, and they are not spread evenly over the province but are likely to reside in a few enclaves in greater Montreal and in the Eastern Townships surrounding the city of Sherbrooke. Only in northern New Brunswick, Montreal, and the urban area of Ottawa-Hull on the border between Quebec and Ontario is

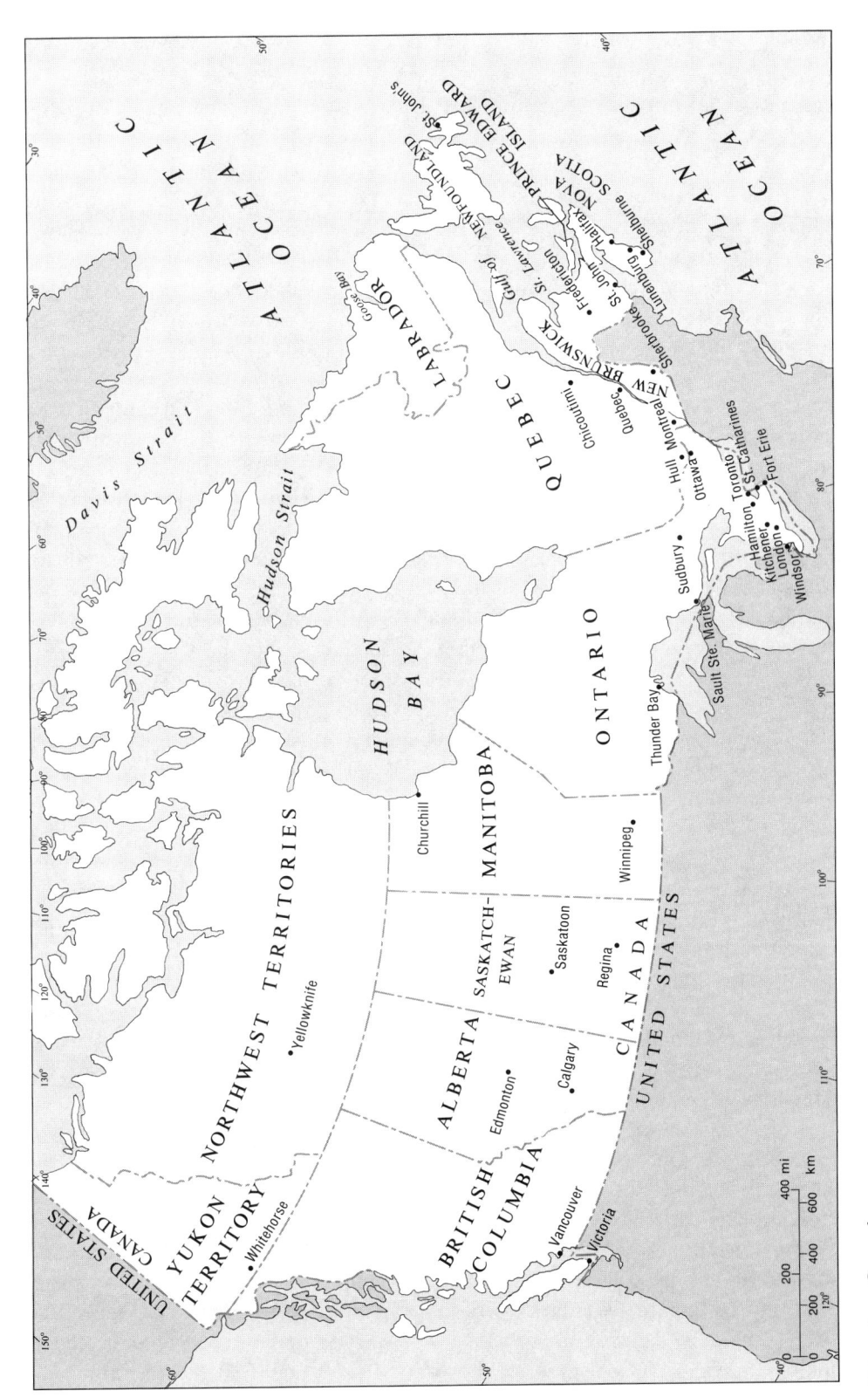

Map 1. Canada

French-English bilingualism common. Farther west, Canada's most populous province, Ontario, dominates the national economy and provides many norms for English-speaking culture through book and magazine publishing, broadcasting, education, and influence on economic development elsewhere in the country. In Ontario, 78.1 percent (6,458,000) of the population have some variety of English as a mother tongue, and only 5.6 percent (462,000) report French as the language of their childhood. The remaining 16.3 percent (1,340,000) were born into homes where some language other than English or French was spoken, a reflection of the continuing influx of immigrants from Europe and Asia to Canada's metropolitan centers.

Spreading in all directions from Hudson and James Bays and continuing to the northern shore of Lakes Ontario, Huron, and Superior is the Laurentian Shield. The Shield is a huge, repeatedly glaciated plateau of thin soil; although mineral and forest resources have continued to provide an important economic base for northwestern Ontario and northern Quebec, the industries that they support resist diversification and require long lines of transportation to the markets of the south and east. Products of the region, at first dominated by the fur trade and later by timber, pulpwood, and the products of iron and nickel mines, move through the waterways of the Great Lakes and the Ottawa and St. Lawrence rivers. Yet, because the Shield is not hospitable to agriculture, farms and farm settlements did not move steadily westward in a continuous line as in the United States, and the Shield acts as a boundary between the urban East and the agricultural Prairies. In the Red River valley of present-day Manitoba, settlers from eastern Canada (including immigrants who proceeded west directly from Scotland) established a colony in the early nineteenth century and soon found themselves in armed conflict with the Métis, long-time residents who still depended on the fur and pemmican trade for their subsistence. Fifty years of conflict between the francophone Métis and the anglophone arrivals culminated in the execution of the Métis leader Louis Riel at Regina in 1885, and while the dispute was fundamentally political, it had important implications for the future roles of English and French in the West. At the same time, settlement of the Prairie Provinces (Manitoba, Saskatchewan, and Alberta) drew settlers north from the Great Plains of the United States; thus farming practices and lines of transportation, both for immigrants and for the export of farm products, extended settlement into Canada without direct connection to the linguistic and cultural norms of the Maritimes, Quebec, and Ontario. Not until restrictive tariffs were imposed by both the United States and Canada in the 1870s did the Prairie Provinces begin to take on an identifiably Canadian character, and not until 1885, when a railroad was completed between Ottawa and Winnipeg, did Canadians in the West have convenient and direct access to the financial centers of Toronto and Montreal and begin to free themselves from American economic and linguistic dominance.

The far West of Canada has its own history, even more distinct in language and culture from the Maritimes of the Atlantic coast than California is from New

English in Canada

England. While James Cook and George Vancouver explored the *canals* (or inlets) of the rugged Pacific shore in the eighteenth century, not until 1843 was Victoria established as a headquarters for the Hudson's Bay Company operations in the West. When gold was discovered in the Fraser River valley in 1856, the area was overrun by American prospectors and entrepreneurs whose greed had not been satisfied in the great California gold rush of 1849. The more rapacious among them attempted to annex the area to the United States, a reassertion of the imperial impulse that had animated the United States presidential election of 1844, and the attempt to include most of Canada's Pacific coast within the United States produced the slogan, "Fifty-four Forty or Fight." Even though many of the miners soon left for other endeavors, the adoption of the name British Columbia in 1866 captures the mixture of the two dominant strains of the early population—the "British" (both immigrants from Great Britain and from eastern Canada) and the "Columbians" (from the United States). Though the eventual penetration of the trans-Canada railroad to the Pacific allowed Vancouver to become the western outpost of Canadian culture, foreign influences from the United States and from trade around the Pacific basin continue to affect the language and culture of western Canada.

The English language first touched the shore of present-day Canada with the exploratory voyage in 1497 of John Cabot, who apparently gave the territory he discovered the name Newfoundland. Cabot was the first of many to probe North America for a passage to Japan and China, but it would be many years before permanent English-speaking settlements were established. The first of these followed the colonizing expedition of Sir Humphrey Gilbert in 1583. But far from raising his flag on a barren coast, Gilbert took "official" possession of the seasonal port at St. John's, Newfoundland, a place already well established as a provisioning and fish-drying center by seamen from France, Portugal, Spain, and the southwest of England who voyaged every summer to fish the waters of the Grand Banks. Hence English provided one more component in the developing vocabulary for the fishing trade. Through contacts along the Grand Banks, it contributed to the growth of an Atlantic creole in which English vocabulary and structure joined with contributions from Breton, French, Portuguese, and Spanish. Little is known of the contact language that developed in northern fisheries, but vocabulary that survives suggests its diversity and constitutes the first of the "Canadianisms" in English: *Baccalaos* (from Portuguese 'codfish'; a term for the entire region of the fishery); *Labrador* (from Portuguese *lavrador* 'worker'); *penguin* (first recorded in 1536 in Hore's *Voyage to Cape Breton* and probably borrowed from a form in the Breton language akin to Welsh *pen gwyn* 'white head'); *caplin* (from French for a bait fish used by codfishermen). Though perhaps never used except in contacts between Amerindians and European fishermen of various nationalities, the language from which these words survive was apparently quite common in the outports and shore stations; according to Lescarbot (in his *Histoire de la Nouvelle France*, 1612), "the local people, to accommodate themselves to us . . . speak to us in a language with which we are more familiar wherein there is much Basque mingled" (quoted by Hancock 1971, p. 512). Later voyagers report terms from the Newfoundland fishing industry that show special uses of existing English vocabulary that in new senses also constitute Canadianisms: *flake* ('drying rack for fish', first attested in 1620), *header* ('worker who beheads cod', ca. 1777), and *stage* ('waterside shed for processing fish', 1620).

During the early years of exploration and settlement, English speakers concentrated their colonies farther south along the Atlantic coast. It was the French, first in the 1520s under Jacques Cartier, and later in the early years of the seventeenth century with the more resolute efforts of Samuel de Champlain, who established permanent and enduring settlements in Canada. Like the British, the French began by searching for the elusive Northwest Passage, but when Champlain founded Quebec in 1608 as a westward outpost of the settlement in Acadia (modern Nova Scotia and New Brunswick), he laid the foundation for a program of trade and missionary efforts that extended linguistic and related French influence westward into the interior of the continent through the drainage basins of the Great Lakes and southward to the mouth of the Mississippi River. The influence on English of these developments in Canada was significant. For a century and a half, English immigrants would find established French inhabitants throughout the interior.

Unlike the English-speaking colonists from Great Britain, the young French *coureurs de bois* enthusiastically traveled south and west into the "bush"—the forested wilderness of the hinterland. There they established themselves in Native American communities to whose language and life-styles they rapidly adapted. Like many of the Amerindian terms that characterize Canadian English, *Canada* itself comes from a native source to English through French and is most reliably traced to the Iroquoian *kanata* 'village'. Many of the borrowings from North American languages that are recorded in the *Dictionary of Canadianisms* (Avis et al. 1967) have been traced to their sources through adaptation by the French traders; among them are such words as *caribou* (first attested in English in 1665), *Eskimo/Esquimaux* (1548), and *toboggan* (1691). It is likely that many of the other words from native sources were influenced by French before their introduction into English in Canada and then dispersed into the word-stock of English around the world: *muskellunge*, *muskrat*, *papoose*, and *pemmican*.

Though the fur trade remained predominantly French for more than a century, the lucrative industry inspired English competition in the established patterns of harvest and export. In 1670, the Hudson's Bay Company was chartered and began to penetrate the heartland of the fur country from Churchill in the far North. A century later, in the wake of the Treaty of 1783, John Jacob Astor's American Fur Company brought yet another influx of English-speaking trappers and traders into the interior of the continent. Nonetheless, the extensive technology of the fur trade retained much of its French and French-adapted Amerindian vocabulary, for whether the furs found their way to Paris, London, or New York, the trappers continued to be francophones. With this history, it was natural for the vocabulary associated with the trade and the topography of the fur lands to enter Canadian English, and many of the borrowed words continue in general use: *batteau* (first attested in 1760), *canoe* (1576), *cariole* (1769), *chute* (1793), *coulee* (1840), *dalle* (1789), *portage* (1698), *rapids* (1770), *sault* (1600), *strong woods* (< French 'bois forts', 1794), and *voyageur* (1793). In addition, Canadian place names, like those along the waterways of the Great Lakes and Mississippi Valley in the United States, show the evidence of the French settlements whose fur trade brought European influence to the interior. Along the route from Michilimackinac and Sault Ste. Marie to Montreal are such places as Deux Rivières, Chapeau, and Portage du Fort. In the region south of Lake Winnipeg in Manitoba are Souris, Boissevain, Beauséjour, and Portage la Prairie. The structural influence of French is also shown in the loan translations of the names of the Great Lakes themselves: Lake Superior, Lake Michigan, Lake Huron, Lake Erie, and Lake Ontario (see Stewart 1945, p. 213). In Manitoba, two of the immense lakes that spread north of Winnipeg are also named according to the French pattern—Lake Winnipeg and Lake Manitoba—and one, a subsidiary lake remote from settled areas, the English pattern: Cedar Lake.

The eighteenth century brought with it decisive events that influenced the shape of Canadian history and its English. In 1713, as a consequence of the Treaty of Utrecht, France surrendered to Great Britain its claims to Newfoundland, the Hudson's Bay Territory, and the established settlements of Acadia. When the territory was captured by the British in 1710 only 1,600 residents lived in Acadia, and these were dispersed throughout the modern provinces of Nova Scotia, New Brunswick, and Prince Edward Island. The benefits of land easily farmed and a profitable fishery had led to a new immigration from France, and the population grew to more than 10,000 residents by the middle of the century. To diversify the growing community of French, the British government fostered a settlement of 3,000 Protestant Germans at Lunenburg in 1753, a community that in its English still retains vestiges of its distinctive history (Wilson 1958). When hostilities between France and Britain broke out, the British began to clear Acadia of its French inhabitants. Between 1755 and 1758, more than 6,000 of the French were deported, leaving their well-developed lands as an attractive inducement to new settlers. Their places were taken almost immediately by English speakers who moved north from New England (Hansen and Brebner 1940, p. 30). So sudden and numerous was this migration that French language and institutions virtually disappeared from British Acadia. According to one historian,

> "every family narrative and every description of institutional development—churches and schools—indicated how completely the new Nova Scotia was a child of New England. Ministers and schoolmasters came along with the farmers and their imprint upon this impressionable society was so deep that the even larger inflow of bitter and determined Loyalists two decades later could not efface it." [Hansen and Brebner 1940, p. 35]

From this foothold, finally achieved 250 years after Cabot's voyage of discovery, English was finally established on the Canadian mainland.

It is difficult to estimate in any detail what the English of these new Canadians was like. The new settlers were doubtless less successful but more ambitious than their neighbors in New England and the Middle Colonies, and their impulse to migrate to the less developed areas of the continent had been checked by government restrictions and Amerindian hostilities west of the Appalachian Mountains. Socially they probably resembled the people who migrated westward in the United States just a few years later into the Western Reserve on the south shore of Lake Erie. Yet the population was also diverse, since opportunities for a settled life in an English-speaking area cleared of stumps and Indians also attracted new migrants from Scotland, Ireland, and England. A few of the displaced French found their way back to Acadia, but by official policy nearly all were dispersed among the colonies of newcomers. For the next quarter century, the community consolidated its schools and churches, established economic institutions, and made English, in a form soon to be recognized as distinct in British North America, the basis for subsequent developments in Canada. Numerically, the English of New England predominated, and of the 18,000 people resident in Nova Scotia in 1768, as many as 13,000 were recent immigrants from New England. Nonetheless, fully one-third of the new population spoke French or German or used the distinctive English already beginning separate development in Pennsylvania and the colonies of the South, or brought with them to the New World the dialects of England, Scotland, and Ireland.

Just a generation later, Canada experienced the second great immigration of English speakers. When the American colonies declared independence from England in 1776, persons sympathetic to the revolutionary cause returned to New England from Halifax and the smaller towns of Nova Scotia. As the war turned against British forces, however, the flow of migration began to move northward. Many of the Loyalists were property owners and professional people who saw little to be gained by separation from Great Britain. Others were farmers and artisans who were sympathetic to the English cause but were not all of British origin; among them were Dutch, Scots, and Germans of the Hudson Valley. Since modern Canadians discern the virtues of probity and patriotism in these Loyalists, there is a tendency to overestimate their numbers and influence. In the Maritimes, as many as 28,000 arrived in central and eastern Nova Scotia, and many soon dispersed to New Brunswick, Prince Edward Island, and Cape Breton Island. Not all of them found the life in Canada congenial, and most depended upon the charity of the established inhabitants while suffering long delays in waiting for a grant of land from the government. As a result, some of the more prosperous migrated to England, where they joined large numbers of other displaced Americans. Still others moved westward in Canada or to the new settlements opening in the Northwest Territories of the United States (Hansen and Brebner 1940, pp. 55–56). As for the influence of the Loyalists on the development of English, it is likely that the settlers who remained in the Maritimes added strength to the influence of the speech of New England and the Middle Colonies already established in the 1760s and perhaps helped to accelerate linguistic changes in progress. Though new towns developed to accommodate the newcomers—particularly St. John, New Brunswick, and its hinterland—many of the Loyalists settled in and around Halifax. For a brief time in 1784, Shelburne on the southeast coast of Nova Scotia had the distinction of being the largest city in British North America, but the concentration of Loyalists soon dispersed. Among this mass of people were 600 families of freed slaves, many of whom were subsequently persuaded to resettle in the newly organized colony of Sierra Leone in Africa. Such a thrust toward uniformity was only an extreme example of the more general process by which the Loyalists "settled" in Canada. Those who were prepared for the rigors of the wilderness pressed northward into New Brunswick (which subsequently became known as the Loyalist Province) and westward to the Eastern Townships in Quebec. Others increased the population of the growing cities or migrated elsewhere on the continent. Certainly the influence of this sudden influx of new citizens left its mark on the language and contributed to the future shape of Canadian English. But probably most Loyalists adapted to the prevailing customs (and presumably to the emerging speechways) rather than importing and rebuilding intact the English and the customs they had left behind in the American colonies.

In Upper Canada, above Montreal in the St. Lawrence waterway, conditions were quite different. From the earliest times of European settlement, the Iroquois confederacy dominated what is now northern New York state and southern Ontario, so much so that the fur trade was forbidden the easy passage through the Lakes and was forced overland from Georgian Bay to the Ottawa Valley and thence to Montreal. But the wars in the West of the 1760s began the decline of Amerindian influence, and the Iroquois' decision to side with the British in the American Revolution led to their defeat in their traditional territory. As a result, southern Ontario, along with the territories to the south, were suddenly available for European settlement. Communities were established upriver from Montreal, along the northern shore of Lake Ontario, on the western banks of the Niagara River, and westward in the area protected by the fort at Amherstburg, near the modern city of Windsor. At first, these colonies were relatively homogeneous, since by official policy land grants were given in blocks to members of disbanded Loyalist regiments. The settlements were fostered by generous grants of supplies and equipment, and by 1785 some 7,000 settlers had established themselves in Upper Canada. Though better organized than the Loyalists in the Maritimes, they were also diverse. Some communities consisted of the German mercenaries who had fought for the British in the American Revolution, while others were dominated by Glengarry Highlanders from Scotland, Mennonites and Quakers from Pennsylvania, and new immigrants from England. The most important source of new population, however, was the eastern part of the United States. Land in southern Ontario was more easily available than in the adjacent areas across the border, and those who had settled for patriotic reasons were soon joined by those who were merely pragmatic. Though some of the "late Loyalists" were deported in the wake of the War of 1812, their enthusiasm for southern Ontario remained undiminished. One such testimonial may stand for many that helped to spread enthusiasm for Canadian settlement:

> First, I am a native of the United States, was born in Pennsylvania, ten miles from Philadelphia, and in the year 1808 moved with my family to the province of Upper Canada, in order to obtain land upon easy terms, (as did most of the inhabitants now there) and for no other reason. I had not long remained in the province till I discovered that the mildness of the climate, fertility of the soil, benefit of trade, cheapness of the land, morals of the inhabitants, and equality of the government so far exceeded my former expectations and the expectations of the public in general, that I deemed it my duty to make known the same; especially when I considered that there were many thousands of my fellow citizens of the United States, who were without land, and prospect of obtaining any in the United States upon such easy terms as they might in Upper Canada. [Quoted by Hansen and Brebner 1940, p. 83]

Such enthusiasm for Canadian settlement led to a massive migration from New York, New Jersey, and Pennsylvania. The pioneer Loyalists of the 1780s were soon overwhelmed by waves of new settlers, and by 1812 the population of Upper Canada had reached 100,000, most of them former citizens of the United States.

The history of Canadian settlement is immensely significant in determining the origins of English in Canada. Only by romanticizing history are present-day Canadians able to trace their linguistic ancestry to the "United Empire Loyalists," but they are not alone in creating a history to support national sensibilities. In the United States, for instance, some anglophones like to imagine a direct connection with Plymouth Colony (if they are Yankees) or with the First Families of Virginia (if they admire the antebellum South). But a history that is partly fictional may nonetheless be socially significant, and national myths can bolster notions of linguistic prestige and thus influence the course of language change in progress. Hence accounts of settlement history must combine the facts of migration with the beliefs that combine with them to create present-day norms of language behavior.

In the Maritimes, there were doubtless social forces that compelled the Loyalist migrants who remained there to conform to the customs of the earlier waves of English-speaking settlers from New England. Social institutions were already established in Nova Scotia along lines familiar to the Loyalist newcomers, and where the new migrants joined established settlements (as they did in southeastern Nova Scotia), the familiar speechways were continued. Even today, southeastern Nova Scotia is a relic area within Canada where the parallels with particular New England communities are strong. In particular, as shown by Wilson (1958, p. 47), Queens and Lunenburg counties have some distinctive vocabulary that links them to southeastern Massachusetts: *porch* 'addition to a house' is a New England relic in these counties; other parts of Nova Scotia have *ell* in this sense. Similar words in which the Loyalist area of the province resembles New England more than the rest of Canada include *earthworm* 'angleworm', *sunup* 'sunrise', and *hay heap* 'haycock'. But these resemblances are by no means general. On the whole they are restricted to isolated communities with traditional life-styles—in Nova Scotia, fishing and farming; in areas of more diverse population and more modern ways, connections with the Loyalists are much less clear.

In all communities, language change is a natural and continuous process. Most striking about English in the Maritimes is that where entirely new settlements were erected after the migrations of 1755—in northeast Nova Scotia, New Brunswick, and Prince Edward Island—the language began to take on a distinctly "Canadian" form. Of all the many linguistic variables that figure in this development, perhaps none is as significant in distinguishing Canadians from other English-speakers along the Atlantic coast as the history of [r] after vowels.[1] The progressive vocalization and deletion of this consonant begins in East Anglia, that part of England north and east of London where Puritanism flourished and whose people provided the impetus for both Cromwell's revolution and the colonization of New England. Naive spellings in seventeenth-century American town records demonstrate the progressive and widespread loss of such [r]: *patchis* 'purchase', *joyney* 'journey', *Passen* 'Parson', *Mach* 'March', *they* 'their', and *fo* 'for' are typical examples (Orbeck 1927, pp. 84–85). As with most sound changes, innovation proceeded more rapidly in certain phonetic environments. Loss of historic [r] was apparently most common before [s] and [ʃ], and in many parts of North America related pairs of words show the effect of *r*-lessness in such positions: *passel/parcel*, *hoss/horse*, and *cuss/curse*. The effect of an initial vowel in a following word, on the other hand, tends to preserve [r] in word final position, even in varieties of English that otherwise lack postvocalic *r*. Hence it is not surprising that almost all informants interviewed in southern and western New Brunswick for the *Linguistic Atlas of New England* (Kurath 1939–43) kept [r] in *far off* (vol. 1, map 48) even though they did not use [r] in *marsh* [mɑ·ʃ] (vol. 1, map 31). Just as *r*-loss begins with [r] before [s] and [ʃ], so, when the process is reversed, the last [r] to be restored is likely to be the one in those environments.

As the American colonies grew in population during the first two hundred years of settlement, [r]-deletion spread to more and more phonetic environments, and newcomers imitated the increasingly established *r*-less pronunciations until American English along the Atlantic coast (with the exception of the area dominated by Philadelphia) was *r*-less from Maine southward to Charleston, South Carolina. The spread of the *r*-less pronunciation was most extensive in eastern New England, both in the range of phonetic environments and across social classes, and it was from New England that most of the Loyalist settlers in the

Maritimes came. Yet *r*-less pronunciations did not generally flourish in Canada, even in the areas of stable population and continuous contact with New England.[2] One reason for the arrest and reversal of change in Canada may be that the changes that took place in New England continued after the departure of the Loyalists. It is, however, quite clear that the loss of [r] was well established by the middle of the eighteenth century, and the *Journal* of Captain Abijah Willard provides useful evidence of the state of the language at the time of the expulsion of the Acadians. Willard, a native of central Massachusetts who assisted in the removal of the French from Acadia, kept a diary of his experiences on the expedition of 1755–56. Through his spellings, he reveals that he did not pronounce [r] at the ends of words (*regulas* 'regulars'), before [ʃ] and [tʃ] (*mash* 'marsh' and *macht* 'marched'), or before front consonants (*fote* 'fort', *boaded* 'boarded', *wam* 'warm'). There is no evidence, however, that Willard deleted [r] before back consonants (as in *work*) or before a following vowel (as in *your aunt*), a change that took place mainly in the colonies farther south.[3] When Willard arrived in New Brunswick as a Loyalist refugee twenty-five years later, he and his companions doubtless had *r*-less pronunciations in many words, but his descendents did not imitate him, and a century later nearly all of New Brunswick was *r*-full (see Kurath, et al. 1939–43, p. 34, chart 16). While the feature continued to spread in eastern New England, its progress was halted and even reversed in Canada.

Two factors doubtless account for the eventual disappearance of New England *r*-less pronunciations in the Maritimes. One must certainly be the migration that brought other varieties of English to Canada. Since most of the newcomers were from northern England, Scotland, and Ireland (where [r] after vowels was and is a systematic feature of pronunciation), they provided an English that competed with that of the American Loyalists, and apparently these migrants were more influential than those from the south of England, where *r*-loss was well established in prestige dialects by the early nineteenth century. But a more important reason is to be found in the growing sense of national identity among the new Canadians. Their institutions may have been American in origin, but as keepers of the true Loyalist faith they despised the rebels and were staunch in their defense against attempts by the United States to annex Canada in the War of 1812. In the years that followed, they continued to resist threats of annexation from the south, and though they had not yet formed a nation, they constituted a community. By maintaining Loyalist traditions, they believed that they were preserving Loyalist language. In fact, they reversed the process of change already well established at the time of their exodus northward. In his studies of the English of the New Brunswick–Maine border in the 1930s, Guy Lowman discovered a contrast between the Canadians of Charlotte County, New Brunswick (where [r] by that time was generally reestablished) and the Americans of Calais, Maine, just across the border (where the *r*-less speech of rural New England was common):

> Many people in Charlotte Co. have a strong aversion to English, Scotch and Irish types of speech and prefer what they regard as their own Canadian speech, i.e., the speech of the old Loyalist families. The speech of Calais, Me., they regard as affected. [Kurath 1939, p. 238]

Lowman's comment on one of his informants in St. Stephen, a housewife then aged eighty-seven years, must stand for many of the Loyalists' descendents: "Thoroughly loyal to the British Isles, though they seem to her as far away and as foreign as they would to a New Englander" (Kurath 1939, p. 238).

Though the contrast of *r*-full and *r*-less pronunciations is the most noticeable feature that distinguished the Maritimes from the New England states to the south, there are other features of colonial speech that developed differently on the two sides of the border. New England "short o" [ɵ] in such words as *whole*, *road*, and *yolk* is rarely found in New Brunswick even though it is current, though increasingly old-fashioned, in Maine and southward through eastern Massachusetts and Rhode Island (Avis 1978a). In vocabulary, New Brunswickers sometimes use *pot cheese* 'cottage cheese' as do some of the descendents of the Dutch settlers of the Hudson River valley of New York; in eastern New England, the same food is commonly called *sour-milk cheese*. But even though such distinctions show the separate development of Canadian English, it must not be assumed that the Maritimes are a uniform dialect region. Even within the same community, several pronunciations or competing synonyms may be found, and speakers may vary their English with audience and occasion. Just one example may suffice to show the extent of this diversity of English in the Maritimes. In a questionnaire circulated by the Survey of Canadian English, adults were asked to name the "hard portion inside a cherry." In Prince Edward Island, 29 percent reported using *pit* and 59 percent replied that they used *stone*; in neighboring New Brunswick, 70 percent gave *pit* as their answer and 17 percent *stone* (Scargill 1974, p. 121). Such variability, even within regions sharing a common history, is the rule rather than the exception in dialect research.

Early evidence of the variability within the English of eastern Canada is provided in the tales that make up *The Clockmaker* by Thomas Chandler Haliburton (1796–1865). In these stories, Haliburton made famous a fictional Yankee peddler, Sam Slick, who travels through Nova Scotia, making shrewd and satirical observations on the manners and customs of the inhabitants. Much scholarly energy has been devoted to the question of the fidelity of Haliburton's use of "Yankee" dialect, but it is perhaps more important that the speech of New Englanders (like Sam Slick) and Nova Scotians was sufficiently distinct by 1836, when Haliburton began to publish the Sam Slick stories in a Halifax newspaper, that Canadian readers could recognize Sam as a familiar type whose English was distinct from their own even in southeastern Nova Scotia, where similarities between the two varieties of English remained strong.

Haliburton himself was a descendent of the first wave of English-speaking immigrants who moved north from Massachusetts to occupy the lands of the displaced French-speaking Acadians. Haliburton's father was, like his son, a resolute Tory who had no sympathy with the American Revolution, and both father and son became respected judges of the Supreme Court of Nova Scotia. Though often using Sam Slick to promote the causes of the British Empire, Thomas Haliburton had a good ear for the variety of voices that he heard around him. Through his stories, modern readers gain some appreciation of the different kinds of English that were widely heard in the province, particularly Slick's "Yankee":

> "I allot," said Mr. Slick, "that the blue-noses are the most gullible folks on the face of the airth—rigular soft horns that's a fact. Politicks and such stuff set 'em a gapin, like children in a chimbley corner listenin to tales of ghosts, Salem witches, and Nova Scotia snow storms; and while they stand starin and yawpin, all eyes and mouth, they get their pockets picked of every cent that's in 'em." [Haliburton 1840, ser. 1, tale 31]

Sam's speech and the speeches of the Nova Scotians he meets show many similarities: both the Yankee and his Canadian customers lack [r] after vowels, both use [n] for [ŋ] in present participles (*starin* 'staring'), and both use *a*-prefixed participles (*a gapin*). Yet the Yankee is distinguished by a few features not used by the Canadians he encounters (e.g., *chimbley*) and by the flamboyance of hyperbole and adage that Haliburton assigns to him. As Sam says, "they all know me to be an American citizen here by my talk" (ser. 1, tale 29).

The variety of characters in Haliburton's stories and the variety of their dialects is an indication of the diversity of English heard in Halifax and surrounding Nova Scotia in the early nineteenth century. Though Haliburton had not traveled abroad at the time he began to publish the Sam Slick stories, he was apparently quite familiar with dialects of English in remote places through his experience of immigrants to the country and from the reports of travelers. In *The Clockmaker*, he imitates the characteristic speech of the Quaker ("Verily, I am sorry for thee, friend" [ser. 2, tale 13]), a Hawaiian queen (whose "Mr. Shleek" captures the raising of [ɪ] to [i] typical of Hawaiian pidgin [ser. 2, tale 12; see Glissmeyer 1973, p. 197]), and of the Dutch ("De ferry teyvil hisself is in te man, and in de trouser too" [ser 2, tale 20]). Such samples by no means exhaust the range of English known to Haliburton and reproduced in the Sam Slick stories.[4]

Two selections from *The Clockmaker* reflect the English of important communities of people in Nova Scotia: the survivors of the Micmac Amerindian population, and the substantial community of black Canadians who arrived with other English-speaking immigrants from the United States or who migrated northward to Halifax from Jamaica. In the dialect Haliburton used in reporting a dispute between Peter Paul, a Micmac, and James McNutt, an immigrant landowner, one of the English-based contact languages widely current in North America is deftly imitated:

> M'Nutt he came to me, and says he, Peter, what adevil you do here, d—n you? I say, I make 'em bucket, make 'em tub, may be basket, or ax handle, to buy me some blanket and powder and shot with; you no want some? Well, he say, this is my land, Peter, and my wood; I bought 'em and pay money for 'em; I won't let you stay here and cut my wood; if you cut anoder stick, I send you to jail. Then I tell him I see what governor say to that; what you plant, that yours; what you sow, that yours too; but you no plant 'em woods; God, he plant 'em dat: he make 'em river, too, for all mens, white man and Injian man, all same. God, he no give 'em river to one man; he make him run through all the woods. When you drink he run on, and I drink, and then when all drink he run on to de sea. He no stand still; you no catch him; you no have him. If I cut down your apple-tree, then send me to jail, cause you plant 'em: but if I cut down ash tree, oak tree, or pine tree in woods, I say it's mine. [Ser. 2, tale 20]

Features of Peter Paul's English are widely reported from throughout the North American frontier and are even approximated in the "Injun talk" of the "me see 'um bad man" type in present-day popular culture. But unlike the highly simplified literary dialect used in western films and novels, Haliburton's representation encompasses a broad range of features: *'em* with transitive verbs; declarative order in questions (compare *you no want some?* with *you no have him*); negation with *no*; equative sentences without copula (*that yours*); pronominal apposition (*God, he plant 'em*); and simplification of grammatical suffixes (*say* 'said', *run* 'runs', and *blanket* 'blankets'). The conversation Haliburton creates is set in Lunenburg County, Nova Scotia, but the variety of English he imitated must also have been current across the continent as Canadians moved westward.[5]

A second sample of Haliburton's dialogue shows that he also recognized the distinctive population of some 3,000 blacks (in a population totaling 58,000 in 1827) that had grown in numbers through natural increase and immigration since 1755 (see Haliburton 1829, vol. 2, pp. 277, 293). In the following passage, he represents the speech of a freedman who had moved north from South Carolina following the "second American war":

> When we drove up to the door, a black man came out of the stable, and took the horse by the head in a listless and reluctant manner, but his attention was shortly awakened by the animal, whom he soon began to examine attentively. Him don't look like blue-nose, said blacky, sartin him stranger. Fine critter dat, by gosh, no mistake.
>
> From the horse his eye wandered to us; when, slowly quitting his hold of the bridle, and stretching out his head, and stepping anxiously and cautiously round to where the Clockmaker was standing, he suddenly pulled off his hat, and throwing it up in the air, uttered one of the most piercing yells I think I ever heard. . . . Oh, Massa Sammy! Massa Sammy! Oh, my

> Gor! Only tink old Scippy see you once more! How you do, Massa Sammy? Gor Ormighty bless you! How you do? . . . O Massa Sam, you no recollect Old Scip? . . . How's Massa Sy, and Missey Sy, and all our children, and all our folks to our house to home? De dear little lily, de sweet little booty, de little missy baby. Oh, how I do lub 'em all! . . . Oh, I grad, upon my soul, I wery grad. [Ser. 2, tale 7]

Once again Haliburton reproduces a variety of features: [d] for [ð], [t] for [θ], and [β] for [v] (in *lub* 'love' and *wery* 'very'); negation with *no* (*you no recollect*); invariant pronouns (*him don't look like blue-nose*); and equative sentences without copula (*I grad, him stranger*). Such samples as these from the days before Confederation suggest a continuing trait of Canadian English: its diversity. Whether in the Maritimes or farther west, Canadians, both recent immigrants and long-settled families, do not speak a single, uniform variety of English.

Settlement in Upper Canada was more rapid than in the Maritimes, and a more temperate climate made farming there less precarious than in the East. As already noted, most of the population of present-day Ontario entered Canada through the United States, and most of these settlers were speakers of American English. Hostilities between Britain and the United States in the War of 1812 began the process by which the Americans who would not pledge allegiance to the Crown returned to their original homes or migrated to the territory south of Lake Erie. But the flow of population back and forth across the border continued, varying as economic opportunities favored settlement in one country or the other. In addition, many of the migrants who settled the American West passed through Canada across the peninsula from Fort Erie in the east to Windsor in the west, and though most did not remain, they provided a continuing American influence on the development of Canadian English. Nonetheless, Upper Canada was a British province, and as the population grew, direct migration from Great Britain increased the influence of the English of the "mother country" on the language of Canada. But though British models and affection for things English may have influenced the more prosperous and those near the centers of government in Upper Canada, the American model continued as the major source of influence. One observer, Dr. Thomas Rolph, lamented the American English he heard in Ontario in 1832 and feared that it would spread to the children of the province:

> It is really melancholy to traverse the Province, and go into many of the common schools; you find a herd of children, instructed by some anti-British adventurer, instilling into the young and tender mind sentiments hostile to the parent state; false accounts of the late war in which Great Britain was engaged with the United States: geography setting forth New-York, Philadelphia, Boston, &c., as the largest and finest cities in the world; historical reading books describing the American population as the most free and enlightened under Heaven; insisting on the superiority of

> their laws and institutions, to those of all the world, in defiance of the Agrarian outrages and mob supremacy daily witnessed and lamented; and American spelling-books, dictionaries, and Grammar, teaching them an anti-British dialect, and idiom; although living in a Province, and being subjects, of the British Crown.[6] [Rolph 1836, p. 262]

Educational reforms were responsive to Rolph's critique, and Egerton Ryerson, a Loyalist descendent who served as Ontario's superintendent of education from 1844 to 1876, helped to ensure that Canadian history and viewpoints would be reflected in the schools (Avis 1973, p. 47). Nonetheless, American publications, including schoolbooks, continued in widespread use in Ontario and elsewhere in Canada, despite an act of the provincial legislature in 1850 restricting their official adoption.

Foreign visitors, especially those from Britain, continued through the nineteenth century to identify the English language of Upper Canada with the Yankee dialects of the United States. Though doubtless exaggerated, a sample of the Canadian English of Upper Canada (present-day Ontario) was recorded by John Howison during his visit to the Thames Valley in 1818–20:

> "How d'ye do, my good lady, how d'ye do?"—"Oh, doctor," cried the patient, "I was wishing to see you—very bad—I don't calculate upon ever getting *smart* again." "Hoity, toity!" return the doctor, "you look a thundering sight better than you did yesterday."—"Better!" exclaimed the sick woman, "no, doctor, I am no better—I'm going to die in your hands."—"My dear good lady," cried the doctor, "I'll bet a pint of spirits I'll *raise* you in five days, and make you so *spry*, that you'll dance upon this floor."—"Oh!" said the woman, "if I had but the *root* doctor that used to attend our family at Connecticut; he was a dreadful *skeelful* man." Here they were interrupted by the entrance of her husband, who was a clumsy, credulous-looking person. "Good morning to you, doctor," said he, "what's the word?"—"Nothing new or strange, sir," returned the doctor. "Well, now, doctor," continued the husband, "how do you find that there woman?—no better, I conclude?—I guess as how it would be as well to let you understand plainly, that if you can't do her never no good, I wouldn't wish to be run into no expenses—pretty low times, doctor—money's out of the question. Now, sir, can *you* raise that there woman?"—"Yes, my good sir," cried the doctor confidently, "yes I can." [Howison 1821, pp. 195–96]

The linguistic features that Howison employs in representing this conversation are the ones that British visitors were likely to despise in all varieties of North American English: words imagined to be Americanisms (*smart* and *spry* are both words long in the English vocabulary, but they flourished in the new senses in the United States and Canada); forms that existed in regional dialects but not in cultivated speech in Great Britain (*I'll raise you in five days*); features that continue to typify folk speech on both sides of the Atlantic (such as multiple negation); various expressions that were already stigmatized as typical of American speech (*I don't calculate, I guess as how*), particularly intensifiers of strained metaphorical force (*thundering sight, dreadful skeelful*); the use of honorifics that reflect, to the visitor, the "leveling" of social distinctions; and new usages that are genuinely North American in origin (*root doctor*).

Not long after the settlement of Upper Canada by English speakers, Canadians and visitors alike began to identify elements of Canadian English that they scorned as "those primitive fabrics in Cannuckian vernacular" (Hultín 1967, p. 244 n.). For the most part, the focus of criticism was restricted to vocabulary, both that derived from Yankee settlers and words developed in Canada itself. In the most sweeping of these early critiques, the Reverend A. Constable Geike collected a list of "Canadian" words that he found particularly contemptible: *boss* 'master', *bug* 'insect', *caucus* 'committee meeting', *chisel* 'cheat', *dicker* 'bargain', *donate* 'give' and *donation* 'gift', *down town*, *first class* 'capable, able', *fix* 'adjust, repair', *limbs* 'arms and legs', *loan* 'lend', *located* 'situated', *make tracks* 'run away', *pants* 'trousers', *rendition* 'performance', *rooster* 'cock', *sick* 'ill', and *store* 'shop'. Such words, Geike wrote, and "a thousand other examples" constitute "a corrupt dialect growing up amongst our population, and gradually finding access to our periodical literature, until it threatens to produce a language as unlike our noble mother tongue as the negro patua, or the Chinese pidgeon English" (Geike 1857, p. 353).[7]

Both foreign observers and native critics generally treated Canadian English as indiscriminately "Yankee" and amply expressed their fears that the separate development of English in North America would loosen the ties of loyalty and culture that kept Canada within the British Empire. Eventually, John Robert Godley, who had traveled on both sides of the border, detected that "the Canadians are neither British nor American." In the same breath, he observed that "they are more American than they believe themselves to be, or would like to be considered" (Godley 1955, p. 144). Modern Canadian opinion continues to note the ebb and flow of American influence: "In periods when the situation in the United States is most menacing, Canadians tend to focus on the features in their own society which distinguish them most from their neighbour and their neighbour's view of man" (Caplan and Laxer 1970, p. 309). While criticisms like Geike's of Canadian English continue, Canadians have often found satisfaction in the distinctive features of their language. In light of their political and cultural independence, Canadians have created for themselves a sense of their past that reduces Yankee influence and asserts kinship with Great Britain.

In modern publications, certain spellings mark a text as distinctively Canadian. Only in Canada is the combination *tire centre* normally encountered, an assertion of independence from the British *tyre* and the American *center*. While such tokens of linguistic independence may strike visitors as less than revolutionary, they are cited by many Canadians as traces of their distinctive past and present status as British North Americans. Nonetheless, such views of the spelling system are not held with equal fervor throughout the country. Adult respondents to the Survey of Canadian English were invited to report the spelling they preferred between *color* (the United States convention) and *colour* (the British):

	color	colour	either
Maritimes	37%	39%	23%
Ontario	14	75	11
Prairies	57	23	20
British Columbia	37	45	18

As most Canadians would predict, Ontario is the focal area for the spelling perceived to be more British (and hence more fitting for Canadians). By means of the books, magazines, and newspapers published in Ontario and circulated throughout the country, Ontarians are able to make their preferences felt outside the province. By contrast, it is not surprising that Albertans confess the greatest influence from the United States, and the practices and dialects of their southern neighbors have been transplanted to the northern plains along with the cattle and petroleum industries. Insignificant as such spelling differences may seem, they arouse in some an intense passion about the "proprieties" of the English language. In 1852, for instance, a writer excoriated *plow* (instead of *plough*) as reflecting "a savage and heretical disregard of everything in the shape of orthodox precedent" (quoted by Hultín 1967, p. 251). Such fervor reminds both Canadians and anglophones abroad of their deep concerns about the state of the language, and even minor details can reflect strongly held feelings. One student from Vancouver suggested this dilemma in his report that, though he says [luˈtɛnənt] *lieutenant* (like 72 percent of male students from British Columbia), he believes that [lɛfˈtɛnənt] is the better pronunciation because it is "more Canadian."

While it is conventional for linguists to speak of a "General Canadian" variety of English, such a term conceals significant regional and temporal differences. As a scholarly fiction, General Canadian does not recognize that *bluff* 'a group of trees' is used by only 3 percent of Canadians in Ontario and eastward but is the preferred term of 54 percent of adults in Manitoba and Saskatchewan, nor can a description on general principles do more than note that *lumbering* is the common term in the East for what Westerners call *logging*. Without the perspective of history, "general" traits of Canadian English do not incorporate most of the terms listed in the *Dictionary of Canadianisms*, many of which are archaic, are restricted to subregions of the country (e.g., *saltchuck* 'body of saltwater connected to the Pacific Ocean', or *skookum* 'powerful, strong, brave'), or have currency only as historical memory keeps them alive (e.g., *Bennett buggy* or *Red River cart*). Yet General Canadian does allow for the description of those features that are found across the country from St. John's, Newfoundland, to Victoria, British Columbia—a distance of 4,700 miles. Such features distinguish Canadians from others in the worldwide speech community of English and encompass both stereotypes ("conscious" Canadian traits) and markers (linguistic identifiers equally distinctive but not easily specified by untrained observers). Most important, General Canadian recognizes that Canadian English, though diverse in communities and variable in the speech of individuals, is not a composite of archaic or rustic features or a potpourri of British and American speechways but a true national language.

In pronunciation, Canadians participate in certain general tendencies that, though sometimes current in Britain and the United States, are differently distributed in Canada, either socially or in terms of their linguistic environments. In answer to the Survey of Canadian English, for instance, 85 percent of respondents from across Canada reported that *cot* and *caught* "rhyme." In Canada, the historic vowels in these words coalesce into either [ɒ] or [ɑ], and the merger extends to pairs of words that are in contrastive distribution in many other varieties of English—for example, *lager/logger, collar/caller, holly/Hawley, Don/dawn,* and *hock/hawk*. Such a merger has not commonly taken place in England, and though the tendency toward making these pairs homophones is rapidly spreading in the United States, Canadians have extended the vowel they use in these words to others where Americans who participate in the merger would have a different vowel: for example, *block, coffee, father, hockey, lost, pot, rob,* and *solder*.[8]

A similar tendency is the change in articulation of [t] from a stop to a flap in intervocalic position (e.g., *pity, patio, setup*) and after [r] before vowels (e.g., *party*). The extent of this change may be age-graded in present-day Canada; in the Survey of Canadian English, 61 percent of adults reported medial [t] in *butter,* but 60 percent of their children believed [d] to be a feature of their pronunciation of this word. In a related change, medial [t] after [n] may be deleted, producing [ˈdɛnɪst] *dentist* and [ˈtwɛni] *twenty* (Gregg 1978, p. 15). Both processes are stylistically variable, and neither change affects citation forms or careful styles of speech. In the popular lore of Canadian English, the process by which [t] is deleted after [n] accounts for the general assumption that the capital city of Ontario is called by its inhabitants "Trntuh," "Toronna," or "Trawna."[9] In many varieties of English, final voiceless stops are accompanied by glottal constriction. When final [t], for instance, is deleted, speakers will produce such pronunciations as [ʃɑʔ] *shop*, [nɑʔ naʊ] *not now,* and [nɑʔ ju] *not you.* Whether glottal stops will take the place of other final consonants, as in working-class Scots, remains to be investigated.

As in most varieties of North American English, the contrast of [hw] and [w] (or, alternatively, [ʍ] and [w]) is seldom a property of informal Canadian speech and is rare even in citation forms. In the Survey of Canadian English, 39 percent of adult women reported that *which* and *witch* have differing initial segments; only 28 percent of their daughters claimed to have this contrast. If the tendency toward merger suggested by these figures continues, it is likely that only those areas of Canada influenced by other varieties of English, where the contrast is preserved, will sustain it. Though generally variable elsewhere, the speech of part of the United States bordering Ontario, northern English, Scots, and Hiberno-English all maintain the contrast in citation forms and careful speaking styles. In Canada, the process by which [w] extends to initial segments affects *which*, *whine*, *wheel*, *what*, *whey*, *whiskers*, and other words with historical [hw].

In 1906, a Canadian writer bewailing the influence of "Yankee" English noted that "in one respect we are not sinners. We seldom say 'noos', 'avenoo', or 'dooty' " (quoted by Hultín 1967, p. 255). In present-day Canadian English, such pronunciations are probably more common than at the turn of the century; in response to the Survey of Canadian English, 58 percent of adults rhymed *new* with *few*, but 34 percent reported rhyming *new* with *do*. Among their children, however, the preference for [u] was 40 percent and only 37 percent claimed to use the [ju] of *few*.[10] In *student*, however, [u] was chosen over [ju] by 55 percent of adults and by 67 percent of their children. Gregg (1978, p. 20) notes that deletion of [j] following [t], [d], and [n] is "found at all social levels in Canada," and the results from the Survey suggest that the preference for [u] instead of [ju] is farthest advanced in New Brunswick and Nova Scotia, perhaps due to the influence of New England speech where [u] is widespread (Kurath and McDavid 1961, p. 74). Yet despite the apparent shift from [ju] to [u] in such words as *Tuesday*, *duty*, and *new*, the [ju] pronunciation retains some of the social significance attributed to it in the past; for those speakers who look to the prestige dialect of southeastern England as a model for their speech, the [ju] pronunciation current in that variety of English reinforces its use in Canada. Whatever the variability of [ju] and [u] following [t], [d], and [n], the use of [u] after other alveolar consonants is virtually universal in Canada (in such words as *absolute*, *pursue*, *resume*, *rude*, and *suit*). But where the [ju] pronunciations occupy a position of prestige (as they do among some social groups in Ontario, for instance), [ju] may be substituted for [u] in environments where neither historical origins nor standard British English provide a model for their use: for example, [mjun] *moon*, [njun] *noon*, and [tju] *too* (Avis 1978b, p. 75).

Of all the features of Canadian English pronunciation, perhaps none has received more attention in both popular lore and linguistic analysis than the diphthongs in such words as *house* and *write*. Both Canadians and Americans recognize that there is something distinctive about these sounds, though Canadians correctly object to the American idea that they say "oot" for *out* and "aboot" for *about*.[11] But whatever the accuracy of the lore, these sounds are sharply differentiated by the United States–Canadian border and thus constitute both stereotypic and actual distinctive features of Canadian English.

Words containing the diphthongs in question derive from Middle English [i] or [u], and as a consequence of the Great Vowel Shift were transformed from monophthongs to diphthongs. While the precise dating of the changes remains a matter of dispute, many varieties of English followed a sequence from Middle English [tid] *tide* and [hus] *house*, to Early Modern English [təɪd] and [həʊs], to Modern English [taɪd] and [haʊs]. Not all varieties of English have carried this process through to completion in the schematic pattern just indicated, and the phonetic environments in which these sounds occur are crucial in explaining the distribution of vowels in these words found in many varieties of English.

What is apparently the first stage in the change, the shift from Middle English [i] and [u] to [əɪ] and [əʊ], accounts for the distinctive feature of Hiberno-English discussed by Michael V. Barry elsewhere in this volume; both diphthongs (with their centralized onsets) occur generally in environments in which the sounds are word-final or occur before either a following voiced or a following voiceless sound. A second pattern of development is illustrated by Scots, in which [əɪ] and [əʊ] may be realized as [aɪ] and [aʊ] in some speech styles in word-final position (e.g., *I* and *how*), before a following vowel, or before a voiced fricative (e.g., *alive* and *mouth* [verb]). A third pattern, represented by Canadian English, employs [aɪ] and [aʊ] in all environments except those where the following consonant is voiceless; in that case [əɪ] and [əʊ] appear. Hence Canadian English is typified by the following contrastive pairs where the diphthong manifests the contrast made in some kinds of American English (for example) by vowel length:

[əɪ]	[aɪ]	[əʊ]	[aʊ]
fife	*five*	*house* (n.)	*house* (v.)
price	*prize*	*bout*	*bowed*
pipe	*pie*	*lout*	*loud*
site	*side*	*mouth* (n.)	*mouth* (v.)

Though a good generalization about Canadian English, the statement that [əɪ] and [əʊ] occur before voiceless consonants omits crucial details. In some varieties, for instance, the selection of diphthongs may vary according to speech style, and for many speakers neither [əɪ] nor [əʊ] are categorical before voiceless consonants. For many Canadians, [aɪ] is consistently used in all environments while [əʊ] is regularly used before voiceless consonants. Another complicating feature can be traced to the influence of Scots and Hiberno-English patterns. In the Ottawa Valley, for instance, the use of [əɪ] and [əʊ] (and above all [əʊ]) in contexts other than before voiceless consonants is associated in the minds of city dwellers with the rustic varieties of Canadian English typical of the Irish-descended people in the surrounding rural areas (Pringle 1979, p. 20; see also Woods 1979).

Further exceptions to the view that [əɪ] and [əʊ] occur systematically before voiceless sounds reveal the complexity of these variables in Canadian English. Though [n] is obviously voiced, it is assimilated to the previous vowel by those Canadians who distinguish [məʊnt] *mount* and [maʊnd] *mound*. For speakers who participate in assimilation in this pair, the selection of the diphthong in *find time* and *fine day* may potentially vary in a similar way. In addition, the usual pronunciation ['rəɪdər] *writer* may be explained by assuming that the voicing of intervocalic [t] "comes after" the conditioning of the diphthong. Similarly, the pronunciation ['həɪskuɫ] *high school* shows a reinterpretation of the compound in which the word boundary is not recognized and the following voiceless sound, [s], selects the diphthong. Yet further complications in the description arise from those varieties of Canadian English in which the effect of a following nasal consonant supports a three-way diphthongal contrast when [ɛɪ] and [ɛu] occur in the vowel inventory:

following nasal:	[bɛɪnd] *bind*	[bɛund] *bound*
following voiced sound:	[bəɪd] *bide*	[bəud] *bowed*
following voiceless sound:	[baɪt] *bite*	[baut] *bout*

With such complexity of phonetic conditioning joined to the factors arising from social meaning and stylistic variety, these "Canadian diphthongs" present a particular challenge to linguistic and social analysis.[12]

In the extensive scholarship that summarizes views of Canadian English, features like the reflexes of Middle English [i] and [u] just discussed are often treated as the residue of one or another kind of "foreign" influence. Avis, for instance, speculates that these diphthongs are derived from Great Britain—"it may well be that Scottish and Northern English influence accounts for this oft-remarked Canadian speech trait" (1973, p. 64)—and it is a commonplace to say that "Canadian usage divides between British and American practice" (Hamilton 1964, p. 457). When one model or the other is not fully realized in Canadian practice, the differences are often attributed to "frequent inconsistencies" (Orkin 1970, p. 128). Neither scholars nor writers in the popular press seem prepared to recognize distinctive developments that have sprung up on Canadian soil except, perhaps, for the vocabulary that has been borrowed from Native Americans or incorporated from other languages that have been spoken by settlers in Canada. What is needed is a description of Canadian English that is not initially contrastive (thus emphasizing departures from American or British models), but is descriptive of actual practices. Such a description needs to take into account the social facts that bear on individual stylistic variation on the one hand and on the distinctive traits of various groups in Canadian society on the other.

The social history of distinctively Canadian English is relatively complex. As noted earlier, such nineteenth-century observers as the Reverend A. Constable Geike spoke of the English of Upper Canada as "a corrupt dialect growing up amongst our population" and attributed all departures from British English—"our noble mother tongue"—to American influence even though some of the features he mentioned were almost certainly of purely Canadian origin. Such hankerings after the prestige dialects of England continued well into this century, and there is some continuing residue of Geike's beliefs among older anglophiles in Toronto and Montreal (see Hamilton 1975). Stephen Leacock, Canada's internationally acclaimed humorist, suggested something of the ambivalence of Canadian linguistic attitudes in a essay published in 1936, "I'll Stay in Canada":

> We used to be ashamed of our Canadian language, before the war, and try to correct it and take on English phrases and say, "What a ripping day," instead of "What a peach of a morning," and "Ah you thah?" instead of "Hello, Central," and "Oh, rather!" instead of "O-Hell-Yes." But now, since the Great War put Canada right on the level with the Portuguese and Siamese and those fellows who come from—ah! one forgets the names, but it doesn't matter—I mean, made Canada a real nation—we just accept our own language and are not ashamed of it. We say "yep!" when we mean "yep!" and don't dare try to make out it's "yes," which is a word we don't use; and if we mean "four" we say so and don't call it "faw." [Leacock 1955, p. 210]

Yet attempts to imitate the English of Great Britain were never commonplace, and it seems particularly doubtful that any large numbers of Canadians cultivated the *r*-less pronunciations Leacock mentions in words like *there*, *are*, or *four*. But Leacock, like Geike, assumed that Canadians sounded more like the English at some earlier time, a view that the linguistic and social history does not support. Despite Leacock's testimony, it is unlikely that large numbers of Canadians have ever devoted much energy to mimicking British models, and more recently it appears that British speaking styles can be a barrier to social success.[13] In linguistic as in other matters, Canadians are inclined to say that they "are conditioned from infancy to think of themselves as citizens of a country of uncertain identity, a confusing past, and a hazardous future" (Frye 1977, p. 1).

In spite of the national uncertainty that Canadians may from time to time express, immigrants both past and present have almost always been obliged to conform to Canadian speechways. In the early nineteenth century, John Robert Godley wrote about the process that was then old and continues today. "Everybody is a foreigner here," he wrote:

> You have the provincial peculiarities of every part of the British Islands contrasted with those of European and American foreigners: one man addresses you in a rich Cork brogue, the next in broad Scotch, and a third in undeniable Yorkshire; the Yankee may be known by his broad-brimmed hat, lank figure, and nasal drawl: then you have the French Canadian, chattering patois, in his red cap, blue shirt, sash, and mocassins; the German, with his blue blouse and black belt; and the Italian, following the usual trades of his country. [Godley 1955, p. 143]

"Here," he concluded, "is a national character in the process of formation." Just as those immigrants had to adapt to the unfamiliar landscape and the new society, so in the process they became Canadians.

Today, the flow of immigration continues, perhaps even more various in its origins than in Godley's day, as newcomers from throughout the Commonwealth settle across Canada (see Fawcett 1979, pp. 16–19). Diversity calls forth pressures to conform, and few of the immigrants resist the expectation that they will acquire the distinctive traits of Canadian English. The experience of many is reflected in the observations of a new Canadian from Sri Lanka (who encountered Canadian English when he established residence in Calgary):

> They speak of culture shock. I had never experienced until I came out here. Calgary was the antithesis of everything I had ever known. The first thing that struck me was disillusionment. I thought "My God, my English is not good enough." I couldn't make myself understood. I was asking for "trousers" when they were saying "pants." Then I found that they couldn't speak the language themselves, using the double negative and so on. So I ended up putting myself in the situation where if I speak with a certain kind of guy, I use the double negative myself. "I do not know nothing." But I wouldn't want to say that to a guy who has some education. It's a question of adapting myself every day to very rapidly changing circumstances. [Montero 1977, pp. 125–26]

With each successive wave of immigration, Canadian society is changed but Canadian English is likely to be reinforced and made more, rather than less, coherent as a national language.

Thanks to the imaginative work of Cornelius Baeyer, it is possible to see Canadian English in a new perspective. Instead of a picture of a nation in which 75 percent of the population lies within 100 miles of the United States border, map 2 (from Baeyer 1976) shows the topography of Canada redrawn as an isodemographic map, one in which the population rather than the surface area of the country is represented. Map 2 shows clearly that Canada is an urban nation and graphically demonstrates what census tables show in a less visual way: more than half of Canadians lived in cities larger than 100,000 inhabitants at the time of the 1976 census. However, the largest cities—Toronto, Montreal, Vancouver, and Edmonton—are the least studied by linguists and dialectologists. Lunenburg, Nova Scotia, has been the subject of detailed investigation for fifty years (see Emeneau 1935); Toronto has been studied systematically only very recently (see Léon and Martin 1979).

In most countries, the cities are the focus of linguistic change, and their influence extends steadily outward to the regions that surround them. Such is probably the case in Canada.[14] Yet, though the results of the Survey of Canadian English are immensely valuable, it is impossible to separate rural from

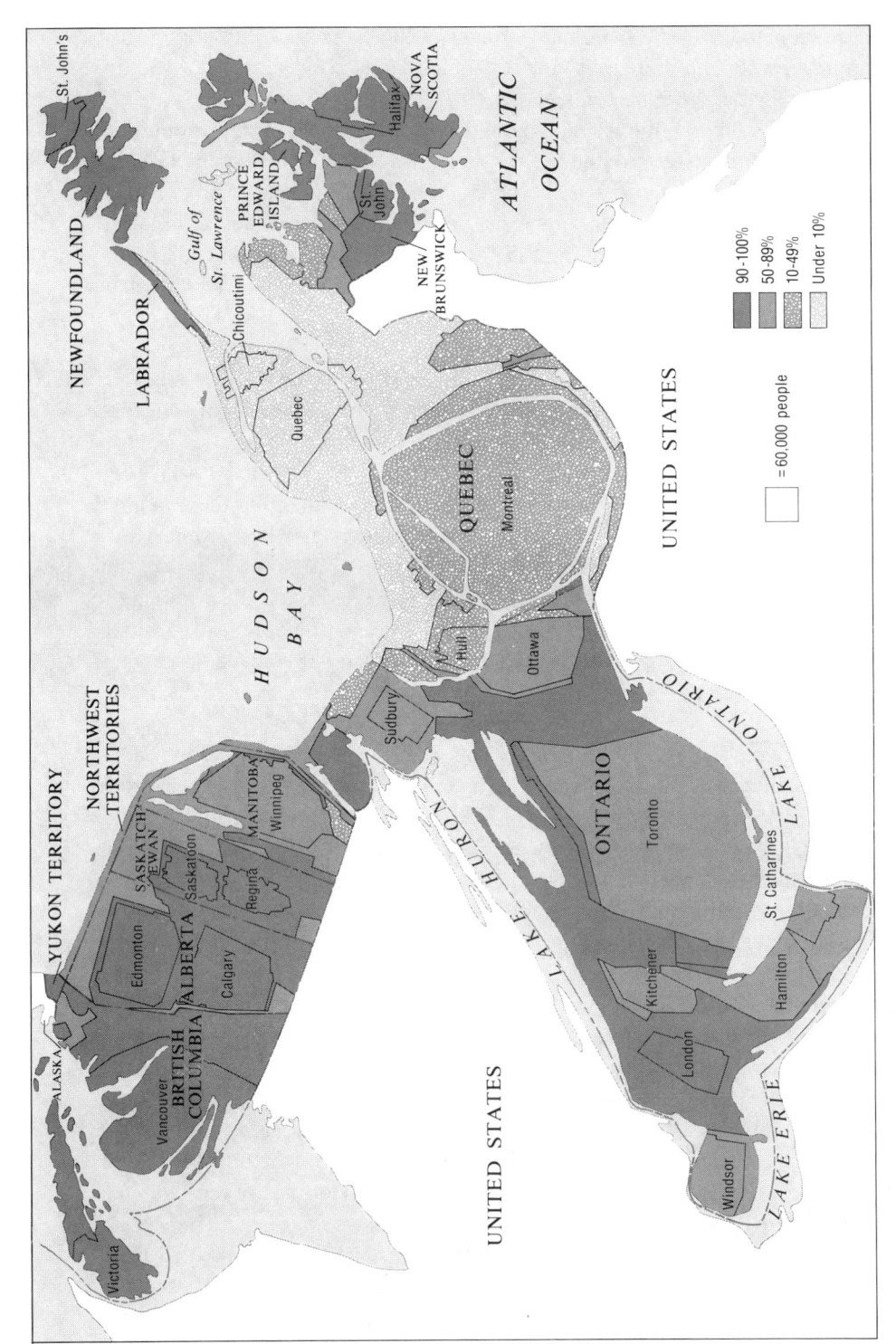

Map 2. English in Canada. Each province and city is shown in proportion to its population. Shades indicate what percentage of the population usually speaks English at home.

urban responses or to identify which variables reflect prestige forms or negative stereotypes. Since the Survey provides separate tabulations for adults and children and for men and women, it may be tempting to suppose that women in Canada (as in some other English-speaking communities) are in the vanguard of change and that the young reflect the leading edge of linguistic changes in progress.

Both suppositions are perilous. In several of the answers to the Survey, men and women differ markedly in their preferences. Across Canada, *dived* and *dove* compete for predominance as the past tense of *dive* in the sentence "He _____ into the pool." Nationally, women preferred *dived* in larger numbers than men (54 percent to 38 percent). From these numbers alone, it might reasonably be guessed that *dived* is increasingly used. Linguistic history can be invoked to bolster this thesis, since *dived* would appear to be yet another instance of the tendency toward leveling strong verbs in English. But analysis of the province-by-province results clouds this clear picture: women select *dived* by substantial margins only in Newfoundland, Prince Edward Island, New Brunswick, Manitoba, and Saskatchewan (64 percent of adult women prefer *dived* and 32 percent *dove*). By an equally decisive margin (56 percent to 39 percent), women in Nova Scotia, Quebec, Ontario, and British Columbia prefer *dove*. There is no reason to suppose that one group of women is more influential than the other, nor is there any obvious historical explanation to account for the distribution of these preferences by province. Further, neither group of women clearly influences the choices made by their children. Thus, what at first may have seemed a tenable hypothesis cannot be supported by the Survey data.

The assumption that children are likely to represent the next generation of Canadian English is similarly dubious. As Scargill (1974, p. 138) observes, the young report more forms that appear to be archaic and conservative than their parents. Twice as many children as parents use *riz* for 'raised', and more students than adults use *yelk* 'yolk of an egg' and pronounce *deaf* to rhyme with *leaf*, *yeast* with *lest*, and *home* with *dumb*. In all cases, the numbers of responses for these apparently old-fashioned variants is small. Yet it is tempting to assume that the preference of the young for such pronunciations as [ˈbʊri] *bury*—14 percent for children in the Prairies versus only 5 percent for adults in the same region—points to a linguistic future in which the minority pronunciation gains adherents. Such an assumption rests on the view that the young are likely to persist in their linguistic habits rather than to adapt gradually to the norms of adults.

Given the perils of extracting from the still photograph of the Survey a moving picture of the dynamism of linguistic change, it is not entirely surprising that some observers have attempted to trace the filiations of various forms in Canadian speech to other kinds of English. Yet similarities elsewhere do not of themselves provide unambiguous evidence of historical influence or contemporary reinforcement through imitation. Consider, for instance, the following facts about present-day Canadian English:

1. About three-quarters of Canadians use [zɛd] rather than [zi] for the name of the letter *z*, and about two-thirds use *bath* (rather than *bathe*) in the expression "to bath the baby."
2. Virtually all Canadians pronounce [r] after vowels.
3. About two-thirds pronounce the *l* in *almond* and three-quarters use *chesterfield* rather than *sofa* or *davenport*.

Evidence of this kind can be marshaled to support any one of three quite different hypotheses: (1) Canadians are like the English (in, for instance, preferring [zɛd] and *bath* as a verb); (2) Canadians are like Americans (in, for instance, the articulation and distribution of [r]); (3) Canadians reflect their own national tradition in the widespread use of forms unknown or uncommon elsewhere (in, for instance, *almond* and *chesterfield*). Each of these linguistic hypotheses implies an assumption about Canada's place in the political world: "Loyalists" in the Commonwealth; "North Americans" by geography; "nationalists" by virtue of separatism and independent growth. Each political assumption and linguistic hypothesis has adherents, but the facts of Canadian English resist unambiguous classification.

On the whole, Canadians are less "British" in their speech than they may imagine: [ɛt] *ate*, whatever currency it may have once enjoyed in Canada, is now barely reported; *schedule* begins with [sk] rather than [ʃ] for 75 percent of adults, and the former is even more commonly used by their children; while *lieutenant* begins with [lɛf] for 43 percent of adult men, only 11 percent of their daughters report using this form; *missile* ends with [l] or [əl] (rather than [aɪl] for 81 percent of respondents to the Survey; only 10 percent prefer *autumn* to *fall*. Most Canadians do not deploy eating utensils by *laying the table* as many Britishers do, nor do they receive letters from the hands of a *postman*. Instead they *set the table* and meet the *mailman*. Canadian anglophiles may treat the British element in their English as symbolically important, but most of their compatriots do not imitate British styles or promote departures from Canadian norms.

Despite their fears of "Americanization," Canadians are likewise resistant to developments in the American English of the United States, and their common border serves to divide both political institutions and linguistic habits. Though Fort Erie, Ontario, and Buffalo, New York, face each other across the Niagara River and traveling from one to the other is convenient and common, each city remains linguistically distinctive. Merger of the vowels of *cot* and *caught* and the centralized diphthongs in *fight* and *house* stop on the Canadian side; the raising of [æ] to [ɛ]—so that the vowel of *pan* and *rather* approaches that of *pen* and *feather*—is virtually restricted to the American shore.[15] Farther west, where Ontario and Manitoba adjoin Minnesota and North Dakota, the boundary is similarly sharp. *Bluff* (for a *clump* or *grove* of trees) is "uniquely and indisputable Canadian" (Allen 1973, p. 138); [tʃ] initially in *Tuesday* and *tube* is also a distinctive Canadianism. In this region, Americans use [hw] in *whoa* and *whetstone* and Canadians do not; Americans pronounce [z] in *raspberry* where Canadians have

[s]; [ves] is the usual American pronunciation of *vase*, but only 16 percent of adults in Manitoba follow that pattern, preferring instead [vɔz].[16] Still farther west, Canadians remain distinct from their American neighbors. On Vancouver Island, [aɪ] in the first syllable of *either* is reported by two-thirds of the Survey respondents; in the cities of the Lower Mainland around Vancouver, one-third report [aɪ] and two-thirds [i]; in the adjoining regions of the United States, [i] is nearly universal.[17] Contrasts like these suggest that Canadians are less like Americans than they sometimes fear themselves to be. If "American English is the present-day language of imperialism" (Fetherling 1972, p. 25), then Canadian English can fairly be said to resist it.

What is distinctly Canadian about Canadian English is not its unique linguistic features (of which there are a handful) but its combination of tendencies that are uniquely distributed. One further example that illustrates this point is the "Canadian eh" (pronounced [e]), a stereotype of Canadians so widely known and recognized that "border officials have come to regard it as a pretty good way to spot a Canadian" (James 1971, p. 11). Yet Avis has demonstrated that *eh* is abundant in British, American, and Canadian English and also occurs in Australia and South Africa (Avis 1978c). In all of these places the functions of *eh* are diverse: as a question tag ("hey, Barry, you have a cold one for me tonight, eh?"), as a reinforcer ("call me Alex, eh?"), and in elliptical statements of various kinds ("see you eh?" and "you won't eh?"). Assuming that the historical attestations are reliable, *eh* does not have its origin in Canada, and in only one function is it more common in Canada than elsewhere—in what Avis calls "narrative *eh*." In this use, which may occur "with disconcerting frequency," *eh* serves in place of a hesitation vowel or, implicitly, as a request for confirmation of the speaker's assumptions:

> He's holding on to a firehose, eh? The thing is jumping all over the place, eh, and he can hardly hold onto it eh? Well, he finally loses control of it, eh, and the water knocks down half a dozen bystanders. [Examples from Avis 1978c]

Though 25 percent of the schoolchildren responding to the Survey of Canadian English said that they would never use an expression like "so that's what he thinks, eh?" (Scargill 1974, p. 30), *eh* is clearly widespread across the country and across social classes. Both by its use in narrative contexts and by its relatively high frequency, it qualifies as a "Canadianism" and serves as one of the "distinctive" features of Canadian English. In fact, a book designed to help new Canadians learn English suggests that "if you want an easy way to sound casual and Canadian, use *eh*" (Baeyer 1976, p. 46).

Though few usages are indisputably typical of all Canadians, the vocabulary of all varieties of English is enriched by elements that have their origin in Canada: *igloo*, *kayak*, and *parka* have been borrowed from the Inuit languages of the Canadian North; *blueline, face-off,* and *puck* use English elements in new meanings; *snye* 'subsidiary stream of river', *joual* [ʤwal] 'colloquial Canadian French', and word order in government-created names (e.g., Parks Canada, Air Canada) show the influence of Canada's other language, French. Canadian political institutions have names with special meanings (for instance, *reeve, riding,* and *sheriff*), and Canadian inventions bear the names given by their creators—for example, *McIntosh apples, kerosene,* and *Hudson's Bay blanket.* Such a list could be extended almost indefinitely. On the principle that a Canadianism "is a word, expression, or meaning which is native to Canada or which is distinctively characteristic of Canadian usage though not necessarily exclusive to Canada" (Avis et al. 1967, p. xiii), the *Dictionary of Canadianisms* provides detailed information about some 10,000 words and expressions that reflect the creativity and vitality of Canadian English.

What constitutes a "distinctive characteristic" of Canadian English depends upon the perspective of the observer (see Avis 1973, p. 63). To Americans, Canadians are likely to seem distinctive by their use of *tap, serviette, braces,* and *porridge* (rather than *faucet, napkin, suspenders,* and *oatmeal*). To the British, *gas, truck, billboard,* and *wrench* seem similarly "Canadian" (instead of *petrol, lorry, hoarding,* and *spanner*). Yet not every speaker of Canadian English uses these words. In Toronto and Victoria, the British synonyms have some currency; in Edmonton and Windsor, the American equivalents are common. The most useful perspective, then, is one in which Canadian English is viewed as a cluster of features that combine in varying proportions in differing communities within Canada. Nationally, *tap,* for example, is the form preferred by 89 percent of adult respondents to the Survey of Canadian English (synonyms in descending frequency include *faucet, spigot,* and *valve* for the plumbing of a kitchen sink), but there are some who differentiate *faucet* and *valve* when speaking of an outdoor water point. Similarly, some Canadians distinguish *frosting* and *icing*—the former for a soft sugary coating of a cake and the latter a firm or hard one—while others use either term whatever the consistency of the substance. Likewise, another of the "distinctive" Canadianisms, *serviette* 'paper napkin' is used by only 48 percent of Survey respondents, but some distinguish a paper *serviette* and a cloth *napkin* while others use one term or the other for both. In each of these cases, both the choice of a synonym and the presence or absence of semantic differentiation indicate the variability of the Canadian speech community.

Canadian English entails systematic sets of probabilities varying according to individual, speech style, social class, regional setting, and responsiveness to native or foreign influence. In the absence of studies that discriminate each factor, it is impossible to describe the conditions that vary with linguistic features. Nevertheless, the results of the Survey of Canadian English show some of the features involved in variation: *again* has [e] as its stressed vowel, rather than [ɪ] or [ɛ], for 63 percent of adults, but only 48 percent of their children share that preference; in the second vowel of the prefixes *anti-* and *semi-,* most Canadians prefer [ɪ] to [aɪ], but there is a tendency for [aɪ] to occur with greater frequency in the former than in the latter; *aunt* and *ant* are homophones (both with [æ]) for 61 percent of adults; *congratulate* has medial [ʤ] rather than [tʃ] for only 23 percent of adults, but 51 percent of their children report using [ʤ] even though that pronunciation is sometimes stigmatized as "nonstandard" in Canadian schools; *film* is pronounced as a single syllable by 63 percent of adults and competes with pronunciations employing an epenthetic vowel (['fɪləm]); another sometimes stigmatized pronunciation, *genuine* with [aɪ] as its third vowel, is used by 76 percent of adults; *guarantee* has three competing vowels in its first syllable—[æ] for 18 percent of adults, [ɑ ~ ɒ] for 31 percent, and [ɛ] for 51 percent; the first vowel of *leisure* is [i] rather than [ɛ] for 68 percent of adults; the first vowel of *lever* follows a similar pattern in that 84 percent of adults prefer [i] to [ɛ]; *progress* alternates between [o] and [ɑ ~ ɒ] with 58 percent of adults reporting the use of [o]; *tomato*, one of the most complex of these variables, has [e] in its stressed vowel for 78 percent of adults and 86 percent of children, but substantial numbers in both groups use [a], [æ], or [ɑ ~ ɒ], and [æ] is likely to be heard in Quebec and the Maritimes and [ɑ] from adults in Newfoundland and Labrador. For the most part, Canadians share the word-stress patterns of other North Americans (in, for example, treating final *-ary*, *-ery*, and *-ory* as full syllables in *secondary*, *dysentery*, and *explanatory* [Gregg 1978, p. 33]), but they are much more likely to use ['dɛkl̩] *decal* rather than [dɪ'kæɫ] as do most anglophones in the United States.

Neither the stylistic range of a single speaker nor social class variation have yet been systematically studied in Canadian English.[18] Regional differences, however, have been sketched in several parts of the country. In British Columbia, for instance, the usages that predominate in the cities of the Lower Mainland (Vancouver, New Westminster, Burnaby, and Richmond) set them apart from Victoria and the other communities on Vancouver Island to the west, the Okanagan and Kootenay valleys to the east, and the Cariboo to the north.[19] The Ottawa Valley of eastern Ontario has long been recognized as a distinctive area—so much so that its speech is known in the folklore of Canadian English as the Ottawa "twang"— and is now being systematically investigated by Ian Pringle and Enoch Padolsky.[20] Thanks to the efforts of scholars at Memorial University, Newfoundland is also becoming better known as a distinctive linguistic area, and scholarship is at last providing substance to the nationally-known stereotype of the "Newfie" dialect.[21] With generous support from the Social Sciences and Humanities Research Council, such studies should continue to prosper and multiply. If the recommendations of the Report of the Commission on Canadian Studies are implemented, studies of Canadian English and the training of scholars to conduct them should also increase in Canadian universities (see Symons 1978).

In the context of present-day variation in Canadian English, it is important to recognize that governments at both federal and provincial levels have taken steps to adapt to Canada's status as a multilingual nation, but relatively few citizens are aware that nearly 40 percent of the respondents to the 1976 census reported as their mother tongue some language other than English. Among the languages most widely mentioned are English (14,122,770 speakers), French (5,887,205), Italian (484,050), German (476,715), Ukranian (282,060), Chinese (132,560), North American languages including Inuit (133,005), Portuguese (126,535), Dutch (114,760), and more than thirty-two other languages that, though they are used by fewer than 100,000 speakers across the country, also constitute viable linguistic communities (e.g., Finnish, with 20,380; Yiddish, with 10,175 speakers in Ontario; and Russian, with 10,085 in British Columbia). As a consequence of this linguistic diversity, several varieties of bilingualism are common in Canada; the main types are English-French, English-German, English-Italian, English-Ukranian, and French-Italian, French-Ukranian, and French-German.[22]

While all of these languages have potential influence on English in Canada, most of them have made little impact on the word-stock, pronunciation, or grammar of Canadian English. With a few exceptions, most of the communities have been obliged to adapt to English in order to participate in the national life of the country. Even though ethnic communities in the cities or "block settlements" in the rural areas may preserve languages other than English from one generation to the next, anglophones have had little motivation to acquire even the limited facility in other languages that is a prerequisite for borrowing. Such loans as there are in Canadian English from Chinese, for instance, are likely to be borrowings (e.g., *chow mein*) or loan translations (e.g., *spring roll*) derived from the restaurant trade. Such contacts as the following, recreating a conversation between an English and a German-descended Canadian in Kitchener (formerly Berlin), Ontario, suggest the constraints on borrowing from other languages into Canadian English:

> At a table not quite midway along the left aisle, downstairs, a short, plump, black-bonneted woman offers little pats of schmearkase wrapped in waxed paper, for a nickel each. I buy a quarter's worth to take home and prepare as she tells me: "you chust mix it with a little salt and plenty sweet cream till it's real smooth, and then you put some in a nappie, pour lots of maple syrup over," she winks and smiles broadly, "and that really schmecks." [quoted by McConnell 1979, p. 185]

From such an exchange, the English speaker may well extract the noun *smearcase* (from German *Schmierkäse*) 'cottage cheese', but the other elements represented here—for instance, *chust* 'just', *plenty sweet cream, pour lots of maple syrup over*, and *schmecks* 'tastes good'—are unlikely candidates for imitation or borrowing. As the passage demonstrates, the German cheese merchant has developed in her English some Canadian features that, taken together, would be unlikely to be learned in another variety of English—*real smooth* 'really smooth' and *nappie* 'serving dish'—and has applied English inflections to German words (*schmecks*). Given the long tradition in which English speakers have acted as employers and customers, while speakers of other languages have been workers and sellers, it is not surprising that there is little in Canadian English that reflects the languages of the many thousands of nonanglophones who have come to Canada as immigrants. Except for communities that remain isolated from Canadian life for religious reasons (such as the Amish and Doukhobors), there are strong pressures to master English and, by the invasion of English elements, many of the linguistic enclaves in Canada are decimated by what one scholar has called the " 'linguicidal' measures which result in the constant decline of the minority languages in Canada" (*Report of the Royal Commission* 1967, p. 164).

Of all the languages apart from English spoken in Canada, it is French that has historically been the most significant, both in numbers of speakers and in shaping the political and social institutions of Canadian life. At the time of Confederation in 1867, one-third of Canadians spoke French, but by the time of the 1976 census, the proportion reporting French as their mother tongue had fallen to one-quarter of the population. Since 1763, French Canadians have struggled to maintain their language and culture against the majority who speak English and who control much of the nation's economic and political power. From the earliest times to the present, anglophones have argued that Canada cannot be unified as a nation as long as separate languages divide the loyalties of the people, and they have not been hesitant to oblige the French Canadian to accommodate unity by giving up French. Such views have been repeatedly stated by anglophone Canadians and English-speaking visitors alike, but the observations of Hugh Gray, who toured Canada in 1806–8, are sufficiently representative of a consistently held perspective to be worth brief quotation. On visiting the seat of government in Quebec in March 1807, Gray found that legislative deliberations were going forward in French:

> The [French] Canadians will not speak English; and Englishmen are weak enough to indulge them so far as to speak French too, which is much to their disadvantage; for though they may speak French well enough to explain themselves in the ordinary affairs of life, they cannot, in debate, deliver themselves with that ease, and with the same effect as in their native language. [Gray 1809, p. 101]

Such unnatural behavior in a British colony, as Gray thought, was intolerable to the sound management of the Empire. But Gray was not so sanguine as to imagine that the French would promptly give up their language and institutions, and so he took it upon himself to persuade them into English:

> What the Canadians ought principally to regard is, that they must infallibly be surrounded by people who speak English, with whom it is their destiny to buy and sell, to traffic, and treat. . . . [English] presses upon them on all sides; so that, on this account alone, it is evidently the *interest* of the Canadians to learn English; not to mention how much it is their *duty* also

to learn the language of the head, and executive part of the government. [Gray 1809, pp. 340–41]

Thanks to continued support for bilingualism, confirmed by the legislature in 1792 and making possible the parliamentary debate observed by Gray during his visit, French continued as one of the two languages of Canadian government, despite various official and unofficial assaults against it in the years before and after confederation. However pragmatic the arguments of Gray and others, French Canadians continue to assert their interests, and their duties, without abandoning their language.

Since English-speaking Canadians achieved a majority of the population in the mid-1840s, French Canadians became a minority constituency in government, though their votes in the national legislature have made possible a series of coalitions that have often dominated national political life. Nonetheless, English has clearly been the language of power and prestige, and the resulting asymmetry of influence is evident in the contrast of present-day Canadian English and Canadian French. In examining Canadian English, it is difficult to identify many borrowings or significant influences from the French of Canada that have entered the language since the mid-nineteenth century.[23] Canadian French, on the other hand, has been invaded by loan words, calques, and artifacts of English phonology. If *franglais* in France itself should excite the anger of academicians and purists, they have only to look at French in Canada to see the impact of the majority English culture. *Wagon* (*ouagine*), *snack, fun, slippers, husting, caucus, sheriff, job, steam, dump* (*dompe*), *mop,* and *sink* are only some of the English borrowings that have replaced French vocabulary (see Vinay 1973, p. 387). Such influences are strongly felt in Quebec, where 85 percent of Canada's French-speaking population is located. For the outposts of French Canadian culture elsewhere in the country, the impact of English is devastating. In southwestern Ontario, for instance, "the ordinary speech of Windsor French [is] incomprehensible to anyone who does not know English" (Hull 1972, p. 258).

Despite the relatively small influence of French on recent Canadian English, anglophone Canadians have contrived a stereotype of the "habitant" that presumes a characteristic pattern of accent and language mixture. Some of the features of this kind of English are captured in anecdotes and poems, among them "The Wreck of the *Julie Plante*" by the Canadian poet William Henry Drummond (1854–1907):

> De win' she blow from nor'-eas' wes',—
> De sout' win' she blow too,
> W'en Rosie cry "Mon cher captinne,
> Mon cher, w'at I shall do?"
> Den de Captinne t'row de big ankerre,
> But still de scow she dreef,

> De crew he can't pass on de shore,
> Becos' he los' hees skeef.
> [Quoted from Gustafson 1967, p. 60]

While some features mimicked in this stanza from Drummond's poem are genuine imitations of French-accented English (e.g., [t] for [θ] and [d] for [ð]), others are contrived from the beliefs of English speakers about the characteristics of such English (e.g., the use of *she* as a generalized pronoun). The "imperfections" of this partly imaginary dialect perpetuate the idea that speakers of Canadian French are not to be given serious consideration as coequal members of Canadian society, and anglophones across the country commonly hold the belief that *joual* and standard Canadian French are essentially the same and essentially inadequate for full participation in modern life.[24]

While English and French have been nominally equal in the national parliament for nearly two centuries, a significant step toward bilingualism came only with the passage of the Official Languages Act of 1969. By assigning English and French "equality of status" in all the services of the federal government, the act has created a significantly increased awareness of French throughout anglophone Canada by means of printed forms and publications, broadcasting services, and signage and announcements in public places (see *A National Understanding* 1977). For most anglophone Canadians outside Quebec, the French they encounter has relatively small significance, though it is a daily reminder of the official recognition of French as a coequal language. Since French-English bilinguals have opportunities denied to the monolingual in the military and the federal civil service, some have seen in the Official Languages Act a conspiracy "to convert Canada from an English-speaking country into a French-speaking country." For alarmists, current language policies are seen as leading to "a Canadian civil war" (Andrew 1977).

Cooler predictions, based on census data, suggest that French and English communities in Canada are growing farther apart, particularly as Quebec separatism threatens to convert the province to a monolingual French community:

> Outside Quebec, French-speaking communities are fading away at an accelerating rate because of massive assimilation. Within Quebec, however, there has been very little net assimilation toward the majority language [i.e., English], and it is the continuing departure of Anglophones that has left French the dominant language almost everywhere in the province outside Montreal; knowing that they have a whole continent in which they can live and work in their own language, most Anglophones find it easier to leave Quebec than to make the effort required to live in French. [Joy 1978, p. 39; see also deVries and Vallee 1977]

Hence, despite governmental efforts to make Canada bilingual, it appears that French will more and more be limited to Quebec and that English—in a distinctly Canadian variety—will prevail as the national language of the rest of Canada.

Like other varieties around the world, Canadian English reflects is distinctive history and unique position through the national standard and its regional and social subvarieties. Canadians may formerly have seen in the differences between their English and that of Great Britain and the United States cause for concern and even distress, but today Canada's sense of linguistic difference is a source of pride and an assertion of independence. As the facts sketched in this essay demonstrate, the emergence of Canadian English as a fully elaborated national variety is now clearly established.

NOTES

This essay could not have been written without the inspiration of the scholarship of the late Walter S. Avis of the Royal Military College of Canada. I am particularly grateful to my students at the University of British Columbia and to Ian Pringle, James Sledd, Thomas E. Toon, Bernard van't Hul, Ralph G. Williams, and H. Rex Wilson for advice and counsel. For a variety of information not specifically credited in this essay, I am glad to acknowledge Brebner and Masters (1970), McConnell (1979), and McNaught (1976).

1. The feature typically described as "postvocalic *r*" is more properly defined as the [r] that occurs at the ends of words (e.g., *better*) and after vowels but before consonants (e.g., *first*). Both rhotic and nonrhotic varieties of English employ consonantal [r] in initial position (e.g., *run*) and between vowels (e.g., *barrel*). The conventional terminology—"postvocalic *r*" and "*r*-less" or "*r*-full" dialects—is used here.
2. While *r*-loss does occur in some limited number of phonetic environments in Nova Scotia, it is most widespread in the areas of German settlement around Lunenburg (Wilson 1958, p. 119), a region in which Loyalist linguistic influence was likely to have been slight since German continued in common use through the middle of the nineteenth century.
3. See Wilson (1972, p. 223) and Kurath and McDavid (1961, map 157).
4. Haliburton's use of dialect has been widely discussed; see, for instance, Bengtsson 1956 and Bailey 1981.
5. See Leechman and Hall 1955. Unfortunately, there is no detailed history of the contact languages used by Amerindians and Europeans on the frontier. Through the nineteenth century, Bungee (a lingua franca combining Cree, French, and English) was used in Manitoba (see Scott 1975). Good written records allow for a relatively full picture of Chinook Jargon, a contact language of the Pacific Coast in which Nootka, Salish, French, and English elements appear. The opening paragraph of the *Kamloops Wawa* (2 May 1891) suggests the features of this language:

   Ookook Pepa iaka nem: Kamloops Wawa. Chi alta iaka chako tanaz. Msaika alke tlap iaka kanawe Sunday.

   [This paper is named: Kamloops Wawa (literally, Kamloops Talk). It is born just now. You will receive it every Sunday.] [Reproduced in McConnell 1979, p. 235]

From Chinook Jargon, Canadian English has borrowed some words that survive in British Columbia (e.g., *mowitch* 'deer') or have even more general currency (e.g., *muck-a-muck* ['dignitaries' < 'banquet' < 'food'] and *potlach* 'gift-giving'). As with other contact languages, the proportion of non-English elements is widely variable. McConnell quotes the following representation of Chinook Jargon from *Many Trails* (1963, p. 75), a memoir by R. D. Symons:

"One tam," Jack told me, "me see um that Ankiti Siwash—me hyu scare—all he dlaid hyu tall—he helo shirt his back; he helo mocassin his feet; helo hat his head stop—just plenty hair like bush. Me no savvy see-um that fellow before—me hyu cumtux him Ankiti Siwash! Me go way that place all same cultus coulee."

In this passage, non-English elements are relatively infrequent, partly because the speech is from a work designed for an English-reading audience and partly because Chinook Jargon underwent the process of re-lexification as its speakers were more and more dominated by anglophones. A partial gloss to the passage reveals the diverse origins of Chinook Jargon: *Ankiti Siwash* 'Indian Giant from Long Ago' (*ankiti* < Chinook *ankutti* 'ancient, long ago' and *siwash* < French *sauvage* 'Amerindian'), *hyu* 'much, many, great, very' (< Nootka *iyahish* or < Tokwaht *aiya*), *helo* 'no, not, none, cumtux* 'understand' (< Nootka *kommetak*), *cultus coulee* 'stroll' (< Chinook *kaltas* 'useless' and < French *courir* 'to run').

6. While this passage has often been quoted (by, e.g., Hodgins 1895, p. 3, Avis 1973, p. 47, and Orkin 1970, pp. 7–8) to illustrate the supposedly insidious influence of American schoolteachers, there is good reason to assume that Rolph exaggerated the difference between Canadian English and the "anti-British dialect and idiom" promoted by the schoolteachers. Rolph wrote of his impressions on first arriving in Canada from England and, though trained as a physician, he sought and in 1839 achieved a position as an "emigration agent" stationed in England to promote settlement in Canada. His next publication, Rolph 1842, was apparently even more laudatory of things Canadian and, if possible, more anti-Yankee than his first effort in 1836.

7. Geike was not opposed to all innovation, and he regarded the terms used in land surveys in Canada as genuinely valuable. As examples, he lists *broken-front* (1793–, 'parcel of land of irregular shape situated along a river or lake'), *concession* (1764, 'division of land containing townships, sections and lots'), *gore* (1791, 'parcel of land remaining after division of land into concessions, townships and lots of uniform size'), *township* (1756, 'division of land containing thirty-six sections'), and *waterlot* (1791, 'piece of land fronting on a river or lake'). "All of these," Geike says, "are definite, universally understood with the same significance [and] some of them at least, will be permanently incorporated into the English language" (Geike 1857, p. 348).

8. These facts are amplified by Gregg (1975, p. 135) and Walker (1975, p. 129). Though a postal questionnaire like the one used in the Survey of Canadian English is unlikely to obtain fully accurate phonetic detail, Rodman (1974, p. 58) noted that in Vancouver Island—reputedly the most "English" of Canada's subregions—the merger of *cot* and *caught* is nearly universal. Gregg (1978, p. 22) notes that "there is no shift from [ɒ] to [ɑ] within the speech of one individual"; either the rounded vowel [ɒ] or the unrounded vowel [ɑ] is selected by Canadians for the words italicized in this paragraph.

Most speakers of Scottish Standard English show the merger of *cot* and *caught* (Abercrombie 1979, p. 72); for many, however, the vowel in these words may be "a moderately close one, [o]" (Aitken 1979, p. 102) so that *cot/coat* and *clock/cloak* are homophones, a tendency not found in Canada.

9. These three spellings reflect attempts by Canadian journalists to capture the pronunciation of *Toronto*; the earliest of them is from 1910. See Avis and Kinloch 1977, items 183, 474, and 539.
10. The remainder in both groups answered that they pronounced *new* "either way" (Scargill 1974, p. 53).
11. See *Time* (Canadian ed.), 24 April 1972, p. 11. The situation along the border is discussed by Allen 1975, p. 107 and Avis 1978*b*, p. 69. Similar claims about these words are sometimes made in reference to tidewater Virginia, where many speakers participate in the rules for these diphthongs noted in Canada.
12. In this brief summary, I am particularly indebted to the work of R. J. Gregg (especially 1973 and 1978). Other discussions that provide additional information on these matters include Chambers 1975*b*, Picard 1977, and Pringle 1979. The connection of these diphthongs with social attitudes is persuasively demonstrated for Martha's Vineyard, Massachusetts, by Labov 1963.
13. See, for instance, a news story from the *Toronto Telegram* headlined "Pure BBC Accent is Handicap Here, English Girl Finds" (Nicholson 1953).
14. Pringle, Jones, and Padolsky (1981), drawing on the survey of 100 informants conducted by Woods (1979), show that this is the case in Ottawa and the surrounding rural areas. They argue that the structural influence of the urban dialect is the first felt in rural areas and then followed by "final phonetic adjustment" toward the urban norm.
15. See Willis 1972 and Labov, Yaeger, and Steiner 1972, vol. 1, pp. 73ff.
16. See Scargill 1974, pp. 58–59; Allen 1973, p. 138; Rodman 1974, p. 56; and Kurath and McDavid 1961, p. 177. The pronunciation of *vase* in Canadian English is highly variable. Nationally, [vɒz ~ vɑz], [ves], and [vez] are the principal variants but [væz] and [vaz] also occur. Results of surveys of Montreal (Hamilton 1975) and Ontario show that [vez] and [vɑz] are the most frequent forms in eastern Canada.
17. See Polson 1969, p. 101 and Stevenson 1976.
18. An exception is the detailed study reported by Pringle, Jones, and Padolsky (1981). They found more conservative patterns in casual speech and more innovative ones in reading styles (both from passages and word lists); women, and particularly younger women, tended to have the greatest difference between casual speech and reading styles. Woods (1979) has also examined stylistic and social variation and includes findings related to age, sex, socioeconomic status, ethnic group membership, and rural/urban background. Robert J. Gregg is now supervising a study of Vancouver and the Lower Mainland that will allow examination of these variables.
19. See Polson 1969, Rodman 1974, and Stevenson 1976. The features that have been investigated in most detail in British Columbia are those that also appear in the Survey of Canadian English: the pronunciations of *tomato, vase, apricot, lever, soot, route,* and *schedule*, and the presence or absence of vocalic contrasts in *father/bother, caught/cot, aunt/ant, leisure/pleasure,* and *bury/furry*.
20. Some characteristics of the Ottawa Valley are described by Chambers (1975*b*): *mind* 'remember', *for to* as a complementizer, the phonetic conditioning of centralized diph-

thongs in the reflexes of Middle English *i* and *u*, and the systematic use of [æ] before [r] in [ˈgærdən] *garden*, [bærn] *barn*, and [ˈmærθə] *Martha*. Pringle and Padolsky (in press) provide further details: loanwords from Gaelic (e.g., *gruamach* 'gloomy, overcast weather') and from German (e.g., *vipple-vopple* 'teeter-totter'), and a variety of phonological relics from Hiberno-English (including palatalization of [k] and [g] in *cart* and *guard* and affrication of [t] and [d] before [r]).

21. The forthcoming *Newfoundland Dialect Dictionary*, edited by G. M. Storey, will be especially welcome. Of interest in Newfoundland English is the treatment of verbal auxiliaries, particularly the uses of *be* that are apparently a relic of connections formerly maintained with the southwest of England:

I bees asked out   'I am asked out'
I do be watching   'I am watching' (emphatic)
I be into bed but I don't be asleep   'I am in bed but I am not asleep'

The association of forms like these with present-day rural speech in England is clearly demonstrated in *The Linguistic Atlas of England* (Orton, Sanderson, and Widdowson 1978, maps M1–M5). In addition, some features of pronunciation apparently reflect connections with the southwest of England and Ireland, whence came many of the early settlers of the province: [v] for initial [f] ([vʌr] *fir*) and [t] for [θ] ([taɪ] *thigh*, [mɔnts] *months*, and [fɪft] *fifth*). See Widdowson 1964.

22. See Statistics Canada 1978, Rudnyckyj 1973, p. 611, and deVries 1977.

23. Ian Pringle reports that many anglophones in Ottawa sprinkle their speech with such French expressions as *d'accord* to show their support for government bilingual programs. Bilingual greetings ("bonjour good morning") are commonplace in the services of the federal government, and *anglophone* and *francophone* are such recent borrowings that they do not appear in the *Dictionary of Canadianisms* (Avis et al. 1967). Resistance to bilingualism among English-speaking Canadians is apparently quite strong (see Andrew 1979).

24. Most anglophone Canadians do not distinguish *joual* from standard Canadian French. (*Joual*, as defined by the *Dictionary of Canadianisms*, is "uneducated or dialectal Canadian French considered as debased or inferior by educated French Canadians, characterized by regional pronunciations, non-standard grammar and often, especially in cities, by numerous English words and syntactical arrangements.")

REFERENCES

Abercrombie, David. "The Accents of Standard English in Scotland." In *Languages of Scotland*, edited by A. J. Aitken and Tom McArthur, pp. 68–84. Edinburgh: W. and R. Chambers, 1979.

Aitken, A. J. "Scottish Speech: A Historical View with Special Reference to the Standard English of Scotland." In *Languages of Scotland*, edited by A. J. Aitken and Tom McArthur, pp. 85–118. Edinburgh: W. and R. Chambers, 1979.

Allen, Harold B. *The Linguistic Atlas of the Upper Midwest*. 3 vols. Minneapolis: University of Minnesota Press, 1973.

———. "Canadian-American Differences along the Middle Border." In *Canadian English: Origins and Structures*, edited by J. K. Chambers, pp. 102–8. Toronto: Methuen, 1975. Reprinted from *Canadian Journal of Linguistics* 5 (1959):17–24.

Andrew, J. V. *Bilingual Today, French Tomorrow: Trudeau's Master Plan and How It Can be Stopped*. Richmond Hill, Ont.: BMG Publishing, 1977.

———. *Backdoor Bilingualism: Davis's Sell-Out of Ontario and Its National Consequences*. Richmond Hill, Ont.: BMG Publishing, 1979.

Avis, Walter S. "The English Language in Canada." In *Current Trends in Linguistics*, edited by Thomas A. Sebeok. 14 vols. Vol. 10, *Linguistics in North America*, pt. 1, pp. 40–74. The Hague: Mouton, 1973.

———. "The New England Short *o*: A Recessive Phoneme" (1961). In *Walter S. Avis: Articles and Essays*, edited by Thomas Vincent, George Parker, and Stephen Bonnycastle, pp. 93–111. Kingston: Royal Military College of Canada, 1978*a*.

———. "Speech Differences along the Ontario-United States Border: Pronunciation" (1965). In *Walter S. Avis: Articles and Essays*, edited by Thomas Vincent, George Parker, and Stephen Bonnycastle, pp. 68–85. Kingston: Royal Military College of Canada, 1978*b*.

———. "So *Eh?* is Canadian, Eh?" In *Walter S. Avis: Articles and Essays*, edited by Thomas Vincent, George Parker, and Stephen Bonnycastle, pp. 172–90. Kingston: Royal Military College of Canada, 1978*c*. Reprinted from *Canadian Journal of Linguistics* 17 (1972):89–104.

Avis, Walter S., and Kinloch, A. M. *Writings on Canadian English, 1792–1975*. Toronto: Fitzhenry and Whiteside, 1977.

Avis, Walter S., et al. *A Dictionary of Canadianisms on Historical Principles*. Toronto: W. J. Gage, 1967.

Baeyer, Cornelius V. *Talking about Canadian English . . . and Canadian French as Well*. Ottawa: Program Development and Consultation Unit, 1976.

Bailey, Richard W. "Haliburton's Eye and Ear." *Canadian Journal of Linguistics* 26 (1981):90–101.

Bengtsson, Elna. *The Language and Vocabulary of Sam Slick*. Uppsala Canadian Studies, no. 5. Copenhagen: Ejnar Munksgaard, 1956.

Brebner, J. Bartlet, and Masters, Donald C. *Canada: A Modern History*. Ann Arbor: University of Michigan Press, 1970.

Caplan, Gerald L., and Laxer, James. "Perspectives on Un-American Traditions in Canada." In *Close the 49th Parallel etc.: The Americanization of Canada*, edited by Ian Lumsden, pp. 305–20. Toronto: University of Toronto Press, 1970.

Chambers, J. K. "Canadian Raising." In *Canadian English: Origins and Structures*, edited by J. K. Chambers, pp. 83–100. Toronto: Methuen, 1975*a*. Reprinted and revised from *Canadian Journal of Linguistics* 18 (1973):113–35.

———. "The Ottawa Valley 'Twang'." In *Canadian English: Origins and Structures*, edited by J. K. Chambers, pp. 55–59. Toronto: Methuen, 1975*b*.

deVries, John. "Languages in Contact: A Review of Canadian Research." In *The Individual Language and Society in Canada*, edited by W. H. Coons, Donald M. Taylor, and Marc-Adélard Tremblay, pp. 15–36. Ottawa: The Canada Council, 1977.

deVries, John, and Vallee, Frank G. *Data Book on Aspects of Language Demography in Canada*. Ottawa: The Canada Council, 1977.

Emeneau, M. B. "The Dialect of Lunenburg, Nova Scotia." In *Canadian English: Origins and Structures*, edited by J. K. Chambers, pp. 34–39. Toronto: Methuen, 1975. Reprinted from *Language* 11 (1935):140–47.

Fawcett, Margot J., ed. *The 1979 Corpus Almanac of Canada*. Toronto: Corpus, 1979.

Fetherling, Doug. "Speak American or Speak English: A Choice of Imperialisms." In *Issues for the Seventies: Americanization*, edited by Hugh Innis, pp. 22–25. Toronto: McGraw-Hill Ryerson, 1972. Reprinted from *Saturday Night*, September 1970, pp. 33–34.

Frye, Northrop. "Canadian Culture Today." In *Voices of Canada: An Introduction to Canadian Culture*, edited by Judith Webster, pp. 1–4. Burlington, Vt.: Association for Canadian Studies in the United States, 1977.

Geike, A. Constable. "Canadian English." *Canadian Journal of Industry, Science, and Art*, n. s. 2 (1857):344–55.

Glissmeyer, Gloria. "Some Characteristics of English in Hawaii." In *Varieties of Present-Day English*, edited by Richard W. Bailey and Jay L. Robinson, pp. 190–222. New York: Macmillan Co., 1973.

Godley, John Robert. *Letters from America*. 2 vols. 1844. Reprinted in *Early Travellers in the Canadas, 1791–1867*, edited by Gerald M. Craig, pp. 142–50. Toronto: Macmillan Co. of Canada, 1955.

Gray, Hugh. *Letters from Canada*. London: Longman, 1809.

Gregg, Robert J. "The Diphthongs *i* and *ai* in Scottish, Scotch-Irish and Canadian English." *Canadian Journal of Linguistics* 18 (1973):136–45.

―――. "The Phonology of Canadian English as Spoken in the Area of Vancouver, British Columbia." In *Canadian English: Origins and Structures*, edited by J. K. Chambers, pp. 133–44. Toronto: Methuen, 1975. Reprinted from *Canadian Journal of Linguistics* 3 (1957):20–26.

―――. "Canadian English." MS, 1978.

Gustafson, Ralph, ed. *The Penguin Book of Canadian Verse*. Harmondsworth: Penguin, 1967.

Haliburton, Thomas Chandler. *An Historical and Statistical Account of Nova Scotia*. 2 vols. Halifax: Joseph Howe, 1829.

―――. *The Clockmaker; or, The Sayings and Doings of Sam Slick of Slickville*. New York: William H. Colyer, 1840.

Hamilton, Donald E. "Standard Canadian English: Pronunciation." In *Proceedings of the Ninth International Congress of Linguists*, edited by Horace G. Lunt, pp. 456–59. The Hague: Mouton, 1964.

―――. "Notes on Montreal English." In *Canadian English: Origins and Structures*, edited by J. K. Chambers, pp. 46–54. Toronto: Methuen, 1975. Reprinted from *Canadian Journal of Linguistics* 4 (1958):70–79.

Hancock, Ian F. "A Survey of the Pidgins and Creoles of the World." In *Pidginization and Creolization of Languages*, edited by Dell Hymes, pp. 509–23. Cambridge: At the University Press, 1971.

Hansen, Marcus Lee, and Brebner, John Bartlet. *The Mingling of the Canadian and American Peoples*. Vol. 1, *Historical*. New Haven: Yale University Press, 1940.

Hodgins, J. George. *Documentary History of Education in Upper Canada*. Vol. 3, *1836–1840*. Toronto: Warwick Bros. and Rutter, 1895.
Howison, John. *Sketches of Upper Canada, Domestic, Local, and Characteristic*. Edinburgh: Oliver and Boyd, 1821.
Hull, Alexander. "The Americanization of French in Windsor." In *The Influence of the United States on Canadian Development: Eleven Case Studies*, edited by Richard A. Preston, pp. 245–59. Durham, N.C.: Duke University Press, 1972.
Hultín, Neil C. "Canadian Views of American English." *American Speech* 42 (1967):243–60.
James, Geoffrey. "Canadian English: It's a Little Different, Eh?" *Time* (Canadian ed.), 4 January 1971, p. 11.
Joy, Richard J. *Canada's Official-Language Minorities*. Montreal: C. D. Howe Research Institute, 1978.
Kurath, Hans; Hanley, Miles L.; Bloch, Bernard; Lowman, Guy S., Jr.; and Hansen, Marcus L. *Linguistic Atlas of New England*. 3 vols. in 6. Providence: Brown University Press, 1939–43.
Kurath, Hans; Hansen, Marcus L.; Bloch, Julia; and Bloch, Bernard. *Handbook of the Linguistic Geography of New England*. Providence: Brown University Press, 1939.
Kurath, Hans, and McDavid, Raven I., Jr. *The Pronunciation of English in the Atlantic States*. Ann Arbor: University of Michigan Press, 1961.
Labov, William. "The Social Motivation of a Sound Change." *Word* 19 (1963):273–309.
Labov, William; Yaeger, Malcah; and Steiner, Richard. *A Quantitative Study of Sound Change in Progress*. 2 vols. Philadelphia: University of Pennsylvania, 1972.
Leacock, Stephen. "I'll Stay in Canada" (1936). Reprinted in *Canadian Anthology*, edited by C. F. Klinck and R. E. Waters, pp. 209–13. Toronto: W. J. Gage, 1955.
Leechman, Douglas, and Hall, Robert A., Jr. "American Indian Pidgin English: Attestations and Grammatical Peculiarities." *American Speech* 30 (1955):163–71.
Léon, Pierre R., and Martin, Phillipe J., eds. *Toronto English*. Studia Phonetica, no. 14. Montreal: Didier, 1979.
McConnell, R. E. *Our Own Voice: Canadian English and How It Is Studied*. Toronto: Gage Educational Publishing, 1979.
McNaught, Kenneth. *The Pelican History of Canada*. Harmondsworth: Penguin, 1976.
Montero, Gloria. *The Immigrants*. Toronto: James Lorimer and Co., 1977.
National Understanding: Statement of the Government of Canada on the Official Languages Policy, A. Ottawa: Minister of Supply and Services Canada, 1977.
Nicholson, Brian. "Pure BBC Accent Is Handicap Here, English Girl Finds." *Toronto Telegram*, 22 July 1953, pp. 1 and 4.
Orbeck, Anders. *Early New England Pronunciation as Reflected in Some Seventeenth Century Town Records of Eastern Massachusetts*. Ann Arbor: George Wahr, 1927.
Orkin, Mark M. *Speaking Canadian English: An Informal Account of the English Language in Canada*. Toronto: General Publishing Co., 1970.
Orton, Harold; Sanderson, Stewart; and Widdowson, John. *The Linguistic Atlas of England*. London: Croom Helm, and New York: Humanities Press, 1978.
Picard, Marc. "Canadian Raising: The Case Against Reordering." *Canadian Journal of Linguistics* 22 (1977):144–55.

Polson, James. "A Linguistic Questionnaire for British Columbia." Master's thesis, University of British Columbia, 1969.
Pringle, Ian. "The Linguistic Survey of the Ottawa Valley." MS, 1979.
Pringle, Ian; Jones, C. Stanley; and Padolsky, Enoch. "The Misapprehension of Ottawa Standards in an Adjacent Rural Area." *English World-Wide* 2 (1981):165–80.
Pringle, Ian, and Padolsky, Enoch. "The Irish Heritage of the English of the Ottawa Valley." *English Studies in Canada*, in press.
Report of the Royal Commission on Bilingualism and Biculturalism. Vol 1, *The Official Languages.* Ottawa: Queen's Printer, 1967.
Rodman, Lilita. "Characteristics of B.C. English." *The English Quarterly* 7, no. 4 (1974):49–82.
Rolph, Thomas. *Observations Made during a Visit in the West Indies and a Tour through the United States of America, in Parts of the Years 1832-3; together with a Statistical Account of Upper Canada.* Dundas, Upper Canada: G. Heyworth Hackstaff, 1836.
———. *Comparative Advantages between the United States and Canada for British Settlers.* London: Smith, Elder and Co., 1842.
Rudnyckyj, J. B. "Immigrant Languages, Language Contact, and Bilingualism in Canada." In *Current Trends in Linguistics*, edited by Thomas A. Sebeok. 14 vols. Vol. 10, *Linguistics in North America*, pt. 1, pp. 593–652. The Hague: Mouton, 1973.
Scargill, M. H. *Modern Canadian English Usage: Linguistic Change and Reconstruction.* Toronto: McClelland and Stewart, 1974.
Scott, S. Osborne. "The Red River Dialect." In *Canadian English: Origins and Structures*, edited by J. K. Chambers, pp. 61–63. Toronto: Methuen, 1975. Reprinted from *The Beaver* 282 (1951):42–43.
Statistics Canada. *Population: Demographic Characteristics (Mother Tongue).* Ottawa: Minister of Supply and Services Canada, 1978.
Stevenson, Roberta C. "The Pronunciation of English in British Columbia." Master's thesis, University of British Columbia, 1976.
Stewart, George R. *Names on the Land.* New York: Random House, 1945.
Symons, R. D. *Many Trails.* Toronto: Longmans Canada, 1963.
Symons, Thomas. *The Symons Report.* Toronto: Book and Periodical Development Council, 1978.
Vinay, Jean-Paul. "Le français en amérique du nord: Problèmes et réalisations." In *Current Trends in Linguistics*, edited by Thomas A. Sebeok. 14 vols. Vol. 10, *Linguistics in North America*, pt. 1, pp. 323–406. The Hague: Mouton, 1973.
Walker, Douglas C. "Another Edmonton Idiolect: Comments on an Article by Professor Avis." In *Canadian English: Origins and Structures*, edited by J. K. Chambers, pp. 129–32. Toronto: Methuen, 1975.
Widdowson, J. D. A. "Some Items of a Central Newfoundland Dialect." *Canadian Journal of Linguistics* 10 (1964):37–46.
Willis, Clodius. "Perception of Vowel Phonemes in Fort Erie, Ontario, Canada, and Buffalo, New York: An Application of Synthetic Vowel Categorization Tests to Dialectology." *Journal of Speech and Hearing Research* 15 (1972):246–55.
Wilson, H. Rex. "The Dialect of Lunenburg County, Nova Scotia." Ph.D. dissertation, University of Michigan, 1958.

———. "From Postulates to Procedures in the Interpretation of Spellings." In *Studies in Linguistics in Honor of Raven I. McDavid, Jr.*, edited by Lawrence M. Davis, pp. 215–28. University, Ala.: University of Alabama Press, 1972.

Woods, Howard. "A Socio-dialectology Survey of the English Spoken in Ottawa: A Study of the Sociological and Stylistic Variation in Canadian English." Ph.D. dissertation, University of British Columbia, 1979.

Geographical Variation of English in the United States

Frederic G. Cassidy

The present essay will focus attention on geographical variations in language, recognizing that these cannot be separated from social factors except arbitrarily. Language reflects the lives of its speakers and would have no existence or function apart from them. It is a matter of interest, therefore, to know what the variations in American English are and to see how they relate to the history of settlement and movements of population. In the few pages at our disposal we shall attempt to sketch this sociogeographic aspect of the English language in the United States.

Consider briefly, to begin with, the state of the English language just before the era of American colonization. The Tudor period had seen the emergence of a nation unified under a strong government centered in London; it saw the language of that part of England, the East Midlands, given prestige by political, commercial, and literary eminence. The other parts, or "dialect areas," still asserting their differences till the end of the fourteenth century, had yielded in the half century before Shakespeare to this prestige, and any writing that pretended to gain a national hearing accepted what might be broadly called "London English"—the standard of the court, the law, the church, and commercial enterprise. People out in the counties continued to speak their local varieties—the gentry as much as common folk. (As late as the eighteenth century, the bumpkin "gentleman" who comes up to London is a figure of amusement to polished "cits.") Broadly, the dialects of Kent, the Southwest, West Midlands, and the North were recognizably distinct, to say nothing of the regions beyond, whose contemporary stereotypes Shakespeare vividly immortalized in his Welshman Fluellen, Irishman Macmorris, and Scotsman Jamy, each speaking his characteristic "national" version of English and all fighting side by side under the English King Henry V. It was but a short time before the beginning of transatlantic colonization that English had attained the status of a vernacular respectable on the world scene, one that literary men and national leaders could use without apology (see Jones 1953, chap. 6), one that so important a figure as Ben Jonson could defend as having some properties and capacities "above all other" languages (1928, p. 27). But though this "standard" type emerged for public use, the local varieties remained very much alive. Speakers of most of these, along with speakers of more standard varieties, were among the American colonists.

In any living language, a degree of conservatism or traditionalism always coexists with a degree of innovation. Dialect features can be remarkably enduring. Features of sound and syntax are the most tenacious: speakers are little aware of them, repeating what they heard in childhood. Even those who are aware of differences in pronunciation or phrase structure seldom consciously attempt to alter their own speech. Less tenacious are vocabulary items; it is normal to expect new words and phrases to be added or to displace older ones, or for meanings to change with society and the way of life. Nevertheless, basic words used every day by Everyman, especially for concrete objects, may resist change for centuries. As the new *Linguistic Atlas of England* (Orton, Sanderson, and Widdowson 1978) testifies, some language differences already present in Anglo-Saxon times persist broadly today, a thousand years later. For example, *from* (< Old English *fram*) is the folk form throughout the South and Midlands; in the North (and Scotland) *frae* (< Old Norse *fra*) is the prevailing form (1978, map L60). *Freckles* (and its variants) is used everywhere except in the Southwest, where *vreckles* preserves the old West Saxon voicing (1978, map L50a). Such homeland differences were inevitably transported to the American colonies, some to be lost, others to hang on persistently.

A remarkable reminiscence of the Danelaw versus Wessex may be heard any day in the United States when people in the central and south Atlantic Coast and the Mississippi Valley and westward, following the pattern of southern England, say "quarter *to* eleven" whereas those in the northern and Scots tradition predominantly say "quarter *till* eleven" (see maps 1 and 2). From Wessex and the Saxons comes *to* (< Old English *to*); from the "Danes" comes *till* (< Old Norse *til*). *Till* is hardly to be found in the north or central Atlantic area; it is strongest in Appalachia and the south Atlantic states, general in the Midlands, especially South Midland. So for the old forms. The new form "quarter *of* eleven" was evidently developed in New England and has spread southward and westward, though it dominates only the northeast and north as far west as Ohio (see map 3). This divided usage clearly illustrates the coexistence of tradition and innovation, with ongoing competition between them.[1]

With few exceptions, people at the top of the social scale do not become colonists; they have no need to, except possibly as a sort of adventure. Colonists are those who leave the homeland because they have no property or other obligation to hold them back; their hope is only to improve their lot in the new land. Thus, the language of American colonists derived from the middle and lower classes and reflected the dialectal features of many parts of Britain. Despite this there was still, in the Jamestown and Plymouth colonies and their overflow, a basis of similarity through the colonial leaders, who were men of some consequence and education (see Hansen 1939). It has been shown, further, that the first colonists were preponderantly from the East Midland counties (Orbeck 1927), were conversant with the life of London, and spoke very much the same kind of English—not of the court, but of the countryside and small-business world. Differences that we find today between Yankee and Southerner have developed in the interim, some being relatively recent. English colonies of the seventeenth century—from the Atlantic mainland to the Caribbean islands—held much in common in their composition and language, despite the many variances they show today.

Forces affecting language change in a colony would include the quite impersonal one of numerical majority, so that the most frequent alternatives would, from sheer weight, tend to impose themselves and to survive. Not impersonal, and probably to a degree contrary, would be the force of prestige, the language of community leaders serving as the natural model. Under both these forces, anomalies would drop away unless reinforced by continuing immigration; homeland influences would gradually be lost. Since the contact with England was generally steady during the colonies' formative years, such differences as developed would be due mainly to the conditions of colonial life.

But underlying these generalities, and harder to assess though of unquestionable force, is the character of a people and its society. Though the assessment will not be attempted here, we should not forget certain questions that it would pose. Is the colonizing group unified, well ordered, conscious of forming a stable community, or is it more individualistic—are the members independent, restless? Contrasts have been pointed out between the Massachusetts Bay colony and that at Plymouth, the one dynamic and aggressive, the other rather passive; or between Massachusetts Bay, religiously tight, dominant, exclusive, and Providence, tolerant and receptive (Hansen 1939, pp. 62-68); or between the Massachusetts Bay and Virginia settlements, a small-farm culture as against a plantation culture, the one with little class cleavage, the other socially hierarchical. To what extent is education sought, and for whom? What role does the press play—one of ferment as in New England, or a more neutral or conservative one, as in Virginia? Such differences in the nature of colonies are inevitably reflected in their way of speech.

But we must return to the language itself. Names for the new things encountered in America had begun to enter English a century before actual colonization, during the phase of exploration—for example, *maiz* or 'Indian corn', and *kanoa*, which settled down as *canoe* after many changes in pronunciation and spelling. These came in before 1555 via Spanish from Caribbean island Indians.[2] The process continued throughout the phase of colonization, with much simplification of Indian sounds to suit European tongues. *Skunk* has lost a first-syllable vowel and a final *w*; *hickory* has lost two initial syllables.[3] Many words had already been simplified by adoption into French or Spanish before coming to English: *cisco* 'Great Lakes herring' is abbreviated from Canadian French *ciscovette* from Ojibwa *pemitewiskawet*; *tomato* is from Spanish *tomate* from Nahuatl *tomatl*, the *-o* of the English word being a pseudo-Spanish touch. When native words were not adopted, new objects or concepts were named from English resources: *backwoodsman*, *squatter*, *deputize*, and thousands more (see Mathews 1951).

Addition of words to the vocabulary, however, is relatively superficial and

Maps 1–4 were computer-made for the *Dictionary of American Regional English*. States are retained in their proper relative positions and something like their geographic shapes. In size, however, they reflect not area but the number of communities investigated in each; these 1,002 communities were chosen according to density of population on a rural-to-metropolitan scale. All informants were local native speakers of American English. The data were gathered from 1965 through 1970.

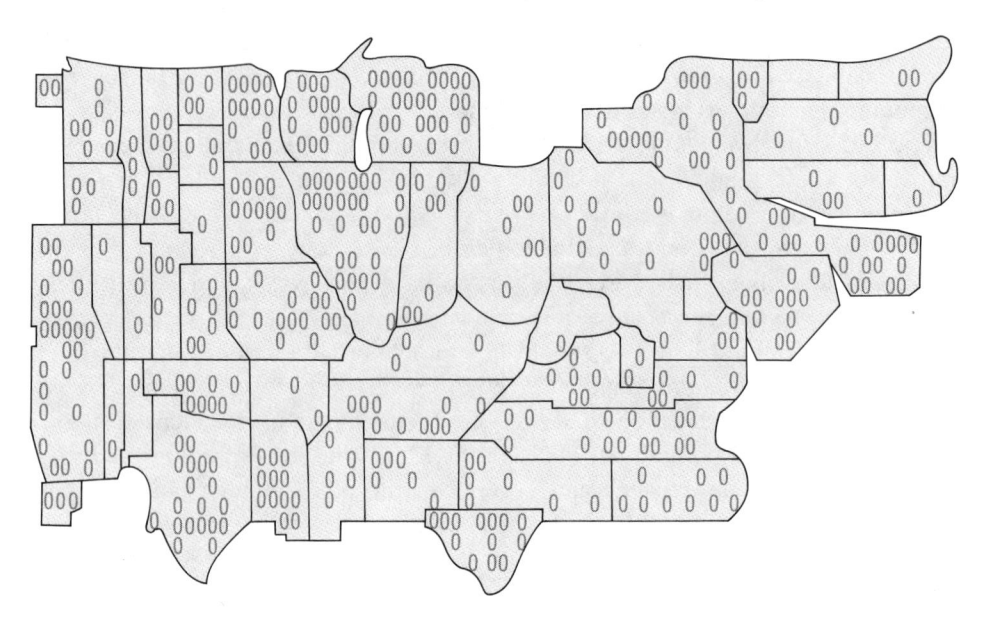

Map 1.   All responses with *to*—412 informants

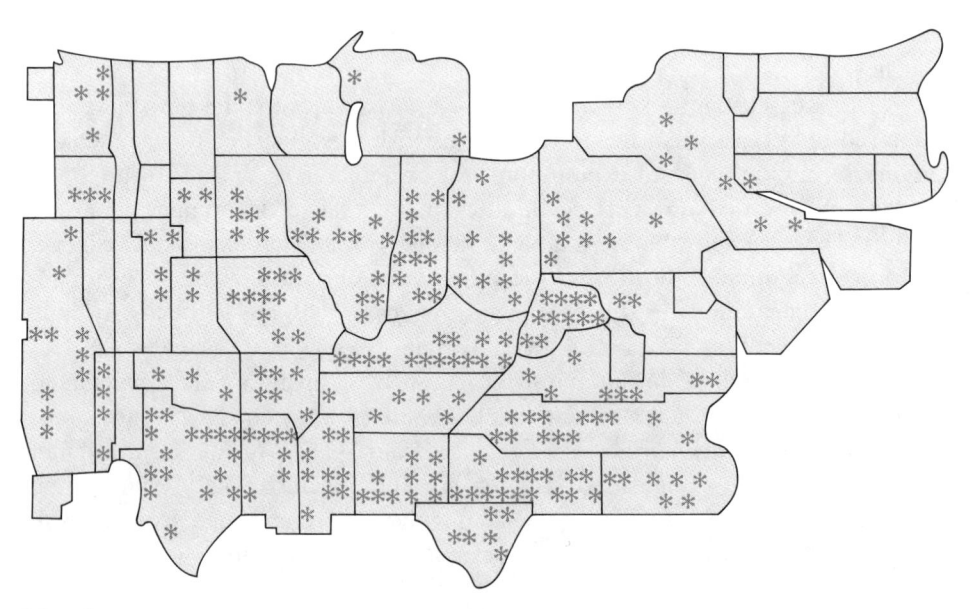

Map 2.   All responses with *till*—241 informants

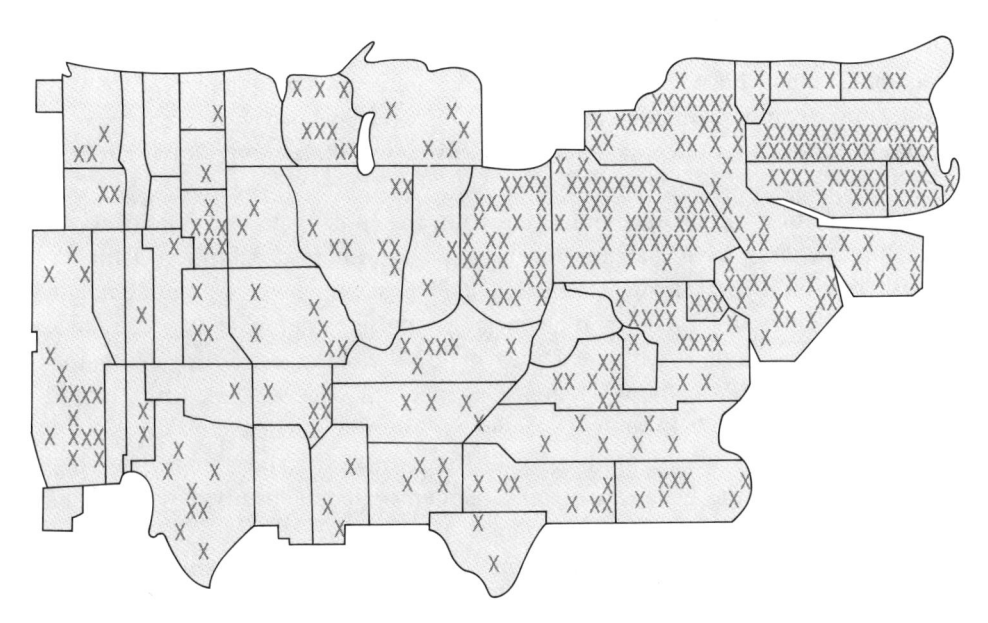

Map 3. All responses with *of*—327 informants

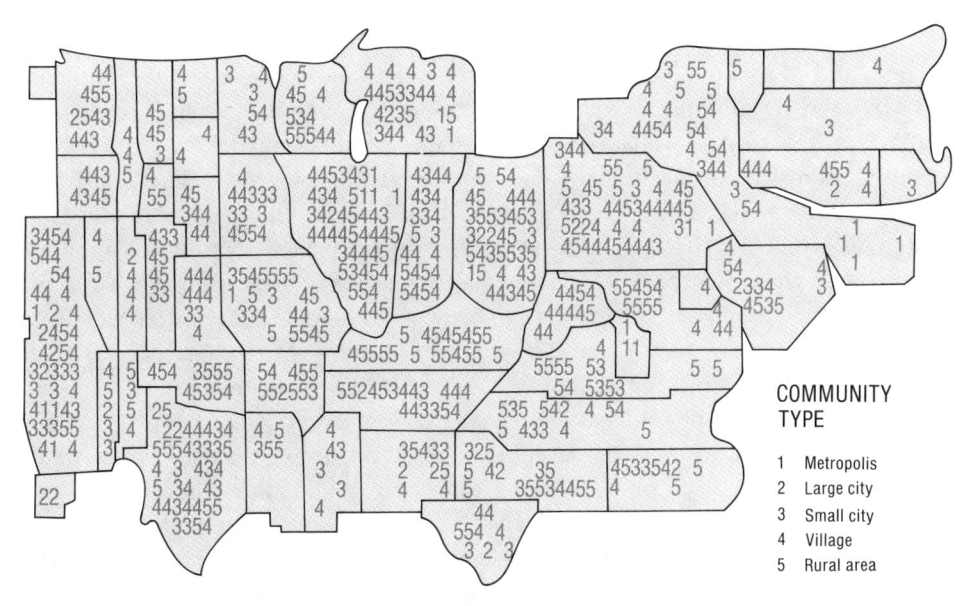

Map 4. [to want] *in, off, out*—845 informants

COMMUNITY TYPE

1 Metropolis
2 Large city
3 Small city
4 Village
5 Rural area

does not greatly affect language structure. Changes or variations in pronunciation and syntax are deep, but in American English they have been few and not profound. Certainly, there have never been changes great enough to impede comprehension in standard, formal or informal. And during the colonial period changes were imperceptible. If a century produced three or four generations, and if (as was the case) the majority of colonists never returned to Britain, the sense of attachment must have been greatly weakened. For colony-born people the "homeland" would seem remote, even to a degree legendary; the actual world was their American world. This feeling had become thoroughly established long before the Revolution.

In addition to language influences from the Indians, the new physical conditions, and change of life-focus from England to America, a further factor was the inflow on non-English-speaking colonists, whose languages were ultimately to make their contribution. This settlement began earlier than many people realize. New Netherland, founded by the Dutch in 1624, yielded to the English in 1664 and became New York, though Dutch language influence remained in the Hudson Valley and Catskill Mountains for a century more, as Rip Van Winkle and Diedrich Knickerbocker remind us (see Irving 1819–20 and 1809). The small Swedish colony on the Delaware River, founded 1638 and absorbed by the Dutch in 1654, went over with New Netherland. The so-called Pennsylvania Dutch—actually Palatine Germans—began settlement after 1638. Relatively slow to assimilate, their present form of English is still notably influenced by German. Acadians deported from Canada somewhat later (1755) took refuge in Louisiana; their English speech today also strongly reflects the French substrate. African slaves were imported—unwilling colonists—from 1619 forward. They, too, had to assimilate linguistically, as many did with success on the smaller plantations of Virginia and Maryland. The large-plantation system, however, as in the Carolinas and Georgia, rapidly increased the importation of slaves. Field hands especially were separated from adequate models; for them, full linguistic assimilation was rendered impossible—and thus was laid the foundation of today's Black English.[4]

For all speakers of languages other than English, then, assimilation was a matter (as with the Africans) of what kind of English they were in a position to adopt—what class of people they associated with; whether their life was rural or urban; whether they came with property or with nothing. An interesting example may be seen in the history of the phrases *want in*, *want off*, and *want out*. These express one's desire to enter or leave a building, a vehicle, or the like: one says to the bus driver, "I want off at the next corner;" or one opens the kitchen door because "the dog wants in." These phrases were once thought to have originated with the Pennsylvania Germans because they were found in common use among them and would translate "Ich will aus" or "er will ein." Later investigation, however, indicates that they existed in earlier English, were preserved in Scotland, and were first noticed in American use in the areas of heaviest Scotch-Irish settlement (see Marckwardt 1948). Today (see map 4) they are in no more than sporadic use along the Atlantic Coast, but south and west of especially western Pennsylvania (the Germans are in southeastern Pennsylvania) they have spread throughout the country.[5] The logical inference is that the Pennsylvania Germans learned their English—or at least these phrases—from the Scots, perhaps adopting them more easily because of their similarity to German phrases.

Map 5 gives at least a gross idea of the establishment and increase of the English colonies until just after the Revolution, at the time of the first census (1790). By the end of the seventeenth century the Massachusetts colony had spread north through coastal New Hampshire into Maine, and southward to join with the Rhode Island, Connecticut, and New York colonies in moving up the valleys of the rivers, especially the Connecticut and Hudson. The coastal areas of northern New Jersey and Delaware and both shores of Chesapeake Bay had been taken up, and the inland movement was well started. South of Virginia there were only beginnings, at the head of Albemarle Sound and north of the Cape Fear River. South of that, only the Charleston settlement, begun in 1670, was notable.[6]

Expansion during the eighteenth century was especially common southward from eastern Pennsylvania; westward movement from that region was impeded by the Appalachian, Allegheny, and (farther south) Blue Ridge mountains. Only after 1770 was any real settlement established west of these mountains. Beginning with the Harrodsburg (1774) and Boonesborough (1775) "colonies," and encouraged by the liberal land policies of Virginia, a large portion of central Kentucky was settled by the end of the century. As the map clearly shows, the Ohio River was an important route of transportation. Indian resistance in Kentucky was continual and often successful; this was, literally, the frontier until the end of the century. Kentuckians became famous as riflemen and did more than their share in the War of 1812 and subsequent "conquest of the West."

The revolutionary struggle, its success, and the new sense of national independence and status released a vital force not fully realized before. The formerly confining mountains had just been breached; now population began to flow into the lands beyond, "the West." Settlement had begun on the Mississippi before the Revolution; by 1800 it too broke into the lands beyond and into the Great Plains—the new "West," which rendered the Mississippi Valley states only "Middle West." Sweeping on to the Rockies, the "Far West," pioneers crossed them to meet the Pacific Coast settlements. Thus "West" kept changing its reference. In the nineteenth century it came to include a huge unbounded territory of mingled parts.

Map 6 shows, grossly by states but reflecting the direction and pace as organized government spread across the continent and beyond, the relatively small area of the original thirteen states, the movement to the Mississippi River by 1820, the crossing, then the northwestern push to the Pacific by 1890. Texas and California entered the Union relatively early; the Southwest otherwise, for lack of sufficient population, could not attain statehood until the present century. Though the main trend was of course westward, it should not be forgotten that

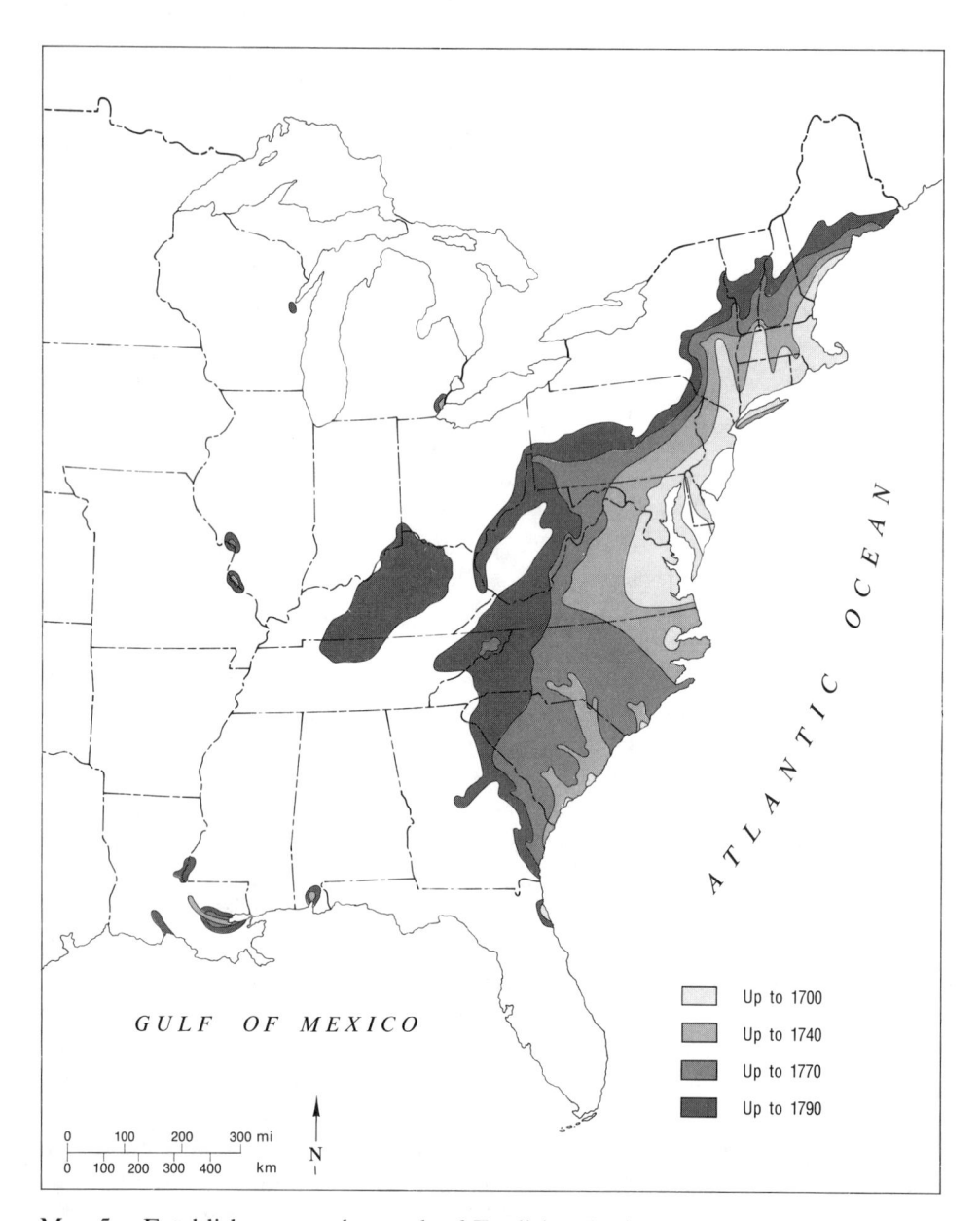

Map 5. Establishment and growth of English colonies

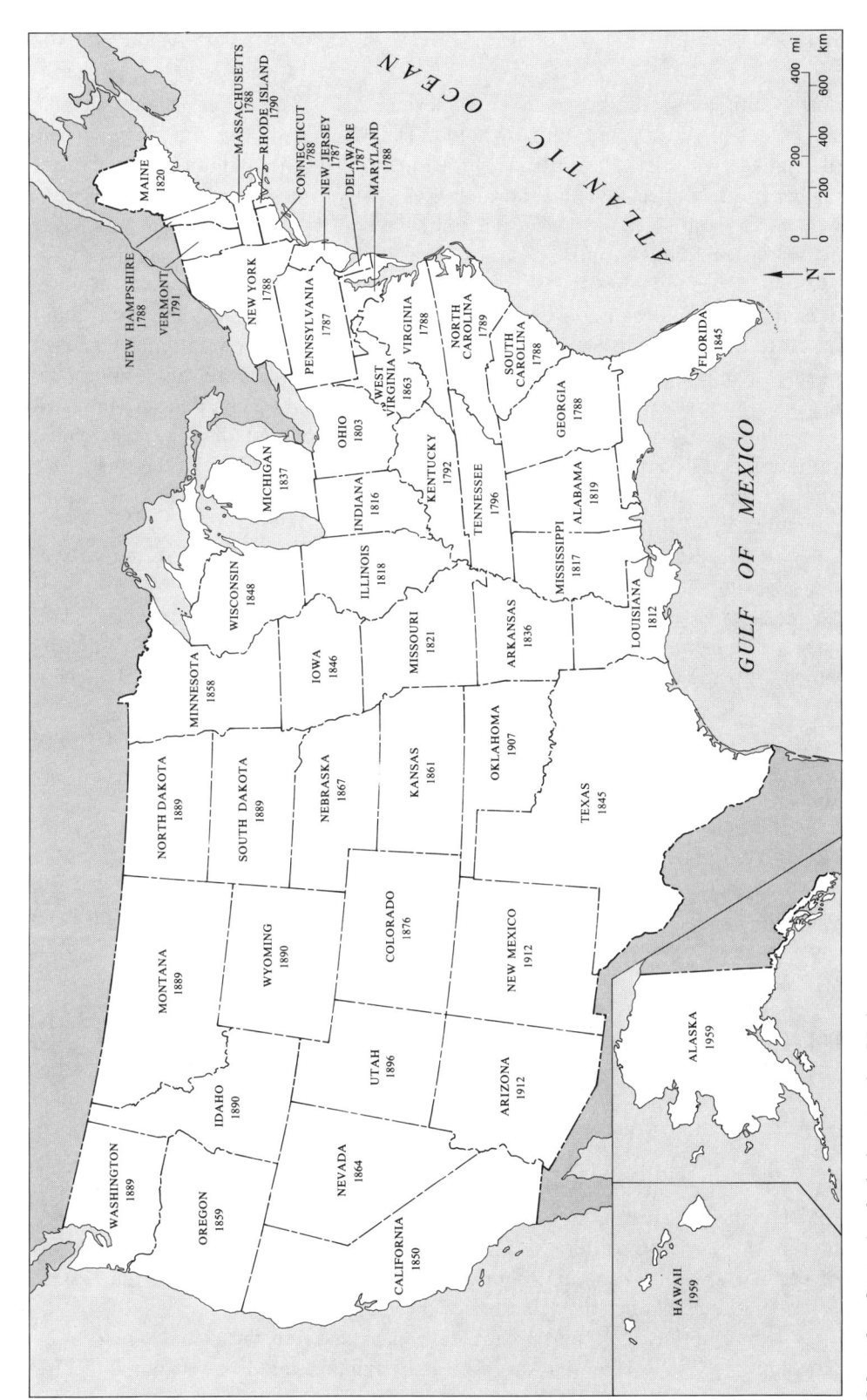

Map 6. States' admission to the Union

north-south movements played an important part.[7] Most conspicuous was the settlement of Appalachia, already noted. The Mississippi, too, the chief highway of relatively easy travel and trade, brought many southern and midland features farther north. Especially after the Civil War, many dispossessed Southerners went west for a fresh start, and from the southwest northward. Settlement was never evenly distributed: the more desirable agricultural land was taken up first, while swampy, poor, and stony areas were skirted. The map does not show this. Neither does it show the urban concentrations that worked reciprocally with farm settlements to fill the territories, the former carrying westward the traditional language of rural living, the latter mingling and obscuring regional features but also producing innovation. During the westward rush between the Revolution and the Civil War, lines of linguistic difference established in colonial days were extended without serious confusion at least as far as the Mississippi. West of the river these lines became entwined and confused, but other features took their place as regional markers.

When did observers begin to be aware that American usage differed from that of Britain? As noted before, the acquisition of new names for exotic things is the most obvious, though by themselves they would not greatly change a language, but merely increase its word-hoard. The colonies' "new way of speech" which drew the comment of travelers was due rather to their changing the meanings of words from those of the homeland, or to shifts in syntax. John Josselyn's comment in 1663 that Americans used the word *ordinary* to mean a tavern whereas it meant a boardinghouse in England, is the earliest known record of a change in meaning (Read 1979). Another American usage that was to be repeatedly pilloried, once it had been noticed (1735), was *bluff* as a topographical term (Read 1979).[8] The word had existed in English use for over a century as an adjective meaning "perpendicular," but its conversion to a noun, or the reduction of "bluff headland" to mere *bluff*, was considered "corrupt." What might have passed in the homeland as a natural development was censured when it occurred in a colony.

Two things are to be noted here: the new meaning had developed in popular and oral use, as language normally does; and the criticism was coming from a writer self-consciously literate, since he considered the new phrase "barbarous English" at just the time when the lack of an Academy in England which could establish "correctness" was being generally deplored, and neologism in any form was being condemned. This distinction between spoken forms and literary ones, though essential, is often overlooked. Neologism, new growth, usually in the spoken language, a sign of its natural vitality, is but charily admitted into literary usage which, conservative and selective, shudders at the livelier inventions of popular speech, accepting them only when they have become so fully established that they can no longer be rejected.

Small differences had already developed between the colonies before the Revolution. First to comment on this was Benjamin Franklin, who noted in 1752 that "Every Colony has some peculiar Expressions familiar to its own People, but strange and unintelligible to others" (quoted by Read 1979). Franklin no doubt had in mind his own observations as a Bostonian transplanted to Pennsylvania, of humble origins but raised to literacy by his own efforts, who therefore knew the whole gamut of social variations within an important part of the country, with its related differences of language. But it was natural also for English and Europeans visiting the colonies, and then the new nation, in the late eighteenth and early nineteenth centuries to comment on differences they observed in the language. Evidently assuming that the colonists would have preserved English dialect features or developed some of their own, the travelers were uniformly surprised to find these lacking. Differences there were, of course, but not at all to the same degree as in the rural, provincial dialects of England. This "sameness" of American English was exaggerated and repeated, becoming a staple commentary—after the Revolution, a point on which Americans vaunted themselves.[9]

This observation of "uniformity" and "purity" has been traced back to at least 1724 (see Menner 1938) and recurred for more than a century. A well-known statement of it is that of Timothy Dwight,[10] who held that Americans speak the language on the whole better than the English do: they pronounce it "more correctly," by which he meant that "the inhabitants at large speak English with a nearer accordance to your [English] standard of pronunciation, than [do] the inhabitants of England" (1821–22, vol. 4, p. 277). Dwight found provincial English almost unintelligible. He stated that throughout the settled part of the country "every American, descended from English ancestors, understands every other, as readily as if he had been bred in the same neighborhood." Several reasons account for this, said Dwight: because there are no distinct orders in society; because the educated mingle freely with the uneducated, then are taken as models by those less polished. For these and other causes, "we have derived a pronunciation; probably more uniform than has ever prevailed in any other country in the world" (1820–21, vol. 4, p. 283). Discounting something for Dwight's patriotic warmth, and remembering that he barred from consideration the speech of the foreign-derived, one may accept his observation broadly. Over the settled one-third of a continent, communication about ordinary matters of life was never in danger. Nevertheless, the regional differences in American pronunciation and word usage were real, and extreme examples were certainly sources of difficulty.

But gradually a clearer distinction emerged: that between dialects as the English and Europeans knew them, and broader regional differences. The earliest known statement of this distinction is noted in the *Journal* of Fannie Kemble Butler, who toured the eastern United States in 1832–34:

> The southern, western, and eastern states of North America, have each their strong peculiarities of enunciation, which render them easy of recognition. The Virginian and New England accents appear to me the most striking; Pennsylvania and New York have much less brogue; but through

all their various tones and pronunciations a very strong nasal inflection preserves their universal brotherhood. They all speak through their noses, and at the top of their voices. Of dialects, properly so called, there are none; though a few expressions, peculiar to particular states, which generally serve to identify their citizens; but these are not numerous, and a jargon approaching in obscurity that of many of our [English] counties is not to be met with. The language used in society generally is unrefined, inelegant, and often ungrammatically vulgar; but it is more vulgar than unintelligible by far. [Butler 1835, vol. 1, p. 164 n; quoted by Menner 1938, p. 9]

This triple division soon became another staple of commentary among writers on the language: they came to think broadly of "New England" (or "Yankee Land"), "the South," and "the West" as having more or less distinctive types of speech. A typical statement is that of the novelist Thomas Low Nichols (1815–1901):

I know of no physiological reason why a Yankee should talk through his nose, unless he got in the habit of shutting his mouth to keep out the cold fogs and drizzling north-easters of Massachusetts Bay.[11] It is certain that men open their mouths and broaden their speech as they go West, until on the Mississippi they tell you "thar are heaps of bar (bear) over thar, whar I was raised." Southern speech is clipped, softened, and broadened by the negro admixture. The child learns its language from its negro nurse, servants, and playmates, and this not unpleasant taint is never quite eradicated. [1864, vol. 1, p. 385]

He continued, contrasting Yankee euphemism and understatement with Western profanity and exaggeration:

Besides peculiarities of articulation and enunciation, there are forms of expression peculiar to and characteristic of each section of the American States. A Yankee does not swear; he says, I vum, I swon, I swow, I vow, darn it, gaul darn your picter, by golly, golly crimus; and uses other mean and cowardly ways of whipping the devil round the stump. The Western man has no trouble with swearing, and has a remarkable breadth of expression. [1864, vol. 1, p. 385]

Nichols was also aware of the Southwest, where boastful magniloquence flourished:

In the south-west is found the combination of Western and Southern character and speech. The south-western man was born in Old Kaintuck, raised in Mississippi, is death on a bar, and smartly on a painter fight. He walks the water, out hollers the thunder, drinks the Mississippi, calculates that he is the genuwine article, and that those he don't like ain't worth shucks. He tells of a fellow so poor and thin he had to lean up agin a saplin' to cuss. He gets as savage as a meat axe. He splurges about, and blows up like a steamboat. Yankees guess everything, past, present and future; Southerners reckon and calculate. All these peculiarities of speech would fill a small volume. Most of the Yankeeisms can be found in the districts of England from which the country was first settled. The colloquialisms of the South and West are more original. [1864, vol. 1, p. 387]

Admittedly, these are one man's generalizations; other observers put the emphasis otherwise. But the following examples from literary texts should better suggest the peculiarities of both place and social type. In the absence of recording machines, we must rely on the accurate ears and faithful reproduction of competent authors who knew their subjects at first hand.

Our first example is from Maine, part of a sea yarn (from the 1850s) being told by an old sailor to others around the stove, of an evening, at Captain Simeon's store.

"Then, thinks I, bedide ef I don't try a trip or two into one o' them timber ships they was all telling about so much.

"I took and put her for Quebec, and run afoul of this 'ere ship the fust thing, all loaded and most ready to sail, she was. Quick's ever I see her I knowed she was Yankee-built fast enough, though there 't was painted on her stern plain 's daylight, 'Falls of Ettrick, Sunderland'; but come to once git aboard, and 't wa'n't only a short time 'fore I'd bated dollars to doughnuts she was the ole Gertrude Spurshoe. They'd turned to and changed her over into full ship rig, and painted her all up diff'rent, and besides that she was nigh buried out o' sight un'neath a tormented great deckload of deals; but still there was quite a few things I twigged pooty quick, so's there wa'n't no doubt in my mind but what she was the ole Gerty for sure.

"There wa'n't ary one of the crew knowed the fust blame' thing about her, mind ye, but soon's ever the chance showed up, I took and sounded the mate on the subjic', and he 'lowed right off 't was jest how I thought.

"Wal, o' course I was nach'ally kind of pleased like to git aboard the ole packet ag'in so fashion, being's how I see her built and launched, and had made r'ally my fust deep-water v'yage into her, let alone bein' so ter'ble well acquainted along o' ole Cap'n Spurshoe ever sence I knowed enough to go. And besides all that, 's I say, she was a grand good, dry, comfor'ble ole creetur to go into, take it most any kind of chance, but ye see it did appear so sort of sing'lar like the way I'd fell in along on her ag'in, that 't was nach'al I should make some consid'ble amount of talk about it forrard there amongst the rest-part o' the crew. [Wasson 1903, pp. 114–15]

The short, clipped "New England" speech is suggested by *'s* for *as*, *'t* for *it*, *'m* or *'em* for *them*; by the aphetic forms *most* for *almost*, *'lowed* for *allowed*, *'fore* for *before*. Ellipsis of *r* as an internal syllable is seen in *un'neath*, *nach'ally*, *consid'ble*. Unschooled pronunciations are *ag'in*, *wa'ant*, *git*, *jest*, and *pooty* (where the non-Yankee would say *purty* or *prit*), and corresponding grammar in *them* for *those*, *this 'ere* for *this*, *see* for *had seen*, though these are not regional but general folk usage. More clearly regional are *took and* plus a verb, and *I'd* for *I would have*. Old-fashioned pronunciations are *v'yage* for *voyage* and *r'ally* for *really*.

The "Yankee settlement area" in upstate New York, and overflow from New England, furnishes another example of northeastern speech. Here a middle-aged small-town banker tells his sister (Polly Bixbee) how he sold a balking horse to Deacon Perkins.

" 'I'll tell ye,' I says, 'you jest git in 'ith me an' go down an' look at him, an' I'll send ye back or drive ye back, an' if you've got anythin' special on hand you needn't be gone three quarters of an hour,' I says,"

"He come, did he?" inquired Mrs. Bixbee.

"He done *so*," said David sententiously. "Jest as I knowed he would, after he'd hem'd an' haw'd about so much, an' he rode a mile an' a half livelier 'n he done in a good while, I reckon. He had to pull that old broadbrim of his'n down to his ears, an' don't you fergit it. He, he, he, he! The road was jest *full* o' hosses. Wa'al, we drove into the yard, an' I told the hired man to unhitch the bay hoss an' fetch out the roan, an' while he was bein' unhitched the deakin stood 'round an' never took his eyes off'n him, an' I knowed I wouldn't sell the deakin no roan hoss *that* day, even if I wanted to. But when he come out I begun to crack him up, an' I talked hoss fer all I was wuth. The deakin looked him over in a don't-care kind of a way, an' didn't 'parently give much heed to what I was sayin'. Finely I says, 'Wa'al, what do you think of him?' 'Wa'al,' he says, 'he seems to be a likely enough critter, but I don't believe he'd suit Mr. White—'fraid not,' he says. 'What you askin' fer him?' he says. 'One-fifty,' I says, 'an' he's a cheap hoss at the money'; but," added the speaker with a laugh, "I knowed I might 's well of said a thousan'. The deakin wa'n't buyin' no roan colts that mornin'."

"What did he say?" asked Mrs. Bixbee.

" 'Wa'al,' he says, 'wa'al, I guess you ought to git that much fer him, but I'm 'fraid he ain't what Mr. White wants.' An' then, 'That's quite a hoss we come down with,' he says. 'Had him long?' 'Jes' long 'nough to get 'quainted with him,' I says. 'Don't you want the roan fer your own use?' I says, 'I guess not. I don't need another hoss jes' now.' An' then, after a minute, he says: 'Say, mebee the bay hoss we drove'd come nearer the mark fer White, if he's all right. Jest as soon I'd look at him?' he says.

'Wa'al, I hain't no objections, but I guess he's more of a hoss than a dominie 'd care for, but I'll go an' fetch him out,' I says. So I brought him out, an' the deakin looked him all over. I see it was a case of love at fust sight, as the storybooks says. 'Looks all right,' he says. 'I'll tell ye,' I says, 'what the feller I bought him of told me.' 'What's that?' says the deakin. 'He said to me,' I says, ' "that hoss hain't got a scratch ner a pimple on him. He's sound an' kind, an' 'll stand without hitchin', and' a lady c'd drive him as well 's a man." '

" 'That's what he said to me,' I says, 'an' it's every word on't true. You've seen whether or not he c'n travel,' I says, 'an', so fur 's I've seen, he ain't 'fraid of nothin'.' 'D'ye want to sell him?' the deakin says. 'Wa'al,' I says, 'I ain't offerin' him fer sale. You'll go a good ways,' I says, ' 'fore you'll strike such another; but, of course, he ain't the only hoss in the world, an' I never had anythin' in the hoss line I wouldn't sell at *some* price.' 'Wa'al,' he says, 'what d' ye ask fer him?' 'Wa'al,' I says, 'if my own brother was to ask me that question I'd say to him two hundred dollars, cash down, an' I wouldn't hold the offer open an hour,' I says."

"My!" ejaculated Aunt Polly. "Did he take you up?"

" 'That's more'n I give fer a hoss 'n a good while,' he says, shakin' his head, 'an' more'n I c'n afford, I'm 'fraid.' 'All right,' I says; 'I c'n afford to keep him'; but I knew I had the deakin same as the woodchuck had Skip. 'Hitch up the roan,' I say to Mike; 'the deakin wants to be took up to his house.' 'Is that your last word?' he says. 'That's what it is,' I says. 'Two hunderd, cash down.' "

"Didn't ye dast to trust the deakin?" asked Mrs. Bixbee.

"Polly," said David, "the's a number of holes in a ten-foot ladder." Mrs. Bixbee seemed to understand this rather ambiguous rejoinder.

"He must 'a' squirmed some," she remarked. David laughed.

"The deakin ain't much used to payin' the other feller's price," he said, "an' it was like pullin' teeth; but he wanted that hoss more'n a cow wants a calf, an' after a little more squimmidgin' he hauled out his wallet an' forked over. Mike come out with the roan, an' off the deakin went, leadin' the bay hoss." [Westcott 1898, pp. 16–18]

Clipped forms are *'ith* for *with* and *c'd* for *could*. Aphetisms are frequent: *'parently*, *'fraid*, *'nough*, *'quainted*, *'fore*. Again we find *git*, *jest*, *critter*, and *wa'al*, and examples of lost postvocalic *r*: *hoss*, *wuth*, *fust*, *dast* for *durst*. Grammatical variants include *knowed*, *done* (for *had done*), *took* (for *taken*), *his'n*, and *I says*. *On* for *of* is an archaism (cf. Shakespeare's *The Tempest*: "We are such stuff as dreams are made on"). Characteristic words and phrases are *reckon*, *hem'd and haw'd*, *fetch*, *squimmidge*, and *crack up* (boast about). The sharp-trading Yankee emerges from the subject and situation, but also from the lively speech.

Leaving the North and moving to Georgia, we next have a sample from a poor-white farmer who comes in to Augusta to sell his cotton and falls victim to a thimblerigger.

>Three thimbles were next produced, and the game began.
>"Now," said the little man, "I am going to hide this little ball under one of these thimbles, all before your eyes, and I want you to guess where it is."
>"Well," said Peter, "go it—I'm ready," and the shifting game began. To the apparent astonishment of the little man, our hero guessed right every time. No matter how rapid the changes, Peter invariably lifted the thimble from the ball, and had begun to grow disgusted with the game, little dreaming how soon he was to prove its efficacy as a source of revenue, when the little man suddenly checked his hand.
>"Wrong," said he, with a friendly smile; "the ball is not under the middle thimble, but under that next you."
>"Darned ef it is though!" responded Peter; "I ain't as green as you Gusty folks think. Blamed ef I don't know whar that ball is jist as well as you does, and dod-drapped ef I don't bet four hundred and fifty-one dollars no cents (the price of the cotton) agin the load o' cotton, that it's under the middle thimble."
>"No, *sir*," said the little man, with another smile, "you are wrong, and I'd hate to win your money."
>That smile deceived Peter—it manifested a friendly consideration for his welfare, which he felt he did not need, and after bullying the "Gimblit-man" for a few minutes, he succeeded in inveigling him (as he thought) into a bet, which was duly closed and sealed, to the entire satisfaction of his *friend*! Alas for poor Peter! he had awakened the wrong passenger. But the idea of being too smart for an Augusty feller, and he was sure he had cornered one this time, was too great a temptation for him to withstand. "Drot it," said he to himself, "I seen him put it under that ere middle thimble, I seen it myself, and I know it's thar, and why not win the old man's cotton back when it's jest as easy as nothin? And ef I do win it, why in course the old man can't claim more'n four hundred and fifty-one dollars, no how. (Peter forgot that the profits to be realized ought of course to belong to the owner of the capital invested.) The time me and that Yankee swapped critters, warn't I thar? Hain't I cut my gums? Don't the old man, yes, and all the settle*ment*, say I'm smart, and then thar's Kitty Brown, I reckon she ort to know, and don't she say I'm the peertest feller in our parts? *I've* bin to Augusty, and this time, dod-drapped ef I don't leave my mark."
>The result we need hardly relate. Peter was tempted—tempted sorely, and he fell. [Lane 1851, pp. 32–34]

Not regional, but indicating social level and lack of schooling are the familiar *that ere, does* for *do, seen* for *saw, jist* and *jest, reckon,* and *agin*. Distinctive of the

English in the United States

South are *ef* for *if*, *in course* for *of course*, final-syllable stress on settlement, and *peertest* for *pertest*. The final unstressed *-a* in names and some words widely pronounced as [i]—here in *Augusty*—was not regional. (The *r* in *ort* is graphic; it was not pronounced.)

An example of the speech of South Carolina whites, one a plantation owner, Captain Porgy, the other a man "on the make," Millhouse, presents contrasts of its own. Millhouse is urging Captain Porgy to marry the widow Eveleigh, who, he says, is willing.

> "Ha! ha! ha! Delightful! 'Pon my soul, Millhouse, you put the case in quite a new and striking point of view. You think I should speak in time to prevent the widow from addressing me, and so spare her blushes."
>
> "In course, I does! That's jest the thing—spar' her blushes!"
>
> "But, suppose she were to propose to me, and I were to—refuse her?"
>
> "Lord love you, cappin, and be merciful to your onderstanding; but you wouldn't be so onkind and outright redickilous, as to do that—and after all that's she's been a-doing for you."
>
> "It would be rather hard-hearted, I confess."
>
> " 'Twould be most monstrous redickilous! But, cappin, you mus'n't wait for her to do the axing. It mout-be she'd come arter awhile, and when she couldn't stan' keepin' in her feelin's any longer; but then it mout-be—it would be—too late, then, to help your sarcumstances. Ef the property was to be sold by the sheriff, what would it bring, I want to know, now, when thar's so little money guine about. Not enough, by half, to pay this warmint, M'Kewn. But, ef 'twas only on account of the lady, it's your business to speak quick. The man has no right to keep the poor woman a-waiting on him. He has no right to keep a-thinking, with pipe in his mouth, while she's a weeping and pining away a-most to nothin'."
>
> "But I don't see that Mrs. Eveleigh shows any such signs of suffering, Millhouse."
>
> "It's all innard, cappin. She's got too proud a stomach, to show outside, in her flesh and sperrits, how much she suffers innardly. Many's the woman that's looked fat and hearty, while her heart's been a-braking in her buzzum." [Simms 1854, pp. 119–200]

Millhouse is a cut above Peter the farmer by having had dealings with gentlemen, but he still uses *a-doing* and *a-waiting*, *jest*, *spar'* for *spare*, and *I does*. Notably southern are his *in course*; *guine*, *axing*, *ef*, and especially *mout-be*. His elliptic or assimilated forms *arter* for *after*, *innard* for *inward*, and *cappin* for *captain* are of a piece with his old-fashioned pronunciations, *sarcumstances*, *sperrits*, *buzzum*, and with *stomach* in the sense of inclination; he also uses Cockney *warmint* for *vermin*. Though he mispronounces them, he is still capable of such words as *ridiculous* and *understanding*. Captain Porgy, of course, talks like a gentleman.

The next example puts into contrast a Southerner (who passes as a gentleman but is a scoundrel) and a rural Midwesterner from Ohio. Captain Lumsden is trying to cheat Kike (nickname for Hezekiah) of his land. Kike at last stands up to him.

> Kike's face was livid, and his voice almost inaudible.
> "Come, come, don't be impudent, young man," chuckled Captain Lumsden.
> "I don't know what you call impudence," said Kike, stretching his slender frame up to its full height, and shaking as if he had an ague-chill; "but you are a tyrant and a scoundrel!"
> "Tut! tut! Kike, you're crazy, you little brute. What's up?"
> "You know what's up. You want to cheat me out of that bottom land; you have got it advertised on the back side of a tree in North's holler, without consulting mother or me. I have been over to Jonesville to-day, and picked out Colonel Wheeler to act as my gardeen."
> "Colonel Wheeler? Why, that's an insult to me!" And the captain ceased to laugh, and grew red.
> "I hope it is. I couldn't get the judge to take back the order for the sale of the land; he's afeard of you. But now let me tell you something, Enoch Lumsden! If you sell my land by that order of the court, you'll lose more'n you'll make. I ain't afeard of the devil nor none of his angels; and I reckon you're one of the blackest. It'll cost you more burnt barns and dead hosses and cows and hogs and sheep than what you make will pay for. You cheated pappy, but you shan't make nothin' out of Little Kike. I'll turn Injin, and take Injin law onto you, you old thief and—"
> Here Captain Lumsden stepped forward and raised his cowhide. "I'll teach you some manners, you impudent little brat!"
> Kike quivered all over, but did not move hand or foot.
> "Hit me if you dare, Enoch Lumsden, and they'll be blood betwixt us then. You hit me wunst, and they'll be one less Lumsden alive in a year. You or me'll have to go to the bone-yard." [Eggleston 1895, pp. 58–59]

Familiar features here are *afeared*, *hoss*, *holler*. *Reckon* allies his speech to the South, as does *pappy*. But *gardeen* for *guardian* was universal, as was *wunst* for *once*. *Injin* (more often *Injun*), testifies to the once common change of *-di-* to *-j-*, which produced *journal* from *diurnal*, and may still be seen in *Cajun*, from *Acadian*, *Bajan* from *Barbadian*, and such pronunciations as *rejuce* for *reduce*.

The next example is of wild "western" talk, from Nevada in the "flush times" of the silver fever. Of this time and place Mark Twain has written:

> . . . as all the peoples of the earth had representative adventurers in the Silverland, and as each adventurer had brought the slang of his nation or

his locality with him, the combination made the slang of Nevada the richest and the most infinitely varied and copious that had ever existed anywhere in the world, perhaps, except in the mines of California in the "early days." Slang was the language of Nevada. [Twain 1872, p. 330]

Our scene depicts a rough named Scotty, whose fellow rough, Buck Fanshawe, has died, attempting to tell the minister about it and get him to conduct Buck's funeral. Scotty's slangy talk is set against the clergyman's formality.

But to return to Scotty's visit to the minister. He was on a sorrowful mission, now, and his face was the picture of woe. Being admitted to the presence he sat down before the clergyman, placed his fire-hat on an unfinished manuscript sermon under the minister's nose, took from it a red silk handkerchief, wiped his brow and heaved a sigh of dismal impressiveness, explanatory of his business. He choked, and even shed tears; but with an effort he mastered his voice and said in lugubrious tones:

"Are you the duck that runs the gospel-mill next door?"

"Am I the—pardon me, I believe I do not understand?"

With another sigh and a half-sob, Scotty rejoined:

"Why you see we are in a bit of trouble, and the boys thought maybe you would give us a lift, if we'd tackle you—that is, if I've got the rights of it and you are the head clerk of the doxology-works next door."

"I am the shepherd in charge of the flock whose fold is next door."

"The which?"

"The spiritual adviser of the little company of believers whose sanctuary adjoins these premises."

Scotty scratched his head, reflected a moment, and then said:

"You ruther hold over me, pard. I reckon I can't call that hand. Ante and pass the buck."

"How? I beg your pardon. What did I understand you to say?"

"Well, you've ruther got the bulge on me. Or maybe we've both got the bulge, somehow. You don't smoke me and I don't smoke you. You see, one of the boys has passed in his checks and we want to give him a good send-off, and so the thing I'm on now is to roust out somebody to jerk a little chin-music for us and waltz him through handsome." [Twain 1872, pp. 331–32]

While characteristic of the West, this kind of slang best illustrates the avoidance of the ordinary words in favor of some colorful, unexpected, or grotesque metaphor. *Gospel-mill*, *doxology-works*, and *chin-music* are the obvious examples, with the technical terms of card play transferred to this totally inappropriate situation.

Though representative enough, this handful of literary examples can give no more than a taste of the variety that existed in American popular and dialect speech of a hundred years ago. Scientific study of the language was in its infancy; it did not come of age until late in the century, culminating in 1889 with the founding of the American Dialect Society (ADS). The society at once began to publish word lists and other studies in *Dialect Notes* (1890–1939). The first volume contains E. S. Sheldon's brief essay "What is a dialect?"[12] which is still worth reading. Sheldon recognized that American conditions for dialect study differ considerably from those in Europe. He emphasized that "the so-called standard language is not a fixed and infallible standard, but is itself constantly changing" (1890, p. 287). He recognized the existence of occupational and social dialects, and even "different dialects of the same individual, according to different circumstances affecting his speech at different times"—what are today called codes.

It is evident that the founders of ADS had in mind from the first an American counterpart to the English Dialect Society. The goal, as Sheldon put it, was the investigation of English dialects in America with regard to pronunciation, grammar, vocabulary, phraseology, and geographical distribution. As the last item indicates, dialect geography was envisioned from the beginning; so also was the production of a dictionary to correspond to the *English Dialect Dictionary*, which Joseph Wright was just then beginning to edit in 1889. Progress of the ADS over the years was slow, since all work was voluntary and financial support minimal. It was not till the American Council of Learned Societies, with the help of several universities, undertook to fund the Linguistic Atlas of the United States and Canada project that progress was at last made toward discovering and mapping the distinctive features which set the types of North American English apart from one another.

The first part of this ambitious plan to be completed was the *Linguistic Atlas of New England* (Kurath et al. 1939–43); since then, other atlases have covered the Atlantic Coast from New Brunswick to Georgia (see Kurath 1949; Atwood 1953; and Kurath and McDavid 1961), and the *Linguistic Atlas of the Gulf Coast* is well along toward completion.[13] Field collecting has been finished in the entire area east of the Mississippi River, and the first trans-Mississippi atlas, the *Linguistic Atlas of the Upper Midwest* (Allen 1973–76), is in print. Other volumes are well advanced for the Pacific Coast states, for Oklahoma, Missouri, and Arkansas; and some work has been done in all the rest. Though this kind of study is expensive and slow, there is a good hope that the entire United States and English-speaking Canada[14] will have been mapped by the end of the century, thus permitting widespread comparisons. The completed portion has already vastly improved our knowledge of the language: its diversity, its development, its social correlates.

That there are, indeed, distinctive New England, southern, and western features has been confirmed, but with considerable redefinition. It has become clear, for example, that there are really two New Englands, separated generally by the Connecticut River, one coastal or oriented coastward, the other

English in the United States

land-oriented and overflowing westward. (Indeed, all the Atlantic states are similarly divided east and west.) Western New England is the eastern base of the entire "Inland Northern" region, which stretches westward, narrowing here and there but continuing unbroken to the Pacific coast. As mentioned before, the lines of regional separation are distinct to the Mississippi River, less distinct beyond it. But many northern features persist and set this region off rather clearly.

This North is linguistic, not political; it must not be thought of in the old popular way (deeply enforced by the Civil War) as somehow corresponding to the Mason-Dixon line. Atlas studies clearly show that, in terms of language, the South comprises chiefly the coastal and piedmont areas of Delaware, Maryland, Virginia, the Carolinas, and Georgia, with the Gulf states including eastern Texas. Between this North and South lies an extensive "Midland" region (itself divisible into North Midland and South Midland) with distinctive features of its own. It includes southern New Jersey and Pennsylvania, northern Delaware, and the mountain regions (the Appalachians) of Virginia, Maryland, the Carolinas, and Georgia, whence it expands westward, taking in a great part of the Southwest. These division lines are all set on the basis of the field study by direct interviews of local inhabitants—in the Atlantic states, more than 1,200 of them. Some 400 local and regional expressions were mapped for pronunciation, word usage, and many grammatical forms.

A few of the distinguishing features of Northern, Midland, and Southern follow.

The southern extent of *pail*, closely matched by the northern extent of *bucket*, makes a line running across southern New Jersey and diagonally, southeast to northeast, through Pennsylvania. *Pail* is clearly the preferred term in the North, *bucket* in the Midland and South. In close agreement with these are the lines for Northern *darning needle* 'dragonfly' setting it off from Midland *snake feeder*, and Northern *whiffletree* or *whippletree* as against Midland *swingletree* or *singletree*. When lines for individual features correspond closely, forming a "bundle," they designate a distinct regional boundary, as the foregoing clearly do.

The Southern and Midland regions are separated similarly. Against Midland *snake feeder* and *snake doctor* is the Southern *mosquito hawk*; against Midland *quarter till* (in telling time) is Southern *quarter to* (and, as noted before, Northern *quarter of*); so with many other features. But the regions often agree, two against the third: Midland *blinds* 'roller shades' contrasts with Atlantic (Northern and Southern) *curtains*, and similarly Northern and Southern *eaves troughs* or *water troughs* (along the edge of a roof) becomes *spouting* in the Midland region. Southern and Midland often agree: *you-all* in general, though *you'ns* competes with it in the Midland area. *Light bread* for white bread made with yeast is universal in the South and Midland. Certain words are found in a single region, others only in part of a region, and some are notably local, limited to a very small area. Examples are:

Northern: *buttery* 'pantry'; *johnnycake* 'corn bread'
Midland: *skillet; smearcase* 'cottage cheese'
Southern: *plunder room* 'storeroom'; *earthworm* 'angleworm'; *lightwood* 'kindling'

Notably local usages:

double runner 'bobsled', *sour-milk cheese* 'cottage cheese'—eastern New England

eavespout 'eavestrough'—northern New England, Cape Cod

tumble 'haycock'—northeastern New England, western Massachusetts

neb 'wagon tongue'—northeastern Massachusetts

pig's squin 'hasslet', *cade* 'pet lamb'—Rhode Island and adjoining Massachusetts

hay barrack 'haystack', *pot cheese* 'cottage cheese'—Hudson River Valley

pightle 'barnyard', *kip!* 'call to chickens'—eastern Long Island

kush(ie) 'call to cow while milking', *tye!* 'call to calves'—northern New Jersey

crib house 'corncrib'—southern New Jersey

toot 'paper bag', *bee!* 'call to chickens'—southeastern Pennsylvania

hap 'quilt,' *chickery* or *grinnie* 'chipmunk'—western Pennsylvania

hot cakes 'pancakes', *bag school* 'play truant'—Pennsylvania, southern New Jersey, northern Delaware

piece 'small quantity of food taken between meals'—Pennsylvania and West Virginia

mongst-ye 'you-all'—Eastern Shore of Maryland, southern Delaware

(sea)-grass sack 'burlap bag'—coastal Maryland, Virginia, Delaware, southern New Jersey

hobby 'corn griddlecake'—southern West Virginia

trumpery room 'storeroom', *co-dubbie* 'call to calves'—northeastern North Carolina

Certain objects have a great variety of names, some widespread, others local. The *freestone peach* (the prevailing term throughout the North and North Midland) is also called

free-seed peach—western West Virginia

open-stone peach—eastern Maryland, western North Carolina

open-seed peach—northern Maryland, northeastern West Virginia

clear-stone peach—southeastern North Carolina, eastern South Carolina

clear-seed peach—eastern North and South Carolina

cleave-stone peach—Cape Cod

open peach—coastal strip, Delaware to South Carolina; southern North Carolina

> *opening peach*—Eastern Shore of Maryland and adjacent Delaware
> *soft peach*—eastern Virginia, northern North Carolina

Geographically restricted terms are likely to be old-fashioned, local survivors against the competition of more favored synonyms. The existence of many local variants argues that they were established early, but not necessarily that they were once in wider use; they may be (for whatever reason) especially tenacious. It is evident that the three major regional divisions do not stand entirely apart from each other: there is coincidence and overlapping. Further, it is evident that focuses of dense population—the cities—are always pressing against the surrounding thinner population, often spreading their usages by sheer social and commercial weight.[15]

The linguistic atlases, when completed, should cover the United States and Canada. But the time span of the usages collected, approximately seventy years, will seriously limit comparability. However, comparison of thousands of items is now possible for the entire nation through field collections made within a less-than-five-year period (1965–70) for the *Dictionary of American Regional English* (*DARE*).[16] (A sample column of the dictionary is shown as fig. 1.) A fresh program of collecting by direct interview in 1,002 communities, using a "Questionair" with 1,847 questions phrased exactly to ensure comparability, has furnished data from which maps are now being computer-made (see maps 1–4). These greatly enlarge our knowledge of word and phrase distributions. Just as "every word has its history,"[17] so each has its geographical distribution. When many agree, one can speak generally of a region. But no two distributions are exactly alike. We shall note here only a few of the more striking regional and local usages that have been mapped.[18] The figure in parentheses following some forms is the number of communities in which that response was given.

> *baby coach* 'baby carriage'—southeastern Pennsylvania and southwestern New Jersey
> *bayou* 'sluggish stream'—chiefly Louisiana
> *bayou* 'without current, slough'—chiefly Mississippi Valley
> *beau dollar* (34) 'silver dollar'—South, and taken North by blacks
> *belly girt* 'bellyband on a horse'—Atlantic states
> *blat* (123) 'the noise made by a calf that is taken away from its mother'—chiefly Northeastern and Northern, as against *blate* (85)—chiefly Southern and Southwestern
> *blind pig* (111) 'a place where liquor is sold and consumed illegally'—Northern, from Michigan to the Pacific Coast, as against *blind tiger* (84)—chiefly Southern and Midland (north to Indiana)
> *cabinet* 'milk shake with ice cream'—Rhode Island and adjoining Massachusetts
> *calling (the) hogs* (61) 'snoring' (jocular)—South Midland and South

A-B-Ab n (From schoolroom repetition of letters and syllables: see quot 1894) Obs. See **abiselfa**.

1 An elementary step in learning to spell.

1894 quot **Romulus NY** (1901 *DN* 2.135), Of course, the a, b, c's were first, then a, b, *abs*, and when the child could put two syllables together and form a word, as bak-er, baker, it was a proud day to the little fellow.

2 Transf. Something simple.

1901 *DN* 2.135, **n&eNY**, "He doesn't know his a b abs" (Of a stupid boy).

abide v, usu in neg constr. *OED* sense 17. Somewhat old-fash. Chiefly **N** and **SE**—see DS II29A.

To endure or put up with (something unpleasant).

1912 Green *Va Folk-Speech* 60. **1965** *Wilson Coll* **csKY**, I just can't abide him and his biggity ways. **1970** *DARE* Inf NY234, [You should] just abide corns [not try to cure them].

able adj.

1 Having the capacity or ability (to do something). See DS BB46.

In various joc phr understating the feeling of good health: quite well.

able to be out, 1967 *DARE* Inf **SC31**.
able to crack corn, 1900–10 *Craven Co NC* (1946 *PADS* 6.33), Humorous understatement in reply to "How are you?"
able to go, 1945 Letter, *Harder Coll* **cwTN**.
able to run around, 1945 Letter, *Harder Coll* **cwTN**.
able to sit up and pick, 1968 *DARE* Inf **PA74**.
able to sit up and take nourishment, 1930's and after, **nOH** etc. (FGC)
able to trot, 1967 *Harder Coll* **cwTN**.

Note: Used also in places besides those named.

2 See quot.

1966 *Wilson Coll*, **csKY**, Able: adj. Rich, well-to-do, powerful.

ace boon coon |'es'bun'kun| n (*ace*, first in importance + *boon*, good + *coon*, fellow [see *DA* coon n, 2]; compare *boon companion*.) Among Blacks.

A number-one or closest friend.

1965 Brown *Manchild* 77, I knew K.B. about a year before we became ace boon coons. K.B. was the first cat I locked with up at Wiltwyck. **1970** *DARE* Inf, 6 responses, all from Blacks—see DSII1.

admire v, before infin with *to*, occas *for to*.

1 To be much pleased, to enjoy.

a1770 J. Mecom *Lett. to B. Franklin* (1859) 194, (1972 *OEDS*), I should admire to come and see and hear all about every thing. **1931** Motte *Charleston Goes to Harvard* (diary) 88, After drinking a glass of soda water, which he admired [to do?] (Yankeeism), we started for Boston. **1917** Gordon *Ommirandy* 149 (*Hench Coll*) **cVA**, I always did admire see you wid dat beaver on. **1927** *Am Sp* 2.347 **cwWV**, She would admire for to see your mother.

2 To wish, to desire strongly.

1876 B. Harte *Gabriel Conroy* IV.i (1972 *OEDS*), 'Why didn't you come into the parlour?' she said . . . 'I didn't admire to to-night,' returned Gavriel. **a1967** *Wilson Coll* **Ozarks**, I'd sure admire to see that girl. **1967** *DARE* Inf **TN11 Jonesboro** (Reported "heard"), I would admire to have been somewheres else.

Fig. 1. Sample column from *DARE*. The treatment is historical, with dated quotations. Pronunciation, part of speech, variant spellings and pronunciation spellings, source, region or locality of use, usage status, definition, cross-references, and notes are given when pertinent.

English in the United States

cap (56) 'the metal circle on a wood-burning stove that lifts out so that wood may be put in'—northern New York, central and northwest Pennsylvania, Michigan; as against *griddle* (41)—chiefly South Midland and Southwest, *damper* (11)—chiefly eastern North Carolina, *cover* (22)—New England, *eye* (147)—South, especially Central South

cowboy (44) 'careless driver'—Northeast

dip (44) 'the sweet liquid poured over pudding'—chiefly North Central states and westward, except Pacific states

dropped eggs (40) 'poached eggs'—New England

ethyl (393) 'high octane gasoline'—Michigan to Florida and westward to the Pacific

ex 'axle of a wagon'—western New England and North to North Dakota

griddle 'round metal piece on wood-burning stove'—chiefly northern New York

jockey box 'glove compartment in a car'—Northwest states

sultry (136) 'humid (weather)'—Mississippi Valley and westward to the Pacific

whicker 'sound made by a horse'—South and Inner South

Little has been said of pronunciation, but this, too, differs, as everyone knows—indeed, the nineteenth-century classification of the country into New England, South, and West was to a great extent based on it. Many studies of single features of American pronunciation have been made, and some good general ones, but until specific field investigation on a wide scale was undertaken by the Linguistic Atlas it was impossible to treat the subject with anything like full accuracy.[19] We now have maps, for example, which show exactly where the *r* in such words as *barn, car, care, far, four, fear, wire, hours* ("postvocalic *r*")[20] is lost, and where it is retained. This *r* is generally lost everywhere along the Atlantic Coast and well inland, except in the area of Philadelphia and the Delaware River (southern New Jersey, Delaware, the Eastern Shore of Maryland). What is the reason for this gap? Postvocalic *r* had begun to be lost in southern England already in the mid-fifteenth century (see Wyld 1953, pp. 398–99). By the time of American colonization in the early seventeenth century, the loss was far advanced, and absence of *r* has continued in the upper-class speech of England (Received Pronunciation [RP]) ever since. The New England and Virginia colonies, keeping close touch and taking their educated usage from the area around London, also lost *r*. Philadelphia, however, was founded and much influenced by Quakers (whose chief strength was in the North of England) and later by Scots, both groups coming from areas in Britain where *r* had not been lost. In New England, *r* is retained west of the Connecticut River valley (western Vermont, Massachusetts, and Connecticut), an area of Scotch-Irish settlement, and in the southern Appalachians for the same reason. And it was these western and mountain settlers, among others, who pushed the frontier ever further westward, retaining postvocalic *r*, so that in the United States

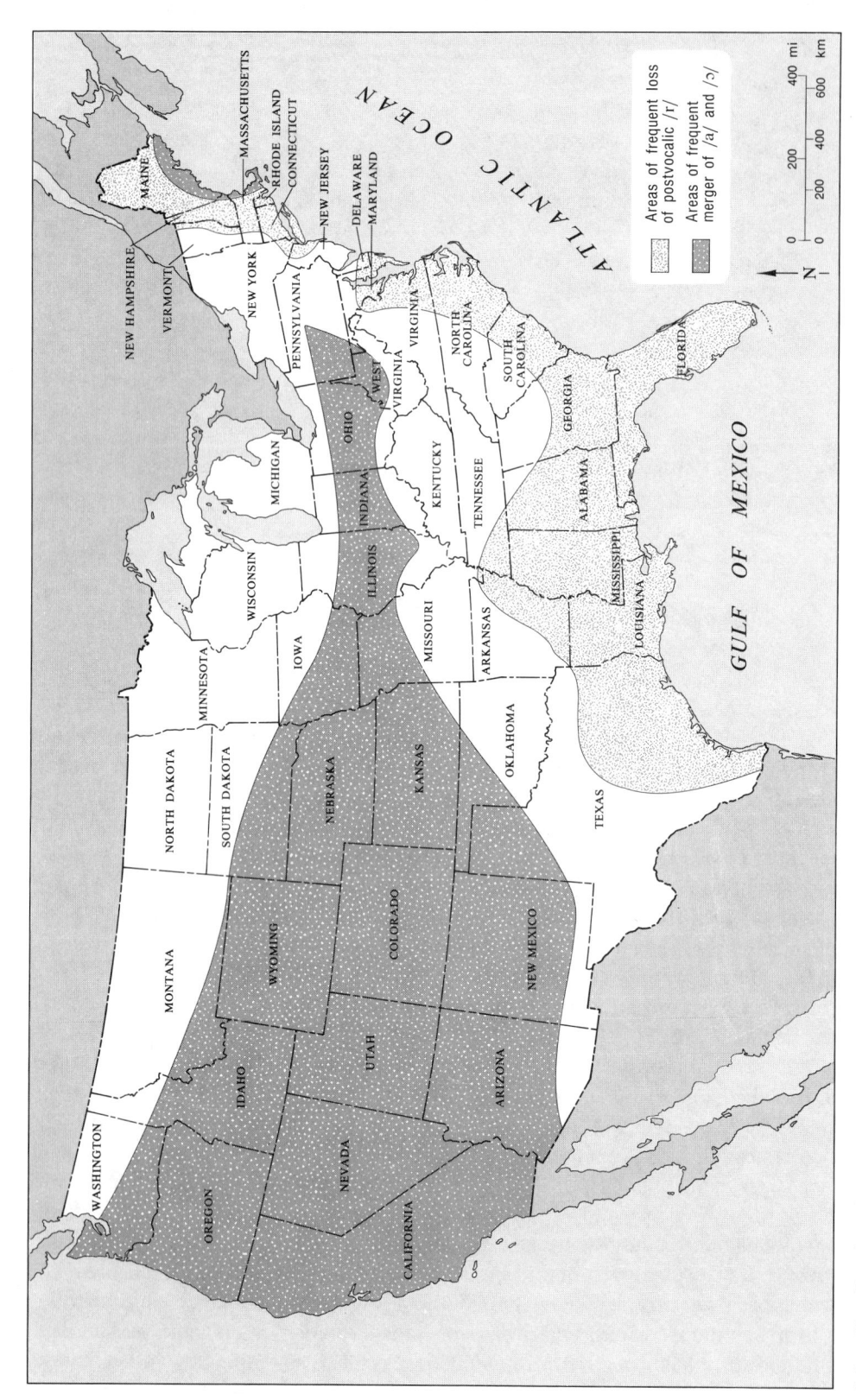

Map 7. Regional differences in pronunciation

today, *r* is retained by the country at large, lost only along that broken Atlantic strip. Recent evidence shows that this provincial English and now more generally American retained *r* is spreading—there is a sort of backwash toward the East. Younger people are restoring *r* in parts of the South, and it is growing in prestige in New York City,[21] a border area.

Other regional differences of pronunciation may be quickly summarized. The "short *o*" in such words as *not*, *got*, and *hot*, said with rounded lips in Britain, had begun to be unrounded to *a* by the time of colonization. The change did not become established in RP, but in America it had some success and is now widespread. To the English, Americans seem to be saying *nat, gat, hat* (actually [ɑ] or [a]). The general contrast between such pairs as *cot/caught*, *tot/taught*, and *don/dawn* has broken down in eastern New England and western Pennsylvania, where [ɑ] and [ɔ] have merged, and the breakdown appears to be spreading in the Midwest and West (see map 7).[22]

Some of the most interesting and characteristic regional differences are found with the diphthongs: *ai* as in *five*, *ride*, and *white*; *au* as in *down*, *out*, and *fowl*; and *oi* [ɔɪ] as in *boil*, *coin*, and *voice*. In the southern half of the United States there is a strong tendency to weaken the glide, often to the point of monophthongization, with the vowel lengthened—contributing to the effect of the so-called Southern drawl. Where the glide element is retained, subregional differences depend on whether it is upgliding or ingliding (for example, [ɔᶦ] or [ɔᵊ]), ingliding being found especially in the Charleston area and the coastal South. When *r* is lost after [ʌ], as in *first*, *third*, and *curl*, one reflex is a high-front glide vowel. Thus [ʌr] becomes [ʌᶦ]—the so-called Brooklyn *r*. This sound is by no means limited to Brooklyn, however; it can be heard as far north as Boston, down the Atlantic coast especially in the cities, and on the Gulf coast as far west as eastern Texas. In "dialect" writing it is usually spelled *oi*, for the lack of any more accurate way of representing it—thus *boid* for *bird*, *coil* for *curl*—though it is definitely not the same as the diphthong in *boil*.

A triple contrast for many years used as a broad test of regionality[23] is that between *merry*, *Mary* and *marry*. In the Southeast, these words have respectively the vowels [ɛ], [e], and [æ]. In the "hill South" (Appalachian uplands) the vowel of *marry* has been raised, so that it falls together with that of *merry*, reducing the contrast to two members. In the Midwest and West generally, *Mary* has lost its distinctive [e] and fallen together with the other words, so that all three are pronounced with the same vowel [ɛ].

Consonantal variation is, of course, much less frequent than vocalic. A striking example is the use of *d* and *t*, respectively, for the initial sounds of *then* and *thin*, making them *den* and *tin*. This is most conspicuous in the speech of blacks, but also of whites (as in South Carolina and Georgia) who have been in constant contact with blacks from childhood. It is also found, however, in foreigners' speech (since these sounds are rare outside of English) and in that of lower-class native white speakers in large cities.

An interesting instance of an intrusive consonant is the *r* added to the vowel in such words as *wash* and *mush* (*warsh, mursh*). This is concentrated in western Pennsylvania, West Virginia, and (somewhat less) the hill South; it is sporadic in upstate New York and western New England. A quite different *r* is that added inorganically at the end of words ending in a vowel when they come before another vowel: thus *law* + *r* in *lawr and order*, *sofa* + *r* in *the sofar upstairs*, or *Anna* + *r* in *Annar at home*. Since in *r*-dropping areas *r* is not dropped before vowels, a pattern is set up by which *r* is "expected" between any adjacent vowels. And this pattern is carried over even when (as with *law*, *sofa*, *Anna*) there never was an *r* to be dropped. Nevertheless, once it has repeatedly been supplied before vowels, it attaches itself permanently—hence *lawr*, *sofar*, *Annar* (not so spelled, but so pronounced). President Kennedy was noted for his *Asiar*, *Africar*, and *Cubar*. This feature agrees with the usage in the East Midlands of England—here New Englanders and other *r*-droppers have followed the same course as speakers in England, and for the same reason.

As this sketch has tried to suggest, the English language in America, or American English—or what some call, with less science than patriotic bias, "the American language"—was already diverse when brought to the colonies, and has continued so, though changing patterns. Many dialectal features came over from Britain—notably the contrasting southern and northern ones; some persisted, others disappeared. New conditions added loanwords, fresh formations, altered meanings. On the other hand, continued contact with Britain and the rapid development of a class of leaders, many of whom got their education in England and generally accepted English standards, prevented any rapid diversion or loss of intelligibility.

The effect of the Revolution and of national independence was tremendous. No less a figure than Noah Webster saw here a great opportunity to cast off the "corrupt" language of England and to rationalize and refine the language for the new nation. The attempt to found an academy for such a purpose, which had several times failed in Britain, was made once again under the leadership of Thomas Jefferson. But other forces were at work—popular forces—which were to have a powerful effect, especially when actual democracy, rather than limited upper-class governance, came to the fore under Andrew Jackson. The surge of population westward, the phenomenon of the expanding frontier in which the restraints and standards of more settled society were thrown off, was reflected in the language. With little or no education, having to cope as best they could with harsh physical conditions, the "conquerors of the West" became freely innovative in their language, ebullient with descriptive and metaphorical inventions—with "tall talk," exaggerated humor, vigor that had no time for refinement. In the East, in the cities, however, education flourished; the leading class had it and it became a national ideal: the mark of progress in any settlement was that a school had been started. Self-education, especially for talented people of humble beginnings, was widely practiced and admired. Public address, often learned in the "school of hard knocks," carried to the people educational ideals and their kudos. Some of the interesting neologisms were the direct offspring of ignorance pretending to be learned. A whole school of humor portrayed its characters as unschooled but practically wise.[24]

The physical frontier is no more. Other conditions and compulsions rule the changing course of American English in this century. Chief among these have been the enormous overturn of life through widespread literacy, industrialization, mechanization, scientization, urbanization. Every census of population shows the rural areas and small settlements losing to the cities, the cities sprawling into suburbia, suburbia transforming outlying villages into "bedroom towns." Attempts to "return to the land" often transport city appurtenances to places where they do not fit—or which they destroy. Language, following the society, grows at a dizzying pace, adding new scientific, technical, and occupational words by the thousands. Vogue-words of many kinds proliferate. Overcommunication, with the same activities described daily, often repeated several times a day, produces insipid formulas. In the attempt to escape this cliché language, writers and "media personalities" invent unexpected, often extravagant, neologisms. Recent immigrants to the cities contribute foreign words—a kind of condiment. Popular language has a voice it never had in former centuries; many of its contributions work their way up through general colloquial use to use in print. Over the past fifty years the writing in our "best magazines"—those addressed to college-educated readers—has steadily become more informal, racier, less academic. The plentifulness and ubiquity of popular expression have muscled in on the language of "good writing," sometimes shouldering it aside. Vigor, liveliness, and "in" phrases are more valued than niceties of style. Change, a natural property of language, is accelerated as the society itself changes more rapidly.

The question often asked is whether the enormous outpouring of language produced by cheap and rapid printing, and especially by radio and television, which reaches into every corner of the land, will not ultimately homogenize American speech—whether, indeed, the process is not already well advanced. Some loss of regional and local difference there surely is, as standardization and nationwide commercialization take their ineluctable course. But the movement is not all in the same direction. Though Americans change their places of residence—their geographical attachment—probably more often than do other people, the greater part of any population "stays home." There is a nucleus of stability. Those who go away and return fall back into familiar patterns because they must deal with the local people. Those who move into linguistically different areas find their children adapting to the new community—which is *their* community—rather than following the parents' patterns which come from places they do not know. Thus at least the broad, basic regional differences are largely unaffected. Movement, in any case, is usually by individual units, not by masses, and those who move must adopt the differences they meet for the utterly practical purpose of communicating.

Local words and turns of phrase are easy enough for the newcomer to adopt. What causes more difficulty is pronunciation. Most people use language as they do any other mechanism, making it "work" without inquiring *how* it works. Only when it breaks down do they become aware of it as such; then they hear queer sounds to which they cannot react in the customary automatic way. They are even forced to notice their own speech. Natural mimics with good ears adapt without knowing it. Some others hear different pronunciations as disturbingly "off," but cannot adapt their own. Features of foreign pronunciation come through into American English and last for generations; they, and some syntactic features, are more tenacious than items of vocabulary. Obviously, large foreign settlements have been slower to acculturate than small units or individuals. Broadcast pronunciation on nationwide radio and television hookups carefully avoids the strikingly regional: the important "commentators" are usually speakers from the Midland area, with their sharp edges rubbed down. If they furnish any kind of model, it is a bland one. But, little imitated, they offer little threat to regional differences. One threat certainly exists: the person whose speech is notably old-fashioned or "ignorant" or "backwoods"—the "hillbilly," for example—will be laughed at, but not imitated by younger people. Even so, some sentimental value is placed on the quaint or salty expressions of past generations, often preserved in memory though no longer in common use. And for the young, those not yet settled in their lifeways, "prestige," real or imaginary or commercially invented, counts for a great deal. It is probably the most important factor in the increasing use of postvocalic *r*—the eastward "backwash" already noted—in the *r*-less Atlantic coastal area. "Prestige" is not accorded to any extreme type of regional speech: prestige is literally eccentric.

With language it is always dangerous to make predictions. What can be said of regional differences in present American English is that they will certainly not disappear suddenly or altogether; that there are strong conservative forces at work; and that the massiveness of the vogue language which washes over the nation does not keep it from being voguish. It, too, soon becomes outmoded and is overborne by the next wave. The basic features of the language remain, with their regional differences. And normal renewal probably counterbalances loss.

NOTES

1. Maps 1 through 4 were made for the *Dictionary of American Regional English*, in progress at the University of Wisconsin at Madison. Maps of this kind will be used throughout the dictionary to illustrate regional and social factor distributions.
2. The *Oxford English Dictionary* quotes from Richard Eden 1555.
3. From Algonkian forms such as Abnaki *segankw* and Virginia *pawcohiccora*.
4. The first United States census (1790) is instructive in showing figures on residents from places other than England (out of a total of 3,938,635):

Scots	188,589	4.78%	
Germans	156,457	3.97%	
Dutch	56,623	1.43%	
Irish	44,273	1.12%	
French	13,384	0.34%	
Blacks	694,330	17.63%	(slaves)
	59,150	1.50%	(free)

5. The phrases are used by people of all ages and all degrees of education. There may be a slight preponderance of rural use.
6. Charleston's first settlers were planters from Barbados, West Indies.
7. A map which shows subordinate directions of settlement well is that of Raven I. McDavid, Jr., 1958.
8. Francis Moore, English traveler, found *bluff* applied to a hill in Savannah, Georgia.
9. See Read 1933.
10. Dwight 1821–22. Dwight was president of Yale College from 1795 to 1817.
11. The climatic or "weather" theory is an ancient one, used to "explain" dialectal differences at least as far back as Dante's *De Vulgari Eloquentia*.
12. *Dialect Notes*, vol. 1 (1890), pp. 286–97. For further references see the bibliographical lists in *Dialect Notes*, vol. 1, pp. 12–16, 80–83, 344–47; idem., vol. 2 (1890–1901), pp. 151–78. See also my recent summary (Cassidy 1973, pp. 75–100).
13. Under direction of Lee A. Pederson, Emory University.
14. Work in Canada has been done by Henry Alexander, Rex Wilson, Murray Wanamaker, R. J. Gregg, and others, and in French-speaking Canada, by Gaston Dulong.
15. A fuller summary of the evidence is given by E. Bagby Atwood 1970, pp. 200–214.
16. Now in preparation at the University of Wisconsin at Madison under my direction, and funded chiefly by the National Endowment for the Humanities and the Andrew W. Mellon Foundation, *DARE* will include regional and folk usages for the entire United States. It is the official dictionary of the American Dialect Society.
17. Jules Gilliéron, director of *Atlas Linguistique de la France*.
18. *DARE* maps show geographical distributions primarily, but also five "social" ones: type of community (urban to rural, see map 4), informants' age, sex, race, and degree of education. Significant correlations among these will be noted in the dictionary. The areas indicated show where features are concentrated, though they may be sporadic elsewhere. I have published some of these maps in previous articles (Cassidy 1977a, 1977b, and 1980).
19. See Kurath and McDavid 1961. Four types of Atlantic States pronunciation are isolated and compared: see especially pages 6–7. For the United States generally, see Hartman (in press), which was prepared for *DARE*.
20. This is also known as "final and preconsonantal r," coming at the ends of words when they do not precede a vowel.
21. See McDavid 1948. See also Labov 1966 and map 7.
22. Map 7 and the discussion given here rely on James Hartman, "Pronunciation of American English," to appear as an introduction to *DARE*. I am glad to acknowledge Professor Hartman's willingness to furnish his unpublished findings.
23. This was skillfully used by Henry Lee Smith in the 1940s in a nationally broadcast radio program, "Where Are You From?"

24. Reference is to the pseudonymous writings of Petroleum V. Nasby, Orpheus C. Kerr, Artemus Ward, Bill Arp, and other "cracker-barrel philosophers."

REFERENCES

Allen, Harold B. *The Linguistic Atlas of the Upper Midwest*. 3 vols. Minneapolis: University of Minnesota Press, 1973–76.
Atwood, E. Bagby. *A Survey of Verb Forms in the Eastern United States*. Ann Arbor: University of Michigan Press, 1953.
———. "Postscript: The Principal Speech Areas of the Eastern United States." In *English Linguistics*, edited by Harold Hungerford, Jay Robinson, and James Sledd, pp. 200–214. Chicago: Scott Foresman, 1970.
Butler, Frances Anne. *Journal*. London: John Murray, 1835.
Cassidy, Frederic G. "Dialect Studies, Regional and Social." In *Current Trends in Linguistics*, edited by Thomas A. Sebeok. 14 vols. Vol 10, *Linguistics in North America*, pp. 75–100. The Hague: Mouton, 1973.
———. "Computer-Aided Usage 'Labeling' in a Dictionary." *Computers and the Humanities* 11 (1977a):89–99.
———. "On-Line Mapmaking for the Dictionary of American Regional English." *Germanistische Linguistik* 3–4 (1977b):107–19.
———. "Computer Mapping of Lexical Variants for *DARE*." In *Theory and Method in Lexicography*, edited by Ladislav Zgusta, pp. 147–60. Columbia, S.C.: Hornbeam, 1980.
Dialect Notes. 6 vols. New Haven: American Dialect Society, 1890–1939.
Dwight, Timothy. *Travels in New England and New York*. New Haven: T. Dwight, 1821–22.
Eden, Richard. *The Decades of the Newe Worlde or West India*. London: Powell, 1555.
Eggleston, Edward. *The Circuit Rider*. New York: Scribner, 1874.
Gilliéron, Jules, and Edmont, E. *Atlas linguistique de la France*. 35 vols. Paris: H. Champion, 1902–10.
Hansen, Marcus. "The Settlement of New England." In *Handbook of the Linguistic Geography of New England*, edited by Hans Kurath et al., pp. 62–121. Providence: Brown University Press, 1939.
Hartman, James. "The Pronunciation of American English." MS, 1981.
Irving, Washington. *A History of New York*. New York: Inskeep and Bradford, 1809.
———. "Rip Van Winkle." In *The Sketch Book*. New York: C. S. Van Winkle, 1819–20.
Jones, Richard Foster. *The Triumph of the English Language*. Stanford: Stanford University Press, 1953.
Jonson, Ben. *The English Grammar*. Edited by Strickland Gibson. London: Lauston Monotype Corp., 1928.
Kurath, Hans. *A Word Geography of the Eastern United States*. Ann Arbor: University of Michigan Press, 1949.
Kurath, Hans; Hanley, Miles L.; Bloch, Bernard; Lowman, Guy S., Jr.; and Hansen, Marcus L. *Linguistic Atlas of New England*. 3 vols. in 6 pts. Providence: Brown University Press, 1939–43.

Kurath, Hans; Hansen, Marcus L.; Bloch, Julia; and Bloch, Bernard. *Handbook of the Linguistic Geography of New England*. Providence: Brown University Press, 1939.

Kurath, Hans, and McDavid, Raven I., Jr. *The Pronunciation of English in the Atlantic States*. Ann Arbor: University of Michigan Press, 1961.

Labov, William. *The Social Stratification of English in New York City*. Washington, D.C.: Center for Applied Linguistics, 1966.

Lane, T. W. "The Thimble Game." In *Polly Peablossom's Wedding*, edited by Thomas A. Burke, pp. 28–40. Philadelphia: Peterson, 1851.

McDavid, Raven I., Jr. "Postvocalic /-r/ in South Carolina: A Social Analysis." *American Speech* 23 (1948):194–203.

———. "Dialect Areas of the United States [Map]." In *The Structure of American English*, by W. Nelson Francis, p. 580. New York: Ronald, 1958.

Marckwardt, A. H. "*Want* with Ellipsis of Verbs of Motion." *American Speech* 23 (1948):3–9.

Mathews, Mitford M. *A Dictionary of Americanisms on Historical Principles*. Chicago: University of Chicago Press, 1951.

Menner, Robert J. "Two Early Comments on American Dialects." *American Speech* 13 (1938):8–12.

Nichols, Thomas Low. *Forty Years of American Life*. 2 vols. London: John Maxwell and Co., 1864.

Orbeck, Anders. *Early New England Pronunciation*. Ann Arbor: George Wahr, 1927.

Orton, Harold; Sanderson, Stewart; and Widdowson, John. *The Linguistic Atlas of England*. London: Croom Helm, and New York: Humanities Press, 1978.

Read, Allen Walker. "British Recognition of American Speech." *Dialect Notes* 6 (1933):313–334.

———. "Milestones in the Branching of British and American English." Lecture presented at Vanderbilt University, 13 March 1979.

Sheldon, E. S. "What Is a Dialect?" *Dialect Notes* 1 (1890):286–97.

Simms, William Gilmore. *Woodcraft*. New York: Redfield, 1854.

Twain, Mark. *Roughing It*. Hartford, Conn.: American Publishing Co., 1872.

Wasson, George S. *Cap'n Simeon's Store*. Boston: Riverside, 1903.

Westcott, E. N. *David Harum*. New York: Appleton, 1898.

Wyld, H. C. *A History of Modern Colloquial English*. 3d ed. Oxford: Blackwell, 1953.

Variation in Contemporary American English

Thomas E. Toon

Language change and language variation have traditionally been studied separately. Historical linguistics has described patterns of change, while dialectology has explored regional variation within single periods. In the United States, however, dialectology was shaped by historical inquiry, and the first major product of American dialect geography, Hans Kurath's *Linguistic Atlas of New England (LANE)*, was a systematic description that correlated dialects and the facts of settlement history. Even so, Kurath recorded information about the informants and their speech that could be used to examine the relation of dialect to social class. Subsequent studies within the tradition established by *LANE*—of which Frederic G. Cassidy's forthcoming *Dictionary of American Regional English* is the most ambitious—retain a regional and historical focus but provide the complementary perspective of variation according to community type, sex, age, degree of education, and race of the informants. Thus, the historical tradition of dialectology usefully complements more recent efforts in the sociology of language variation.

With growing interest in the relation between speech variety and such variables as occupation, age, sex, race, and ethnic origins, we have begun to account for the social consequences of language variation and the social influences on that variation. Methodological changes in fieldwork recognize that individuals alter their speech to match their perception of the demands of varying situations. While dialect geographers summarize their findings in isoglosses that delimit the regional boundaries of speech types, sociolinguists measure the frequency of individual variants used in defined contexts and attempt to relate those frequencies to extralinguistic demographic factors.

From antiquity, some members of a language community have used the evidence of dialect variation to shape the destiny of others. In Biblical times, the army of Jephthah demanded that soldiers crossing the Jordan River pronounce the word *shibboleth* 'stream'; those who said *shibboleth* were allowed to cross unharmed, while those who said *sibboleth* were recognized as enemies and put to death (Judges 12:5–6). On 24 May 1692, similar inquisitors in Salem, Massachusetts, asked Mrs. Nathaniel Cary to recite the Lord's Prayer:

> How wonderfully the devil twisted her tongue when she tried, "hollowed" instead of "hallowed," tricks which the unobservant might not notice but which converted holy litany to hellish parody. [Starkey 1969, pp. 139–40]

Mrs. Cary's dialect thus led to her trial for witchcraft, and if the consequences of language variation are not always so dramatic, it is nonetheless clear that the use of our language is closely connected to our social, economic, and political status. We make a place for ourselves in our society by learning the varieties and uses of language, and those varieties keep us in our place.

Our education in the linguistic facts of life begins in the cradle. While most models of the acquisition of language by children have concentrated on the linguistic system, Halliday has argued that models must also consider the developing command of the uses of language:

> The child knows what language is because he knows what language does. The determining elements in the young child's experience are the successful demands on language that he himself has made, the particular needs that have been satisfied by language for him. He has used language in many ways—for the satisfaction of material and intellectual expression of feelings and so on. Language in all these uses has come within his own direct experience, and because of this he is subconsciously aware that language has many functions that affect him personally. Language is, for the child, a rich and adaptable instrument for the realization of his intentions; there is hardly any limit to what he can do with it. [Halliday 1969, p. 27]

Through games, riddles, and private codes, children establish close peer associations that exclude the adult world. The rules and formulas for these language acts are conveyed to children by other children and remain stable for long periods of time, perhaps even for centuries.[1] Consider some of the formulas used for the termination of a game of hide-and-seek:

> Olley, olley ottsinfree!
> Olley, olley oxen free!
> Olley, olley outs in free!
> Olley, olley in free!
> Olley, olley, ee!
> Olley, olley, Oxford free!

The many variants of this rhyme probably evolved slowly and over much time from something like "all ye, all ye, outs in free!" Such examples illustrate both the continuity and social importance of prescribed verbal behavior.

As children, we receive our first introduction to slang and use it to build solidarity through language behavior. Sexual and excretory euphemism, pejorative terms for teachers and school, and naming (and nicknaming) are group reactions to perceptions of power structures. Usually, these linguistic habits are age graded. They are useful for only a limited period of our lives; we outgrow them and in most cases forget we ever knew them. Occasionally, however, children initiate linguistic change and influence future states of the language. The current American extension of the verb *go* to mean 'say' is apparently such a case. The following examples of this use would, until recently, have been found only in the speech of preadolescents:

> "You see, I'm puttin' a frog in Jeannie's lunch bag and in walks the teacher, and he goes, 'What are you doing, Sally?' and I go, 'Gettin' an apple outta my lunch.' That was a close one, huh?"

That such usage is heard among today's university undergraduates illustrates the diffusion of a linguistic innovation.[2]

The close study of the language-learning abilities of young children leads to a startling observation about social conditioning:

> Through the preschool years and in the early school years, girls exceed boys in most aspects of verbal performance. They say their first word sooner, articulate more clearly and at an earlier age, use longer sentences, and are more fluent. By the beginning of school, however, there are no longer any consistent differences in vocabulary. Girls learn to read sooner, and there are more boys than girls who require special training in remedial reading programs; but by approximately the age of ten, a number of studies show that boys have caught up in their reading skills. Throughout the school years, girls do better on tests of grammar, spelling, and word fluency. [Maccoby 1966, p. 26]

Competing explanations for such differences give varying weight to social and biological factors, and after puberty men's and women's voices are distinguished by pitch (the male larynx tends to be larger and the vocal cords tend to be longer and thicker). But before puberty, children in English-speaking America are likely to develop sex-linked language styles. In general, boys' voices are likely to be more nasal and girls' more oral; children imitate adults and mimic the tendency for men "to talk as though they were bigger and women as though they were smaller than they actually may be" (Sachs, Lieberman, and Erickson 1973, p. 75). In middle-class American homes, vulgarity and boisterous language may be tolerated in boys but stigmatized in girls. As Mary Ritchie Key notes, " 'masculinity' and 'femininity' are behavioral constructs which are powerful regulators of human affairs" (1975, p. 22). Children of both sexes are conditioned to define their speech in terms of differing social roles (listener versus hearer), modes of speech (quiet versus rowdy), and subjects (ladylike versus gentlemanly).

Feminist leaders over the past decade have identified sex-linked language differences and spurred important changes in American written English. Persons who reject *Ms.* as a generic female title have nonetheless been obliged to recognize that the contrast of *Miss* and *Mrs.* implies that marital eligibility is somehow more important in mentioning women than it is in referring to men. As a result, newspapers and magazines now use surnames without prefixed titles for a wide spectrum of reporting (though earlier there was a tendency to use surnames for women of low status or those convicted of serious crimes—"Wragg is dead"). The same trends have speeded the decline of the so-called generic *he/him* and hastened the spread of *they/them*, despite the supposed illogicality of matching plural pronouns with such "singulars" as *everyone* or *anyone*. Other changes involve the revision of job titles that imply that only men are employed: *foreman* is being replaced by *supervisor*, *postman* by *mail carrier* or *carrier*, *fireman* by *firefighter*, and *workman's compensation* by *worker's compensation*. Since written usage is regulated by a relatively small number of people, these changes have taken place quite rapidly as the result of political pressures from the women's movement.

A variety of scholars have claimed that men and women differ in their use of American English. Robin Lakoff (1975), for instance, has asserted that women use certain expletives not used by men (e.g., *oh fudge*, *dear me*), select some adjectives that men seldom use (e.g., *adorable*, *charming*, *sweet*, *lovely*, *divine*), make greater use of tag-questions and rising intonation in assertions (*the president vetoed the bill, didn't he?*), and employ the intensifier *so* more often than men (e.g., *That sunset is so beautiful!*). All of these usages convey the impression that "ladylike" English is the language of the subservient, the powerless, and the irrelevant. Such empirical studies as have been done, however, do not sufficiently distinguish the variables of gender and power. As Susan Ervin-Tripp has pointed out, "it is a necessary control to include in these studies comparisons within sex that contrast differences in power. It would be quite awkward to a theory that tag questions represent hedging and fear if, in fact, male bootlickers do not use such forms, nor do women addressing more powerful women" (1976, p. 9).

As more research is conducted, the complexity of sex-linked language differences becomes more and more apparent. Though the evidence is not clear-cut, men and women appear to play quite different roles in advancing or retarding linguistic change. In Britain and the United States, women tend to be more aware of standard usages and to correct their speech toward the perceived standard. In words like *talking*, *working*, and *learning*, middle-class women in Detroit used [n] for [ŋ] 15.3 percent of the time; men from the same class used [n] in such words in 63.8 percent of the possible occurrences. Social class constitutes a major variable in the proportion of such "nonstandard" usages, but sex differences are regularly apparent within each class. In the use of multiple negation (e.g., *I don't have none*), the same Detroit survey (Shuy, Wolfram, and Riley 1967) revealed important differences in the use of nonstandard negative constructions:

	Lower Middle Class	Lower Working Class
Women	1%	59%
Men	32	90

Such different patterns of usage illustrate how sex roles act as "powerful regulators of human affairs."

A strong strain of prescriptivism has long pervaded the American educational system and influences the linguistic education of American children. Charles C. Fries's comment of 1940 still holds true:

> English maintains its place as the most frequently *required subject* of our schools and college curriculums because of the unanimous support given it both by the general public and by education authorities. This support rests upon the general belief that the mastery of *good English* is not only the most important asset of the ambitious, but also an obligation of every good citizen. There is, however, in many quarters, a very hazy idea of the specific elements which make *good English*. A great deal of vigorous controversy ignores all the larger problems of effective communication and centers attention upon the criteria to be applied in judging the acceptability of particular words and language forms. [Fries 1940, p. 1]

"Effective communication" is measured very differently in schools and in the world outside schools. Attention to a few unsystematic rules of "usage" in the classroom often conveys the idea that there is a body of arcane lore that governs good English, and many otherwise confident adults fear that they violate linguistic conventions and lapse into unwitting error. But despite these insecurities, Americans persist in using the language of power and solidarity within their communities. The workplace provides a technical jargon, while family and social relations support the continuity of regional and social varieties of English. Though it is commonplace for Americans to assume that national broadcasting or widespread literacy have reduced the disparities among dialects, there is little evidence to suggest any such levelling effect. It is true, of course, that the number of features distinguishing the subvarieties of American English is small relative to the variation of English as a world language; nonetheless, the social meaning that attaches to the varieties provides powerful support for the sex, class, racial, ethnic, and regional divisions in American society.

A few generalizations may introduce the more specific consideration of some of the distinctive ethnic varieties of English. In general, English in the United States is most uniform in the domain of syntax and most variable in pronunciation. Southern and South Midland features tend to lack prestige outside their locales, but in certain domains (e.g., in broadcasts on citizen's band radios) they are recognized as worthy of imitation by outsiders. Northeastern speech patterns, as exhibited by Presidents Roosevelt and Kennedy, are often associated with prestige and power, though outsiders seldom attempt to mimic them. Inland Northern varieties are regarded as generally attractive, and national broadcasters tend to adjust their regional or social dialect to include some of the pronunciations of that region.

Stylistic variation, class membership, and regional origin often affect the same features of English, making any generalization about usage quite complex. The following features are likely to enter into speech that is regarded as more informal, more typical of speakers with limited education and low status, and more "dialectal" (i.e., typical of the Eastern Seaboard or South and Southeast).[3]

Phonology
The merger of [ɪ] and [ɛ] before nasal consonants, rendering *pin* and *pen* homophones [pɪn], is becoming increasingly common throughout the United States. It is least common in the North and Northeast where it is stigmatized and associated with southern migrants to the area.

Deletion or reduction of weakly stressed syllables has a long history in English (e.g., *'lectricity* for *electricity*, *fence* from *defense*, *daisy* from *day's-eye*) but the extension of this process is sometimes stigmatized: ['terəz] *potatoes*, ['ʃoəns] *insurance*.

Various processes affect the realization of [θ] and [ð]. *Toity-toid Street* 'Thirty-third Street' is a stock phrase used by New Yorkers to mimic the stigmatized speech of their city, and in that region the place of articulation remains the same (i.e., the consonants are dentals) but the manner has been shifted from fricative to stop. In *bathe* and *bath*, however, other varieties have moved the place of articulation to a labial while retaining the fricative quality. In general, shift in either place or manner of articulating [θ] and [ð] is regarded as informal or nonstandard.

Many words that in Early Modern English were stressed on their second syllable are now pronounced with first-syllable stress: *character*, *illustrate*, *concentrate*, and *reconcile*. Varieties of American English that have added to the inventory of fronted-stress words are, however, likely to be stigmatized: ['hotɛl] 'hotel,' ['sigar] 'cigar,' ['ditrɔɪt] *Detroit*.

Morphology
Phonological processes that affect inflections are generally treated as serious departures from "standard" English. Among the features particularly stigmatized are deletions of the plural and possessive markers (e.g., *I see two book there; that's John book*), of the inflection for third-person singular present tense (*he walk to school every day*), and of the [t] and [d] used to form the past tense of weak verbs (*she burn herself yesterday*).

Various modifications of the pronoun and demonstrative system are also stigmatized: *they hurt theirselves; she was with them girls yesterday*.

Verb morphology is variable according to region and social class. Some varieties retain archaic (or archaic-sounding) past tense forms and past participles: *driv* for *drove*, *drug* for *dragged*, *bit* for *bitten*, *friz* or *froze* for *frozen*. Others employ weak inflections where standard varieties retain strong forms: *catched* for *caught*, *throwed* for *threw* or *thrown*, *stoled* for *stole* or *stolen*.

A few common irregular verbs may be subject to restructuring in nonstandard varieties: *do* (*he done it but he shouldn't have did it*); *be* (*John and me was gonna go there; Alice ain't home now*); *go* (*we would have went there if we'd had the time*).

Syntax

Multiple negation is often stigmatized, and most attention is given to constructions involving indefinites: *I don't have no money* versus *I don't have any money*. Some forms of multiple negation are common in standard varieties (e.g., *The consultant was not unhelpful in reviewing the project*), and others are subject to only mild social pressure (e.g., *she couldn't hardly finish the job*).

The formation of indirect questions varies in structure, but the distinction in types only occasionally rises to social consciousness: *she asked him did he do it; she asked him whether he did it; she asked him if he did it*.

Selection in the pronoun system enters into distinguishing standard and nonstandard speech. *Joe and me are going* is somewhat more stigmatized than *Me and Joe are going,* probably because of the increased distance between the pronoun and the verb that governs its selection. Similarly, *Alex gave the money to she and Alice* is more likely to be stigmatized than *Alex gave the money to Alice and she* because of the increased distance between *to* and *she*. In general, the personal pronouns used in the nominative case tend to have a more positive social meaning than those in the accusative case, resulting in generalization of *I*, *she*, *he*, and *we* to positions in verbal or prepositional objects.[4]

Such examples do not exhaust the range of features that enter into the perception of "standard" and "nonstandard" speech, but they do indicate the kind and nature of variants that have social meaning. Other variables, such as the merger of *cot* and *caught* or the incidence of *r* after vowels, present a more complex picture. As Cassidy notes in the preceding essay, these variables do enter into the distribution of regional and social dialects of American English, but they do not generally have a well-defined social value that enhances or diminishes the perceived status of those who do (or do not) use them in their speech.

In general, an integrated community will speak an integrated language—one that does not greatly vary in pronunciation, morphology, or syntax. But in a society of separate communities where interaction across social or regional boundaries is rare, linguistic separatism will emerge and remain. To illustrate this point in American society, we will examine in turn some of the well-defined subcommunities of our nation and illustrate the varieties of English characteristics of each: Native Americans, Hispanics, blacks, and Appalachian whites.

The English of Native Americans

Native Americans form a relatively small and widely diverse ethnic minority; in the 1970 census, some 800,000 identified themselves as "Native American Indians" and claimed membership in eighty-four tribal groups (though fully one-fifth did not specify any tribe). Only about one-quarter of the total live east of the Mississippi River, and of this number most are urban dwellers. In the West, there are major concentrations of Native Americans in Arizona (96,000), California (91,000), Oklahoma (98,000), and New Mexico (73,000). Until recently, this diffuse group lacked a common political voice and was largely ignored in present-day national life, though western fiction and films have promoted a romantic past in which Native Americans play a prominent role. About one-quarter of Native Americans live on reservations and maintain their independent languages and cultures. Some, such as the Navajo and Hopi, live on their traditional lands; others were forcibly removed during the "reservation period" of American history (1867–87) and relocated far from their homelands. Oklahoma, formerly designated as "Indian Territory," is the center for widely diverse groups: the "Five Civilized Tribes" (the Cherokee, Chickasaw, Choctaw, Creek, and Seminole) of the Southeast, the Comanche of Wyoming and Nebraska, the Wichita of Kansas, and the Potawatomi of Michigan.

When Europeans first came to the New World, they encountered hundreds of separate Amerindian languages far more diverse in structure than the languages of Europe. Since the Europeans offered a desirable material culture in axes, firearms, and other hardware and claimed dominion over Native American lands, it was natural that Native Americans were obliged to learn French, English, or Spanish to negotiate with the newcomers. From the earliest times, Native Americans became bilinguals, and today those who maintain their languages are commonly bilingual, with widely varying proficiency, in English or Spanish. English was receptive to loans from Amerindian sources, particularly in the names of animals, plants, and objects unknown in Europe. While some of these words are now obsolete, dozens continue in common use (e.g., *chipmunk*, *moose*, *pecan*, *squash*, and *woodchuck*). Many loans were adapted through shortening and phonetic approximation; others were borrowed into English from other European languages (for instance, *toboggan* from Micmac through French and *chocolate* from Nahuatl through Spanish). Loan translations also entered English: *warpath*, *paleface*, *firewater*, and *peace pipe* are typical examples. Since early settlers came to associate "falseness" with the term *Indian* itself, some compounds still in use preserve this connotation (for example, *Indian summer* 'a mild season in late autumn', *Indian giver* 'one who gives something and then takes it back'). But the asymmetry of relations between the two cultures necessarily resulted in relatively few borrowings into English; English invaded the Native American languages and, where their speakers survived, English structure and vocabulary overwhelmed most Amerindian languages and drove them to extinction.

Relatively early in the contact between the two cultures, a pidgin language apparently developed based almost entirely on English elements. Early records of settlement and traveler's reports suggest some of the features of this variety of English: *Umh, umh poo Ingismon, mee save yow Life, mee take yow to Captain*

Mosee and *he be ver strong Man for he die* are typical examples from such sources.[5] With the development of popular fiction in which Native Americans figure as characters, a literary convention arose in which a variety of this pidgin was widely used. Doubtless the literary dialect contains more fiction than fact, but it provides the basis for many of the stereotypes associated with Native Americans by members of the mainstream American culture (see Miller 1967).

In present-day society, most Native Americans in the eastern United States have little command of their ancestral languages, and their English is usually not distinct from other Americans of like social class, age, sex, and occupation. In the West, however, social isolation (whether in urban centers or on reservations) has helped to maintain Amerindian languages. "Indian English" varies from one linguistic group to another, but there are sufficient similarities to justify the belief held by Native Americans and outsiders alike that there is a pan-tribal variety of English that unites disparate peoples. Casual observation may support the assumption by teachers and others who view this English that it is merely nonstandard, and indeed its features are shared with other nonmainstream dialects described in this essay—word-final consonant-cluster reduction, some patterns of multiple negation, use of an uninflected *be*, and lack of subject-verb agreement, among other traits.[6] Close analysis, however, reveals that these processes function under different constraints in Indian English; they produce similar surface phenomena but are the products of different grammatical systems. In apparent failures of subject and verb concord, for instance, there may be a process influenced by the Amerindian language requiring both subject and verb to be marked in the same way; hence *some peoples comes in* and *this ritual take place in June*.

Since English has traditionally been the language of reservation education, community attitudes toward Indian English and standard English reflect a complex mixture of attitudes relating to self-identity, Indian ethnicity, and the demands of "American" life. Use of an Amerindian language is, of course, the essence of tribal identification, but when not all members of the community are equally fluent, Indian English may come to be a vehicle for group solidarity:

> Effective use of Indian English styles can receive positive validation in its own right. Speakers at the annual meetings of Indian interest groups are heard to employ it most convincingly as an attention-getting device, in their addresses to the assembled participants. Not infrequently, people who return home after several years away from the community are chided if their speech departs from the local Indian English norms. Too much standard expression can place you, as one pueblo Indian noted in a discussion of this point, "too deep in the apple orchard."[7] [Leap 1977, p. 13]

Such observations suggest that Indian English is emerging as a fully developed social dialect with favorable connotations in the group and as a distinctive trait of ethnic pride in contact with outsiders.

Hispanic American English

Considering that the 1970 census recorded some nine million Hispanic Americans, the scant attention paid to them and their varieties of English is remarkable. This neglect is a symptom of a more general reluctance of the monolingual majority to acknowledge the social and linguistic facts of the bilingual lives of a large minority of Americans. Anglophones often incorrectly assume that a Spanish accent marks only a Spanish speaker.

> The Southwest today includes many hundreds of thousands—perhaps millions—of people whose native language is a special variety of English with a Spanish sound to it. The curious thing about this Spanish accent is that it is often heard from people who have no ability to speak or understand Spanish, people who are monolingual as well as perfectly fluent in English. [Metcalf 1979, p. 1]

On a continuum from the Spanish-accented English of anglophones to the limited English of Spanish speakers there are a great many intermediate stages. Even persons who are fully fluent in both languages may show evidence of one of their languages in speaking the other, and diglossia or code-switching are commonplace in conversations within the Hispanic community. Further, there is considerable dialectal variety in the Spanish-influenced English spoken in the United States, ranging from the Chicano English of California, the Puertoriqueño English of the urban Northeast, and Cubano English of Florida to the varieties of "Tex-Mex" English spoken along the border with Mexico. All of these factors combine to present a complex pattern of language choice and language variation within the national Hispanic community (see Teschner et al. 1975).

The linguistic and social consequences of contact between Spanish- and English-speaking communities is well documented for the American Southwest. Map 1 shows the distribution of Hispanic population in Texas, a typical border state.[8] As a result of such population concentrations, Texas English has incorporated what Atwood termed a "lexicographical pilón" of borrowings from border varieties of Spanish; indeed, many of these borrowed terms have come to enjoy a more general currency through Western novels and films. The following selection gives the flavor of the social and cultural relations between Anglo-Americans and Hispano-Americans in the Southwest:

> *arroyo* 'creek or stream'
> *wrangler* < *caballerango* 'a ranch employee who takes care of the saddle horses', more broadly 'cowboy'
> *frijoles* 'cooked beans'
> *mott* < *mata* 'a clump of trees'
> *mesa* 'high, flat land'
> *olla* 'earthenware crock or pot'

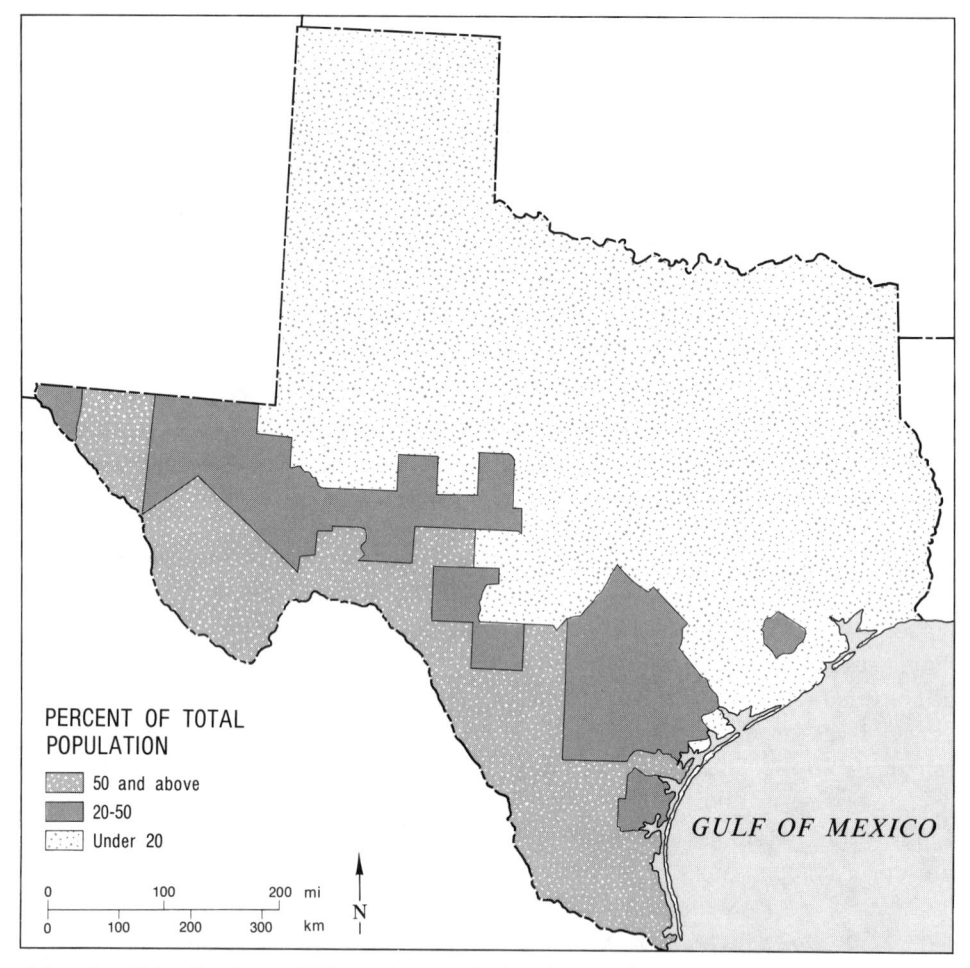

Map 1. Distribution of Hispanic population in Texas

> *pelado* 'Hispanic American', commonly used in Spanish with a derogatory meaning, implying that a person is ill-bred, unmannerly, or vulgar
> *pilón* 'something extra, a gift, lagniappe'
> *vaquero* 'cowboy'

When English speakers arrived in Texas, they needed words for aspects of the unfamiliar terrain and borrowed them from those who had already settled there. Spanish-American agricultural practices formed a model for the development of the western cattle industry. Ranching terms of Spanish origin describe ranch employees and the staple of their diet. The word *ranch* itself, which has come to embody the western approach to agriculture, has an interesting social history. Mexican Spanish *rancho* originally meant 'the place where ranch employees live', itself a development in the Americas of the European Spanish word meaning 'mess hall'.

The sociolinguistic aspects of bilingualism in one southwestern community are documented in Janet B. Sawyer's study of San Antonio, Texas. She studied the extent to which English and Spanish have influenced each other in an area where speakers run the gamut of the bilingual continuum and where a complex society includes both descendants of the original *colonial* Spanish populations and more recent *immigrants*:

> In a city like San Antonio, Spanish is the first language of almost half the population. It was spoken by the first permanent settlers brought by the colonial government from the Canary Islands. Spanish was still the language of the three Texas outposts when the first English-speaking settlers arrived in 1821. When the real flood of immigration began to fill the territory in 1865, over twenty-seven percent of the settlers were from Mexico, and since 1910 the volume of Mexican immigration has steadily increased.
>
> Unlike the typical immigrants who form a small cultural island cut off from their home culture, the Spanish speakers represent an extension of Mexican culture thrusting far north into Texas. Maintaining constant contact with their homeland, the people retain their Mexican peasant culture in the life of family, neighborhood, church, and even generally in their occupations; the American state government makes its only effort toward acculturation with the schools, handicapped by the fact that the Spanish-speaking community regards segregation for language training as a form of discrimination. [Sawyer 1971, p. 571; see also Sawyer 1973]

Sawyer studied fourteen second-generation, permanent residents of San Antonio: seven native speakers of English—*Anglos* in local usage—and seven "immigrant" *Latins*. Three of the seven Latinos she classified as *unilingual* because they usually spoke Spanish and because their English showed extensive interference from the linguistic structure of Spanish. Four *bilinguals* had substantial contact with the Anglo community and spoke English with ease.

The Anglo informants shared eleven (generally Southern and South Midland) phonological features:

1. Diphthongal [ɔᵘ] in *saw*, *fog*, and *bought*
2. [aⁱ] monophthongized to [a:]
3. Loss of postvocalic *r*
4. Palatalization following alveolars in *Tuesday*, *duty*, and *new* (e.g., ['tjuzde])
5. [ɨ] in the unstressed syllables of *Dallas*, *Texas*, and *haunted*
6. Fronting to [æ] of the first element of the [aᵘ] diphthong (e.g., [mæutn̩] *mountain*)
7. [ɔr] and [or] distinct in *horse* and *hoarse*, *forty* and *fourteen*
8. Merger of [ɪ] and [ɛ] before nasals (e.g., [pɪn] *pin*, *pen*)

9. [z] rather than [s] in *grease* and *greasy*
10. [u] rather than [ʊ] in *roots*
11. [ɒ] in *fog*, *hog*, and *frog*

Except for item 10, which coincides with the structure of Mexican Spanish in which there is no [ʊ], these regional features never occurred in the speech of unilingual speakers and were only beginning to become apparent in the bilingual speakers. Sawyer's findings thus suggest that the unilinguals, for whom Spanish was the primary language of home and family, did not acquire the local Anglo dialect but drew on models of English typical of other regions of the United States.

In the following excerpt from a work of fiction, we see an accurate reflection of unilingual speech (and its social consequences) put into literary use. The dialogue is an "interview" between an Anglo police officer and an old Latino farm laborer:

"You José Amadda Contreras?"
The old fellow nodded. "Jou go' 'rest me?" he whispered.
Burns was inclined to whisper, too, but it seemed somehow beneath him, and he asked aloud, pointing to the other man:
"Who's that?"
"Este? mi amigo. Se llama Juan Dombraski."
Dombrowski. That was the one, all right. "He spik English, savvy?"
"Inglés, no. Nada, nada—not!" he emphasized.
"How about you? You spik English—"
"Lettla beet, no muncho [*sic*]."
"Listen. I'm standing out in the street. I hear a man say in English, 'Don't shoot, that's my son.' And something about a bad foot. It wasn't you?"
"Me? No, no. Me slip." He pantomimed sleep. "Him slip too." He made a snoring noise. "Puede ser otra casa," he suggested hopefully. . . .
"Jou lukin' for Ramón Arce, qué no? Ramón no here. Aw gone—psht!" He laughed with glee, skidding one palm off the other, to suggest how fast Arsy had skipped. "No ketch. Ramón go psht." [Lawrence 1954, pp. 249–50]

The author effectively communicates a sense of the old man's background and social position by means of his difficulties with English.

Tense and lax high vowels are merged and the realized vowel is a compromise between the two; i.e., [i] and [ɪ], [u] and [ʊ] are not distinct and are pronounced with a vowel that Anglos hear as the tense alternative. Consequently, in the sample text, we find *beet* for *bit*, *slip* for *sleep*, *luke* for *look*, and *spik* for *speak*.

The systems of consonant contrast in the two languages compete. Hispanic English alternates [ʃ] and [tʃ]; *church* can be heard as *shurch*, *chursh*, or *shursh* in Spanish-influenced English. Similarly, [j] and [ʤ] are not contrasted in many varieties of Spanish (*yolk* = *joke*); hence, *Jou* for *You* in the text. Interference is not, however, a one-way street. Anglos hear the Spanish bilabial fricative [β] as [v] and reproduce words like *sabe* 'you know' as *savvy*.

Spanish does not contain the English sounds [æ] and [ə], and both are usually realized as [ɑ] in Hispanic English; *tab* and *tub* are pronounced [tɑb].

Written English provides few resources for representing intonation contours, and the sample text is not obviously distinctive of Hispanic English in this respect. As Metcalf notes, however, "at the end of a declarative sentence, the pitch and loudness do not fall off as rapidly [in Spanish-influenced English] as in other dialects, sometimes giving an outsider the false impression that the speaker is unfinished, uncertain, or asking a question" (1979, p. 7). In real-life conversation, the police officer might well have been mollified by the half-fall intonation contour—with its English connotations of tentativeness and passivity—of the farm worker's declarative sentences.

The sample text successfully displays the social pressures which often confound Anglo-Latino communication. The old man responds (initially, with a full English sentence) in whispered terror, but immediately collects his wits, and realizes that it is not in his best interests to display full command of the language of the more powerful. He lapses into a simplified Spanish which he knows the Anglo is likely to understand but punctuates his Spanish with the English *not* when communication is essential. After he realizes that he is in no real danger, he confidently returns to an English style of communication.

It would be a mistake to assume that Hispanic English in any of its styles shows all of the traits characteristic of the "errors" of Spanish-speakers learning English. Despite the stereotypes of fiction and film, Hispanic English does not contain the use of *she* or *he* for inanimate objects as a carry-over from the gender system of Spanish nouns; it does not contain syntactic patterns that are word-for-word translations of Spanish structures (e.g., **Is round this?* 'is this round?', **Bill saw to Mary* 'Bill saw Mary'); multiple negation may be used but it follows the pattern of English rather than Spanish (i.e., *Sarah didn't talk to no one* occurs, but not *Sarah no talk to no one*). The distinctive features of Hispanic English generally involve matters of pronunciation and intonation, not vocabulary and syntax. As a variety of English, it serves the functions of social solidarity and supports cohesiveness in the community. To a considerable extent, its distinctive features are conventionalized and, increasingly, acquired by children whose main or only language is English.

Among many Hispanics, the language of social solidarity involves a mixture of Spanish and English in diglossia and rapid code-switching. While generally restricted to spoken language, a few such patterns of language mixture are becoming institutionalized, particularly in what the poet Miguel Algarín calls "Nuyorican" (a blend of *New York* and *Puerto Rican*):

>my NUYORICAN being
>my eagle knife caution
>filled mind reads your neon
>signs AQUÍ YOUR CREDITO ES GOOD
>and I feel sad that in school,
>we're forced to reach for standards
>do you know what I mean?
>standards like
>>STANDARD ENGLISH
>>STANDARD SPANISH
>
>but meanwhile your neon
>signs tell the real truth:
>you are bilingual Puerto Rico
>you are NUYORICAN on
>your own home soil,
>your schools scold me for illiteracy
>while your Cuban/American bankers
>sell me the island in spanglish
>
>>[Algarín 1975, p. 140]

The disparity between presumed standards and actual linguistic behavior continues to be a source of conflict within the Hispanic community and in relations between Hispanics and the Anglo culture.

The English of Black Americans

In the past fifteen years, black Americans have asserted their just claims to full participation in American society—in education, in employment in a wider range of jobs in both public and private sectors, and in all of the domains of social and economic life. As they organized and asserted political power, blacks became the subject of intense study by social scientists, and if some myths about black life have been debunked (or replaced by other myths), it is also true that a great deal of substantial information has been accumulated about the separate and still unequal cultures that divide America along racial lines. Black English has gone from being neglected and understudied (as Hispanic English now is) to being the single most fully studied of the varieties of American English. The recent impetus in research has been fired by a changing social climate in the United States, by the innovations of William Labov's approach to language analysis, and by the still smoldering debates about the origins of Black English and its place in the American speech continuum. In 1967, William A. Stewart proposed that linguists study black speech not from a perspective of similarity to southern white speech but from a perspective of difference, and he hypothesized that Black English emerges from

> a variety of English which was in fact a true creole language—differing markedly in grammatical structure from those English dialects which were brought directly from Great Britain, as well as from New World modifications of these in the mouths of descendants of the original white colonists. [Stewart 1972, p. 96]

In support of Stewart's claim, Rickford has argued that the weight of linguistic evidence makes the case for "the prior creolization of B[lack] E[nglish] very likely indeed" (Rickford 1977, p. 215) and supports Wolfram's important and generally heeded plea that the collection and analysis of empirical data of black speech take precedence over speculations about origins (Wolfram 1971).

While Black English was first studied by field-workers in the southern states, recent major attention has focused on the speech of black communities in northern cities: Labov, Cohen, Robins, and Lewis (1968) in New York City, Wolfram (1969) in Detroit, and Fasold (1972) in Washington, D.C. Such studies acknowledge the major migration since 1940 as blacks left the rural South and moved to the urban North and West. As this movement has taken place, linguists have noted, Black English has changed as a consequence of contacts with other dialects and a shift from agrarian life to industrial employment in cities. Map 2 illustrates the direction and magnitude of the shift of black population.

Black English, like other varieties discussed here, is neither uniform nor invariable. Some black Americans make only occasional use of its features for stylistic effect; some whites in regular contact with black communities may command the full range of features and, when heard on tape, be consistently identified as black. Nonetheless, it is generally acknowledged that Black English is a coherent and fully developed language system widely used in the black community and recognized as distinctive by both blacks and whites. Though there is continuing dispute involving the name *Black English* itself—some competing labels are *Ebonics* and *Black English Vernacular* (*BEV*)—the dialect is acknowledged by all to exist even if there are profoundly differing evaluations of its importance and value in American life.

The lexicon of Black English consists mainly of words and phrases shared by other varieties of American English, though some have proposed fanciful etymologies that emphasize the contribution of African languages to black vocabulary. In his important study of Sea Island Creole (known to outsiders as Gullah), Turner found 251 words (other than names) of African origin. Most of these are unknown outside the Sea Islands of Georgia and South Carolina; a few of them, however, have spread to the English of both blacks and whites: *gumbo*, *guba* (*goober* 'peanut'), *juke* (as in *juke-joint, -box*), *kuta* (*cooter* 'turtle'), *wudu*

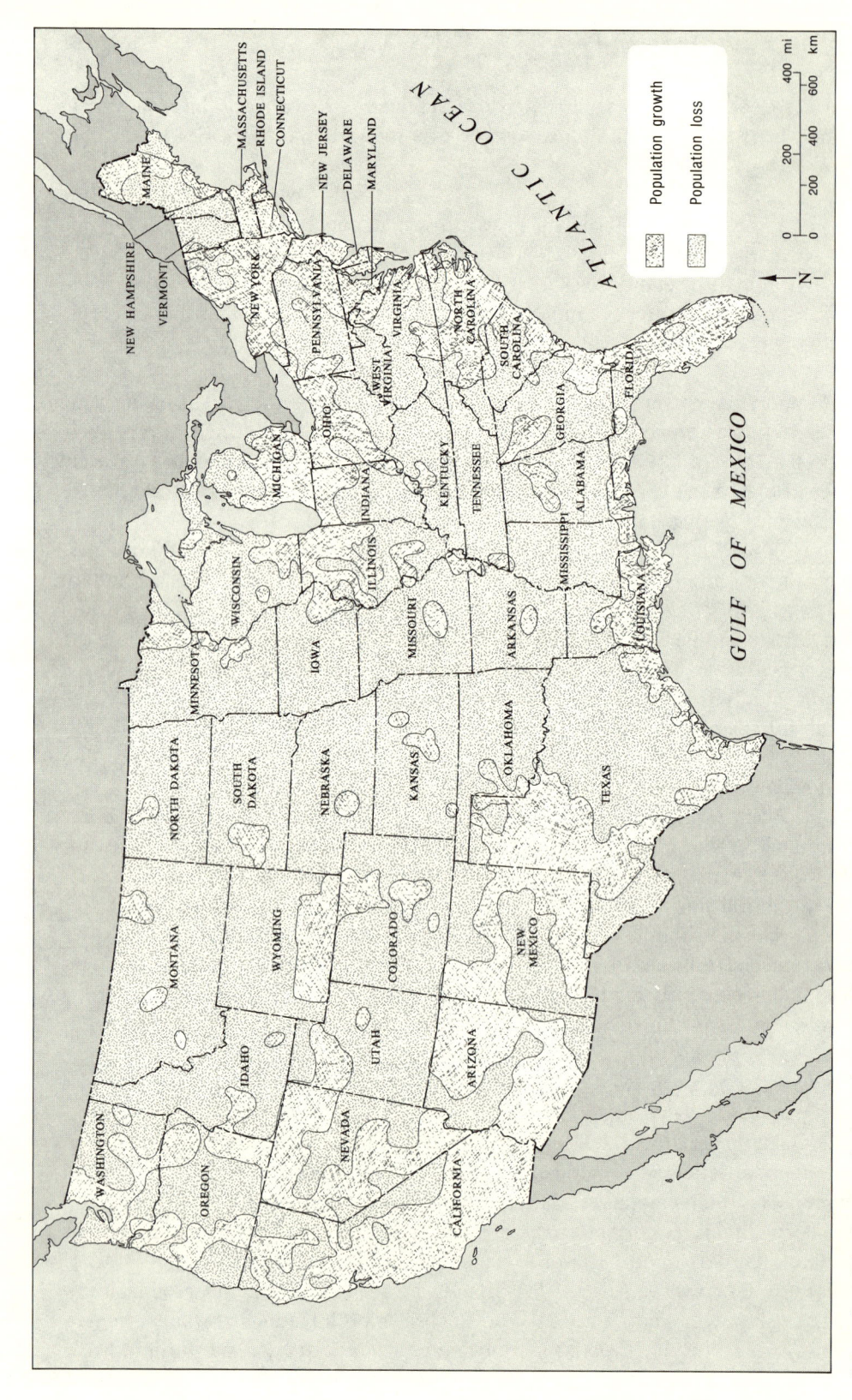

Map 2. Black population change, 1940–60. See Department of Interior 1970, p. 258.

(*voodoo*), and *yam*. Black richness in lexical innovation has especially influenced the language of those fields in which American society has encouraged black participation. The speech of black musicians is one notable area.

> The most original and revolutionary art form in North America . . . has been black music. And out of the life-styles of the people who make it comes the vernacular that has made possible certain functional concepts—such as *bad* meaning good; *hard* having a positive connotation; *kill* to mean: affect strongly, to fascinate; *love letter* to mean: a bullet; and *murder* to express approval of something excellent. [Major 1970, pp. 13–14]

Major's *Dictionary of Afro-American Slang* gives full treatment to these and other elements of the black lexicon.

While the full extent of black contributions to American English is only now being fully appreciated, it is also true that blacks participate in the variable features of English found in other communities, and patterns of borrowing and influence regularly cross racial lines. Nonetheless, many blacks participate in the features that will be identified here as Black English. As in other varieties, most of the distinctive qualities are found at the level of pronunciation.[9] Though the regional and social patterns of intonation have not been systematically studied in American English, contrastive investigations attest to the fact that blacks often use higher pitch levels (and a much wider range of pitch), more frequently approach a falsetto register for stylistic effect, and tend to use rising and level final contours more frequently (Wolfram and Fasold 1974, pp. 147–48). Since observations of the "musical" quality of black speech were reported quite early, it is fair to assume that these intonation characteristics arose as blacks developed their distinctive variety of English on American soil. Some have speculated that these features are survivals from the tone languages of West Africa, but whatever the historical explanation, blacks continue to exploit a broad range of pitches and make use of rising and level contours in distinctive ways. Blacks also participate in the tendency to shift word stress to initial syllables and to delete weakly stressed initial syllables as do other varieties of American English; informal observation, however, suggests that these features are likely to be categorical in Black English (i.e., stress-shifts and syllable restoration are less likely to occur as stylistic variants).

Black English follows the pattern of *r*-less American dialects in which postvocalic [r] is lost or replaced by [ə], as it usually is in the Northeastern and Southern pronunciation of such words as *farm*, *part*, and *park*. Postvocalic and word-final [r] deletion occurs, as it does in the South, before words beginning with a consonant and a vowel. In the North final [r] is retained before words beginning with a vowel. The Southern tendency is generalized in black speech so that mid-morpheme, intervocalic [r] is lost more frequently than in general Southern speech (italicized consonants are lost or vocalized):

New England: My father is here, but his brother Harold isn't.
Southern: My father is here, but his brother Harold isn't.
Black: My father is here, but his brother Harold isn't.[10]

In most dialects, *r*-loss is a matter of degree and is often limited to a few lexical items.

Like [r], the related liquid consonant [l] is frequently vocalized (becoming a vowel off-glide) and is often deleted postvocalically in American English dialects. The phenomenon can be viewed as a continuation of the historical process which produced the *l*-less pronunciations of such words as *walk* and *talk*. Because of the influence of spelling, an *l* is being reintroduced for many Americans into a large subsegment of the lexicon—e.g., *calm*, *palm*, and *balm*. In his fieldwork, Labov has observed:

> The loss of *l* is much more marked among the black speakers we have interviewed than among whites in northern cities, and one therefore finds much greater tendencies toward such homonyms as
>
> *toll* = *toe*   *all* = *awe*
> *help* = *hep*   *Saul* = *saw*
> *tool* = *too*   *fault* = *fought*
> [Labov 1973, p. 246]

A process widely common in the languages of the world is the weakening of final consonants, especially stops. In most varieties of American English, final voiceless stops are realized phonetically as glottal stop plus the voiceless stop: *Mack*, *map*, and *mat* are pronounced [mæʔk], [mæʔp], and [mæʔt]. Some speakers sometimes pronounce *mat* as [mæʔ], and one hears young speakers from all social classes occasionally apply the same process to the final [p] and [k]. For them *Mack*, *map*, and *mat* are all pronounced [mæʔ]. That tendency is even commoner in black speech and may extend to the loss of glottal stricture. Since the voiced stops [d], [b], and [g] are frequently devoiced finally in black speech and can then undergo further reduction, Labov reports the following as possible homonyms:

boot = *boo*   *seat* = *seed* = *see*
road = *row*   *poor* = *poke* = *pope*
feed = *fee*   *bit* = *bid* = *big*

Stop consonants are regularly deleted from word-final consonant clusters under certain predictable (yet variable) conditions. The first and invariant condition is that the stop agree in voicing with the segment which precedes it; both must be either voiced or voiceless. The phonetic condition which governs the *degree* to which deletion occurs is whether the first segment of the next word is a

Contemporary American English

consonant or a vowel. As in the case of [r] and [l] deletion, consonants favor deletion and vowels hinder it. There is a further nonphonetic constraint which also affects the degree to which reduction occurs. Consonant clusters ending in *t* or *d* can be inherent in the morpheme (as in [mɪst] *mist*); or they can be the result of past tense formation, and the consonant cluster is formed across a morpheme boundary (as in [mɪst] *missed*). Because of a regularity in English morphophonology, the past tense or past participle marker always agrees in voicing with the segment which immediately precedes it. Wolfram and Christian (1976, p. 34) offer the following compilation of clusters and illustrative examples.

Phonetic Cluster	Type I	Type II
[st]	*text, post, list*	*missed, messed, dressed*
[sp]	*wasp, clasp, grasp*	
[sk]	*desk, risk, mask*	
[ʃt]		*finished, lashed, cashed*
[zd]		*raised, composed, amazed*
[ʤd]		*judged, charged, forged*
[ft]	*left, craft, cleft*	*laughed, stuffed, roughed*
[vd]		*loved, lived, moved*
[nd]	*mind, find, mound*	*rained, fanned, canned*
[md]		*named, foamed, rammed*
[ld]	*cold, wild, old*	*called, smelled, killed*
[pt]	*apt, adept, inept*	*mapped, stopped, clapped*
[kt]	*act, contact, expect*	*looked, cooked, cracked*

Such deletions are not categorical but are a matter of degree. They can be quantified and a frequency level can be determined; the phenomenon is highly regular and, with close study, one can predict the degree of deletion which is to be expected within a given community. Not only is the linguistic variation predictable, but the extent of deletion can be correlated with social class, age, and sex. The following data for the frequency of deletion are taken from Wolfram's study of black speech in Detroit.

Environment	Upper Middle	Lower Middle	Upper Working	Lower Working
Following vowel Final member is *-ed*	7%	13%	24%	34%
Following vowel Final member is not *-ed*	28	43	65	72
Following consonant Final member is *-ed*	49	62	73	76
Following consonant Final member is not *-ed*	79	87	94	97

(Social Class)

These data clearly demonstrate the extent to which social class can influence even subconscious linguistic variation, making the variation linguistically *and* socially significant. Without knowing we do it, we define our group memberships by learning such patterns. The behavior is highly regular even across social class: phonetic environment is always a stronger influence than the grammatical category of the morpheme. More importantly, the rate of deletion parallels social stratification; the higher one's social class, the less one deletes *t* and *d*. Notice the similarities when the above data are compared with northern urban white speakers.

Environment	Middle Class White Detroit	Working Class White New York City Adolescents
-ed, vowel following	3%	3%
Inherent, vowel following	12	19
-ed, consonant following	36	23
Inherent, consonant following	66	67

In both the Northern and Southern contexts, blacks delete in every environment at a higher rate than whites. In both cases, black and white speech form a regional whole, rather than black speech following one pattern in both regions against a white pattern seen in both regions.

The consonant cluster [ks], usually spelled *x* in English, is regularly reduced to [k] in black speech, so that *six* is pronounced the same as *sick*, *Max* as *Mack*, and *box* as *bock*. There is a related reduction involving the pluralizing morpheme, the possessive morpheme, and the third-person present tense morpheme. Since each of these three morphemes undergoes different patterns of deletion and because the deletion is independent of the following phonetic environment, the process is best viewed as governed by grammatical rather than phonological factors. The plural morpheme, predictably [s] or [z] according to the voicing of the immediately preceding segment, is deleted at a maximum rate of about 10 percent of the time. Reduction is favored by the presence of a quantifier—that is, when the plural marker is redundant information: *I see four book*. There is an interesting apparent irregularity in black plural formation. We find [ɪz] suffixed on such stems as *test*, *desk*, *wasp*, and similar words. These words, which undergo loss of the final stop, are analyzed as ending in sibilants and are treated as such according to the pattern of American English by adding [ɪz]—['tɛsɪz], ['dɛsɪz], and ['wɑsɪz] for *tests*, *desks*, and *wasps*. Deletion of the possessive marker is common since possession is unambiguously marked by word order: *that's the man hat*. Categorical reduction is rare, although it has been reported for some Southern black speakers. Loss of the verb inflection is frequent for most speakers of Black English and categorical for some. Labov found the following facts of *s*-deletion before consonants in New York City black adolescents: plural—8 percent, possessive—58 percent, present tense—67 percent (Labov, Cohen, Robins, and Lewis 1968, p. 249). It is clear from this sketch of [s] and [z] deletion, however, that it exhibits none of the highly structured and phonologically based statistical regularity of *t/d* loss.

The dental fricatives [θ] and [ð] are variously altered in black speech, as they are in many American varieties (and in the speech of young children). When they occur initially, they are realized as the voiceless and voiced stops—[t] and [d]—so that *den* = *then* and *thigh* = *tie*. The initial [θr] cluster is frequently heard as [fr], yielding *three* = *free*. A similar process affects what is [θ] and [ð] in white speech intervocalically and finally after vowels. *Brother* can be pronounced ['brʌvər] in black speech; *either* is ['ifər] and *Ruth* and *tooth* are [ruf] and [tuf]. In the proximity of nasals, [θ] becomes the corresponding stop [t]: [tɛnt] for *tenth*, ['rɪtmɑtɪk] for *arithmetic*. Of course, final [t] can be deleted altogether.

The black treatment of nasals is also an extension of processes evident in some varieties (particularly Southern) of American speech. The -*ing* suffix, a stylistic variation in most American colloquial styles, is regularly pronounced as [ɪn]. While this feature has traditionally been described as "dropping the *g*," the process actually involves the substitution of the alveolar nasal for the velar nasal. It is interesting to observe that this feature was once a socially prestigious one (and continues to be in some varieties), and as such is found represented in the speech of Dorothy Sayers's Lord Peter Wimsey.[11] Further, nasals often receive no oral closure in black speech. The preceding vowel is nasalized, but the nasal consonant itself is not formed. Consequently, *dumb*, *dun*, and *dung* are all pronounced [dʌ̃].

Several vowel developments are characteristic of Black English. All are present in other varieties of American English but are found more frequently or have been generalized to include new environments in black speech. The merger of [ɪ] and [ɛ] before nasals—*pin* = *pen*, *bin* = *Ben*, and the like—is general among black speakers, and in parallel fashion [i] and [eɪ] merge before [r] and [l]: *beer* = *bear*, *cheer* = *chair*, *steer* = *stair*, *peel* = *pail*. Likewise [u] and [o] merge before [r] in Black English and in many other American varieties: *poor* = *pour*, *sure* = *shore*, *moor* = *more*. Most black speakers participate in an urban tensing of [æ] after which an inglide develops: *mad* [mæəd] and *bad* [bæəd]. The vowel nucleus is often concomitantly raised to [ɛ], [e], [ɪ], and sometimes even [i]. Black English also reflects the Southern tendency to realize [ɔ¹] before [l] (e.g., *boiled*, *spoiled*, *oil*) as an upgliding diphthong: [oə]. Those who do not participate in this process, including some blacks in the North, believe that *oil* and *all* rhyme in these dialects, though many speakers of Black English (like many Southerners) contrast the two diphthongs through the degree of roundedness of the vowel nucleus. Before voiceless consonants, [aɪ] is often monophthongized—in [fa:t] 'fight' or [na:s wa:f] *nice wife*; this process extends the general Southern tendency to reduce this diphthong before voiced segments—[də'fa:d] *defied*. Similarly, blacks monophthongize the [aʊ] diphthong to a low central vowel, whereas most

Southern varieties alter this diphthong by fronting or centralizing the first element. Even though vowel contrasts many be retained, the shift of points of articulation may lead outsiders—especially Northerners—to imagine that blacks and Southerners have merged such sets as *rat*, *right*, and *riot*. Hence Labov (1973, p. 249) has identified the following homophones in Black English as heard by Northern whites:

> *find = found = fond* *boil = ball*
> *time = Tom* *oil = all*

Discussion of homophony in Black English would be purely academic except that these facts have wide ranging social significance. Black children are often subjected to tests supposedly designed to determine whether or not the child can hear certain contrasts. Pairs of similar sounding words are read to test whether the child can hear a difference. Of course, some pairs of words like *pin-pen*, *sheaf-sheath* and *clothe-clove* (actual examples from the Wepman Auditory Discrimination Test) may be different for the tester but are not different for a speaker of Black English. The black child does not need a speech therapist, the usual prescription, but a school system which takes into account the facts of normal language variation.

The following speech sample is a transcription of an interview with a black woman born in slavery (1852). For ease of reading, it is offered in a modified, standard spelling which reflects pronunciation variants; *ta*, *de*, *dem*, and *wid* are "pronunciation spellings" of [tə], [deɪ], [dɛm], and [wɪd] for *to*, *they*, *them*, and *with*. Deleted or vocalized sounds—*r*, *l*, *t*, and *d*—are italicized. Through the drama of her understated style and ease, "Sweet Ma" Perry gives us a glimpse of the nature of linguistic and social interaction between blacks and whites in the slave South:

> Well, my fathe*r* belonged to chu*r*ch, understan*d*. Luke Lancaste*r* hired my, uh, Robe*r*tson to go ta the wa*r* for him. And put my daddy to watch ove*r* his wife, 'til the wa*r* ended. Afte*r* the wa*r* ended, understan*d*, t'was the trouble. I got a half-white brothe*r*. You understan*d* me? By a whi*t*e 'oman! I watch he*r*. He done mighty well. But a*ll* de colo*r*ed folks, I tell you, had ta do what the white folks said ta do—didn't ca*r*e what dat was. An*d* do like dey say. But afte*r* while da wa*r* come. When, when, when, Robe*r*tson come back, understan*d*, my fathe*r* continued to stay aroun*d* the Bud Robe*r*tson's plantation. My mothe*r* was belongin' to Tom Harris. Margaret Ha*rr*is is my mothe*r*, understan*d*, and she was Mary Harris— Tom Ha*rr*is' wife was her aunt. Tom Ha*rr*is' wife mothe*r* was my mammy's grandmothe*r*. Took away from he*r* mother whe*r*e she was bo*r*n—in de house and raised he*r* wid de white folks and didn't let he*r* stay wid nigge*r*s. They was rich folks, you see. Didn't let 'em stay.

[What happened when he went to war?]

Well, you know, the baby come! I*'ve* got a brothe*r*—I*'ve* got de brothe*r*, uh, Sidney Robe*rt*son. My brothe*r*, Sidney Robe*rt*son, he's down he*r*e at Littleton No*r*th Ca*r*olina, my brothe*r* Sidney Robe*rt*son, he came an*d* so, uh, she uh, he*r* husban*d* tol*d* he*r* dat she—if she got rid of the child she could stay. She gave my fathe*r* the child. My fathe*r* got a lady to take the child and take ca*r*e of it—an*d* raised 'im.¹²

Such a narrative makes clear why Black English shares so many of the patterns of Southern speech. Black Americans first spoke English in the South. That is, blacks and whites were members of the same speech community—a community far more complicated than the stereotyped view of the master-slave relationship usually admits. The text further attests a historical continuity in the processes of Black English phonology (the intervocalic loss of *r* in *Harris*, for example) and demonstrates the variable nature of [r], [l], [t], and [d] deletion.

The morphological structure of Black English is greatly influenced by the phonological processes described above. The verb paradigm is most strongly affected. For most speakers the following is a possible, though variable, paradigm for both the simple present and past:

I talk   *we talk*
you talk   *you talk*
he/she/it talk *they talk*

Deletion of the third-person present indicative marker in some styles may result in a generalized insertion of *s* throughout the paradigm in more formal styles: *I, you* (singular), *we, you* (plural), and *they talks*. The hypercorrected *s* is even extended to nonfinite forms—*he want to talks all the time*. Because of the consistent loss of postvocalic *l*, the contracted forms of the paraphrastic future and conditional can be reduced and become homophonous with the reduced past and present forms:

I'll talk = I'd talk = I talk
you'll talk = you'd talk = you talk
he'll talk = he'd talk = he talk

Gonna ['gɔ:nə] has become a frequent marker for future in black speech, as in *I gonna talk*. The contracted forms of the present perfect auxiliary, *have* and *has*, are also amenable to further reduction. *I've talked three hours* becomes *I talk three hours*, which could also mean *I talked three hours* or *I* (habitually) *talk three hours*. The merger of this contrast is, however, balanced by a greater use of the past perfect construction in narratives by Black English speakers, so *I had talked three hours* carries the perfective meaning in contrast with the imperfect *I talk three hours* (Fasold and Wolfram 1972, p. 69).

Like Southern nonstandard varieties, black speech has a completive aspect not found in standard speech; *I done talked myself tired* emphasizes the completedness of the activity. A remote time aspect is peculiar to black speech. *I been talked myself tired to that old man* communicates the added information that the action had taken place a long time ago. Both the completive and remote aspect constructions are rare in Northern black speech and appear to be disappearing everywhere.

Through the convergence of phonological, morphological, and syntactic factors, the verb *be* has radically different forms and functions in Black English. To begin with, Black English shares with other nonstandard varieties a strong tendency to regularize this most irregular paradigm of English. For many speakers, especially children and rural Southern blacks, *is*, *was*, and the negative *ain't* are used for all persons and numbers (Wolfram and Fasold 1974, p. 157). A second feature of Black English, the regular deletion of the copula, makes data collection on forms of *be* difficult. Labov has shown *be* deletion to exemplify what he has termed *inherent variability*—deletion is present in all speakers but categorical in none. He presents the following examples of the syntactic environments in which *be* is regularly lost:

> Before a noun phrase:
> *She the first one started us off.*
> *Means he a faggot or sump'm like that.*
> Before a predicate adjective:
> *He fast in everything he do.*
> *I know, but he wild, though.*
> Before a locative:
> *You out the game.*
> *We on tape.*
> Before a negative:
> *But everybody not black.*
> *They not caught.*
> Before Verb-*ing* forms:
> *He just feel like he gettin' cripple up from arthritis.*
> *Boot always comin' over my house to eat, to ax for food.*
> Before the "gonna" future:
> *He gon' try to get up.*
> *'Cause we, we gon' sneak under the turnstile.*
> [Labov 1972a, pp. 67–68]

On the other hand, forms of *be* are usually present in the following contexts:

In the past tense constructions:
> *I was small; I was sump'm about one years o'baby.*
> *She was likin' me . . . she was likin' George too.*

In *ain't* constructions:
> *It ain't no cat can't get in no coop.*
> *My sons, they ain't but so big.*

In first-person singular constructions:
> *I'm tired, Jeannette.*
> *I'm not no strong drinker.*

In the reduced forms *I's*, *tha's*, and *wha's* (from *it's*, *that's* and *what's*):
> *I's a real light yellow color.*
> *Tha's my daily routine: women.*
> *Wha's a virgin?*

In nonfinite forms:
> *You got to be good, Rednall!*
> *His wife is suppos' a be gettin' money for this child.*

In imperative constructions:
> *Be cool, brothers!*
> *Don't be messin' with my old lady!*

With emphasis:
> *Allah is God.*
> *He is a expert.*

In yes/no questions:
> *Is he dead? Is he dead?—Count the bullet holes in his motherfucking head.*
> *Are you down?*

In tag questions:
> *Is that a shock? or is it not?*

In clause final positions:
> *(You ain't the best sounder, Eddie!) I ain't! He is!*

After ellipsis in comparative constructions:
> *He is better than the girls is, now.*
> *It always somebody tougher than you are.*

In embedded questions with WH-attraction:
> *That's what he is: a brother.*
> *I don't care what you are.*

[Labov 1972a, pp. 70-72]

These examples show that deletion of forms of the verb *be* are subject to different kinds of linguistic factors. Phonological processes constitute one form of constraint; loss of final [z] and [r] would be predicted from Black English phonology, but final [m] would not be lost. Not all instances of [z] and [r] are deleted (as in *he is* and *I don't care what you are* above). It is interesting to note that Black English does not delete in just those cases in which contraction is impossible for speakers of mainstream varieties (**yes, he's* and **I don't care who you're* are impossible constructions in both varieties). The quantitative analysis of *is* and *are* deletion yielded the following results. *Are* is lost twice as frequently as *is* in the speech of black youth in New York City (Labov 1972a, p. 52): *is*, 40–50 percent; *are*, 75–90 percent. But *is*-deletion is not governed by linguistic variables alone:

> As we move from single, face-to-face interviews to spontaneous group sessions, we find that the percentage of all forms generally increases. The feature which is correlated with style shift from single to group sessions is the ratio of deleted to originally contracted forms. . . . In other words, BEV speakers do not necessarily contract more in excited interaction, but they delete more of the forms which have been contracted. These stylistic shifts are minor effects among the preadolescent and adolescent peer groups and only begin to assume importance with older adolescents and adults. [Labov 1972a, p. 83]

There is a convergence of linguistic and social variables such as group membership, contextual style, and age. Peer group membership is defined and maintained by means of language behavior.

The most distinct trait of Black English morphology is an aspect of the copula system. In addition to the irregularly inflected forms of *be* (Labov's be_1), Black English possesses a morphologically invariant *be* (be_2). The meaning of be_2 has been variously interpreted:

> The invariant *be* in *He be always fooling around* generally indicates "habitual" behavior: durative or iterative depending on the nature of the action. [Labov 1972a, p. 51]

> This type of invariant *be* occurs because *be* is possible in Vernacular Black English with a meaning something like "object or event distributed intermittently in time." This use of *be*, as in *Sometime he be here and sometime he don't*, occurs only in Vernacular Black English and is usually misunderstood by Standard English speakers. [Wolfram and Fasold 1974, p. 161]

Black speakers vary greatly from one to another in the extent to which they use the invariant be_2. Older Northern black speakers are uncomfortable with be_2 and, in fact, misuse it, often to the amusement of their children. The invariant be_2 is a recent importation into the speech of black Americans in Salt Lake City, where there has been an isolated black community since the 1847 Mormon immigration into the Great Basin. While the origins of this feature will probably remain clouded, two observations are in order. First, the occurrences of be_2 are closely related to constructions with *will* and *would* (both of which regularly undergo contraction and deletion). *I be good* could be the reduced form of *I will be good* and *I would be good* as well as the peculiarly black *be₂*. Second, Labov notes the relationship of black *be₂* to the standard *be₁*:

> The habitual *be₂* illustrates again a certain systematicity in BEV rules. We find that it occurs two to five times more often in environments where other dialects have *are* than in *is* environments. . . .
>
> There may be good semantic reasons for this. We may speak of habitual actions by plural subjects more often than singular ones. But we cannot ignore the fact that *are* is deleted about twice as often as *is*. . . .
>
> The deletion of *are* has reached such a high point that it is effectively zeroed out for many speakers. The morpheme *be₂* cannot be affected by the phonological processes that attack *are*, so that *be₂* naturally falls into the hole left by *are*. To put it more simply, it is easier to put something in where something is not than where something is.[13] [Labov 1972a, p. 52]

Because [s]-[z] deletion is less frequent than [t]-[d] deletion, Black English noun morphology departs less radically from general American usage than does its verb morphology. There is a tendency to regularize plural formation—*tooths, gooses, deers*—and double plurals are common as well: *teeths, geeses, policemens*. Since the possessive marker is deleted something over half the time, one would expect great uncertainty about its use among black speakers. In fact, considerable hypercorrection occurs, especially with personal names as in *Jack's Johnson's car* or *Jack's Johnson car*. The contrast between the possessive and subject pronoun pairs *your/you* and *their/they* is lost because of extensive *r*-lessness:

> In rapid speech, one cannot distinguish *you* from *your* from *you-all*. This seems to be a shift in grammatical forms, but the relation to the phonological variables is plain when we consider that *my*, *his*, *her*, and *our* remain as possessive pronouns. Speakers of the BE vernacular do not say *I book*, *she book*, or *we book*, though there are reports of such forms from young children, especially where there has been heavy West Indian influence or other Creole influence. *He book* is not as uncommon among young children, though again it seems to be concentrated heavily in certain areas. This form is subject to the same phonological processes as those [noted for *you book* and *they book*], though the phonetic motivation is much weaker than with *their* and *your*. [Labov 1972a, p. 24]

Speakers of Black English share the major syntactic patterns of general American speech. Even the divergences follow patterns developed in other nonstandard varieties. The most important, and best-studied, area of difference is in negative formation. Black English, like most nonstandard American varieties and like earlier varieties of English, makes extensive use of multiple negation. Standard varieties, of course, allow only one negative element in a negative sentence:

I don't have any money.
I have no money.

Black speech tends to place a negative wherever one is possible: **I don't have no money*. In the standard English pattern, a nondefinite subject must be negativized:

Nobody has any money.
*Anybody doesn't have any money.
*Anybody has no money.

The equivalent in black speech is: *Nobody don't have no money*. While multiple negation is optional in most nonstandard varieties, there is evidence that it is obligatory in Northern black speech (Wolfram and Fasold 1974, p. 165).

Black English makes use of the construction *it is* where other varieties employ *there is*: *it's a house on the corner of the street* is equivalent to *there's a house on the corner of the street*. This construction was current in Middle English but, according to the *Oxford English Dictionary*, was replaced by *there is* in the seventeenth century. (The most recent *OED* citation, from 1617, exactly parallels Black English usage today: "it is no living with them.") Whether the modern usage in Black English is a survival of the earlier form or a separate innovation cannot be known, but black children in New York were found to use the *it is* construction from 60 percent to 80 percent of the time (Labov 1972a, p. 281), though among adults in the same community *there is* was almost universally used.

Black speech extends the range of negative modal inversion, a feature common among nonstandard dialects of southern origin (Wolfram and Fasold 1974, pp. 169–70). The following examples have the inverted form of questions but they are uttered with statement intonation patterns:

Ain't nothing happenin' 'n' shit.
Ain't nobody gon' let you walk all around town to find somebody to whup them.
Ain't no white cop gonna put his hands on me.
Ain't nobody in my family Negro.
Don't nobody break up a fight.
Doesn't nobody really know that it's a God, you know.
Can't nobody tag you then.
[Labov 1972a, p. 60]

In a related phenomenon, black speakers along with many others regularize direct and indirect question formation by extending the direct question pattern into the embedded context: *I asked her how did she do it* frequently is used in place of *I asked her how she did it*.

The following is a Black English version of the Nicodemus story adapted from the Gospel of John.

> It was a man named Nicodemus. He was a leader of the Jews. This man, he come to Jesus in the night and say, "Rabbi, we know you a teacher that come from God, cause can't nobody do the things you be doing 'cept he got God with him."
>
> Jesus, he tell him say, "This ain't no jive, if a man ain't born over again, ain't no way he gonna get to know God."
>
> Then Nicodemus, he ask him, "How a man gonna be born when he already old? Can't nobody go back inside his mother and get born."
>
> So Jesus tell him, say, "This ain't no jive, this the truth. The onliest way a man gonna get to know God, he got to get born regular and he got to get born from the Holy Spirit. The body can only make a body get born, but the Spirit, he make a man so he can know God. Don't be surprised just cause I tell you that you got to get born over again. The wind blow where it want to blow and you can't hardly tell where it's coming from and where it's going to. That's how it go when somebody get born over again by the Spirit."
>
> So Nicodemus say, "How you know that?"
>
> Jesus say, "You call yourself a teacher that teach Israel and you don't know these kind of things? I'm gonna tell you, we talking about something we know about cause we already seen it. We telling it like it is and you-all think we jiving. If I tell you about things you can see and you-all think we jiving and don't believe me, what's gonna happen when I tell about things you can't see? Ain't nobody gone up to Heaven 'cept Jesus, who come down from Heaven. Just like Moses done hung up the snake in the wilderness, Jesus got to be hung up. So that the peoples that believe in him, he can give them real life that ain't never gonna end.[14] [Wolfram and Fasold 1969, pp. 150–51]

The text is faithful to the oral narrative styles of many black speakers and illustrates a number of linguistic features—*it* for *there*; copula deletion; negative modal inversion; multiple negation; third-person singular *s* loss; *gonna* as a future auxiliary; and perfective *done*.

Appalachian English

Some perspective on the degree of difference between Black English and other varieties can be gained from looking closely at Appalachian English. The geography of the hills of Appalachia encompasses a variety of communities with separate histories, varied employment, and differing dialects. The coal miner of West Virginia has a linguistic kinship with the farmer of northern Georgia, but it would be a mistake to posit uniformity in their speech. The following summary of features is taken from Wolfram and Christian's (1976) detailed study of Mercer and Monroe counties in southern West Virginia and can only be extrapolated to Appalachia as a whole when additional studies have been completed. The data are based on extensive spontaneous interviews with informants "who were typically of the lower socio-economic classes and who were lifetime residents of the area" (Wolfram and Christian 1976, p. 11).

Appalachian speakers exhibit a variety of [t] and [d] deletion which compares interestingly with those already discussed (ranges for six speakers and an average in parentheses are given):

-ed before a Vowel	Inherent before a Vowel	-ed before a Consonant	Inherent before a Consonant
3–6%	9–29%	56–71%	65–81%
(5)	(17)	(67)	(74)

Source: Wolfram and Christian 1976, p. 36.

The relatively high frequency of deletion of *-ed* before a consonant reflects an Appalachian innovation toward higher rates of deletion. There is little [s] and [z] deletion in the area, although there is a characteristic plural formation of words ending in *sp, st,* or *sk*: *deskes* ['dɛskɪz], *ghostes* ['gostɪz], and *waspes* ['waspɪz] for *desks, ghosts,* and *wasps.*

There is also a distinct pattern of *r*-lessness in Appalachia. *R*-loss before a consonant (words like *farm, born, turn*) is rare. It is more common in word-final positions and is, of course, enhanced by a following consonant, but the strongest determiner of *r*-deletion is whether the final syllable is stressed (*before, prepare, four*) or unstressed (*father, camper, regular*). Below are the ranges for ten speakers with average rates in parentheses.

| | Word-final Stressed Syllable || Word-final Unstressed Syllable ||
Within a Word	Before a Vowel	Before a Consonant	Before a Vowel	Before a Consonant
0–7%	0–7%	0–13%	0–27%	13–73%
(1)	(3)	(3)	(14)	(39)

Source: Wolfram and Christian 1976, p. 47.

An intrusive *r*, [ər], is also found in words ending in [o]—*holler* for *hollow, tobaccer* for *tobacco, yeller* for *yellow,* and *winders* for *windows.* Since it is one of the stereotypes of Appalachian speech, this feature occurs with increasingly lower frequency in the speech of younger speakers. Prevocalic *r*-lessness is also observed in selected lexical items: *throw* and *through* but not *three* or *prone* and occasionally in unstressed syllables—*p'ofessor*, *p'otect*. As one might expect, *l* is also vocalized and lost:

> If the following segment is a labial sound such as *p*, *b*, or *f*, *l* may be completely deleted. This occurs in items such as *wolf*, *help* or *shelf*, making words such as *woof* and *wolf*, *hep* and *help*, or *chef* and *shelf* homophonous. [Wolfram and Christian 1976, p. 48]

The sounds [θ] and [ð] receive special treatment in Appalachian speech. Initially they are pronounced as the corresponding dental (not alveolar) stops, but at a lower frequency than in other nonstandard varieties. Medially and finally, [θ] becomes [f].

> He shoots this juice stuff in your *mouf* and it nums your *mouf*.
> . . . If I get back *wif* 'er.
> I had a *birfday* party.
> . . . in a phone *boof*.
> [Wolfram and Christian, p. 49]

As in other nonstandard dialects, initial [ð] may also be deleted, but again with substantial differences:

> Demonstratives (*this*, *that*, *these*, *those*)
> > I don filled up on *'is* ham.
> > And this boy grabbed a great big cinder block—'bout like *'at* and throwed *'at* in on me.
> > She's get on *'ose* skates.
> Third person plural forms
> > You could pick *'em* good while *'ey* was hot.
> > But *'ey* wasn't right *'at* day.
> Comparative *than*
> > You can't bat more *'n* one eye at a time.
> > I mean things are gettin' worser anymore *'n* what they used to be.
> Locative and existential *there*
> > *'ere's* 'at high priced knife, Chester.
> > They said they's gonna ride up *'ere*, get on Sukis, push 'em up to the top of the hill up *'ere*.
> [Wolfram and Christian 1976, p. 54]

Deletion of [ð] is more frequent in Appalachian English than in other varieties and is even found in some formal styles. Further, it is regularly deleted both in stressed positions and in sentence-initial position, where such deletion is highly constrained in other varieties:

> You wanna use '*is* or you wanna use '*at.*
> '*at* was Daddy's mother.
> '*ere's* '*at* high-priced knife, Chester.
> [Wolfram and Christian 1976, pp. 54–55]

Since *r*-deletion occurs less frequently in Appalachian speech than in Black English or Southern white speech, deletion of contracted *are* is much less common—*we here* for *we're here*. In Wolfram and Christian's study, deletion of contracted *are* occurred only with pronouns and never with other subject noun phrases. Deletion of the contracted [z] of *was* and *is* never occurred as it so often does in Black English. Nonetheless, the paradigm of the *be* verb has been substantially modified in Appalachian English. *Was* for *were*—in such examples as *we was going*—was reported by Atwood (1953, p. 29) as "nearly universal" among the less cultivated speakers in the region, and Wolfram and Christian (1976, p. 77) found that *be* did not follow the conventional patterns of concord in 80 percent of past tense uses. In the present tense, however, *be* did not show concord in only 21 percent of the usages (*they is very good* for *they are very good*). Lack of concord may extend to other verbs, especially in the following environments:

> Conjoined Noun Phrase
>   Me and my sister *gets* in a fight sometimes.
>   A boy and his daddy *was* a-huntin.
> Collective Noun Phrase
>   Some people *makes* it from fat off a pig.
>   *People's* not concerned.
> Other Plural Noun Phrase
>   . . . no matter what their parents *has* taught 'em.
>   The cars *was* all tore up.
> Expletive *there*
>   *There's* different breeds of 'em.
>   There *was* five in our family.
> [Wolfram and Christian 1976, p. 78]

Contracted forms of *will* and *have* are deleted, and thus the Appalachian future closely resembles patterns of Black English: *tomorrow I be going*. *Have*-deletion is especially common when *have* combines with *been*, although it is also lost with other verbs:

> First time I ever *been* out in the woods with a gun.
> I think she *been* down here maybe twice.

> Well, I've just been lucky I never *been* bit.
> I seen several pictures in the paper where people *been* snake-bitten.
> I've got a horse, saddle horse and we take it and I *got* another horse, quarter horse. . . .
> [Wolfram and Christian 1976, p. 44]

Verb morphology is also different because of two other constructions. The *done* perfective forms occur in Appalachia as they do in other varieties of southern origin:

> . . . because the one that was in there had *done* rotted.
> If she had, she woulda *done* left me a long time ago.
> We thought he was *done* gone.
> [Wolfram and Christian 1976, p. 86]

Progressive constructions with *a*-verb-*ing* are also very common:

> I knew he was *a-tellin'* the truth but still I was *a-comin'* home. . . .
> My cousin had a little brown pony and we was *a-ridin'* it one day.
> Well, she's *a-gettin'* the black lung now, ain't she?
> . . . and he says, "who's *a-stompin'* on my bridge?"
> This man'd catch 'em behind the neck and they'd just *be a-rattlin'*.
> [Wolfram and Christian 1976, p. 70]

The Appalachian English pronoun system is also distinctive. As in other varieties, object forms are often found in subject positions, especially in compound constructions: *me and him went together*. Southern *y'all* is common, and the archaic *hit* is preserved among older speakers (and *h* is found before *ain't*):

> When the winter set in *hit* set in, *hit's* just like in a western.
> *Hit* was these three billy goats.
> I *hain't* got none now.
> I said I *hain't* a-gonna do it.
> [Wolfram and Christian 1976, p. 58]

In some ways, Appalachian English is exemplary of the features regarded as nonstandard in American English. One translation of Aristophanes' *Lysistrata* employs it to render the Doric Greek of the original (see Parker 1964, pp. 69–71); television comedies with some international circulation also draw upon Appalachian English for comic effects (e.g., "The Beverly Hillbillies"). Among the additional features given particular currency in such efforts are the analogic reflexive pronouns *hisself* and *theirselves*; *here* or *there* added to a demonstrative (e.g., *this here bonded stuff*); possessive pronouns with *-n* rather than *-s* (*yourn*, *hisn*, *hern*, *ourn*, and *theirn*); and multiple negation. Appalachian English also participates in the use of expletive *it* for *there*:

> King cobra 'posed to be 'bout the deadliest snake *it* is.
> *It's* a lotta them does that.
> *It* was a fly in it.
> [Wolfram and Christian 1976, p. 126]

Such features combine to form a coherent and easily recognized stereotype, both for outsiders and for the Appalachian English speakers themselves. Like other nonstandard varieties, Appalachian English is subject to official disapproval in schools and some employment offices, but for its speakers it reflects the virtues of warmth and a "down-home" style. Such an opinion is manifested in the following selection from a collection of oral narratives describing the cold welcome Appalachian English speakers often find in northern cities:

> I told im, "Now if you find somebody from West Virginia, or the South somewhere, down in Alabama or someplace like that, they're ready to talk to you." But the original ones that live here, you can ask em anything. Maybe they'll say something or they'll turn their head and look the other way. I had em do me that way lots a times. Settin in a beer garden, you know, drinkin. Maybe I'll go in and get me a mug o' beer, say somethin-or-other to a guy: it's pretty cold out there, or somethin, or pretty warm, or somethin like 'at. "Yep"—he'll just turn his head over, turn right on the stool, turn and look the other way. [Gitlin and Hollander 1970, pp. 197–98]

In the following spontaneous narrative, a sixty-seven-year-old retired Appalachian miner tells his best raccoon hunting story:

> Him and me and Jack Stern, we went to Bath County, Virginia, coon hunting. Went up to Leroy Buzzie's. . . . He used to be an Army man, the old man Leroy Buzzie, see, he's dead now. He was a retired Army man, and, we went up 'ere and John supposedly had a sack to put the coon in if we caught one. We's gonna try to bring it back alive, so we tromped through the woods 'til along about six o'clock in the morning. The dogs treed up a big hollow chestnut oak, and we proceeded to cut the thing down. It's about three or four inches all the way around. About four foot through the stump. We tied the dogs and cut the thing down. Well, we cut it down and turned one dog loose, and he went down in that thing, way down in the old hollow of the tree and it forked, and we couldn't get up in there so he backed out and he tied 'im. And we's a-gonna chop the coon out if it was in there, I's a kinda

halfway thought maybe it just treed a possum or something. Well, I chopped in and lo and behold, right on top of the dang coon. Eighteen pounder, Jack Stern says, kitten coon. I run in with the axe handle down in behind him to keep him from getting out or backing down in the tree. He reached, fooled around and got him by the hind legs and pulled that thing out. It looked big as a sheep to me. Turned 'im loose, he said "kitten, Hell." We had an old carbide light and he turned that over and the lights were . . . that's all the light we had. And, we had to hunt it then and the dogs took right after the coon right down the holler and the dogs caught it and Jack beat us all down there. Went down there and he's a-holding three dogs in one hand and the coon in the other hand. And they's all a-trying to bite the coon and the coon a-trying to bite Jack and the dogs, and Jack pulled out a sack and it wasn't a dang thing but an old pillow case that Maggie had used, his wife, it was about wore out. So we fumbled around 'ere and finally got that coon in that sack and he aimed to close the top of it and the coon just tore the thing in half, in two, and down the holler he went again. With that sack on him, half of it and we caught that thing, and you know, E. F. Wurst finally pulled off his coveralls and we put that thing down in one of the legs of his coveralls and tied that coon up. He's tearing up everything we could get, we couldn't hold him he's so stout. And I brought that thing home and kept 'im about a month, fed 'im apples and stuff to eat so we could eat 'em. Well, I did, I killed him and tried eat that thing, I'd just soon eat a tomcat or a polecat, I wouldn't make much difference. And, that's about the best coon hunt I believe I was on. [Wolfram and Christian 1976, p. 181]

While this transcription does not attempt to be faithful to the phonological aspects of Appalachian speech, it does contain an intrusive [r] in *holler* for *hollow* and several examples of the deleted initial [ð]—*'ere* for *there*. The use of object pronouns in compound subjects can be seen in the first line—*Him and me and Jack Stern, we went. . . .* Lack of subject-verb concord is the rule, especially with forms of *be* where the contracted *'s* of *is* is generalized to all persons—*I's, we's,* and *they's.* It also contains a *gonna* future in *we's gonna try* and several examples of the *a*-verb-*ing* construction—*he's a-holding three dogs* and *they's all a-trying to bite the coon.*

Conclusion

The data of this chapter illustrate the dimensions which sociolinguistic inquiry has recently added to traditional dialect studies. The relationships between social class and speech variety are becoming clearer, and more importantly, the study of variation enables us to view standard and nonstandard varieties of American

English as parts of a pluralistic speech continuum. Such study allows us to focus more clearly on the social aspects of language—what a speaker of a social, economic, or sexual variety of American English *does* in choosing to speak that variety. Thus far, the examples cited have described the nature of synchronic variation in contemporary speech patterns, but the comparison of recent studies with the earlier work of the atlas linguistic geographers has yielded a new direction of study—the study of sound change in progress.

Thirty years after Guy Lowman had collected data for *LANE*, Labov returned to the island of Martha's Vineyard to reinitiate investigation of the speech of the island's permanent residents:

> The Vineyard is best known to linguists as an important relic area of American English: an island of *r*-pronouncers in a sea of *r*-lessness. With a 320-year history of continuous settlement, and a long record of resistance to Boston ways and manners, the island has preserved many archaic traits which were probably typical of southeastern New England before 1800. [Labov 1972b, p. 6]

Labov began a study of the social forces at work in this conservative community's resistance to mainland speech habits. While the Vineyard is a beautiful place to live, it is both expensive and a hard place to make a living. Many of the local residents have been forced to leave their homes to find jobs or to make room for the influx of "summer people." Labov discovered that the feature most typical of the island's linguistic isolation was most frequent among middle-aged fishermen—fishing is one of the few occupations available to those who have decided to live permanently on the island:

> This age group has been under heavier stress than any other; the men have grown up in a declining economy, after making a more or less deliberate choice to remain on the island rather than leave it. [Labov 1972b, p. 30]

The linguistic consequences of this choice became clear when the speech of adolescent males was examined. Adolescents split dramatically into two groups. Those who planned to leave the island after school were adopting mainland speech habits; those who planned to remain or to return to the island after college imitated the speech of middle-aged fishermen.

Like the Vineyarders, all Americans express their position in society and their aspirations through their speech. We change our speech to meet the demands of our audience, adapt it to new circumstances, and try to retain through it the respect and affection of peers and family. Social and regional dialects thrive through our allegiance to our neighbors; national standards emerge as we strive to broaden our linguistic horizons.

NOTES

1. See Opie and Opie 1959 and Knapp and Knapp 1976.
2. The use of *go* in a broad sense of 'make a sound' is, of course, quite old in English—*the duck goes quack*—but the extension of this meaning to human speaking is not recorded in the *OED* or its recent supplement.
3. See McDavid 1972 for a more detailed account of these features. McDavid notes that "we are all ethnocentric after our own fashion" (1972, p. 136), and different linguistic features may carry contrary social meanings in different communities. Chicagoans, he says, regard *r*-loss in *barn* as "lower class"; Southerners associate the *r*-full pronunciation as a trait of "poor-white" speech.
4. As the *OED* notes, the use of *I* after a verb or preposition was "very frequent" in the sixteenth and seventeenth centuries; recent citations in the 1976 *OED Supplement* suggest that the usage is now mainly found in spoken English.
5. Both examples date from 1675–99; see Leechman and Hall 1955.
6. A major source for the study of this variety is Leap 1977.
7. *Apple orchard* in this quotation draws upon recent slang in which *apple* is applied contemptuously to a Native American who affects the manners or ideals of Anglo society; an *apple* in this sense is "red on the outside, white on the inside" (see Barnhart, Steinmetz, and Barnhart 1980, p. 35). In conception, *apple* parallels American black usage of *oreo*, literally a chocolate cookie with a vanilla cream filling (see Barnhart, Steinmetz, and Barnhart 1973, p. 335).
8. The map and the examples that follow are drawn from Atwood 1962.
9. The following discussion relies especially on Fasold and Wolfram 1972 and Labov 1973.
10. Some individual lexical items show the long history of *r*-deletion in mid-morpheme (e.g., the nickname *Hal* for *Harold*). Black English tends to extend this process to new environments.
11. Sayers's use of this feature doubtless reflects her belief in the preservation of archaic features among aristocrats. According to Wright and Wright (1924, p. 107), "Many educated speakers still preserve the dental [n], but through the influence of spelling the guttural [ŋ] began to be restored again in the early part of the nineteenth century, and has now become the regular pronunciation with most educated speakers, as *evening, living, morning, walking*, etc."
12. This text is representative of one of the many "slave narratives" collected by fieldworkers employed under the Works Progress Administration in the 1930s; a version of it is published in Purdue, Barden, and Phillips 1976, pp. 224–25. A phonograph record of this selection was deposited in the Library of Congress, and the text quoted here was prepared with the help of that recording.
13. As other contributors to this volume show, a form resembling *be* is current in the southwestern dialects of England (see Orton, Sanderson, and Widdowson 1978, map M5 and elsewhere), in Ireland, eastern Canada, and elsewhere. The question of whether these forms arise from a common source or are independent developments in widely separated varieties remains unsettled.
14. A version of this same passage in Scots English is quoted by Suzanne Romaine, p. 64.

REFERENCES

Algarín, Miguel, and Pinero, Miguel, eds. *Nuyorican Poetry*: *An Anthology of Puerto Rican Words and Feelings*. New York: William Morrow, 1975.

Atwood, E. Bagby. *A Survey of Verb Forms in the Eastern United States*. Ann Arbor: University of Michigan Press, 1953.

———. *The Regional Vocabulary of Texas*. Austin: University of Texas Press, 1962.

Barnhart, Clarence L.; Steinmetz, Sol; and Barnhart, Robert K. *The Barnhart Dictionary of New English since 1963*. Bronxville, N.Y.: Barnhart, 1973.

———. *The Second Barnhart Dictionary of New English*. Bronxville, N.Y.: Barnhart, 1980.

Ervin-Tripp, Susan. " 'What do Women Sociolinguists Want?': Prospects for a Research Field." In *Sociology of the Languages of American Women*, edited by Betty Lou Dubois and Isabel Crouch, pp. 3–16. San Antonio: Trinity University, 1976.

Fasold, Ralph W. *Tense Marking in Black English*: *A Linguistic and Social Analysis*. Washington, D.C.: Center for Applied Linguistics, 1972.

Fasold, Ralph W., and Wolfram, Walter A. "Some Linguistic Features of Negro Dialect." In *Contemporary English*: *Change and Variation*, edited by David L. Shores, pp. 53–85. Philadelphia: J. B. Lippincott, 1972.

Fries, Charles C. *American English Grammar*. New York: Appleton-Century Co., 1940.

Gitlin, Todd, and Hollander, Nanci. *Uptown*: *Poor Whites in Chicago*. New York: Harper and Row, 1970.

Halliday, M. A. K. "Relevant Models of Language." *Educational Review* 32 (1969):26–37.

Key, Mary Ritchie. *Male/Female Language*. Metuchen, N.J.: Scarecrow Press, 1975.

Knapp, Mary, and Knapp, Herbert. *One Potato*, *Two Potato*: *The Folklore of American Children*. New York: W. W. Norton, 1976.

Kurath, Hans; Hanley, Miles L.; Bloch, Bernard; Lowman, Guy S., Jr.; and Hansen, Marcus L. *Linguistic Atlas of New England*. 3 vols. in 6 pts. Providence: Brown University Press, 1939–43.

Labov, William. *Language in the Inner City*: *Studies in the Black English Vernacular*. Philadelphia: University of Pennsylvania Press, 1972*a*.

———. *Sociolinguistic Patterns*. Philadelphia: University of Pennsylvania Press, 1972*b*.

———. "Some Features of the English of Black Americans." In *Varieties of Present-Day English*, edited by Richard W. Bailey and Jay L. Robinson, pp. 236–55. New York: Macmillan Co., 1973.

Labov, William; Cohen, Paul; Robins, Clarence; and Lewis, John. *A Study of the Non-Standard English of Negro and Puerto Rican Speakers in New York City*. Report on Cooperative Research Project 3288. New York: Columbia University, 1968.

Lakoff, Robin. *Language and Woman's Place*. New York: Harper Colophon Books, 1975.

Lawrence, Lars. *Morning Noon and Night*. New York: Putnam, 1954.

Leap, William L. "The Study of American Indian English: An Introduction to the Issues." In *Studies in Southwestern Indian English*, edited by William L. Leap, pp. 5–20. San Antonio: Trinity University, 1977.

Leechman, Douglas, and Hall, Robert A., Jr. "American Indian Pidgin English: Attestations and Grammatical Peculiarities." *American Speech* 30 (1955):163–71.

Maccoby, Eleanor E. *The Development of Sex Differences*. Palo Alto: Stanford University Press, 1966.

McDavid, Raven I., Jr. "A Checklist of Significant Features for Discriminating Social Dialects." In *Culture, Class, and Language Variety*, edited by A. L. Davis, pp. 133–39. Urbana, Ill.: National Council of Teachers of English, 1972.

Major, Clarence. *Dictionary of Afro-American Slang*. New York: International Publishers, 1970.

Metcalf, Allan A. *Chicano English*. Arlington, Va.: Center for Applied Linguistics, 1979.

Miller, Mary Rita. "Attestations of American Indian Pidgin English in Fiction and Nonfiction." *American Speech* 42 (1967):142–47.

Opie, Iona, and Opie, Peter. *The Lore and Language of Schoolchildren*. Oxford: Oxford University Press, 1959.

Orton, Harold; Sanderson, Stewart; and Widdowson, John. *The Linguistic Atlas of England*. London: Croom Helm, and New York: Humanities Press, 1978.

Parker, Douglass, trans. *Lysistrata*. Ann Arbor: University of Michigan Press, 1964.

Purdue, Charles L.; Barden, Thomas E.; and Phillips, Robert K., eds. *Weevils in the Wheat*. Charlottesville: University Press of Virginia, 1976.

Rickford, John R. "The Question of Prior Creolization in Black English." In *Pidgin and Creole Linguistics*, edited by Albert Valdman, pp. 190–221. Bloomington: Indiana University Press, 1977.

Sachs, Jacqueline; Lieberman, Philip; and Erickson, Donna. "Anatomical and Cultural Determinants of Male and Female Speech." In *Language Attitudes: Current Trends and Prospects*, edited by Roger W. Shuy and Ralph W. Fasold, pp. 74–84. Washington: Georgetown University Press, 1973.

Sawyer, Janet B. "The Speech of San Antonio, Texas" [1959]. In *A Various Language: Perspectives on American Dialects*, edited by Juanita V. Williamson and Virginia M. Burke, pp. 570–82. New York: Holt, Rinehart and Winston, 1971.

———. "Social Aspects of Bilingualism in San Antonio, Texas" [1964]. In *Varieties of Present-Day English*, edited by Richard W. Bailey and Jay L. Robinson, pp. 226–33. New York: Macmillan Co., 1973.

Shores, David L., ed. *Contemporary English: Change and Variation*. Philadelphia: J. B. Lippincott, 1972.

Shuy, Roger; Wolfram, Walter A.; and Riley, William K. *Linguistic Correlates of Social Stratification in Detroit Speech*. Washington, D.C.: U.S. Office of Education, 1967.

Starkey, Marion L. *The Devil in Massachusetts*. Garden City, N.Y.: Anchor Books, 1969.

Stewart, William A. "Continuity and Change in American Negro Dialects." In *Contemporary English: Change and Variation*, edited by David L. Shores, pp. 96–106. Philadelphia: J. B. Lippincott, 1972.

Teschner, Richard V.; Bills, Garland D.; and Craddock, Jerry R., eds. *Spanish and English of United States Hispanos: A Critical, Annotated, Linguistic Bibliography*. Arlington, Va.: Center for Applied Linguistics, 1975.

Turner, Lorenzo D. *Africanisms in the Gullah Dialect*. Chicago: University of Chicago Press, 1949. Reprint. Ann Arbor: University of Michigan Press, 1974.

U. S. Department of the Interior. *The National Atlas of the United States*. Washington, D.C.: Government Printing Office, 1970.

Wolfram, Walter A. *A Sociolinguistic Description of Detroit Negro Speech*. Washington, D.C.: Center for Applied Linguistics, 1969.

———. "Black-White Speech Differences Revisited." In *Black-White Speech Relation-*

ships*, edited by Walter A. Wolfram and Nona H. Clarke, pp. 138–61. Washington, D.C.: Center for Applied Linguistics, 1971.
Wolfram, Walter A., and Christian, Donna. *Appalachian Speech*. Arlington, Va.: Center for Applied Linguistics, 1976.
Wolfram, Walter A., and Fasold, Ralph W. "Toward Reading Materials for Speakers of Black English." In *Teaching Black Children to Read*, edited by Joan C. Baratz and Roger W. Shuy, pp. 138–55. Washington, D.C.: Center for Applied Linguistics, 1969.
——. *The Study of Social Dialects in American English*. Englewood Cliffs, N.J.: Prentice-Hall, 1974.
Wright, Joseph, and Wright, Elizabeth Mary. *An Elementary Historical New English Grammar*. London: Humphrey Milford, 1924.

English in the Caribbean
David L. Lawton

Like pieces of a giant puzzle, the islands of the Caribbean lie roughly to the south of the English-speaking North American continent, to the east of the Central American republics, and stretch away as Leeward and Windward groups arching down to the tip of Venezuela. The figure of a giant puzzle is apt not only as a geographical description, but as a linguistic one. Overrun by the Spanish, French, English, Portuguese, and Dutch, the islands and some bordering areas of the Central American coast retain the linguistic flavor of each marauder together with that of the native inhabitants (where they still remain) and the descendants of West African slaves brought by Europeans to work the plantations of the islands and coasts.

The linguistic milieu that draws our greatest interest, however, is that of English in all its variation and chameleon guises. These varieties stretch from "Caribbean Standard" to the contact developments known variously as "creoles," "patois," and "broken talk." The map shows the geographical distribution of areas where English is in contact with other languages, or English with its English-based creole form coexists. Table 1 gives population and other demographic information.

In addition to the areas given in the table, there are pockets of settlement around the Caribbean and in other not-well-charted places where English in one form or another has provenance. Indeed, one can spot some areas only with a nautical chart since they are not mentioned on popular maps. With great justification, Allsopp (1972) writes of the anglophone Caribbean with its identifying phonology and syntax which extends beyond the islands and territories where British traditions are firmly rooted. For example, the linguistic situation in Guyana, South America, reflects in significant ways that of Jamaica, and in less important ways that of Belize, where Spanish, English, and Carib come together (Le Page 1978; Escure 1979).

The history of English in the Caribbean involves, as a matter of course, the history of the islands themselves. Jamaica, the largest of the English-speaking islands, was first a Spanish possession, and later an English one by virtue of conquest in the seventeenth century. With the advent of sugar cane, Jamaica became one of the wealthiest islands in the sun, with a substantial slave population drawn from West Africa. The number of slaves increased as the result of continued importation and breeding until the slaves far outnumbered the nonslave inhabitants. Never reconquered by Spain, whose Cuba lay ninety miles to the north, nor overwhelmed by France, whose Haiti was a fast day's sail to the east,

TABLE 1. LINGUISTIC AND DEMOGRAPHIC FACTS

Country	Official Language	Other Languages	Population/ Ethnic Groups	Political System/ Education
ABC Islands (Aruba, Bonaire, Curaçao, St. Eustatius, Saba, St. Maarten)	Dutch / French (Northern St. Maarten)	English, Papiamentu, Spanish, Sranan	250,000: white, black, mixed, other	Constitutionally on level with Netherlands
Barbados	English	English-based creole	250,000: 5% white; 90% black; 5% mixed	British Commonwealth system; 97% literate
Belize (formerly British Honduras)	English	Spanish, English-based creole	No official data	British Commonwealth; self-governing
Cayman Islands	English	English-based creole	11,500	Dependency of Jamaica within British Commonwealth system
Cuba	Spanish	possible Spanish-based creole	9,600,000: white, black, mixed	Socialist republic
Colombia	Spanish	Palenquero: Spanish-based creole; Indian languages	25,640,000: white, 20%; mestizo, 58% white and black, 14%; Indian, 1%	Republic
Dominican Republic	Spanish	No data	5,120,000: white, black, Carib, mixed	Republic; 68% literacy
Guadaloupe	French	French-based creole	370,000; mostly black	Department of France
Haiti	French	French-based creole	4,830,000: 95% black; 5% mixed	Republic; 10% literacy
Jamaica	English	English-based creole; some Spanish; some Hakka	2,090,000: 85% black; 10% mixed; 5% Caucasians, Chinese, East Indians, Lebanese, Jews (Sephardic), Latinos	British Commonwealth; self-governing; 86% literacy
Leeward Islands (British; including Antigua, St. Kitts, Nevis-Anguilla, Montserrat, Virgin Islands)	English	English-based creole	150,000: mostly black	Self-governing and associated status within British Commonwealth system
Martinique	French	French-based creole	370,000: mostly black	Department of France

Mexico	Spanish	Indian languages	66,940,000: 60% mestizo; 30% Indian; 10% Caucasian	United Mexican States; 82% literacy	
Nicaragua	Spanish	English; English-based creole (Bluefields)	2,400,000: 70% mestizo; 17% Caucasian; 9% black; 4% Indian	Republic; 57% literacy	
Panama	Spanish	English; English-based creole	1,830,000: 70% mestizo; 13% black; 10% Caucasian; 6% Indian; 1% other	Republic; 79% literacy	
Puerto Rico	Spanish and English	None	3,358,000: 99% Hispanic	Commonwealth of Puerto Rico	
Trinidad and Tobago	English	English-based creole; Hindi	1,130,000: 43% black; 36% East Indian; 2% white; 1% Chinese; 18% mixed	Republic (1976); 90% literacy	
Venezuela	Spanish	Indian languages	13,120,000: 70% mestizo; 20% Spanish, Portuguese, Italian; 8% black; 2% Indian	Republic; 82% literacy	
Windward Islands (British: St. Vincent, St. Lucia, Dominica)	English	Island Carib (Dominica); English-based creole	100,000: mostly black	St. Lucia and Dominica, self-governing; St. Vincent, British Commonwealth	

Note: Where figures are given, the information is obtained from *The World Almanac* (New York: Doubleday, 1980, pp. 513–94, 703). Often, the information is not consistently patterned, so that occasionally *Caucasian* is given and at other times *white* is used. *Mestizo* is used to refer to an ethnic group composed of Caucasian and Indian persons; *mixed* is used to refer to any other combination of persons but, generally, refers to Caucasian and black.

The heading *country* is used with the idea of conveying "political entity" in the case of the Cayman Islands and Puerto Rico, as well as in that of the French departments of Guadaloupe and Martinique.

For Colombia, the offshore islands of San Andrés and Providencia are not listed since they could not be placed under *country*. Their importance lies in the use of an English-based Creole on both islands. In other instances, research is not available or incomplete on linguistic and demographic facts. It may well turn out, for example, that cases will come to light that are similar to those of *Palanquero* (Bickerton and Escalante 1970) and Dutch Creole in the American Virgin Islands (Sprauve 1976).

The official ethnic information for Puerto Rico is flawed (*World Almanac*, p. 703) since *Hispanic* is used as a cover term to include *black*. Puerto Rico is so thoroughly integrated ethnically that census figures do not discriminate as do those of the United States mainland. Further, ethnic designations in the Caribbean are largely *color* determined rather than *racially* determined. Additional information is derived from Taylor 1977, Hymes 1971, and Cave 1976.

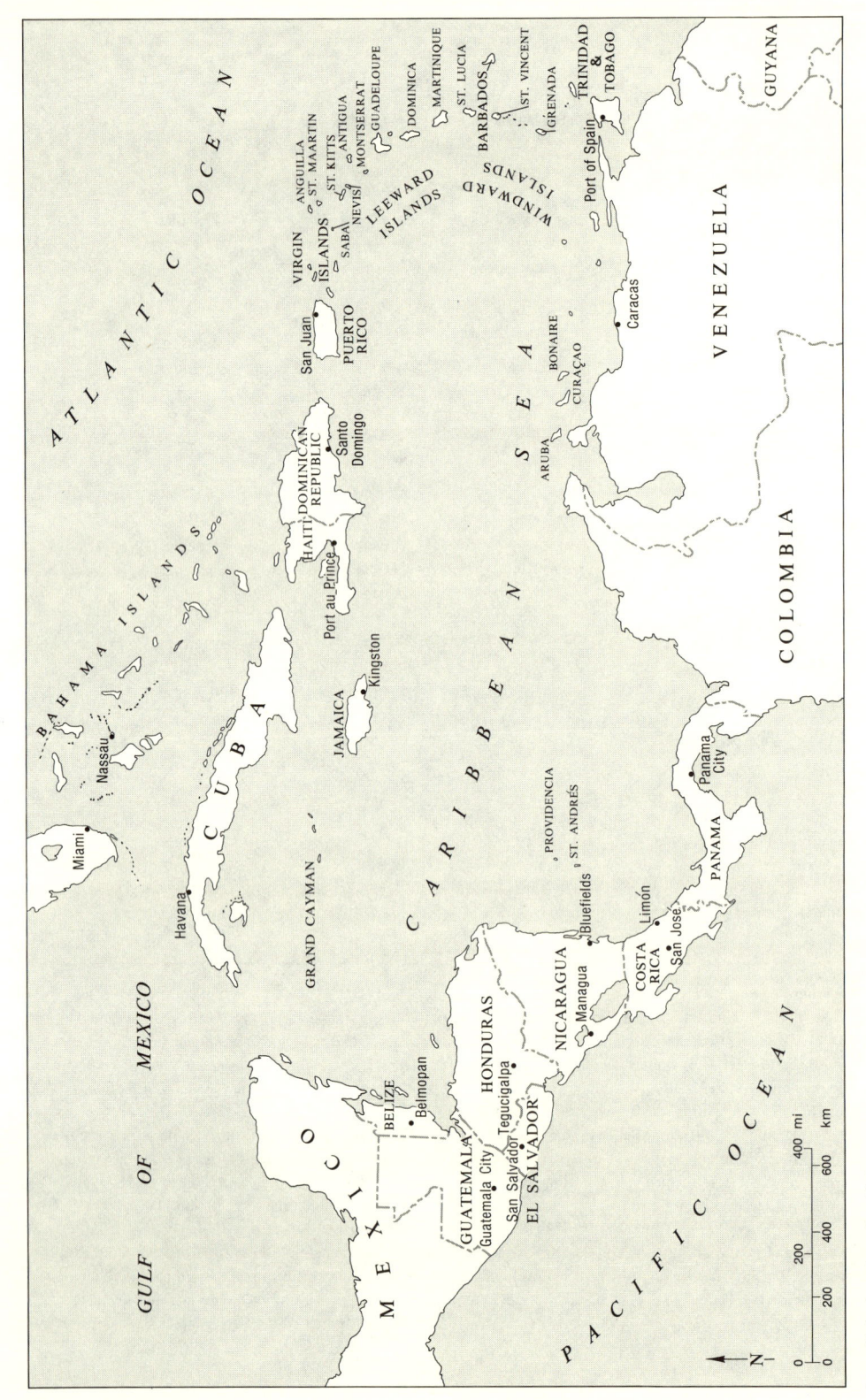

English in the Caribbean

Jamaica has retained an unbroken tradition of English as the official language until the present day.

Concomitant with different kinds of British English, there arose another language in Jamaica formed from the contact of English with West African languages. These West African languages were brought by the thousands of slaves who worked the sugar plantations. The result of English in contact with West African languages is the development of a third language, Jamaican Creole. The inception and development of Jamaican Creole has been a constant source of speculation among linguists. In none of the other islands of the Caribbean has English enjoyed quite the same development, although analogs may be found. In Trinidad, for example, Spain, France, and England have all played an important role in linguistic history through colonization and settlement. Although France never took Trinidad by formal conquest, Eric Williams (1964, p. 4) is close to the truth when he suggests that Spain ruled but France governed. Of course, there are other linguistic influences which have played a distinctive role in Trinidad, particularly Hindi and Tamil, whose speakers were imported as cheap labor in the nineteenth century. Hindi in contact with English has been made a vehicle for humor in the novels of Vidia Naipaul, whose stature is international. In Jamaica, however, although Hindi and Tamil speakers were brought in during the same period of their immigration to Trinidad, the linguistic influence has not been perceptible in either Jamaican Creole or Jamaican English.

English has been a dominant force in the Caribbean, and migrations have been particularly frequent among some of the islands and to the Central American mainland. But the English that prevailed was British English in such places as Dominica, Belize, and Panama, the latter country drawing a great many Jamaicans to work on the Canal during the first decade of the twentieth century. Many Jamaicans remained in Panama and formed a pocket of English and Jamaican Creole speakers in an otherwise Spanish environment. The major language contact situation, however, came about not through the further spread of British English, but through conquest of Puerto Rico by the United States during the Spanish-American War in 1898. The influence of American English provides a unique case of two different varieties of a major European language in contact in the Caribbean where the prevailing contacts had been Spanish with West African and Amerindian languages, and French and English with West African languages. The result of language contact in the Jamaican situation has been much modified by changing social and political conditions since independence was achieved in 1962, whereas Puerto Rico has been emancipated neither from its commonwealth status with the United States, nor from the dominance of American English in an otherwise Hispanic environment. Jamaica and Puerto Rico thus provide separate focuses from which one can draw some linguistic conclusions about languages in contact.

Jamaican English is not substantially different from RP at the segmental level; it is a variety of English in which there is no postvocalic *r*, and intrusive [r] appears under the same conditions as RP. The chief differences between Jamaican English and RP lie in the prosodic features: Jamaican English has syllable timing akin to Spanish rather than English. If one compares the vocalic segments of Jamaican English and Jamaican Creole, crucial differences become clear:

Jamaican English	Jamaican Creole
[æ] *bat* /æ/	[ɑ] *mata* 'matter' /a/
[ɑ:] *path* /a/	[ɑ:] *path* /aa/
[i] *feet* /i/	[i] *feet* /ii/
[eɪ] *bait* /e/	[ɪe] *bait* /ie/
[ɛ] *bet* /ɛ/	[ɛ] *bet* /e/
[ɑɪ] *bite* /ai/	[ɑɪ] *bite* /ai/
[ə] *mother* (final syllable) /ə/	
[ʌ] *cut*	[o] *bird* /o/
[ɒ] *hot* /a/	
[ʊ] *hood* /ʊ/	[ʊ] *tutu* 'male sexual organs' /u/
[u] *choose* /u/	[u] *choose* /uu/
[ɑʊ] *out* /aʊ/	[ɵʊ] *out* /au/
[ɔ:] *cause* /ɔ/	
[ɔɪ] *loiter* /ɔi/	
[jʊ] *you* /ju/	[jʊ] *you* /yu/
[oʊ] *joke* /oʊ/	[ʊo] *joke* /uo/

Both Jamaican English and Jamaican Creole lack *r*-colored vowels. Where *r*-colored vowels do appear in speech, they are due to the speaker's having acquired an Americanized idiolect. One has to distinguish quite clearly between idealized patterning of Jamaican English and Jamaican Creole while treating all other phonetic differences as variant forms deriving from outside influence. With the advent of World War II and subsequent large migrations by Jamaicans to Great Britain as well as the United States, substantial phonetic variation has crept into "standard" Jamaican English. But Jamaican Creole has remained remarkably stable. The people who go away to other countries have often returned in small numbers to Jamaica to work in the professions and broadcast media, but they are seldom able to eradicate all salient features of basic Jamaican English or Jamaican Creole, depending on which of the two was their first language.

With respect to the consonants, Jamaican Creole shows significant and systematic differences from Jamaican English. In Jamaican English, the consonants are the same as in RP. Jamaican Creole has no *th* sound in any position; [β] substitutes for [v] between vowels and sometimes for [b] at the end of a word not under emphasis. In words like *garden*, the initial consonant is the voiced palatal stop, [ɟ]; and the vowel of the first syllable is geminated to give [gjaadn̩] (Cassidy and Le Page 1967, pp. xxxix–lviii). Note that [ɹ] is deleted and final [n] is syllabic. Just as [g] is palatalized, so is [k] before low back vowels as in [kjãã] *can* or *can't* depending on the tonal contrast. The tildes symbolize nasalization of the final vowels. The palatal nasal [ɲ] appears in a few words such as [ɲjam] *to eat*. With respect to [r], there is alternation between [l] and [r], unattested for English dialects but fully attested for some West African languages (Cassidy and Le Page 1967, p. lxi): for example, [flitaz]/[fritaz] *fritters*. Both [t] and [k] are in alternation in words like *little*. Sometimes final nasals are assimilated to the preceding vowel before another nasal, as in [fra maanin] *from morning*, and [gwãi] in [gwãi kom] *going to come*. Note also that initial [g] is labialized.

Initial clusters beginning with [s] in Jamaican English have [s] deleted before voiceless stops and velars, as in [tomok] *stomach*, [pwaɪl] *spoil*, [troŋ] *strong*, [kin] *skin*. Before nasals, [s] is followed by an epenthetic vowel of very short duration resembling [ɨ] as in [sɨmaal] *small*. Cassidy and Le Page have attributed deletion of [s] in initial clusters to West African substratum influence, particularly that of Twi (1967, p. lxii). The more research done in Jamaican Creole phonology, the more insights one obtains into the systematic differences between idealized Jamaican English and Jamaican Creole. Assimilation and metathesis operate in Jamaican Creole to produce new morphological forms, as in [aaredi] *already*, [brenot] *breadnut*, [flim] *film*, [slandaz] *sandals*. Other changes occur across morphological boundaries, as in [sidoŋ] *sit down*, where [t] is assimilated and the final nasal is velarized. The clear identification of phonological features of Jamaican Creole from Jamaican English allows one to describe code shifting between both languages on a phonological level; some steps have been taken in that direction by Velma Pollard (1978, pp. 16-31). Code shifting at the phonological level, however, is not paralleled consistently by morphology or syntax.

So far, in the examples of phonological differences between Jamaican English and Jamaican Creole, the reader will note that no prosodic features have been marked. For example, [kjãã] *can't* or *can* is distinguished by a tonal contrast in which the form for *can* carries a high, level tone and the form for *can't* carries a high, falling tone. Tonal contrasts, which are represented by a very small sample of minimal pairs in Jamaican Creole, provide crucial evidence of West African reflexes. These reflexes serve to differentiate, partially, Jamaican English from Jamaican Creole. Stress has no contrastive function in Jamaican Creole. The sentential rhythm depends on syllable timing in Jamaican Creole and Jamaican English. Although the Spaniards occupied Jamaica from the last decade of the fifteenth century until the 1650s, there is no credible evidence to support Spanish influence and thus account for syllable timing. Rather than a Romance-language influence, there is increasing evidence from historical and psychological research to support retention of West African prosodic features (Carter 1979, p. 15) in creole communities of the Caribbean.

Representing the three tonal contrasts which I postulated (1963) as high (ˊ), mid (ˉ), and low (unmarked), one can observe their distribution on sample lexical forms in Jamaican English where they replace English stress: *rēcōgníze*, *contamīnáte, addréss*. The even syllabic rhythm and the glide of tones from one level to another account for the impression on the part of the native English speaker from North America or England that Jamaican English is cadenced but "flat," the flatness accounted for by a lack of stress contrasts to which the native English speaker from outside the Caribbean is accustomed. Specific prosodic distinctions that illustrate the case for tonal Jamaican Creole are found in examples such as *rúudnís* 'sexual intercourse'; *rúudnis* 'rudeness'; *kiss mi nóh* 'I dare you to kiss me'; *kiss me nōh* 'I want you to kiss me'.[1] The first utterance ends on a rising pitch glide; the second, on a falling one.

At the morphological level, a number of lexical forms illustrate non-English formations frequent in Jamaican Creole but absent from Jamaican English except where code shifting takes place. Allsopp (1976) and Rickford (1976) point out several examples where "actor" and "agent" combine to form what is given in English as a single free morpheme: for example, *eye-water*, Jamaican Creole *yaiwáata* 'tears'. In Twi, the pattern *ani-suo* 'eye-water' suggests calquing in Jamaican Creole and other English-based creolized languages; other examples are Fante *enyiwa + nsu* 'eye-water'; Yoruba *omi-oju* 'water eye'; Igbo *anya-miri-akwa* 'eye water flowing' (Allsopp 1976, p. 12). Common in Jamaica and other parts of the English-speaking Caribbean are constructions which suggest calques formed on a West African model such as *to grow a big man* 'to become an adult'; *bad mind* [bad máɪn] '(to have) evil intentions'; *mōut wáata* 'saliva'; *hand middle* [haŋ migl] 'palm of the hand'.

Jamaican English, like standard varieties of North American English and RP, follows a subject-predicate syntactic order. Jamaican Creole, however, does not follow a consistent subject-predicate order. Observe the following examples:

1. *wān shīf mi hab rāta kōt ī*
2. *a di wan shíf mi hab rātā kóti* } '[the] only shirt I have, rats have got it'
3. *ā gáan mī gáan man*
4. *mī de gáan man/mī gáan man* } 'I'm really going now/I must go now'

In the first example, there is no explicit definite article. *Wan* includes the meaning of 'the only'; *mi hab* carries the full functional load of the relative clause, 'that I have'; *rata* is an implied plural explicitly marked in Jamaican Creole with *-dem*; *kot* is unmarked for tense or aspect, and *i* is nasalized and a variant of 'it'. In the second and third examples, *a* has the force of 'it is'. One could almost render the third sentence 'it is going, I'm going, man', and it would be an identical rendition of one English dialectal phrasing. But even if one were inclined to stretch the imagination for that example, neither the second nor the third example resembles any form of English syntax in arrangement or morphology. Both the third and fourth examples are intentionally emphatic in urgency. Emphasis is shown by repetition of *gaan*. A formally literal sequencing of items in the last example would be *me I am going, man/me going, man*. The second alternative in the last example is particularly interesting since *mī gáan* would contrast with *mí gaan*, the latter meaning 'I am going, not someone else'. The tone of *gáan* would end on an upglide, whereas *gaan* would terminate on a downglide. One function of tone, then, is to distinguish grammatical meaning in Jamaican Creole.

To examine in further detail the difference between Jamaican English and Jamaican Creole, observe the following text by F. McKnight from the *Daily Gleaner* (13 February 1978):

> Some people say it must be duppy that controlling the gunmen who shooting up the country. And don't worry try telling these people what the psychologists, sociologists and criminologists say about it because these people are convinced that is duppy controlling the society in general.
>
> They say that is the duppies from all of those people who we use to hang and baby duppies we did trample up at the stadium and from the babies some mothers used to throw in pits. Is those duppies gang up and running the society wild.
>
> Then there are the other people who believe that is "A certain sort of Madness" that controlling all of us. They say well what else can explain why the gunmen wouldn't even take a day off on Christmas day or why they start to take out people finger nails even though finger nails don't have any value. Don't tell them what the experts or any "ologist" have to say about it. They are sure as fate that is "A certain sort of Madness."

Rather than "fate" or some abstract mystical source of resolving matters beyond easy mortal interpretation, *duppy* is the *deus ex machina* held accountable for actions not otherwise explainable in rational terms. Cassidy and Le Page (1967, p. 164) gloss *duppy* as *dopi/dopii*; Edwards (1974, p. 10) attributes *duppy* to Adangme *adope* 'ghost', a West African spiritlike, ethereal essence. A duppy is not, however, to be equated with a poltergeist, although duppies may be harmful or beneficent, depending on the circumstances. Like the oracle at Delphi, they bear much interpretation in their pronouncements, which are often given in a high, falsetto key by storytellers.

Regardless of the actions of duppy, which may well lead one astray from the main task of linguistic explanation, it is the grammatical facts which prove of overwhelming interest. This interest derives from the interplay of Jamaican Creole and Jamaican English not at the phonological, but at the syntactic level. In the first sentence of the first paragraph of the preceding quotation, the noun phrase complementizer is omitted before *it*. *It* has subject function in the embedded sentence. The appropriate *be* form is left out before *-ing* forms. Additionally, the noun phrase complementizer is excluded before *gang*, a form which may be read in translation as either an unmarked past tense or an unmarked *-ing* form. If the first interpretation is accepted, then no noun phrase is needed; however, the omission of the noun phrase before verbal *-ing* forms where progressive *be* is missing is a regular feature of Jamaican English where code shifting from Jamaican Creole is in operation. In the last line of the first paragraph, a noun phrase occurs before copula *be*, but the subject slot is empty where standard English would have *it*. The matrix sentence has no overt subject in the last sentence of the second paragraph, but patterns instead on Jamaican Creole, which would give *a di dopidem a gang up an a ron di sosaiiti wail*. Rather than accounting for absent *it* as subject deletion, and an element of the mythical continuum, the syntactic construction exemplifies code shifting from Jamaican Creole. Copula *a* permits subject incorporation as "understood" in the same way that English imperatives permit subject deletion.

In "baby duppies we did trample . . ." *did* occurs as a past tense marker before unmarked *trample*. Standard English permits *do* where emphasis is intended, but no emphasis is intended in the Jamaican English version. Code shifting provides the most natural explanation from Jamaican Creole *done trample* or, simply, *trample*. With *did*, the "correctness" principle is in operation so that rather than deleting *do* and marking *trample* for past, *do* is marked for past. *Start*, in "they start to take out people finger nails," is unmarked for past tense, a characteristic of Jamaican Creole and other creolized languages.

"Some people say it must be duppy" clearly illustrates code shifting from Jamaican Creole to Jamaican English, since Jamaican English would have *duppy* preceded by an article, or *duppy* pluralized in the normal manner. The grammar of the sentence provides a compromise between Jamaican Creole *it a dopidem* and Jamaican English *it must be duppies* by creating a "generic" category *duppy*. Observe that further on in the selection, "generic" *duppy* is given in "these people are convinced that is duppy," but formally pluralized in "Is those duppies . . ." Nonstandard English of either British or American origin would have *dem* or *them* before *duppies*. In Jamaican English, however, the correct demonstrative applies, but code shifting applies either through article deletion before *duppy*, or through subject deletion of *it*. The type of code shifting exemplified above has not been described before in "if . . . then" terms so that one can claim unequivocally that wherever nouns are pluralized according to standard English norms, code shifting to Jamaican Creole is illustrated by subject deletion. In Jamaican Creole, however, subject deletion is quite common in such statements as *is Mievis briŋdem kom* '[it] is Mavis who brought them here'.

Further on in the selection, one can see two other peculiarities consistent with Jamaican Creole and other English-based creoles: the regularity of unmarked past tense and the lack of formal possessive markers as in ". . . people finger nails . . ." for 'people's finger nails' or 'the finger nails of people'. *Nails*, of course, is not Jamaican Creole, but the contiguous arrangement of two nominal forms before a third where the first nominal indicates possession is normal in Jamaican Creole. Quite clearly, there are grammatical features of Jamaican English which correspond in their underlying forms with other varieties of standard English. The "deviations" from Jamaican English within the selection exemplify

English in the Caribbean

the interaction of two grammatical systems, Jamaican English and Jamaican Creole. By closely observing and understanding a creole society, one can see from the selection, fragmentary as it is, that implicit constraints apply which control topic, rhetorical device, grammatical constructions, and lexical choice and therefore account for code shifting.

The example we have been discussing deals with the increase in banditry and violence in Jamaica. The author conceives of *duppy* as the cultural vehicle understood by the entire society, without regard for ethnic differentiation, to be explanatory on different levels: the satirical and unreal, the folk mythology, and the cultural *deus ex machina*. The operation of code shifting can be effective only through the audience's perception of the well-known rhetorical devices. These devices trigger lexical choice and grammatical structures which appeal to a middle-class audience. The middle-class audience understands both Jamaican English and Jamaican Creole. The use of "generic" *duppy*, subject deletion, absent possessive markers, and deleted progressive *be* indicate that the explanation for violence given in the selection cannot be accounted for through the past and the belief in *duppy*. Further, the *duppy* is rejected by the middle class as a "creature" from a West African milieu. The compromise in code shifting, in which use is made of Jamaican Creole devices without producing all the syntactic arrangements of Jamaican Creole, makes the selection acceptable to an audience that would reject pure Jamaican Creole on the one hand and pure Jamaican English on the other.

The incorporation of Jamaican Creole forms is deliberate, not unconscious. The focus of shifting from Jamaican English to Jamaican Creole is created by the event described, an event which evokes images and beliefs rooted in the folk experience which distinguishes between social acts limited by man-made laws and acts over which the common law has no control. Although one important constraint on code shifting is audience, one can observe that the following example from *Peenie Wallie* (1976, p. 19) shows no evidence of code shifting:

> It is commonly believed that followers of Ras Tafari are all members of the lower classes, poor and generally uneducated. This opinion does not seem to be true and evidence points to the religion spreading and gaining many followers among young middle class high school and university students.

Peenie Wallie, a name taken from the commonplace name for the firefly in Jamaica, is a college publication in the west of the island and is directed at the intellectual. In past years, the Ras Tafari movement had no appeal to intellectuals, since one of the claims of the movement was that Haile Selassie of Ethiopia was their leader, and that all members derived from Ethiopia and owed allegiance to that country. With a focus on the ideational content of the movement and the development of an "in language" of reference and identification, the language of wider communication became Jamaican English because only through Jamaican English could the Ras Tafari movement gain followers in the power elite. Jamaican English is the language of abstraction and respectability and, therefore, the vehicle chosen in the selection from *Peenie Wallie* to publicize the movement. But if Jamaican English is used to appeal to the intellect, Jamaican Creole is increasingly used at the lexical and syntactic level in the creation of verbal art. Poverty and deprivation on the one hand, and the world of property and power on the other, are cogently spliced with the deft use of both Jamaican Creole and Jamaican English to correlate with each phrase of the social scene. For illustration, take the following poems from the *Jamaica Daily News Magazine* (28 March 1977, p. 7):

14 and pregnant

Fourteen and pregnant—Jesus Christ!
What Mama goin seh?
Well, dat wi haffi stop
in about six months or so
Even if dem would allow me in
mi nah walk roun wid belly
mek dem pickney laugh at me
No sah, no school!
An dat mean no "0" Levels
nex year neider
Dat mean domestic work
Jesus Christ!

[Michael Reckord]

Caviar and Sky Juice

Lancies of light strike
the polished chrome of the Rolls Royce
that glided unseen through customs.
Power steered downhill
with effortless ease
by a manicured finger
it glides past the bundle of fined rags
who is compiling a treasury of waste paper.
It lik a pot 'ole
one "polish tin" wheel fly
offa de hand cart
dat did mek outa
ole boawd
"trow-way" tin
and Foreshore Road rubba

English in the Caribbean

de sky-juice dat sell
an 'im did tief de steering wheel.
The finger curves the chrome round
a corner han' and body strain to tun
de steering wheel chrome and cart
lik up!
Sky juice fly in de face of chrome
car door opens, polished shoe
tests the ground
dutty barefoot step offa de rubba!
pure palava
FM plays "we shall overcome."

[Jennifer Brown]

Why,
Why not?

The desert is dry:
on the surface:
dig it deep
to find running water.
Why, why not?
The belly is full:
on the surface:
search it deep
to find enduring hunger.
Why, why not?
The body is dead:
on the surface:
slit it open
to find a bleeding heart.
Why not?

[Iro Eweka]

Although we have well-established conventions for English spelling, British or American, we have none for Jamaican Creole. At least, we have none that is so overwhelmingly prestigious as to win wide acceptance. Each writer of Jamaican Creole adapts the English system of spelling to suit his own representation of the phonetic facts. Since the audience knows Jamaican Creole, whatever deviations from writer to writer may obtain, the word and meaning are clear. The notion of prestige opens up another issue, and that is that Jamaican Creole has no official prestige or acceptance even though its use in speech and writing is more prevalent than ever. The fluctuations of pitch, the leveling of stress, the cadence and rhythm all go unmarked before the reader as either faultless Jamaican Creole or terribly convoluted English. That English spelling is adapted to the needs of Jamaican Creole presents no problem to the indigenous audience clearly able to distinguish between two codes. To the non-native speaker, however, the text may be incomprehensible or, if seemingly comprehensible, only so at a trivial level. The fact that a word or phrase is recognizably "English" on paper or in speech has little relationship to its semantic extension in Jamaican Creole. For example, *bot di cháil doan íit* 'the child won't eat' would be misinterpreted by the unilingual English speaker as 'the child doesn't eat' on the basis of surface representation. To demonstrate some of the phonological differences between Jamaican Creole and Jamaican English, consider the short phonemicized transcription below of a section from "Caviar and Sky Juice":

ɪt lík a pātúol
wan pālɪshtīn wíil flái
áaf dɪ hānkyáat
dat dīd mek óutā
úol búod
trúowe tīn
an fúorshúor rúod rōba
di skáijúus dat sēl
an ɪm did tīef dɪ stéerīng wíil.

[It (the Rolls Royce) struck a pot hole,
A polished tin wheel flew
off the hand cart
That was made out of
old boards,
discarded pieces of tin
and pieces of inner tubes and old tires
found on the Foreshore Road.
(Such was the construction of the handcart whose vendor sold beverages.)
And the steering wheel that controlled
the handcart was stolen (from somewhere).]

Grammatically, the transcribed verses conform to all the rules of Jamaican Creole grammar except in two lexical items: use of *it* and *a* in the first line for *im* and *wan*, respectively. Where English uses *she* or *it* to refer to an automobile, Jamaican Creole often uses *ī* or *im*. For *a*, Jamaican Creole uses *wan*. The variation within the poem at the lexical level is permissible because of the rhythm of the verse. Tenses are unmarked; periphrastic expressions are not used in such expressions as *fúorshúor rúod rōba* 'rubber from the Foreshore Road'. Plurals are unmarked, as in *úol búod* 'old boards'. I have marked the transcription for pitch, however, to illustrate the prosodic features that characterize Jamaican Creole speech patterns. Note also the two uses of *do* which do not in any way correspond with Jamaican English *do*. In *did mek*, *did* functions as a perfective marker in the sense of English 'was made'. In the case of *did tief*, however, *did* functions simply to reinforce the fact that the steering wheel was stolen. The phrase in which *did tief* occurs conveys the passive idea without any other formal arrangement of lexical items.

The variation in syntax between Jamaican English and Jamaican Creole in "Caviar and Sky Juice" is not free, but controlled by the realities of a binary creole world view. I use *creole* in the sense of subsuming all social classes within creole society. That the first eight lines of "Caviar and Sky Juice" conform to Jamaican English is no accident, but is intended to represent the world of the upper middle class where Jamaican English prevails. Conversely, Jamaican Creole is the world of the street vendor of "sky juice." The writer of the poem controls both Jamaican Creole and Jamaican English and makes very few compromises in syntax to accomplish her objective.

In "14 and Pregnant," the syntax is preponderantly Jamaican Creole, with *even if* and *would allow* from English. But there are some constructions in the poem which reveal another crucial difference from Jamaican English. The protagonist is moving from one social stratum to another. The first social stratum, that of the milieu of Jamaican Creole, is to be leavened through attendance at one of the secondary schools where English is the official medium of instruction. The schoolgirl of the poem will be unable to attempt the transition from Jamaican Creole to Jamaican English, however, for reasons the poem makes obvious. Code shifting shows up in the suppositional clause beginning *Even if*. Consider the negative function in the line *mi nah walk roun wid belly* 'I am not going to walk around with a belly', more freely translated as 'I am not going to walk around pregnant'. *Mi nah walk* employs a subject noun phrase followed by the negative marker immediately preceding the simple form of the verb. In *mi nah walk*, there is no progressive marker but two other variants are possible, both of which contain it: *mi no go walk* and *mi no a go walk*.

It is interesting to examine the form *no* (represented variously as *noh* or *nah*) because there is a distinction between *no* as negative marker and *no* as tag. In most varieties of English, the tag copies the auxiliary or makes use of a form of *do* with polarity opposite the main clause: *he has left the room, hasn't he?*; *Ruth doesn't like fishing, does she?* In Jamaican Creole, however, tags pattern more like Spanish than like English: *im no líiv di rúum, nó?* 'hasn't he [already] left the room?'/'he has [already] left the room, hasn't he?'; *Rúut a fish, nó?* 'Ruth has been fishing, hasn't she?'/'Ruth is fishing, isn't she?' (Spanish: *el no sale del cuarto, ¿verdad? Rut pesca, ¿verdad?*) *No* in Jamaican Creole, like *verdad* in Spanish, appears in the tag. It is immaterial whether *no* appears in the main sentence or not. *No*, however, has other semantic characteristics than as simple tag. Take, for example, *dat no im fáadá* 'that is indeed his father' and *dat no im fáada* 'that's not his father'. The contrast between high tone and low tone on the final syllable distinguishes between assertion and negation in Jamaican Creole (Christie 1979). *No* can be deleted in the same construction given above as in *dat ím fáadá* (assertive) and *dat im fáada* (implicit negation). High tone contrasts with low on *im* and on the final syllable of *faada* (Lawton 1963).

Tonal contrasts, which operate mainly at a grammatical level in Jamaican Creole, operate differently in Jamaican English. Relative pitch functions in Jamaican English over utterances the way stress functions in standard English. In Jamaican English, stress is level in unemphatic utterances. Unfortunately, the written word does not convey prosodic features. Nevertheless, both "14 and Pregnant" and "Caviar and Sky Juice" demonstrate crucial differences between Jamaican English and Jamaican Creole at the segmental level. In "Why, Why Not?", the syntax is obviously in conformity with standard English. Although formal and informal English can be unambiguously differentiated, there is no such thing as formal versus informal Jamaican Creole. When Jamaican Creole and Jamaican English are used within the same stretch of discourse, the linguistic process involved is that of code shifting. In an oral interchange among speakers who command both Jamaican English and Jamaican Creole, phonological shifts from one code to the other are often accompanied by lexical shifts, or by both lexical and syntactic ones. The example given below is quoted from the remarks of a local citizen speaking at a formal meeting of the mayor and town council of Kingston:[2]

Wen it keim aut dat di faia chiif mied a vizit in disemba an lied daun sərtən ruulz tu disemba it wəz nat den wid di nalij əv di taun klaak so dat dier wəz dis vækyum dat noub adj nyu dat di faia chiif had mied diiz vizits ən lied daun diiz ruulz dat giev di sinimәz taim tə karek diiz tiŋz dat iz in disemba piirəd.

[When it came out that the firechief made a visit in December and laid down certain rules to December, it was not done with the knowledge of the town clerk. So that there was this vacuum that nobody knew that the firechief had made these visits and laid down these rules that gave the cinemas time to correct these things—that is in December period.]

The transcription is in a quasi-phonemic style similar to that of Frederick Cassidy and Robert Le Page's transcription in the first edition of the *Dictionary of Jamaican English* (1967). No agreed-upon writing system yet exists for Jamaican Creole. The contour lines represent a phonetic distribution of relative pitch; the utterance is syllable-timed with stress. Note that Jamaican English diphthongs [ɪe] are replaced by Jamaican Creole [ie]: [ei] becomes [ie]; [ə] replaces [a] in some instances ([a] occurs in Jamaican Creole and [ə] in Jamaican English). *Th* is absent and is represented by *d*, [d]. The foregoing phonological differences between Jamaican English and Jamaican Creole illustrate in a simplified way the result of code shifting on the phonological level. The replacement of Jamaican Creole [a] by Jamaican English [ə] does not represent "interference," since "interference" assumes that no language contact situation exists, and that variation is free or unconscious in a speaker's performance. For example, a Puerto Rican speaker learning English will say *I want to assist your class*, or *I want to assist to your class*. Spanish *asistir a* 'to attend' is a false cognate of English *assist*, but the closeness of the form to English *assist* produces a wrong sentence in the first instance, and a totally incorrect one in the second. The sentence intended is *I want to attend your class*.

The point of the example is that "interference" results from a language-learning situation. The Jamaican English speaker *knows* Jamaican Creole and knows what linguistic compromises to make based on the situation and the participants. Use of either [θ] or [ð] would be too formal in a "mixed" audience and be immediately recognized as "putting on airs." The use of [ə] is acceptable since it is not as distinctive a sound in free discourse as are interdental fricatives. The one area of discourse where "interference" does enter is at the prosodic level, the most difficult to change or modulate at will—particularly so after a speaker has passed the "critical" period for language acquisition. The speaker moving from Jamaican Creole to Jamaican English carries over the prosodic pattern from Jamaican Creole. Two-syllable and three-syllable words have rising pitch on final syllables. The shift back to Jamaican Creole from Jamaican English has the "constant" of the prosodics which functions contrastively within a non-Jamaican English syntax.

The relation of Jamaican English to Jamaican Creole has sparked a great deal of controversy about the nature of linguistic variation within a creole society:

> The term "post-creole continuum" [describes] . . . a lack of a sharp distinction between a creole language and the standard variety of one of the donor languages [English]. Instead of a complete break between the two systems, there is a continuous range of speech varieties. This is the result of the creole gradually merging with the standard language [English] changing slowly over time and acquiring many features of the standard [Jamaican English]. [Day 1974, p. 38]

The foregoing statement, an accurate reflection of a current position, assumes a static view of language in one respect and a dynamic view in another. The acceptance of a "creole language" which does not have a sharp distinction suggests the dynamic view. Languages do not have to have "sharp distinctions" for them to be defined as languages. Flemish and Dutch are good examples. As Richard E. Wood writes, "Czech and Slovak are two because the Czechs and Slovaks so consider them, though they are in some ways closer than American and British English."[3]

Wood's view makes the business of language definition one of national opinion rather than of linguistic design. Nevertheless, sharp breaks in phonology and lexicon are not necessary for separating Jamaican English from Jamaican Creole. Lexicon changes rapidly in language development, followed by phonology and syntax, with prosody last. The crucial elements of distinction between Jamaican English and Jamaican Creole lie in syntax and prosody. Day's "speech varieties" (1974, p. 39) do not describe Jamaican Creole in contact with Jamaican English, although they could describe the differences between Canadian English and those of the midwestern United States or between Midland and Midwestern American English. The differences between Jamaican Creole and Jamaican English are analogous to the differences between Portuguese or Spanish and between French and Haitian Creole. The claim of Jamaican Creole merging with English and changing "slowly over time . . . acquiring many features of the standard [Jamaican English]" (Day 1974, p. 38) is not a linguistic fact, but a hypothesis, a hypothesis no longer tenable in the light of events in Jamaica. The political shift to democratic socialism, the flight of the old middle class, and the inability of government to carry out a coherent school policy have placed Jamaican English in an even more limited role than it had before these social changes took place. Additionally, the focus on Jamaican Creole as worthy of study, and the fact of a developing literature in Jamaican Creole coupled with developments in the theater, music, and dance have all operated to improve the acceptability of Jamaican Creole as a medium of communication. Concurrently, other areas of the anglophone Caribbean have their own developments in their "standard" variety of English as well as in their creole vernaculars. In spite of the improving status of Jamaican Creole, however, there is still an ambivalent attitude toward the full, communicative role of Jamaican Creole, a language in as wide a use as Papiamentu in the islands off the Venezuelan north coast. To facilitate language planning, Jamaican Creole and Jamaican English must be viewed in a binary relation. Without a binary view of language in Jamaica, problems of education, intrasocial communication, and industrial relations become impossible to resolve.

The view of urban versus rustic "varieties" of language may be allowable for Guyana, but not for Jamaica, where automobiles have replaced bicycles on an island no larger than Rhode Island. The open market common in the less developed countries of Latin American has been largely replaced by the "supermarket" of Jamaica. The flow of traffic from one part of Jamaica to another is as intense as ever even though gasoline has increased in price from less than one dollar to more than four Jamaican dollars per imperial gallon. Most of the population is under twenty-five years of age, with a large proportion functionally illiterate. Identity has become an important issue. The one aspect of identity which is ineradicable is speech, and a phonological distinction between Jamaican English and Jamaican Creole is one aspect of code shifting which operates to place an individual within Jamaican culture and within a particular social class. Phonological code shifting accompanied by lexical and syntactic shifts is social rather than demographic, vertical rather than horizontal: social in the sense that code shifting is not constrained by geographic region but by the social demands of interaction within a bilingual speech community; vertical in the sense that code shifting is a phenomenon of middle-class language behavior. Only the socially secure can shift without adverse consequences. Code shifting takes place within the same social group, generally, but it also operates in speech between employer and maid, and between political candidates and their constituencies.

Code shifting is diglossic in the sense that Fishman (1971, p. 52) uses the term; that is, the shift serves an intragroup purpose. In addition, certain types of quasi-religious ceremonies call for Jamaican Creole rather than Jamaican English. The telling of folktales and the Christmas pantomime call for Jamaican Creole. In short, Jamaican Creole does have a ritualistic function as well as a larger social role. It is in the role of ritual that Jamaican Creole has a diglossic function. The Anancy story is the best example of an art form in which Jamaican Creole is requisite. Riddles, proverbs, and poems of the kind offered in this discussion as examples of code shifting are all forms of the diglossic function of language in Jamaica.

One of the major problems that arises in a discussion of Jamaican Creole is that the preponderant number of its lexemes are drawn from English and, therefore, we refer to Jamaican Creole as an English-based creole. As more and more work is done on creolized languages by native linguists who have studied in West Africa, West African reflexes of prosodic features, calques, and sentence patterning become more obvious than hitherto. The linguist is still hampered, however, by the dearth of attested historical evidence for West African sources of creoles. Customarily, Jamaican Creole employs words of English derivation in a non-English manner, and arranges these words sententially in a similar non-English manner. For example, observe the following sentences.

5. *Dem duon buot mama yet* 'my mother hasn't voted yet' (literal: 'dem don't vote Mama yet').
6. *Dem gwain to buot mi aanti fram kontri* 'my aunt from the country is going to vote' or 'my aunt from the country is going to be permitted to vote' (literal: 'dem going to vote my aunt from country').
7. *Dem sen mi tek an bai pensil* 'they send me to buy pencils' (literal: 'they send me take and buy pencils').
8. *Mi win Debi kom daun and Debi win kom op* 'I won the race with Debbie going one way, and Debbie won the race going the other way' (literal: 'me win Debbie come down and Debbie win me come up').
9. *Mi wiek suun mek shi kyãã wiek mi* 'because I woke up early, she didn't have to wake me' (literal: 'me wake soon make she can't wake me').
10. *Di boddem kyã iit* 'the birds can be eaten' or 'the birds are edible' (literal: 'the birds can eat').

Reliance on the literal translation provides no adequate clue to meaning in the examples of Jamaican Creole syntax. Reliance on word order alone will give either the wrong meaning or an ambiguous one. Tentatively, one may conclude that the speaker is using a pidgin or else is a second-language learner in trouble. Neither tentative conclusion is correct, since the language exemplified is a speaker's first language. Because word order is not crucial to meaning, Jamaican Creole is different in one crucial way from Jamaican English and any other variety of English. For Jamaican Creole, lexicon and prosody provide syntactic meaning. Lexical items which are cognate with English are often false cognates. In example 7, *sen mi tek* is really a single semantic unit having the force of 'command'. Since *pensil* 'pencil' can be marked with -*dem* for plural, or left unmarked as it is in the example, one must *know* in some way that a plural is intended. Disambiguation of a noun plural from a noun singular is obtained through "implicit context"—the knowledge the speaker/hearer has of the social situation. The social situation involves an understanding of how some actions are carried out, how items are purchased, and the force of the total discourse. Sometimes "explicit context," the linguistic environment which conditions the form or function of a linguistic unit, applies, as in *bring mi wan bok, man* 'bring me a book, man'. Example 8 requires the hearer to understand that *win* means 'to beat someone at something'. *Kom daun* and *kom op* are understood through implicit context. Example 9 opens with a conditional clause, unmarked by any conventional means of English marking. *Mek shi* actually operates as the conditional clause marker, but follows rather than precedes the subordinated part of the sentence. Example 10 seems to be an unmarked passive. The key is *kyāā* 'can't'. There are some problems with claiming "passive," however, since it is not possible to claim that *di boddem kyā iit* is the same as *di boddem kyā iit* (*di fuud*) 'the birds can't eat the food'. There is no linguistic mechanism for reversing subject and object nominals. To differentiate between *the birds can be eaten* and *the birds can eat something*, the whole Jamaican Creole sentence must be rephrased, substituting *fiid* 'feed' for *iit* 'eat'. It is possible to have two different meanings for the sequence *di boddem kyāā iit*, but the difference will be '*the birds can be eaten* versus *the birds can't be eaten*. The difference in meaning is made by tonal contrast: (1) *di boddēm kyā̄ā íit* ↓ 'the birds can be eaten', and (2) *di boddēm kyáā íit* ↑ 'the birds can't be eaten'.

These examples are differentiated by the presence or absence of high tone on *kyāā* and rising or falling tone at the end of the sentence. In addition, the overall pitch of the second sentence is considerably lower than that of the first, so that in addition to the contrast between *kyáā* and *kyāā*, there is a difference in the spread of pitch over the entire utterance. The closest approximation of this pitch spread in English is the sarcastic *No* of unbelief. In example 5, *mama* is the object not of *buot* but *duon*. The sequence *dem duon buot* has the force of 'they have not permitted [my] mother to vote'. *They* is unspecified, and *my* is implied from the larger unit of discourse surrounding the example, but not given. If one translates *dem duon buot* as 'they don't vote', the translation will make no sense and therefore cannot be equated with English sentential patterning. In example 6, *dem gwain to buot* indicates that Auntie is going to be permitted to vote, rather than that Auntie be voted into some office. Quite clearly, one can see from the limited but substantive evidence given that Jamaican Creole is systematically different from Jamaican English and from English generally. Claims made for a single language in Jamaica with a postcreole continuum are made almost entirely on the grounds of phonological data divorced from lexicon and syntax and without regard for the development of a third language—Jamaican Creole—from contact between an Indo-European language, English, and non-Indo-European languages of West Africa. Rather than view the language situation in Jamaica as a single continuum, one can see evidence of language change in Jamaican English and in Jamaican Creole. In Jamaican English, the change is chiefly lexical. In Jamaican Creole, the change is lexical and semantic. The semantic change lies in the extension of meaning given to pronominal forms such as *I and I*, a locution of the Ras Tafari group but picked up by the general run of Jamaican Creole speakers. *I and I* reinforces the idea of self, physical and intellectual, and introduces a new way of using old forms to convey special meanings. The new development taking place within Jamaican Creole is not sufficiently established yet for detailed analysis, but it suggests a vibrant and living vernacular rather than one moving toward assimilation with Jamaican English.

Comparisons between the language situation in Jamaica and elsewhere in the Caribbean are hampered by there being no dictionary of the anglophone Caribbean, nor a usable grammar of the standard forms of English and their related vernaculars. Certain spoken phrases, idioms, and words are peculiar to the Caribbean in general, and others to specific island or regions on the Central American mainland. *To take in with someone, to dance calypso, to grow a big man*, and *pay him no mind* are some of the expressions current in the Caribbean. Some date from earlier English usage, while other forms of expression seem to be West African calques in English guise. Such words as *trouble, upstairs*, and *trust* have their own West Indian significance (Allsopp 1972, pp. 14–15).

The distinctions that one must make in the Caribbean are distinctions among English and, in the case of Jamaica, Jamaican English and Jamaican Creole. Tourists may never encounter the latter unless they stray from the usual path. If they do stray, they will find themselves in a speech community vaguely familiar but essentially different and strange—different because of non-Anglo social behavior, and strange because of a predominant vernacular, Jamaican Creole. If one is particularly fortunate, one may witness the code shifting and wordplay on several levels of interaction: between members of the middle class and those of the lower or working classes, or among members of the middle class themselves. The latter kind of interaction is the most difficult for the outsider to observe since the middle class likes to preserve the fiction of total ignorance of Jamaican Creole and variously refer to it as patois, broken talk, or "labrish."

The Jamaican language situation represents a remarkably stable situation between Jamaican English and Jamaican Creole in form and function—remarkable because Jamaica is surrounded by islands whose first language is Spanish. Both Hispaniola and Cuba are only a short distance away. The Central American mainland lies reasonably close and within the trade lanes of Jamaica. Until the advent of Castro in Cuba, there was some movement back and forth between Jamaica and Cuba of people to work the sugar plantations, and travelers used Cuba as a way station to the United States. There were also pockets of Jamaicans and other English-speaking people living in Cuba. During World War II, Spanish-speaking refugees were brought from Gibraltar by the British and lodged in Jamaica. In spite of the early history of Spanish settlement in Jamaica and the continued contacts and movement of people between Jamaica and the Spanish-speaking countries of the Caribbean, Spanish remained a discrete language in Jamaica, spoken by a relatively small group of persons, although the secondary schools sought to reinforce the use of Spanish by making it a requirement. Louise Bennett, a well-known folk poet and a "tradition" in Jamaica, makes fun of the contact between Spanish and English in Jamaica in "Jamaica Patois":

> Is wha Miss Liza she dah-form,
> Dah-gwan like foreigner!
> Because her sister husban get
> One job up at Mona!
> You want hear her cut Spanish, like
> She jus come out from sea!
> So till dem bwoy start fe call her
> De dry-lan refugee!
>
> Toder mornin me go ask her
> Wat she tink about de war,
> She gi out "Ah tink de war is
> Muyee malo me amar"
>
> [Bennett 1966, p. 87]

In what is a particularly good example of code shifting, Bennett ridicules the social aspirations of a non-Spanish-speaking Jamaican who seeks to improve her social status by aping the speech of a Spanish-speaking refugee's *muy malo mi amor*. Bennett, depicting a situation that took place some forty years ago, hardly contemplated that Spanish would be introduced into Jamaica during the 1970s as a second language. Quite regularly, the *Daily Gleaner*, an English-language newspaper with a large circulation in Jamaica, prints part of the news in Spanish. Recently, too, the political and social liaison with Cuba has grown, with cultural interchanges and a large Cuban embassy in Kingston. Whether enforced contact with Spanish will result in a trilingual Jamaica is dependent on political and social developments on the island and in the Caribbean in general.

English in the Caribbean

The one instance of language contact in the Caribbean where both Spanish and English survive side by side is that of Puerto Rico. Because of the different social and political conditions that obtained in Puerto Rico, a hybrid language has not developed as quickly as it is supposed to have done in the purely anglophone world. One can argue that the conditions were not ripe for hybridization or creolization of Spanish and West African languages in Puerto Rico. Spain's policy toward African slaves in Puerto Rico was markedly different from that applied in the British colonies of the Caribbean. Further, the proportion of "slave" to "free" in Puerto Rico never became such that slaves outnumbered nonslaves as in Jamaica and the rest of the British Caribbean colonies (Mintz 1971). The policy in the Spanish colonies also favored progressive acculturation, so that all the inhabitants were expected to embrace Catholicism and the Spanish language. As a result, the slave had no incentive for developing an intra-language or creole.

With the influx of the United States into the Puerto Rican environment, conditions were present for a language situation resembling in some overt features that of incipient creolization: American cultural dominance, a condition of conquest and occupation, and a population with ambivalent ties to Spain. Most of the people lived in very poor circumstances with a high degree of unemployment and illiteracy. In a survey conducted in Puerto Rico during the 1920s, it was reported that 8 percent of the children did not remain in school long enough to become functional in English (Cebollero 1945, p. 17). In spite of a high degree of illiteracy among Puerto Ricans, the dominance of the United States in political and cultural areas made it necessary for Puerto Ricans to acquire some English even though the conditions for such acquisition were far from ideal. Since the important matters of state and business were conducted in English, the elite acquired proficiency in English, and the unschooled majority acquired sufficient English as was necessitated by economic factors. This "sufficient English" is best observed today in a wide range of English lexical items adapted to Spanish phonology with morphological changes which often do not correspond fully to the linguistic rules of Spanish or English: *el fanbelt* for *la correa de ventilador*. In the following examples, "standard" Spanish occurs on the left and Puerto Rican "anglicized" Spanish on the right.

11.	A los mejicanos les gusta decir	Lo mejicano gusta decil
12.	Las estrellas que influyen en el amor	Un amol influenciada po[r] la ehtreya
13.	Yo escojo ésta	Yo pico éhta
14.	Renuncié el trabajo	{ Me quitié el trabajo { Me quitié el work
15.	Esa caja no pesa nada de todas maneras	Eha caja no pesa nada anyway

In example 11, *gustar* is intransitive in standard Spanish and the sentence corresponds to English 'one likes to say to the Mexicans'; in anglicized Spanish *gustar* is transitive and the sentence means 'The Mexicans like to say'! The pattern of sentence is anglicized by word ordering; *s* is deleted from *lo* and *mejicanos*; *gustar* loses *r*, and *decir* has *l* in place of final *r*. In example 12, Puerto Rican Spanish transforms the active voice to the passive voice and thus changes *the stars that influence love* to *a love influenced by stars*. The *influenced by* is adapted into Puerto Rican Spanish as *influenciada por* in place of the correct Spanish *influída en* or *influída sobre*. Both the morphological form of *influír* and the change from *en* to *por* reflect language contact with English. The phonological replacements of *r* by *l* and *s* by *h* arise from non-English influences. In place of such Spanish verbs as *escoger* 'to choose' (example 13) or *renunciar* 'to resign' (example 14), Puerto Rican Spanish uses *quitiar* from English 'quit' and *picar* from English 'pick, choose'. At one level of language contact of English with Spanish, the morphological English forms are adapted to Spanish morphological patterns. The foregoing examples have implications for language change where English reflexes show up in one dialect of Spanish in the same way West African reflexes appear in Jamaican English. These reflexes may very well indicate a process of creolization in which a third language evolves from contact between English and Spanish (Lawton 1973, pp. 193–94).

The result of language contact in Puerto Rico, however, is that the bilingual Puerto Rican code-shifts between English and Spanish. This code shifting is diglossic in that it is motivated by social and cultural constraints. Whether shifting is conscious or subconscious (Blom and Gumperz 1972, p. 432) is a moot point. Consider the following from Miguel A. Santín in *El Mundo* (San Juan, 5 August 1969).

> No, no more Three Kings' Day. *Ahora los regalos* are placed in stockings *en* Christmas Eve that in the old days *era conocida como Noche Buena*. *Pero* that's all past, *casi todos los* houses *tienen* fireplaces *donde se cuelgan las medias llenan de juguetes*, you follow me?

Although phonological shifts are not represented in this example, one can point out the salient ones. In *no*, [o] is a monophthong, not diphthongized as in English. All occurrences of *th* are [d̪]. In final *-st* clusters, *t* is deleted. The rhythm is syllable-timed, and the intonation is Spanish rather than English. Code shifting from Spanish to English in the example employs Spanish phonology and Spanish syntax for topical references: *los regalos* 'the gifts', *conocida como Noche Buena* 'known as *Noche Buena*', *llenan de juguetes* 'filled with toys'.

Santín is a well-known satirist, and he does justice to the interaction, the code shifting, between Spanish and English. This code shifting is not relegated to the semiliterate, but also takes place among well-educated persons who want to confirm to each other their competence in English. Rodolfo Jacobson (1977) has noted similar behavior among Mexican-Americans. Sometimes, code shifting operates as a put-down between participants, one of whom is less proficient than the other in English. Conversely, a New York Puerto Rican in Puerto Rico may be put down in Spanish since New York Puerto Ricans often have a much more restricted performance in acceptable Spanish than Puerto Rican residents of the same age and comparable schooling. Code shifting in Puerto Rico is further complicated by the social structure. For the most part, Puerto Ricans who have gone to the mainland United States have been those at the bottom of the social scale, with little education and no employment skills. Those who have been successful on the United States mainland sometimes return to take up residence in Puerto Rico. When they return, however, they are often proficient in English and their children are unilingual in English. Their behavior is that of Anglos rather than that of islanders. They are therefore rejected by the middle class in Puerto Rico and also by the working class from which they have come and, therefore, form a separate social structure within Puerto Rico. Most of these returnees operate entirely in English. Since there is no similar migration to the Spanish-speaking countries or to Spain, there is little reinforcement for Spanish.

Playing on the nature of code shifting in Puerto Rico and focusing on the nature of idiomatic translation and its relation to "literal" representation, María Esther M. de Febles, writing in the *San Juan Star* (1 April 1968), submitted the following:

> I am answering your card that appeared in the San Juan *Star*, and I want to tell you that I unscrewed and stretched myself from laughing.
>
> I accompany you in your sentiments by the disgrace that you had in your family. I wait that at the reading of this card Candidito is like coconut.
>
> My exit of the English idiom I accredit to my with-father who gave me something called a dictionary. It might not be the better one but to a given horse you don't look in the tooth. Besides I have many friends that are good in the English idiom and he who approximates himself to a good tree a good shadow will shelter him.
>
> My only advice to you is that the next time you want to go for a couple of sticks you go with your male breadfruits, so your wife will not give you of rice and mass.
>
> I was going to write you more early, but the first card, my son, flew it and he painted himself and took the mountain.
>
> Mr. Flower, please don't sleep yourself in the straw, because shrimp that sleeps will be carried by the current.
>
> I hope to see you at the return of the corner.

Some of these constructions seem very familiar to one who knows the language situation in Puerto Rico. There are false cognates literally transferred from Spanish as well as idiomatic forms pertinent to the island culture. For example, *by the disgrace* is rendered in Spanish as *por desgracia* 'unfortunately'; *my exit* is confused with *éxito* 'success'; *I accredit to my with-father* is a distortion of *acreditar* and *compadre*, the latter word having a wider range of meaning than simply 'godfather'. *To look a gift horse in the mouth* becomes *a given horse you don't look in the tooth*, where *given* seems to have been formed on analogy with *gift*. *Good in the English idiom* is another example of cognate confusion; Spanish *idioma* 'language', does not correspond to English *idiom*. Another interesting turn of phrase is *to go for a couple of sticks* where *sticks* (palitos) means 'drinks' in the sense of *going for a couple of drinks*. The idioms which are taken from Puerto Rican Spanish and translated literally into English may be as confusing to the bilingual Puerto Rican as they are to the unilingual English speaker, but Febles's parody is a good caricature of practices common in Puerto Rico.

Pérez Sala (1973, pp. 55–56) reports on calques which seem to reflect, conversely, the influence of English on Spanish in Puerto Rico: *haga Ud. consciente a sus amigos* 'make your friends conscious' for *entere a sus amigos*; *el está supuesto a venir* 'he is supposed to come' for *se supone que venga*; and *nos unimos en simpatía con Usted por la partida de su sobrina* 'we join you in sympathy . . .' for *le acompaño en el sentimiento por la muerte de su sobrina*. The kind of language transfer illustrated by Pérez Sala is concomitant with code shifting similar, if not identical, to the patterned shifting of Chicano speakers. A good illustration is reported by Pacífico (1977–78, p. 669).

> When I hear music I see images inside my head . . . *Tengo la mente cuando voy para hacer un trabajo y es el del pasado, yo tengo el don que yo puedo entrar en ese pasado y sentir las cosas y verlas de nuevo.* . . . I wrote as I matured. . . . Well, I have found that because you have religion, catholic and protestant, and different divisions in ideologies—left, right, and middle. And in business, forget it! In politics, *olvídate*. I decided I would rise, *porque soy un pajarito*, rise above all that.

Although the author grew up in New York City, the shifting back and forth from English to Spanish is precisely the same as that found in San Juan. The influence from New York is growing and cannot be neatly set aside as a passing phenomenon. The first shift is a detailed repetition of the theme in the first sentence and is addressed to a bilingual/bicultural audience in Puerto Rico. The other italicized items are "cues" rather than restatements—cues of opinion: *olvídate* 'forget [it]'; *porque soy un pajarito* 'because I am [like] a little bird'.

Looking at the examples of language contact in Puerto Rico, one can see that English and Spanish seldom appear as completely discrete systems in any but the most studied performances, oral and written. In speech [θ] and [ð] are replaced by [d̪] in English. The vowels are approximations of Spanish vowels—Puerto Rican dialect—rather than of English; final *r* is replaced by [ə] in variation with [a]. The prosodic pattern of English is replaced by that of Puerto Rican

English in the Caribbean

Spanish, and the rhythm is syllable-timed. When the bilingual language act is captured on paper in Puerto Rico, the written representation is in the standard form of either English or Spanish. Thus, the reader may very well miss the strategy of language interaction which has both an oral and a written dimension (Lawton 1977).

Looking at the anglophone Caribbean, one tends to divide the linguistic situation in the islands and on the eastern littoral of Central America into English, Spanish, French, and "other". It comes as something of a surprise to note that English is a contact language with Spanish in Puerto Rico, particularly, and that processes of change involving language adaptation, borrowing, calquing, and relexification are continuing in such a way as to modify our views about language development. Our focus on Jamaica on the one hand, and on Puerto Rico on the other, is meant not to minimize developments elsewhere in the Caribbean, but rather to treat English from a much-studied and influential base. Jamaican English and Jamaican Creole, however one regards their linguistic relationship, have influenced other forms of English in places as close as Limón, Costa Rica (Herzfeld 1976) and as far away as Sierra Leone. Jamaican English has been little influenced by Spanish or French in spite of Jamaica's being but a relatively short distance from Hispaniola to the east and Cuba to the north. Actually, pockets of Jamaicans existed in Cuba, Panama, Costa Rica, and Belize, and still do to this day. In some instances, they have retained the tradition of English much modified by Spanish (Herzfeld 1976).

Grammatical features current and variant in Jamaican Creole and Jamaican English show up elsewhere in the Caribbean. Alleyne (1976), in a discussion of Trinidadian English, reflects on "habitual aspect forms of adjectival predicators":

16. *hi dʌ bi sik* 'he's usually (or always) sick'
17. *hi go bi sik* 'he'll be sick'
18. *hi mʌs bi dʌz siŋ* 'he probably (or always) sings'

In Jamaica, however, I observe differences among Jamaican English *he is sick, man/he is sick all di time, man* and Jamaican Creole *hi(m) sik aal di taim* 'he's usually (or always) sick'. Contrastively, Trinidadian English's *hi go bi sik* becomes Jamaican Creole *hi(m) gwain sik/a sik/hi(m) gwain sik*. Example 18 from Trinidadian English has no exact counterpart in Jamaican Creole; the closest equivalent would be *a tiŋk se him siŋ*.

Cases like example 19 from Trinidadian English show *get* functioning as a passive marker.

19. *it get breek* 'it was (has been) broken'

Examples 20–22 show alternative expressions in Jamaican Creole, and both a passive meaning and a simple past coexist in each.

20. *it don briek* 'it was (has been) broken'
21. *it brok(op)* 'it was (has been) broken'
22. *a brok it brok* 'it was (has been) broken'

Trinidadian English's *mi faada hat* 'my father's hat' is identical in construction and semantics with Jamaican Creole; however, Trinidadian English's *a ẽ goin* 'I'm not going' differs from Jamaican Creole's *mi no go/mi no a(de) go/mi no gwain go*. In Jamaica, as in other parts of the anglophone Caribbean, *be* occurs unmarked for tense, person, or number distinction, as in *we/I is going. Dem a go/dem going/dei going/they are going* also occur as socially constrained variations. Alleyne points out that in Trinidad, Barbados, and Guyana habitual aspect with *do* occurs, as in *we does live in the city*. Topicalizing *be* is also common, as in *is who do it? Is Harry do it?* The latter two examples can be treated as calques from Creole with West African reflexes, on analogy with *a hu duwit? a hari duwit?* In addition, *ẽ*, which varies with *ent* 'ain't', occurs everywhere in the Caribbean except Jamaica. In Trinidad, *ent* occurs in such expressions as *he dʌz ẽnt sing/he ẽnt dʌz sing* 'he is not in the habit of singing'.

Undoubtedly, one could list far more similarities than dissimilarities in syntax and phonology among the varieties of anglophone English in the Caribbean. The anglophone of the Caribbean, however, is oriented toward British norms of speech even though North American influence is more pronounced than it was twenty-five years ago. Allsopp (1972, p. 1) feels that the major problem is lexical and to this end proposes a dictionary that would encompass the entire anglophone Caribbean rather than any single specific area. A related problem is that variant meanings of the same lexical forms occur in different parts of the region. The situation in the regions where British influence is predominant or was predominant in the immediate past is grossly different from that obtaining in Puerto Rico, but there are analogical developments in English contact with Puerto Rican Spanish and English contact with Chicano Spanish in the continental United States. These developments must be viewed in the total context of English in the Caribbean. Linguistic changes in the English of the Caribbean have not only a linguistic dimension but social and political dimensions which exert strong pressures toward or away from a normative standard. As people move back and forth through the Caribbean and extend their itinerary to Canada and the United States, variations at all levels will arise and be incorporated into several dimensions: creole, in the case of those regions where creole is current; local standard forms of English prevailing among the middle and upper middle classes; and both Spanish and English in Puerto Rico.

NOTES

1. This particular example was contributed by Walter Edwards of the University of Guyana.

2. This example was recorded on tape in 1975 from a radio broadcast.
3. Richard E. Wood, personal communication, 3 October 1978.

REFERENCES

Alleyne, Mervyn C. "Dimensions and Varieties of West Indian English and the Implications for Teaching." *TESL Talk* 7, no. 1 (January 1976):51–55.

Allsopp, Richard. "The Problem of Acceptability in Caribbean Creolized English." In *UWI/UNESCO Conference on Creole Language and Educational Development*, pp. 1–20. Barbados: University of the West Indies at Cave Hill, 1972.

———. "The Case for Afro-Genesis." In *New Directions in Creole Studies*, edited by George N. Cave, pp. 1–21. Turkeyen, Guyana: University of Guyana, 1976.

Bennett, Louise. *Jamaica Labrish*. Kingston, Jamaica: Sangster's, 1966.

Bickerton, Derek, and Escalante, A. "Palenquero: A Spanish-Based Creole of Northern Columbia." *Lingua* 24 (1970):254–67.

Blom, Jan-Petter, and Gumperz, John J. "Social Meaning and Linguistic Structure: Code Switching in Norway." In *Directions in Sociolinguistics*, edited by John J. Gumperz and Dell Hymes, pp. 407–34. New York: Holt, Rinehart and Winston, 1972.

Carter, Hazel. *Evidence for the Survival of African Prosodies in West Indian Creoles*. Society for Caribbean Linguistics Occasional Paper, no. 13. St. Augustine, Trinidad: University of the West Indies, School of Education, 1979.

Cassidy, Frederick G., and Le Page, R. B. *Dictionary of Jamaican English*. London: Cambridge University Press, 1967. 2d ed. 1980.

Cave, George N., ed. *New Directions in Creole Studies*. Turkeyen, Guyana: University of Guyana, 1976.

Cebollero, Pedro A. *A School Language Policy for Puerto Rico*. San Juan: Imprenta Baldrich, 1945.

Christie, Pauline. *Assertive "No" in Jamaican Creole*. Society for Caribbean Linguistics Occasional Paper, no. 10. St. Augustine, Trinidad: University of the West Indies, School of Education, 1979.

Day, Richard R. "Decreolization: Coexistent Systems and the Post-Creole Continuum." In *Pidgins and Creoles: Current Trends*, edited by David DeCamp and Ian F. Hancock, pp. 38–45. Washington, D.C.: Georgetown University Press, 1974.

Edwards, Jay. "African Influences on the English of San Andrés Island, Colombia." In *Pidgins and Creoles: Current Trends*, edited by David DeCamp and Ian F. Hancock, pp. 1–26. Washington, D.C.: Georgetown University Press, 1974.

Escure, Genevieve, J. "Linguistic Variation and Ethnic Interaction in Belize: Creole/Carib." In *Language and Ethnic Relations*, edited by Howard Giles and Bernard St. Jacques, pp. 101–16. Oxford: Pergamon Press, 1979.

Febles, María Esther M. de. Letter to the Editor. *Star* (San Juan), 1 April 1968.

Fishman, Joshua. *Sociolinguistics: A Brief Introduction*. Rowley, Mass.: Newbury House, 1971.

Herzfeld, Anita. "Second Language Acrolect Replacement in Limón Creole." In *New Directions in Creole Studies*, edited by George N. Cave, pp. 1–21. Turkeyen, Guyana: University of Guyana, 1976.

Hymes, Dell, ed. *Pidginization and Creolization of Languages*. Cambridge: At the University Press, 1971.
Jacobson, Rodolfo. "The Social Implications of Intrasentential Code Switching." *New Scholar: New Directions in Chicano Scholarship* 6 (1977):227–56.
Lawton, David L. "Suprasegmental Phenomena in Jamaican Creole." Ph.D. dissertation, Michigan State University, 1963.
―――. "Code Shifting in Jamaica Creole." In *New Directions in Creole Studies*, edited by George N. Cave, pp. 1–25. Turkeyen, Guyana: University of Guyana, 1976.
―――. "Tag Questions in Jamaican Creole." Paper presented to the Michigan Linguistic Society at Central Michigan University, 10 October 1973.
―――. "Bilingual Strategies of Communication: Evidence from the Text." *The Fourth LACUS Forum*, edited by Michel Paradis, pp. 218–25. Columbia, S.C.: Hornbeam Press, 1977.
Le Page, Robert B. *Projection, Focussing, Diffusion*. Society for Caribbean Linguistics Occasional Paper, no. 9. St. Augustine, Trinidad: University of the West Indies, School of Education, 1978.
Mintz, Sidney W. "The Socio-Historical Background to Pidginization and Creolization." In *Pidginization and Creolization of Languages*, edited by Dell Hymes, pp. 481–89. Cambridge: At the University Press, 1971.
Pacífico, Patricia. "Piri Thomas Talks at Inter American University." *Revista/Review Interamericana* 7, no. 4 (1977–78):666–73.
Peenie Wallie. Montego Bay, Jamaica: Cornwall College, 1973. Reprint. Kingston: Jamaica Periodicals, 1976.
Pérez Sala, Paulino. *Interferencia lingüística en el Español hablado en Puerto Rico*. Hato Rey, Puerto Rico: Inter American University Press, 1973.
Pollard, Velma. "Code Switching in Jamaican Creole: Some Educational Implications." *Caribbean Journal of Education* 5 (1978):16–31.
Rickford, John R., and Rickford, Angela E. "Cut-Eye and Suck-Teeth: African Words and Gestures in New World Guise." *Journal of American Folklore* 89 (1976):294–309.
Santín, Miguel A. "Trasfondo." *El Mundo* (San Juan, Puerto Rico), 5 August 1969, editorial page.
Sprauve, Gilbert A. "Chronological Implications of Discontinuity in Spoken and Written Dutch Creole." In *New Directions in Creole Studies*, edited by George N. Cave, pp. 1–22. Turkeyen, Guyana: University of Guyana, 1976.
Taylor, Douglas M. *Languages of the West Indies*. Baltimore: Johns Hopkins University Press, 1977.
Williams, Eric. *History of the People of Trinidad and Tobago*. New York: Praeger, 1964.

The English Language in West Africa

Loreto Todd

For the purposes of this article, West Africa lies between seventeen and ten degrees of latitude south of the equator. It includes fourteen countries: Senegal, Gambia, Guinea-Bissau, Guinea, Mali, Sierra Leone, Liberia, Ivory Coast, Upper Volta, Ghana, Togo, Benin (formerly Dahomey), Nigeria, and Cameroon. No one is quite sure how many indigenous languages exist in this area of stratified multilingualism, but informed opinion—Berry and Greenberg (1971) and Treffgarne (1975)—puts the number at between one and two thousand. With such diversity, West Africa is one of the most linguistically complex regions in the world.

Apart from the local vernaculars which serve the mass of the people in their everyday domestic pursuits, several languages are also employed to facilitate interethnic communication. These include English, French, and Portuguese (in both standard and pidginized forms), Arabic, and vehicular forms of Manding and Hausa. In spite of the usefulness of Manding and Hausa as languages of wider communication, however, neither these nor any other West African vernacular is officially sanctioned as a language of state. This role is fulfilled by Portuguese in Guinea-Bissau; by French in Senegal, Guinea, Mali, Ivory Coast, Upper Volta, Benin, and Togo; and by English in Gambia, Sierra Leone, Liberia, Ghana, and Nigeria. Cameroon, which has been called "Africa in miniature," has two official languages—French and English. Thus, of the seven nations originally involved in extensive trading with West Africa (Portugal, Spain, Holland, Denmark, France, England, and Germany), only three have left a linguistic legacy in West Africa.

In the nineteenth century, the European powers divided West Africa as if it were something inanimate, a mere territory on a map without people, traditions, or organized patterns of government. European politicians paid scant attention to tribal systems and ethnic sensibilities. It was easier to draw a boundary that followed the course of a river than to take people and their traditions into account. It is true that the languages of the colonizers helped to bring socioeconomic efficiency and a sense of national identity to individual West African countries, but the patchwork-quilt effect of different European languages and a legacy of differing colonial governments have left many West African countries unable to communicate with their neighbors unless they acquire a second European language.

The Portuguese were the first Europeans to visit and establish settlements on the West African coast, but from 1481 onward the English showed some interest in the area. William Hawkins made three visits to West Africa between 1530 and 1532 (Beeching 1972, p. 51). By 1553 English ships had reached Benin

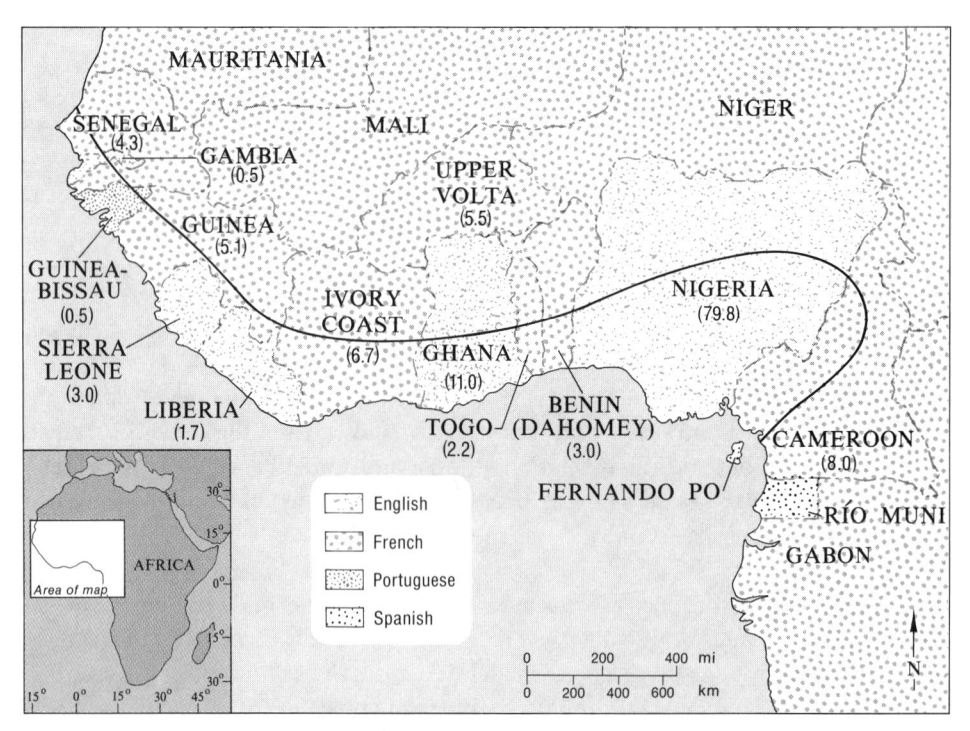

West Africa's colonial language legacy. Figures give the population in millions of individual countries on the basis of recent counts or estimates. The dark solid line indicates the approximate extent of the use of Pidgin English along the coast as a lingua franca.

in Nigeria and established a trade in ivory, pepper, and indigo; as early as 1555, John Lock had brought a group of African slaves to England (Beeching 1972, p. 68). From this date onward Africans were regularly taken to England, taught English, and then used as interpreters along the West African coast.

Although there is no textual evidence about what language was used as a means of communication between English and African traders at this early date, it seems likely that some words of English were heard on the West African coast in the sixteenth century. It also seems reasonable to assume that some form (or forms) of English was spoken in and around the six fortified settlements that the British had established on the coast of Ghana by 1663. Later on, several references to English being used as a trade language can be found in Jean Barbot's *Description of the Coasts of North and South Guinea*. With regard to the Sierra Leone region, for example, we are told:

> Most of the *Blacks* about the bay speak either *Portuguese* or *Lingua Franca*, which is a great convenience to the Europeans who come hither, and some also understand a little *English* or *Dutch*. [Churchill and Churchill 1732, vol. 5, p. 103]

There was at least some English on the Gambian coast in 1738 when Moore wrote: "The English have in the River Gambia much corrupted the English Language, by Words or literal Translations from the Portuguese" (Moore 1738, p. 294).

Probably the strongest claim for the use of English on the West African coast was made by Labarthe (1803, p. 70) when he claimed that the English language was spoken in all coastal areas with the result that the British had an enormous trading advantage.

By the early part of the nineteenth century, English was certainly spoken and perhaps even written from Gambia to Fernando Po.[1] It was even sufficiently well established in Calabar to allow a local Efik chief, Antera Duke, to keep a diary in a variety of English from 1785 to 1788. His entry for February 5, 1785, is as follows:

> about 6 am in aqua Landing with Little fog morning so I go Down for Landing after . . . clock noon wee 3 go to Egbo Young house Liverpool Hall for share 3 keg powder soon wee hear news ship com up so wee Run for Landing for gett 5 great guns Redy for firs sam time wee see Little canow Com & till wee his be Captin Loosdan Tender. [Forde 1956, p. 80]

> [About 6 A.M. at Aqua Landing with a little morning fog, so I went down to the landing; after . . . noon we three went to Egbo Young's house "Liverpool Hall" to share three kegs of gunpowder. Soon we hear the news that a ship is coming up [the river] so we run for the landing to get five guns ready to fire. At the same time we see a little canoe coming and he tells us he is Captain Loosdam's tender.] [Forde 1956, p. 28][2]

From this time onward English became increasingly well-established in ports along the West African coast. In the nineteenth century, as missionary activity increased, it became a language of education and advancement in the territories under British jurisdiction.

British varieties of English were not the only types to exert an influence on West Africa. Throughout the eighteenth century, an antislavery campaign grew, and many felt as Granville Sharp did that it was desirable to repatriate freed slaves to Africa.[3] Accordingly, in 1787, Sharp planned a settlement in Sierra Leone as a home for slaves freed in England. In the same year, 351 freed slaves sailed from Portsmouth and established Freetown. In 1792 John Clarkson, who was appointed the first governor of Freetown, brought 1,131 ex-slaves of American origin from Nova Scotia—they had fought for the British against the Americans in the American War of Independence—to join the original settlers, and these were further augmented in 1800 by the arrival of 550 Jamaican Maroons.

In 1808, the settlement was taken over by the British government as a crown colony, and it became a base for the British campaign to prevent slave trading on the West African coast. Many ships containing cargoes of human beings were captured by the British, and the slaves, often referred to as "recaptives," were taken to Freetown. Many of the recaptives chose to remain there, thus expanding the settlement so that, by 1834, it is estimated that there were 32,000 Creoles in Sierra Leone (Isichei 1977, p. 129).

The language of the original manumitted slaves was an English-based creole, subsequently called Krio. Since Krio speakers had prestige throughout West Africa as Christians, teachers, and clerks, their creole had a marked influence on many varieties of English throughout West Africa. Indeed, Fyfe (1956, p. 118) states that

> By the middle of the [nineteenth] century Creoles could be found from the Gambia to Fernando Po; by the end of it, they filled the government offices of Nigeria and were scattered as far away as the Cape of Good Hope.

When the Baptist Society of Britain established a mission station in Cameroon, 29 percent of the missionaries were Krios, either directly from Freetown or via Fernando Po (Gwei 1966, pp. 140–44). Today, Krio is spoken by about 120,000 people in and around Freetown and is acquired as a second language by many others (Hancock 1977, p. 375).

Liberia was also established as an African homeland for freed slaves and, like Sierra Leone, part of its population speaks a variety of English as a mother tongue. This settlement for freed American slaves of African origin was begun in 1821–22. It was subsequently enlarged by other groups of American slaves, and when Liberia became an independent republic in 1867, there were more than 11,000 Afro-Americans living there. The variety of English spoken by the original settlers seems to have had much in common with American Black English (Hancock and Kobbah 1975, p. 248), and American English has continued to exert a marked influence on Liberian English mainly through educational, cultural, and economic ties.

It is important to stress that each West African country had unique contacts and an individual history, yet at this stage it may be useful to distinguish four types of West African English.

First, the most common is *Pidgin English*, varieties of which can be found in coastal areas from Gambia to Equatorial Guinea. It seems likely that this chain of Pidgin Englishes came into being in the seventeenth and eighteenth centuries to facilitate trade with the British and that such forms of English were restricted to the vicinity of the ports.[4] This useful form of communication has survived largely unaffected by later colonial languages and has in various mixed communities become creolized. There has been some debate as to the interintelligibility of the coastal variants, and it is undoubtedly true that regional differences exist. Nigerians do not always understand Cameroon Pidgin and Krio speakers experience initial difficulties with Gambian Pidgin English, but speakers of all varieties are capable of adjusting their performances to guarantee mutual intelligibility.[5]

It is perhaps worth emphasizing that Pidgin English is a linguistic system and is not to be confused with Broken English, which is unsystematic and consists of little more than strings of English words.

Second, *second-language English* is often acquired at school and is strongly influenced by the mother tongue(s) of the speakers. The mother-tongue influence varies according to the linguistic abilities of individual speakers but can be seen at all linguistic levels.

Third, a definitive study has not yet been made of *standard West African English,* although studies of Ghanaian and Nigerian English exist. It is a written standard based mainly on British norms, although it reflects West African culture especially in vocabulary. Standard English is, for the moment, the only variety of English in West Africa with a recognized orthography, and the aim of most educated West Africans is that their use of the standard language should differ in no fundamental respect from standard British usage.

Fourth, *francophone West African English* is widely taught in French-speaking West Africa largely because of the growing need in francophone countries for a trained cadre capable of using English in foreign affairs, trade, banking, tourism, agriculture, science, and health care.

The English of West African francophones often illustrates influence from French, mainly at the levels of lexis and syntax though occasionally at the phonological level as well. The following examples show the carry-over of French habits into English and were all taken from the written English of francophone Cameroonians. Three main types of error are involved:

1. Selecting an English word which is similar in form to a French one but different in meaning. Thus:
   I wanted to demand *some help.*
   I need some essence *for my car.*
2. Selecting the wrong English equivalent:
   At the bottom (< *au fond*) he is a naughty (< *méchant*) somebody.
3. Carry-over of a French pattern:
   I cannot do it without to know (< *sans savoir*) *the reason.*
   They love themselves (< *ils s'aiment* 'they love each other').

Frequently, several types of error occur in the same sentence.

Many francophones learn English because it is a useful accomplishment in the fields of diplomacy and finance. Petty traders likewise find a knowledge of English valuable even though their English need only serve very restricted needs. In his dissertation on *The Status of English in the Ivory Coast* (1972, p. 37), Kone Souleymane explains that many Ivorian traders "have acquired a kind of telegraphic language necessary for their business." Included in their repertoire are such phrases as *come see*; *fine goods*; *you want?*; *O.K. pay*; *I sell good price*; *how much you give/want/pay?*; *what price you pay?*; *this fine dress*; *it suit you*; *it fit you*; and *pay it*. Interesting, though not so central to our theme, is the fact that some English vocabulary items are to be found in the indigenous languages of the Ivory Coast. As examples, Souleymane (p. 47) lists *school ba* 'school boy', *matches* 'box of matches', *maket* 'market', *kow-tow* 'kneel', and *to* 'toe nail'.

British English, dialectal as well as standard,[6] has helped to mold West African English, even though, as we have seen, some varieties did not derive directly or exclusively from it. Nevertheless, from the nineteenth century, British models became prestigious because highly regarded Africans like the Krios identified strongly with Britain.[7] Kofi Sey, writing about Ghanaian English, insists that even today "the educated Ghanaian would not 'accept' anything other than educated British Standard English" (1973, p. 7). With the exception of Liberia, it would be accurate to claim that in most West African states, standard English is equated with British norms.

Today, English is an official language in six West African countries and is the most widely taught second modern language in francophone territories. But standard English is not widely spoken, even by the inhabitants of anglophone West Africa. Sey suggests that in Ghana standard English is spoken only by those Ghanaians who have "completed a course of formal instruction in primary and middle schools" and adds that according to "recent figures only about 22% of the adult population . . . are educated" (1973, p. 1). Bamgbose claims that the figure is perhaps as low as 5 percent of the population of Nigeria (see Spencer 1971, p. 38). It is, of course, extremely difficult to assess how many West Africans speak standard English. Statistics for present-day students receiving full-time education give only a vague approximation of how widely standard English may be understood in the future. Often one finds that West Africans who have received several years of primary education have a very uncertain knowledge of English, whereas certain uneducated workers like taxi drivers and traders may have an excellent command of the limited range of English required in their work. It is probably true that standard English is and will remain a minority language even in anglophone West Africa until all children receive at least primary education, and even then, the English will not necessarily be equatable with standard international English.[8]

In each West African country where English is an official language, we find a continuum of English ranging from a local standard, through a set of L_1-influenced English and pidgin/creole-influenced English to a very basic sort of English (often associated with market mammies[9]) consisting of little more than lexical strings augmented by gesture: *buy okra, okra fine, bring money, what of banana?* We shall examine each of these varieties in some detail, with the exception of the rudimentary trading English which is highly unstable and very limited in range. In addition, in order to avoid producing a very superficial overview, we shall generally limit our analysis to three main areas: Ghana, Nigeria, and Cameroon.

English in West Africa   287

Phonology

Most of the textbooks used in West Africa for teaching the phonological features of English describe Received Pronunciation, and yet virtually no African speaks RP. In Nigeria, for example, Igbos are often recognized by the vowel harmony that they carry over from their mother tongue; thus *follow* is realized as [fɔlɔ]. Hausa speakers tend to introduce intrusive vowels into nonhomorganic consonant clusters; thus *screw* is realized as [sᵘkᵘru]. Yet, in spite of regional and educational differences, certain generalizations can be made about the pronunciation of West African English largely because West African languages are fairly similar in structure. As Dalby puts it,

> Divergences in their structures, i.e., in their grammatical, phonological and semantic systems, are frequently less extensive than their divergences of vocabulary, and—relative to the structures of European languages—West African languages are found to share many widespread structural features. As a result, Africans are often well experienced in operating divergent sets of vocabulary, as they master a variety of local languages, but in doing so are able to retain many of the grammatical, phonological and semantic rules which they have acquired as part of their original mother-tongue. [1970, p. 6]

English in West Africa has fewer vowel contrasts than RP. Most West Africans utilize seven monophthongs and either three or four diphthongs ([eɪ] being rare in colloquial speech):

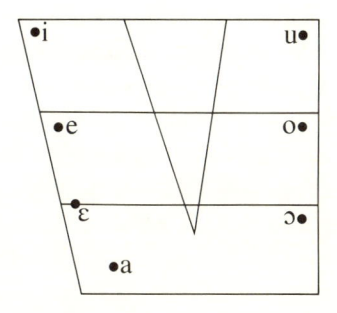

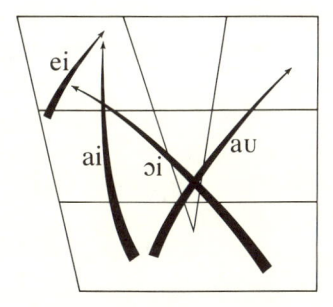

Qualitative distinctions between such vowel sounds as those in *beat* and *bit* are rare, although many educated Africans make a distinction in length: [biːt] *beat*, [biˑt] *bit*; [wuːd] *wood*, [wuˑd] *would*. Central vowels and centralizing diphthongs are virtually nonexistent in West African English. Words which end in [ə] in RP have [a] in the final syllable: *smoother* is realized as [smuθa], [smuda], *beer* as [bia]. Words like *chair*, *hair*, and *wear* are pronounced as [tʃe], [he], and [we] by acrolectal speakers and often as [tʃia], [hia], and [wia] by people who have not received much formal education in English. The long central vowel of such words as *bird* is fronted to [ɛ], thus [bɛːd]. The [ʌ] sound which occurs in the RP pronunciation of *but* is replaced by [ɔ]; hence [kɔla] *color*.[10] The [æ] sound of *hat*, *rat*, and *bad* is realized as [a], and there is usually only a quantitative difference between: [hat] *hat* and [haˑt] *heart*.

With its smaller inventory of vowels, West African English naturally has more homophones, especially in the speech of the less highly educated members of the community who make no phonological distinctions among *cut, cot,* and *court* [kɔt]; between *bed* and *bird* [bɛd]; and between *duck* and *dock* [dɔk]. West African English tends to be syllable-timed, not stress-timed, and therefore reduced vowels and weak forms are rare: RP [aɪv 'sin hɪm tə'deɪ] versus West African English [ai hav siˑn him tude].

Educated West African speech contains essentially the same inventory of consonants as other international varieties of English, though like RP it is non-rhotic. Syllabic consonants are extremely rare; *bottle* is realized as [bɔtul] or [bɔtɛl] and *lesson* is realized as [lɛsɔn]. Initial, nonhomorganic clusters tend to be split up by intrusive vowels.

If one judges by the speech of old pidgin speakers, West Africans found all English clusters difficult. *Trouble* was realized as [tɔrɔbu] or reduced to [tɔrɔ], and clusters beginning with *s* either lost the *s*—[tɔrɔŋ], [trɔŋ] *strong* and [kwis] *squeeze*—or had an intrusive vowel inserted: [sᵘmɔl] *small*.

Lexis and Syntax

Many writers refer to "Ghanaian English," "Nigerian English," "Sierra Leone English," or "Gambian English" as if local standards exist (e.g., Grieve 1964). It is certainly true that a Nigerian can recognize a Ghanaian by his speech just as an Irishman can spot an American, but although a West African standard may exist, there is little evidence that each anglophone country has its own standard.

Some West African vocabulary (e.g., *okrika* 'secondhand clothing') is found throughout the region, while some is peculiar to individual countries: *okyeame* 'head spokesman' and *penin* 'elder' from Ghana; *chi* 'personal god' and *oga* 'headman' in Nigeria; *fon* 'chief' and *nchinda* 'spokesman of the chief' in Cameroon.

Some semantically changed items are similarly general: *balance* 'change' ("You did not give me any balance"); *bata* 'sandals, shoes, footwear'; *branch* 'make a stop on a journey' ("When we go to Port Harcourt we will branch at Aba"); and *bush* 'unpolished, rural' ("He's a proper bushman"). Others are again peculiar to individual countries: *airtight* 'metal box' and *steer* 'steering wheel' in Ghana; *gallops* 'potholes' and *go-slow* 'traffic jam' in Nigeria; *bending corners* 'sharp bends' and *woman's belly* 'large bag, hold-all' in jocular usage in Cameroon.

English vocabulary has been extensively modified in the domains of childbearing and marriage. All of the following have been taken from Cameroon English, but comparable sets are found throughout West Africa: *move with* 'court, go out with' ("Did you know that Richard is moving with Eunice?"); *wedding bells* 'invitation to a wedding' ("Why have you not sent out your wedding bells?"); *take in* 'become pregnant' ("My wife has taken in"); *be in state* 'be pregnant' ("She has many children and is again in state"); *deliver* 'give birth to' ("My wife has delivered"); *offsprings* 'children'; *germinate* 'reach puberty' ("My daughter has germinated").[11]

A number of West African idioms have arisen, among them: *give kola* 'offer a bribe'; *have a godfather* 'be related to an influential person'; and *have long legs* 'have influence'. Numerous calques also occur, often varying from region to region: in Ghana, *chewing sponge* 'something to chew in order to clean one's teeth', *cover shoulder* 'type of blouse', *enskin* or *enstool* 'enthrone a chief'; in Nigeria, *chewing stick* 'stick for cleaning one's teeth', *chop box* 'food box'; and in Cameroon *head tie/tie head* 'scarf', *cry die* 'wake, funeral rites', *throw water* 'offer a bribe'.

The majority of syntactic patterns in educated West African English are identical with those found elsewhere, but some West African phrasal verbs have developed: *cope up with* 'cope with'; *plan up* 'draw up a plan'; *voice out an opinion*. Prepositional usage does not always coincide with international norms: *It was my first time of going to Lagos*; *He drove around with a view to picking passengers*. The tags *isn't it?* or *not so?* are very common: *he loves you, isn't it/not so?*; *it doesn't matter, not so/isn't it?*[12]

As in other varieties, one observes an occasional failure to distinguish between countable and noncountable nouns (*an advice, behaviors, firewoods*). A few patterns reflect the structure of the vernaculars: *I am coming* 'I'm going away now but I'll be back soon', *sorry* (used as an empathy formula), and *I can hear an awful smell*. Other influences, including hypercorrection, produce a variety of distinctive usages:

> With a drainage system that leaves its gutters *widely* open to the elements and therefore allows a very nauseating stench to evaporate. [*Ghana Daily Graphic*, 29 November 1977]

> When he becomes sick or has a court case he will be well off and will not need the services of the *immatured* and the *boastfuls*. [*Ghana Pioneer*, 2 November 1977] [Italics added]

Such usages occur generally in the speech and writing of educated West Africans and, in combination, are probably sufficiently distinctive to warrant their being called standard West African English. These variants give a local coloring to the English spoken in West Africa, but differences at the syntactic level are rare and, with more widespread education, may diminish. Many West Africans pride themselves on the correctness of their English, and Kofi Sey sums up their attitude to local variants thus:

> The linguist may be able to isolate features of Ghanaian English and describe them. But once these are made known to him, the educated Ghanaian would strive to avoid them altogether. The surest way to kill Ghanaian English, if it really exists, is to discover it and make it known. [1973, p. 10]

Yet West African English is often more flamboyant, more literary, more influenced by the Bible than its equivalent form in Britain. The following short extracts from Nigeria, Ghana, and Cameroon suggest these traits:

> There was a palm-tree at the centre of the plot. Tall grass with richly tasselled apexes encircled the tree, to a height of about eight feet. A squadron of birds, darting across the plot, perched on the grass and began to peck. They were very small and very clever with their beaks as well as with their wings; and they had a most serene combination of colours in their plumage, including a frontal white, like a waistcoat, or a tabard, and a blue rear. [Munonye 1973, p. 123]

> At one stage, Alex was determined to report the matter to Mr. Tuffuor. But he thought of what the repercussions could be—a possible forthright dissolution of their marriage. And since he did not want to wreck anybody's marriage, he refrained from telling him.
> But the temptation continued, with Janet writing love letters to him in Accra whenever he had not been to Kumasi for say a week. And since the spirit is always willing but the body is weak, Alex's body, naturally, gave way and began to have some sympathetic feelings for Janet which later developed into latent love. But he never made it manifest to Janet though it was there and growing steadily, fanned and nursed by Janet's constant temptations and secret proposals. [Mickson 1968, p. 62]

> I believe in this country's destiny. And from the vantage coign of its present re-awakening, I can see the Cameroons of tomorrow looming like a distant vision: it looks to me more beautiful than the hills look in Bamenda; it beggars in solid strength the mountain dome at Buea.
> I believe in the youth: they feel more deeply over a country's misery; they fall in love more readily with its hopes and aspirations; they rally round more eagerly to fight for a noble cause: on them a lot depends.
> I believe that, if we could but fill the mind of the country's youth with sound and solid learning;—if we could fill their hearts with eager love for all that is good and true and beautiful, if we could but teach their hands to love the salutary dirt of labour; then to the future we can look with hope and confidence.
> I believe in the power of clean lives; in the strength of unity, and in the

might of right. We cannot overlook the importance of these and hope to reach the best success. [Fonlon 1971, pp. 70–77]

In addition to local varieties of standard English, we find in West Africa a cline of English differing in the extent of influence by the vernacular languages. An extreme example of this influence can be found in Gabriel Okara's *The Voice* (1969) which is close to being a relexified version of his mother tongue, Ijaw, but L_1-influenced English can be found in the popular literature of West Africa and can be seen in the following extract from an Onitsha market novel, *Rosemary and the Taxi-Driver*:

> The sun flickered over her cannon-ball head, with the hairs on her forehead, heightened like onboard type of shaving. She resoluted to follow the train at the earliest declining hour of the day. At down [*sic*, 'dawn'], she got ready to march with all the guts of the times, besides her romantic love. She sang many love poems to them, while they twist, wiggle-waggle and utter many love incantations, worthy of marring all the lively zests of any woman folk.
> She was in her maiden form and had remained untampered, since her generate days. Even to meddle with her zestful glamour of beauty, nobody had ever succeeded. The grim enthusiasm of her ardent lust was bubbling on her romantic face, and her youthful glances of shyness. She had got all the zests of the West and mettled her senses, to bolster up alertly, to crack love, romance and joke, up to the highest mediocre of acme. It was a day for love maniacs to come and a day for Rosemary to travel too.
> Reaching the town station on April ten, Rosemary delved into an undisturbed romance, with her boyfriend, who was sobering, with mournful bunch of derangement, sending love expressions with quakeful Arctic chill, over her love conscious intensive unnerves. He tossed her, to stop crying for her departure and urged her to beat her heart throbs and vibrating mind, quite at its intensive urgent, with the incidence. He tossed, managing to serene her temper; cleaning with affection, all the bitter tears of love, which were journeying down her retroussed pug-nose. [Albert 1963, pp. 6–7][13]

The Pidgin-Creole Continuum

Apart from the locally modified standard language and L_1-influenced English, we find in many parts of West Africa a pidgin or creole English. There can be no neat linguistic distinction between a creole and a pidgin here because many West Africans learn a so-called pidgin as one of their mother tongues. A fairly stable continuum of pidgin and creole English is found from Gambia to Cameroon, and although regional, social, and educational variation occurs, the varieties remain mutually intelligible.[14] Ghana has a pidgin English but it is fairly restricted in use and so, in this section, we shall take our samples from three regions where a pidgin or creole plays an important role in everyday life: Sierra Leone, Nigeria, and Cameroon.

Sierra Leone Krio

Krio is a mother tongue and the only mother tongue of the descendants of the manumitted slaves who founded Freetown. It is also acquired as a second language by many who live and work in the Freetown area. Our samples from Sierra Leone are: (1) a set of five proverbs recorded by Mrs. Millie Smith in Leeds, 1979; (2) an original poem by Thomas Decker (1971, pp. 88–89); and (3) a translation of Mark Antony's speech from *Julius Caesar* (Decker 1965, p. 74)[15]:

> *At nɔto bon* 'heart no bone': "Mercy should season justice."
> *Babu dai, babu kam* 'baboon die, baboon come': "Nobody is indispensable."
> *Bɛl no gɛt glas* 'belly no get glass': "It is impossible to know what someone else is thinking."
> *Da bɔd we gɛt hia na in fut nɔ fɔ jɔmp faia* 'that bird who get hair on his foot no for jump fire': "One should consider one's limitations carefully before undertaking a task."
> *Dɔg we nɔ trɔs in wes nɔ go swɛla big big bon* 'dog who no trust his anus no go swallow big big bone': "Know your limitations."

slip gud	**Sleep Well**
Slip gud o, bebi-gial!	[Sleep well, baby girl
opin yai lilibit	Open your eyes a little
ɛn luk mi wan minit	And look at me for a moment
bifo yu slip.	Before you sleep.
A wan fɔ si da tin	I want to see that thing
we kin de shain insai	That shines deep
insai yu fain-fain yai	Deep in your beautiful eyes
ɛn kɔt mi at.	And tears at my heart.
So! sɛt yu yai nau nɔ	So! close your eyes now please
a tink se a dɔn si	I think I've seen
wetin a wan fɔ si.	What I wanted to see.
Gudnait! Slip gud.	Good night! Sleep well.]

> *Antoni: Padi dɛm, kɔntri, una ɔl we de na Rom. Mek una ɔl kak una yes. A kam bɛr Siza, a nɔ kam prez am.*

English in West Africa 293

> Dɛm kin mɛmba bad we pɔsin kin du
> lɔng tɛm afta di pɔsin kin dɔn dai.
> Bɔt plɛnti tɛm di gud we pɔsin du
> kin bɛr wit im bon dɛm. Mek i bi so
> wit Siza. Bra Brutɔs dɔn tɛl una
> se Siza na bin man we want pas mak.
> If i tɔk tru, na badbad ting dis ya.
> ɛn Siza dɔn gɛt im bad pe fɔ dat.
> A tek pamishɔn frɔm Bra Brutɔs dɛm[16]
> fɔ kam tɔk na Bra Siza im berin.
> ɛn Bra Brutɔs na ɔnarebul O!
> Dɛm ɔda wan sɛf na ɔnarebul.

Nigerian Pidgin English

There are no statistics for the number of Nigerians who use Pidgin English, but it is likely that Pidgin speakers outnumber speakers of standard English.[17] Pidgin is widely used in ports and towns and is especially prevalent among Igbo traders and members of the police force and the army. Our samples from Nigeria are: (1) part of a spoken narrative by a seventeen-year-old Oyibo girl recorded by Paul de Quincey in 1978 (de Quincey 1979); (2) an original poem by Frank Aig-Imoukhuede (1963, pp. 128–29); and (3) an extract from a gossip column in the *Lagos Weekend*, a popular weekly which devotes almost a full page to lighthearted pidgin humor in a column entitled "Walkabout."

> an a wan tel una wan ting. na advais tu una. mek una dɛ du samting in taim o. oyibo pipul dɛ spik am se una mek he wail di sɔn shain.[18]
>
> i kɔm gɛt tu gɛlz we dɛm jɔs nia aua haus wɛl-wɛl. dis tu gɛlz dɛm[19] de praimari siks. dɛm kɔm pe kɔmɔn ɛntrans. dea hɛdmasta kɔm giv dɛm nɔmbaz. dis gɛl dɛm se—di wan we gɛt sɛns, i kɔm kip in nɔmba jejeje fɔ gud ples. di ɔda wan i jɔs kɔm i[20] trowe di nɔmba fɔ eniwea kari fud i it. di nɛks de wɛn de wan go du di kɔmɔn ɛntrans, di wan we gɛt sɛns i jɔs wash in klos wɛl-wɛl, aiɔn dɛm pakpakpak,[21] kip dɛm sɛprɛt sɛprɛt jejeje.

[And I want to tell you plural something. It is advice to you. Do things in time o. The Oyibo people say that you should make hay while the sun shines.

There were two girls who lived very close to our house. These two girls were in primary 6. They came to pay the Common Entrance fee. Their headmaster came and gave them their numbers. These girls said—the one who was wise, she kept her number very carefully in a good place. The other one just came and threw her number into any old place and took her food and ate it. The next day when they wanted to go and do the Common

Entrance, the wise one she just washed her clothes nicely, ironed them carefully, kept them nicely apart from other things.]

One Wife for One Man[22]

I done try go church, I done go for court
Dem all dey talk about di 'new culture':
Dem talk about 'equality', dem mention 'divorce'
Dem holler am so-tay my ear nearly cut;
  One wife be for one man.

My fader before my fader get him wife borku
E no' get equality palaver; he live well
For he be oga for im own house.
But dat time done pass before white man come
Wit 'im
  One wife for one man.

Tell me how una woman no go make yanga
Wen 'e know say na 'im only dey.
Suppose say—make God no 'gree—'e no born at all?
A' tell you dat man bin dey crazy way start
  One wife for one man.

Jus' tell me how one wife fit do one man;
How man go fit stay all time for him house
For time when belleh done kommot.
How many pickin', self, one woman fit born
  Wen one wife be for one man?

Suppose, self, say na so-so woman your wife dey born
[Suppose, even, that it was only girls your wife gave birth to]
Suppose your wife sabe book, no' sabe make chop;
[Suppose your wife can read, but can't cook]
Den, how you go tell man make 'e no' go out
Sake of dis divorce? Bo, dis culture na waya O!
  Wen one wife be for one man.[23]

E don happen for my friend[24]
[It happened to my friend]

I get one friend wey we dey call Duro. Nobody know im real name but na bicos e dey too much like to stand, das why we say make we call am Duro.

By di time wey e first begin dey chop life, e no get chair for im house. So, any visitor wey go visit am na stand dem dey stand,[25] *if di person no fit siddown for ordinary cement. Na since dat time all im friend don begin dey call am Duro.*

[I have a friend whom we call Duro. Nobody knows his real name but it's because he really likes to stand, that's why we decided to call him Duro.

At the time when he first began to taste life, he hadn't a chair in his house. So, any visitor who visited him had to stand if that person wasn't able to sit on ordinary cement. It was from that time all his friends began to call him Duro.]

Cameroon Pidgin English

Cameroon is an area of extreme multilingualism, and it has an estimated 100 to 200 languages for a population of under 8 million. There are two official languages—English and French—and in parts of the Muslim north, Arabic is highly respected as a language of religion and as a vehicle for an extensive literature both sacred and secular.

In Cameroon today, in spite of the fact that most children receive at least some education, Pidgin English continues to thrive. It is still the most frequently used language of the Catholic church in the anglophone zone, and Pidgin has also proved its usefulness as a lingua franca between anglophone and francophone politicians[26] and as one of the languages used by police, gendarmes, and soldiers.[27]

Three samples from Cameroon are: (1) a conversation between a worker in the American embassy and a teacher, (2) an example of liturgical Pidgin, and (3) a sample of Pidgin written by a francophone in a gossip column.

so, i bin bi yɛstade, mi an ma masta wi girap fɔ go fɔ wɔk[28] *fɔ Brikɛteri, fɔ go luk sɔm haus fɔ sɔm waitman we wata i no de fɔ i haus an lam i bin dɔn lɔs fɔ i haus. wi go fɔ ripiram. wi wan kam, shofe i tek motu i kil smɔl dɔg fɔ rod.*
 Kenjo: i kilam fɔ usai?
 i kilam fɔ Brikɛteri. hau i kil smɔl dɔg fɔ rod, ma masta tɔk se[29] *i no go chɔp fɔ dat de fɔseka se i de . . . (laughter) . . . i se i de fɔ sɔm rɛlidʒɔn we i no wan si ting we i dai fɔ i ai.*

[So, yesterday, my employer and I got up to go to work in Briketerie, to go and look at a house for a European who had no water in his house and the light had also gone out in his house. We were going to repair it. As we were going, the chauffeur took the car and killed a small dog on the road.
 Kenjo: He killed it where?
 He killed it in Briketerie. Because he killed a small dog on the road, my master said he wouldn't eat for the rest of the day because he is . . . (laughter) . . . he says he belongs to a religion where he does not want to see a thing that is dead with his eyes.]

The following sample is a translation of part of St. Paul's epistle to the Romans (13:11–13). It is anglicized in syntax and uses a slightly modified orthography.

My brothers, una savy say, time e done catch for wake up for sleep. Time for go for heaven e done near now pass for time whe we begin for believe. Night e done go before, and sun time e done near. So, make we lef them thing, whe man he de make'm for dark time. Make we use dem strong, whe light e de give we.

[My brothers, you know that the time has come to wake up from your sleep. The time to go to heaven is closer now than at the time when we began to believe. Night has already gone, and dawn is near. So, let us leave the things, which men do in the dark. Let us use the strength, which the light gives us.]

Massa Tchakala[30]

Some peple bi bin tok dam plaba, dèm thing dasso sé na play. Djèss no, oll man don bikin op eye. Bikoss i no dé waka again. Di plaba we oll don sabiyam. From last iyè fossikop plaba "one point" wédon kill Caïman today, équip fo Akwa, dan wish "Ngando"[31] bin shine[32] séi "if Union no daï lèkey nyiso, dèm most tok dasso fo diwala don finish."

[Mister Unfixit]

[Some people have been talking about this problem, they think it's only a joke. Just now, everybody has begun to open their eyes. Because it's not going right again. We all know the problem. Since last year because of the problem of the "one point" which has destroyed Caiman today the Akwa team, whose witch Ngando claimed, "If the Union team is not to die like it, they must say so for Douala is finished."]

I have described the various forms of English that occur in West Africa as if they were discrete entities. Often different social conditions will trigger the use of one variety rather than another. A public speaker, for example, may lecture in the standard language, although he might slip in a phrase or two in Pidgin for comic effect. An urban doctor, on the other hand, when examining a workman who does not share his mother tongue, may use Pidgin to get his meaning across. The variants are not always mutually exclusive, however. Often the educated West African, especially in relaxed circumstances, will blend mother tongue, English, and Pidgin. Occasionally, too, a writer will move from one variety to another. Soyinka, for example, shifts between Yoruba and English in his novel *The Interpreters* (1965, p. 58):

Hours and hours later, or perhaps only a few minutes, and a small sharp face, cicatrized, approached him for the seventh time. "Yes, yes, bring another. Whiskey this time."

"*O ti sah.* Madam *ni npe yin.*"

"Enh?"

"Madam. *Won ni npe yin wa.*"

Egbo looked round wildly, hardly daring to believe. Simi was no longer there. Angrily he gripped the boy by the ear, pinching him on the lobe. "Are you trying to joke with me?"

The boy twisted in pain, protesting.

"Go on. Which madam? Where? Where?"

"*Nta. Won na nnu* taxi."

In his play *The Trials of Brother Jero* (1973, vol. 2, pp. 159–60) Soyinka shifts between standard and Pidgin English:

Chume [*stammering.*]: Father . . . forgive her.
Congregation [*strongly.*]: Amen.
   [*The unexpectedness of the response nearly throws Chume, but then it also serves to bolster him up, receiving such support.*]
Chume: Father, forgive her.
Congregation: Amen.
   [*The penitent continues to moan.*]
Chume: Father forgive her.
Congregation: Amen.
Chume: Father forgive am.
Congregation: Amen.
Chume [*warming up to the task.*]: Make you forgive am. Father.
Congregation: Amen.
   [*They rapidly gain pace, Chume getting quite carried away.*]
Chume: I say make you forgive am.
Congregation: Amen.
Chume: Forgive am one time.
Congregation: Amen.
Chume: Forgive am quick quick.
Congregation: Amen.

The English of West African Literature

Since the seventeenth century, there has been some literature written in European languages by West Africans, but only since the 1950s has that literature been produced in large quantities. In West Africa a writer must make one of three choices in selecting the medium in which he creates. He can write in his mother tongue, knowing that his audience will be a limited one; for instance, Obiajunwa Wali has chosen to write in Igbo; D. O. Fagunwa in Yoruba; and other writers in a variety of West African languages including Twi, Akan, Hausa, Manding, and Douala. Wali, defending his decision to write in Igbo, puts the case for using indigenous languages as follows:

> . . . the whole uncritical acceptance of English and French as the inevitable medium for educated African writing is misdirected, and has no chance of advancing African literature and culture. In other words, until these writers and their western midwives accept the fact that any true African literature must be written in African languages, they would be merely pursuing a dead end, which can only lead to sterility, uncreativity, and frustration. [Wali 1963, p. 14]

Although Wali published his creative writing in Igbo, his apologia for using his mother tongue was in English.

A second alternative is to relexify one's mother tongue, using English vocabulary but indigenous structures and rhythms. Gabriel Okara's *The Voice* (1964) is probably the most consistent attempt to preserve the patterning of an African mother tongue while using English vocabulary.[33] Okara consciously attempted to reproduce Ijaw syntax and idioms, as can be seen from the following extract:

> Wonder held Izongo, held Abadi, and held all the Elders. They looked at each other. Izongo his head shook vigorously like a stunned man trying to clear his head.
>
> As wonder held them so, Okolo threw his back at them and walked away. But he had gone only a little way when running feet he heard, coming behind him. [1964, p. 29]

Such attempted relexification produces linguistically interesting structures and occasional lyrical patches, but it has so far failed to result in sustained literary creation.

The third option—the use of English—is the one espoused by Ghana's Armah and Awoonor, by Nigeria's Achebe and Soyinka, and by Cameroon's Jumbam. These writers use English in the full awareness that English is no longer just the language of Britain, the United States, and the old Commonwealth but is also part of the linguistic heritage of many Africans. Such writers believe that it is part of their role as novelists and poets to mold the English language, making it capable of expressing their creative impulse and their cultural associations. Achebe puts the case in this way:

> The African writer should aim to use English in a way that brings out his message best without altering the language to the extent that its value as a

medium of international exchange will be lost. He should aim at fashioning out an English which is at once universal and able to carry his peculiar experience. [1965, p. 29]

West African writers who write in English have, over the past twenty-five years, been "fashioning" a language capable of expressing their culture and their inspiration. In doing so, they have contributed to the vitality of international English.

Such a brief survey cannot do justice to the scope and vitality of West African literature in English, but it helps to show that the varieties of English found in West Africa are not limited to trade or education, religion or tourism, but combine to form a code capable of expressing the innermost thoughts and creative impulses of its poets and playwrights, its novelists and critics.

The many varieties of English are vitally important in the everyday life of West Africa. In education, commerce, trade, bureaucracy, in the sciences, and in literature, these varieties permit communication and interaction. It is hard to say what the future holds for the many languages in West Africa. Increasing numbers of educated West Africans insist on the value of their mother tongues, and more vernacular languages are being standardized now than at any time in the past. On the other hand, more children are being educated, and thus more and more West Africans are being exposed to English. English has become an African language and has been adopted and modified to suit its new users. Many Africans already use English more extensively than they do any other language, and many more will probably echo the sentiments expressed by Achebe:

> ... for me there is no other choice. I have been given this language [i.e., English] and I intend to use it. I hope, though, that there will always be men, like the late Chief Fagunwa, who will choose to write in their native tongue and ensure that our ethnic literature will flourish side by side with the national ones. For those of us who opt for English there is much work ahead and much excitement. [1965, p. 30]

In the future, it seems likely that the standard West African English that has already evolved will become more widely recognized. I do not see each country developing individual standards, but regional, social, and stylistic variation will remain. English has been and continues to be woven into the linguistic fabric of West Africa, and English users throughout the world will become increasingly aware of the vitality and richness of this Africanized language.

West Africa is an enormously complex linguistic area in which stratified multilingualism is the rule rather than the exception. One example from Cameroon may make this point clearer. In Djottin, a little village in the anglophone zone, an illiterate village woman would speak Noni with her family, Lamnso at the nearby market town of Kimbo, Pidgin English in the confessional and in matters relating to the church, and vehicular Hausa when buying milk from the nomadic tribe, the Cattle Fulani. Her children would acquire English in primary school and French in secondary school. The monolingual African is as rare as the multilingual Englishman, and for nearly every African, some knowledge of a European language is becoming increasingly essential.

It is not really possible to talk about *the* English language in West Africa unless we are aware that we are using a shorthand expression. Under the umbrella title of English are found a local standard, L_1-influenced English, L_1-influenced-French-influenced English, and a whole spectrum of pidgin and creole Englishes. But these headings are idealizations, because the subvarieties influence each other and are influenced by other world varieties of English. Standard British English still has prestige in most areas but, because of the Peace Corps and films, records, books, and magazines from the United States, the American norms also make an impression.

NOTES

1. The island of Fernando Po, where the official language is Spanish, is not included in our survey of English in West Africa because reliable data from Equatorial Guinea (which includes Fernando Po) are not available. We know that in the nineteenth century, Fernando Po was important to the British as a center for suppressing the slave trade. According to Gwei (1966, p. 8), "Between 1827 and 1840 there grew up on the island a large colony of freed slaves of various African tribes, but all speaking English as the lingua franca." We also know that in this century, possibly as many as 70 percent of the islanders understood and used Pidgin English. In the 1960s the island was a favorite tourist resort for expatriates working in Nigeria and Cameroon, and on a visit to Fernando Po in 1966, I discovered that virtually every trader in Santa Isabel was proficient in Pidgin English. Many of these traders, however, were from the coastal regions of Nigeria and Cameroon, and large numbers of these have left Fernando Po since 1968 when Rio Muni and Fernando Po became the independent territory of Equatorial Guinea.
2. Duke's diary shows some features which still occur in the pidgin English of East Nigeria and Cameroon. In particular, one notices the unmarked verb forms, the multifunctional preposition *for,* and the lack of possessive markers. One also sees some influence from Efik in that the modifier follows the noun in *fog morning.* The "translation" following the original text was prepared by Rev. Dr. A. W. Wilkie (see Forde 1956, p. ix).
3. This was not the first time that the repatriation of Africans had been considered. As early as the closing years of Elizabeth I's reign there had been a certain amount of agitation for the return of Africans to their own continent, but the eighteenth-century movement was more philanthropic in motivation.
4. Later, this chain of Pidgin Englishes was reinforced and modified by Krio and, to a lesser extent, by Liberian Settler English. Thus, Creole Englishes form part of the coastal chain.
5. In October 1979 I had an interesting proof of this. A group of mature West African

students, attending an education course at Leeds University, was conversing in anglicized Pidgin. The group included one Cameroonian, two Togolese, one Gambian, one Sierra Leonean, and me. There was some amusement at regional variants (such as the Cameroon use of [fɔ] as a multipurpose preposition) but the variants used were clearly interintelligible.

6. It seems likely that the earliest types of English heard in West Africa were nonstandard dialects. Little work has been done on this aspect of West African English, although it is touched on in the Ph.D. dissertations of Hancock (1971) and Todd (1975). Dialect influence on vocabulary may be seen in such items as *juke/chook* 'pierce', *lappa* 'loincloth' from *lap* meaning 'wrap', *outside child* 'illegitimate child', and the use of *do* in such sentences as *I do eat them*. Dialectal English may also have influenced the development of *di/de* in such Pidgin English sentences as *a di chɔpam* 'I eat them'.

7. Isichei (1977, p. 132) tells us, for example, that Krios "took pride in the name black Englishmen, called England 'Home' and called Queen Victoria 'our mother' (in Krio, 'we mammy')."

8. In West Africa, some primary school teachers have received only eight or ten years of formal education. It is not unusual to hear them produce such sentences as the following, all of which were recorded in Cameroon classrooms: *we are having a president in Cameroon; I have not seen him of recent;* and *we are packing into our new house*.

9. The term *Mami* is used throughout West Africa as a term of respect to a woman who has had children. In 1975, I heard an educated Cameroonian woman address an old school acquaintance as "Theresia" only to be reprimanded as follows: *Yu no di si pikin fɔ ma bak?* ('Don't you see the child on my back?') This use of *Mami* as a courtesy title goes back at least eighty years. Writing in 1897 about the social groups in Sierra Leone, Mary Kingsley explained: "The ladies are divided into three classes; the young girl you address as 'teetee', the young person as 'seester', and the more mature charmer as 'mammy' " (Kingsley 1897, p. 17).

10. In many parts of West Africa *color* and *collar* are homophones, and so it was natural for one Cameroonian student to write about the advantages of being a "white color worker."

11. Pidgin English has a related set of vocabulary items. In Cameroon Pidgin, for example, we find: *gif bele* 'make pregnant'; *gɛt bele* 'be pregnant'; *spɔil bele* 'abort'; *waʃ bele* 'last child'; *bɔn pikin* 'give birth to a child'; *gɛt flawa* 'get one's period for the first time'; *si mun* 'have one's period'.

12. Pidgin English also has the tag *no bi so?* and it may have influenced the use of *not so?*

13. This novel was written by "Miller O. Albert" and was published in Onitsha in 1963 by Chinyelu Printing Press. See Obiechina 1972 for the background and readership of this type of literature; he also prints a larger extract from this novel, pp. 135–38.

14. In Cameroon, for example, many children learn the local pidgin as one of their mother tongues. In 1976 I recorded three children at play (Lisa, aged three, her brother Kenneth, aged five, and a neighbor Michael, also aged three). The first two children normally spoke English at home while Michael spoke Bakweri. Lisa was organizing the game. She asked her brother, "All right? We'll do it?" and then, turning immediately to Michael asked, "i ɔ rait? wi go duam?"

15. A translation or gloss is provided where the meaning is not obvious, and, since there is

no official orthography, the conventions of the Fyle and Jones (1980) *Krio-English Dictionary* will be employed. Though Krio is a tone language, the tones are not indicated here. The Fyle and Jones conventions are as follows:

/ɲ/	= ny	e.g., /ɲaɲam/ = *nyanyam* 'food'
/ŋ, ŋg, ŋk/	= ng, nk	e.g., /tɔŋ/, /traŋga/, /dɔŋkɔ/ = *tɔng* 'town', *tranga* 'hard', *dɔnkɔ* 'fool' respectively
/ʃ, ʒ/	= sh, zh	e.g., /ʃumeka/, /laʒɔ̃/ = *shumeka* 'shoemaker', *lazhɔn* 'money' respectively
/tʃ, dʒ/	= ch, j	e.g., /tʃɔtʃ/, /dʒɔdʒ/ = *chɔch* 'church', *jɔj* 'judge' respectively
/θ/	= th	e.g., /baθrum/ = *bathrum* 'bathroom'
/ʁ/	= r	e.g., /ʁɔd/ = *rod* 'road'
/j/	= y	e.g., /jaj/ = *yay* 'eye'
/ai, au, ɔi/	= ay, aw, ɔy	e.g., /bai/, /laud/, /tɔis/ = *bay* 'buy', *lawd* 'loud', *tɔys* 'toy' respectively
/Ṽ/ (nasal vowel)	= V + n	e.g., /sɛ̃s/, /pamãi/, /bɔ̃s/ = *sɛns* 'sense', *pamayn* 'palm oil', *bɔns* 'bun' respectively.

The alphabetical order adopted follows the recommendations of the *Practical Orthography for African Languages* (1930) and is as follows:

a b c d e ɛ f g h i j k l
m n o ɔ p r s t u v w y z.

16. *Bra Brutɔs dɛm* means 'Brother Brutus and his friends'. The use of the plural marker *dem* in this context is found throughout West Africa and the West Indies, e.g., Jamaican *Jaan dem* 'John and his (group)' and Cameroon *Maria dem*, 'Mary and her associates'.
17. Nigerian Pidgin has no recognized orthography but, since it seems likely that the Krio orthography of Fyle and Jones will become the basis of the writing systems of all English-based West African pidgins and creoles, I shall use it for my transcription of oral texts.
18. The influence from English is clearly marked in this passage largely because the narrator was a schoolgirl. We see the influence in the use of such a proverb as "Make hay while the sun shines" and in the use of marked forms, e.g., *gɛlz* 'girls', *dea* 'their'.
19. Plurality in Pidgin is normally either implicit from the context or marked by the use of *dem* which follows the noun. This speaker marks plurality in three ways: in the English way (*tu gɛlz*); in a combined English and Pidgin way (*tu gɛlz dem*); and in the Pidgin way (*dis gɛl dem*).
20. Often in Pidgin the pronoun *i* precedes and follows verbs of motion, e.g., *i kɔm i* 'he comes, came'; *i go i* 'he goes/went off'. It is conceivable that this tendency gave rise to the literary convention (found as early as in the writings of Defoe) of adding *-ee* to words, especially verbs, e.g., *masa, if yu lashee, lashee an if yu prishee* [preach], *prishee, but no lashee prishee*.
21. This speaker uses a number of duplicated (e.g., *wɛl-wɛl*) and triplicated (e.g., *pakpakpak*) forms for emphasis.

22. I have used the orthography employed by the poet in reproducing this poem. His use of the normal English orthography has the effect of making the poem seem easier to understand but also of making Pidgin seem like an inferior form of English.
23. *so-tay* 'until'; *borku* 'plenty'; *oga* 'lord, master'; *yanga* 'vanity'; *make yanga* 'put on airs and graces'; *pickin* 'child, children'; *bo* 'friend'; *na waya o* 'is a terrible thing'.

    Although the poet normally spells words in the English way, he occasionally modifies his orthography. *Belleh* pronounced [bele] is from 'belly' and *kommot* pronounced [kɔmɔt] is from 'come out'.
24. Once again, I have used the orthographic conventions of the original.
25. Pidgins and creoles related to African languages often use foregrounding for emphasis. The sentence *a go waka* 'I'll walk' can be transformed into *na mi a go waka* '*I*'ll walk' and *na waka a go waka* 'I'll *walk*, not run or go by car'.
26. It is widely reported in Cameroon that in the late 1960s and early 1970s President Ahidjo and Vice-President Foncha communicated in Pidgin English.
27. It is no longer true to say that Pidgin is the chief language of these forces in Cameroon. Manasseh Ngome visited various headquarters and living quarters of policemen and soldiers in 1979 and found that most of the men addressed their wives in their shared mother tongue or French; that they addressed other women almost exclusively in Pidgin; that the women used Pidgin or French when speaking to each other; and perhaps most interesting of all, that the children used only French. His findings, related to me in a personal communication, were based on visits to Douala and Kumba.
28. I have transcribed this passage using the Fyle and Jones conventions (see note 15 above).
29. Verbs of talking and of mental processes are often followed by *se*, e.g., *i tɔk se* 'he said'; *a tink se* 'I think'; *wi bin mɛmba se* 'we remembered'.
30. [tʃakala, tʃakara] means *to break up into small pieces*. This gossip column, published in *Le Courrier Sportif des Sept Provinces*, prides itself on being able to focus on contentious issues. The theme in the present article is falling standards in football.
31. *Ngando* means 'crocodile, alligator'. Ngando is a Douala god.
32. Literally 'signed'.
33. Much of Amos Tutuola's work, including *The Palm Wine Drinkard*, can be regarded as relexified Yoruba. Tutuola, however, set out to recreate Yoruba folklore in English and the influences from Yoruba's syntactic patterns were unintentional.

REFERENCES

Achebe, Chinua. "English and the African Writer." *Transition* 18 (1965):27–30.

Aig-Imoukhuede, Frank. "One Wife for One Man." In *Modern Poetry From Africa*, edited by Gerald Moore and Ulli Beier, pp. 128–29. Harmondsworth: Penguin African Library, 1963.

Albert, Miller O. *Rosemary and the Taxi-Driver*. Onitsha: Chinyelu Printing Press, 1963.

Armah, Ayi Kwei. *The Beautyful Ones Are Not Yet Born*. London: Heinemann, 1969.

———. *The Healers*. London: Heinemann, 1979.

Awoonor, Kofi. *Night of My Blood*. Garden City, N.Y.: Doubleday, 1971.

———. *This Earth, My Brother: An Allegorical Tale of Africa*. Garden City, N.Y.: Doubleday, 1972.

Bamgboṣe, Ayọ. *Language and Society in Nigeria*. Stanford: Stanford University Press, 1973.

Beeching, Jack, ed. *Richard Hakluyt: Voyages and Discoveries*. Harmondsworth: Penguin, 1972.

Berry, Jack, and Greenberg, Joseph H., eds. *Linguistics in Sub-Saharan Africa*. Vol. 7 of *Current Trends in Linguistics*, edited by Thomas A. Sebeok. 14 vols. The Hague: Mouton, 1977.

Churchill, Awnsham, and Churchill, John. *A Collection of Voyages and Travels*. 6 vols. London: John Walthoe, 1732.

Dalby, David. *Black through White: Patterns of Communication*. Bloomington: Indiana University Press, 1970.

Decker, Thomas. "Julius Caesar in Krio." *Sierra Leone Language Review* 4 (1965):64–78.

———. "Slip Gud." In *The English Language in West Africa*, edited by John Spencer, pp. 88–89. London: Longman, 1971.

de Quincey, Paul. "The Pre-verbal Tense and Aspect Markers in Nigerian Pidgin." Master's thesis, University of Leeds, 1979.

Fonlon, Bernard. *As I See It*. Buea: Catholic Press, 1971.

Forde, C. Daryll. *Efik Traders of Old Calabar*. London, New York, and Toronto: Oxford University Press, 1956.

Fyfe, C. H. "European and Creole Influence in the Hinterland of Sierra Leone before 1896." *Sierra Leone Studies*, n.s. 6 (1956):113–23.

Fyle, C. N., and Jones, Eldred. *Krio-English Dictionary*. London: Oxford University Press, 1980.

Grieve, D. W. *English Language Examining*. Lagos: African Universities Press, 1964.

Gwei, Solomon Nfor. "History of the British Baptist Mission in Cameroon, with Beginnings in Fernando Po." B.D. thesis, Rüschlikon-Zürich, 1966.

Hancock, Ian F. "A Study of the Sources and Development of the Lexicon of Sierra Leone Krio." Ph.D. dissertation, University of London, School of Oriental and African Studies, 1971.

———. "Appendix: Repertory of Pidgin and Creole Languages." In *Pidgin and Creole Linguistics*, edited by Albert Valdman, pp. 362–91. Bloomington: Indiana University Press, 1977.

Hancock, Ian F., and Kobbah, E. "Liberian English of Cape Palmas." In *Perspectives on Black English*, edited by J. L. Dillard, pp. 248–71. The Hague: Mouton, 1975.

Isichei, Elizabeth. *History of West Africa since 1800*. London: Macmillan and Co., 1977.

Jumbam, Kenjo. *The White Man of God*. London: Heinemann, 1980.

Kingsley, Mary H. *Travels in West Africa*. London: Macmillan and Co., 1897.

Labarthe, Pierre. *Voyage à la côte de Guinée*. Paris: Debray, 1803.

Mickson, E. K. *Woman is Poison*. Accra: State Publishing Company, 1968.

Moore, Francis. *Travels into the Inland Parts of Africa*. London: E. Cave, 1738.

Munonye, John. *A Wreath for the Maidens*. London: Heinemann, 1973.

Obiechina, E. N., ed. *Onitsha Market Literature*. African Writers Series, no. 109. London: Heinemann, 1972.

Okara, Gabriel. *The Voice*. London: A. Deutsch, 1964.

Sey, Kofi A. *Ghanaian English: An Exploratory Survey.* London: Macmillan and Co., 1973.

Souleymane, Kone. "The Status of English in the Ivory Coast." B.A. thesis, University of Lagos, 1972.

Soyinka, Wole. *The Interpreters.* London: Panther Books, 1965.

——. *The Trials of Brother Jero.* In *Collected Plays*, vol. 2, pp. 142–71. 2 vols. London: Oxford University Press, 1973.

Spencer, John, ed. *The English Language in West Africa.* London: Longman, 1971.

Todd, Loreto. "Base-Form and Substratum: Two Case Studies of English in Contact." Ph.D. dissertation, University of Leeds, 1975.

Treffgarne, Carew. *The Role of English and French as Languages of Communication between Anglophone and Francophone West Africa States.* London: Africa Educational Trust, 1975.

Wali, Obiajunwa. "The Dead End of African Literature." *Transition* 10 (1963):13–15.

English in East Africa

Ian F. Hancock and Rachel Angogo

English and its uses have developed differently in East and West Africa. West Africa, it has been said, owes a debt to the mosquito for having been spared extensive European settlement, and West Africans had relatively little exposure to native speakers of English, even in the cities. In eastern Africa, native English speakers were present in considerable numbers, had great influence in government, and filled a higher percentage of teaching posts. Another difference is that anglophone West Africa very early developed a separate stream of English—Pidgin—which made the use of English as a lingua franca less essential in many circumstances,[1] but no comparable language developed in eastern Africa as a result of European influence.[2] Because of the continued reinforcement of British standards in the schools, East African English never strayed far from the prestige dialect of England.

This last observation may appear to be an overstatement when English teachers such as Frederick Welch of Kenya's Alliance High School are moved to state that "much of the English used in East Africa—and not only by Africans—is so stilted and archaic as to be almost unintelligible."[3] Though such extreme opinions are often voiced by English expatriates, East African English differs from international English mainly in phonology, lexicon, and idiom, the same criteria which distinguish, say, New Zealand English from that spoken in Canada. With the exception of such varieties as Zambianized English, English in eastern Africa does not differ radically from English spoken anywhere else in the world.

Although there are many locally born anglophone whites in eastern Africa, they constitute only a small fraction of the total English-speaking population. English in eastern Africa functions for the great majority of its speakers as a second language, and the influence of their native languages must be considered in a description of their distinctive varieties of English. Where do learners' errors stop and legitimate features of a local English begin? Can we accept Hocking's position that "what is considered correct in a language is just what native speakers of the language say" (1974, p. 58)? In order to address this question, we must distinguish East African English from imperfectly learned English.

In another paper (Angogo and Hancock 1980), we divide English in eastern Africa into four types:

1. the native English of expatriates and African-born whites;
2. the native English of Africans;

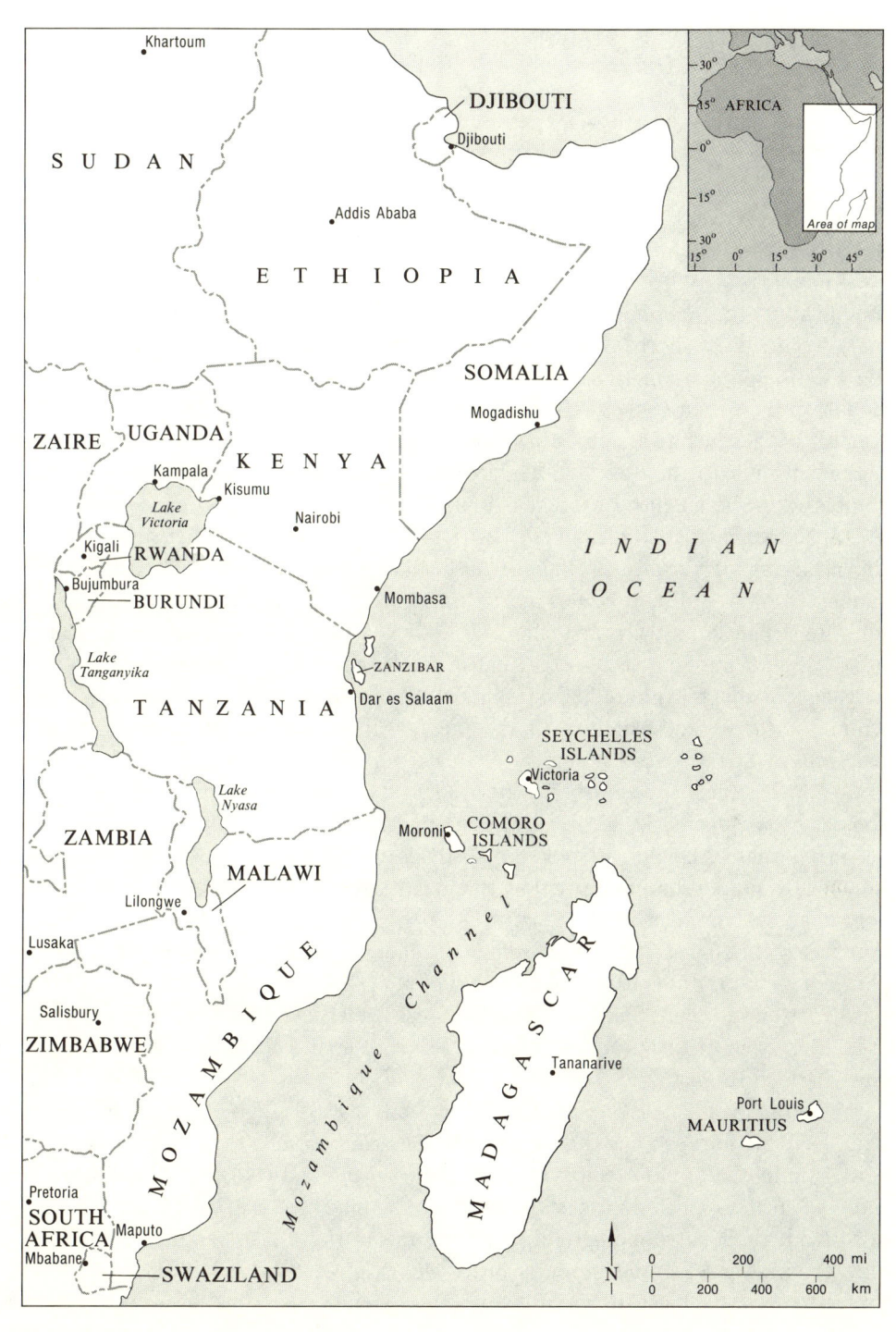

East Africa

3. nonnative English spoken fluently as a second language; and
4. nonnative English spoken imperfectly as a foreign language.

The native English of expatriates is usually British and only occasionally Canadian, American, or some other variety. Its speakers usually return to their countries of origin and have no significant effect upon East African English. Movies, music, and television programs probably have a more lasting influence upon the local idiom than do the expatriates themselves, and several American colloquialisms have become current through such media, sometimes with semantic modification (e.g., *dough* 'money', *bucks* 'shillings', *guy* 'a young male or female'). The locally born whites who form the bulk of the permanent native-speaking English population range from rural farmers to the most prestigious professionals in the urban centers—Lusaka, Kampala, Dar es Salaam and Nairobi. The English of these white residents has undergone the normal process of change from one generation to the next and has acquired a distinctly "colonial" quality when compared to the English of Great Britain.

Native English of locally born Africans is restricted to a rather small group: the offspring of racially or linguistically mixed marriages. If such unions are supported by wealth and homes in urbanized areas, the children will usually grow up with English as their first language. They attend racially and linguistically mixed fee-paying schools where English is the medium of instruction and the language of the playground. English is also commonly used in the home, both within the family and when guests are entertained. However, due to the constant daily interaction between members of this group and others outside of the home environment, their speech is characterized by extreme style shifting from a near-standard to a specifically local variety of English.

Nonnative English is spoken fluently as a second language by an increasing number of middle- and upper-class urbanized Africans, all of whom tend to share certain social characteristics: the nature of their professions, the incidence of their contacts with English-speaking foreigners (including expatriate professional Africans), their aspirations to upward social mobility, and to a restricted degree their participation in linguistically mixed marriages, itself a class-marked phenomenon. It is the speech of this group which may be taken as the norm for the varieties of East African English.

Nonnative English is spoken imperfectly as a foreign language by those who have acquired some knowledge of English through their schooling, but who usually have no need for it in their social and working environment. Others, such as porters and stewards, may acquire a basic knowledge of English from their surroundings (e.g., tourist resorts) and command enough to be able to transact essential business in it. Other languages, such as German and Swedish, may be learned in the same way. Members of this group are often, though not always, working-class and may eventually move into the preceding group.

European Contact with Eastern Africa

By the end of the sixteenth century, English ships had begun to visit the east coast of Africa. These were the forerunners of the British East Africa Company which, with the Dutch East India Company, gradually managed to oust the Portuguese traders from the area, except along the Zambezi coast. Ties were strengthened in 1810 when the British government in India formed an alliance with the reigning sultan on the coast, Seyyid Saidi. These contacts became official with the Moresby Treaty of 1882, which recognized Saidi's power and declared Mombasa a protectorate of the Crown. With a base thus established on the coast, British expansion began, initially with exploratory ventures into the hinterland by Sir Richard Burton, David Livingstone, John Speke, and others. The Americans signed a commercial treaty with Seyyid Saidi in 1833 and four years later opened a consulate in Zanzibar. Although Saidi had been a powerful factor in the coastal slave trade, one of the conditions of the Moresby Treaty had been that slavery be reduced; it was not, however, until Saidi's death in 1856 that slavery began to decline noticeably.

The Germans colonized Tanganyika and Zanzibar (today unified as Tanzania) until the First World War. Their language policy was to encourage the use of kiSwahili, already well established along the coast and the inland slaving routes. Thus, when the English took over, there was already an effective lingua franca, and today kiSwahili is still employed in Tanzania in many of the social roles for which English is used for which in Uganda, Kenya, and Zambia. English is widely known and taught in Tanzania, especially in the capital, Dar es Salaam. In Tanzania there is little stigma attached to the use of kiSwahili; in Kenya and Uganda, on the other hand, it still has not attained full recognition, and English is the lingua franca with greatest prestige.

"The distinctive feature of the first half [of the twentieth] century was the attempt to turn British East Africa into a 'white man's country' " (Marsh and Kingsnorth 1972, p. 112). Until about 1900, most Europeans, with the notable exception of the missionaries, were settled on the coast, but they knew that many parts of the interior were more suitable for white settlement and for the potential development of cash crops such as coffee, tea, wheat, and sisal. The area around Lake Victoria in Uganda was especially attractive to the Europeans, and by 1902 a railway had been constructed between Mombasa, on the Kenya coast, and Kisumu on the lake.[4]

> Difficulties began with the need for European settlers, if the railway was to pay. . . . Sir Charles Eliot arranged for the attractions of East Africa to be made known in South Africa, where he hoped that the unsettled, poverty-stricken state of the country at the end of the Anglo-Boer War might mean that South Africans would be tempted by the opportunities offered in East Africa. The good response surprised the government. [Marsh and Kingsnorth 1965, pp. 165–66]

Thus in the whole of eastern Africa, English was established earliest and most permanently away from the coast, and while political events in the past few years have seen a mass exodus of native-speaking English from Uganda, it remains widely known and taught there.

In Zambia, "often the only language in which Africans speaking different vernaculars may communicate is English. . . . Because of the absence of linguistic domination by any African language in Zambia, it seems plausible that English will eventually become the national language" (Kaplan et al. 1969, pp. 100–101). The Europeans numbered about 70,000 in Zambia in 1970, but

> . . . less than one fifth of their numbers are Zambian-born, and these are mainly children. South Africa has provided the bulk of the European immigrants, nearly one half, and an additional quarter are British-born. . . . All whites, regardless of place of birth, are considered European. [p. 96]

In Malawi, according to the 1966 government census, 190,473 persons above the age of five could speak and understand English, and it is reasonable to suppose that this number has grown in the past fifteen years. Most of the English speakers belong to the 5 percent urban population. According to Phiri (1976, p. 11), there is a very high motivation among students to learn English since it carries connotations of sophistication and intellectualism.

Very few data are available about the situation in Ethiopia or Somalia. The Ford Foundation survey for Ethopia (Bender 1971) does not discuss the characteristics of the English used there. However, the report concludes that "English has a negligible number of native speakers in Ethiopia, but at the present time it has a crucial position in education, commerce, government and international communication, and from this point of view it can be regarded as a major Ethiopian language" (p. 12). The decline of Western influence that has occurred since the Ford Foundation survey was made will doubtless affect the status of English in Ethiopia.

English is not used to any appreciable extent in the Comoros, where French is the language of colonization and Shimayore the local vernacular language. Even kiSwahili is not widely employed (African Inland Mission 1976). In the Seychelles, where creole is now the official language, English is the home language of only 1 percent of the population and scarcely used in public outside the Legislative Assembly and a few administrative and commercial settings. One of the two daily newspapers is in English, and the Anglican church provides an equal balance of services in English, French, and Creole French (Bollée 1977, p. 12).

In Mauritius, English has been the official language since 1810 and is the language of government and the courts. Though regularly used in business, English is not common as a mother tongue, but it is widely taught in schools and employed in broadcasting (10 percent of radio and about 50 percent of television is in English). According to Baker (1969, p. 81), "those whose mother tongue is not French often prefer to speak imperfect English rather than imperfect French in circumstances calling for a 'status' language. One reason for this is that Mauritians generally are far more aware of errors made in French than in English." Baker did not identify characteristics of "Mauritian English," but he did note loan translations and other influences from other languages, especially French and Kreol.

The uses of English for various functions throughout the region are displayed in table 1.

TABLE 1. DOMAINS OF ENGLISH IN EASTERN AFRICA

	Kenya	Tanzania	Uganda	Zambia	Malawi	Zimbabwe	Ethiopia	Somalia	Seychelles
National status	N	N	Y	N	Y	Y	N	Y	Y
High court	Y	Y	Y	Y	Y	Y	N	N	Y
Local court	S	?	S	S	S	S	N	N	S
Parliament	Y	N	Y	Y	Y	Y	N	N	Y
Civil Service	Y	N	Y	Y	Y	Y	N	Y	Y
Secondary school	Y	Y	Y	Y	Y	Y	Y	Y	Y
Primary school	Y	N	Y	Y	Y	Y	N	N	Y
Radio	Y	N	Y	Y	Y	Y	Y	Y	Y
Newspaper	Y	Y	Y	Y	Y	Y	Y	Y	Y
Local novels	Y	Y	Y	Y	Y	Y	Y	?	Y
Local records	Y	N	Y	Y	Y	Y	N	N	N
Local plays	Y	N	Y	Y	Y	Y	N	S	Y
Movies (not dubbed)	Y	Y	Y	Y	Y	Y	N	Y	Y
Advertizing	Y	Y	Y	Y	Y	Y	N	Y	Y
Road signs	Y	N	Y	Y	Y	Y	N	Y	Y
Shop and vehicle signs	Y	Y	Y	Y	Y	Y	N	Y	Y
Business correspondence	Y	Y	Y	Y	Y	Y	Y	Y	Y
Personal correspondence	Y	Y	Y	Y	Y	Y	S	S	Y
Use in the home	Y	N	Y	Y	Y	Y	N	N	N
British council classes	Y	Y	Y	Y	Y	Y	Y	Y	Y

Note: Y = English used; N = English not used; S = English sometimes used

The Transmission of English in Eastern Africa

It is clear that English is not transmitted to any great extent at the present time by direct contact with native speakers. As Kaplan has pointed out, for most native speakers, "British society and culture have dominated their lives" (1969, p. 96). Even the white farmers (in Kenya) or miners (in Zambia), who are locally born and often of working-class background, do not socialize to any great extent with Africans. Yet English is widely spoken by Africans today, and it was obviously acquired by their ancestors at some time during the past century from native speakers.

The significance of the missionaries from Britain should not be underestimated. They were among the earliest English speakers in eastern Africa and continue to live in close contact with Africans today. Primarily through their influence, the basis for East African English is clearly British English. Even the early missionaries from countries other than Britain all spent time in England, undergoing English-language training before leaving for Africa, and it was these same missionaries who controlled the educational system. Later on, the British government introduced school systems similar to those in Britain, and most English teachers in government schools during the period of colonization were imported from Britain.

Some influence from South African English appears, especially the farther south one travels. All East African varieties have a more or less discernible substratum of South African English phonology, though with readily identifiable influence from British and Bantu phonology. In fact, the phonological similarities to South African English may be better attributed to the influence of a common Bantu substratum than to direct influence from South African English, since the many farmers who emigrated from the Cape to all parts of eastern Africa early in this century settled on the land and had no contact with the schools. More significant is the fact that the majority of them were Boers and did not speak English as their first language. They acquired and helped perpetuate the Kenyan pidgin *kiSetla,* which they used in their interactions with the local population. Even today, there are unsubstantiated reports that the use of Afrikaans survives among some of these settler families.

Acknowledgement should be made of the non-African segments of the population who are not native speakers of English: Greeks, Lebanese, Swedes, and others, who are fairly numerous—a quarter of the whole European population of Zambia, for example. Their linguistic impact upon East African English is probably negligible, although German and Swiss missionaries during the early period may have influenced African phonology through teaching their own accented English. The largest non-English, non-African community, however, consists of the Asians—especially East Indians—mainly of Gujerati origin, who maintain their languages and customs and whose English is distinctly ethnolectal. Indians have had long contact with the eastern coast of Africa, and several lexical items of Indian origin are identifiable in both kiSwahili and East African English.

Some Characteristics of East African English

Phonology

Throughout the whole area, mother-tongue interference is more or less apparent. While this is most characteristic of group four, certain such features have become institutionalized in the speech of group three speakers.

Bantu speakers, except those fluent in kiSwahili, generally lack [ð]/[θ] and may substitute [s]/[z] ([zis siŋ] *this thing*), or less commonly [t]/[d]. The devoicing of [b] and [v], as well as some hypercorrect voicing of [f] and [p] in urban areas, have been noted from Zambia, Tanzania and Kenya: [laf] *love*, [ˈlaviŋ] *laughing*, [kab] *cup*. Vowel raising in such items as [rɛn] *ran* (versus [ran] *run*) may be due to the lack of phonemic contrast between [æ] and [ʌ], which have collapsed in /a/ in East African English. Though this same pattern is common in South African English, no hypothesis about origins can account for its occurrence in, for example, the widespread pronunciation [roˈmɛns] *romance*.

Speakers of specific languages may be recognized by their ethnolectal features. Gikuyus tend to introduce a homorganic nasal before stops: [ˈtembo] *table*, [ˈndandi] *daddy*, or to lose it through hypercorrection: [maɪd] *mind*. Embu, Gikuyu, and a number of other groups lack an [l]/[r] distinction. In Kamba, [h] is nonphonemic, yielding such forms as [ˈhapo] *apple*, or [aus] *house*. [ʃ] and [tʃ] are not distinguished in Meru ([ʃaʃ] *church*); Meru also lacks [f], and its speakers substitute [p] in English words: [ˈpaya] *fire*. Some Luyia and Luganda speakers tend to affricate [kj] or [tj] and hence say [vɛˈnatʃula] *vernacular* in English.

Non-Bantu speakers are similarly identifiable. Those with dhoLuo as their mother tongue tend to drop final vowels, especially after [k]: [bek] *bake, baker*, [biˈyut] *beauty*, and to substitute [s] for [ʃ] since [ʃ] is not present in their language: [ˈsuga] *sugar*, [sat] *shut*.

For all speakers, intrusive vowels may be heard between consonants, especially in the environment of /n/—[əˈgenəst] *against*, [ˈkɔnɪfɪdɛns] *confidence*, [risˈpɔnɪs] *response*—and finally, especially after /l/: [ˈwaɪli] *while*, [ˈrili] *real*. Speakers for whom such intrusive vowels are stylistically variable may overcorrect and produce forms that contain the intrusive schwa but eliminate final [i]—for example, [ˈkidənz] *kidneys*. In addition, tense and lax vowels are not generally distinguished; Hill quotes the following written example: "By 1980, all expatriates are expected to live [i.e., 'leave'] the country. They will be replaced by Tanzanian expats[5] who leave [i.e., 'live'] here" (1973, p. 5).

Bantu tone or kiSwahili stress affects not only assimilated English words (e.g., kiSwahili *daktari* < 'doctor', *hospitali* < 'hospital'), but also the distribution of stress (e.g., [misˈtʃivəs] *mischievous*, [ˈsapraiz] *surprise*, [proˈtɛstant] *protestant*). Thus, for many East Africans, there is no contrast between English items distinguished by stress: [ˈrɛkɔd] *record* (n. and v.).

Asian speakers of East African English have a tendency to retroflex alveolar sounds ([ɖoṇt] *don't*, [ˈṇɔːṭi] *naughty*); to collapse [v] and [w] to /v/ ([vaːṭ] *what*); and sometimes to introduce a glide before initial /i/: [jif] *if*, [ˈjiŋgəland] *England*). Their speech also contains a higher proportion of Indian-derived lexical items, and they are characterized by their own variety of kiSwahili.

Within East Africa, there is a widespread sense of a distinctive African-influenced English often called jocularly "Swalengleza" (i.e., kiSwahili-English). In the following parody of this English, the speaker is presumed to be influenced by Meru:

On the twelofth of December, I shall be going on reave andi you can condact my assistant if you lun into any ndifficulties. Ip you go in epery oppice, you pind a notice "Apana kaji—No pacancy" den, tell, vat to do? I rilly like to recture in the shocial deveropment department. You nini, hii njunst ngo lound thi kona ani you wiro see the Nashono Ntheata andi ninio, you come acloss a white building and nthat is the exanct prace you wand.

[On the twelfth of December, I shall be going on leave and you can contact my assistant if you run into any difficulties. If you go in every office, you['ll] find a notice: "*Apana kaji*—no vacancy"; then tell [me], what [is there] to do? I really like to lecture in the Social Development department. You, er, should just go around the corner and you will see the National Theatre, and, er, you['ll] come across a white building, and that is the exact place you want.][Blake 1974, p. 18]

That such parodies appear at all suggests considerable awareness of the distinctive features of the English of East Africa.

While this is not the place to compare East African English with other varieties of English around the world, we have noted elsewhere (Angogo and Hancock 1980) that it is reasonable to postulate a general African Vernacular English encompassing both East and West African varieties. To a large extent the difference between these two subvarieties is intonational, West African generally being more "tonal" than East African English—a natural consequence of the carry-over from the speakers' mother tongues in the two regions. The following chart illustrates the vowels of British English with their West and East African English reflexes:

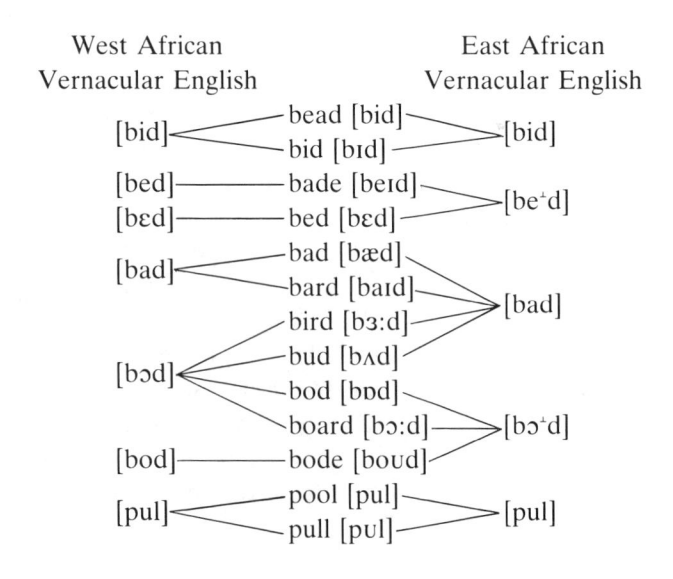

West African Vernacular English	British English	East African Vernacular English
[bid]	bead [bid] / bid [bɪd]	[bid]
[bed] / [bɛd]	bade [beɪd] / bed [bɛd]	[beˑd]
[bad]	bad [bæd] / bard [bɑɪd] / bird [bɜːd]	[bad]
[bɔd]	bud [bʌd] / bod [bɒd] / board [bɔːd]	[bɔˑd]
[bod]	bode [boʊd]	
[pul]	pool [pul] / pull [pʊl]	[pul]

Data from throughout sub-Saharan Africa suggest that African Vernacular English phonology is now well established and generally institutionalized.

Appended to this paper are some extracts from occasional writings and fiction that reveal something of the informal styles of East African written English. The following transcriptions suggest some of the attributes of careful spoken varieties, in this case the styles used by group three speakers in reading from a written sample:

1. West Africa (Nigeria), educated male speaker of Igbo
[dìà à sɔ́m pìpùl hù ágjù dà:t ìf wí à: tù jùz íŋglìʃ ðɛn ì:d mɔ́z bī bêst ɔn ði kwínz íŋglìʃ | ðàt íŋglíʃ wē:dz ʃūd ā:v àìdéntíkúl mínìz ìn làndɔ̀n àn náiróbì | àn dàt dì bíbìsì prɔ̀nànséʃɔn ʃùd bìkɔ́m ði stándàd fɔ ɔl spí:kàz ɔv ðát láŋwèʤ || fɔ mí ðēn | gud íŋglíʃ ìz ðát íŋglíʃ wìʃ ìz ɔ̀ndàstándàbùl ànd ɛnʤɔ́ìàbù bàì dì íst áfríkàn lìsnà || ìt íz ði íŋglíʃ lāŋwèʒ ɛ́ríʃt bàì ði kɔ́seps àn àìdíàz ɛmbédéd ìn àù lókál láŋwēʒ àn lítrètʃà]

2. West Africa (Sierra Leone), educated male speaker of Temne
[dè à sɔ́m pípùl hù ágjù dàt ìf wí á tù jús íŋglìʃ dèn ìt mɔ̀s bì bêst ɔn dì kwíʃ íŋglìʃ | dát íŋglíʃ wɔ́dz ʃùd áv àìdéntìkùl mínìns ìn lɔ́ndɔ̀n ɛ̀n nàròbì | ɛ̀n dàt dì bìbìsí prɔ̀nɔ̀nséʃɔ̀n ʃùd bìkɔ́m dì stándàd fɔ ɔl spíkàs ɔf dát láŋwèʤ || fɔ mí dén | gúd íŋglíʃ ìz dát íŋglíʃ wìtʃ ìz ɔ̀ndàstándèbùl àn ɛnʤɔ́ièbùl bàì dì ís áfrìkàn líʃtìnà || ìt ìz dì íŋglìʃ láŋwèʤ ɛ̀nrítʃt bàì dì kɔ́seps ɛ̀n àìdíàs ɛmbèdèd ìn àùà lókàl láŋwèʤ ɛ̀n lìtrétʃɔ]

3. East Africa (Kenya), educated female speaker of Luyia
[ðèr á: sàm pípùl hù á:gjù ðàt ìf wí: ā tū júz íŋglīʃ ðɛn ìt màs bì bèst ɔ̀n ðɔ̀ kwíns íŋglìʃ | ðɛt íŋglìʃ wáds ʃùd hàv àìdéntíkùl mínìŋs ìn lándàn àn nàìró:bì | àn ðàt bíbìsí prɔ̀nàùnzéʃɔ̀n ʃùd bìkàm ðɔ̀ stándàd fɔ ɔl spìkàz ɔf ðát láŋwèʤ || fɔ mí ðēn | gúd íŋglìʃ ìz ðát íŋglíʃ hwìʃ ìz àndàstándèbù ànd ɛnʤɔ́ièbù bàì ði ìst áfríkàn líznà || ìt ìz ði íŋlìʃ làŋwèʤ ìnríʃt bàì ði kɔ́nzèps ànd àìdíàz ɛmbédèd ìn àù lókò láŋwèʤez àn lítrètʃɔ̀]

There are some people who argue that if we are to use English, then it must be based on the Queen's English, that English words should have identical meanings in London and Nairobi, and that BBC pronunciation should become the standard for all speakers of that language. For me, then, good English is that English which is understandable and enjoyable by the East African listener. It is the English language enriched by the concepts and ideas embedded in our local language and literature.]

These three samples suggest the considerable diversity that divides East and West African English, a result of the substratal influences of the African languages in the two regions. It remains to be seen whether the differences between the two will remain stable, increase as local standards emerge, or decrease through pan-African contacts and teaching based on the "book dialect" of written English.

Grammar and Lexicon

Grammatical characteristics of East African English contain no examples of restructuring (except in calqued expressions), but some surface-form modifications are quite common. Among these are the nonoccurrence of particles in phrasal verbs:

> Her name *cropped* in the conversation ['cropped up'].
> I *picked him* outside his house and he *dropped* at work ['picked him up' and 'dropped off'].
> We should *leave* that word ['leave out' or 'leave in'].

Conversely, several verbs in East African English take *with* where it does not occur in other varieties:

> I'm going to *stay with* this dress but you can have the rest ['keep'].
> You *remain with* this until I come back ['keep'].
> *Go with* this and give it to Mr. Mjinga ['take'].
> Don't forget to *come with* your pencil as well ['bring'].

Some English words in Kenyan and Tanzanian colloquial speech have a plural form but are treated as singulars: *behaviours, bottoms, breads, bums, laps, minds, nighties, noses, popcorns*. In "My noses are stuffed up," the influence of Bantu is clearly apparent since there is in Bantu no single word for *nostril*. In other varieties of English, *trouser* and *trousers*, *panty* and *panties*, co-occur, but the tendency appears to be more pronounced in East Africa than elsewhere: "I was wearing my nighties when three visitors showed up."

Whereas most forms of East African English do not differ grammatically very much from varieties of English spoken elsewhere in the world, "Zambianized English" (Fortman 1978) appears to be an exception. Though Fortman provides very little discussion of the dialect, she says that the forms in her data were classified as Zambianized English "when they appeared with Bantu grammatical affixes" (1978, p. 186). Thus she treated *olanges* 'oranges' as English but *maoranges* or *maolanges* (with the *ma-* pluralizing prefix) as "Zambianized English." Similarly, *cipoto* 'pot' and *cablack* 'black' have Bemba class 4 nominal prefixes *ci-* and *ca-*; *ateacher* 'teacher' has the *a-* third person singular subject pronoun that also occurs in *awashes* 'she washes' and *adriver* 'he drives'. Similar examples collected by Fortman include *mafingers* 'fingers', *mabanana* 'bananas', *maeggs* 'eggs', *cileaf* 'leaf', *maleaves* 'leaves', and *ancita bye bye* 'they said bye bye'.

The lexicon and idioms of East African English fall into a number of categories: words from indigenous languages, calqued forms based upon indigenous languages, international English forms with local interpretations, locally coined forms, and slang.

Practically any local word can turn up in East African English. Some, such as *matoke* 'banana' (Gusii, Luganda) are of limited currency and are not known outside of their area of origin, while others are known and used by much of the population. Thus in Kenya and parts of Tanzania are found *sima* or *ugali* 'cornmeal paste', *khanga* 'cloth wrapper (as an item of clothing)', *panga* 'machete', *sufuria* 'cooking pot', and *pole* as an expression of sympathy. In Tanzania a *foforu* car is a fancy one, and in Uganda *waragi* is the common name for banana gin. Some such items have even passed into international currency: *safari*, *simba* 'lion', *bwana* 'master', *jambo* 'hello'.

It is not always possible to know whether borrowings remain consciously as loanwords for their users or have become assimilated and are thus regarded as English. In general, phonology provides a guide, and in many loanwords both anglicized and African patterns occur:

African vocalic values	*Anglicized vocalic values*
['paŋga]	['pæŋgə] or ['pʌŋgə]
[sufuria]	[sufə'rijə]
[ʤambɔ]	['ʤæmbou]
[bwana]	['bwɑːnə]

The anglicized pronunciations are said to be typical of European speakers of East African English, but among all groups the loanwords typically acquire English inflections even when the words derive from Bantu zero-plural forms (e.g., *two sufurias*).

Calques are fairly common, both lexically and syntactically. Hocking (1974) gives many examples of the latter. The use of *medicine* has been extended to include 'laboratory chemicals', *get down* for 'get out of (a vehicle)', *dry coffee* for 'coffee without milk or sugar', *slowly by slowly* for 'take it easy' (as an exhortation), *hear* for both 'feel (a pain)' and 'understand (a language)', *beat* for 'take (a photograph)', and *clean heart* for 'without guile'. All of these are direct translations from Bantu, especially kiSwahili.

Though not always exclusively East African, many usages are current in the region that have more restricted distribution elsewhere: *box* for 'suitcase', *live* for 'stay (even temporarily)', *impregnated* 'made pregnant' (e.g., "my sister was impregnated by her supervisor"), *friend* 'sweetheart', *compound* 'area around a house', *duty* 'work, occupation', *cane* 'hit (not necessarily with a cane; cf. West African English *flog*)', *face towel* 'washcloth', *Negro* 'Afro-American'. Locally coined words and expressions are *poor money* 'money for the poor', *tea sieve* 'tea strainer', *sundowner* (in Zambia and Zimbabwe and in South African English) 'evening drink; cocktail party', *combi* (< German *Kombi*) 'combination van; VW van', *mono* 'a first-form student', *architect's pencil* 'propelling pencil' (British English), 'mechanical pencil' (American English), *baby-belly* 'state of pregnancy', *jumbo sale* 'jumble sale' (British English), 'rummage sale' (American English), *off head* 'by heart'. By analogy with *overhear* is *overlisten* 'eavesdrop' and as a backformation from *unkempt* is *kempt* 'neat and tidy in appearance'. Examples like these in which international English words are used in special senses account for the bulk of lexical differences between East African English and other varieties; a complete list would fill many pages.

Slang and colloquial terms are rather hard to define in the absence of an acknowledged local standard. One striking feature of some slang terms is that they often appear to be restricted to specific areas, in particular boarding schools such as Ng'iya, Ienana, Cardinal Otunga, and Mary Hill in Kenya, where until recently signs were posted warning pupils to "leave your [native] language outside the gate" and where only English was to be tolerated. Like slang generally, the terms cover such semantic areas as sex, money, illicit activity, and bodily functions; for example, from just one Kenyan girls' school come *georging* 'using the toilet', *rolling* 'menstruating', and *cigarette* 'tampon'. Slang and colloquial expressions more generally known include *block* 'fellow' (cf. British English *bloke*), *escorter* 'something edible to accompany a beverage', *sophi* 'sophisticated, citified', *take off* 'take time off, go on leave', and *(be) on tarmac* 'in the process of finding a new job'.

In addition, some general observations might be made about East African English. British forms prevail over other varieties: in pronunciation (['vitəmin], [tə'mɑto]) as well as in lexical choice: the *boot* 'trunk', *bonnet* 'hood', and *bumpers* 'fenders' of a car, an *engaged* telephone line, *thick* (witted), *petrol* 'gasoline', *knickers* 'panties', *sweets* 'candy', *ladder* 'run in one's nylons'. Spelling pronunciations are not unusual, since few English words are acquired from the mouths of native speakers and many are known only from the printed page—for instance, ['laɪnedʒ] *lineage* and ['dʒumbo] *jumbo (jet)*. Misreadings of the written word are similarly common: [ɪn'dɪgnɪəs] *indigenous*, ['strenɪəs] *strenuous*. Mixed forms include *cope up*, *impunge*, and *trend of thought*.

Freedom in the creation of new forms is especially noticeable and may be found at all social levels. One may walk about *joblessly*, tolerate an *impressment* (i.e., 'a burden', possibly of Biblical origin, like many East Africanisms, rather than a newly created form), or *pedestrate* rather than *drive*. One may be a *native of sima*—that is, eat sima as part of one's ethnic diet, and persons who wish to recall their local diet may say that they can *quote from sima* quite easily.

Conclusion

The future of English seems to be reasonably well assured throughout eastern Africa both because it forms a link with the rest of the continent and with the rest of the world, and because textbooks and other educational materials at the higher levels are available only in that language. In addition, English has a prestige value not shared by other languages in eastern Africa. Some people do not see this as necessarily a good thing; Mwangi Wa-Njau (1970) for instance, remarks:

> English itself is the language of the elite in East Africa. It has created an elite group, separated from the other people by a language barrier. English has, up to this date, perpetuated a colonial elite who regard English as the gateway to becoming a black Englishman. [P. 43]

But English—in Kenya, at any rate—was put firmly in its place very early. The 1925 Commission on Education decreed that

> In secondary schools and further, English and only English should be the medium of education. When English is taught, it must be taught thoroughly and completely, and only to such pupils as are undergoing a period of school life long enough to enable English to be learnt properly. [Quoted by Whiteley 1974, p. 411]

This same policy was reaffirmed in 1929 by the Department of Education: "it is the policy of the Government to establish English as the lingua franca of the colony as soon as possible" (quoted by Gorman 1974, p. 417).

In Ethiopia, Somalia, and Tanzania, English will probably continue to be used by only a relatively few people, since local languages—Amharic and kiSwahili—are generally spoken. In Uganda and Kenya, even with the improving status of kiSwahili, English seems to be permanently established and even growing among a native-speaking African population. A similar extension of English is even more likely in Zambia and Malawi where English is now the principal unifying language.

Yet despite these differing circumstances, neither Africans nor the English language will remain unchanged. In discussing a novel by Samuel Kahiga, Edgar White notes that "British English is for Britain":

> What language would Mumtaz [an Asian] use in speaking to Matthew Mbathia? Not Kikuyu for certain. Probably English, possibly Swahili. And when Matthew uses the occasional slightly non-English use, we accept that also as natural to the context. British English is for Britain. Mbathia and his friend Kago may speak English or Kikuyu to each other, but Kago has one or two terms, vaguely slang American, lifted from the stereotype of the sharp business operator, which is what Kago is. The use of two or three languages, and not only of languages but levels of language, is possible because even though the culture is changing, people are at home in the change, are part of the change, and language is naturally part of the total picture. [1976, p. 116]

Though Kahiga's novel is fictional and his characters imaginary, he has captured an important aspect of East African culture: "the melting pot has language as one of its ingredients" (White 1976, p. 116).

APPENDIX: *Sample Texts*

The following are excerpts from a selection of personal letters all written by high-school students in their late teens living in Dar es Salaam, Tanzania.[6]

>Dearest Suzie: thanks a lot for the beautiful card, it was great to know that you still remember me. Well, how is life treating you down at that end? I've heard that you are really grooving life nowadays. It's really nice to know that you have settled down and adapting yourself to American life. I saw your photographs you look changed and your brother-in-law is really huge eh!

>Dear Suzy: I hope you are alright just as it leaves us over here. Thanks very much for your lovely postcard extended to us recently. We read its contest [*sic*] with zeal, we were happy to learn from you after all that long silence. As a matter of fact I never knew I would have such a good sister like you and so thanks indeed for remembering us. Few months back we wrote to you having addressed our letter with the care of Anita, the address given to us. I wonder if you had received them or not, could you please inquire from Anita if she had the mails? Suzy I have no hot news to deliver at the moment, DSM [Dar es Salaam] is in its high pace, just as you left it no change yet.

>Dearest Suzy, how are you? It's long days ago when you leave us. Although you leave me alone it is not your expect. But I feel bad when you forget us completely. Sure Suzy it will be difficult to forget you wherever I go. Also I'm not forget your mother and my brother David. All are good mood except the danger about house to be fire a few days ago. Are you get information? It is one day when wave of lamp be fire and make danger for somethings in your house.

>Dear Suzie, greetings as usual. It is a long time since you left us for USA and I had heard nothing of you. I don't know why it is like that. I hope you are well progressing with you usual routine. Here we are all well, succeeding with our studies. Several weeks ago I asked your friend Elly about your address, but she kept me waiting impatiently, but fortunately Fatima gave it me and so I decided to mail you. Because it is my first letter to you I want to know if you'll be real interested in such correspondence.

> After your reply to confirm your stand, I will be either totally or partially in correspondence with you. Your former house was burnt due to electrical faults and caused no human injury.

> Dear Suzy, hey! how are you babie! How are you going with your studies down there? Here it is quite OK and I am going well with my studies. I heard that you are now in USA. Why didn't you write to me or inform me that you are in USA. How is everybody there. Myself I'm still remember you and I won't stop remember you Suzie that's why I decided to break the silence which was a strong one. Here in Dar now it is very hot we are all sweating like anything. How is the climate of USA, please I would be glad if you would inform me more about USA cause may be one day I will be able to visit you down there.

The following is a passage from a manuscript novel, *The Entire Cast*, by Tanzanian writer Douglas Kavugha.[7]

> I thought about complaining to Ngoka as soon as we were seated inside, but he was busy moving from one table to another talking to his visitors. He had a charm planted on his face for such a long time that you would think it was real. By the time he got to our table, I had given up the idea. I knew he would not spare the gate keeper. The sudden change from poverty to riches had made an impact on him that changed his attitudes and behaviour on many things. He would very easily bark to his workers words like "I will break your head! I will call the police! I will reduce you to nothing! You worthless pig, you have no brains!" . . . His favourite was "you are fired!"

Next is an example of over-elaborate style found in a Nairobi club newsletter:

> Salutations and felicity from us to you and all, joint and severally. After decades of silence and seclusionism, and after being roused from this posture by your generous beckonings, we now have the greatest pleasure to respond positively. First, we thank you for the aforesaid beckonings. Second, we seize the offer with zeal, joy, and immeasurable enthusiasm.

Finally, here are examples from various short stories by East African writers published in the *East Africa Journal*:

> "The landing of the giant VC-10 had sprung everyone on the gallery to life."

> "My bloody dusty business to make sure you are all provided for."

"He never went late to duty, he never absented himself from duty, unless it was a life-and-death affair."

"More of rivals than friends."

"A flare of honks."

"I want to give you a secret. It is a top secret, and I do not want even a bird to hear it."

NOTES

1. See Todd's description of the functions of West African English elsewhere in this volume. It has been suggested (Moore 1969, p. xxi) that a pidginized English has not arisen in eastern Africa because kiSwahili became established there in a similar function.
2. It may be that Pidgin Portuguese existed on the coast at one time. Schuchardt (1889) lists several areas around the Indian Ocean, from Africa to Persia to India, where it was once spoken.
3. In a talk given at the 1974 annual general meeting of the Kenya Language Association.
4. Duran (1974, pp. 49–50) also summarizes the history of European settlement in eastern Africa:

> Originally, the British had little interest in Kenya itself; it was simply the gateway to Uganda, to the Great Lakes region, and, through Uganda, to the headwaters of the Nile. The Germans, however, were consolidating their hold over Tanganyika and Ruanda-Urundi to the South. To consolidate their own hold on Uganda and the surrounding regions, the British constructed a railroad across Kenya, from the port of Mombasa on the Indian Ocean to what is now the port of Kisumu. The railroad, completed in 1902, transformed Kenya. European settlers were brought in from Britain and South Africa to develop commercial agriculture along the rail line. The bulk of the settlers were settled in a broad area including sections of the Rift Valley Highlands and the intervening Rift Valley floor—an area later known as the "White Highlands." . . . With the coming of independence to Kenya in 1963, and the disappearance of legal restrictions on settlement, the situation changed drastically. Europeans and Asians were given the choices of taking Kenyan citizenship or leaving the country eventually. Many Europeans left Kenya altogether, leaving their farms to be purchased by the Kenyan government or by interested citizens. Many Asians chose to claim British citizenship and vacated businesses in urban centers as African citizens, assisted by government regulations and loans, bought them out. Meanwhile, large numbers of Africans moved to the larger African urban centers, especially Nairobi, which underwent a period of great expansion, together with its hinterland.

5. *Expats* is generally found in colonial English, but among nonnative speakers it is pronounced [εks'pats] rather than [εks'pæts] as in British English.
6. We thank Ms. Suzie Sharp of Austin, Texas, for allowing us to print portions of her letters.
7. Printed with Mr. Kavugha's kind permission.

REFERENCES

African Inland Mission. *Outreach Report: Strategy in Comoro Islands*. Nairobi: African Inland Mission, 1976.

Angogo, Rachel M., and Hancock, Ian F. "English in Africa: Emerging Standards or Diverging Regionalisms?" *English World-Wide* 1 (1980):67–96.

Baker, Philip. "The Language Situation in Mauritius." *African Language Review* 8 (1969):73–97.

Bender, Lionel, ed. *Language in Ethiopia*. London: Oxford University Press, 1971.

Blake, Philip. "Swalengleza: Kenya's Unofficial Language." *Kenya Institute of Administration Newsletter* 5 (1974):18.

Bollée, Annegret. *Le Créole français des Seychelles*. Tübingen: Max Niemeyer, 1977.

Duran, James J. "The Ecology of Ethnic Groups from a Kenyan Perspective." *Ethnicity* 1 (1974):43–64.

Fortman, Clasina de Gaay. "Oral Competence in Nyanja among Lusaka Schoolchildren." In *Language in Zambia*, edited by Sirarpi Ohannessian and Mubanga E. Kashoki, pp. 182–206. London: International African Institute, 1978.

Gorman, T. P. "The Development of Language Policy in Kenya, with Particular Reference to the Educational System." In *Language in Kenya*, edited by W. Whiteley, pp. 397–453. London: Oxford University Press, 1974.

Hill, Trevor. "The Pronunciation of English Stressed Vowels in Tanzania." *Bulletin of the Language Association of Tanzania* 4, no. 2 (1973):4–13.

Hocking, B. D. W. *All What I Was Taught, and Other Mistakes*. Nairobi: Oxford University Press, 1974.

Kaplan, Irving, et al. *Area Handbook for Zambia*. Washington, D.C.; Government Printing Office, 1969.

Marsh, Zoë, and Kingsnorth, G. W. *An Introduction to the History of East Africa*. Cambridge: At the University Press, 1965.

———. *A History of East Africa*. Cambridge: At the University Press, 1972.

Moore, Gerald. *The Chosen Tongue*. London: Longmans, 1969.

Ohannessian, Sirarpi, and Kashoki, Mubanga E., eds. *Language in Zambia*. London: International African Institute, 1978.

Phiri, Anacklet G. "The Language Situation in Malawi." MS. University of Texas at Austin, 1976.

Schuchardt, Hugo. "Allgemeineres über das Indoportugiesische (Asioportugiesische)." *Zeitschrift für Romanische Philologie* 13 (1889):476–516.

Wa-Njau, Mwangi. "Teaching Swahili Is Not a Waste of Time." *East Africa Journal* 7, no. 1 (1970):43.

Wanjohi, G. J. "The Oddities of Kenya English." *Lugha* 4, no. 1 (1974):27–28.

Welch, F. "The Danger of De-standardizing English." *Lugha* 4, no. 1 (1974):12–16.

White, Edgar. "The Bilingual, Bicultural African Writer." In *The Commonwealth Writer Overseas: Themes of Exile and Expatriation*, edited by Alastair Niven, pp. 107–19. Brussels: Didier, 1976.

Whiteley, W., ed. *Language in Kenya*. London: Oxford University Press, 1974.

English in South Africa

L. W. Lanham

History and the Consequences of History

In 1652, colonists from Holland arriving at the Cape of Good Hope made Dutch the first European language to become indigenous in southern Africa. Not until 1806, when Britain invaded the Cape for strategic reasons, was English established. For the next fourteen years, most English speakers were transient and served as administrators and in the military. Some settled permanently in Cape Town and its environs. In this, the first city in southern Africa, society rapidly came to be dominated socially and economically by the English speakers, a minority among the predominantly Dutch- (Afrikaans-) speaking European community. The aftermath of the Napoleonic Wars boosted the numbers of permanently settled English speakers and distributed them more widely in the Cape Colony. In fact, South African English as a mother-tongue variety of world English has its origins in the speech of the "1820 settlers." This group consisted, at first, of between four and five thousand men, women, and children who landed and settled in the eastern Cape in an area which today has Grahamstown and Port Elizabeth as the main cities.

A significant event in the history of English in South Africa[1] was a proclamation in 1822 by Lord Charles Somerset, the governor, making English the only official language of the Cape. Somerset furthered his intention of "facilitating the acquirement of the English Language in all classes of society" by importing from Britain schoolmasters and parsons (the latter from Scotland) to fill the empty pulpits and teaching posts in schools. In consequence of the steps to anglicize the predominantly Dutch-speaking society and of the social, economic, and political control exercised by English speakers (including a few high-status Dutch families who became English in everything but name), Dutch yielded to English in all domains of public life including law, education, entertainment, and the press except on the remote dorps and farms. English did not, however, supplant Dutch in the domains of home and religious life. English fulfilled a need in an isolated frontier society, culturally and educationally deprived. The descendants of the Dutch colonists accepted—but were not subverted by—the great tradition of the English language, life, and letters. Reports of the time indicate a highly competent English-Dutch (Afrikaans) bilingualism—except for accent, which was obviously Dutch-based, reflecting the tenacity with which group identity and value-system allegiance were maintained. The Great Trek of 1836 (of Dutch colonists moving north away from British rule) took Afrikaans English, as a competent second-language variety, into the Boer Republics of the north, where positive attitudes toward English were retained and bilinguals continued to be regarded as *geleerdheid* ('well educated').

In the eastern Cape, British colonists, and a first generation locally born who knew nothing of Britain, were being remolded as a society in an unfamiliar and hostile environment. They were influenced, too, by contact, admittedly restricted, with the Dutch, who after a century and a half had become an African society. Impoverished and embattled—a succession of wars with the Xhosa continued until the 1870s—they had themselves become a frontier society. The linguistic consequences of the changed social conditions were predictable. Social leveling produced a homogeneous form of speech within a generation or two. In the playgrounds of numerous small schools on farms and in villages, there emerged an accent showing nothing of most of the twenty or more English regional dialects present among the settlers, other than the lower-middle- (or lower-) class speech of the Home Counties. To these, a few variables deriving from Afrikaans phonology were added as products of early intermarriage between English men and Dutch women. Vocabulary loans from Afrikaans were becoming naturalized and semantic shifts were shaping English to its new environment. Cape English in the mouths of children even presented some problems of intelligibility to British travelers in southern Africa (Rose 1829).

After 1820, British settlers arrived in the Cape in comparatively small numbers; the English-speaking cities of Cape Town, Port Elizabeth, and Grahamstown have their origins in the period. The next organized British settlement in large numbers took place beyond the borders of the Cape, in Natal, over the period 1848–62. In some important respects, Natal settlers had different origins from the 1820 settlers, and their settlement differed in character. The Natal settlers were, in larger proportion, middle or higher in social class; Pietermaritzburg in the 1850s was "a city of impecunious aristocrats" and Natal "swarmed with half-pay or retired officers of the Army and Navy" according to Hattersley (1940, chap. 3, and 1950). Regionally, the Midlands, Yorkshire, and Lancashire were more strongly represented than the Home Counties. The Natalians were successful in considerable degree in realizing their ideal of creating a corner of Victorian England on alien soil. Forces similar to those that had simplified the social order and life-style of the Cape settlers operated in Natal, but less drastically. There were no frontier wars involving civilians, less poverty, far less contact with the Afrikaner; but a higher density of population, ready access to fashion-setting urban centers, and social distinctions based on position and rank were maintained. In Natal the distinctive accent of the first generation comprised only British English variables; some of these from Yorkshire and Lancashire became hallmarks of the Natal accent in this century. In vocabulary, the impact of Africa was different in item and degree from that of the Cape. A further noteworthy difference was that diversity was maintained in the English of Natal. Standard British English remained more or less intact, largely as a social-class correlate. In

Natal, if not in the wider society, Natal English became recognized as a local variety low in social prestige.

Two second-language varieties of English emerged in the period ending in the 1870s. The pattern and tradition of African English (or Black English) was set in the great mission institutions, first of the Cape Colony and later Natal, founded with missionary zeal at the time of the earliest white settlement. In 1875 the Superintendent General of Education in the Cape reported 22,245 students in mission schools, including many white English-speaking children. According to Shepherd (1971), the white children attended because of the "superior English, classical and mathematical education given." Mission education was elitist, with significant consequences. In providing an authentic learning context for English in and outside the classroom, the attrition of norms of international English was prevented in the displaced context of the African environment; South Africa today has nothing of the pidgins of West Africa. Until the 1950s the highest levels of competence in English in anglophone countries of Africa were found among black South Africans. Schoolteaching absorbed a majority of mission products, more extensively in this century than the last, and, because young blacks have always had their first learning experience of English in school rather than in society, the black teacher has been the main agent in propagating English. A second consequence of mission education is the continuing sense of the "great tradition" of English literature that helps to explain why English is assigned the highest prestige in multilingual South Africa by black South Africans (see Schuring 1977, reporting on the analysis of the latest survey of English and Afrikaans in the black community). Less obvious in the period when missions provided most of the education for blacks, but increasingly so in the past thirty years, Black English has emerged as a speech pattern influenced in pronunciation, grammar, idiom, and usage by African mother tongues.

The Coloured community (of ethnically mixed ancestry) has traditionally been part of the Dutch- (Afrikaans-) speaking speech community and antedates British settlement in the Cape. Its members participated in Dutch-English bilingualism whenever they lived in proximity to concentrations of English speakers, particularly in Cape Town and Port Elizabeth. Church schools, mainly Anglican, provided a small number with English education, and there is early evidence of socioeconomic advancement coinciding with a switch in home language to English. In colloquial style, Coloured South Africans have long had amazing English-Afrikaans proficiency and often indulge in random code switching at a bewildering rate; many are in fact multilingual and control a Bantu language far more fluently than any other European-descended group.

In 1860 Indians began arriving from India as indentured laborers on the sugar estates of Natal; since this early immigration, Indians have come to South Africa in much smaller numbers. The economic life of the Indian community has been mainly in English-speaking Natal, and the Indian schools there have provided an English education little different from that of English-speaking South

Africans. The Indian community accepted the utilitarian value of English as the dominant language of the society, but resisted its threat to the Indian identity and cultural heritage, which they sought to preserve in the home and in religious life (Bughwan 1970). Only in recent generations have Indian dialects and languages been overwhelmed by English in, for example, child rearing in the family. Indian English is characterized by an accent carrying the hallmarks of Indian English elsewhere in the world, but it is extremely fluent and far more intelligible outside its community than many local varieties of African English or than the extreme Indian English of India.

The mineral revolution of the 1870s heralded the industrial age in South Africa; the mining-industrial cities which arose on the diamond and gold fields exercised an influence which radically changed the pattern of rural and small-town life of the "old colonials" in South Africa. In fact, every ethnic-descent group in South Africa was drawn to the Witwatersrand (Johannesburg and its satellite towns), bringing major changes in life-style and values. Sociolinguistic patterns involving English took on a new form. The pursuit of wealth and social status resulted in a stratified society which was familiar to the 400,000 immigrants who arrived between 1875 and 1904 (more than double the white population in 1875), mainly from Britain and eastern and western Europe (Salomon 1964). Far less competent than the newcomers in understanding and negotiating a desired place in a society of this kind were the "colonials" from the Cape and the Afrikaners, both drawn reluctantly, but inexorably, into the cities. Natalians were better placed: their memories of Britain were still fresh (in comparison to the Cape settler descendant), and they were better prepared for a society in which the home-born, upper- or middle-class Englishman was the authority figure. Natalians were often better educated and had more to offer in industrial skills, and above all they were "more English." The Cape colonial had grown close to his fellow frontiersman, the Afrikaner, in most social attributes—even in speech—and it is clear that Cape English was not differentiated from Afrikaans English in the ears of the majority in the mining city. (Afrikaners there had low status; Horton [1968] reports that 800 children in the slums of Johannesburg in 1896 were mainly Dutch-speaking.) White social types perceived in the heterogeneous mining society were: British, colonial, Dutch (employees in one of the major industries were categorized in this way until the 1940s), and European Jew. These social identities mingled in a society far more class-stratified than old-colonial and Afrikaner society had been. Social power rested in the mining plutocracy (most effectively, in their wives!), a group defined by association with the great mining houses which controlled the economy of South Africa. The home-born upper-class Englishman was the reference figure in the society and represented the target of the mining plutocracy's aspirations, and some achieved the highest forms of recognition: the Honours List, a residence in London's West End and a country house in England, and children attending one of the great public schools. In South Africa the main agents in propagating the attitudes and social values of

Victorian Britain were the exclusive Anglican private schools, the Anglican church, and, of course, the mining houses.

This is the social context in which varieties of English in South Africa acquired social meaning. Until the Second World War, white South African society generally disseminated the ideals of the mining plutocracy that live on in the mind of society until the present day. In the postwar period, political change (and consequent social change) has had its effect on sociolinguistic patterns involving English, but available evidence indicates that young adult South Africans of the white descent groups get much the same social information from varieties of English as their grandparents.

British immigrants entered all social strata in the mining-industrial society. Many in the upper class would not have qualified for that status in Britain, but in South Africa they met the criteria of wealth, occupation, and social competence in appropriate "English" behavior—which could be had for the buying from elocution teachers drawn from members of British drama companies who remained in South Africa and from other teachers of the social graces. Louis Cohen, a shrewd observer of the social scene, writes of Johannesburg early in the century: "Johannesburg is very British . . . , loyal to Empire. . . . English manners and traditions appear to be lovingly enshrined in the hearts of the citizens" (Cohen 1924, p. 306). British upper-class speech symbolically conveyed the attributes of the power group: social sophistication, British nationalism, leadership and authority, good education, correctness, and knowledge of the proprieties. The social identity was that of the authentic upper-middle-class Englishman. Some of his attitudes disseminated as norms in English-speaking society are of importance, particularly his denigration of things local (including the colonials from the Cape and Natal) and the ascription of quality and excellence to what was British. This explains why standard British English remains the standard expected from news readers on South African radio and television, and why obviously local speech is rejected in this role by influential English-speaking South Africans.

Until the 1930s, the Natal colonial in the mining-industrial city appears to have played a special role in the development of accent types in South African English and their social meaning (see Lanham and Macdonald 1979). While Natal English was certainly not standard British English, it was not discerned as significantly different from it by other descent groups: European Jew, Afrikaner, and the old colonials of the Cape whose sensitivities to the fine detail of British behavior had faded. For these latter groups, the Natal Englishman was an accessible reference figure, and upward social mobility accompanied by growing sensitivity to society's overt values (Labov 1966) brought certain Natal English variables to characterize a local, informal standard in a society which today accepts a dual standard in South African English speech: Conservative South African English (near British English) and Respectable South African English (incorporating Natal English variables).

The European Jewish community, prominent users of Respectable South

African English, appear to have been primary agents in promoting this local standard in the mining-industrial society. Arriving in South Africa from 1880 onward, mainly as a consequence of the pogroms, eastern European Jewish immigrants lacked language and social competence in a British-dominated society. But they had advantages such as a driving ambition for higher education and experience in economic life that colonials lacked. At a time when the authentic upper-middle-class Englishmen were losing their social and economic power, the first and second locally born generations in the eastern European descent group were rising on the crest of upward social mobility in a socially restructured, more diversified industrial society. (In a sample taken by Watts [1976], families originating in Russia and Lithuania have more than twice the number of university graduates than the general average in the English-speaking sample.) "Fronted ai," a defining variable in Natal English, more than doubled in quantity in Witwatersrand female speech among those socialized after the Second World War, according to evidence offered by Lanham (1978). The eastern European descent group is today concentrated mainly on the Witwatersrand.

Among second-language varieties of English in the period from 1870 to 1940, Afrikaans-English was a low-status, stigmatized variety. (All those of Afrikaner descent did not necessarily use this variety, and it was not entirely confined to that descent group.) English in the Afrikaner community declined in quality and quantity largely in consequence of the rise of Afrikaans as a product of Afrikaner nationalism. In this period the gulf along the line of language loyalty—English versus Afrikaans—deepened in white South African society. English was identified as the "language of the enemy" and ceased to exist in the social life of many Afrikaans-speaking rural communities and towns. Firm evidence of the decline is supplied by the official report of the Public Service Commission in 1953 which noted "a grave decline in standards of English" in entrance examinations, which was not the case with Afrikaans. Census returns in 1950 showed for the first time that there were more Afrikaners than English speakers unable to use the other official language.

Blacks, as well as whites, were attracted to the mining cities, but in the early years the job setting was the only place for them to acquire a smattering of English. As stability and growth came to Johannesburg and adjacent urban areas, blacks came increasingly to learn English in schools. For a privileged minority, church schools took up the mission tradition in the new cities and inspired high levels of competence in English among the black community. The industrial city certainly promoted the quantity of English in this community.

Coloured South Africans, in more extensive contact with English speakers, came to use more English in their daily lives, and Coloured English was certainly spoken more widely. The mining-industrial city did not, however, draw them in anything like the numbers of blacks, and sociolinguistic patterns relating to Coloured English do not appear to show great change under the impact of the urban-industrial society in its early stages.

Similar conditions affected Indians. The bulk of the Indian population remained in Natal. English was the dominant language of the society in which they lived, and it certainly began to exert greater pressure in a period of growing urbanization and spatial mobility. English began making inroads in Indian homes during this period, a process greatly accelerated in the postwar years.

The third significant period in the history of English in South Africa is that following the Second World War. Political and economic change, with social changes in train, have promoted greater contact and social mingling among ethnic-descent groups using different varieties of English and have brought English more deeply into the daily life of communities using it as a second language. The industrial city is the locale where a segregated and divided, yet economically integrated society brings the different varieties of English into juxtaposition. Here, English takes on new social meaning and new functions; as a second language it penetrates new domains with consequent change through mutual contact and adaptation to a new environment.

The Afrikaner provides a good example of extensive urbanization breaking down the regional isolation of different ethnic-descent groups which, in the first 100 years, effectively maintained the distinctiveness of different varieties of English in South Africa. The following list shows the growth of the Afrikaner population in South African cities:

1911: 200,000 (29 percent of the Afrikaner population)
1926: 391,000 (41 percent)
1936: 535,000 (50 percent)
1960: 1,369,000 (75 percent)

The Witwatersrand has by far the largest urban-industrial population, although Durban, Port Elizabeth, and Cape Town (of the "English cities") are also heavily industrialized. In 1896 about 14 percent of Johannesburg's population were Afrikaners; in 1946, 35 percent of the Witwatersrand was Afrikaans-speaking (from Van Jaarsveld 1972). The 1970 census shows this number increased to approximately 42 percent.

This last period in the history of English in South Africa has seen the British presence removed and political power passing to the Afrikaner. Social power and influence in the industrial cities has, however, remained with those who are "English" in a broad South African sense (i.e., not "British"). In the economic life of South Africa, the Afrikaner has advanced rapidly, but is still far from securing the balance of power. Under these conditions, it is to be expected that more typically South African speech patterns supply the norms of the higher socioeconomic strata in urban-industrial society and displace the predominantly British-English norms of generations socialized and educated before the Second World War. The analysis of data from the Human Sciences Research Council's Language Survey of 1973[2] (hereinafter HSRCLS) below shows this to be the case, but the particular South African English variables favored in the shift are interesting: Natal English variables have advanced spectacularly in what is defined as Respectable South African English, coinciding with a retreat from Cape English variables (Extreme South African English). The latter are the most obviously local of South African English norms and are socially rejected in what white society recognizes as the most stigmatized form of speech. Afrikaans-English variables have associations with the stereotype of the "typical local man" and in idiolects are not infrequently intermingled with Extreme South African English variables as a consequence of the intimate social contact more likely to take place in lower socioeconomic strata (see Hauptfleisch 1977 and 1978, and Watts 1976). White society does not, however, perceive a clear difference between Extreme South African English and Afrikaans-English except perhaps, for the most deviant forms of the latter.

It is suggested in Lanham and Macdonald (1979) that sociolinguistic change in English-speaking society does not represent a major change in values, a disregarding of a British tradition in social values and a British identity in favor of those obviously South African. The deep cleavage in white society along lines of language loyalty remains today as the inheritance of opposing nationalisms of the last century, and language choice accompanies religious, political, ideological, and similar affiliations (see the sociological analysis of "white elites" in Van der Merwe et al. 1974). Standard British English retains its social meaning as "standard"—equatable with high social prestige and correctness—with even greater consensus in English-speaking South African society today than in Britain. But in present-day South Africa, it is inaccessible as a model, particularly for those whose links with Britain are remote or nonexistent—a majority in the higher socioeconomic strata. Originally taken as a local substitute for authentic standard English, Natal English is, in the form of Respectable South African English, accepted as an informal, local standard expressing high social status if not correctness in English speech. Standard British English is today only acquired in childhood as a peculiarly individual social experience. Respectable South African English is the viable standard, and it expresses symbolically the antithesis of "typical local man" with his obviously local speech and his values inherited from the frontier.

A sociological analysis of white English-speaking society (Schlemmer 1976) gives support to the analysis offered above. Schlemmer identifies between 10 percent and 20 percent of English speakers as "anglophiles" who

> ... value highly their links with the wider Anglo-Saxon world, reject South Africanism ... [and are to be] ... characterized by ... rejection of and hostility towards Afrikaners. [1976, pp. 131f]

He concludes that anglophiles are "... not a dying imperial fragment, but seem to be the result of a self-renewing tradition" (1976, p. 132).

A variety of factors have in the 1960s and 1970s reversed the decline in the quality of Afrikaans-English (i.e., of mother-tongue Afrikaans speakers) and have increased the quantity of English used in daily life. Afrikaners have established themselves in the cities (including the English cities) and, socially and economically, are upwardly mobile in the manner recalling that of the eastern European a generation or two before. Negative attitudes to English have been mollified as its speakers no longer represent a serious political threat, although sensitivities to them as a social threat remain. Negotiations with an increasingly hostile international community demand English, as does higher education and travel abroad. Under these conditions English used by Afrikaners of high socioeconomic status undergoes some noteworthy changes. Van der Merwe et al. (1974) note the trend to anglicization away from "unilingual orientation" on the part of Afrikaners moving to the highest socioeconomic status in industrial cities (i.e., the social threat which worries the church and the Nationalist Party). English culture "has an attraction for a segment of the Afrikaner group, while Afrikaans culture has little to recommend it to the English-speaker" (Van der Merwe et al. 1974, chaps. 2 and 10). In support of this claim is the switch in language loyalty (or at least to complete bilingualism in the home) in both Van der Merwe's and the HSRCLS samples. It is predominantly Afrikaners who change identity in this way (to the extent of 19 percent of the "elites"). The form of English has changed in that the completely bilingual high-status, well-educated Afrikaner often has few traces of Afrikaans-English and may even have an accent profile close to Conservative South African English. Elite Afrikaners commonly display very high levels of competence in English, while high-status English speakers are commonly incompetent in Afrikaans. Extreme forms of Afrikaans-English and low levels of proficiency in the use of English—which are not necessarily mutually predicting—correlate mainly with low status, poor education, and life in a predominantly Afrikaans-speaking community.

The cities and large towns of South Africa potentially provide a milieu which brings English into the lives of young blacks far more extensively than the rural environment. (The estimate of black urban dwellers in 1975 was 6,240,000 [*Survey of Race Relations in Africa* 1978].) The "English city" and town do this more effectively, although even in black townships near Pretoria, an "Afrikaans city," English is reported to have been more prominent than Afrikaans in the youth of those who are now over fifty years old. Then, as now, English came through advertising, the cinema, comics, and the newspaper apart from what was learned in school. Until the Bantu Education Act of 1954, when all black schools passed to government control, Afrikaans had received little attention in the school curriculum. English was the medium of school instruction after the fifth year and a subject receiving considerable emphasis before that. Even after 1954 it was difficult to meet policy demands for the teaching of Afrikaans and its use as medium for subject teaching because many teachers, particularly the more senior, were the products of missions and church schools and could not speak Afrikaans.

Dr. E. Mphahlele, a prominent black South African writer in English and a teacher in the 1950s, speaks of the "love and esteem for English" on the part of teachers and pupils, and their delight in memorizing and quoting long passages from Shakespeare (personal communication 1979). It is as the object of black South African admiration that English receives its greatest boost in the black community.

Some factors have limited the quality and potential growth of Black English. For young blacks growing up in large urban townships, English is not to any degree the language of the street and is not heard in the home. Residential segregation means that in the formative years, including the middle teens, contact with a mother-tongue English speaker is not a common occurrence. Even in the work situation, contact with whites is more likely to be with Afrikaans speakers acting as foremen or overseers for workers in the manual and unskilled jobs largely filled by blacks. Schuring, reporting on a recent language survey of black South Africans, gives nearly twice the number of blacks speaking Afrikaans in the work situation as English. Hence, blacks wish Afrikaans to remain a subject in school "because of practical considerations" (1977, p. vii).

While increasing greatly in quantity, the quality of Black English has declined seriously in the past thirty years. In black-white interaction, the intelligibility of Black English to whites and the comprehensibility of South African English by blacks poses problems. Recently a white teacher was dissuaded from using a Soweto class for a demonstration lesson because "his English would not be understood!" The communicative incompetence in English of black students now coming to English-speaking universities in growing numbers is a problem receiving urgent attention; black students who enrolled in the "open universities" before 1954 posed no such problem. Teachers are the primary agents for propagation of English among young blacks, and the great majority today are the products of circumstances and a system which have eliminated authentic English as a model for black learners. These circumstances include a vast increase in school-going population and in the number of teachers, while the mission tradition has virtually disappeared and white teachers are only rarely found in black schools. Today the most intelligible and widely consumed form of authentic English on the part of blacks is the newspaper. Some newspapers of white English society have more black than white readers, and several of South Africa's best-known papers run special editions or supplements for their black readers. Periodicals such as *Drum* and newspapers such as the *World* cater only to black readers.

A larger proportion of the Coloured community has always been closer to English than is the case for blacks—closer through many generations of contact with mother-tongue English speakers, especially in the Cape, and through the use of English in the home and a tradition of unselfconscious bilingualism in the cities and small towns of the Cape. Urbanization of the past forty years and the attraction of the industrial cities have affected the Coloured community. Occasions for using English have multiplied and the quantity of Coloured English has consequently increased. Even in the industrial cities, however, the Coloured community remains relatively self-contained and retains its own norms in behavior, attitude, and social values. The distinctive form of Coloured English remains unmodified in the formative years of childhood and early teens. (This statement is based on observations of Coloured children in fee-paying church schools on the Witwatersrand.) Some upward mobility has, however, swelled the higher socioeconomic ranks, and high status appears to coincide with greater use and proficiency in English and suppression in some degree of certain salient accent features of Coloured English. This variety of English in South Africa retains strong support from the social values of the community, and there is no wholesale retreat from it in contact with other varieties or from the stigma assigned to Coloured English. In some degree it symbolizes a social stratum which there is no apparent desire to discard. Coloured English is almost universally paired with Afrikaans in competent bilingualism and, therefore, its many characterizing properties deriving from Afrikaans are not easily eradicated.

Indian English has certainly increased greatly in quantity corresponding to the change in economic life; industry, commerce, and the professions in the cities now occupy many more Indians than half a century ago. The social milieu for Indian English, mainly in Natal, is predominantly English-speaking, and the effect on Indian languages in the home is revealed in Bughwan's study (1970). Her statistics show an increase of over 60 percent in the amount of English used with parents between two most recent generations. Of nonwhite communities, Indians are by far the best educated, and the proportion of university graduates greatly exceeds that of black and Coloured communities. The quality of Indian English has certainly improved in the past forty years, and a noteworthy feature of the best-educated, most influential sector (particularly younger university graduates) is the receding prominence of characterizing linguistic features of that variety. In accent this means a shift toward Conservative South African English, certainly not toward a more typical South African speech.

Demography of English-Speaking South Africa

The South African English community is predominantly urban. In 1974, 76 percent of the population (from Watts's sample [1976]) lived in the cities, with the "English cities" (where 65 percent or more were English-speaking in 1960) claiming the great majority. The mother-tongue English speaker in rural areas and small towns lives mainly in Natal and the eastern Cape, the settlement areas of the settlers of the last century. The province of Natal, as a region, is "more English" than any other major area in South Africa. In Watts's survey two-thirds of the English-speaking sample have a family origin in Britain or Ireland; the Jewish descent group from eastern Europe must be assumed to make up a large proportion of the remainder. Of the total sample, 36 percent have Afrikaans-speaking ancestors, and of these the greater concentration is at the lower end of

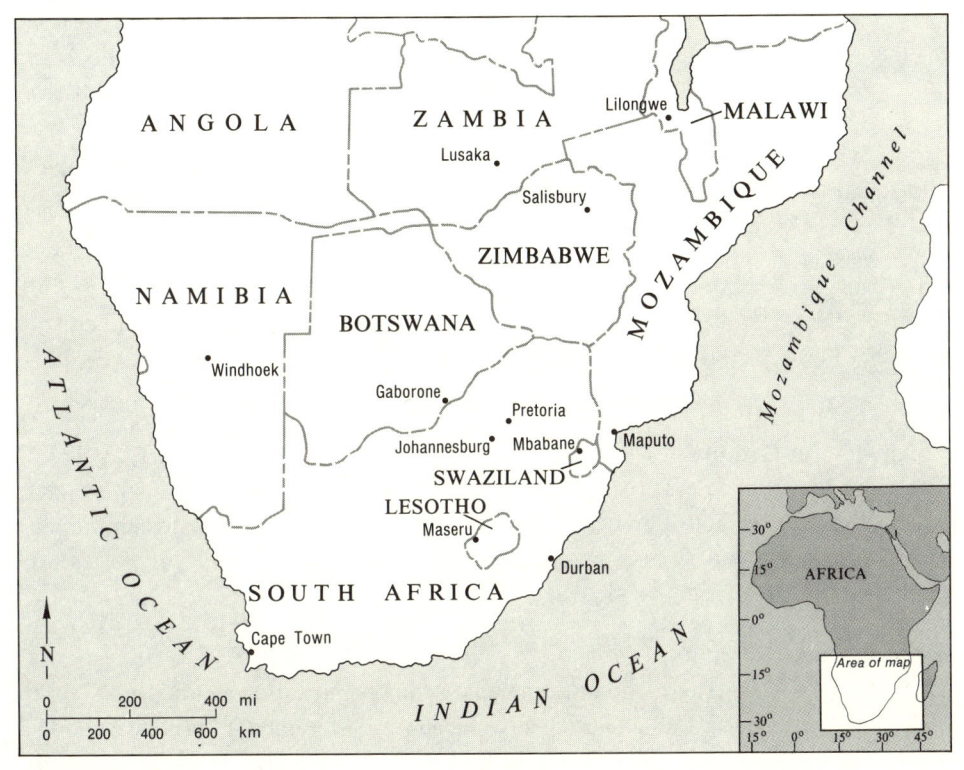

Southern Africa

the socioeconomic scale. In other words, Afrikaner ancestors increase as one "proceeds down the occupational hierarchy," as do low levels of education (Watts 1976, p. 78). In 1948, only 15 percent of directors, managers, and merchants in South Africa were Afrikaans-speaking, but the proportion is certainly much larger now. The social-class distribution of English and Afrikaans in the HSRCLS sample is shown in the following table (Hauptfleisch 1977):

	Upper	Middle	Lower
Afrikaans	30.6%	41.1%	28.3%
English	42.9	39.9	17.2

As Watts suggests, English-speaking white South Africans have "the highest social status in South Africa." White South African society is divided according to language loyalty—English versus Afrikaans—and thus retains the inheritance of the conflict between Boer and Briton which culminated in the Anglo-Boer war of 1899–1902.

English and Afrikaans are by statute the official languages of South Africa. Van Wyk (1978) found in the HSRCLS sample that only 9.6 percent of mother-tongue English speakers claim to be fully bilingual (versus 13.5 percent of

Afrikaners). As many as 22.4 percent of the English speakers reported little or no competence in Afrikaans, but only 12.9 percent of the Afrikaners claimed little or no English.

Within the South African English community the following demographic and social variables are major determinants of accent (see Lanham 1978).

Social class

Three social classes are distinguished, but categorizing is difficult. There are no South African English-speaking manual laborers. Wealth, occupation, and education are the main differentials (as judged by the elites in Van der Merwe's 1974 study).

Ethnic-descent Group

The main divisions are British (divided into recent versus a second, third, or later generation born in South Africa), Afrikaner (at least one parent or two grandparents), and European Jewish. As social types, these three major categories are perceived as part of the social structure of white South Africa.

Associations with Britain

Singly, or in combination, the criteria constituting "associations with Britain" are: education in one of the exclusive, Anglican, high-fee-paying private schools; upper class; attendance at a public school, "old" university, drama school, or similar institution in Britain. As a social experience this variable provides the motivation and the exposure required to adopt Conservative South African English or standard British English.

Age (older or younger than forty-five in 1975)

Socialization and early education before or after the Second World War have significance because of such sociopolitical changes as the dissolution of Empire, the rise to political and, in some degree, social power of the Afrikaner, and the disappearance of the upper-class Englishman as the authority figure in the society.

Sex

Women are more assiduous in acquiring standard speech, and standard British English or Conservative South African English is, among South Africans under forty-five, more a feature of women's than of men's speech. The advance of Respectable South African English on the Witwatersrand appears to be mainly due to the support of women.

The major correlations between linguistic and social variables are:

> Conservative South African English: upper class; over forty-five; recent British descent; associations with Britain; female
> Respectable South African English: middle or upper class (any class in Natal); female; European Jewish descent

Extreme South African English: lower class (in the "English cities," but not necessarily in the Cape); Afrikaner descent

Some opposing systems of social values cut across the grouping of demographic and social variables presented above. Extreme South African English may be adopted as a colloquial style by young men of the middle and even upper classes, to express a social meaning of the kind Labov (1966) associates with a "covert" value system: masculinity and disdain for the proprieties in social behavior. These values have special appeal in South Africa as an inheritance of the frontier society of the not too remote past.

White Afrikaans speakers who are likely to claim competence in English number 1,772,000 (a figure projected from Van Wyk's estimate [1978] that 83.7 percent of Afrikaners have average to excellent command of English). Levels of competence among this group are likely to be high in the English-speaking cities, among those with kinship ties to English-speakers, and among managers and executives in commerce and industry. English speech in these groups may well be a variety of South African English (i.e., a mother-tongue variety) rather than Afrikaans-English. Among the least proficient of the white Afrikaans speakers are those who use English in only a few domains (e.g., low-status government workers). The Afrikaans-English of such speakers is caricatured in the South African English community and is a target of the ire of language-sensitive English speakers.

The Coloured community has 123,000 using English as mother-tongue (according to Van Wyk 1978, using the "latest official figures"). Watts, using 1960 census figures, gives 432,000 (52 percent) as having an "ability to speak English"; his projection into 1974 shows a rise in this number of 7 percent. The highest levels of competence in English in the Coloured community are predicted by residence in the "English cities" and high socioeconomic status. Outside this group, many who claim an ability to use English are single-style speakers who employ a distinctive colloquial style to reinforce group identity and who find their English a distinct handicap in education.

Official figures for competence in English among black South Africans are, in our view, generally an underestimate—if the level of competence is set no higher than "an ability to understand/speak/read English at a level higher than 'weak'." Using this criterion, the latest survey of language in the black community (Schuring 1977, pp. 11–13, based on a random sample of 3,653) gives the following comparative figures:

	Understand	Speak	Read
English	38.4%	33.1%	38.1%
Afrikaans	36.7	29.3	30.4

If we average these three estimates, we can include 5.5 million of South Africa's black population of 15 million in the English-using population.[3] Social factors determining the highest levels of competence in English are: older than forty-five years of age; residence in the English cities; high school education or higher. The strongest predictor of high competence is close social contact with white English speakers in the teens or young adult life.

The Indian community can now (following Watts 1976) almost all be considered to be speakers of English. This group, numbering about 387,000, are mostly resident in Natal. Watts calculates the growth rate of English as home language among Asians—the great majority of whom are Indians—to be almost 13 percent. This growth rate will make English the home language of all South African Indians by 1990. Indian English is, in social interaction, generally highly competent. High-status occupation and university education are probably the main predictors of the highest levels of competence in English.

Linguistic Properties of South African English

Like standard British English, South African English is *r*-less, but shows in some varieties the influence of *r*-full Afrikaans. Where they are adequately perceived, British norms shape the overt standards of usage and other varieties of international English have little influence. In general, phonological variables define the accents of South African English and correlate with social types (see Lanham 1978).

Except for Conservative South African English, which is treated here as a norm, lects (accent profiles) are aggregations of variables in different mixes, with features having varying degrees of prominence. Conservative South African English is a variety close to standard British English and has in accent none of the variables listed below, except perhaps some vowel retraction before /l/ in such words as *belt*, *bill*, and *cold*; centralized /u/, especially following /j/ in such words as *new* and *due*; raised /oᵊ/ in, for example, [bo:d] *bored* and [po:z] *paws*; and stress-raised word-final weak syllables (e.g., *wanted*, *broken*, *money*). These traits, however, tend to be below the level of social consciousness.

In an attempt to identify the defining variables of the accent profiles of other major varieties of South African English, I group them as follows (Lanham and Macdonald 1979).

Cape English

Obstruent /r/: The tip and rim of the tongue approximate the postalveolar region with brief contact (i.e., a tap and not the trill of Afrikaans-English). Especially favored environments are initial /r/ and such clusters as /θr/, /kr/, /tr/, /dr/, and /gr/ (e.g., [grin] *green*).

Back-raised and glide-weakened /ɒɪ/: Especially before /l/, /m/, and /n/, there is a barely discernible upglide resulting in such pronunciations as [tʰɒᵊm] *time*.

Backed and raised /a:/: In eastern Cape schoolboy speech, *kite* and *cart* are barely distinguished, since the variable above reduces the diphthong of *kite* to a near monophthong and the vowel of *cart* is raised and backed. Such pronunciations as [hɒ·t] *heart* are common but subject to style shifting toward [a:].

Fronted and glide-weakened /æʊ/: In such words as [kæˠ] *cow*, Cape English follows the pattern of Australian English and other international varieties, but considerable consciousness of this variable has led to hypercorrection (e.g., [kɑu]).

Natal English

Vowel retraction before /l/: In Natal but also in young upper-class speakers in Johannesburg, vowel nuclei—especially /ɛ/, /ɪ/, and /əu/—are backed and lowered before /l/, resulting in such pronunciations as [bæˑl] *bell*, [bɤld] *build*, and [kʰɒld] *cold*.

Fronted and glide-weakened /aɪ/: Before /l/, /m/, /n/, /v/, /z/, and /s/ especially, the historic diphthong /aɪ/ may be realized as a fully front, tense [a] though some glide may be retained. Such pronunciations as [fa:t] *fight* are typical.

Raised /ə:/: *Stir* may be realized as [stɜ:] in the most advanced variant of the raising of /ə:/, and such words as *earth* and *Durban* are also affected. Hypercorrection may result in the use of /ʌ:/ among those sensitive to standard British English. *Year* with the advanced [ɜ:] is a shibboleth associated with Natal.

Centralized /u:/: Especially favored by preceding /j/, /u:/ may be centralized to [ʉ] (e.g., [jʉ:] *you*).

General South African English

Backed and lowered /əɪ/ and /əʊ/: Though extensively corrected and involved in style shifting, these two variables are prominent in all varieties of South African English, particularly in the Extreme type. Typical pronunciations are [mʌᵉ] *may* and [gʌˠ] *go*.

Raised /ɛ/: Tensing and raising result in [bed] *bed*, and the process is most apparent in [jes] *yes*. In general, the movement toward cardinal vowel [e] in such words has not come to a conscious level of social awareness.

Raised /æ/: Linked to the previous variable is the raising of /æ/ toward [ɛ˔] (e.g., [mɛ˔n] *man*). The most advanced varieties are found in the English cities among working-class children.

Raised and glideless /eə/: Even in open syllables, /eə/ is raised to the position of cardinal [e] and is glideless (e.g., [ke:] *care*). With lower tongue height, in the less advanced varieties, the glide returns.

Low schwa resulting from a polarization of the allophones of /ɪ/: Under the influence of Afrikaans, South African English has expanded the phonetic space between /ɪ/ and /ə/. The result is that some allophones approach cardinal vowel [i] (e.g., [kis] *kiss* and [wig] *wig*) while others are realized as low schwa (e.g., [pən] *pin*). Low schwa occurs in the final syllables of *wanted* and *chicken* and as the final three vowels of *consequences*. With the stress-raising of word-final syllables noted above as a feature of the Respectable variety, low schwa is particularly prominent as a feature.

These variables are illustrated in the specimen transcriptions at the end of this essay.

Analysis of the HSRCLS sample (Lanham 1978) revealed the distribution of salient variables. The dominant accent profile for those under forty-five (in 1973) has a combination of Cape English, Natal English, and General South African English variables (at least one from each group with a high index score). In Natal, however, variables from Natal English and General South African English predominate in the younger group. Accent profiles without any of these variables are found mainly among females over forty-five except in women of the working class. Older speakers—those over forty-five—generally differ in a strong tendency for either Cape English or Natal English to dominate with less mixing of the variables from other varieties. Older working-class males are the most prominent exponents of Cape English variables, followed closely by older males and females in the eastern Cape. Natal English predominates among the older male and female subjects in Natal and among older females on the Witwatersrand.

Accent types which are differentiated in the society and convey well-defined social meaning are identified in Lanham (1978) as:

1. Conservative South African English: defined above
2. Respectable South African English: Natal English variables in prominence particularly [ai > a:], often co-occurring with General South African English variables and stress-raised word-final syllables
3. Extreme South African English: Cape English or Cape English and General South African English; co-occurring Natal English variables do not affect the social identity of this accent
4. Afrikaans-English: Prominent variants of the following variables: obstruent or trilled /r/; raised /æ/ as in *man*, and low schwa (as in General South African English); raised fronted /i/, /i:/ in *kiss*, *see*; high diphthongal glides in [səi] *say*, [təu] *toe*, [mai] *my*; de-aspiration of stops; [j] for [h] as in [jil] *hill*, [jə·] *here*

A rich source of lexical variables is found in Branford (1980). *Location* 'black residential area near white town or city' and *robot* 'traffic light' are General South African English in the sense that they are not strong social differentiators. However, many items of early Afrikaans origin have associations with Extreme South African English: *padkos* 'snacks for consumption on a journey' and *papbroek* 'coward'. Other lexical variables of British origin differentiate Afrikaans-English and Extreme South African English from Conservative South African English: *bioscope* 'cinema' and *ride* 'convey water, produce, etc., by cart or motor vehicle'. These items are not likely to co-occur with Conservative and Respectable South African English accents.

The peculiarly South African English vocabulary is characterized by semantic reformulation of English words with international currency and loans, many of which are from Afrikaans. In a study of 300 items, it was found that 47 percent came from Dutch or Afrikaans, 14 percent from Nguni, 4 percent from Xhosan, and 3 percent from Malay (see Branford 1980, p. 298). Many of these loans have reached international English and appear in the Oxford dictionaries: *aardvark* 'anteater', *blesbok* 'highland antelope', *kloof* 'ravine, valley', *kraal* 'enclosure for livestock', *trek* 'organized migration' (especially in "The Great Trek"), *tsetse fly*, and *veld* 'unenclosed land of Southern Africa, (more generally) rural areas'.

Terms reflecting the social impact of South African politics and ideologies during recent years include: *apartheid* 'policy of racial separation'; *Book of Life* 'comprehensive personal identity document for white South Africans, in use since 1971'; *citizenship certificate* 'document certifying voting rights for residents of a homeland'; *classify* 'to assign an individual to a particular racial group'; *endorse out* 'to be officially ordered to leave an urban area on account of lacking correct endorsements in a reference book'; *exit permit* 'a permit to leave the country without the right to return'; *homeland* 'area set aside for an African people under the policy of separate development'; *Immorality Act* 'law providing for the prosecution of black and white who attempt to marry or whc cohabit'; *job reservation* 'the restriction of certain kinds of employment to particular racial groups'; *reference book* 'an identity document carried by all Africans'; and *separate development* 'the policy of developing homelands where Africans are allowed some measure of self-rule'.

In general, grammatical variables are few in number; those that do exist generally derive from Afrikaans and are thus associated with Extreme South African English. Many of them are found in other varieties of English around the world: deletion of *-ed* in such phrases as *pickle onion*, *long-sleeve shirt*; deletion or reduction to [ə] of *-re* following *we*, *you*, and *they* (e.g., *we working on it now; you looking tired*); deletion of object nouns or pronouns in elliptical sentences (e.g., *Q: "I was looking for some shoes in town." A: "And did you find?"*); omission of *to*, *at*, *in*, etc., after such verbs as *explain*, *reply*, or *lecture* (e.g., *Granny didn't reply me; what are you lecturing this term?*); deletion of third-person singular present tense marker, especially among speakers of Afrikaans (e.g., *I'm no musician but the wife play*). Since Afrikaans *leen* means both 'borrow' and 'lend', the two English verbs may be interchanged (e.g., *he borrowed his book to me*). *How goes it?*, though current in other varieties of English, is probably a translation of Afrikaans *hoe gaan dit?* Afrikaans influence is also apparent in phrases where Afrikaans employs the preposition *op* (e.g., *to propose a toast on someone*, *on the moment* 'at the moment'). Other prepositions similarly reflect Afrikaans usage (e.g., *over* 'about' [*parents anxious over boy*], *with* [*she has insisted that Tom Jones come with*]).

Afrikaans-English has two varieties, one normally found in speakers for whom English is a second language, and the other among bilinguals or monolinguals who acquire English as a mother tongue. The distinction is mainly one of the degree of deviation from standard South African English, and the number of variables may be very large. In addition to those already mentioned, these variables include the substitution of [j] for [ʤ] in *judge*, lack of concord (e.g., *has you got a license?*), and a variety of preposition substitutions (e.g., *I'll be by the house* 'I'll be at home'). In the popular press, the speech style combining English and Afrikaans elements is sometimes called *Anglikaans* in imitation of *Franglais,* which is applied to the invasion of English loans into French. Many literal translations from Afrikaans give this variety its typical flavor: *bell* 'to telephone' (e.g., *I'll bell some of the chicks*); *busy* as an adjective denoting progressive aspect (*this dreadful cattle disease* [rinderpest] *had swept down Africa and was now busy decimating their herds*); *drink* 'swallow medicine or tablets' (*it's such a nuisance to leave my office to drink a pill every four hours*); *give* 'teach' (*what subjects do you give?*); *just now* 'in a little while' (*I'm coming just now*); *otherside* 'on the other side of' (*the post office is otherside the road*); *overseas* 'abroad' (*during the weekend we relaxed into the quietude of our peaceful existence, untroubled by thoughts of overseas*); *rather very* 'somewhat, a bit' (*since I saw you I've been rather very ill*).[4]

Certain salient Black English variables in pronunciation are identified in Lanham and Traill (1965) as points for correction because of their effect on intelligibility:

1. No long-short contrasts appear in vowel nuclei (a highly functional opposition in South African English): *tick* = *teak*, *head* = *haired*, *pull* = *pool*.
2. No schwa quality vocoids exist; thus, *bird* = *bed*, *teacher* = [tiʃa].
3. /e/ : /æ/ opposition is lost.
4. Stress contrasts are obscured.

Other pronunciation features contributing to the Black English accent are an overly tense basis of articulation and diphthongs such as [əɪ] and [əu] which tend toward monophthongs.

Grammatical variables in Black English are usually "mistakes" deriving from the mother tongue and subject to correction in the classroom; hence the extent of their presence is itself a variable relating to competence in English. Lexical variables which mark Black English more clearly and generally include semantic extension, such as *late* used attributively and predicatively meaning 'dead', and neologisms such as *staffrider* 'a suburban train rider who clings to the outside of coaches out of bravado'—or to avoid the *tsotsis* ('muggers') in the compartments.

The extreme form of Coloured English greatly favored for purposes of caricature in stage and radio presentations is not too remote from the language of the street: slangy, rich in contemporary image and simile, with a stock of fixed expressions and turns of phrase that reinforce ethnic identity, although probably more representative of the lower social strata. Not unexpectedly, in view of the Afrikaans tradition of the Coloured community, Coloured English in this form is marked by advanced variants of Afrikaans English (including, especially, the use of [j] initially in *judge* and the devoicing of word-final stops in such words as *hand*). Lexically, this variety of Coloured English displays many borrowings from Afrikaans and also employs features of Cape English, a reflection of earlier cultural contacts with English speakers in that region. Intonation contours are especially distinctive: little use of falling pitch in statements and a tendency for pitch to rise in final accented syllables. Formal styles in Coloured English show fewer of the stigmatized variables, but even well-educated persons use the phonological features of Afrikaans English in all styles (especially the high diphthongal glide characteristic of that variety).

Indian English, as already mentioned, shares the features found in the English of India and in Indian immigrant communities in Britain, the West Indies, and Canada: merger of [v] and [w]; retroflexion of alveolar stops and resonants; and realization of /ei/ and /ou/ as short [e] and [o]. A variety of terms are not known outside the community of Indian English speakers, particularly vocabulary describing clothing, cooking, and food. Indian restaurants are self-described as *lounges* (e.g., *Bhagat's Vegetarian Lounge*), and in commercial uses, *goodself* is sometimes used to avoid the direct form 'you' (e.g., *your esteemed favour of even date to hand and we beg to thank your goodself for same*). Lexically, grammatically, and in usage, Indian English does not deviate greatly from the norms of mother-tongue English in South Africa. Increasing education in English in Natal and extensive contact with English speakers have generally worked to reduce the distinctive characteristics of Indian English among younger members of the Indian community.

Social Information Expressed by Accents and Varieties

Language loyalty marks the deepest division in white South African society. English and Afrikaans as home languages determine distinctly different attitudes, behavior, and values. The respective speech communities can, at the point of maximum social distance, be said to represent different cultures, in spite of a considerable number of mutually exchanged norms acquired through participation in a common public and, in varying degrees, social life. For their white "elites" Van der Merwe et al. (1974, chap. 2) assert that "home language provides the key to most of the internal differences within the elite group, be they attitudinal or otherwise." They continue: "Ethnic background, religious preference and political preference (i.e., ideological allegiance in the specific South Africa sense) are strongly differentiated." Social identities (social types) are perceived as patently different and hence, mutual expectations as to behavior and attitude are different when the two social types interact.

Conflict in social values implied in the language confrontation—a common experience in white South African society—is one way of stating the symbolic content of each of the white languages. These are more easily formulated for Afrikaans than English. English society has, in this respect, changed much more radically in the past forty years than that of the Afrikaner and is far more heterogeneous in origin. Central in Afrikaner beliefs is the sense of nation and mission located entirely in Africa, and the associated ideology embraces the religious as well as the political. The value system symbolized in Afrikaans reflects behavior, beliefs and attitudes and defines the differences between the "South African tradition" and the "British tradition" in English-speaking South Africa. The former is associated with English speakers closest to the Afrikaner and is the present-day inheritance of the frontier tradition arising from English settlement, mainly in the Cape, in the last century. This tradition is a product of the exigencies of frontier life in Africa, and, of course, contact with the Afrikaner as fellow frontiersman. The two value systems can be defined in the following oppositions.

1. Sensitivity to connotations of the respectable, refined, and sophisticated versus concern for physical self-image (e.g., toughness, manliness) rather than intellectual image
2. Selective and exclusive in social relations versus gregarious and egalitarian
3. Nonconformist versus strongly conforming to in-group attitudes and norms
4. Positive attitudes toward standards and attitudes which are English—at least in origin—versus insensitive to the distinction between the English and un-English, or rejection of the former in favor of the obviously local
5. Weak in local loyalties versus strong in local loyalties

Social values stated as extreme contrasts cannot be more than generalizations reflected more or less obviously in behavior. Moreover, they represent the expectations of the out-group, and the upper-class Afrikaner will deny their force (especially as stated in [1] above).

For those who choose to be "English South Africans" (i.e., specifically not "South Africans") or "British" (48 percent of Schlemmer's sample), Afrikaans expresses "typical local man" as an exponent of the values and ideology indicated above. Negative properties of the stereotype (e.g., intolerance and aggressiveness) untempered by the experience of contact with individual Afrikaners, are most heartily endorsed by those at maximum social distance from the Afrikaner. In particular, "anglophiles" are likely to emphasize the negative stereotype, especially those who are upper-class, resident in the English cities, and of recent British descent. This is the group with the "greatest resistance to Afrikaans." In respect Schlemmer adds another significant group to those with negative attitudes toward Afrikaners and, by implication, Afrikaans: young English speakers between sixteen and twenty-four years of age. For the anglophile, English symbolically represents the rejection of the Afrikaner identity and what it expresses. For many older anglophiles "English" is still "British," but younger ones feel less strongly. The closer English-speaking society moves toward the Afrikaner through social class, family history in South Africa, and kinship ties with Afrikaners, the less likely the individual is to subscribe to the negative aspects of the Afrikaner image. Whatever their attitudes and beliefs, however, English-speaking South Africans recognize in English the antithesis of the Afrikaner identity and associated ideology and values. This is the dominant facet of the social meaning of English as it is perceived by all ethnic-descent groups in South African society.

There is no general stereotype of the English speaker in the eyes of white South Africans. In this view we agree with Schlemmer: ". . . the English language-group identity among Whites is a *composite* phenomenon. In terms of a widespread and coherent group-consciousness there are *no* English South Africans" (1976, p. 131). Stereotypes of those who speak English as a mother tongue in South Africa are found mainly in association with the social groups that correlate with varieties of South African English. The one most clearly defined is the most obviously local Extreme South African English speaker—the one who most nearly approaches the Afrikaner. Extreme South African English is not strongly differentiated from Afrikaans-English. This is revealed in Macdonald's inquiries, in which she explored the correlates of South African English accents in terms of behavioral vignettes manifesting the social values described above. University students (English- and Afrikaans-speaking) judged the Extreme South African English stereotype as follows: "he is not a leader, he is uneducated . . . unsophisticated, gregarious and physically strong" (Macdonald 1975, p. 14). Penn and Stafford's inquiry (1971) reveals the South African English community's expectations that low-status occupations are associated with an Extreme South African English. Lanham and Macdonald (1979) cite circumstantial evidence of the social stigma conveyed by Extreme South African English in action taken by government officials against stage and radio presentations reinforcing in caricature the Extreme South African English speaker. It would appear that officials overreacted because "both protesters and officials find a good deal of their own perceived social identity in caricatured 'local man'."

It is possible to elicit from audiences of white South Africans the following correlates of Conservative South African English or standard British English (the two are only differentiated by British-born South Africans): sophistication, high social status, leadership and authority, and good education (see Macdonald 1975).

The social meaning of Respectable South African English implies no well-defined stereotype, except for one existing mainly in caricature: the "Kugels" whose speech reveals their identity. "Kugels" are seen as "pretty, often rich girls . . . who only go to college to hunt for a rich husband . . . wear a uniform of too-tight denims and too-high heels. . . . Jewish but anyone can join up" (*Johannesburg Sunday Times*, 19 September 1976). Such stereotyping is possibly trivial in a statement of social information conveyed by South African speech, but it does identify a group which exceeds the norm in pursuing Respectable South African English and, because of their present-day social significance, plays a major role in promoting this accent. Lanham and Macdonald (1979) suggest that Respectable South African English expresses respectability and high status to those who endorse standard British English as the formal standard but cannot discriminate British norms and have no personal contact with authentic British models. It serves, therefore, as a coexisting, informal, "local standard" mainly outside Natal (from where it has spread). Respectable South African English lacks respectability and high status for old Natalians and those sensitive to British speech norms. In an experiment measuring teacher attitudes to Conservative South African English and Respectable South African English, Macdonald (1977) found that teachers predicted a higher scholastic achievement for pupils speaking Respectable South African English than those speaking Conservative South African English.

Schlemmer's findings (1976) show that the Afrikaner generally feels less alienated from English South Africans than *vice versa*. Afrikaners who need to project an image of high status tend to accept the prestige norms of the English community and to imitate certain South African English variables. The Natal variable, vowel retraction before *l*, is not infrequently prominent in the Afrikaans of women television announcers and in the male voices used in advertising shorts on film and television. According to Van der Merwe et al. (1974, chap. 2), the Afrikaner who achieves high status in the cities becomes much more prone to "anglicization," to move toward an English identity and associated behavior, values and attitudes. For some Afrikaners, socially remote from English South Africans, English in some sense still expresses the "old enemy." More generally, however, English symbolically rejects the Afrikaner and his cause, and in these terms white society is of a common mind in the symbolic content of language choice. The Afrikaner can be said to see in English the betrayal of true South Africanism and the white man's mission in southern Africa.

Black South Africans generally recognize English and Afrikaans as symbols of the same political-ideological conflict acknowledged in the white community, but the extent of their perceptions has not been investigated in detail. In contradistinction to the view in white society, English presents a clear stereotype to blacks which Vorster and Proctor (1976) define in part in a study of black student attitudes. Using a matched guise technique, they opposed English to Afrikaans in certain social attributes and a number of nonpejorative personality traits. They found that "the English stereotype is not seen as taller or stronger than his Afrikaans counterpart, but he is much better looking, has a higher-status job, is more likeable, more sociable, and kinder. In short, then, the English stereotype is of a 'nice' person, whereas the Afrikaans stereotype could be of a 'strong' person" (1976, p. 108). In this connection it is important to note Dr. E. Mphahlele's recent warning that the English speaker might no longer be seen by a majority of blacks as a committed liberal, sympathetic to black aspirations. In social meaning, therefore, the English language probably needs to be separated from the white South African speaker of English. There is little doubt as to what English per se expresses: prestige and a passport to higher education and hence economic advantage and political power. The particular significance of English in education is supported by Edelstein's (1972) finding that 88.5 percent of black parents chose English as the language in which they wanted their children educated.

There is little empirical evidence of the extent to which black South Africans can discriminate between varieties of English in South Africa and find social meaning in them, or of whether the social information conveyed by each variety is similar to that recognized in the white community. Informal tests of attitudes among black teachers conducted by this writer in the middle 1960s revealed firm approval of the "Queen's English" which the teachers desired for themselves and their children while, nevertheless, having little sensitivity in discriminating between British and less extreme South African English. Extreme forms of Afrikaans-English were, however, identified. There is little evidence of Black English being flaunted as a symbol of identity in the black-white social encounter, or even of solidarity in the black community. There is, in fact, not much evidence that the characterizing variables of Black English have risen to a point of conscious awareness on the part of black English speakers; none qualify as stereotypes in Labov's sense (Labov 1966). Black English is, however, cultivated as symbolic expression in black creative writing in English, particularly in recent poetry for which periodicals such as *Staffrider* serve as vehicle. In this context Black English expresses social identity, the voice of protest, and the black man's plight, socially and politically, in white-controlled urban society. The black English press, it must be noted, is not obviously written in a non-mother-tongue variety; its intended audience is revealed mainly in favored social themes in black society and some of the fixed expressions and turns of phrase of Black English.

The domains of English in black society are education, business, and commercial and professional life. Committee meetings in sporting clubs and other urban institutions are likely to be conducted mainly in English. The parish council of an Anglican church in Soweto conducts its meetings mainly in English, but its church services are nearly always in a Bantu language. With few exceptions among professional families, English is not a language of the home. Written English in great quantity comes to black users of English in the newspaper, even those who otherwise speak little English in their daily lives. In the postwar years of social and political turmoil at home and abroad, the black reader has come to regard the English newspaper as a source of full and accurate information.

The recent language survey of black South Africans (Schuring 1977) reveals patterns of preference between English and Afrikaans. Those responding reported attending social gatherings where English was used (12.1 percent versus only 4.7 percent for Afrikaans), listening to English radio broadcasts (18.3 percent versus 3.2 percent for Afrikaans), and writing personal letters in English (11.2 percent versus less than 1 percent for Afrikaans). Half of those with five or more years of schooling read English newspapers, but less than 5 percent of the same group read Afrikaans newspapers.

White South Africans readily perceive Coloured English and Indian English as distinct varieties and assign largely negative social and personal stereotypes to speakers with the most pronounced accents. Nevertheless, Mann (1963) found that whites upgraded "Hindus" on traits collectively amounting to social attractiveness (e.g., friendliness) in a comparison with themselves. Caricatures of both types in stage and radio presentations are not uncommon.

There is little evidence that Indian English expresses group solidarity for its speakers. When there is a clear need for such expression, an Indian language in some form is likely to be used. While generally retaining their cultural identity in private domains, Indians seek acceptance in the social and public life of whites. Domains which most strongly predict the use of English among Indians are preeminently education and economic life. The encroachment of English in the home is indicated by statistics based on Bughwan's (1970) sample: 62 percent of high school pupils used only English with siblings and 52 percent only English with parents (84 percent of parents used an Indian language with their children's grandparents). Only 11 percent of the same sample could communicate in writing in an Indian language. Only in religious life and social institutions specifically intended to maintain Indian culture does English give way to an Indian language.

Coloured English, on the other hand, seems to be cultivated and to symbolize group identity and solidarity. Its use supports the social image of the "South African Cockney" and some of the positive attributes associated with the traditional Cockney. White society is aware of this image and demonstrates some affection for the stereotype, while nevertheless stigmatizing Coloured English strongly in terms of overt values. The Coloured community, particularly in the Cape, has long occupied a low socioeconomic stratum, and the need to reinforce "covert values" in group norms is compelling even in adult life. The extent to which Coloured English represents defiance and rejection of the power structure in South African society needs to be studied and, because of recent political events, might be stronger today than it has been in the past. An HSRC study of sociolinguistic patterns in the Coloured community is currently underway and the role and function of English in the daily life of the community are now only supported by impressionistic evidence. Even when English is predominant in the home, the community remains extensively bilingual, and there is no clear diglossic distribution of English and Afrikaans.

The future of English in South Africa is thus likely to remain diverse, since various kinds of English serve differing functions and reflect varying overt and covert values. For some, only prestige varieties closely resembling standard British English are acceptable; for others, more specifically South African varieties carry connotations of group solidarity and national identity.

APPENDIX: *Typical Features of "Colloquial Style"*

The following specimens show typical features of the "colloquial style" that distinguish four of the groups discussed in this essay.

Afrikaans English: very fluent colloquial style; male; about forty-five years old; poorly educated but with extensive contact with South African English speakers:

ðɛtsrait . . . . nəu . . . . nɔt θru æfrikə ɛni mɔ: stu mɐʃ prɒbləms jɐ bˀt aid laik tu gəu ərɛˑʳunt hɒlənd ɛn dɛmaˑʳk ɔn mai nɛˑks trəp ṇ prɒbəbli tu saibiəriə ṇ rɐʃə . . . jɛːs in nainti əiti

[That's right. . . . No. . . . not through Africa any more (there)s too much problems here, but I'd like to go around Holland and Denmark on my next trip and probably to Siberia and Russia . . . yes, in 1980.]

Extreme South African English with Cape English and Natal English variables prominent: colloquial style; male adolescent; lower middle class:

mɐˑ dɛˑdz frɛn ṇ ɐˑ wɛn ðɛˑ . . . . ṇ tr̥ɐˑ'ṇ dᵘ sˀm fɪʃiŋ . . . s ɛnihɛˑʳˣ wᵉn wɪ gɛt ðɛˑ ɐ soˑs ləl gʌli ðɛˑ . . . lɐk sodəvə æˑˣtlɛt fr'm ðə dɛˑm . . . ṇ ɐ ɒˑs mᵉ frɛn z ðɛt kwɐt ə gud pʰlʌɪs tˀfɪʃ . . . . sˀ hi sɛd nɐː . . . srʌbɪʃ pʰlʌɪs . . . . gɛrəwʌɪ fm̩ jɜ . . . . tr̥ɒˈsʌmwe æˑ ls

[My dad's friend and I went there . . . and try to do some fishing. So, anyhow, when we got there I saw (thi)s little gully there . . . like sort of a outlet from the dam . . . and I asked my friend: Is that quite a good place to fish? So he said: No. (It)s a rubbish place. Get away from here. Try somewhere else.]

Black English: slow formal style (but speaker has little style variation); female; Grahamstown; twenty-two years old; primary school teacher. Note that stress differences between syllables are small, and no syllable is weak to the degree of an English unstressed, schwa syllable. A clear open juncture marks all word boundaries.

ði tʃɪlrɛˑnz maˑðaˑ noᵘ ðat ðeⁱ maˑst goᵘ tu skul . . . . mai oldaˑ sɪstaˑ steⁱs wɪθ maˑðaˑ ɛˑt hoᵘm . . . ʃi is stɪl goʷɪŋ tu skul . . . hɛ neⁱm is dɔːraˑ . . . . dɪ tʃaɪld hɛˑs stɔpt kraɪɪŋ wɛˑn it siːs his maˑːða

[The children's mother know that they must go to school. . . . My older sister stays with mother at home . . . she is still going to school . . . her name is Dora. . . . The child has stopped crying when it sees his mother.]

Coloured English: colloquial style; female; Johannesburg; over forty years old; a health visitor

bikɔs ʃi sɛ⁺d it kudn̩t muːv eni moˑ ɛn jet inə mɒniŋ ðəi fainim in frɐntᵊv ðə doˑ . . . ɛ⁺n waili kikim (di kənərs maː di grap). . . . səu ʃi sɛ˺d ju mɐs təik nəut ɔv ðə nɐmbə bikɔs iˑz gɔt ə lain næ⁺u

[Because she said it couldn't move any more and yet in the morning they find him in front of the door . . . and while he kick him (*Afrikaans:* the children make a joke). . . . so she said you must take note of the number because he's got a line now.]

NOTES

1. South Africa of this title refers to the total society resident within the borders of the Republic of South Africa, including the Transkei and other semi-independent black territories. Our analysis and description can be applied with little modification to users of English in Botswana, Lesotho, and Swaziland providing that recently established international communities of United Nations advisors, Peace Corps, and other voluntary service organizations are excluded. Population statistics cited here do not include these three territories. A sociolinguistic survey of Namibia (South West Africa) was undertaken by the Human Sciences Research Council (HSRC) in 1976, but its results are not yet available. Samples from the data of this survey indicate that of the white languages spoken by blacks, Afrikaans clearly predominates; positive attitudes to English (connoting good education, social prestige, etc.) are, however, the same as in the Republic. Zimbabwe was first settled by whites drawn in the majority from South Africa, many of whom had been reared in white South African society. In consequence, variables which define varieties of South African English (other than Afrikaans-English) characterize the speech of Africa-born white Zimbabwians. There are, however, some differences in their social distribution and some phonological variables as phonetic trends are less advanced (e.g., those of Natal English). No survey data from Zimbabwe are available, and Black English in that society may be qualitatively different and follow different sociolinguistic patterns from those of the Republic of South Africa. Zambia lies within the sphere of influence of English of both East and South Africa; lacking information on this society, we exclude it from this discussion (however, see Ohannessian and Kashoki 1978).
2. This survey provides a completed questionnaire and recorded interview for some 1,607 white South Africans (about two-fifths are South African English speakers) representing a 1-in-375 random sampling of the voters' roll in centers with populations over 10,000.

3. Schuring states that the sample is adequately representative of: those aged fifteen through fifty-four years; both sexes; ethnic (tribal) groups; and rural and urban areas in the Republic and "homelands." He warns, however, that the sample is biased in the direction of those with secondary-school education; hence our estimate is, on this basis, an overestimate in some degree. Using census data, Watts (1976) suggests that 16.1 percent of blacks have an "ability to speak English" and 28.1 percent have an "ability to speak Afrikaans."
4. These and other examples quoted in the preceding paragraphs are drawn from Branford 1980.

REFERENCES

Branford, Jean. *A Dictionary of South African English*. 2d ed. Cape Town: Oxford University Press, 1980.
Bughwan, D. *An Investigation into the Use of English by Indians in South Africa with Special Reference to Natal*. Ph.D. dissertation, University of South Africa, Pretoria, 1970.
Cohen, Louis. *Reminiscences of Johannesburg and London*. London: Robert Holden, 1924.
Edelstein, Melville L. *What Do Young Africans Think?* Johannesburg: Institute of Race Relations, 1972.
Hattersley, Alan F. *Portrait of a Colony*. Cambridge: At the University Press, 1940.
―――. *The British Settlement of Natal*. Cambridge: At the University Press, 1950.
Hauptfleisch, T. *Language Loyalty in South Africa: Bilingual Policy in South Africa—Opinion of White Adults in Urban Areas*. Pretoria: Human Sciences Research Council, 1977.
―――. *Language Loyalty in South Africa: Using and Improving Usage in the Second Language—Some Opinions of White Adults in Urban Areas*. Pretoria: Human Sciences Research Council, 1978.
Horton, J. W. *The First Seventy Years, 1895–1965, Being an Account of the Growth of the Council of Education, Witwatersrand*. Johannesburg: Witwatersrand University Press, 1968.
Labov, William. *The Social Stratification of English in New York City*. Washington, D.C.: Center of Applied Linguistics, 1966.
Lanham, L. W. "South African English." In *Language and Communication Studies in South Africa: Current Issues in Research and Inquiry*, edited by L. W. Lanham and K. P. Prinsloo, pp. 138–65. Cape Town: Oxford University Press, 1978.
Lanham, L. W., and Macdonald, C. A. *The Standard in South African English and Its Social History*. Heidelberg: Groos, 1979.
Lanham, L. W., and Traill, A. *Pronounce English Correctly*. Cape Town: Longman, 1965.
Macdonald, C. A. "An Investigation of the Responses to Four South African English Dialects, and of the Values Esteemed by White South African University Students." Unpublished research report. Witwatersrand University, Johannesburg, 1975.

———. "Accent—Its Role in the Evaluation of Scholastic Ability." B.A. honors thesis, Witwatersrand University, Johannesburg, 1977.

Mann, J. W. "Rivals of Different Rank." *Journal of Social Psychology* 68 (1963):11–28.

Ohannessian, Sirarpi, and Kashoki, Mubanga E., eds. *Language in Zambia*. London: International African Institute, 1978.

Penn, C., and Stafford, S. "The Importance of Dialect in the Perception of Occupation in South Africa." *Journal of Behavioral Science* 1, no. 3 (1971):113–16.

Rose, C. *Four Years in Southern Africa*. London: Henry Colburn and Richard Bentley, 1829.

Salomon, Laurence. "The Economic Background to the Rise of Afrikaner Nationalism." In *Boston University Papers in African History*, edited by Jeffrey Butler, vol. 1, pp. 217–42. Boston: Boston University Press, 1964.

Schlemmer, Lawrence. "English-Speaking South Africans Today: Identity and Integration into the Broader National Community." *English-Speaking South Africa Today*, edited by André de Villiers, pp. 91–135. Cape Town: Oxford University Press, 1976.

Schuring, G. K. *'n Veeltalige samelewing: Afrikaans en Engels onder swartmense in die RSA* [A multilingual society: Afrikaans and English among black people in the Republic of South Africa]. Pretoria: Division for Sociolinguistics, Human Sciences Research Council, 1977.

Shepherd, R. H. W. *Lovedale, South Africa 1824–1955*. Alice, South Africa: Lovedale Press, 1971.

Survey of Race Relations in South Africa 1977. Johannesburg: South African Institute of Race Relations, 1978.

Van der Merwe, H. W.; Ashley, M. J.; Charton, N. C. J.; and Huber, B. J. *White South African Elites*. Cape Town: Juta, 1974.

Van Jaarsveld, F. A. *Die verstedeliking van die Afrikaner* [The urbanization of the Afrikaner]. Johannesburg: South African Broadcasting Corporation, 1972.

Van Wyk, E. B. "Language Contact and Bilingualism." *Language and Communication Studies in South Africa: Current Issues and Directions in Research and Inquiry*, edited by L. W. Lanham and K. P. Prinsloo, pp. 29–52. Cape Town: Oxford University Press, 1978.

Vorster, Jan, and Proctor, Leslie. "Black Attitudes to 'White' Languages in South Africa: A Pilot Study." *Journal of Psychology* 92, no. 1 (1976):103–8.

Watts, H. L. "A Social and Demographic Portrait of English-Speaking White South Africans." *English-Speaking South Africa Today*, edited by André de Villiers, pp. 41–89. Cape Town: Oxford University Press, 1976.

South Asian English

Braj B. Kachru

I shall use the term South Asian English to refer to the variety of English used in what has traditionally been called the Indian subcontinent. The label *South Asian English,* unlike *English in South Asia,* suggests a parallelism with variety-oriented[1] terms such as *American English* or *British English* and implies a historical tradition and institutionalization, as well as distinct formal and functional characteristics. As an institutionalized variety, South Asian English is distinguished from performance varieties[2] which are used as foreign languages in highly restricted functions such as English is used in, for example, Japan and most of Europe.

In terms of language and cultures, the Indian subcontinent has several shared features, and on the basis of its shared linguistic features, South Asia has been defined as a "linguistic area" (see Masica 1976). In political terms, however, South Asia is divided into the following countries: India (population 683.8 million), Bangladesh (88.6 million), Pakistan (82.4 million), Sri Lanka (14.7 million), Nepal (14 million), and Bhutan (1.2 million).[3] The total population is 884.9 million, and of this, the largest number (77.3 percent) live in India, and the smallest (0.14 percent) in Bhutan. South Asia comprises about one-fifth of the total human population and is culturally and linguistically pluralistic. The number of languages and dialects spoken in the region is very large, and the sociolinguistic situation is complex. Four major language families are represented: Indo-Aryan, Dravidian, Tibeto-Burman, and Munda. The two major families are Indo-Aryan and Dravidian.[4]

The Diffusion and Current Status of English

The history of British colonization of South Asia and the introduction of bilingualism in English in the region are closely interlinked. The initial document establishing the British contact with the Indian subcontinent was the Charter of December 31, 1600, granted by Queen Elizabeth I to some merchants of London who formed the East India Company. This charter granted them a monopoly on trade with India and the East and opened the region to British contact and domination. The introduction of bilingualism in English can be described as having three crucial phases.[5] Each phase is, in a sense, independent, and all three are important in understanding the diffusion and impact of English on South Asia.

The first phase—the missionary phase—was initiated around 1614 by Christian missionaries of various persuasions who volunteered to go to South Asia to proselytize. The second phase involved "local demand" and has been

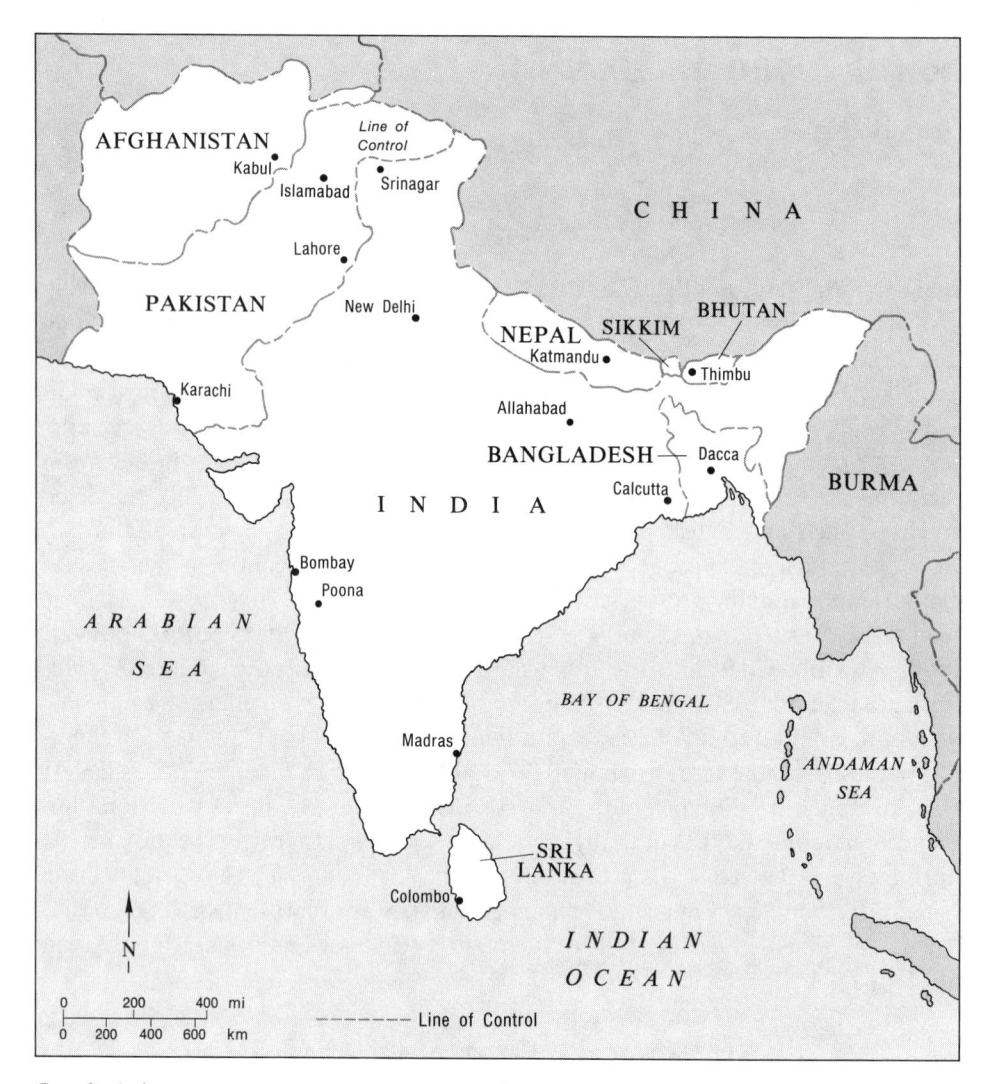

South Asia

considered vital by some scholars who believe that the spread of English was the result of the demand of local people and their willingness to learn it. Chaudhuri ridicules the view that English "was imposed on a subject people by a set of foreign rulers for the sake of carrying on their alien government" (1976, p. 91). The prominent spokesmen for English were Raja Rammohan Roy (1772–1833) and Rajunath Hari Navalkar (ca. 1770). Their aim was to persuade the East India Company to give instruction in English, since Sanskrit, Arabic, and the "Indian vernaculars" did not allow young Indians access to the scientific knowledge of the West. In a letter to Lord Amherst (1773–1857), Raja Rammohan Roy expressed disappointment in the establishment of Sanskrit schools in Calcutta and urged him to allocate funds for employing European gentlemen of talent and education to instruct the natives of India in mathematics, natural philosophy, chemistry, anatomy and other useful sciences, which the natives of Europe have carried to a degree of perfection that has raised them above the inhabitants of other parts of the world. [Quoted in Kachru 1978a, p. 545]

Roy's proposal set off a controversy about Indian educational policy that resulted in the third phase. This phase began after 1765 and resulted in controversy over the merits of different educational systems for India. Two principal groups were involved in the controversy: the anglicists and the orientalists. The anglicists included Charles Grant (1746–1823), Lord Moira (1754–1826), T. B. Macauley (1800–1859); and the spokesman for the orientalists was H. T. Prinsep (1792–1878). In the beginning, the colonial administrators did not agree on a simple educational policy for the subcontinent, but by 1835, Prinsep and others who shared his views could not stop the far-reaching Minute of Macauley from passing. That Minute proclaimed the need to form a subculture in India: "a class who may be interpreters between us and the millions whom we govern, a class of persons, Indians in blood and colour, but English in taste, in opinion, in morals and in intellect" (Sharp 1920, p. 101). The Minute was given final approval by Lord William Bentick (1774–1839), and an official resolution was passed. This resolution is rightly considered epoch-making, and it eventually resulted in the diffusion of bilingualism in English on the Indian subcontinent.

The British *Raj,* or sovereignty (1765–1947), established English firmly as the medium of instruction and administration. The first three universities, modeled after British universities, were established in Bombay, Calcutta, and Madras in 1857. By the end of the century two more were added in Lahore (now in Pakistan) and Allahabad.[6]

Even after Macauley's Minute had been adopted, the debate about the medium of instruction continued in various commissions and subcommissions.[7] Now, after years of controversy and acrimony, Indians seem to have settled for what is known as the "three language formula." This formula was proposed in the 1960s with the pious hope that it would satisfy all three language pressure groups in India: the pro-English group, the pro-Hindi group, and the pro-regional-languages group. In short, this formula entails introducing English and the local regional language. It was expected that in the so-called Hindi area (the *madhyadeśa* [Central India]) a Dravidian language would be introduced so that all the "school-going children" (to use an Indianism) throughout the country would have an equal language load. This formula was an attempt to use an "integrative approach" to India's language planning, but it has not been a success.

Language planning and the role and status of English in Bangladesh, Pakistan, Nepal, and Sri Lanka has not been much different from India. The literature on this topic for these countries, however, is not as profuse as that of India, but a number of studies are available to help in making a comparative study.[8]

In spite of debates and controversies about the position of English in South Asia, English has attained the status of an important intranational and international language in the area. A quantitative profile of South Asian English is not easy to provide, since figures for all the functions of English in all the regions are not available. The following figures, however, are illustrative, though in most cases these apply only to India.

In the five South Asian countries (excluding Bhutan), 24.4 million students are enrolled in English classes. The English-knowing population is distributed in practically every state of India. English newspapers are published in twenty-seven of the twenty-nine Indian states or union territories, and they command the highest circulation in terms of the total reading public (23 percent). The number of English-knowing bilinguals in South Asia is close to or larger than the number of speakers of several South Asian languages which have been recognized as "scheduled" languages—for example, Assamese (1.63 percent), Kannada (3.96 percent), Malayalam (4 percent), Oriya (3.62 percent), and Punjabi (3 percent). English is the state language of two states in eastern India: Meghalaya and Nagaland. There is a pan–South Asian reading public for English books, and in India, for example, the number of books published in English has been significant for a long time, increasing from 33 percent to 45 percent from 1969 to 1973. This percentage is higher than the number of books published in any other language in the area. In 1971, 74 percent of India's scientific journals and 83 percent of the nonscientific journals were published in English. English continues to be the language of the legal system (especially that of higher courts), a major language in Parliament, and a preferred language in the universities and all-India competitive examinations for senior administrative, engineering, and foreign service positions. These examples are not exhaustive, but they certainly indicate the intranational functions of South Asian English.[9]

Varieties of South Asian English

My use of the term *South Asian English* is not to be understood as indicative of linguistic homogeneity in this variety nor of a uniform linguistic competence. It refers to several broad regional varieties such as Indian English, Lankan English, and Pakistani English.

There are basically two subvarieties within educated South Asian English, each providing a continuum from Pidgin English or broken English on the one hand to educated (or standard) South Asian English.[10] Some speakers of educated South Asian English even aim at Received Pronunciation, but this goal is not always achieved in performance. Two parameters, which are not mutually exclusive, may be used to label these subvarieties: *contextual* and *acquisitional*. The contextual parameter refers to the use of categories derived from the South Asian context, for example, regional, ethnic, or occupational (see Kachru 1978*a*, pp. 482–84). The acquisitional parameter refers to the various linguistic performance levels acquired in the second language in a specific school system or educational setup. A tenth grade student in a rural high school does not have the same exposure to English as does, for example, a student in Colombo, Katmandu, New Delhi, or Islamabad.

These parameters are crucial for the concept of the "cline of bilingualism."[11] The cline has three "measuring" points: the ambilingual point, the central point, and the zero point. On the basis of these three guiding points, further quantitative and attitudinal categorization is possible. The attitudinal labels such as *Babu English*,[12] *Butler English*, *Bearer English*, *Burger English*, and *Kitchen English* refer to such categorization. The spectrum of variation is reflected in South Asian newspapers. On the one hand, highly localized newspapers—such as the *Poona Daily News* (Poona), *Kashmir Times* (Srinagar), and *The Rising Nepal* (Katmandu)—are linguistically low on the cline. On the other, there are several national papers with an international circulation—for example, *The Statesman* (New Delhi), *Dawn* (Lahore), and *The Bangladesh Observer* (Dacca). On studying these, one is immediately struck by the range in the presentation, language use, and content.

Speakers of South Asian English seem to recognize such variation within the standard (or educated) variety of their language. In my study of speakers of English from Indian universities, only 16 percent thought that Indian English constituted one uniform variety. Almost 35 percent indicated that the variability might be expressed by two to three distinct varieties, and nearly half felt that Indian English includes between four and ten varieties (see Kachru 1976, pp. 233–34).

The subvarieties and registers are directly related to language function, and one must therefore consider the functions that English performs in the multilingual and multicultural context of South Asia. The importance of English and its continued use in South Asia have to be related to the complex ethnic and linguistic pluralism of this region. Each South Asian country is multilingual and multiethnic. In India there are as many as 1,652 languages and dialects, depending on whose figure one accepts (see Pattanayak 1971).[13] The smaller South Asian countries, Nepal and Bhutan, also are multilingual. It was therefore convenient during the colonial period to use English as a "link" language, and that role of English has not changed in recent years. English has now acquired four major functions: instrumental, regulative, interpersonal, and innovative (or creative).[14] The instrumental function refers to the use of English as the medium of learning at various stages of education. As the language of the legal system and pan-Indian (or pan–South Asian) administration, English performs what might be called a regulative function. The most important role of English, however, is to provide a code of communication to linguistically and culturally diverse groups for interpersonal communication. In this capacity, English has aided regional and national mobility for a certain stratum of society. However, its use in this role also symbolizes elitism, prestige, and modernity, and the opponents of English point to this symbolism as one argument against the continued use of English. The use of English has also resulted in the development of a significant body of South Asian English writing in various genres. This nativized, innovative (or creative) use of English will be discussed in a later section of this essay.

"South-Asianness" at Formal Levels

There are three main factors which contribute to the distinct "South-Asianness" in South Asian English. First, English is primarily a second language in South Asia. A small fraction of the English-using population claims that English is their first language, but this fraction is so small that for the purpose of the present discussion it can be ignored. Most of the English users are at least bilinguals, and in a majority of cases it is even difficult to say which is their dominant language. However, all such users of English have a language repertoire in which English dominates in some functions and one or more South Asian language in others. "South-Asianness" within this group, then, is typified by features of transference.[15]

Second, English is an *acquired* language, and "South-Asianness" reflects the conditions under which it is acquired in various parts of the subcontinent. The introduction of English into the school curriculum varies from one country to another, and within a country it varies from one state to another. In acquiring English, a student is generally presented with, for example, an Indo-Aryan, a Dravidian, or a Munda model of English. The models may further be language-specific—Tamil English, Kashmiri English, Newari English, or Sinhala English. These models are not uniform, since they depend on the training, experience, and competence of the teacher. The number of schools, colleges, or universities where a native speaker of English teaches, or where technological aids are available, are negligible. Chaudhuri is therefore expressing the view of most South Asian users of English when he writes:

> It is my pride today that the English I write, whatever it might be—and I have my opinion of it—was not learnt from any Englishman, Scotsman, Irishman, or American in the flesh, though my debt to the great dead writers of English can never be repaid. [1976, p. 15]

The third factor which contributes to the "South-Asianness" of South Asian English is the fact that English is taught through the written medium in South Asia. The curriculum does not make any special provision for spoken English. It is therefore natural that many features of "South-Asianness" in pronunciation are based on spelling (see Krishnamurti 1978). Spoken models are exclusively Indian, and the written models are provided by the classics of English—mostly of the eighteenth and nineteenth centuries—which Indian graduate students relish.

Phonetics and Phonology

It would be impossible to provide here a detailed phonetic description of the total lectal range of South Asian English with its language-bound, area-bound, ethnic, and other subvarieties.[16] Therefore, I shall only enumerate some general characteristics of the sound system. These are mainly the features of what has been termed transparent South Asian English and, taken together, they may be used to identify a South Asian English speaker.

At the phonetic level we may identify these features on the basis of what I have earlier termed *series substitution*, *systemic differences*, *distributional differences*, and *prosodic differences*.[17] Series substitution involves, for example, the substitution of retroflex consonants for the alveolar series; for example, [ṭ] and [ḍ] are substituted for English [t] and [d]. Systemic differences refer to the elements which constitute a phonological unit such as a syllable. In most of the South Asian languages consonant-vowel-consonant (CVC) morpheme structure is possible, as it is in English. One might then claim that this feature is shared among, say, Hindi-Urdu, Sinhalese, and Kashmiri. But this does not tell the whole story, since these languages (like most other South Asian languages) and English show differences in the elements which operate in the positions consonant, vowel, and consonant in the CVC structure. For example, South Asian language speakers do not use [f], [θ], or [ð], and they do not distinguish between the "dark" and "clear" varieties of [l]. The sounds [f], [θ], and [ð] are generally realized in South Asian English as [ph], [t̪h], and [d̪] or [d̪h], respectively.

The identical consonant-vowel-consonant structure therefore does not presuppose that the inventory constituting the system is identical. Distributional differences entail a different type of transfer. A South Asian language may share items in vowel or consonant inventory, but the distribution of the item may not be identical.

The consonant clusters *sk*, *sl*, and *sp* are present in several South Asian languages, but they do not occur in initial position in, for example, Hindi-Urdu. Therefore there are differences in regional South Asian English pronunciation in the following lexical items: [ɪskul] *school*, [ɪsteʃan] *station*, [ɪspitʃ] *speech*, and [ɪslot̪h] *sloth*.[18]

Prosodic differences make South Asian English markedly distinctive, since transfer from syllable-timed South Asian languages results in a similar rhythm in place of the stress-timed rhythm of British English. Passé (1947) claims for Lankan English that it has comparatively weak stress (since stress—or force accent—is weak in Sinhalese and Tamil); no vowel reduction; and no distinction between strong and weak forms. What is true of Tamil speakers in Sri Lanka also applies to Tamil speakers in India. The stress pattern in northern Indian pronunciation is not significantly different from these Tamil-influenced varieties.

Grammar

The identification of grammatical characteristics of South Asian English inevitably leads to complexities. The attitude toward grammatical deviations is not identical to the attitude toward deviations in pronunciation. Since there has not been any serious attempt at codification of such grammatical characteristics, it is naturally difficult to distinguish a deviation from what may be considered a mistake. In grammar, therefore, the idealized norm continues to be a native prescriptive model. Perhaps the largest number of users of Fowler's *Modern English Usage* are in South Asia. South Asians are also addicts of Nesfield and Jespersen and read their grammars with delight. But in spite of such respect for linguistic authority, there are several characteristics of South Asian English which are productive and may be regarded as South Asian features. The characteristics presented hereafter are only indicative of such tendencies, and they are not in any way codified. They also will not win general approval from a prescriptivist teacher.

It has impressionistically been claimed that there is a tendency in South Asian English to use complex sentences which result in large-scale embeddings. One is inclined to trace this tendency to the preference of the educated South Asians for the *śiṣṭa* 'learned' style which is characteristic of literary style in South Asian languages. This trait is then transferred to South Asian English.

The transfer (or "interference") from the first languages also results in deviant constructions in, for example, interrogative sentences and the formation of tag questions. There is a tendency to form interrogative constructions without changing the position of subject and auxiliary items: *what you would like to read?* or *when you would like to come?*

In English, the structure of tag questions is composed of a statement and a tag attached to it. In such structures there is contrasting polarity; a positive main clause is followed by a negative tag and vice versa. In Hindi-Urdu, the parallel structure consists of a single clause with a postposed particle which is invariably *na*. Transfer thus results in South Asian English constructions such as *you are going tomorrow, isn't it?* and *he isn't going there, isn't it?*

Other differences in South Asian English are the result of the extension in selection restrictions in syntax and semantics as, for example, in the use of stative predicates. There are English verbs which are ungrammatical when used in the progressive form (*is having, seeing, knowing*). Therefore the following constructions, transferred from the first language of South Asian English bilinguals, are unacceptable to a native speaker of English:

> *Mohan is having two houses.*
> *Ram was knowing that he would come.*
> *I am understanding English better now.*

South Asian English

The use of articles in South Asian English has been discussed in detail with reference to Indian English. All three exponents of the article (i.e., definite, indefinite, and zero) are present in South Asian English, but their distribution is erratic. In his excellent studies on this topic, Dustoor has aptly classified South Asian (primarily Indian) use of the articles as "missing," "intrusive," "wrong," "usurping," and "dispossessed."

Reduplication of items belonging to various word classes is a common feature of South Asian English and is used for emphasis and to indicate continuation of a process. Raja Rao, for example, uses reduplication to create the effect of colloquial speech and to develop particular character types. Consider the following example from his short story "Javni": "With these very eyes, with these very eyes, I have seen the ghosts of more than a hundred young men and women, all killed by magic by magic . . ." (R. Rao 1978, p. 84). In this selection, Rao has used larger units for reduplication, but at other places he uses single lexical items: *hot, hot coffee*; *long, long hair*. The use of reduplication is also common in Pakistan, Sri Lanka, and Nepal. Consider, for example, Lankan English *to go crying crying*, *small small pieces*, and *who and who came to the party?*[19]

Collocations

A South Asian English collocation may be defined as South Asian on the basis of its semantic or syntactic characteristics. Such collocations are the result of one or more of the following. Words or phrases of a South Asian language may be translated into South Asian English; *the confusion of caste* or *twice-born* are English translations of the Sanskrit *varṇa sankara* and *dvija,* respectively. In Lankan English the following formations entail such translations: *to buy and give, to jump and run, to run and come (home), to take and come* (Passé 1947). In addition, there are formations which are extensions or analogies derived from English: *black money* on the analogy of *black market*. The most productive class consists of collocations which are formally nondeviant but are culture-bound, context-bound, or register-bound: *brother-anointing ceremony, caste-mark, cow-worship, cousin-sister, rice-eating ceremony, nose-screw* 'a decorative gold or silver ornament for the nose used by women', *waist-thread* 'a ritualistic thread tied around the waist'.

Underlying regular syntactic processes are involved in forming such collocations. In one such productive syntactic process, a unit of higher rank is reduced to a lower rank. Thus, where a native speaker of English might use a clause or a nominal group, a South Asian English user prefers a formation with *modifier + head + (qualifier)* structure. Consider, for example, a preference for *welcome address* as opposed to *an address of welcome*, or for *England-returned* instead of *one who has been to England* (cf. *been-to* in African English used in the same sense). This regular tendency has been characterized as "phrase-mongering" (Goffin 1934) and as "wrong compounding" (Whitworth 1907). Passé considers such formations as "errors of expression that have become more or less fixed in Ceylon English and which the user would be startled and shocked to hear stigmatized as un-English" (1947, n. 4). Other such formations include *god-son* (Sanskrit, *deva-putra*), *Himalayan-blunder*, *nation-building,* and *dumb-millions*. Formations such as the following in Lankan English also fall in the same pattern: *to break rest, bull work,* and *to give a person bellyfull.*

Lexis

South Asian English is the only variety of nonnative English in which there is a long and continuous tradition of lexicographical studies. This interest dates back to the nineteenth century, culminating in *Hobson-Jobson* (1886),[20] which has provided linguistic entertainment by its lexical explanations, ethnographic asides, apt etymological clues, and abundant citations to generations of administrators of the *Raj*, to indophiles, and to indologists.

In our discussion here, we are primarily concerned with two types of lexical items. One type comprises a comparatively small number of items, and the other a large lexical stock. The smaller group includes those lexical items which are shared with British English, and to a lesser degree with American and other native Englishes. A number of them have steadily made their way into the standard lexicons such as the *OED*, the Merriam-Webster dictionaries, and the *Random House Dictionary of the English Language*.[21]

In recent years, there has been a renewed interest in lexicographical research on South Asian English.[22] *The Little Oxford Dictionary* contains a twenty-nine-page "supplement" by R. A. Hawkins which lists about 1,500 Indian English lexical items, and in Nihalani, Tongue, and Hosali (1978) a considerable part of the book has been devoted to the usage of English in India (see Kachru 1980).

Single lexical items vary in their frequency of occurrence. They are essentially register-dependent and therefore are normally used when referring to contexts which are typically South Asian. If such references are aimed at an audience outside the region, it is normal to provide glossaries for them. Consider, for example, the following excerpts from daily newspapers.

> Dharmavati was chosen for Ragam, Tanam, and Pallavi. Singing with an abandon, M.S. set off the distinct character of the mode and followed with methodically improvised Pallavi. The swaraprastara was full of tightly knit figures. [*Daccan Herald*, 26 July 1977]

> Urad and moong fell sharply in the grain market here today on stockists offerings. Rice, jowar and arhar also followed suit, but barley forged ahead. [*Times of India*, 23 July 1977]

Fish stalls in many small markets have nothing for sale. Rohu costs Rs 16 a kg. while bekti, parshe and tangra are priced between . . . Hilsa, which is the most popular among the Bengalis in the rainy season. [*Statesman*, 17 August 1979]

In Karachi Quran khawani and fateha was held at the Cifton residence of late [sic] Mr. Zulfikar Ali Bhutto to mark his "Chehlum" today. [*Pakistan Times*, 12 May 1979]

In South Asian English newspapers such lexical items are also used as captions or headings:

Panchayat system upholds ideals of human rights [*Rising Nepal*, 17 December 1978; three columns]
More subsidy for gobar gas plants [*Hindustan Times*, 5 July 1977; one column]
Krishi bank branch needed [*Bangladesh Observer*, 21 June 1979; one column]
Shariat courts for attack [*Dawn*, 12 March 1979; one column]
Disbursement of zakat: law and order situation [*Dawn*, 14 March 1979; two columns]

The second type of lexical innovation, again very productive, is hybridized and contains at least one item from a South Asian language and one item from English: *janta meals*, *lathi charge*, *tiffin carrier*.[23] Hybrids may be subcategorized into two types on the basis of the constraints which apply to such formations: open-set items without grammatical constraints on the selection (*British sarkar* or *tonga-driver*)[24] and closed-system items involving bound morphemes and showing certain grammatical constraints: *-wala* (*vala*) in *policewala*; *-hood* in *brahminhood*; *-dom* in *cooliedom*; *-ism* in *goondaism*.[25] Some hybrid formations are semantic "reduplications"; an example is *lathi stick*, in which *lathi* (Hindustani) and *stick* (English) have identical meanings. Other such examples are *cotton kapas* and *curved kukri*.[26] A small number of formations were at first restricted to a specific area: *coconut paysam*, *jibba pocket*, and *potato bonda* began in the Dravidian area;[27] *yakka carriage* and *religious diwan* started as innovations in the Indo-Aryan area.[28]

Rhetorical and Functional Styles

In the cultural and linguistic network of South Asia, English is used as an additional communicative tool in a number of contexts. It is, therefore, natural that various linguistic devices are exploited to develop functional or communicative styles relevant to social, literary, and cultural contexts of South Asia. These devices are then organized into what speakers of South Asian English consider appropriate rhetorical styles. Appropriateness is determined by several factors, the native literary and cultural traditions being very important. Above all, the notion of a "proper" style in a particular context is derived from languages such as Sanskrit, Persian, and Arabic. In all these languages, stylistic embellishment is highly valued. These *native* rhetorical styles are then imposed on an "alien" language which results in functional and communicative varieties in South Asian English distinct from other Englishes. The reaction of native English speakers to such "deviant" communicative styles and rhetorical devices has not been one of acceptance or of understanding, as exemplified by the use of attitudinally marked terms such as *Latinity, phrase-mongering, polite diction, moralistic tone,* or *bookishness*. Such labels, however meaningful, ignore the fact that in South Asian English the *text* and the *context* are nativized in order to make the text "meaningful" in new situations in which it functions. As standards of appropriateness and acceptance develop for discourse types in South Asian English, native norms emerge. One consequence of such acculturation for South Asian English is that the more culture-bound it becomes, the more distinct it grows from other varieties of English (see Kachru 1965, p. 409).

The range of South Asian English text types is large. The texts vary primarily on two dimensions: their contextual range and acquisitional range. For each context, texts may be differentiated on the basis of the English used in them, ranging from educated South Asian English to Pidgin English.

The following examples illustrate some typical South Asian English functional texts. I will first consider matrimonial advertisements, since these provide an example of highly contextualized English lexical items with semantic nativization in reference to the caste, color, region, and subcaste (see also Mehrotra 1975).

Well-educated settled Kayastha boy around 28 for Srivastava M.A. Wheatish fair slim girl. [*Pioneer*, 31 December 1978]

Wanted suitable match for fair-complexioned, good looking Christian girl (Protestant) knowing . . . educated Christian (Protestant) youths to apply. [*National Herald*, 31 December 1978]

Wanted well-settled bridegroom for a Kerala fair, graduate Baradwaja gotram, Astasastram girl . . . Subsect no bar. Send horoscope and details. [*Hindu*, 1 July 1979]

Non-Koundanya well qualified prospective bridegroom below 20 for graduate Iyengar girl, daughter of engineer. Mirugaserusham. No dosham. Average complexion. Reply with horoscope. [*Hindu*, 1 July 1979]

> Match for my younger son Khanna, Khatri noble family . . . girl main consideration of respectable family. Highly educated, homely, gracefully [sic], attractive, sweet tempered, smart, fluent English, well-versed in household, cooking, tailoring. Talented in fine arts, crafts, painting, music and driving. [*Hindustan Times*, 20 May 1979]

Announcements of deaths are just as culture-specific. The *Hindustan Times*, for example, announces "the sad demise" or "the sudden and untimely demise of" persons who have "left for heavenly abode," adding that there will be "kirtan and ardasa for the peace of the departed soul" or that a "uthaoni ceremony will take place on" a specified day.[29] If the dead person is a Muslim, "his soyem Fateha will be solemnized" and "all the friends and relatives are requested to attend the Fateha prayers" (*Dawn*, 14 March 1979). These are specimens of highly restricted culture-dependent uses of a nonnative language.

Personal letters in South Asian English often exemplify transfer of rhetorical style. The structure of such letters involve not only the "etiquette" of the first language, but also re-creation of the situation from one's own culture into another language. These letters are often read by users of native Englishes with great amusement, and often the intent of the letter is misunderstood. For example, the relationship in a letter is established by phatic communion, as in the following:

> I am quite well here hoping the same for you by the virtue of mighty god. I always pray to God for your good health, wealth and prosperity. [*Tribune*, 22 November 1978]

Typically South Asian functional styles will be made clearer by the three Indian English texts, which represent three distinct register types. The first is an example of Indian legal language (from Hyderabad) and is taken from what Indians call a "surety bond":

> Know all men by these presents that _____ s/o _____ resident of H. no. _____ in the District of Hyderabad at present employed as a permanent _____ in the Department of _____ (hereinafter called the surety) bind myself firmly to the Registrar, Osmania University (hereinafter called "the Osmania University" which expression shall unless excluded by or repugnant to the subject or context include his successors in office and assigns) in the sum of Rs _____ (Rupees _____ only), to be paid to the Osmania University for which payment to be and truely made I hereby bind myself, my heirs, executors, administrators and representatives firmly by these presents and witness my hands this _____ day of _____ 1980.

Legal language in Indian English has a shared characteristic with that of other Englishes in the sense that it is practically unintelligible to the layman.

The second specimen, a letter published in the *Indian Express* (Madurai, 19 March 1962), is—according to Dustoor (1968, p. 122)—an "average" specimen of "English as written in Indian today":

> Sir—I am one of those poor devotees who are touched on the raw by the way the police handled the crowd at the Krithigai festival in Triuvannamalai. I have visited many pilgrim centres in the North as well as South during festival times, but nowhere have I witnessed such a scene.
>
> The huge temple gates at the foothill are kept open till 5:30 P.M. and whoever comes after that has to wait at the entrance. After the lights are lit at the hilltop the doors are flung open and the crowds from inside and outside the temple dash against each other in the most disorderly fashion. Neither the police nor the temple authorities had made any arrangements for separate entrance and exit of the devotees and being unable to control the crowd, the police began to lathi-charge without any warning.
>
> It was a terrible scene to witness the devotees seeking dharsan of the Lord being meted out a raw deal at the hands of the police. It is most unbecoming of both the police and the devasthanam not to have made any proper arrangements. [N. Rangaswami]

The third specimen is from the administrative register still in use by the Indian bureaucracy:

> H. E.'s P. A. has written D. O. to the A. S. P. about the question of T. A.'s. The D. C. himself will visit the S. D. O. P. W. D. today at 10 A. M. S. T.

Such profusion of "initialisms" in administrative language has not changed since Goffin (1934) first noticed it. The letter intends to convey the following message:

> His Excellency's Personal Assistant has written a demi-official letter to the Assistant Superintendent of Police about the question of Travelling-Allowances. The Deputy Commissioner himself will visit the Sub-Divisional Officer of the Public Works Department today at 10 a.m. Standard Time.

South Asian English Literature

A wide range of stylistic experimentation is found in creative writing in South Asian English, and one's understanding of South Asian English will be limited without considering its large and growing body of literature.[30] Many studies during the last decade have overemphasized either the linguistic or literary aspect of South Asian English. This artificial dichotomy prevents one from viewing South Asian English as a living language functioning as any other nativized language in the South Asian sociolinguistic context. An integrative approach provides a more realistic view of the relationship of language and its use. Such an approach is desirable for South Asian English, since, as an institutionalized variety of English, it has developed a *local* body of writing in various literary genres. In South Asia, English, and to a lesser degree Sanskrit, are the only two pan–South Asian languages. In functional terms Sanskrit is, of course, highly restricted and therefore does not compare favorably with the present functional range of English. English has provided an important pan–South Asian link language, and South Asian English writing is the only writing which has some market (and a reading public, however restricted) in the whole of the subcontinent and outside of it. South Asian English writers still stand out in the literary mosaic of South Asia, since they have more than their share of enthusiastic supporters and equally vocal critics.

Among the South Asian countries, the most active, productive and well-discussed group of writers in English is in India. I will therefore discuss South Asian English writing with a focus on India; however, selected references will be provided for other countries, especially Sri Lanka and Pakistan.[31]

"South Asian English literature" refers to the fast-developing body of literature written by South Asians who use English primarily as a second language. Their writing is now recognized as one of many manifestations of South Asian creative talent and literary aspirations. What Iyengar says about India is certainly true of Sri Lanka and Pakistan:

> Indian writing in English is but one of the voices in which India speaks. It is a new voice, no doubt, but it is *as much Indian as others*. [Emphasis added, Iyengar 1962, p. 3]

That this voice is "as much Indian as others" has upset the nationalistic sensibilities of some Indians and has therefore resulted in great polemics. The study of such polemical writing is useful for understanding the relationship between language and nationalism, language and ethnicity, and language and development.[32]

The short history of South Asian writing in English, particularly that of Indian writing in English,[33] has been one of controversy and search for identity (see Lal 1969, pp. i–xliv). Two early writers, both from Bengal, are Kashiprasad Ghosh and Sochee Chunder Dutt. Ghosh's collection, *The Shair and Other Poems*, was published in 1830 and is considered "the earliest work of Indian poetry in English to have been reviewed in England and which, presumably, is the earliest extant work of its kind" (Bose 1968, p. 31). In the *New Monthly Magazine* (June 1831), published in England, Ghosh received the following commendatory notice:

> Our new poet, Kasiprasad Ghosh [*sic*], describes himself as the "first Hindoo who has ventured to publish a volume of English poems." . . . The Shair [the Persian term for minstrel] is a poem of considerable length and

of varied merit. . . . A great deal of poetical feeling may be discerned in parts of the poem, richness of imagery, and elegance of language, the whole requiring polish and cultivation, but evincing considerable natural powers, and exciting throughout a strong feeling of interest for the writer. [Quoted by Bose 1968, p. 31]

The first fiction in English by an Indian writer was published by Sochee Chunder Dutt in 1845. In him we have one of the first creative writers who "translated Indian terms instead of their pure English equivalents to maintain the Indian local colour as well as to add a distinct Indian flavour" (Sarma 1978, p. 329).

A few years after Dutt, another Bengali, Lal Behari Day, excelled his predecessor in Indianizing the English in his novels. The following passage is a stylistic precursor of Mulk Raj Anand or Khushwant Singh:

> "Come in," said Badan, and jumped out of the verandah towards the door. "Come in, Acharya Mahasaya; this is an auspicious day when the door of my house has been blessed with the dust of your honour's feet. Gayaram, fetch an *asan* (a small carpet) for the Acharya Mahasaya to sit on." [Day 1913, p. 48; quoted by Sarma 1978, p. 330]

Day is apologetic for making his Bengali peasants speak "better English than most uneducated English peasants" in 1874 and explains to his "gentle reader":

> Gentle reader, allow me here to make one remark. You perceive that Badan and Alanga speak better English than most uneducated English peasants; they speak almost like educated ladies and gentlemen, without any provincialisms. But how could I have avoided this defect in my history? If I had translated their talk into Somersetshire [*sic*] or the Yorkshire dialect, I should have turned them into English, and not Bengali, peasants. You will, therefore, please overlook this grave though unavoidable fault in this authentic narrative. [Day 1913, p. 61; quoted by Sarma 1978, p. 332]

The predicament of creating a style range in South Asian English fiction continues even now.

The initial attempts at creative writing in South Asian English not only gave rise to literary traditions but gradually developed a significant body of writing. Among the earlier poets to achieve an international reputation were Aurobindo Ghosh (1872–1950), Manmohan Ghosh (1869–1924), Toru Dutt (1859–77), and Sarojini Naidu (1879–1949).

The use of a colonial, "alien" language for expressing local sensibility and native contexts has been suspect, and even the integrity of such South Asian writers has been challenged. But, in spite of suspicion, polemical controversies, and a restricted although growing reading public, the body of South Asian English writing has been steadily increasing in poetry,[34] fiction,[35] literary criticism,[36] and drama.[37]

Political writing is another important genre with a tradition dating back to Rammohan Roy (1772–1833). English continued to be a medium which various political leaders used for national awakening and the freedom struggle. It was used effectively during the struggle against colonialism and continues to be used now for any issue which has an "all-India" or "pan–South Asian" implication. Such writers include Mohandas K. Gandhi (1869–1948), Bal Gangadhar Tilak (1856–1920), Mahomed Ali Jinnah (1876–1948), Jawaharlal Nehru (1889–1964), and C. Rajagopalachariar (1879–1972).

The story of South Asian English writers in the 1970s is much different from what it was in the 1930s—both in the attitude toward them and in their impact. In 1934, Singh was not only indifferent to the Indian writers in English, but also rather apologetic about their performance:

> Indian writers and story-tellers on the whole do not compare favourably with Anglo-Indian writers. That they write in a foreign tongue is a serious handicap in itself. Then few of them possess any knowledge of the art of fiction. . . . In plot construction they are weak, and in characterization weaker still. [Singh 1934, p. 306]

Contrast this with an observation made exactly thirty years later by Gokak, a critic, creative writer, and an eminent educationist:

> Indo-Anglian [Indian English] writing is direct and spontaneous—like creative writing in any other language. It is conditioned in many ways by the peculiar circumstances of its birth and growth. . . . Gordon Bottomley is said to have described typically Indo-Anglian poetry as "Matthew Arnold in a *sari*." He should rather have referred to it as Shakuntala in skirts. [Gokak 1964, p. 162]

Why do educated South Asians write in English when their own languages provide fine means of expression with a rich literary tradition? The question is naturally most vocally asked by those South Asians who are creative writers in their first languages and has been debated in South Asia with various degrees of intensity at literary and political forums. One such debate of interest to sociolinguists, language scholars, and literary critics is presented by Lal in his *Modern Indian Poetry in English*. In this 594-page anthology of 132 (mostly post-1947) "practising poets," we have specimens of "two decades of revolt, experimentation, and consolidation by the younger poets" (1969, p. iii). The poets' responses to the following questions are also included in the anthology: (1) What are the circumstances that led to your using the English language for the purpose of writing poetry? and (2) Do you think English is one of the Indian languages? I shall consider the answers of some of the more prominent and established poets. They have understandably answered these questions with varying degrees of seriousness and detail. A. K. Ramanujan does not consider it a matter of controversy "whether people can, will, or should write in a particular language." In his view, "people who write in a particular language don't have a choice in the matter" (Lal 1969, pp. 444–45). For Kamala Das, "Why in English?" is a "silly" question: "English being the most familiar, we use it. That is all." And she rightly adds, "The language one employs is not important. What is important is the thought contained in the words" (Lal 1969, p. 171). Kamala Das previously articulated her feelings about her choice of language in an often-quoted poem:

> ... I am Indian, very brown, born in
> Malabar, I speak three languages, write in
> Two, dream in one. Don't write in English, they said,
> English is not your mother-tongue. Why not leave
> Me alone, critics, friends, visiting cousins,
> Every one of you? Why not let me speak in
> Any language I like? The language I speak
> Becomes mine, its distortions, its queernesses
> All mine, mine alone. It is half English, half
> Indian, funny perhaps, but it is honest,
> It is as human as I am human, don't
> You see? It voices my joys, my longings, my
> Hopes, and it is useful to me as cawing
> Is to crows or roaring to the lions, it
> Is human speech, the speech of the mind that is
> Here and not there, a mind that sees and hears and
> Is aware. ...
>
> [Das 1973, p. 128]

More than South Asian English poetry, fiction from this region demonstrates the formal and functional nativization of the English language. Raja Rao's fiction provides a good example of such nativization. He has been successful in transferring the "rhythm" of his mother tongue—Kannada—into his English, and the devices he uses are much more subtle than the linguistic devices used by Mulk Raj Anand, Khushwant Singh, and others. Consider the following passage from his novel, *Kanthapura*:

> The day rose into the air and with it rose the dust of the morning, and the carts began to creak round the bulging rocks and the coppery peaks, and the sun fell into the river and pierced it to the pebbles, while the carts rolled on and on, fair carts of the Kanthapura fair—fair carts that came

from Maddur and Tippur and Santur and Kuppur with chilies and coconut, rice and ragi, cloth, tamarind, butter and oil, bangles and kumkum, little pictures of Rama and Krishna and Sankara and the Mahatma, little dolls for the youngest, little kites for the elder, and little chess pieces for the old—carts rolled by the Sampur knoll and down into the valley of the Tippur stream, then rose again and groaned. . . . [1963, p. 39]

The novelist Mulk Raj Anand (among others) "transcreates" native situations into English by using native lexical items, hybridization, new collocations, and contextually marked translations of Punjabi or Hindi-Urdu clauses and sentences. Although Anand's Punjabi characters (e.g., a coolie, an untouchable, and a washerman) would be distinguished from one another by their dialects, style ranges, and diction in Punjabi, they lose these distinguishing features in the translation to South Asian English. Because of this uniformity and because such individuals do not actually speak English, Anand's characters sound artificial, a little unreal, and almost comic to an Indian, but that is the price one pays for using an "alien" language in contexts in which it does not ordinarily function. Consider the following as a typical example of Anand's stylistic device:

"Ari, you bitch! Do you take me for a buffoon? What are you laughing at, slut? Aren't you ashamed of showing your teeth to me in the presence of men, you prostitute?" shouted Gulabo, and she looked towards the old man and the little boys who were of the company.

Sohini now realized that the woman was angry. "But I haven't done anything to annoy her," she reflected. "She herself began it all and is abusing me right and left. I didn't pick the quarrel. I have more cause to be angry than she has!"

"Bitch, why don't you speak! Prostitute, why don't you answer me?" Gulabo insisted.

"Please don't abuse me," the girl said, "I haven't said anything to you."

"You annoy me with your silence, you illegally begotten! You eater of dung and drinker of urine! You bitch of a sweeper woman! I will show you how to insult one old enough to be your mother." And she rose with upraised arm and rushed at Sohini.

Waziro, the weaver's wife, ran after her and caught her just before she had time to hit the sweeper girl.

"Be calm, be calm; you must not do that," she said as she dragged Gulabo back to her seat. "No, you must not do that." (Anand 1935, p. 37)

The Muslim novelist Ahmed Ali provides an example of such contextualization in a typical middle-class Muslim family:

Dilchain had, in the meantime, discovered a small earthen doll buried under the oven when she was cleaning it one day. She went and showed it to Begam Kalim and Begam Habib.

"It is the effect of witchcraft," she said, "which is responsible for Mian's illness."

The tender hearts of women were filled with dread. They sent Dilchain to Aakhoonji Saheb, who wrote verses from the Koran on seven snow-white plates in saffron water. The plates were to be washed with a little water, and the water from one plate was to be taken for three days, a drop in the morning. . . .

But strange things happened inside the zenana. A pot full of ill-omened things came flying in the air and struck against the bare trunk of the date palm whose leaves had all fallen. Another day some cooked cereal was found lying under the henna tree. . . .

Poor women from the neighbourhood came, fluttering their burqas and dragging their slippers under them, and sympathized. . . .

Thus they came and sympathized and suggested cures and medicines. One said to Begam Habib:

"You must go to the tomb of Hazrat Mahboob Elahi and pray. . . ."

"You must give him water from the well at Hazrat Nizamuddin's tomb," another suggested. "It has magical qualities and has worked miracles. . . ."
[Ali 1966, pp. 278–79]

Anthologies of South Asian poetry include a wide range of styles and genres (see Gokak 1970 and Parthasarathy 1976). The following poets, among others, have not only contributed to anthologies but have also published one or more individual collections in South Asia or the West: Keki N. Daruwalla (born 1937), Kamala Das (born 1934), Nissim Ezekiel (born 1924), Shiv K. Kumar (born 1921), P. Lal (born 1931), R. Parthasarathy (born 1934), and A. K. Ramanujan (born 1929). There are more than half a dozen novelists in South Asia who have created a small but slowly increasing reading public for themselves, both nationally and internationally.[38] South Asian English writing is now hesitatingly but definitely being recognized as part of the indigenous literary traditions in South Asia. It is one of the important voices in which South Asian creative writers express themselves. This body of writing has over the years developed an interested reading public outside South Asia, and it constitutes an important part of what is termed "Commonwealth writing in English" or "world writing in English."

Attitudes Toward South Asian English

The labels which speakers of native Englishes attach to nonnative Englishes are often attitudinally revealing. Such labels have been applied to South Asian English as a whole (as in the case of Prator 1968) and to particular South Asianisms.[39] Equally interesting, however, are the attitudes of South Asian English users toward their own variety of English. Have South Asian English users accepted what has been termed the "ecological validity" of their local or native English?

In South Asia, there has been a traditional conflict between linguistic behavior and linguistic norm. The hypothetical norm continues to be British English, especially RP, although this norm is seldom available and even more seldom attained. Actual linguistic behavior shows use of characteristic South Asian English features varying according to the competence of the user. The following tables show the attitude of students majoring in English, and their teachers, toward various models of English.[40]

Undergraduates' Preferences
for Various Models of English

Model	Preference I	Preference II	Preference III
American English	5%	13%	21%
British English	68	10	1
Indian English	23	18	11
"I don't care"		5	
"Good" English		1	

Faculty Preference for Models
of English for Instruction

Model	Preference I	Preference II	Preference III
American English	3%	14%	26%
British English	67	13	2
Indian English	27	26	12
"I don't know"		5	

In the study of language attitudes, "self labeling" of one's variety provides an important indication about the attitude of a user of a variety toward other varieties. In this study, the graduate students (majoring in English) used the following "identity-marking" terms for their own varieties of English: Indian English, 56 percent; British English, 30 percent; American English, 3 percent. The rest used labels such as "mixture of all three," "I don't know," and "good English."

South Asian English and Other Englishes

In presenting a variety-oriented description, one tends to focus on the differences between the variety in question and other native (or nonnative) varieties. The differences at various linguistic levels are part of each variety and have resulted in variety-specific labels such as *Americanisms*, *Australianisms*, *Canadianisms*, or *Indianisms*. On the other hand, the nonshared differences in the nonnative Englishes have either been viewed pedagogically with reference to second-language acquisition or in a pejorative sense. Whitworth, for example, considers Indianisms as "linguistic flights . . . which jar upon the ear of the native Englishman" (1907, p. 6).

Little research has been done on the shared features among the nonnative Englishes—for example, African English, South Asian English, or Caribbean English. A number of such productive and shared processes in grammar, lexis, and in communicative and functional styles are present in several nonnative Englishes, specifically in African and South Asian English (see Richards 1979). The reasons for linguistic and contextual nativization of English in these two areas also seem to be identical. A few examples intended to illustrate the point follow.

The deviant use of such function words as definite and indefinite articles is shared by several nonnative Englishes.[41] In grammar, several tendencies—especially in the uses of the verb phrase—are common to African, South Asian, and Caribbean English. One feature common to African English and South Asian English, for example, is what has been called "yes-no confusion" (see Kachru 1969, pp. 652–53): the response of *no* where a native speaker would expect *yes*. In several languages (e.g., African, South Asian, Russian, and Japanese), the choice of *yes* or *no* in response to a question depends on the *form* of the question and the *facts* of the situation. If the form and the facts have the same polarity (both positive or both negative), the answer is positive. If the polarity is not the same, (i.e., if the question is in the positive and the situation is in the negative), the answer is negative (and vice versa). In standard English, on the other hand, the response *yes* or *no* depends only on the facts of the situation: in a positive situation, the answer is *yes*; in a negative situation the answer is *no*. Consider the following illustrations from English in Africa (from Bokamba 1982):

Q. Hasn't the president left for Nairobi yet?
A. Yes, the president hasn't left for Nairobi yet.

Q. Didn't you see anyone at the compound?
A. Yes, I didn't see anyone at the compound.

Q. I hope you won't have any difficulty with your fees next term?
A. I hope so [i.e., I hope what you have said will indeed be true].

Parallel examples are found in South Asian English.

Q. Didn't I see you yesterday in college?
A. Yes, you didn't see me yesterday in college.

Q. You have no objection?
A. Yes, I have no objection.

Lexis, collocations, and semantic extension and restrictions in the nonnative Englishes are even more similar. The goal of such nativization is to contextualize the language.

Two other similarities between South Asian and African English deserve mention here. The first refers to what constitutes a "grand" style in South Asian English. "Appropriateness" in various rhetorical and communicative styles is conditioned by the native literary traditions and cultures. The African and South Asian concepts of style therefore conflict with the current western notion of "good" style. In Africa, as Sey says, "flamboyance of English prose style is generally admired" (Sey 1973, p. 7). The speaker or writer

> who possesses this style is referred to in the vernaculars in such terms as "the learned scholar who, from his deep mine of linguistic excellence, digs up on suitable occasions English expressions of grandeur, depth and sweetness." [1973, p. 7]

The same is true of South Asia. Gokak observes that those

> who are true to Indian thought and vision cannot escape the Indian flavour even when they write in English. Their style is, in a great measure, conditioned by the learned vocabulary of the subject on which they write, philosophy, sociology, literary criticism and the like. Even when they write fiction, they depend, for their effect, on picturesque Indian phrases and their equivalents in English. [1964, pp. 162–63]

The "Indianized" style is found in the creative writing of, among others, Mulk Raj Anand, Raja Rao, and G. V. Desani. Anand has argued that the King's English is inadequate for an Indian writer (Anand 1948). But Raja Rao is emphatic that

> English is not really an alien language to us. It is the language of our intellectual make-up—like Sanskrit and Persian was before—but not of our emotional make-up. . . . We cannot write like the English. We should not. We cannot write only as Indians. We have grown to look at the large world as part of us. Our method of expression has to be a dialect which will some day prove to be as distinctive and colorful as the Irish or the American. Time alone will justify it. [1963, p. vii]

The esteemed African writer Chinua Achebe (1965) considers whether African writers can "ever learn to use it [English] like a native speaker," and concludes, "I hope not. It is neither necessary, nor desirable for him to do so." Achebe is in favor of "a new English, still in communion with its ancestral home, but altered to suit its new African surroundings." Many South Asians believe that English is equally adaptable to the South Asian context.

The second characteristic which cuts across nonnative Englishes is the development of code-mixed varieties of English. Code mixing is a result of language contact and code switching and has to be distinguished from lexical borrowing. By code mixing I mean the use of one or more languages for consistent transfer of linguistic units from one language into another which results in a new restricted—or not-so-restricted—code of linguistic interaction (see Kachru 1978b).

The implications of code mixing are important from the point of view of language attitude, elitism, and language change.[42] The code-mixed varieties of English are part of the verbal repertoire of the nonnative users of English and play an important role functionally and formally in various contexts. The process of mixing is not restricted to one unit, but ranges from lexical items to full sentences and embedding of idioms from English:

> mujhe is bat mē bilkul *doubt* nahī̃ hai, *rather I am sure* ki *this year B. Sc. examination* ke *results* bahut kharāb haĩ. kuch to *examiners* ne *strictness* kī aur kuch *papers* bhī aise *out of way* āye ki *students* to *unexpected questions* ko *paper* mē *set* dekh kar *hall* kī *ceiling* hī *watch* karte reh gaye. [Quoted by Bhatia 1967]

There are various motivations for code mixing, the main ones being role identification, register identification, and elucidation.

The study of such cross-variety features of nonnative Englishes is of both theoretical and pedagogical interest. There are at least three areas of research on which such studies may throw some light: second-language acquisition, the nativization of English and the processes used for it, and the impact of English on native languages and literatures.

Conclusion

In this survey, the characteristics of South Asian English have been related to the linguistic and cultural aspects of the South Asian countries. In spite of the apparently overwhelming complexity of linguistic and cultural pluralism and varied political systems, there is an underlying linguistic and cultural unity in the region.

The growing body of South Asian writing in English has been considered here as an integral part of the literary spectrum of the region—native and nonnative. Given the shared range of features and styles, it is not surprising that two prominent creative writers from two separate continents—one Indian and the other African—have almost identical attitudes toward English and its nativization. The Indian novelist R. K. Narayan presents the position of many South Asian English writers when he says:

> We are not attempting to write Anglo-Saxon English. The English language, through sheer resilience and mobility, is now undergoing a process

of Indianization in the same manner as it adopted U.S. citizenship over a century ago, with the difference that it is the major language there but here one of the fifteen listed in the Indian Constitution. [Quoted by Press 1965, p. 123]

The African novelist Chinua Achebe rightly feels that "the English language will be able to carry the weight of my African experience," and he expects English to be "a new English, still in communion with its ancestral home, but altered to suit its new African surroundings" (Achebe 1965).

I hope that this study has shown that the English language is already successfully carrying the "weight" of the South Asian "experience" which manifests itself in the South Asianization of its form and functions.

NOTES

This paper was written during my tenure as associate in the Center for Advanced Study at the University of Illinois (1979–80). I am grateful to the Research Board of the Graduate College and the Center for International Comparative Studies—both of the University of Illinois—for their earlier and recent support of my research on various aspects of English in South Asia.

This paper draws heavily on my earlier research on this topic, especially from Kachru 1965, 1966, 1969, and 1978a (a revised and updated version of the 1969 article). There is a large body of scholarly and popular literature on various aspects of South Asian English, especially Indian English. Readers are encouraged to consult the following bibliographies for references pertaining to specific areas of South Asian English: Aggarwal 1981; Kachru 1978a, pp. 523–37, and 1982a; Central Institute of English and Foreign Languages 1972. Terms such as *rank*, *register*, *system*, and *structure* have been used as in systemic linguistics and are explained in Kachru 1965 and 1966.

1. The term *variety* has been used in the same sense in which it is used in Kachru 1965, 1966, 1969, and 1978a.
2. This distinction was first suggested by Randolph Quirk. See also Kachru 1979.
3. These figures are taken from Fochler-Hauke 1981.
4. For details, see Pattanayak 1971.
5. For references on the history of English in South Asia, see Aggarwal 1982 and Kachru 1978a, pp. 478–83, and 1982a.
6. Pakistan was part of undivided India until 1947, and Bangladesh was part of Pakistan until March 1971, when it was proclaimed an independent state.
7. There is a large body of literature supporting and opposing the use of English in present and future language planning in South Asia. For detailed bibliographical references, see Aggarwal 1982, Kachru 1978a, pp. 514–21, and 1982a.
8. See, for example, for Nepal: Kansakar 1977 and Malla 1977; for Pakistan: Dil 1966; for Sri Lanka: Kandiah 1964.
9. See also Kachru 1979a, Mehrotra 1977, and Sridhar 1979. As we know, it is difficult to define *bilingual person*. Therefore, one cannot provide a clear definition of an

"English-knowing bilingual" in South Asia. One may tentatively define such a person as one who can use English (more or less) effectively in a situation. The intelligibility with a native speaker of English is not necessarily the main criterion. The educational level can also provide some indication about the competence of a person (see Kachru 1978a, pp. 488–89). It is generally believed that South Asia has an English-knowing population of approximately 3 percent. This figure naturally varies with area and country. Sri Lanka has a higher percentage than other parts of South Asia. At present no reliable statistics are available. (For further discussion see Kachru 1978a.)

10. The term *Indian English* has been used to refer to the educated variety in several earlier studies; see Kachru 1965, 1966, and 1969; Masica and Dave 1972; Passé 1947. Passé says, "For practical and other reasons the almost certain course will be the teaching of the Ceylonese [Sri Lankan] variety of 'Modified Standard' English" (p. 34).

Note that almost a century ago, when English was a highly restricted *foreign* (not *second*) language in India, the German scholar Hugo Schuchardt developed a cline of "Indo-Englishes" ([1891] 1980). I am grateful to Glenn Gilbert for bringing this valuable work to my attention in 1978.

11. This term was first used in this sense with reference to Indian English by Kachru 1961, and further explained in Kachru 1965, pp. 393–96 and 1978a, pp. 485–86.

12. The term *babu* (Hindi-Urdu *bābū*) is mainly used for clerks who have reasonable competence in various administrative registers of South Asian English. (For full discussion see Kachru 1981.)

13. The "family affiliation" of these languages is as follows: unclassified, 601; Indo-Aryan, 532; Austric, 53; Dravidian, 148; and Tibeto-Chinese, 227. This list also includes nine languages of Sikkim. See Pattanayak 1971, p. v. Note that the itemized figures given in Pattanayak do not add up to the total figure of 1,652.

14. I have borrowed these terms from Basil Bernstein (1971) but have used these in a slightly different sense from his. See also Kachru 1981.

15. The term *transference* is used in the sense of *interference* or *transfer* from the mother tongue (L_1) to an additional language (L_2), in this case L_1 being a South Asian language, and L_2 English. It is interesting that the transplanted varieties of South Asian English continue to show such transference even in places such as South Africa. In South Africa (see Lanham 1978, pp. 24–25), "the Indian South African needs an Indian . . . language for religious ritual—and that not always—and possibly for communication with his elders, but English for all the other needs of his daily life. His children are taught in the English medium, his newspapers are printed in English, his legal affairs are conducted in English; if Hindi speaking, he converses with his Tamil- or Gujarati-speaking neighbour in English, and in his employment he is utterly dependent on English."

It is claimed that in pronunciation South African Indian English has "many of the features which mark general Indian English of India . . . South African Indian English is further marked by peculiarities of grammar, vocabulary, idiom and turn of phrase, many with an obvious source in Indian languages" (Lanham 1978, pp. 24–25; see Bughwan 1970).

16. A selected list of such studies is given in Kachru 1978a, pp. 523–37.

17. See Dustoor 1968, especially pp. 180–263, and Kachru 1978a.

18. This statement applies primarily to the South Asian English speakers whose first language is Hindi-Urdu.
19. See Passé 1947 and Kachru 1978a, pp. 502–3.
20. See Yule and Burnell [1886] 1968. The phrase *Hobson-Jobson* ". . . may be taken as a typical one of the most highly assimilated class of Anglo-Indian *argot*, and we have ventured to borrow from it a concise alternative title for this glossary" (1968, p. 419).
21. A detailed study of South Asian borrowings in South Asian English and native varieties of English is given in Kachru 1975 and G. Rao 1954. According to the following sources, the extent of South Asian lexical items in English varies from 188 items to 26,000 items depending on the size and focus of a dictionary: (1) Fennell (1892, p. xi) lists 399 words. These are divided among Hindoo [sic] (336), Sanskrit (32), and Dravidian (31). (2) The *Oxford English Dictionary* includes 900 words of South Asian origin. This number does not include many thousands of derivatives from these words. (3) Wilson ([1855] 1940) lists 26,000 words. (4) Serjeantson (1935, pp. 220–60) lists 188 words. The *Random House Dictionary of the English Language* includes over two hundred words of Indian origin. The largest group involves the nonshared items. They are nonshared in the sense that they belong to South Asian English registers (e.g., those of agriculture, caste, or rituals), and are therefore culture-bound. Wilson is correct in his observation about such items:

    > *Ryot* and *Ryotwar*, for instance, suggest more precise and positive notions in connection with the subject of the land revenue in the South of India, than would be conveyed by cultivator, or peasant, or agriculturalist, or by an agreement for rent or revenue with the individual members of the agricultural classes. [(1855) 1940, p. 1]

22. For a detailed discussion on the history of the dictionaries of South Asian English see Kachru 1973 and 1980.
23. *janta* 'the people, the masses'; *lathi* 'long iron-bound stick, baton' (used to control a mob, usually by police); *tiffin* 'snack, light meal'.
24. *sarkar* 'government'; *tonga* 'two-wheeled horse-drawn open carriage'.
25. *vala*, used as an agentive suffix in Hindi-Urdu; *coolie* 'hired labor'; *goonda* 'a hooligan, a rowdy person'.
26. *kapas* 'cotton'; *kukri* 'curved'.
27. *paysam* 'pudding' (a dish made of coconut); *jibba* 'loose shirt'; *bonda* 'savory fritters'.
28. *yakka* 'pony-trap'; *diwan* 'religious recitation common among the Sikhs'.
29. See the *Hindustan Times*, 20 May 1979; 20 June 1979; 28 June 1979; and 30 June 1979.
30. For a detailed discussion and bibliographical references, see Kachru 1981 and 1982a.
31. For India: see Narasimhaiah 1976, pp. 47–53 and Kachru 1982a; for Sri Lanka: see Abeysinghe and Abeysinghe 1970, Goonewardene 1970, Halverson 1966, Kandiah 1971 and 1981, and Obeyesekere and Fernando 1981.
32. For anti-English comments and articles see, for example, *Organiser* (Delhi); for pro-English views see *Swaraj* (Madras).
33. In the literature a number of terms have been used to refer to this body of writing, e.g., *Anglo-Indian*, *Indo-Anglian*, *Indo-English*, and *Indian English*. See Kachru 1978a, pp. 504–5.
34. See Lal 1969 and Parthasarathy 1976.
35. See Mukherjee 1971.

36. See Naik, Desai, and Amur 1968, and Ramakrishna 1980.
37. See Naik and Mokashi-Punekar 1977.
38. For example, Mulk Raj Anand, Anita Desair, Manohar Malgonkar, R. K. Narayan, Raja Rao, Khushwant Singh, and Nayantara Sehgal.
39. As in, for example, Goffin 1934, and Whitworth 1907.
40. Figures in the two tables result from a study of 700 undergraduates and 196 faculty at major universities in India; percentages do not sum to 100 percent since the numbers are based on the total sample, whether or not respondents answered these questions. For more details of this study, see Kachru 1976.
41. See Bokamba 1982, Kachru 1981, Kirk-Green 1971, and Sey 1973. The reduplication of word classes is extensive in several nonnative Englishes and is also used in some native varieties of English such as Black English in North America. In Kenyan English, reduplication is used the same way as in South Asian English: *small small one*; *small small whiskey*; *long long one*.
42. The West African and the Philippine situations have been discussed by Ansre (1971) and Bautista (1977), respectively.

REFERENCES

Abeysinghe, A., and Abeysinghe, I. "Some Thoughts on the Contemporary Ceylonese Literature in English." *New Ceylon Writing*, 1970, pp. 4–7.
Achebe, Chinua. "English and the African Writer." *Transition* 18 (1965):27–30.
Aggarwal, Narindar K. *English in South Asia: A Bibliographical Survey of Resources*. Gurgaon and New Delhi: Indian Documentation Service, 1982.
Ali, Ahmed. *Twilight in Delhi: A Novel*. 1940. Reprint. Bombay: Oxford University Press, 1966.
Anand, Mulk Raj. *Untouchable: A Novel*. London: Wishart Books, 1935.
———. *The King-Emperor's English*. Bombay: Hindi Kitabs, 1948.
Ansre, Gilbert. "Language Standardization in Sub-Saharan Africa." In *The Translation of Culture*, edited by T. O. Beidelmann, pp. 680–98. London: Tavistock, 1971.
Bautista, Ma Lourdes S. "The Noun-Phrase in Tagalog-English Code-Switching." *Studies in Philippine Linguistics* 1 no. 2 (1977):1–16.
Bernstein, Basil. *Class, Codes and Control*. 3 vols. Vol. 1, *Theoretical Studies Toward a Sociology of Language*. London: Routledge and Kegan Paul, 1971–75.
Bhatia, Kailash Chandra. *A Linguistic Study of English Loan Words in Hindi*. Allahabad: Hindustani Academy, 1967. In Hindi.
Bokamba, Eyamba. "The Africanization of English." In *The Other Tongue: English across Cultures*, edited by Braj B. Kachru, pp. 77–98. Champaign: University of Illinois Press, 1982.
Bose, Amalendu. "Some Poets of the Writers' Workshop." In *Critical Essays on Indian Writing in English, Presented to Armando Menezes*, edited by M. K. Naik, S. K. Desai and G. S. Amur, pp. 31–50. Dharwar: Karnatak University, 1968.
Bughwan, D. "An Investigation into the Use of English by Indians in South Africa with Special Reference to Natal." Ph.D. dissertation, University of South Africa, 1970.
Chaudhuri, Nirad C. "The English Language in India—Past, Present and Future." In *The*

Commonwealth Writer Overseas: Themes of Exile and Expatriatism, edited by Alastair Niven, pp. 89–106. Brussels: Didier, 1976.

Central Institute of English and Foreign Languages. *A Bibliography of Indian English.* Hyderabad: Central Institute of English and Foreign Languages, 1972.

Das, Kamala. *The Old Playhouse and Other Poems.* New Delhi: Orient Longman, 1973.

Day, Lal Behari. *Bengal Peasant Life.* 2d ed. London: Macmillan and Co., 1913.

Dil, Anwar S. "The Position and Teaching of English in Pakistan." In *Pakistani Linguistics: Shahidullah Presentation Volume*, edited by Anwar S. Dil, pp. 185–242. Lahore: Linguistic Research Group of Pakistan, 1966.

Dustoor, P. E. *The World of Words.* Bombay and New York: Asia Publishing House, 1968.

Fennell, C. A. M. *The Stanford Dictionary of Anglicized Words and Phrases.* Cambridge: At the University Press, 1892.

Fochler-Hauke, Gustav, ed. *Der Fischer Weltalmanach 1982.* Frankfurt: Fischer, 1981.

Goffin, R. C. *Some Notes on Indian English.* Society for Pure English Tract, no. 41. Oxford: Society for Pure English, 1934.

Gokak, V. K. *English in India: Its Present and Its Future.* Bombay and New York: Asia Publishing House, 1964.

———. *The Golden Treasury of Indo-Anglian Poetry.* New Delhi: Sahitya Akademi, 1970.

Goonewardene, James. "Ceylonese Writing in English and British Literary Traditions." In *National Identity*, edited by K. L. Goodwin, pp. 148–52. London and Melbourne: Heinemann, 1970.

Halverson, J. "Prolegomena to the Study of Ceylon English." *University of Ceylon Review* 24 (1966):61–75.

Iyengar, K. R. Srinivasa. *Indian Writing in English.* Bombay and New York: Asia Publishing House, 1962.

Kachru, Braj B. "An Analysis of Some Features of Indian English: A Study in Linguistic Method." Ph.D. dissertation, Edinburgh University, 1962.

———. "The Indianness in Indian English." *Word* 21 (1965):391–400.

———. "Indian English: A Study in Contextualization." In *Memory of J. R. Firth*, edited by C. E. Bazell, J. C. Catford, M. A. K. Halliday, and R. H. Robins, pp. 224–87. London: Longman, 1966.

———. "English in South Asia." In *Current Trends in Linguistics*, edited by Thomas A. Sebeok. 14 vols. Vol. 5, *Linguistics in South Asia*, pp. 627–78. The Hague: Mouton, 1969.

———. "Toward a Lexicon of Indian English." In *Issues in Linguistics: Papers in Honor of Henry and Renée Kahane*, edited by Braj B. Kachru, pp. 352–76. Urbana: University of Illinois Press, 1973.

———. "Lexical Innovations in South Asian English." *International Journal of the Sociology of Language* 4 (1975):55–74.

———. "Models of English for the Third World: White Man's Linguistic Burden or Language Pragmatics." *TESOL Quarterly* 10 (1976):221–39.

———. "English in South Asia." In *Advances in Societal Multilingualism*, edited by Joshua A. Fishman, pp. 477–551. The Hague: Mouton, 1978*a*.

———. "Toward Structuring Code-Mixing: An Indian Perspective." In *Aspects of Sociolinguistics in South Asia*, edited by Braj B. Kachru and S. N. Sridhar, pp. 27–46. The Hague: Mouton, 1978*b*.

---. "Models of 'Non-native English': Origin, Development and Use." Paper presented at Conference on Language Planning: International Perspective, Wayne, N.J.: William Paderson College, 20 April to 1 May, 1979.

---. "The New Englishes and Old Dictionaries: Directions in Lexicographical Research on Non-native Varieties of English." In *Theory and Method in Lexicography: Western and Non-western Perspectives*, edited by Ladislav Zgusta, pp. 71–101. Columbia, S.C.: Hornbeam Press, 1980.

---. "The Pragmatics of Non-native Varieties of English." In *English for Cross-Cultural Communication*, edited by Larry E. Smith, pp. 15–39. New York: St. Martin's Press, 1981.

---. *The Indianization of English: The English Language in India*. New Delhi: Oxford University Press, 1982*a*.

---. "Meaning in Deviation: Toward Understanding Non-Native English Texts." In *The Other Tongue: English across Cultures*, edited by Braj B. Kachru, pp. 325–50. Champaign: University of Illinois Press, 1982*b*.

Kandiah, Thiru. "The Teaching of English as a Second Language in Pakistan." *Transactions of the University of Ceylon Linguistic Society*, 1964, pp. 61–75.

---. "New Ceylon English." *New Ceylon Writing*, 1971, pp. 90–94.

---. "Lankan English Schizoglossia." *English World-Wide* 2 (1981):63–81.

Kansakar, Tej K. "The Teaching of Spoken English in Nepal." In *Report of the Second National Convention of the Teachers of English*, pp. 85–102. Katmandu: Tribhuvan University, 1977.

Kirk-Green, Anthony. "The Influence of West African Languages on English." In *The English Language in West Africa*, edited by John Spencer, pp. 123–44. London: Longman, 1971.

Krishnamurti, Bh. "Spelling Pronunciation in Indian English." In *Indian Writing in English*, edited by Ramesh Mohan, pp. 129–39. New Delhi: Orient Longman, 1978.

Lal, P. *Modern Indian Poetry in English: An Anthology and a Credo*. Calcutta: Writers Workshop, 1969.

Lanham, L. W. "An Outline History of the Languages of Southern Africa." In *Language and Communication Studies in South Africa*, edited by L. W. Lanham, pp. 13–28. Cape Town: Oxford University Press, 1978.

Malla, Kamal P. *English in Nepalese Education*. Katmandu: Ratna Pustak Bhandar, 1977.

Masica, Colin P. *Defining a Linguistic Area: South Asia*. Chicago: University of Chicago Press, 1976.

Masica, Colin P., and Dave, P. B. *The Sound System of Indian English*. Hyderabad: Central Institute of English and Foreign Languages, 1972.

Mehrotra, R. R. "Some Registral Features of Matrimonial Advertisements in Indian English." *English Language Teaching Journal* 30, no. 1 (1975):9–12.

---. "English in India: The Current Scene." *English Language Teaching* 21 (1977):163–70.

Mukherjee, Meenakshi. *The Twice Born Fiction: Themes and Techniques of the Indian Novel in English*. New Delhi and London: Heinemann, 1971.

Naik, M. K., and Mokashi-Punekar, S. *Perspectives on Indian Drama in English*. Madras: Oxford University Press, 1977.

Naik, M. K; Desai, S. K.; and Amur, G. S., eds. *Critical Essays on Indian Writing in English Presented to Armando Menezes*. Dharwar: Karnatak University, 1968.

Narasimhaiah, C. D., ed. *Commonwealth Literature: A Handbook of Select Reading Lists.* Delhi: Oxford University Press, 1976.

Nihalani, P.; Tongue, R. K.; and Hosali, P. *Indian and British English: A Handbook of Usage and Pronunciation.* New Delhi: Oxford University Press, 1978.

Obeyesekere, Ranjini, and Fernando, Chitra, eds. *An Anthology of Modern Writing from Sri Lanka.* Tucson: University of Arizona Press, 1981.

Parthasarathy, R., ed. *Ten Twentieth Century Indian Poets.* Delhi: Oxford University Press, 1976.

Passé, H. A. "The English Language in Ceylon." Ph.D. dissertation, University of London, 1947.

Pattanayak, Debi Prasanna. *Distribution of Languages in India, in States and Union Territories.* Mysore: Central Institute of Indian Languages, 1971.

Prator, Clifford. "The British Heresy in TESL." In *Language Problems of Developing Nations*, edited by Joshua A. Fishman, Charles A. Ferguson, and Jyotirindra Das Gupta, pp. 459–76. New York: John Wiley and Sons, 1968.

Press, John, ed. *Commonwealth Literature: Unity and Diversity in a Common Culture.* London: Heinemann, 1965.

Ramakrishna, D., ed. *Indian English Prose: An Anthology.* New Delhi: Arnold-Heinemann, 1980.

Rao, G. Subba. *Indian Words in English: A Study in Indo-British Cultural and Linguistic Relations.* Oxford: Clarendon Press, 1954.

Rao, Raja. *Kanthapura.* London: G. Allen and Unwin, 1938. Reprint. New York: New Directions, 1963.

———. *The Policeman and The Rose.* Delhi: Oxford University Press, 1978.

Richards, Jack C. "Rhetorical and Communicative Styles in the New Varieties of English." *Language Learning* 29, no. 1 (1979):1–25.

Sarma, Gobinda Prasad. *Nationalism in Indo-Anglian Fiction.* New Delhi: Sterling Publishing, 1978.

Schuchardt, Hugo. "Indo-English" (1891). In *Pidgin and Creole Languages: Selected Essays by Hugo Schuchardt*, translated by Glenn G. Gilbert, pp. 38–64. London: Cambridge University Press, 1980.

Serjeantson, Mary S. *A History of Foreign Words in English.* London: K. Paul, Trench, Trübner and Co., 1935.

Sey, K. A. *Ghanaian English: An Exploratory Survey.* London: Macmillan and Co., 1973.

Sharp, Henry, ed. *Selections from Educational Records.* Calcutta: Bureau of Education, Government of India, 1920.

Singh, Bhupal. *A Survey of Anglo-Indian Fiction.* London: Oxford University Press, 1934.

Sridhar, Kamal K. "English in the Socio-Cultural Context of India." *Studies in Language Learning* 2, no. 2 (1979):63–79.

Whitworth, George Clifford. *Indian English.* Letchworth: Garden City Press, 1907.

Wilson, H. H. *A Glossary of Judicial and Revenue Terms, and of Useful Words Occurring in Official Documents Relating to the Administration of the Government of British India.* 1855. Reprint. Calcutta: Eastern Law House, 1940.

Yule, Henry, and Burnell, A. C. *Hobson-Jobson: A Glossary of Colloquial Anglo-Indian Words and Phrases, and of Kindred Terms.* London: J. Murray, 1886. Reprint. New York: Humanities Press, 1968.

English in Singapore, Malaysia, and Hong Kong

John T. Platt

The functions and characteristics of English in Singapore, Malaysia, and Hong Kong may be described in one essay so that similarities and differences may become obvious. All three areas were part of the British Empire, and in all three English was the main language of administration and of the legal system, the language needed for advancement in many types of government and private employment and, therefore, the main language for the type of education which might lead to such advancement.

In all three areas, a Chinese ethnic group was either numerically dominant or, as in the case of the Malay States, the numerically dominant urban group and the group from which most of the pupils at the English-medium schools came. One could reasonably expect, therefore, some similarities in the type of English which developed. A more careful look at the three situations, however, reveals certain differences, not only in the type but in the status and functions of English. In Singapore and what is now Malaysia, English served as a lingua franca among those who had been educated at English-medium schools, not only for Chinese, Malays, and Indians but for Chinese of different Chinese "dialect" backgrounds. Among the English-medium-educated, it was a prestige lingua franca in which topics of any kind could be discussed, whereas the pidgin lingua franca, Bazaar Malay, was appropriate only for humble, basic matters like bargaining in markets or instructing workers.

In Hong Kong, however, the population was, and still is, overwhelmingly Chinese- and predominantly Cantonese-speaking. Therefore, although English served as an avenue to careers and professions, it did not serve a broad range of functions, and because of its more limited use in Hong Kong, it did not develop the type of systematic characteristics that appeared in the Malayan region.

In recent years, because of different government policies, the status and functions of English in Singapore and Malaysia have been moving apart. In the Republic of Singapore, both the sounds and the visual impact of English are common, but in Malaysia, English is being replaced more and more in all spheres of life by Malay, although it remains important as an international language and communicative link with world science and technology. In Hong Kong, English plays an increasingly important role but almost entirely in its written form.

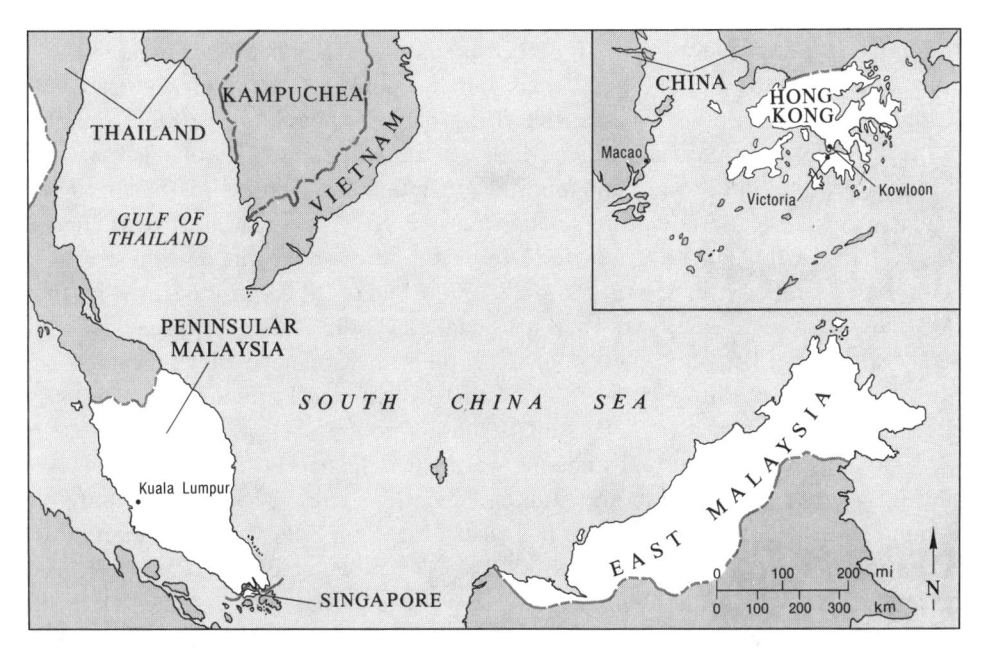

Singapore and Malaysia; Hong Kong

Singapore and Malaysia

Singapore is a small country of 587.6 square kilometers situated at the southern tip of the Malay peninsula. It consists of the main island, about two dozen inhabited islets, and about forty uninhabited ones. Its population at the end of June 1975 was estimated at 2,250,000, 76 percent being Chinese, 15 percent Malays, 8 percent of Indian, Pakistani, or Sri Lankan ethnic background, and 2 percent of other ethnicity. Malaysia consists of West Malaysia, a peninsula situated between Thailand to the north and Singapore to the south, and the East Malaysia states of Sabah and Sarawak on the island of Borneo. The total area is 332,000 square kilometers, of which the East Malaysian states make up about 60 percent. The population in 1975 was estimated at 10,385,000 in peninsular Malaysia and 1,864,000 in East Malaysia. In peninsular Malaysia, the population is approximately 53 percent Malay, 35 percent Chinese, and 1 percent Indian. In Sabah, the Chinese form about 22 percent of the population, the rest being Malays and indigenous people. In Sarawak, there are about 30 percent Chinese, 18 percent Malays, 31 percent Ibans (an indigenous people), and the rest other indigenous groups. (The census reported in 1980 now estimates the population of Malaysia to be 13,436,000.)

English has had a comparatively long history in Singapore and Malaysia, although it is only in the last few decades that it has been taught to virtually all school children.[1] The area is highly complex linguistically, largely as a result of nineteenth- and twentieth-century immigration. The Malays were overwhelmingly the main ethnic group until the nineteenth century. They lived mainly along the coast and river estuaries and in the coastal plains of areas like the present states of Kedah and Kelantan, where extensive rice growing is possible. The more remote areas were sparsely populated by various aboriginal peoples. As far back as the fifteenth century, there were communities of Indian and Chinese merchants, particularly in Malacca. Some of the Chinese settled there, taking Malay wives. Their descendants, who generally married ethnic Chinese, spoke (and in the case of some older people, still speak) a creole, Baba Malay. Malacca was ruled by the Portuguese from 1511 to 1640 when it was taken by the Dutch, who ruled it until 1824, when the British gained control through an exchange for Bencoolen in Sumatra. There is still a small group of ethnically mixed Portuguese in Malacca, speaking among themselves a Portuguese-based creole.

It was after the establishment of British influence in the area, however, that large waves of Chinese and Indians began to arrive. The British colony of Penang was established by Captain Francis Light in 1786, and Singapore was established by Sir Stamford Raffles in 1819. These two colonies, along with Malacca and the island of Labuan off the coast of Borneo, later became a British crown colony, the Straits Settlements, an entity which lasted until the Japanese occupation in 1942. It was in Penang, Singapore, and Malacca that English was most important, and consequently where its acquisition was felt to be an advantage. The three colonies grew rapidly—Singapore, according to Raffles, from a population of 150 (80 percent Malays and 20 percent Chinese) to 5,000 in four months.

British influence over the Malay states themselves extended gradually, and by 1891 the four states of Perak, Selangor, Negri Sembilan, and Pahang were grouped into the Federated Malay States with British Residents as "advisers" to the sultans. Kuala Lumpur became the capital of the federation, and the use and importance of English increased with the development of the British administrative and judicial system. By 1914, Britain had extended its influence over the other states which, however, remained unfederated. The importance of English increased in these states too, particularly in their capitals, but not to the extent that it did in the Federated Malay States or the Straits Settlements.

In the Malay states, the immigration of Chinese increased rapidly in the late nineteenth century in the form of indentured labor for the tin mines. From the early twentieth century there was also a considerable influx of southern Indians, mainly Tamils, who came as indentured labor to work on rubber estates. A pattern of population distribution developed which has persisted until today, although present policies are bringing about changes. The towns became overwhelmingly Chinese, with minorities of Indians, particularly in the larger ones. Typically the Indians would live in different parts of a town according to religion (Muslim or Hindu) and their regional or ethnic background. Malays remained predominantly rural, engaging in rice farming, fishing, and, later on, in the running of small rubber plantations. In areas of larger rubber plantations, there were many Tamils living in coolie lines on the estates. In tin mining areas, Chinese (mainly Cantonese and Hakka) lived in settlements near the mines, and some Chinese also engaged in market gardening and other rural pursuits.

Besides using their own languages within their own communities, these various groups also needed speech varieties for communication with other groups. Among the Chinese, there was (and is) typically a dominant Chinese "dialect": in Penang, it is a variety of Hokkien, while in Kuala Lumpur and Ipoh, and generally in the tin-mining areas, it is Cantonese.

Interethnically, the lingua franca was Bazaar Malay, a pidginized form of Malay still used in interethnic communication in Malaysia if at least one of the participants in a speech situation has not been educated in English or in Bahasa Malaysia. A local English-based pidgin did not develop, no doubt because a pidginized Malay had been used since the earliest contact with Indians and Chinese. In fact, British residents of Malaya (now West Malaysia) and Singapore had to acquire some competence in Bazaar Malay in order to communicate with lower-rank employees, some servants, and in their transactions in small shops. A type of basic Pidgin English was used only in communication with Europeans who "passed through." Merchants in Change Alley near the Singapore waterfront, for example, used it to converse with Europeans who paid brief visits en route elsewhere, and it was used by some Chinese *amahs* 'house servants' from the Canton area.

The Development of English-Medium Education

English-medium education began in 1816 with the establishment of Penang Free School by the colonial chaplain of Penang. This was followed by other free schools (so called because no restriction was placed on the entry of pupils because of race or religion), and by mission schools. By 1931, there were eighty-two English-medium schools in the region with a total enrollment of 28,071. Only about 0.65 percent of the total population (possibly 2 percent of school-age children) then had attended or were attending an English-medium school. Attendance at these schools was also very unevenly distributed, both regionally and ethnically. Among the Malays, the opportunity to attend them was virtually limited to the sons of royalty and the aristocracy. Most Malay children received only a few years of education in rural vernacular schools, as did the children of Indian rubber tappers; most of the poorer Chinese could not afford any education for their children. Many other Chinese had strong feelings about the need for their children to become literate in Chinese, and to retain Chinese cultural values, and sent their children to Chinese schools.

With the expansion of the British colonial administration and of British commercial enterprises, employment for English-medium educated Asians became more and more available, although higher positions were filled almost exclusively by staff sent out from Britain. Asians with an English-medium education were also admitted to universities in Britain, and an increasing number of students studied there. Tertiary English-medium education became available in Singapore with the opening in 1905 of the Singapore Medical School, which in 1915 became the King Edward VII College of Medicine. Raffles College was opened officially in 1929 and provided courses in arts and science.

English-medium education was increasingly recognized by some sections of the community—especially among the upwardly mobile urban Chinese and Indians—as a prerequisite for higher-paid employment and the professions. For most, the acquisition of English was instrumental rather than integrative, although there were, as in many colonial situations, those who acquired a genuine love of the language and of English culture.

The Development of a Distinctive Singapore-Malaysian English

Singapore-Malaysian English[2] developed through the school system and not through a pidgin as in West Africa, the Caribbean, and New Guinea. Several reasons can be advanced for the development of Singapore-Malaysian English and its extensive use:

1. The English-medium schools did not teach local languages. If any other language was taught at all, it was typically Latin.
2. The use of English was strongly encouraged both in and out of the classroom and, in fact, there were often sanctions in the form of small fines imposed on pupils using another language at school.
3. Headmasters and headmistresses, and often other senior staff, were usually from Britain.
4. Although most pupils were Chinese, there were also Indians and Eurasians. It is likely that junior pupils used Bazaar Malay at first in interethnic communication, but soon found English an appropriate language for the expression of more complicated ideas.
5. For almost all pupils, English was the only language in which they were literate.

For various reasons, Singapore-Malaysian English developed distinctive characteristics. The native speech varieties of the learners had their influence; however, some characteristics are no doubt to be attributed to teaching strategies. The influence of Indian teachers on the English of Singapore has since been mentioned by Ramish (1970) and, because India came under British influence earlier than Singapore, many English-educated Indians—especially Tamils and Malayalis—were employed in teaching, as well as in clerical work.

The typical older English-educated Indian of Singapore or Malaysia (although not speaking an altogether Indian English) had certain "Indian English" characteristics of intonation and articulation: for example, retroflex articulation of

English alveolar plosives in some positions. Younger English-educated Singaporeans and Malaysians of all ethnic and family language backgrounds speak more and more alike. However, with the implementation of the national language policy of Bahasa Malaysia as the national language of Malaysia and as the language of instruction (except in the case of Chinese- or Tamil-medium primary schools), both the functions and characteristics of English in the two nations are diverging.

Recent Language and Educational Policies

In 1956 an all-party committee in Singapore recommended bilingual primary and secondary education, and this became the practice. If English was the language of instruction, then Chinese (Mandarin), Malay, or Tamil was to be the second language. If one of these were the language of instruction, then English was the second language. There was a steady increase in English-medium education from 46.7 percent of all school children in 1957 to 64.8 percent in 1972. Trends since then have been even more toward enrollment in English-medium schools or "streams." Because attendance has steadily decreased at other schools, the majority of which are Chinese-medium, there has been a tendency lately to promote bilingual education by having some subjects taught in English and some in the other language.

Thus, in Singapore, the three Asian languages are considered as symbols of Asian culture and, particularly in the case of Chinese (Mandarin) and Malay, as important for their practical value in international communication. English is recognized for its utilitarian value and as an interethnic unifying force, and in the long run it is hoped that "through the utilitarian value of English, instrumental attachments will eventually strengthen legitimacy of the state and further sentimental attachments, thus facilitating the emergence of a supra-ethnic national identity" (Kuo 1978).

The trends have been different in Malaysia. Until 1962 there was a steady increase in enrollment in English-medium secondary schools, reaching 90 percent in that year but falling to 69.1 percent in 1967. The enrollments at Malay-medium secondary schools increased rapidly from 4.1 percent of secondary school pupils in 1956 to 30.9 percent in 1967. Malaysia achieved self-government in 1957, but even before that the Malayan government had worked toward the establishment of Malay as the national language. With independence, Malay-medium secondary education was established, and Malay became a compulsory subject in all other schools. English was also to be compulsory because of its utilitarian value. In Chinese- and Tamil-medium primary schools both English and Malay were required as second languages. In 1970, the Ministry of Education announced that the first-year level at English-medium elementary schools would change to Malay-medium in 1971, and a gradual conversion would be completed in 1982 (Wong and Ee 1975).

The National Language Policy of Malaysia has also been steadily implemented in other spheres of life—government service, radio, television, and the universities. Thus, the functions of English are rapidly decreasing in Malaysia, although it is recognized as an important international language for commerce and communication and the language in which much important scientific and technical literature is written. In fact, in some quarters, there has been a trend toward emphasis on reading ability rather than overall competence in English.

For some Malaysians (most Eurasians and even some Indians and Chinese), English has been a first language; for many others, it has been more than simply a second language. Even though it may have been acquired after one or two other speech varieties, in the past it has been a prestige language used in government, education and, for some, in employment. More colloquial varieties of Malaysian English were used with friends and in various kinds of transactions. English covered a continuum from first language through second language to a foreign language. Bahasa Malaysia is replacing English in most of its previous functions, but English may be expected to remain as a continuum from second to foreign language according to the background and occupation of the speaker.[3]

In Singapore, de facto norms have developed more than in Malaysia. Although in both nations English is in some respects exonormative, with the written standard being a British standard and the spoken standard wavering somewhat uncertainly between RP and an educated local variety, there is no doubt that in everyday communication a local de facto norm has developed—to such an extent that it is considered highly inappropriate for a local speaker to speak with friends in RP. As the functions of English diminish in Malaysia, the local norm may be expected to disappear; in Singapore, a local variety of English will continue to develop.

Use of English in Singapore

The growing proportion of Singaporeans who have had English-medium education and have used English for many activities is reflected in the increased literacy rate and claimed comprehension of English. Kuo (1977) gives figures for a 1975 survey showing the percentage of the population aged fifteen years and over who claimed to understand English as follows:

Age Group	Percent Claiming to Understand English
15–20 years	87.3%
21–30	71.7
31–40	44.9
over 40	27.5

An investigation of the use of English within the family revealed considerable variation in the claimed use of English with various family members and a difference according to the age of the speaker, as shown in the following table.

CLAIMED USE OF ENGLISH WITHIN THE FAMILY

Age Group of Speaker	With Father	With Mother	With Spouse	With Siblings	With Children
18–35	29.3%	11.7%	66.7%	75.4%	80.0%
35–55	23.5	5.6	51.4	43.8	96.2

Adapted from Platt and Weber 1980.

Considerable differences were also obvious with regard to the medium of education of the speaker. For example, although 35.7 percent of English-medium-educated Singaporeans claimed to use English with their fathers, none of the Chinese-medium-educated did, and although 71.0 percent of the English-medium group claimed to use English with siblings, only 34.8 percent of the Chinese-medium-educated did.

Level of education is also an important factor in the use of English. In speaking with fathers, 11.8 percent of those with less than four years of secondary school claimed to use English, but 46.2 percent of those with six or more years of secondary education did so.

In speaking with friends, the percentages for use of English by the group with six or more years of secondary education were:

Age Group of Speaker	English-Medium-Educated	Non-English-Medium-Educated
18–35	58.5%	24.0%
35–55	61.3	27.1

Adapted from Platt and Weber 1980.

The slight decrease for the younger group is attributable mainly to an increased use of Mandarin.

In transactional situations such as shopping, banking, and traveling by public transport, English is widely used in larger stores, banks, and modern smaller shops in the newer shopping complexes. There are, however, larger stores in which varieties of Chinese are used, for instance, in the People's Park complex. In smaller provision shops, with bankers, and at newspaper kiosks, English appears to be used when the vendor is Indian and the shopper does not speak the same language. If, in such interethnic situations, one of the interlocutors has little or no competence in English, then Bazaar Malay is used.

In employment, the use of English varies from very high in government offices, non-Chinese banks, the administration of the large international hotels, and larger businesses to virtually no use in some traditional Chinese-type businesses and in some factories. Newspapers in all four of the official languages are published in Singapore: four in Chinese, two in English, one in Malay, and one in Tamil. By 1976, the daily circulation figure for English-language newspapers was 206,000 (Kuo 1978). In addition, there are, of course, English-language periodical publications, both popular and scientific.

Kuo (1978) reports that Radio Television Singapore (RTS), which is government operated, broadcast in English 25 percent of the time, but of the 32.3 percent of those interviewed who claimed to have listened to the radio the previous day, only about 20 percent said they listened to English-language broadcasts as opposed to 40 percent to Chinese-language broadcasts. For television, weekly broadcast hours in 1975 totalled 55 percent in English, 25 percent in Chinese, 11 percent in Malay, and 9 percent in Tamil (Kuo 1978). However, there has been an increasing tendency over the last few years for a greater use of Mandarin and English in certain locally produced programs. For cinema attendance in 1975-76, Kuo (1978) estimates 28.6 percent for English-language films and 65.7 percent for Chinese.

Use of English in Malaysia

In Malaysia, the use of English is less common than in Singapore and is likely to decrease steadily with the implementation of the national language policy. However, English still remains as a language of considerable importance and is still being used in various spheres of everyday activity.

Within the family, an investigation of ethnically Chinese Malaysians (Platt 1976a) revealed a considerable difference in claimed use of English between those having English-medium education (E) and those with Chinese-medium primary education and English-medium secondary education (C) as shown by the following percentage figures:

Claimed Use of English with:	E	C
Mother	6%	0%
Father	39	0
Siblings	84	0

Use of English by Indians with secondary education was found to be higher, but with Malays the trend was toward greater use of Malay—even among those with English-medium education.

Claimed use of English with friends by the same ethnically Chinese group mentioned above was 90 percent for the E group and 58 percent for the C group (Platt 1976a). The use of English by English-medium-educated Indians could be expected to be at least as high as for the E group, but its use was obviously decreasing among the English-medium-educated Malays.

In transaction situations, English is used considerably less than in Singapore, but it is still used to some extent in more fashionable shops, airline booking offices, and some banks and hotels, especially, of course, in interaction with tourists from Australia, the United States, and Europe. In a week-long investigation of speech variety use between vendors and customers at markets in Penang, the observed use of English ranged from 27 percent at Pulau Tikus market, frequented by expatriates and the upper socioeconomic group of Penang residents, to 0.5 percent at Chowrasta market in the inner metropolitan area (Afendras 1979).

Although competence in Bahasa Malaysia is required for positions in the government and in many private firms, English is still an important language requirement for many positions. An investigation of newspaper advertisements in the English-language press in August 1975 showed that of 264 positions advertised, 57.2 percent made no mention of language requirement. Of the rest, 30.1 percent mentioned English as against 51.3 percent Bahasa Malaysia, 15.9 percent Chinese dialects, and 2.7 percent Mandarin. Particular jobs requiring English (and other languages) included almoner with a medical insurance organization, a position with a freight forwarding company, secretary to a general manager, and apprentices with the Royal Malaysian Navy.

There are four main daily newspapers in peninsular Malaysia, and their total circulation is approximately 257,000 (computed from *Malaysia Singapore Media Annual* 1976–77). For the whole of Malaysia, including Sabah and Sarawak, the approximate weekday circulation according to language is: Malay, 108,000; English, 319,000; Chinese, 718,700; Tamil, 27,600. Radio dan Talivisyen Malaysia (RTM) is run by the Ministry of Information. The main language used for radio broadcasts is Bahasa Malaysia, but English is used for some news broadcasts as well as for some advertisements and programs by advertisers on one of the four networks. Although the music played on RTM is mainly American popular music, it is announced in Bahasa Malaysia. There are two television channels. News broadcasts are given in Bahasa Malaysia, English, Mandarin, and Tamil but most locally produced programs are in Malay. However, a considerable amount of English-language material is imported, such as feature films and series.

Average attendance at English-language films at cinemas varies from state to state—over 28 percent in Kelantan (a predominantly Malay state), for example, and nearly 23 percent in Penang (a predominantly Chinese area) (based on figures in *Malaysia Singapore Media Annual* 1976–77).

While English remains the language of government and the law in Singapore, there has been a progressive change toward the use of Bahasa Malaysia in Malaysia. Visible manifestations of the change are seen in the use of Bahasa

Malaysia for street signs (e.g., *Jalan Sahala* 'one-way street'), street names (e.g., the change from *X Road* to *Jalan X)* and on shop signs, where it is required that Bahasa Malaysia be given prominence. In Singapore, street names are in roman letters, terms such as *Road, Street,* and *Avenue* are generally used, and shop signs in various languages or language combinations are seen: English only, English and Chinese, or English and Tamil, with use of English—alone or in combination—being virtually universal.

Variation in Singapore-Malaysian English

I shall refer to the speech continuum which exists in Singapore and still continues to some extent with English-medium-educated Malaysians as Singapore-Malaysian English. Singapore-Malaysian English is clearly a speech continuum, and certain variables may be shown to be *implicational* in the sense used by DeCamp (1971), Bickerton (1973, 1975), and others. Certain characteristics must be considered as variables, with considerable differences in occurrence from the basilect (the subvariety lowest in prestige) through mesolects (medium-status) to the acrolect (the prestige subvariety). In general, the higher the educational standard and employment status of the speaker and the more formal the situation, the closer his or her speech is to the acrolect. Thus, a business executive in a formal meeting is likely to speak a variety which in syntax approaches standard British English, although lexical choices are likely to contain some Singapore-Malaysianisms, and phonology will be marked by a tendency to monophthongize some diphthongs and to reduce consonant clusters. An acrolectal speaker is not likely to replace nearly all final stops by glottal stops or to have a high proportion of verbs unmarked for past tense, as would the basilectal speaker. However, in informal situations with friends, the same business executives are likely to drop a long way down the continuum, and their speech will be characterized by the same phonological, syntactic, and often lexical features of those who cannot reach higher than the basilect or lower mesolects.

Some Phonological Variables

In our investigation of final consonant cluster reduction or modification by a group of English-educated speakers, we found that reduction or modification occurred in 71 percent of words which end in a two-consonant cluster in standard British English. For example, a word like *recent* was frequently reduced to *recen*. Reduction or modification ranged from about 12 percent for the speaker of highest social status to 97 percent at the other end of the scale. With words ending in a single consonant in standard British English, the same group of speakers had less than 18 percent nonoccurrence or replacement by a consonant with a different place of articulation (e.g., a glottal stop). However, glottal stop substitution was common for final k (47 percent of cases) or t (50 percent of cases).

Variation in the articulation of standard British English [ð] and [θ] is common in many varieties of English—for instance, Irish English or Black American English. In an examination of the speech of a group of speakers, a score of 0 was given for the standard fricative form (e.g., [θɪŋk] for *think*, [ðen] for *then*), 1 for an affricated form (e.g., [tˢɪŋ] for *thing*) or a variant fricative (e.g., [zɪs] for *this*), and 2 for a stop (*t* or *d*) (e.g., [dɪ] for *the*). Low overall scores mean frequent use of the prestige form; high scores mean the opposite (observed scores have been multiplied by 100). For those speakers with at least the General Certificate of Education (taken at the end of the fourth secondary school year) the mean score was 87, whereas for the group with lower levels of education, the overall mean score was 180.

Speakers of Singapore-Malaysian English are inclined to shorten their vowels; *see*, for example, is pronounced [si] or [sɪ]. Very noticeable, too, is the use of a monophthong where a diphthong is used in RP: [ɔ] for RP [əu] or [ou] and [ɛ] for RP [eɪ]. A study which divided speakers into two subgroups according to level of education revealed that monophthongization of diphthongs is common, particularly with speakers of the lower subvarieties of Singapore-Malaysian English.

Variations in stress—for example, *educáted* for *éducated* and *criticísm* for *críticism*—are very common. In a sample of 210 words of three or more syllables, 72 deviations from the RP norm in regard to stress occurred, and of these, 69 had a stress shift to a later syllable. If primary stress is on the final syllable in RP, the Singapore-Malaysian English stress-pattern is not likely to vary from it, but of 64 three-syllable words in the sample having primary stress on the first syllable in RP, 26 had syllable shift (e.g., *preférence*), and of 30 four-syllable words with primary stress on the first syllable in RP, 24 had stress shift (e.g., *educáted*).

Whereas RP is stress-timed, with primary stress recurring at roughly even intervals through a sentence, Tay (1979) refers to Singapore English as being basically "syllable-timed," that is, all syllables are separated by equal time intervals. However, there is a greater stress on the final syllable of word groups and particularly on the sentence final syllable, and visitors who are not familiar with Singapore-Malaysian English may think that contrastive stress is being used when in fact the speaker does not wish to convey contrast at all (e.g., "I give the ticke(ts) to *hím*"). Another noticeable feature of sentence intonation and stress is the lack of liaison between words. This feature, as well as the syllable-timed rhythm, gives outsiders the impression of a staccato style.

Lexical Items

Some lexical items are peculiar to Singapore-Malaysian English and others probably occur in other of the "newer" Englishes, particularly Indian English. Still others are words used in the international varieties that have special senses in Singapore-Malaysian English.

It is not possible within the scope of this chapter to give more than a few representative examples of typical Singapore-Malaysian English expressions. Some of them come from the background languages, especially from Malay and its pidginized form, Bazaar Malay (e.g., *kampong* 'a village, a small settlement', *makan* 'food'). The word *(h)ulu* in Malay means 'upstream, the upper part of a river' or the area upstream, which was often a more backward region than the settlements near a river estuary. In Singapore-Malaysian English it has come to mean an outer area, away from the town center, 'a place where there isn't much going on': *'cause this is quite an ulu area, y'know* (a comment made by a speaker about an outer area of Singapore).

Other words come from Chinese, particularly Hokkien, as for instance the word *towkay* (from Hokkien *thâu-ke* meaning 'an employer of labor, a businessman', usually fairly well-to-do). In Singapore-Malaysian English it has come to mean 'a Chinese businessman', usually wealthy: *lot of towkay use to live in this street*.

Some expressions of Portuguese origin most likely date back to the Portuguese occupation of Malacca in the sixteenth century. Although their use may not be confined to the Singapore-Malaysia area, they have often taken on a special meaning in Singapore-Malaysian English. *Peon*, for example (from the Portuguese *peão* 'farm hand'), signifies in Singapore-Malaysian English an office attendant or messenger who is usually ethnically Malay or Tamil: *you ask the peon, he take your letter*. The Portuguese *ama* 'nurse' became *amah*, 'a nurse or female domestic servant': *my amah, she don(t) speak English*.

Many British English expressions have taken on a different meaning in Singapore-Malaysian English. *Alphabet(s)*, for example, has come to mean the 'letters of the alphabet' as against the whole inventory of symbols: *Pla(tt)? You write your name with three alphabets or four?*, and *deep* is sometimes used in Singapore-Malaysian English to refer to the educated or formal subvariety of a particular language or Chinese dialect: *the deep Hokkien I cannot speak* (used by a Malaysian Chinese of Hokkien background).

Other expressions relate to different styles of living or different sociocultural backgrounds, for example, *coffee-shop, hawker (centre), shophouse*. In many more established varieties of English, *hawker* refers to an itinerant seller of various, usually portable, goods. In Singapore-Malaysian English, a hawker is typically someone running a stall which sells food (in particular) or other goods. *Hawker centre* is quite common and refers to a cluster of various stalls, usually selling food of different kinds—Chinese, Indian, Malay, and others. Some centers are semipermanent; others are used by day as car parks: *this hawker centre better; also got Indian food*.

Speakers of Singapore-Malaysian English tend to use some lexical items which in established varieties of English would be considered inappropriate because of social criteria (e.g., the use of *missus*) or because of stylistic criteria (e.g., the use of *converse, occupy,* or *presume* in colloquial speech). In British English, for example, *missus* is considered as a very low prestige word with reference to someone's wife, but in Singapore-Malaysian English *missus* is often considered more polite than the word *wife*. Thus, *your missus coming down?* was a polite inquiry by the manager of a large hotel. This is possibly an influence from Chinese, where the same word may be used for *wife* and the title *Mrs.* (e.g., Mandarin *taitai*).

Common to all varieties of English is the use of abbreviations and the use of the initials for various organizations and companies. However, the use of initials for place names is a noticeable feature of Singapore-Malaysian English: *K.L.* for Kuala Lumpur, capital of Malaysia, or *J.B.* for Johore Bahru, capital of the Malaysian state of Johore. The use of abbreviated forms of names is also common in newspaper headlines, e.g., *Raja* for Mr. Rajaratnam, the foreign minister of Singapore, or *Raza* for Razaleigh Hamzah, a minister in the Malaysian government. Such shortenings are limited to the names of Indians or Malays having long, polysyllabic names.

Morpho-syntactic Features of Singapore-Malaysian English

With lexical items, it has been possible to give some typical examples but not to deal with them quantitatively as with some of the phonological variables. With morpho-syntactic features one can again consider quantitative aspects of variation.[4]

Past Tense Marking
Variable marking of past tense is a well-known feature of several varieties of English and of English-based postcreole continua (Bickerton 1973, 1975; Fasold 1972; Labov 1972a, 1972b). Past tense marking by a group of forty-two English-educated speakers with different levels of education is described in Platt 1977c. Occurrences were classified according to four verb classes and four common irregular verbs. The verb classes were:

1. Vowel change (e.g., *break*, *come*) and also irregular types involving vowel change (e.g., *buy/bought*)
2. *Vowel + d* (e.g., *try*, *play*)
3. *Consonant + ed* (e.g., *depend*, *start*)
4. *Consonant + d/t* (e.g., *pass*, *move*)

The four irregular verbs were *get*, *be*, *have*, and *go*. *Get* is of particular interest because in Singapore-Malaysian English, particularly at the more basilectal end of the continuum, there is also a verb *got* used possessively (*I got two brother, one sister*), or as an existential or locative (*here got many people* 'there are many people here'). Not surprisingly, *get* in the sense of 'obtain' and 'become' was the verb most commonly marked for the past tense (as *got*), presumably because of the influence of *got*. When an implicational scale was constructed, the implicational relationship was: *consonant + d/t*; *vowel change*; *vowel + d*; *have*; *go*; *consonant + ed*; *be*; and *get*, with an overall scalability of 90 percent. Scores were obtained for the whole group of speakers and further analyzed in terms of two subgroups: group 1, with more than four years of secondary education and higher status occupations, and group 2, with up to four years of secondary education and lower status occupations. The percentage scores are presented in table 1 (adapted from Platt 1977c).

TABLE 1. PAST TENSE MARKING BY ENGLISH-EDUCATED SPEAKERS WITH DIFFERENT LEVELS OF EDUCATION

	get	*be*	*go*	consonant + *ed*	*have*	vowel change	vowel + *d*	consonant + *d/t*
Whole Group								
Percentage	92.9	79.2	77.2	70.4	65.4	63.5	41.8	26.6
order	1	2	3	4	5	6	7	8
Group 1								
Percentage	100	100	87.0	100	73.3	90.9	60.0	54.3
order	1	1	5	1	6	4	7	8
Group 2								
Percentage	92.0	70.8	73.2	61.1	62.2	55.1	37.8	19.4
order	1	3	2	5	4	6	7	8

The two subgroups differed considerably in their overall percentage scores and in their overall and implicational ordering. As suggested by Platt (1977c), a fairly high degree of past tense marking for some verb types appears to be acquired early and then increases fairly slowly. In other cases such as the vowel change or the *consonant + d/t* types, level of education has a marked effect. The relatively low degree of past tense marking for the latter verb type, even for group 1, is largely attributable to consonant cluster reduction. The background languages of Singaporeans and Malaysians do not have final consonant clusters, and, in fact, the various Chinese varieties restrict which consonants may appear in word-final position. The low degree of marking in the vowel change and *vowel + d* categories by group 2 speakers is obviously attributable to the fact that in the background languages there is no marking of tenses but a use of aspect markers where necessary. Thus, examples like *My mum, she come from China many years ago* and *I start here last year* are common.

Third Person Singular Present Tense Marking

The background languages of Singaporeans and Malaysians have no system of subject-verb agreement for person or number. Nonmarking of third person singular is a common feature of English-based creoles. Variable marking is common in varieties such as Black American English (see Fasold 1972; Labov 1972a), but it is also a feature of the less socially prestigious lects of some other varieties, for example, Norwich English (see Trudgill 1974).

For the group of forty-two English-medium-educated speakers already referred to, the overall percentage of third person singular present tense marking was 43 percent, with an overall score of 72 percent for those with higher socioeconomic and educational backgrounds and 23 percent for the others. Examples such as *this radio sound good* and *my mother she work very hard* with present reference are common, more so at the basilectal end of the continuum. This deletion is largely due to consonant cluster reduction (e.g., *sounds-sound*), but the lack of verb marking in the background languages clearly is an important factor.

Be as a Copula or Auxiliary

Variable use of *be* is another characteristic of English-based creoles and Black American English. For a group of fifty-nine speakers—forty with English-medium education and the rest with Chinese- or Malay-medium education—the implicational ordering was (1) pre-adjective (*this coffee house very dirty*), (2) pre-predicate nominal (*my car a Toyota*), (3) pre-*verb* + *ing* (*my sister also not working*), and (4) pre-locative (*my auntie in America*), with an overall scalability of 91 percent. The number of speakers having 100 percent *be* occurrence for each of the four syntactic environments was as follows: (1) zero out of fifty-nine, (2) seventeen out of fifty-eight, (3) twenty-eight out of fifty-eight, and (4) thirty-four out of fifty-six (some speakers did not use certain constructions).

These uses reflect the structure of the background languages to a great extent; however, some characteristics of variation can be attributed to developments within the variety itself.

Aspect Markers in Singapore-Malaysian English

As already mentioned, Malay and Chinese have aspectual systems but no obligatory tense. Bickerton (1974) has claimed that creoles typically have an aspectual system indicating anterior, irrealis, and nonpunctual actions and states. Whether or not this is a universal, it is certainly the case that Singapore-Malaysian English, especially at the more basilectal end of the continuum, marks anterior or completive (with *already*) and nonpunctual or habitual actions or states (with *use to*) without necessarily marking tense.

At the lower end of the Singapore-Malaysian English continuum, *already* is very commonly used to indicate that an action or state has been operative up to the present or is completed. Often, *already* co-occurs with an unmarked form of the verb but may co-occur with a past tense form: *my father already pass away* 'my father has passed away'; *I stay in X seventeen years already* 'I've lived in X for seventeen years'.

Use to ([justU]) frequently occurs in Singapore-Malaysian English and has no necessary connotation of past action or state, although it may be used with past reference. The following examples refer to habitual or general actions: *all Europeans use to go there*; *Indian shop, we use to speak English*.

The common occurrence of *would* where *will* would normally occur in other varieties of English is a striking feature of Singapore-Malaysian English. Tongue (1974, p. 31) lists sentences which exemplify this feature: for example, *I hope the government would take action to put a stop to this practice* and *I trust that his son would retain his zest for the game*. Tongue reports that when this peculiarity is pointed out to local speakers of Singapore-Malaysian English, they "often reply that they have always understood that *would* was more polite than *will*." However, it appears that *would* is characteristically used when the speaker is referring to a state or event which is not actually so and will not definitely be so but could be so. Thus, at higher levels of the Singapore-Malaysian English continuum, it appears that the tense-aspect system of English has been restructured so that *would* marks any unrealized state or action. At lower levels of the continuum, unmarked verb forms frequently occur when an unrealized action or state is indicated: *I hope you come again*; *I see you tomorrow, I show you* 'if I see you tomorrow, I'll show you'.

The Noun Phrase

In the background languages of speakers of Singapore-Malaysian English, nouns are not marked for the plural by affixation. In Chinese a plural classifier may be used and in Malay reduplication may occur, but there is nothing comparable to the system in English. Thus, sentences such as *how many bottle?* and *my house got two bedroom* are hardly surprising.

Definite articles occur more frequently than indefinite articles. An investigation of twenty lower mesolectal and basilectal English-medium-educated speakers (Platt 1977c) revealed not only that the overall mean score for *the* was higher (87.9 percent) than the overall mean score for *a* and *an* (71.7 percent), but that the score for *the* was higher for each individual speaker. Again, this distribution tends to reflect both the lack of indefinite articles in the background languages and the fact that in Chinese, definiteness and indefiniteness are sometimes differentiated by variation in sentence structure. Thus, sentences like *I don(t) have ticket* are quite common, especially at the more basilectal end of the scale. Interestingly, there is frequent use of a demonstrative where it would not occur in, for example, British or Australian English: *is just at the back of this Sago Lane*; *some, they buy these perfume*.

Subject and object pronoun deletion is particularly noticeable at the more basilectal end of the scale: *(I) speak Cantonese also*; *we don(t) have (it/them)*. An investigation of twenty-five speakers of different socioeconomic backgrounds showed that, although the overall occurrence of subject pronouns was 95 percent, only six of the twenty-five *always* used a first person pronoun; eleven always used the third person; and fifteen always used the second person. When the subject pronoun of a verb other than *be* would have been *it*, the overall rate of occurrence for the twenty-five was only 35 percent. Thus, sentences like *(it) depends on the person* were very common. With *be*, the rate of occurrence of *it* was even lower—71 out of a possible 394, or 18 percent. Only one of the twenty-five speakers *always* used *it* in such structures, so that sentences like *(it) is very cheap* are very common. This trait does not appear to be a case of phonetic reduction, since *is* occurs usually as [ɪz] and not [ɪs].

Further structural characteristics include:

1. Preposing of objects, time phrases, etc.: *one subject they pay for seven dollars*; *is very interesting I find geography*
2. Pronoun copying (very frequent): *but the grandson, they know to speak Malay*; *some customers, they disapprove if you speak to them in English*
3. Invariant tag questions (an almost universal feature): *you want Mary, is it?*; *you check out now, is it?*; *you like Carlsberg, isn't it?*
4. The *la* particle (one of the most noticeable features of Singapore-Malaysian English): *then I get a job there as a part-time la*[5]
5. Coordination without *or*. The influence of Chinese structures is evident in examples like *after two, three times she gave up*
6. Coordination without *and* (more common at the basilectal end): *he go in the room, talk to my sister*
7. Conditional clauses. At the basilectal and lower mesolectal end, the lack of *if* is noticeable; it is sometimes replaced by *supposing* and sometimes merely by a juncture after the conditional clause: *supposing that a student was to fail . . .* ; *you go by meter, you got to pay*; *stay longer, they have to over charge* ('charge extra')
8. Several uses of *so* (particularly in the more basilectal varieties): *if the age is under, so* ('then') *they stay another year*; *so* ('if') *you come late, you don(t) know where to park*; *no, I don't think so* ('that') *my English is that good*; *so* (sentence introducer) *it depend la*.

Some Singapore-Malaysian-English Features along the Lectal Continuum

I have suggested that Singapore-Malaysian English is a continuum and have given examples of phonetic, lexical, and syntactic variation. Table 2 suggests the relationship of some syntactic features to lects along the continuum. As mentioned earlier, the speaker with a command of higher lects will drop down the continuum in appropriate situations (see Platt 1977*a* and 1978*b*). Richards (1979) also gives examples which distinguish acrolectal and basilectal speakers in terms of modals, clause sequencing, and lexicon. However, some of his examples of basilectal usage (e.g., invariant tag questions and *use to* as a habitual aspect marker) are also characteristic of mesolectal and even acrolectal speakers.

TABLE 2. SELECTED SYNTACTIC FEATURES RELATED TO LECTS IN THE SINGAPORE-MALAYSIAN ENGLISH CONTINUUM

	Acrolect	Mesolect	Basilect
Past tense marking	occasional *d/t* deletion after consonants	frequent *d/t* deletion after consonants; some deletion after vowels; some *-ed* deletion	*d/t* almost invariably deleted after consonants; frequent *d* deletion after vowels; frequent *-ed* deletion after *d/t*; vowel change verbs often in present tense form
Third person present tense marking	nearly categorical	variable	nearly categorical nonmarking
be as copula or auxiliary	some deletion pre-adjective	more deletion pre-adjective; some deletion pre-nominal or *vowel+ing*	variable to categorical deletion in all positions
Aspect markers			
already	none	some use	frequent use
use(d) to	occasional use	moderate use	frequent use
would	some use	quite frequent use	infrequent or no use

Singapore-Malaysian English in the Press

Although the linguistic features discussed above sometimes appear in print (e.g., omission of noun plural marking or third person singular marking), these features are relatively rare in the local English-language press and more likely reflect printer's errors rather than the journalist's style of writing. A few constructions distinctive to Singapore-Malaysian English appear in print—topicalizing and the use of *very* in, for example, "Although the animals are *very* safely separated"—but printed English in the English-medium press resembles standard British English. Likewise, some local vocabulary is used in the discussion of local subject matter (e.g., *belukar*, a Malay word for 'secondary jungle'), while other local colloquial expressions (e.g., *makan* 'food') appear only occasionally in articles written in a jocular style or in those quoting local dialogue.

Printed advertisements sometimes consist of English texts with a local flavor. These are often advertisements for smaller local stores or manufacturers and are more likely to be found in the more popular press than, for instance, in such papers as the *Straits Times* (Singapore) and *New Straits Times* (Malaysia). For example, nonrealization of definite or indefinite articles occurs occasionally (e.g., *with every purchase of cooker . . .*), as does nonmarking of past tense constructions or noun plurals, (e.g., *all our shop reopen last week*; *prawn cracker in colored packet*; *Marie biscuit*; *sardine in tomato sauce*).

Singapore-Malaysian English in Literature

The history of literature in English by Singaporean and Malaysian writers, naturally enough, is not a very long one. Even though education in English goes back well into the nineteenth century, the atmosphere during the colonial era was not one conducive to the writing of poetry, short stories, novels, or plays. The emphasis in the schools was on English literature written in Great Britain, and it is unlikely that there would have been a market for locally written works. There were short stories and novels by Europeans resident in the region (e.g., Frank Swettenham and Sir Hugh Clifford) and also by visitors to the area such as Joseph Conrad and Somerset Maugham, but it is really only since 1945 that locally written English literature has developed. The most common genre has been poetry. For example, Edwin Thumboo's anthology *The Second Tongue* (1976) contains 175 poems by thirty-eight Singaporean and Malaysian writers. Short stories have also been quite common but novels and plays less so.

Most writers have used a standard English with few or no examples of typical Singapore-Malaysian features. Poets, in particular, rarely give the flavor of colloquial Singapore-Malaysian English in their work although many poems have to do with the atmosphere and life of the area. An example of locally flavored verse is the following from Mervin Mirapuri's "Eden 22" (1974):

> i send an invitation
> come
> we dig together
> you came
> but doorman say
> no digging here
> your host
> he grows beard
> his club illegal
> but car waiting
> to take madam
> to cultural festival
> with nice
> nice person

In his essay, "Poetry in English in the Seventies," Robert Yeo suggests that poets may attract an audience "by using a public language that appeals to as many of the English-educated in Singapore. And by a public language I mean one that uses English as spoken and written here in Singapore at present—with its distinctive pronunciation, grammar, vocabulary and common phrases" (Yeo 1977, p. 16). It will be interesting to see whether more poets try to capture the quality of Singaporean English.

It is easier to find examples of local colloquial English in prose writing, especially, of course, in dialogue. Catherine Lim's short story "The Taximan's Story" consists of a taxi driver's dialogue with a lady passenger, and captures the flavor of basilectal Singapore English. For example, on the subject of family planning, the taxi driver says:

> In those days, where got Family Planning in Singapore? People born many, many children, every year, one childs. Is no good at all. Today is much better. [Lim, 1978, p. 76]

Other features of local speech emerge when he discusses the behavior of some schoolgirls:

> They tell their Mum got school meeting, got sports and games, this, that, but they really come out and play the fool. Ah, madam, I see you surprise, but I know, I know all their tricks. I take them about in my taxi. They usuall is wait in bowling alley or coffee house or hotel, and they walk up, and friend, friend, the European and American tourists, and this is how they make fun and also extra money. Madam, you believe or not when I tell you how much money they got? [Lim 1978, p. 77]

A good example of a play using local varieties of English in dialogue is Edward Dorall's *A Tiger Is Loose in Our Community* (1972), where the characters display English that ranges from the acrolectal speech of the middle-class Eurasians—Mr. and Mrs. Reade and their son Philip—down to the basilectal speech of the residents of a squatter settlement on the outskirts of Kuala Lumpur. The following is from a scene where Philip and his Chinese girl friend Helen are sitting in the Lake Gardens in Kuala Lumpur. There is a marked contrast between Philip's speech and Helen's:

> *Philip*: Helen.
> *Helen*: Ah?
> *Philip*: What's it like—in your home?
> *Helen*: Ah? What for you want to know?
> *Philip*: Hoong said I know nothing about you really, how you feel and how you live.
> *Helen*: What you mean, how I live? Same as other people.
> *Philip*: You hardly talk about your mother.
> *Helen*: I don't see her enough. My mother works in a coffee shop. We got a cousin who got a coffee shop, so she work there. Very long hours, you know. Sometime she so tired she sleeps there, don't come home for two or three days.

More basilectal speech is used in a conversation involving Pillai (a Tamil Indian), Siew and Low (Chinese), and Hashim (a Malay), all residents of the squatter settlement:

Pillai: Hey—I got a great idea.
Siew: Ah?
Pillai: How to settle that Tiger gangster. Properly.
Siew: Very funny! Tell 'nother joke lah!
Pillai: No. Listen. Very soon Tiger going to fight that idiot. Isn't it?
Hashim: And then? I think he beat him up.
Siew: Kali can't fight. Too stupid.
Pillai: Yes. Yes. But listen. If Kali get a knife, a nice, sharp knife in his hand—
Low: Where he get knife? You think his father give him?
Pillai: No lah. *I* give him.

Robert Yeo has suggested that "English as spoken here should be used more"; whether this advice will be heeded for poetry, prose, and drama is difficult to predict. The idea of deviating from the "standard English" norm is distasteful to some, while others have obviously sensed that the use of local lects gives added realism to dialogue. An article in *Asia Week* (1 December 1979) sums up the role of English in creative writing in Singapore: "English is clearly about to become *the* medium of creative writing in Singapore" and "it is only English-language works that can rise above communal barriers and give artistic shape to the entire range of the city's multi-cultural experience." For Malaysia, however, the article states that "many onlookers believe that English literature is moribund in Malaysia." Naturally, since Bahasa Malaysia is the national language and the main medium of education, the readership for English literature may be expected to diminish.

Hong Kong

The British crown colony of Hong Kong is situated on the China coast about 120 kilometers south of the Tropic of Cancer. It consists of the island of Hong Kong itself, which was ceded to Britain in 1842; Kowloon on the mainland opposite the island, which, with Stonecutters Island, was ceded in 1860; and the New Territories, which were leased from China in 1898 for ninety-nine years. The total area is 1,046 square kilometers, made up of Hong Kong and adjacent islands (76 square kilometers), Kowloon and Stonecutters Island (11 square kilometers), and the New Territories (959 square kilometers). The island itself is very hilly and unsuitable for agriculture. Most of the coastal strip and much of the hillside land is heavily built up and densely populated. The New Territories area is mostly steep, hilly country, but almost all the lower land not occupied by buildings is given over to farming and market gardening.

The population has grown rapidly from 840,000 at the 1931 census to an estimated 4,500,000 in mid-1972. More than 98 percent of the population are Chinese, and 89 percent were born in Hong Kong.

Before World War II, only a small proportion of children attended school, but it is estimated that now nearly a third of the population is enrolled in schools, colleges, and education centers. By 1971, free primary education was available, and subsidized secondary education is becoming progressively available.

Formerly, English was the official language of Hong Kong, but now English and Chinese officially have equal status. Street names and signs, official forms, and government publications are now in (or available in) both languages. English is the main language of business correspondence, but Cantonese is overwhelmingly the main spoken variety, not only within the family and with friends but also in many other areas of verbal communication. Twenty-five percent of the population aged ten years and over understand English (according to *Hong Kong's Population* 1978), but, of course, "understanding" may cover skills that range from the ability to converse easily to the ability to undertake only such simple transactions as selling food.

The use of English in Hong Kong goes back to the beginning of British administration, although for quite a time its use was restricted to those who had come from Britain for business reasons or who served in the administration or military forces. However, China Coast Pidgin had been in use in the area for much longer and continued in Hong Kong among Chinese of different dialect backgrounds; it has diminished greatly during this century, especially with the increasing availability of education, so that there are now few speakers of it. Nowadays a kind of unstable interlanguage is used by Chinese with little or no education in English—for example, by shop assistants or by taxi drivers when speaking to Europeans.

As in Singapore and Malaysia, the value of competence in English for better employment became more and more obvious. For some Chinese—as was the case in other parts of the British Empire—there was a real desire to become familiar with western culture. As Lord (1978) puts it, "in colonial days the learning of English had become what some experts have called an *integrative* venture. In other words the learner was encouraged to identify as closely as possible with the culture and life of the home country." As Lord continues, "But all that has gone. The need now is utilitarian, pragmatic. English is needed not for cultural identification, but for a range of practical pursuits, not necessarily all prosaic, and some of them requiring considerable intellect and imagination." English has changed its status "from colonial to international."

The Functions of English in Hong Kong

Education is available through the medium of English or Chinese with the other language being taught as a subject. The spoken variety of Chinese is mainly

Cantonese, although the written language usually reflects Mandarin structure. The most common pattern is Chinese-medium primary education followed by English-medium secondary education for those who continue at school. According to Kwok and Chan (1972), of the two most common types of secondary school, the Anglo-Chinese English-medium schools have more than three times as many pupils as the Chinese schools. The five-year courses of both types of schools lead to the Hong Kong Certificate of Education Examination, in which most of the subjects are examined in either English or Chinese, but English language, English literature, French, typewriting, and shorthand are examined in English only.

At the tertiary level there are the University of Hong Kong, where the medium of instruction is English (except for most courses in the Department of Chinese); the Chinese University; the Hong Kong Polytechnic; and the Colleges of Education (teacher training institutions), one of which, Grantham College of Education, offers courses in both English and Chinese (Cantonese).

Within the family, Cantonese is overwhelmingly the dominant speech variety used, even when one parent is of another Chinese dialect background. The use of English appears to be very limited, even among those of more advanced or even tertiary education. Kwok and Chan (1972), when investigating the language use of 100 undergraduate students from both the University of Hong Kong and the Chinese University, found a similar pattern. They state that most students from both universities never speak English to their parents but claimed to use it frequently with siblings, depending on the topic under discussion. According to Kwok and Chan, the questionnaires revealed that most of the parents of the students questioned did not speak English.

My own investigations showed that even those with a considerable amount of English-medium education appear to use Cantonese with friends except when there is a need for particular lexical items to express some concept or refer to some object for which they do not know the Cantonese terms. Some who were more fluent in English claimed that they used English with Indian friends (there is a small but important Indian community in Hong Kong) "because it's a matter of respect that we speak to people in their own [sic] language."

Many university students talking together in the corridors of the University of Hong Kong appeared to be doing so almost entirely in Cantonese. This is quite a contrast to Singapore University, where many students would be talking to each other almost exclusively in Singapore-Malaysian English. In fact, students at secondary schools in Singapore often use English together when walking to and from school.

In employment, English is essential for all higher paid positions in larger firms. As one secretary put it:

No matter whether you can speak English really well or whether you jus(t) manage to do it—they will insist that you speak English [meaning "are *able to* speak it"]. In advertisements you see "Secretary wanted: *English* and Chinese." They never say "Chinese and English." And if a girl has good personality and she cannot speak English really well—then I think that will have to depend on the kind of company that is employing her. Suppose it's only a smaller company or if the boss is Chinese—then maybe he wouldn't really mind but I think what is really necessary is that no matter how badly you do English you mus(t) do it—you mus(t) be able to speak it.

However, just as in communication with friends, it seems that Cantonese is the main medium of communication among Chinese employees in shops and offices. If, however, a European is involved in the situation, then English will usually be used.

In transaction situations, Cantonese again predominates, and even in fashionable boutiques the competence in English of the sales personnel is often very limited. In Tsimshatsui, where most of the tourist hotels are located, shopkeepers and assistants use English in communication with customers, but few use English with the fluency of Singaporeans in similar situations. Similarly with regard to hotels, although the reception personnel are able to deal with English-speaking guests, it was noticeable that at a large hotel, a switchboard operator answered first in Cantonese. In a number of large firms it is the policy that everyone should answer the telephone in English, but it is quite common practice after that for the Chinese employees to switch to Cantonese if appropriate.

In the media and entertainment, English plays a minority role in terms of volume of output, but that role is nevertheless important. In 1977, there were 118 newspapers, including four English-language dailies (*The Media in Hong Kong* 1977). These English-language newspapers are mostly read by Chinese of higher educational and socioeconomic levels. However, among a group of tertiary students, only a few claimed to read an English-language newspaper regularly. Several claimed that the family took an English-language newspaper on Saturdays, the day on which most employment vacancies are advertised.

There are two radio broadcasting organizations: Radio Television Hong Kong (RTHK), the government organization, and Commercial Radio. RTHK broadcasts on two channels in English and two in Chinese (Cantonese) from 6 A.M. to 3 A.M. daily. Commercial Radio has two Chinese channels and one English channel. All announcements on the latter channel are in English. Broadcasting times for all three channels are from 6 A.M. to 1 A.M., but listener numbers vary considerably. Of those in the highest income bracket, 15 percent listened to the English channel, whereas of those in the lowest income brackets only 1 percent listened to it.[6]

There are two commercial television stations: HK-TVB and RTV, both having English and Chinese channels. Broadcasting time is longer on the Chinese channels. HK-TVB, for instance, transmits an average of 115 hours a week on its Chinese channel (Jade) and 76.5 hours a week on its English channel (Pearl).

The legal system is based on the British one; English is its official language.

Some Features of Hong Kong English

English performs a more restricted range of functions—or rather a lower proportion of each function—as compared with Singapore. As English is not an important everyday means of oral communication on a wide range of topics for many Hong Kong Chinese, it does not appear to have the kind of "understood" rules of appropriateness that are characteristic of usage in Singapore. Typically, a Hong Kong Chinese with some English-medium education will try to use his or her "best" English in communication with Europeans and will not "drop down the continuum" for stylistic purposes as Singaporeans (and some English-medium-educated Malaysians) do in informal situations. The Hong Kong Chinese I interviewed had received a high degree of exposure to English in education and the business environment and often spoke good English, but it was a learner's language, a developmental continuum rather than a lectal and developmental continuum as in the case of Singapore English.[7] At present there is probably less justification for speaking of a Hong Kong English than of a Singapore English as a variety in its own right. Nevertheless, certain typical characteristics appear to be emerging.

Phonetic Features
Vowels: As in Singapore-Malaysian English, there is a tendency to replace diphthongs by monophthongs, and long by short vowels: [tɛks] *takes*, [dʒɔkɪŋ] *joking*, [ʃʌks] *sharks*.

Consonants: Reduction of consonant clusters and deletion of final consonants is common: *one thousan(d) dollar(s) a mon(th)*; *we canno(t) affor(d)*; *ol(d) priva(te) apar(t)men(ts)*. Unlike Singapore-Malaysian English, where a glottal stop frequently replaces [t] or [k], there appears to be a complete deletion in the case of [t] and variable replacement of [k]: [snɛ], [snɛʔ] *snake*. Replacement of [l] by flapped [r] is common: [ɪŋgrɪʃ] *English*, [kɔrɛdʒ] *college*; but initial [r] and [r] after initial [t] is sometimes replaced by [w]: [wɛlwɛ] *railway*, [twɛn] *train*. Syllabic [l̩] as in *people* is typically replaced by [əl].

Stress and intonation: As in Singapore-Malaysian English, there are tendencies toward even stress (*Néw Térritóries*), main stress later in the word (*footbáll, populáted, usuallý*), and sentence- or phrase-final stress even when no contrastive stress is intended (*where all de movie come fróm*; *you give money to hím*).

Morpho-syntactic Features
Lack of noun plural marking (variable for many speakers): *he give all de picture(s) to you*; *where de movie(s) all come from*; *his four wive(s)*.

Lack of third person singular marking (also variable): *he like(s) de boy(s) better den de girl(s)*.

Lack of copula (variable): *de Vietnam people (are) smuggle(d) ou(t)*; *English (is) main language of instruction*.

Nonmarking of past tense (varying according to the level of English-medium education and to phonetic factors): *Mandarin, I learn(ed) it privately*; *X (name of firm) give me a good training*; *I don't learn at secondary school* (the speaker was no longer at school).

Nonoccurrence of subject, especially of *it*: *here (it) is not allowed to stop the car*; *doctor? (he) spea(ks) also Cantonese*.

Nonoccurrence of object pronoun (variable when the reference is obvious from the context): *Q. And you finished M (name of book)? A. Yes, finish. Q. You liked it? A. I don't like*.

Variable occurrence of definite and indefinite article: *I don(t) have (the) patience to learn*; *say you're doing (a) receptionist job*; *you can see de China ri(ght) across*; *I can ta(ke)* ('eat') *de sna(ke) but I can(t) ta(ke) de dog mea(t)*.

Pronoun copying (apparently very frequent): *our Chinese people, we like fishing very much de shrim(ps)*; *de farmer(s) dey do de gardening ou(t)si(de) dere*.

Idiosyncratic features: A learner's language has a certain amount of structure. However, as mentioned in Platt and Weber (1979), the more an interlanguage is still on the threshold between a foreign and second language, the more idiosyncratic features one is likely to encounter in it. In the English of speakers in Hong Kong, particularly those speakers who use English infrequently, a great number of idiosyncratic features could be observed: *so that's was my firs(t) job*; *because I'm learned do science subjec(t)s*; *all our rices we have to impor(t)*.

Conclusion

The language situation in general varies considerably among the three regions under discussion. The differences are reflected not only in the *position* which English holds within each region, but also in the *type* of English which is spoken by the local residents.

In Malaysia, where Bahasa Malaysia, the official variety of Malay, is gaining a more and more important position, the role of English has changed from its earlier status as the prestige language of the colonial era and the decades after World War II to a second language. At the moment it is still considered important as an international code to be used for diplomatic and commercial negotiations and as a language necessary in many fields of tertiary study and research. It is still used by non-Malays, particularly those with an English-medium education, in everyday communication on certain topics in certain situations. It appears to be used less and less by Malays, whether English-medium-educated or not, and by the younger sector of the community who have had a Bahasa Malaysia education. There are indications that the type of English that was spoken in the region and that bore a close resemblance to the type of English spoken in Singapore is on the wane, and that it is being gradually replaced by a more Malay-influenced type of English which would have, at best, second-language status and characteristics. Future developments will depend to a great extent on government educational policies and opportunities for using English outside the classroom.

In Singapore, English is without doubt the most prestigious and important of all the four national languages and still has a wider range of functions and overall status than the second important official language of the republic, Mandarin. Recently there has been emphasis on bilingual education and efforts to promote the other three official languages—Mandarin, Malay, and Tamil—for their cultural and "Asian" values, in order to counterbalance the influence of certain western values. It may be expected, then, that the status of these languages will rise and that their range of functions will increase, particularly in the case of Mandarin. However, this development is unlikely to affect the use of English but rather to reduce the scope of the native Chinese dialects.

With most of the younger sector of the population acquiring competence in English, it can be assumed not only that the functions of English will increase further, but also that Singapore English will continue to develop, particularly in its spoken form, as a variety of English in its own right, that certain idiosyncratic features will slowly disappear, and that the structure of a speech continuum with sociolectal divisions will develop further. The norm of British English, which is still ambivalently hovering in the background, will give way to a local norm modeled on the speech of educated Singaporeans, just as has happened in Australia, where now, in many circles, an educated Australian English is preferred to a British way of speaking.

As far as Hong Kong is concerned, it is still too early to forecast the future position of English with any certainty. There is no doubt that the position of Cantonese is very strong, and it has a great variety of functions from private to public and informal to formal. While many Malaysians or Singaporean Chinese have an attachment to their native dialect, they are often aware that it serves only limited functions, and they have other speech varieties, often more prestigious ones like English and Mandarin, at their disposal. To many Hong Kong Chinese, Cantonese *is* Chinese, a native language which is more than just a dialect, although many acknowledge the pragmatic value of English and wish they could speak it "better." Unlike some English-medium-educated Singaporean Chinese, they consider it not as a substitute for Cantonese but rather as a language in addition to it.

NOTES

The Singapore-Malaysian research was supported by Australian Research Grants Committee grants A68/16801 and A77/15359 and the Hong Kong research by Monash University Special Research Grant A35/79. Thanks for their cooperation are due to many government departments, members of tertiary institutions, and the staff and management of private enterprises in Singapore, Malaysia, and Hong Kong—and above all to those many local residents who agreed to be interviewed.

1. For a fuller discussion of many of the statements in this article, see Platt and Weber 1980.
2. When speaking of the *development* of English in what was formerly Malaya, one should actually refer to *Malayan English,* since the nation of Malaysia came into being only in 1963.
3. As the functions of English diminish in Malaysia, it is to be expected that even the English of these speakers may change, reflecting lower levels of use.
4. During recent years, I have investigated a number of variables, and the results of these investigations appear in Platt 1976*b*, 1977*a*, 1977*b*, 1977*c*, and Platt and Weber 1980.
5. Richards and Tay (1977) make a convincing case for the Hokkien origin of this particle and for its being a marker of rapport, familiarity, and informality. We have noticed that it was used in our interviews only by persons with whom there was good rapport in an informal situation, except in the case of some Chinese-medium-educated speakers who had not, as Richards and Tay suggest, "mastered the sociolinguistic rules for *la.*"
6. This information was supplied by the courtesy of Commercial Radio.
7. Corder (1976) defines *development continua* as being "characterized by increasing complexity towards some particular target in the case of a language learner" and *lectal continua* as being "characterized by equal complexity but oriented towards some reference norm." In Platt 1977*b*, I suggest that Singapore English quite clearly displays two-dimensional characteristics, that is, *lectal* by using lects along the continuum as functional values and *developmental* by displaying a dynamic movement toward a target language.

REFERENCES

Afendras, E. A. "Multilingual Communication in the Market Place: A Comparison of Malaysia and Singapore." Paper presented at the International Symposium on Language in Context and Conflict, Brussels, 8 June 1979.

Bickerton, Derek. "On the Nature of a Creole Continuum." *Language* 49 (1973):640–69.

———. "Creolization, Linguistic Universals, Natural Semantax, and the Brain." *Working Papers in Linguistics* (University of Hawaii) 6, no. 3 (1974):125–41.

———. *Dynamics of a Creole System.* London: Cambridge University Press, 1975.

Corder, S. Pit. "Language Continua and the Interlanguage Hypothesis." Paper presented at the Conference on the Notion of Simplification, May 1976, at the University of Neuchatel.

DeCamp, David. "Towards a Generative Analysis of a Post Creole Speech Continuum." In *Pidginization and Creolization of Languages,* edited by Dell Hymes, pp. 349–70. London: Cambridge University Press, 1971.

Dorall, Edward. *A Tiger Is Loose in Our Community.* In *New Drama One,* edited by Lloyd Fernando, pp. 1–81. Kuala Lumpur: Oxford University Press, 1972.

Dulay, Heidi C., and Burt, Marina K. "Creative Construction in Second Language Learning and Teaching." *Language Learning,* Special issue no. 4 (1976):65–79.

Fasold, Ralph W. *Tense Marking in Black English*. Arlington: Center for Applied Linguistics, 1972.
Hong Kong's Population. Hong Kong: Government Information Services, 1978.
Kuo, Eddie C. Y. "The Status of English in Singapore: A Sociolinguistic Analysis." In *The English Language in Singapore*, edited by William Crewe, pp. 10–31. Singapore: Eastern Universities Press, 1977.
———. "Multilingualism and Mass Media Communications in Singapore." *Asian Survey* 18, no. 10 (1978):1067–83.
Kwok, Helen, and Chan, Mimi. "Where the Twain to Meet: A Preliminary Study of the Language Habits of University Undergraduates in Hong Kong." *General Linguistics* 12, no. 2 (1972):63–82.
Labov, William. *Language in the Inner City*. Philadelphia: University of Pennsylvania Press, 1972*a*.
———. *Sociolinguistic Patterns*. Philadelphia: University of Pennsylvania Press, 1972*b*.
Lim, Catherine. "The Taximan's Story." In *Little Ironies: Stories of Singapore*, edited by Catherine Lim, pp. 76–79. Singapore: Heinemann Educational Books, 1978.
Lord, R. "Language Quandary." *South China Morning Post*, 19 December 1978.
Malaysia Singapore Media Annual. Singapore: Association of Accredited Advertising Agents in Singapore, 1976–77.
Media in Hong Kong. Hong Kong: Government Information Services, 1977.
Mirapuri, Mervin G. "Eden 22." In *Singapore Writing*, edited by Chandran Nair, pp. 65–69. Singapore: Woodrose Publications, 1974.
Platt, John T. "Speech Repertoires and Societal Domains of Malaysian Chinese." *Speech Education* 4, no. 1 (1976*a*):18–28.
———. "Implicational Scaling and Its Pedagogical Implications." *Working Papers in Language and Linguistics* (Tasmanian College of Advanced Education), no. 4 (1976*b*):46–60.
———. "The Sub-Varieties of Singapore English: Their Sociolectal and Functional Status." In *The English Language in Singapore*, edited by William Crewe, pp. 83–95. Singapore: Eastern Universities Press, 1977*a*.
———. "The 'Creoloid' as a Special Type of Interlanguage." *Interlanguage Studies Bulletin* 2, no. 3 (1977*b*):22–38.
———. "English Past Tense Acquisition by Singaporeans: Implicational Scaling Versus Group Averages of Marked Forms." *ITL: Review of Applied Linguistics* 38 (1977*c*):63–83.
———. "Sociolects and Their Pedagogical Implications." *Regional English Language Centre Journal* 9, no. 1 (1978*a*):28–38.
———. "The Concept of a 'Creoloid'-Exemplification: Basilectal Singapore English." In *Papers in Pidgin and Creole Linguistics*, vol. 1, pp. 53–65. Pacific Linguistics, ser. A, no. 54. Canberra: Australian National University, 1978*b*.
Platt, John T., and Weber, Heidi. "The Position of Two ESL Varieties in a Model of Continuity and Tridimensionality." In *New Varieties of English, Issues and Approaches*, edited by Jack C. Richards, pp. 112–30. Regional English Language Centre Occasional Papers, no. 8. Singapore: Regional English Language Centre, 1979.
———. *English in Singapore and Malaysia: Status—Features—Functions*. Kuala Lumpur: Oxford University Press, 1980.

Ramish, Lucille M. "An Investigation of the Phonological Features of the English of Singapore and the Relation to the Linguistic Substrata of Malay, Tamil and Chinese Languages." Ph.D. dissertation, Brown University, 1970.

Richards, Jack C. "Rhetorical and Communicative Styles in the New Varieties of English." *Language Learning* 29 (1979):1–25.

Richards, Jack C., and Tay, Mary W. J. "The *La* Particle in Singapore-English." In *The English Language in Singapore*, edited by William Crewe, pp. 68–82. Singapore: Eastern Universities Press, 1977.

Tay, Mary W. J. "The Uses, Users and Features of English in Singapore." In *New Varieties of English, Issues and Approaches*, edited by Jack C. Richards, pp. 91–111. Regional English Language Centre Occasional Papers, no. 8. Singapore: Regional English Language Centre, 1979.

Thumboo, Edwin. *The Second Tongue*. Singapore: Heinemann Educational Books, 1976.

Tongue, R. K. *The English of Singapore and Malaysia*. Singapore: Eastern Universities Press, 1974.

Trudgill, Peter. *The Social Differentiation of English in Norwich*. Cambridge: At the University Press, 1974.

Wong, Francis Hoy Kee, and Ee, T. H. *Education in Malaysia*. 2d ed. Kuala Lumpur: Heinemann Educational Books, 1975.

Yeo, Robert. "Poetry in English in the Seventies." In *Singapore Writing*, edited by Chandran Nair, pp. 14–16. Singapore: Woodrose Publications, 1977.

English in Australia and New Zealand

Robert D. Eagleson

The European settlement of Australia began in 1788 when Great Britain established a penal colony at Sydney to relieve the pressure on its overcrowded jails. The "first fleet" sailed into Botany Bay, conveying 717 prisoners and almost 300 officials, soldier-guards, wives, and children. In the fifty-two years that the convict system persisted, some 130,000 prisoners were transported to be the predominant element in the formative years of the colony. It was not until after 1840 that free settlers outnumbered those with convict origins. Until 1816, free settlers required special permission to enter the colony, and by 1820 they numbered only 1,300. In that same year 16,000—half the population—were still in servitude, while another 8,000 were released or emancipated convicts. Nevertheless, by then the free population, along with the convicts who served them, had proved the enormous potential of Australia as a producer of wool, and by attracting the attention of British capital and industry, they had assured the continuation of a British presence in Australia.

Unofficial European settlement, mainly by whalers, began in New Zealand as early as 1792, but it was not until 1840 that an official colony was established when the British government signed the Treaty of Waitangi with the Maori chiefs. From the beginning, New Zealand was set up as a free rather than a penal colony, although, as with Australia, many of its early settlers came to its shores on assisted passages.

Since those early days, the European populations of the two countries have grown only slowly and still continue to be small in relation to the huge land mass of Australia and the substantial size of New Zealand:

Year	Australia	New Zealand
1788	1,030	
1800	5,200	100
1820	33,500	200
1840	190,000	2,050
1850	405,000	25,000
1900	3,750,000	770,000
1950	8,300,000	1,800,000
1960	10,400,000	2,400,000
1970	12,600,000	2,750,000
1980	14,500,000	3,500,000

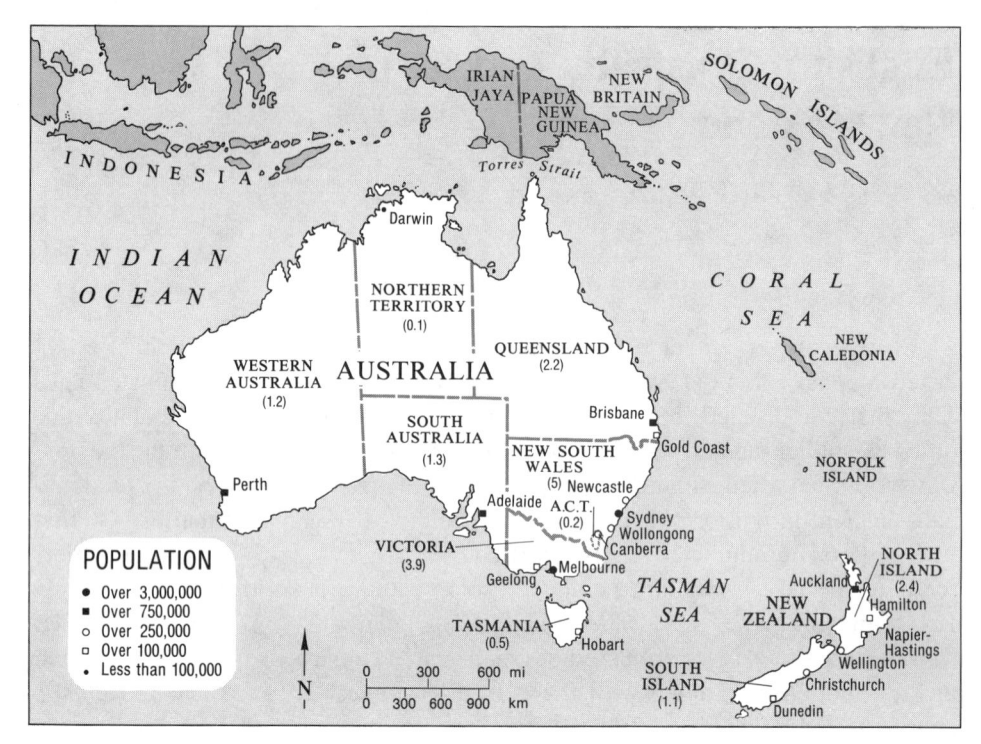

Australia and New Zealand. Figures give the population in millions. A.C.T. is the Australian Capitol Territory.

Until the mid-twentieth century, with the exception of periods of gold rushes, the source for immigrants has mainly been the United Kingdom. During the convict period in Australia, the southeast region of England was the major source, though between 1789 and 1805, almost 2,000 Irish political prisoners were transported and at one time constituted a third of the population.

Despite the small numbers of European settlers, there was an early and rapid spreading out into all habitable regions in both countries. There was no consolidation of one region, to be followed by a slow expansion outward. Instead, under the impetus of pastoralists seeking land for their rapidly increasing flocks and herds, the occupation of the land was rapid. What has followed since has been stagnation and even retraction in the rural areas and the development of large cities. From 1871, when only 27 percent of the population lived in the capital cities of Australia, the situation has changed so that 65 percent now reside in those seven locations. Sydney, with 3.5 million people, and Melbourne, with 2.9 million, contain between them 45 percent of all Australians, and the community must be regarded as most urbanized.

Urbanization reflects a shift in the activities of the people. Particularly since the Second World War, Australia has become an industrialized nation, and while primary products and mineral resources still figure importantly in its economy, the majority of its people are engaged in ever-expanding and varied secondary industries.

Especially in Australia, Europeans face a natural environment which is immensely different from their homelands. Here is a country of vast dimensions, its 7,687,000 square kilometers being thirty times larger than Great Britain. Half of it lies within the tropics and experiences long, hot, and frequently very dry summers. It contains the largest desert area outside the Sahara in North Africa, and one-fifth remains unoccupied and possibly uninhabitable. One-third of the land receives less than 250 millimeters of rainfall per year. On the other hand, there are seemingly endless stretches of rich fertile land, bearing crops and fruits of all descriptions and supporting an enormous population of sheep and cattle which dwarfs the human population.

So alien were the conditions which faced the early settlers that not only did the land compel them to adjust their habits of life and modify their methods of agriculture, but it also forced adjustments to their language. These people called upon the resources they already had in English and by the straightforward and well-established procedure of combination fashioned names for new experiences. Such compounds as *drop-rail* (a crudely but easily constructed gateway in which rails were inserted into mortises in upright posts and simply dropped out when one wanted to pass through) enabled them to link the new with the known, while *back run* (land at the back of a property, away from the river, the front or best part of the property being on the river) and *sly grog* (illicit alcohol) point to distinguishing characteristics of the items referred to.

In the early days some words were brought into constant service in compounding. Two such words are *bush* and *native*, giving rise to *bush dray*, *bushfire*, *bushman*, *bush mechanic*, *bush scab*, and *bush telegraph* on the one hand, and *native bear*, *native dog*, and *native pear* on the other. The latter are less than imaginative, and many of the early compounds incorporating *native* have since been replaced.

Later compounds are *outback* (the remote districts inland, the "back of beyond"), *flying doctor* (a medical service established in the outback where people were scattered over immense distances, in which the doctor attended patients by airplane), and a series with *cocky* as the last element—for example, *cow-cocky* 'dairy farmer' and *sheep-cocky* 'sheep farmer'.

From New Zealand we have such compounds as *share milker* (a farmer who works a dairy and shares the profit with the owner of the property), *bush skiddy* (a worker who keeps forest tracks cleared in the timber industry), and, as names for birds and trees, *waxeye*, *fantail*, *lancewood*, and *thousand jacket*. As in Australian English, *bush* is a popular element in compounds, occurring in, for example, *bush hawk* and *bush warbler*.

Within the area of word formation there is also the construction of such derivatives as *bathers* 'swimming costume'. *Ropeable* had its origins in the cattle station and was initially applied to animals which were so wild or intractable that their legs had to be tied with rope before they could be branded. In time its use came to be figuratively transferred to human beings in the sense of 'extremely angry, so furious that one should be tied up'. A popular word in New Zealand nowadays, *bach* 'a holiday cottage or weekender' (immediately from *bach* 'live as a bachelor'), offers an instance of shortening.

Another change was the expansion of the meaning of lexical items. *Paddock*, which in England had referred to a small, enclosed field, in Australia came to be used far more loosely to refer to a field of any size. In fact, *paddock* has become the general term, and *field* is somewhat restricted to such environments as *playing field*. *Brush* was extended from a thicket of small trees and shrubs to an area containing larger timber, and especially to a thick, dense stand of trees; *bush*, among other possibilities, has come to represent the country as opposed to the city.

In New Zealand English *gully* has impinged on the semantic domain of *valley* and has virtually acquired all its senses, replacing *valley* on most occasions. *Section* now incorporates the sense of 'a plot of land in a town or city suitable in size for the erection of a house'. In this sense the word is in constant use, though it has also retained meanings shared with British English.

In both countries *crook* has widened in sense to encompass 'ill, unwell' on the one hand, and 'angry, ill-tempered' on the other. One can thus *feel a little crook* 'feel slightly unwell' or *go crook at someone* 'speak angrily to them'. It is also possible to have *crook weather* 'bad weather' and a *crook time* 'unhappy or unpleasant time'. In both countries, too, especially up to the 1950s, *home* had the additional sense of 'Great Britain', and even third and fourth generation Australians would speak of *going home* as much as *going to England*.

There are times when the sense which a word originally had in Great Britain persists in Australia and New Zealand alongside any extension of meaning it has undergone in these two countries. Such is the case with *station*, which is standard in such contexts as *railway station* and *police station*, but which also may occur to refer to places where animals are raised: *sheep-station*, *cattle-station*. The slang term *wog* is still very much a pejorative term for a foreigner, but in Australia it has also received a figurative extension to denote particularly a gastric illness, especially one whose cause cannot be diagnosed exactly (an implication presumably that the sufferer has a foreign body in his system). Sometimes the special extension becomes predominant, so that the mention of *lifesaver*, for example, will first and foremost bring to mind to an Australian a person who is trained to rescue surfers from drowning and who belongs to a club for this purpose, although he knows of other kinds of *lifesavers* and *lifesaving drugs*. At other times, the original British sense has disappeared in popular usage; this has happened with *creek*, which would always be used for a small river and not "a narrow inlet in the coastline of the sea or the tidal estuary of a river" (*OED*).

A less felicitous outcome of the linguistic activities of the early pioneers is the unfortunate naming of some of the flora and fauna. Not altogether unnaturally, they allowed superficial resemblances to guide them in naming what were quite different species. An Australian tree was called *oak*, for example, though it really belongs to the genus *Casuarina* and not *Quercus* to which the British counterpart belongs. In the same way the Australian *broom* is not the same shrub as the *broom* in Britain. *Beech* in *New Zealand southland beech* is a misnomer. The beefwood tree was regularly called a *cypress* in the early days because of similarities in the timber, and the Australian *cedar* received its name because of likeness in color and grain, though it does not bear cones. This practice leads to no ill effects if one is confined to Australia, but there is potential for ambiguity when one tries to communicate with those from another region.

In the extremely sparsely populated country that Australia was in the nineteenth century, a full series such as *hamlet-village-town-city* was far too precise. No doubt *town* and *city* would have been more familiar terms to most early Australians, but to be realistic, the young colony could have coped with just one term. *Town* seems to have been most commonly used at first, though in their application of the term to a particular settlement early writers often had in mind its future rather than its existing condition. As they grew larger, some towns were promoted to cities, a population of 15,000 being set as the minimum to qualify for the status of city. But "towns" which just failed to fulfill any promise were not demoted, and *hamlet* and *village* have never played a role in the classification of Australian settlements, with the result that *town* today may still refer to a cluster of four or five houses and some commercial enterprise such as a general store-cum-post office, a hotel, or a garage. *Village*, however, is today undergoing something of a revival in urban areas. It is a fad term with a certain snob appeal and is applied to small shopping complexes discreetly tucked away in exclusive residential areas. It has also been attached to fashionable and expensive shopping centers.

Another approach to coping with immediate lexical needs was to derive a new lexical form from a proper name. It was perhaps natural that a genus of shrubs should be called *Banksia* after Sir Joseph Banks, a botanist who had accompanied Captain Cook, and *Boronia* is a similar adaptation of the surname of an early French explorer. In Australian English *granny smith*, a type of apple first grown by Mrs. Maria Smith, a grandmother who lived in a suburb of Sydney, and *bundy*, a mechanism incorporating a clock which automatically registers an employee's time of arrival at work, are further examples. In dispute is *pavlova*, a dessert with a meringue base with a soft marshmallow center, topped with whipped cream and fruit. Everyone agrees that the original *pavlova* was made in honor of the famous Russian ballerina, but both New Zealand and Australian cooks claim the invention, demonstrating how the history of Australia and New Zealand English is in places closely intertwined.

Buckley's chance, which is often reduced to *Buckley's*, is a case where folk etymology has intervened to confuse the pedigree of a term. Many now trace it to a convict who escaped from Port Phillip in 1803 and managed to survive in the bush for over thirty years by living with Aborigines. But Baker (1966, p. 269) suggests that the expression more likely comes from a play on the name of a Melbourne firm, Buckley and Nunn: "There are just two chances, Buckley's and none."

Folk linguistics has also played quite a part in the development of another word. One kind of parrot was initially called *rosehill parrot* after the district in which it was first sighted. This title was developed into *rosehiller*, whence through misunderstanding and no doubt an attempt at a scientific form, it was converted into *rosella*! This shows how quickly Australian English has been swept into the lines of development that older forms of language have experienced.

To understand the manner in which Australian English developed, one must take into account not only the distinctive attributes of the geographical environment, but also the character of the original British immigrants. These were not idealists or exiles seeking religious or political freedom, or the ambitious looking for a better way of life. On the contrary, as already indicated, the majority in the early decades came as convicts, transported as punishment for their crimes. Most were members of the lower classes, victims of the Industrial Revolution who had eked out pitiful existences in the major cities. Largely uneducated and generally illiterate, they were speakers of nonstandard social dialects. Moreover, the soldiers who guarded them were of the same class. The exceptions were the governors, some officers, administrative officials, a few better-educated free settlers, and an occasional professional person serving a prison sentence.

The social pressures on behavior in general, and language behavior in particular, were somewhat different from those in Great Britain. The very composition of the early settlements in Australia, allied with the harshness of the life and the brutal treatment of the convicts, would have meant that the usual social norms were disturbed. There would have been less obvious respect for the classes usually regarded as prestigious and far less concern for the niceties and refinements of life. In this milieu there was opportunity for nonstandard speech to exert a more potent influence, and it found its way quite naturally into popular writings, as the old ballad *Click Go the Shears, Boys* (McAuley 1975), which has enjoyed a recent revival, testifies:

> Out on the board the old shearer stands,
> Grasping his shears in his long, bony hands,
> Fixed is his gaze on a bare-bellied "joe,"
> Glory if he gets her, won't he make the ringer go.
> Chorus:
> Click go the shears boys, click, click, click,
> Wide is his blow and his hands move quick,

> The ringer looks around and is beaten by a blow,
> And curses the old snagger with the blue-bellied "joe."
> ....
> Now Mister Newchum for to begin,
> In number seven paddock bring all the sheep in;
> Don't leave none behind, whatever you may do,
> And then you'll be fit for a jackeroo.

It must not be imagined, however, that the standard dialect vanished from the colonies. There was still the bureaucracy issuing commands and preparing reports in official English. Very quickly a wealthy class began to establish itself with aspirations for recognition as the local gentry. There were those who tried to preserve the customs of the homeland and to declare their great worth by doing so, and there were always those seeking to join what they saw as the prestigious class. Many a term became fully acceptable in Australian English even if restricted in Britain to informal usage. A number of these terms had to do with arguments, fights, and general disturbance, such as *barney*, *shivoo*, and *turn-up*; others dealt with flattering or deceptive talk, such as *carney* and *guiver*.

There was a whole set of names for the inhabitants of the new settlement. Convicts only recently transported were *new chums*, while those who had served some time were *old chums*. *Croppy* initially referred to an Irish convict, so named because a number of them had had their hair cut short. The word came to be applied to any convict and especially to a runaway one. Those born in the colony were known as *currency*, while those born in England were given the name *sterling*. A number of these terms persist and with the passing of the convict system have entered more general usage. *New chum* became the name for a recent immigrant, especially from Great Britain. *Cockatoos* continue to be posted in the vicinity of illegal betting shops and *two-up schools* to warn of approaching police. A *shivoo* may be just a boisterous party at which there may be a lot of friendly *chiacking*.[1]

Many a writer tries to capture this informal quality in representing the speech of Australian characters, though their efforts usually suffer from exaggeration:

> I heard Herb come in after this and greet Peggy:
> "Is the big bloke in, Peggy?"
> "Come in, smacker," I yelled.
> "How're you, boss?"
> "Never felt better," I said. "Like my new watch?"
> He picked it up, looked at it for several minutes and dangled it by its chain.
> "It's a beaut!"

> "You bet!" I said. "How's tricks?"
> "Good," he said, "but the old trout's getting lemony. Says I'm taking up too much room and stops her serving customers."
> "I'll push her ears back," I said. "She'd be mucking well bankrupt before this if we hadn't given her a free ad. Did you tell yer how lucky she is we chose her shop?"
> "Yes," he said, "I've told her." [Stivens 1959, p. 78]

In the early days, not only were nonstandard speakers more numerous, but other forms of English were not known. Australians were pressed into duties which were unfamiliar to them and which in England had been performed by others who had both the skills and the associated language for them. The result has been the loss of many rural dialects and the special vocabularies of trades and occupations. Essentially from the urban setting, most of the first Australians were ignorant of the many distinctions in waterways. In consequence, *brook*, *stream*, *rivulet* and such terms have disappeared from general use in Australia and would be recognized only as literary and non-Australian usage. In their place there is the simple binary classification of *river* and *creek*, the latter, as noted earlier, modified in its sense. Other terms of a like nature not brought from England were *dale* and *meadow*. The nonrural background of the early population probably also contributed to the replacement of *flock* and *herd* by *mob* in Australia.

In confirmation of this assessment of the human factors behind the development of Australian English, it is interesting to recall the observations in early descriptions of the colony. Wakefield (1929, p. 51), for instance, remarked in *A Letter from Sydney* (originally published in 1829) that

> bearing in mind that our lowest class brought with it a peculiar language, and is constantly supplied with fresh corruptions, you will understand why pure English is not, and is not likely to become, the language of the colony.

Not all differences in Australian and New Zealand English can be attributed to the environment or the background of the inhabitants. Geographical separation, no doubt, must also account for some of the variations that have taken place in the use of terms. *Kerosene* and *paraffin* in Australian English, for example, refer to different petroleum products. *Washer* may also have the sense of 'face cloth'; *identity*, especially *an old identity*, may indicate a well-known person in the community. A *lay-by* has nothing to do with highways or expressways, but instead indicates a method of purchase, whereby the buyer makes an initial partial payment, and then completes the transaction by paying a number of installments over a given period. In the meantime, the shopkeeper "lays the goods by" and does not hand them over until the final installment has been paid.

As time has passed and distinctive social structures have emerged in Australia and New Zealand, their forms of English have shifted away from other types. Because the separate Australian states eventually came to unite in 1901 in a system of federation, with a federal and commonwealth government on top of the individual state governments, the terms *prime minister* and *premier* came to be given discrete areas of use. Unlike the situation in Great Britain, they are not synonymous in Australia, *prime minister* being reserved for the leader of the federal government and *premier* for the leader of a state government. So, too, there is a *governor general* as the queen's representative at the federal level, and a *governor* at the state level. In the area of industrial relations, the rights of workers are established and protected by sets of *awards* which are determined by the Arbitration Court, part of the judicial system of the country. *Award rates* and *award wages* are levels of salaries which are compulsory for employers to pay, depending on the industry and the type of work carried out.

While members of other English-speaking communities may not be readily able to distinguish Australian and New Zealand speakers, Australians and New Zealanders can recognize each other by their accents. In pronunciation they have diverged from each other, just as both have diverged from other varieties of English. But the differences lie mainly in the realization of individual sounds and not in a more fundamental variation in system. Despite the comedian's oft-repeated joke about the Australian in London being interpreted by the locals as saying "I came here to die" when he was actually indicating that he had just arrived, Australians do differentiate between *day* and *die*. *Day* might be articulated as [dʌɪ] and so appear more like [daɪ] to a non-Australian, but by the same token the same Australians would pronounce *die* as [daɪ]. For them there is no possibility of confusion between *day* and *die*. Indeed, the various accents in Australian English and New Zealand English may be seen as forming a continuum with the Received Pronunciation of Great Britain, each one, including RP, simply being a variant along the line. In the articulation of most sounds, especially the consonants, there would be close agreement, and because the documentation on RP is widely available, it will be conveniently taken in what follows as the base for comparison, and only those features in which Australian and New Zealand English vary markedly from it will be described.

The most comprehensive investigation of the Australian accent is the one conducted by Mitchell and Delbridge (1965) in the late 1950s and early 1960s. It confirmed some earlier observations (especially by Mitchell) on the varieties within Australian English and clarified and greatly enhanced our understanding of them. The results of the survey pointed to three major varieties of Australian English: Broad, General, and Cultivated. These may be recognized only at the diaphonic level, and their differentiation hinges largely on the production of six sounds:

	Broad[1]	General[1]	Cultivated[2]
beat	[ə˕ˈɪ]	[əɪ]	[ɪi], [i]
boot[2]	[ə˕ˈʊ]	[əʊ]	[ʊu], [u]
say	[ʌˈɪ], [ʌ˖ɪ]	[ʌɪ]	[ɛɪ], [eɪ]
so	[ʌˈʊ], [ʌ˖ʊ]	[ʌʊ]	[oʊ], [ɛ˖ʊ]
high	[ɒˈɪ]	[ɒɪ]	[aɪ]
how	[æˈʊ], [æ˔ʊ]	[æʊ]	[aʊ], [a˖ʊ]

1. ˖ indicates an advanced vowel; ˕ indicates a more open vowel; ˈ indicates stress on the following vowel.
2. Bernard (1967) has since proposed the following set of diaphones instead: [u˖], [u], [u˔].

The following passage offers a good illustration of the Broad accent. It is transcribed from the conversation of a girl in a large country town and was collected by Mitchell and Delbridge during their survey. As they comment, "her speech is broad, with noticeable assimilation and contextual nasality" (1965, p. 88):

> ʌm | las wikɛn mɒɪ | an n pɛːrn̩s wɛnt æ˔·ʊt bɪ təʊ lɪzmɔː bikəz | mɒɪ ant wəz sɪ·k | n ðʌɪ brɔt hə dæ̃·ʊn ʃəɪ hæd ɒpθælmɪk ʃɪŋglz ænd | ðə dɒktə sɛd ət wz ðə wɜs kʌ·ɪs ðt he˕·ɪd ɛvə sə˕ˈɪn | ænd wɛn ʃəɪ kʌ˖˔m dæ̃ʊɪn | ʃə˕ɪ wd | hæβ ʌʊnləɪ bəɪn æ˔ˈʊt əv hɒspətl lɪtl wɒɪl æn ʃə˕ˈɪz vɛrəɪ ta·d frm trævlɪŋ | ænd | wɪ ə gɒt kwɒɪt ə ʃɒk təʊ sə˕ˈɪ hɜr ɪn əz ʃə˕ɪ wɒz ||

> [Um . . . last weekend my . . . aunt and parents went out bi . . . to Lismore because . . . my aunt was sick 'n they brought her down she had ophthalmic shingles and . . . the doctor said it was the worst case that he'd ever seen . . . and . . . when she came down she would . . . have only been out of hospital little while and she was very tired from travelling . . . and we er got quite a shock to see her in as she was . . .] [Mitchell and Delbridge 1965, pp. 26, 85]

Mitchell and Delbridge found that the distribution of speakers across these three varieties was: Broad Australian, 34 percent; General Australian, 55 percent; Cultivated Australian, 11 percent. They would not, however, want these figures to be taken too literally, as suggesting that the Australian community is divided into three neat compartments. There are borderline cases between Broad and General, General and Cultivated, and instead of watertight segments one should think in terms of a continuum with speakers being found at every point along the scale. The figures quoted for each variety are thus only suggestive of the relative tendencies within Australian speech. In their conclusions, Mitchell and Delbridge state:

> Our account of the sounds of Australian English implies a single phonemic segmental structure with a range of diaphonic variations that are socially meaningful throughout the continent. [1965, pp. 86–87]

Delbridge (1970, p. 20) has since elaborated these conclusions:

> Statistically, at least, one can say that the choice a person makes of a speech variety is affected by a complex set of factors, chief among which are the sex of the speaker, the type of school attended, his family background, and his residence either in the city or the country. Girls tend towards Cultivated and General forms, boys towards General and Broad. Cultivated speech correlates significantly with the higher occupations, independent schools, and city life. But there emerged no geographical or cultural boundaries for diaphones, and speakers of each of the main varieties could be found anywhere within the same city or town, the same school and even the same family. One feels some confidence in believing that what emerged from the inspection of this limited corpus would reappear in a still wider investigation, were it to be undertaken, though the category proportions would no doubt reflect the altered sample.

No equally comprehensive survey of New Zealand pronunciation has been made, but it would appear to have divisions with characteristics very similar to Australian English, though the broad accent is perhaps not quite as marked. New Zealanders can be differentiated from Australians, however, by their practice of centralizing [ɪ] so that the contrast between [ɪ] and [ə] is blurred, if not lost altogether, with the result that [tɪn] is articulated as [tən].[2] The starting point for [ɪə] also seems to be higher, and the diphthong approaches [iə]. In addition to these diaphonic or realizational differences, there are a number of distributional differences which distinguish Australian and New Zealand English from RP. One is the sound at the end of such words as *happy* and *pity*, which is articulated as [əɪ] in Broad and General, moving to [i] in Cultivated, but not [ɪ] as in RP. The unstressed vowel in *pocket*, *painted*, and *buses* occurs as a central [ə].

That studies so far have not uncovered distinct regional varieties in Australia is to some degree surprising, given the isolation of the early settlements—Perth was two months' sailing from Sydney—and the continued relative isolation of some small communities today. Some members of the general public would refute this view and claim that they can recognize from what state an individual comes. But this evidence is scanty and based on occasional differences. They will argue that South Australians can be recognized by the way they pronounce *school* ([skul] instead of [skəul]), or Victorians by the fact that they say [kæsl] and not [kasl]. These same people, however, overlook the fact that not all South Australians or Victorians have these features, and their limited experience blinds them to the fact that these pronunciations may be heard elsewhere in Australia as well.

Moreover, these pronunciations are restricted to one or two words. Those who substitute [æ] for [a] in *castle* still preserve [a] in *park* and *ta*. Concrete evidence for regional varieties in Australia is not available at present, and far more work needs to be done.

Hawkins (1973, p.3) argues that much the same situation obtains in New Zealand English.

> There is remarkably little regional variation within New Zealand itself; there is no Auckland accent for example, which is characteristically distinct from a Wellington or Christchurch or Napier accent. The exception is a uvular fricative [r] found in parts of Southland and Westland, a throwback to the Scottish ancestry of the inhabitants of these wild and remote outposts of the country.

Several theories have been advanced to account for the rise of a distinctive Australian accent. There is the folk myth that it is the product of climate and terrain, the result especially of efforts to combat dust and flies. A more serious explanation sees the Australian accent as flowing from an amalgam and leveling of all the various British dialects that were transported to Australia, a leveling which was encouraged by the fact that the majority of early Australians came from the same southeastern area of England and by the mobility of the early population among the main areas of settlement. Lacking more positive evidence, this theory has come to be accepted by most, though it is also realized that it has certain deficiencies. In particular, it leaves unexplained why the same result came to be produced in widely scattered settlements, some of which in the early history of the country were quite isolated. What we can say with certainty, however, is that a distinctive form of pronunciation developed very early, within two or three decades at most. This is confirmed by comments in early descriptive accounts of Australia, which also suggest that the dialects of London were making a major contribution. Cunningham, for instance, observed that "the London mode of *pronunciation* has been duly ingrafted on the colloquial dialect of our Currency youths"(1827, vol. 2, p. 60).

As for the origin of the varieties within Australian English, it is critical to understand exactly the significance of *Cultivated* as a label for one of the accents of Australian English.[3] J. R. L. Bernard (1967, p. 648) comes close to the mark in his proposal that Cultivated Australian arises from an attempt on the part of its speakers to emulate RP. It is, then, to a large extent an acquired accent, a deliberate attempt motivated by social aspirations to modify one's initial accent. That it is not exact RP is explained by this origin, and in support of this contention is the telling point that many Australians regard the Cultivated variety as affected. In this view, then, the Broad accent may be seen as the historical base, with the General and the Cultivated growing out of it.

Australia and New Zealand still await thoroughgoing investigations of variation at the lexical and grammatical levels, similar to those conducted in Great Britain and the United States. In the meantime, what seems to be the preeminent characteristic of these two forms of English is their overall uniformity, particularly on a regional basis, which may partly be explained by the heavy concentration of the population in a few centers. But there is not complete homogeneity. One buys an *ice-cream soda* in some areas, but a *spider* in others. What is called a *pusher* in South Australia is known as a *stroller* in New South Wales. Queensland stores still advertise *duchesses*, which are called *dressing tables* elsewhere. Strawberries are sold in *punnets* in Sydney and *chips* in Melbourne. *Port* is a more common variant of *suitcase* in some regions. *Deli* (an abbreviation of *delicatessen*) and *stubie* (an electric light pole) seem to be restricted to South Australia. *Dinner* in country regions is more likely to be the midday meal, whereas in urban areas the clash between *dinner* and *tea* for the evening meal is a social matter. In the middle of the morning at school, children are given a recess, and what is eaten at that time is known variously as *play lunch*, *little lunch*, and (mainly in Western Australia) *morning piece*. The piles on which a house is built in Queensland to raise it well above the ground for circulation of air are called *stumps*. In tropical Queensland, *evening* refers to any time after midday. An ice cream carton holding a small portion is a *pixie* in Victoria but a *bucket* in New South Wales.

Both Australia and New Zealand share the term *southerly buster* to refer to a particular type of wind, but many districts have their own special names for local features of the weather. Although in Sydney one normally hears *southerly buster*, in the old days the term *brickfielder* was used from the fact that a brickfield lay to the south and the wind would blow dust from it over the township. In Freemantle a cooling afternoon sea breeze is known as the *Freemantle doctor*. In the north of Australia a cyclone will be referred to as a *cockeye bob*, while in Greymouth, New Zealand, the *barber* is a cutting, unpleasant wind.

There have always been close ties between Australia and New Zealand and a constant flow of people in both directions. In earlier times, seasonal workers would move from country to country pursuing their trade, as the "season" normally began earlier in Australia. It is not surprising, therefore, that the two forms of English should share so much in common. But differences may also be found. The Australian *weekender* is likely to be a *bach* in New Zealand. A building site for a home is a *section* in New Zealand but a *block* or *lot* in Australia; houses erected by the government are known as *state houses* in New Zealand but *housing commission houses* in New South Wales. Then, too, the presence of Maori borrowings in New Zealand and Aboriginal borrowings in Australia serves to set the two forms apart.

The innovation of an indigenous style of football, known officially as Australian National Football but more commonly as Australian Rules by supporters of other codes, has led to a number of new terms being developed (e.g., *behind*, *ball-up*) alongside others taken over either unaltered or slightly modified in sense from established football games. Though less than a century old, there has developed in association with the game considerable variation in terminology from state to state (see Eagleson and McKie 1968–69). In Victoria and South Australia, for instance, *check-side* is used for a kick designed to make the ball curve in flight, but the term is not in use in other states nor does it appear in official publications. On the other hand, *knock ruckman* and *left centre* occur in New South Wales and South Australia but not in Victoria.

The Australian dried fruit industry operates in the three states of New South Wales, South Australia, and Victoria. Despite the fact that the growing areas are dependent on the same Murray River and are not too widely separated from one another, Sharwood (1974), in an investigation of the terminology of the industry, came across considerable regional variation. What is a *silly plough* in New South Wales becomes a *crazy plough* or a *gooseneck* in Victoria and a *cranky plough* in South Australia. These two studies demonstrate the latent possibilities in wider-ranging investigations of regional variation in Australia and New Zealand.

Certain industries and activities in both countries have developed, as might be expected, specialist terminologies mainly known by those engaged in them. To take just two illustrations, there are the many specialist terms connected with the shearing industry, such as *boggi*, the name for a shearer's handpiece which arose because of a resemblance in shape with the boggi lizard, *gun shearer* 'the fastest shearer in the shed', and *wets*, *dags*, and *snobs*, all names for different types of sheep. From the well-known Australian form of gambling, *two-up*, which is also called *swy* (based on German *zwei*), comes *ringie*, the man in charge of the ring around which the gamblers assemble; *spinner*, the person who tosses the coins; and *kip*, the thin piece of board used to toss them. If an industry operates only in one part of the country, such as sugarcane growing, then the terminology is also on the whole regionalized, so that *screw down* as the term for a particular type of railway truck is not used and hardly known outside northern New South Wales and Queensland.

In the discussion of pronunciation above, it was observed that the accents in Australian English were socially determined. Not until the last decade, however, has any serious attention been given to discovering whether social groupings within the community had characteristic markings in other areas of language. My recent work (Eagleson 1976) has shown that such grammatical structures as the following may be heard among the poorer, less educated sections of the community:

> Tommy *brang* his dog to school.
> He said "No, but it's *wrote up* out there."
> It's the way they *been* brought up.
> . . . had it *have been* the boot on the other foot.
> *You was* at work a lot with Lynn.
> Then she *weren't* served any more.

The water *don't* go far.
Her and Malcolm were mates.
He turns his face and *won't* have *nothing* to do with a person, *doesn't* he?
They're *more harder* to clean where the English bikes are *more simpler*.
Then they seen *them* dummies.

The evidence suggests that there is a group of people for whom these patterns are the regular and constant practice. They cannot be regarded simply as a series of errors, a substandard form of the language. They are more ingrained and occur in writing as well as in speech. They have all the strength of a nonstandard dialect, and many of them figure in distinguishing social class in other varieties of English around the world.

It would seem, then, that in Australia we should give recognition to the existence of a nonstandard social dialect alongside the standard one. Given the background of the population, its presence is hardly exceptional, and its existence today might well be seen as a preservation of an old rather than the creation of a new form of Australian English.

As already noted, Australia and New Zealand were established as British colonies, and for most of their history they remained for all intents and purposes British. While there were immigrants from other countries and even a few national settlements such as the Germans in the Barossa Valley, South Australia, and an Italian community around Innisfail in north Queensland, these additions to the basic British stock were minute and had no influence on the character of English. Since 1950 and the commencement of the postwar immigration policy, there has been a dramatic shift. Today 20 percent of Australians—some 2.5 million people—were not born in an English-speaking country or have at least one parent of non-English-speaking origin. These recent migrants have come with a variety of language backgrounds: Latvian, Yugoslav, Greek, French, German, Italian, Dutch, and more recently Turkish, Lebanese, and Vietnamese, to mention but a part of the total. Until recently, most have been scattered through the community; it is only in the past few years that one has become conscious of national groupings forming in some of the major cities. Moreover, there has been pressure on these people both self-imposed and from society at large to learn to use English.

As a result of these factors and because of the short period of time involved, this marked change in the linguistic makeup of the Australian community has not yet had any significant influence on Australian English itself.[4] The only obvious effect so far lies in the contribution of new terms connected with items of living which the migrants have introduced to the native-born Australians and which have now been absorbed into the general way of life. Not surprisingly most of them are names of various foods and beverages: *sauerkraut, ravioli, pizza, espresso, gelato, goulash, schnitzel, cappucino, tambourlie, bolognese, tambora,* and *spumoni*.

Greater competition has probably existed among the different branches of English than between English and foreign languages. There has been a tension in particular between American and British English. American English made a contribution from the beginning but indirectly via British English. The British in general, and the civil service in particular, had acquired many terms in governing the American colonies. *Bushranger*, *land shark*, *location*, and *squatter* are most likely to have entered Australian English in this way, though they have acquired a local coloring since.

During the gold rushes in the mid-nineteenth century, Americanisms entered Australian English directly, introduced by the miners from California and other North American goldfields. To the American gold diggers we might trace *prospect* and *bowie knife*. America and things American have been growing in prestige, particularly since the close contact between the nations in the Second World War. The United States was seen as the hub of modernity and progress, and Australians and New Zealanders have been open to influence, while some have sought actively to imitate and adopt Americanisms. In consequence, Australian and New Zealand English have a fair share of American terms: *babysit*, *windbreak*, *level with*, *punk*, *beach buggy*, *neck* 'kiss, caress', *jazz*, *heel* 'cad', *troubleshooter*, and *sundae* are just a few of the total complement. Perhaps the most ironic borrowing of all from American English is *kangaroo court* 'a self-appointed court without legal constitution'.

What is especially interesting in this context is the conflict which has sometimes arisen between a British and an American term in Australian English. *Lorry*, for instance, was once the regular term, but it has now been all but displaced by *truck*. *Lift* is giving way to *elevator*, especially on signs in modern skyscrapers. Modern highways are called *expressways* and sometimes *freeways*, but never *motorways*, the British term. *Motorway*, however, is used in New Zealand. But not always has the American rival won out. *Biscuit*, *dole*, *chemist*, and *nip* still retain local allegiance instead of *cookie*, *welfare*, *drugstore*, and *shot*. Australian and New Zealand cars still have a *boot*, not a *trunk*, and are filled with *petrol*, not *gas*. One can come across Australian *beauticians*, and *undertakers* now style themselves *funeral directors* rather than *morticians*. *Diaper* (instead of *nappie*) may be heard, though infrequently, from a few under the influence of American films and advertisements, but *faucet* would never be used instead of *tap*. Sometimes terms of different origins seem to be in a state of coexistence. Such pairs are *kiosk* and *snack bar*, *ring me* and *phone me*, *let* and *lease*, *convenience* and *rest room*, *bubbler* and *water fountain*, *alternative* and *alternate*, *holiday* and *vacation*. On the other hand, Australians have preserved some independence and have adopted neither *underground* nor *subway* in connection with their urban railway system. The British *register one's luggage* and American *check one's baggage* have been evenly merged into *check one's luggage* in New Zealand (see Turner 1972).

Both Australia and New Zealand had been settled by other races before the British arrived, but in neither case were the original inhabitants very numerous. In Australia, the Aborigines, it is estimated, numbered 200,000. They were scattered over the vast continent and lived a nomadic existence grouped into some 600 tribes, each with its own language or distinctive dialect. It is now accepted that there were about 200 different languages, although these are now seen as belonging to five main language families. In New Zealand, the Maoris also numbered about 200,000 at the beginning of the nineteenth century. They inhabited mainly the warmer northern island.

Both races suffered at the hands of the white men. Their numbers seriously declined during the nineteenth century as a result of killing and susceptibility to disease introduced by the Europeans. By 1900, for instance, the Maori population had fallen to 50,000. Gradual enlightenment among the white population and improvement in policies have produced a halt to this diminution in recent decades, and today the population figures are 161,000 Aborigines and 270,000 Maoris, with the Aborigines now being the fastest-growing section of the community in Australia.

Given the lexical needs of the early settlers, it is perhaps surprising that the number of borrowings from the languages of the peoples who already inhabited Australia and New Zealand is quite small. In Australia there were several obstacles to more extensive borrowing from the Aboriginal languages. The way of life and the pursuits of the races were completely different. The Aboriginal languages were not geared to help those who wanted to introduce European agriculture and industry. Whites, as was typical in the eighteenth and nineteenth centuries, generally despised the Aborigines because of their black coloring and their way of life. More were concerned with driving the Aborigines away than with learning from them. The Aborigines were essentially nomads, and contact was intermittent; they congregated in small tribes, and each tribe had its own dialect or separate language. There was no one uniform Aboriginal language to which the white settlers were continually exposed, with the result that their knowledge of Aboriginal languages in the formative period of the white settlement was flimsy, and the presence of variants led to uncertainty and hesitation in using any one form.

Despite these obstacles to borrowing, as the customs and practice of the inhabitants were strange to the British, it is perhaps not quite unnatural that in this direction at least the British would take over some terms from the indigenous languages: Aboriginal words such as *corroboree* 'a ceremonial dance', *boomerang* 'a curved throwing stick', *woomera* 'a wooden stick with a hooked end used for throwing a spear', and *gunya* 'hut', in Australian English, and such Maori items as *haka* 'war dance', *pa* 'fortified village', *hongi* 'form of greeting', and of course *Maori* itself in New Zealand English. As the pioneers came to learn something of the native languages, so also they began to take over their names for flora and fauna. *Waratah*, *wallaby*, *koala*, *kurrajong*, *mulga*, and *quandong* were all borrowed from Australian Aboriginal languages. From the Maoris came such names as *kauri*, *tutu*, *mategowrie*, *moa*, *kiwi*, and *katipo*.

Contact with the original occupiers led to a small number of more general terms also finding their way into English. Perhaps the best known from Maori is *pakeha* 'European' or 'white', but *paua* 'a shellfish used in jewelry', *whare* 'a small house', and *toheroa* 'a shellfish from which soup is made', are also in regular use. In Australian English, there are *gibber* 'stone, boulder', *bung* 'useless, ruined, bankrupt', *bombora* 'dangerous eddying of water caused by a concealed reef of rocks', and *coo-ee* 'the call used to attract attention'. *Coo-ee* has become so well established that it has largely displaced *hail* in such collocations as *within hail*, most if not all Australians now preferring *within coo-ee*.

From the early days there has also been a good sprinkling of Maori and Aboriginal place names, such as *Rotorua*, *Waikarenoana*, *Moana*, and *Tauronga* in New Zealand, and *Goodooga*, *Panitya*, and *Porongerup* in Australia. In more recent years, there have been conscious efforts to use more such names and where feasible to revive ones which had been discarded. But leaving place names out of account, it must be recognized that the borrowing from the native languages has been relatively slight.

Sometimes the borrowings from the Aboriginal and Maori languages were not immediate, and a purely English invention was first employed as a name. Thus in early writings we can come across, for example, *settler's clock* or *laughing jackass*[5] and *native dog*. Then for a period these coinages existed alongside, and only subsequently gave way to, the Aboriginal *kookaburra* and *dingo*. In New Zealand *parson bird* has finally been overcome by the Maori name *tui*.

As for the acquisition of the English language by Aborigines and Maoris, one finds the full range from broken and Pidgin English, through a creole to nonstandard to a complete mastery of standard English. In the outback areas where tribal groupings can be relatively isolated from the white community, Aboriginal languages continue in daily use. Among such people a type of Pidgin English is also employed. In the Roper River area, for example, it has been discovered that the younger generations have all but abandoned their fathers' tongue and have creolized an earlier pidgin. Its features are reflected in the following transcript of part of a story told by a member of the local tribe:

dijan—de bin alde go. de bin alde luk dat bigwan. big tri bin jandab. belam—blam tri. diswan. de bin libam dat big tri. ledi jandab. de bin alde luk dat yaŋ tri, e? pilam. de bin luk an bletnim, bin kadim. de bin kadim an grebam. grebam, megi lilwan. megi flatwan prabli. gidim redwan, megim baya. megim baya an barnim. megim jilagwan, bindimbak an pudim dat ton ek.

[This (tree)—they always went to one. They always looked for a big one, a big tree standing, a plum tree, this one. They left the big trees, let (them) stand. They always looked for a young tree, see? A plum. They found one and flattened it, (and) cut (it). They (would) cut (it) and scrape (it), scrape (it) (and) make (it) small, make (it) really flat. (They would) get a hot coal (lit. 'red one'), (and) make a fire, make a fire and heat (it). (They'd) make it flexible (slack), bend it back and put the stone axe (head) (on it).] [Sharpe and Sandefur 1976, p. 71]

Elsewhere in northern Australia different groups have developed what might be recognized as Aboriginal English. The pronunciation is marked by a retroflexive quality which reflects the influence of Aboriginal languages, and the grammatical structure exhibits such features as:

1. *bin* as marker of past tense: *(h)e bin find a big fat one*; *that man bin come inside bar*
2. Omission of copula: *we just playing*; *he half-caste*
3. Absence of plural number inflection: *how many huncle you got?*
4. Absence of possessive marker: *one little boy trouser*

Except for the very old, Aborigines in an urban setting have lost their indigenous languages. For the most part they speak a nonstandard form of English with virtually the same characteristics as the nonstandard variety of English spoken by whites; most would also speak largely with a Broad accent. At the poorer end of the socioeconomic scale they find their dwellings and their occupations among whites of a similar status and naturally adopt that form of English to which they are exposed. The contemporary Aboriginal writer, Robert Merritt, captures some of the flavor of the Aborigine living in regular contact with whites in his play *The Cake Man*:

Look, I'll tell you something. No laughing, you're not allowed to laugh but you gotta try to listen and not call me a liar or laugh. I'm not no liar . . . ask Rube, ask my missus, she'll tell you that's one thing about me, that I ain't a liar . . . one thing I'm not. . . .
    [pause]
You every heared of a eurie-woman? You say it like that, eurie-woman. No? Never heared of one a' them? Well listen, then, I'll tell you what's a eurie-woman, and what it is I want here.
    I was working at Killara Station . . . after I had me feed, I went an' laid down on me bed an' started readin' this gubba book I had . . . [Wide-eyed] . . . an' all of a sudden I heerd this emu drummin' somewhere close, I got up an' wen' outside an' stoked up the fire, an' all the time this emu was still drummin'. I's tryin' to hear 'zactly where it was so I could find that nest . . . then the drummin' started closer to the tent. I was just sorta curious, like, y'know?

Not all Aborigines and Maoris use the sort of English imitated by Merritt, and many have acquired standard varieties through the schools. But standard English is not necessarily recognized as a prestige variety within the Aboriginal community, and it is sometimes called *flash language* with pejorative overtones. While children and teenagers may be expected and even encouraged to learn the standard, they will also be expected to use a nonstandard variety in the home and related social situations, and they will "talk flash" only in non-Aboriginal settings.

Although its practice may be uncertain and its understanding less than precise, in principle the whole community in both New Zealand and Australia holds that standard English is the only form of the language which is acceptable in serious or formal situations: education, government, and commerce. Its witting displacement in writing would only be condoned if it served some artistic purpose—to amuse, parody, ridicule, or reveal. There is no dispute about this, and those who consider their mastery of the standard imperfect still maintain its importance.

At a more abstract level when Australian English per se is considered, however, there are conflicting opinions within the community. Even in the early days of the settlement, the quality of Australian English seems to have been a matter of debate. Visitors and officials frequently commented on it. To Dixon (1822, p. 46), a visitor to both New South Wales and Tasmania, it was "purer, more harmonious, than is generally the case in most parts of England," but to Cunningham (1827, vol. 2, p. 60) it was corrupt.

As time passed Australians themselves came to express opinions about their language. The accent in particular has been condemned by many members of the general public. Typical of this outlook is the following extract from a letter to a Sunday newspaper:

> It is safe to say that however it [the Australian accent] came about, no greater millstone was tied around the neck of any nation.
> The Australian accent at its worst brands every one of us whether we speak it or not, as uncouth, ignorant and a race of second-class people. [*Sydney Sun-Herald*, 3 February 1974, p. 78]

Much of this popular condemnation reflects, no doubt, a characteristically colonial false sense of inferiority, an outlook which regards the mother country as the source and center of culture, the preserver of refinement. There may be a touch of snobbery, a pretense that one has more taste than one's countrymen, or a servile acceptance of the brash judgments of British visitors for fear of appearing uncultured. Despite the strengthening awareness of national independence, especially since the 1940s, it is interesting to see that unfavorable remarks are still being made and seem to be as common as ever.

The situation has been confused by the invention of *strine* in the mid sixties (Lauder 1965). *Strine* is in essence a party game, a brain teaser, depending for its success on the inadequacies of normal English orthography to represent sounds in combination: *ebb tide* 'hunger, desire for food', as in "I jess dono watser matter,

Norm, I jess got no ebb tide these dyes" (Lauder 1965, p. 16). It amounts to a caricature of the assimilations and sometimes excessive elisions which occur in rapid, informal speech in all countries. It purportedly arose from an experience of a visiting British novelist, who, while autographing copies of her novel in a city department store, misinterpreted an Australian's query "Emma Chisett" (the strine representation) as her name, rather than as a version of *how much is it?* The item *strine* itself is supposed to indicate the way many say *Australian*.

A proportion of the general public have taken the parody seriously and have come to believe that *strine* is a true representation of how Australians speak most of the time. The publication of examples of strine served only to confirm them in their belief that Australians are slovenly in articulation. Although the active invention of strine items and jokes has ceased, the term has been kept alive by journalists as a way of referring to the distinctive quality of English in Australia. In current use it is rather vague in sense and imprecise in application but most frequently carries an implication of disapproval.

At the level of lexis, however, one is more likely to find the reverse attitude. Here there is almost a jingoistic pride in the capacity of Australians who are lauded as extraordinary linguistic innovators. Highly influential was Sidney Baker, who in the first edition of *The Australian Language* gave strong voice to the *inventiveness* of Australians and wrote of their "linguistic revolution."[6] But Baker was not alone in this thinking, and others have either echoed or independently propounded similar views. Gunn (1970, p. 54) writes of the "Australian love of the truncated term" (e.g., the reduction of *fiddley did* to *fiddley* or even *fid*) and the "love of the familiar diminutives" (e.g., *wharfie* 'wharf laborer' and *garbo* 'garbage man'). Many in the population hold that Australians are particularly creative in the realm of rhyming slang, such as *Joe Blake* (= *snake*), *trouble and strife* (= *wife*), *Uncle Willie* (= *silly*), and *butcher's hook* (= *crook*, i.e., *sick* or *bad*). Perhaps there is a kind of inverted snobbery operating in this glorifying of slang and less respectful expressions.

This view of lexis, like the one which condemns the accent as ugly, is more sentimental and emotional than rational. It simply asserts but never produces concrete evidence to establish that Australians are more inventive than English speakers in other countries; and its claimants are naively ignorant of the English language elsewhere, frequently boasting of items which actually originated (as some of the examples above testify) in the United Kingdom or North America.

The sad fact about these unenlightened discreditors and enthusiasts is that they have served to distract the community from a proper assessment of the contribution that English speakers in Australasia have made to world English. The emphasis has fallen too much on the informal aspect of the language, on glorying in such expressions as *come the raw prawn*, *full as a goog*, *fit as a Mallee bull*, *stone the crows*, and *this side of the black stump*. Too little attention has been given to meaning extension, although this process adds at least as much to creating a distinctive form of language. The result has been a lack of concerted support for a serious investigation of English in the region, and efforts at balanced descriptions of Australian English have been largely individual and extremely spasmodic.

For all the expansions and changes that have been described, by far the largest proportion of Australian and New Zealand English would be uniform with British English. There may have been additions, deletions, and modifications, but by far the strongest force has been retention. Nowhere is this more clearly seen than in grammatical structure, where the changes have been minuscule. Moreover, most of the growth at the levels of lexis and grammar that has taken place in the English language in Great Britain since 1788 has also been transported to Australia and New Zealand. It is not that, once parted from their homeland, the speakers in these two countries pursued a completely separate linguistic development. Instead there has been a constant interplay and exchange. The stages in semantic extension through which *module*, for example, has passed in recent years in Britain and the United States have been duplicated in New Zealand and Australia.

That there has been this preservation and continuity of so much has a natural explanation: culture, occupations, and life-styles are essentially British and European. Australians and New Zealanders have never attempted to adopt the life-styles of the Aborigines or the Maoris, but simply recreated as much as they could the traditions and ways of life of their homeland. For decades, and until recently, textbooks used in schools were mainly produced in Great Britain and tended to perpetuate the British tradition. On the other hand, the exchange has not always been one way, and words and meanings devised in the Southern Hemisphere have passed into the speech of those in the north. Obvious examples are the borrowings from the Aboriginal and Maori languages, such as *wallaby*, *boomerang*, and *kiwi*, but there are internal claimants as well, such as *finalize* and *ropeable*. British items—for example, *larrikin* and *barrack*—have occasionally been refurbished in the south and returned home again in a revitalized form.

The English language in Australia and New Zealand, then, is very similar to the English in other major English-speaking countries, but it is not the same. We may definitely recognize Australian English and New Zealand English as separate entities, but still very much part of the family—forms of English making their own special contribution to world English.

NOTES

1. *Cockatoos* are lookouts posted to warn of the arrival of the police at *schools* or sites where *two-up*, a gambling game involving betting on the outcome of spinning pairs of coins, is played. A *shivoo* (cf. Anglo-English *shindy*) was formerly a more riotous event; *chiacking* involves teasing or, sometimes, ridicule.
2. Hawkins (1973, pp. 4–5) argues that "the evidence strongly suggests that [ɪ] and [ə] should be merged as a single phoneme" and observes that this development comes close to amounting to a systemic difference between RP and New Zealand English. Australians recognize New Zealanders by this feature especially.

3. Early descriptions had used the label *educated*, but this was abandoned because it was open to misinterpretation, suggesting to some that the accent was the prerogative and the mark of the educated.
4. For example, Sharwood (1965) showed that there was little Italian influence on the phonology of local Australian English beyond the first generation, even in the long-established settlements in Innisfail and Ingham.
5. The name *settler's clock* arose because the kookaburra welcomes first light with its piercing laugh and so served to wake the settler to his daily labor.
6. To be fair to Baker, he tempered his remarks somewhat in the second edition.

REFERENCES

Baker, Sidney J. *The Australian Language*. Sydney: Angus and Robertson, 1945. 2d ed. Sydney: Currawong Press, 1966.
Bernard, J. R. L. *Some Measurements of Some Sounds of Australian English*. Ph.D. dissertation, University of Sydney, 1967.
Cunningham, Peter Miller. *Two Years in New South Wales*. 2 vols. London: Henry Colburn, 1827.
Delbridge, Arthur. "The Recent Study of Spoken Australian English." In *English Transported*, edited by W. S. Ramson, pp. 15–31. Canberra: Australian National University Press, 1970.
Dixon, John. *Narrative of a Voyage to New South Wales and Van Diemen's Land*. Edinburgh: John Anderson, 1822.
Eagleson, Robert D. "The Evidence for Social Dialects in Australian English." In *Australia Talks: Essays on the Sociology of Australian Immigrant and Aboriginal Languages*, edited by Michael Clyne, pp. 7–27. Canberra: Australian National University Press, 1976.
Eagleson, Robert D., and McKie, Ian. "The Terminology of Australian National Football." *Australian Language Research Centre Occasional Papers*, 12(1968):1–24; 13(1968):1–27; 14(1969):1–26.
Gunn, J. S. "Twentieth-Century Australian Idiom." In *English Transported*, edited by W. S. Ramson, pp. 49–68. Canberra: Australian National University Press, 1970.
Hawkins, P. "The Sound Patterns of New Zealand English." In *AULLA Proceedings 15*, edited by Keith I. D. Maslin, pp. 13.1–13.8. Sydney: Australasian Universities Language and Literature Association, 1973.
Lauder, Afferbeck [pseud.]. *Let Stalk Strine*. Sydney: Ure Smith, 1965.
McAuley, James. *A Map of Australian Verse*. Melbourne: Oxford University Press, 1975.
Merritt, Robert J. *The Cake Man*. Sydney: Currency Press, 1978.
Mitchell, A. G., and Delbridge, Arthur. *The Speech of Australian Adolescents*. Sydney: Angus and Robertson, 1965.
Sharpe, Margaret C., and Sandefur, John. "The Creole Language of the Katherine and Roper River Areas, Northern Territory." In *Australia Talks: Essays on the Sociology of Australian Immigrant and Aboriginal Languages*, edited by Michael Clyne, pp. 63–77. Canberra: Australian National University Press, 1976.

Sharwood, J. *Spoken English in the Two Areas of Italian Settlement in North Queensland.* Master's thesis, University of Queensland, 1965.

———. *A Study of Terms Employed in the Dried Fruits Industry of Victoria.* Ph.D. dissertation, University of Melbourne, 1974.

Stivens, Dallas. *Jimmy Brockett: Portrait of a Notable Australian.* Sydney: Angus and Robertson, 1959.

Turner, G. W. *The English Language in Australia and New Zealand.* 2d ed. London: Longman, 1972.

Wakefield, Edward Gibbon. *A Letter from Sydney.* London: Everyman's Library, 1929.

Tok Pisin in Papua New Guinea

Peter Mühlhäusler

The southwestern Pacific is an area of great linguistic diversity. Seven hundred languages are said to be spoken in Papua New Guinea alone, and Laycock (1969) estimates that more than a quarter of the world's languages are spoken in this area. Some of these linguistic systems have come into being during the last 150 years, and in this area perhaps the largest number of varieties of Pidgin English were and are spoken. The main consequence of these various offsprings of English has been to reduce the number of linguistic barriers and to allow people from various backgrounds to enter into communication and thus build new societies.

One can distinguish three main types of pidgin according to the social functions they have fulfilled in the various parts of the southwestern Pacific: jargons used in short-term communication between Europeans and South Sea Islanders; pidgins that sprang up in various plantation areas; and pidgins transported from plantations to the main recruiting areas (nativized pidgins). Such a division can at best be only an abstract ideal since in reality much more complex configurations of forces shaped the individual varieties. The distinction between jargon plantation pidgin and nativized pidgin is not just social but is also reflected in a number of linguistic characteristics of these languages. Thus, one can conceive of a scale of both stability and complexity ranging from unstable impoverished jargons to fully fledged expanded pidgins. While jargons constitute individual attempts at communication across linguistic boundaries (e.g., by means of baby talk or ad hoc simplifications), true pidgins are socially sanctioned linguistic systems.[1]

The diverse character of the individual languages labeled English-based pidgins has led to the failure of attempts to determine their number and to draw clear boundaries among them, particularly for the less stable jargons, which exhibit a great deal of fluctuation. Observers such as London (1909) and Churchill (1911) subsume all such varieties under the label *Beach-La-Mar*. Jargonized varieties of English have been reported from numerous parts of the southwest Pacific including Micronesia (Hall 1945), the Gilbert and Ellice Islands (David 1899), and New Zealand (Baker 1941, pp. 71–92) as well as such other areas as Samoa, the New Hebrides, and New Guinea, where the jargonized varieties were later supplanted by a true pidgin. Churchill speaks of "sporadic foci of evolution of some mongrel dialects, each narrowly restricted in essential conditions to one or at most two white men, and the few communities of islanders with which they were in intimate contact" (1911, p. 8). While at this stage we only have an incomplete

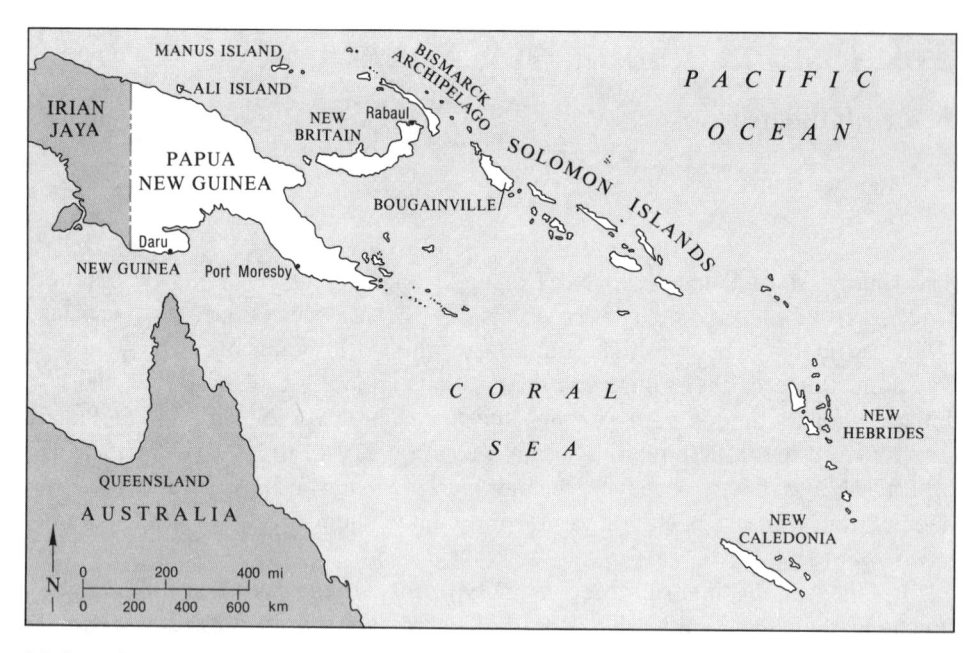

Melanesia

documentation of jargonized English, work currently being carried out by Clark promises to lead to important insights (see Clark 1977).

The pidgins that emerged in a number of plantation centers were not much better documented until recently. Schuchardt (1881 and 1889) provided some information on Samoan and New Caledonian Pidgin English, but little work was done until my recent study dealing with Samoa (Mühlhäusler 1976*b* and 1978) and Hollyman's work on New Caledonia (1976). Both Hollyman's and my own work involved scrutinizing a large body of literature—in particular, documents written in German and French which had been neglected by earlier observers. Dutton and I have begun similar work on Queensland "Kanaka Pidgin," the remnant of the former Queensland Plantation Pidgin.[2]

While both the early jargons and the various plantation pidgins have almost disappeared, three nativized pidgins—pidgins carried home by the plantation workers—survive: Bichelamar in the New Hebrides; Solomon Islands Pidgin or Neo-Solomonic; and Tok Pisin of Papua New Guinea. All three have undergone considerable structural and functional expansion since they were first brought to these respective areas. Of all the English-based pidgins and creoles of the southwestern Pacific, Tok Pisin is the variety that is both linguistically most developed and socially most firmly institutionalized. According to census figures from 1971, it is the dominant lingua franca in Papua New Guinea. The other two official languages, English and Hiri Motu, are much less widely used, as the following figures show:

Home Language	Males	Females
English	23,381	12,267
Pidgin	67,366	24,627
Motu	1,496	631
Other	728,045	731,780

Languages Spoken	Males	Females
English	24,266	25,429
Pidgin	287,633	162,118
Motu	33,512	21,488
English/Pidgin	131,035	63,331
English/Motu	18,420	14,241
Pidgin/Motu	13,172	2,793
English/Pidgin/Motu	37,913	9,114

Tok Pisin has been known by a number of names in the past, among them New Guinea Pidgin, Neomelanesian, and Tok Boi. Its present name, Tok Pisin (literally, *talk pidgin*), reflects the linguistic independence of its speakers. Unlike some pidgin languages, Tok Pisin cannot be regarded as a relic from a colonial past. This article will outline the developments that have led to the linguistic and social independence of Tok Pisin.

Although Tok Pisin is little more than a hundred years old, much of its early history has remained a matter of guesswork until very recently. Theories about its origin included the contention that the language was invented by the Germans in order to keep the natives in their place, that it was brought to New Guinea by Chinese plantation laborers, that it is a continuation of Queensland Plantation Pidgin English, and that it originated from a spontaneous development triggered by certain situational stimuli. Recently, I have demonstrated that probably the single most important factor accounting for the development of a Pidgin English in New Guinea is the fact that thousands of indigenes were sent to the German plantations in Samoa between 1879 and 1913, where they acquired an already stabilized form of Pidgin English (Mühlhäusler 1976b).

Other influences, of course, were operational at various stages in the life of Tok Pisin, including influences from Chinese Pidgin English, as Wu recently demonstrated (1977, pp. 1047–56). It is impossible to reconstruct all factors operative in the development of Pidgin English in the southwestern Pacific; however, the interrelations between the numerous varieties spoken in the 1880s can be represented, tentatively, in figure 1.

The Origin and Development of Tok Pisin

In discussing the internal and external history of Tok Pisin we are dealing with a special kind of linguistic system—a complex configuration of lects ranging from

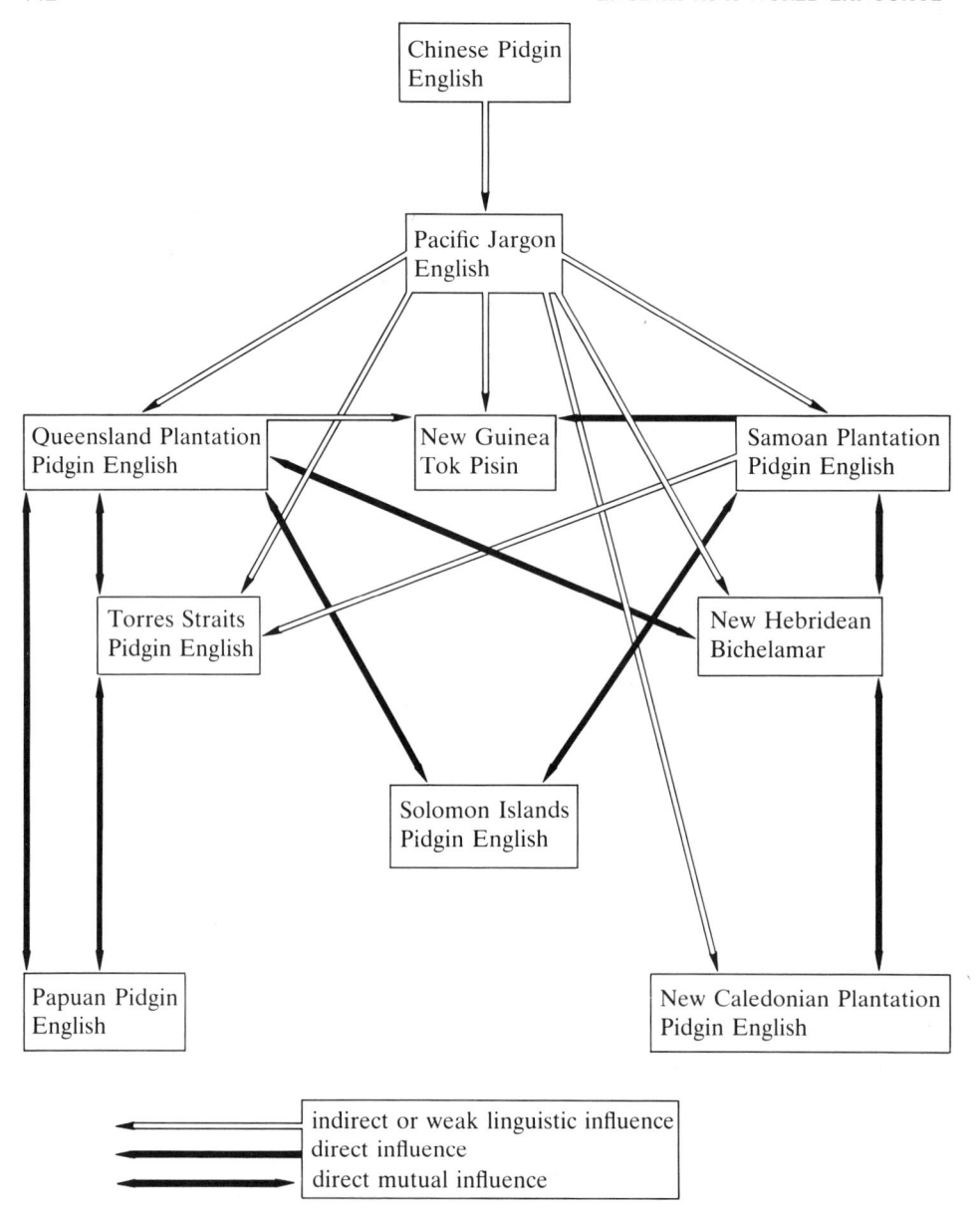

Fig. 1. Interrelations among varieties of Pidgin English spoken in the 1880s

unstable pidgin to fully fledged creole varieties. I use the terms *pidgin* and *creole* in the following senses. A pidgin is a contact language used among people who have no other language in common. It is a second language for those who use it, and its use is restricted to a limited number of situational contexts such as trading, plantation life, or military operations. Since a pidgin is used in a small number of contexts, its lexicon is smaller and its grammar less complex than languages with native speakers. Grammar and lexicon are derived from many sources, including the superimposed (superstratum, often a European) language, local (substratum) languages, and universal grammar. A creole develops if parents from different linguistic backgrounds use a pidgin to communicate at home and if their children grow up speaking this pidgin as their first language. If this happens in many households of a community, the nativized pidgin can become the language of the community. This process is known as creolization. A creolized pidgin, or creole, is structurally more complex than a pidgin, as it has to meet all the communicative requirements of native speakers. The structural complexity of a creole is comparable to that of any other natural language. These definitions may suggest that pidgins and creoles are somehow static systems and are therefore in need of repair. In reality, pidgins are continually changing and expanding. Their dynamic character will now be discussed with reference to the life cycle of Tok Pisin.

The life cycle hypothesis was first proposed by Hall (1962, pp. 151–56). More recent studies usually distinguish five qualitatively and quantitatively different stages in the development of a pidgin language. These stages closely correspond to the stages found in child language acquisition and second-language acquisition. For this reason all three phenomena are sometimes grouped together as developmental continua. The factors in the development of a pidgin include:

1. Jargon phase: language contact, imperfect learning on the part of the subordinate group, use of "foreigner talk" by superordinate group, various communication strategies
2. Stabilization phase: universal simplification tendencies, substratum influence, selective reduction of variation
3. Expansion phase: internal development, i.e., expansion from language-internal resources, some borrowing
4. Creolization phase: universals of language development, some borrowing
5. Postpidgin/postcreole phase: contact of stable pidgin or creole with its original main lexifier language, heavy borrowing and mixing

In less than 100 years Tok Pisin has completed the entire life cycle for some of its speakers, although other speakers still use varieties representative of earlier stages (i.e., its entire history is still synchronically present). Before discussing this fascinating aspect of the language, I will discuss the social and linguistic developments accompanying each stage.

The Jargon Phase

Contact between Europeans and South Sea Islanders led to the development of a large number of unstable jargons in many parts of the Pacific. While jargonized varieties of English were found in a number of areas of New Guinea and the Bismarck Archipelago that had been visited by European traders and adventurers before 1880, their importance for the later development of Tok Pisin is rather restricted. The fact that a fully functioning and stabilized pidgin was imported from Samoa may have led to a quick absorption of the local jargons by the more developed Samoan Plantation Pidgin.

A jargon is characterized by its instability, its impoverished structure, and its heavy dependence on the nonlinguistic context for disambiguation. The following conversation between a labor recruiter and a Buka tribesman illustrates a number of jargon features.

> "Me like boys" sagt der Weisse zu den Schwarzen, "plenty kai kai (Essen)," "no fight (keine Prügel)?" fragen die Schwarzen; "yes, plenty kai kai and no fight" antwortet der Weisse. "What you pay me?" fragt nun der Besitzer eines Sklaven oder der Häuptling. "One fellow anikow (ein Beil)," erwidert der Anwerber. [Reported by Ribbe 1903, p. 223]

The following linguistic features are present in this conversation:

1. The presence of the plural -s in the speech of the recruiter;
2. Incomplete sentences;
3. The lexical item *anikow*, illustrating heavier borrowing from local languages at the beginning of the life cycle;
4. The question *what you pay me?* The preferred word order in Tok Pisin is *yu peim mi wanem*, with the *wh*-pronoun appearing question-finally.

Many features of the various jargonized varieties of English are no longer found in later stages of Tok Pisin. However, similar ad hoc simplification and borrowing can still be encountered in areas where Tok Pisin has only recently been introduced.

The Stabilization Phase

Stabilization of a pidgin language is the result of the development of socially accepted language norms. Such norms develop when none of the languages in contact serves as a target language. Whinnom (1971, pp. 91–115) suggests that stable pidgins are not likely ever to have arisen out of a simple bilingual situation. Instead, they owe their stability to the fact that a jargon (secondary hybrid) is used as a medium of intercommunication by people who are not speakers of the original lexifier language. For Tok Pisin this means that the first stabilization occurred among the ethnically and linguistically diverse plantation workers on the Samoan plantations of the Deutsche Plantagen- und Handelsgesellschaft, and subsequently on the plantations belonging to various German firms in the Bismarck Archipelago and the New Guinea mainland.

An important factor for the continued stability of Tok Pisin over a period of several decades was that from 1884 to 1914 northeastern New Guinea and the Bismarck Archipelago were under German control. This meant that the language of the socially superior group was not identical with Tok Pisin's main lexifier language—English—and most Germans regarded it as a language in its own right that had to be learned as a foreign language. In the same situation, native speakers of English would have been much more likely to resort to ad hoc simplifications of their own language, as a comparison with Solomon Islands Pidgin English (Young 1976) and Papuan Pidgin English (Mühlhäusler 1979a) will show, for instance, in the pronoun system:

	Papuan Pidgin English (1920)	Tok Pisin (1920)
Singular		
First person	ai, mi	mi
Second person	yu	yu
Third person	hi, him, em	em
Plural		
First person inc.	yumi, wi	yumi
First person exc.	wi	mipela
Second person	yu, yu all	yupela
Third person	oltugeta, dei	em ol

The development of linguistic norms was further helped because the economic and the administrative center of the colony were both located in the Gazelle Peninsula of New Britain after 1899. Thus, the Rabaul variety of Tok Pisin, a variety influenced by Tolai and related languages, became the prestige variety. Influence from the local languages of the Gazelle Peninsula area is still felt in many areas of Tok Pisin's vocabulary, particularly those that are related to local customs, fauna, and flora. Loanwords from Tolai in present-day Tok Pisin include *mal* (< *mal*) 'bark loin covering'; *tultul* (< *tultul*) 'messenger, assistant village chief'; *muli* (< *muli*) 'citrus fruit'; *umben* (< *ubene*) 'fishing net'; *muruk* (< *murup*) 'cassowary'.

The German presence provided stimuli not only for the stabilization but also for the linguistic growth and geographic expansion of the language. In 1880 Tok Pisin was restricted to recruiting, trading, and plantation contexts, but by 1914 it was used in many new domains—for instance, in the police force, in domestic contexts, in the developing shipbuilding industry, and in the courts. Attempts to replace Tok Pisin with simplified German failed (cf. Mühlhäusler 1975 and 1977); however, German influence was strongly felt in the vocabulary associated with these domains, as the following examples show. At one time, 250 out of a total of about 1,000 lexical bases were of German origin, though this is an example of adlexification rather than relexification: Tok Pisin *sutman* (< *Schutzmann*) 'policeman'; *hauman* (< *Hauptmann*) 'captain'; *hebsen* (< *Erbsen*) 'peas'; *sarang* (< *Schrank*) 'cupboard'; *sparen* (< *Sparren*) 'rafter'; *git* (< *Kitt*) 'caulking'; *strafe* (< *Strafe*) 'punishment'. The following passage illustrates stabilized

Tok Pisin. The speaker is Fritz from Ali Island, West Sepik Province, about seventy-five years of age when the recording was made in 1973.

> Na bruder em tu i stap wantaim. Mi stap long kuk tu, mi stap long tisa tu, orait, mi bosim ol boi tu, givim kaikai. Na pater oltaim i stap long helpim skul tu, i wokabaut go Suain kam bek Ulau. Sapos i go Yakamul i go, mi, mi holim ki, olgeta ki bilong rum bilong pater mi holim. Pater i laik go we, em i go, olgeta pater laik i go we, ol i go i kam bek, mi givim bek ki, ki bilong rum. Haus bilong pater i gat tupela rum, wanpela rum spaisesima, wanpela rum bilong slip.

> [And a religious Brother also stayed there at the same time. I stayed there as cook, I also stayed there as teacher, well, I supervised the indigenous workers, I gave them food. And the priest always helped with the school, he walked to Suain and returned to Ulau. If he went away to Yakamul, I had the keys, I held all the keys for the priest's rooms. If the priest wanted to go somewhere, he went and if all the priests wanted to go, they then came back, I returned the keys, the keys to the rooms. The priest's house had two rooms, one room was the dining room, one room was the bedroom.]

A number of linguistic features distinguish this text from the previous one.

1. Optional plural marking by means of *ol* (from *all*) as in *ol boi* 'indigenous workers'
2. Complete sentences but few subordinate sentences; instead, juxtaposition is used, sometimes reinforced by discourse-structuring elements such as *orait* 'well'
3. Adjectives and transitive verbs marked by the suffixes *-pela* and *-im* respectively
4. Some German items such as *bruder* 'religious Brother' and *pater* 'priest' in the stable core lexicon. *Spaisesima* 'dining room', on the other hand, is an ad hoc loan.
5. Relatively stable syntax with little variation in word order

The Expansion Phase

The development of Tok Pisin from a stable but simple pidgin in the 1910s into the complex language of the 1960s and 1970s illustrates the principle that expansion of the social functions of a language results in its structural expansion. It appears that this expansion occurred, by and large, without any significant amount of creolization.

The first stimulus for the expansion of Tok Pisin was the gradual "pacification" of New Guinea. In its wake, intercommunication across tribal boundaries became important, first on the government stations but subsequently in the pacified areas as a whole. Tok Pisin became nativized; that is, its primary function shifted from vertical communication between colonizers and colonized to horizontal intertribal communication. This development is characterized as follows by Mead:

> But perhaps the greatest change is that he [i.e., the European] has given to Melanesia, the most disorganized and linguistically diverse district in the world, a new culture. The small hatreds of one valley for another are being obscured under the more exacting conditions which require that all natives shall deal with the white man. Under the stimulus of white contact, thousand-year differences have been forgotten, and the richly different idioms which the local dialects have developed, are now being poured back into a common speech." [1931, p. 191]

A second important stimulus for the expansion of Tok Pisin was the decision by a growing number of missionary groups to use Tok Pisin as a mission lingua franca. The first official policy favoring the use of Tok Pisin was that of the Catholic missions in the mid-1920s, while the Lutheran missions only adopted the language in the 1960s. The result of these mission policies was that the domain of nontraditional religion became firmly associated with Tok Pisin, culminating in the publication of the *Nupela Testamen* 'New Testament' in 1969. Mission involvement with Tok Pisin at the same time resulted in a fair amount of standardization and vocabulary planning.

The Second World War and the years immediately thereafter brought a third stimulus. During the war, large-scale propaganda campaigns in Tok Pisin were carried out by both the Japanese and the Allied forces. Millions of leaflets were dropped over the country, and Tok Pisin was used in radio broadcasts for the first time. The war also created the need for scientific descriptions of the language on which language teaching programs could be based. Hall's comprehensive structuralist description of Tok Pisin (1943) was written for just that purpose. The following extract is from a pamphlet dropped on Bougainville toward the end of the war in New Guinea. Note the names for modern war machinery:

> Mipela givim dispela tok long yu.
> Soldia bilog yumi i kisim pinis Wiwiak nau ol soldia bilog Japan i ronwei long bik bus. Balus bilog yumi pondaun long ples balus bilong Maprik. Long Bik Buka soldia bilog yumi i winim Japan long bik rot bilog Buin nau oldei oldei planti bam bilong yumi i kilim Japan olsem tang nau bikpela masket.

> [We bring you the news.
> Our forces have captured Wewak and are driving the Japanese back into the country beyond. Our planes now land on Maprik airstrip.

In Bougainville the Japanese are being driven back along the Buin Road and every day more and more are killed by our bombs and tanks and heavy artillery.]

The years following World War II brought two important new developments: first, the opening up of the New Guinea Highlands and the spread of Tok Pisin into this most populated part of New Guinea; and, second, the gradual breaking down of social barriers between expatriates and indigenes. The status of Tok Pisin was changed from that of a low-caste language to one promoting equality and democratization of the society. Tok Pisin emerged as the language of local government. A number of Tok Pisin newspapers aimed at spreading democratic ideas also began to appear after 1945. In addition, Tok Pisin was taught in a number of government and mission schools.

Official support for Tok Pisin was withdrawn after 1954, but unofficially its spread into new functions and domains could not be stopped. In the wake of self-government and independence in the 1970s, its expansion was accelerated. Tok Pisin became the main language of debate in Parliament; it was used more and more by the news media; its use in primary education was permitted again; and creative writing in Tok Pisin became an important part of the cultural life of independent Papua New Guinea. The increased use of the language is illustrated by the percentages of transactions carried out in Tok Pisin by the House of Assembly (quoted from Noel 1975, p. 78): 1964–68 legislature, 40 percent; 1968–72 legislature, 60 percent; 1972–73 legislature, 95 percent. The rapid growth of the urban populations and accompanying culture change have also had a tremendous impact on the development of Tok Pisin: "As might be expected, urban centres have promoted the most complex growth. The city dweller who is forced to enact different roles, and to modulate different identities, is also forced into a more enterprising use of language" (Brash 1975, p. 322).

To sum up, the following general tendencies can be observed during Tok Pisin's expansion:

1. Beginning with a mere communicative function, Tok Pisin gradually began to be used for integrative and expressive purposes. It became the symbol of a new culture and its speakers began using it to express their inner feelings and desires. Without being a native language, it became the principal language for many of its speakers.
2. Tok Pisin was used in an ever-increasing number of domains, such as religion, economy, agriculture, education, aviation, modern warfare, and parliamentary transactions.
3. Tok Pisin began to be used in the media, including radio broadcasting, pamphlets, newspapers, books, and, more recently, films and theater plays.
4. Tok Pisin today no longer is supplementary to the traditional vernacu-

lars but is beginning to take over their functions, thus leading to the functional and structural decline of vernaculars in some areas.
5. Although Tok Pisin is a second language for most of its speakers, this fact has not slowed down its expansion, since it is far more useful than either English or the local vernaculars.

The expansion of Tok Pisin is manifested in a dramatic increase in structural complexity. An examination of the newly developed structures suggests that developments have sprung from internal resources rather than from borrowing, as has been shown for a number of syntactic constructions by Sankoff (e.g., 1975) and for the word-formation component by Mühlhäusler (1976a). The most outstanding structural innovations are as follows:

1. Derivational depth has developed—mainly through embedding.
2. Grammatical categories such as tense and number have become compulsory (Sankoff and Laberge 1973 and Mühlhäusler 1976c).
3. The language has acquired a word-formation component which enables speakers to create new names for new things. (For an exhaustive account of this development, see Mühlhäusler 1976a.)
4. The language developed mechanisms for structuring discourse, such as focusing devices, pro-forms, and a complex set of deictic markers.
5. Stylistic differentiation developed.

While these developments are of great importance for a general theory of language change, it is impossible to discuss details in this article. Instead, some of the complexities of present-day expanded Tok Pisin will be illustrated with the following text from Bom, formerly Stephansort, a village that began to use Tok Pisin around 1900. The speaker is about thirty years of age:

Tumbuna ol i *bin* toktok *olsem* olgeta pis bilong solwara ol i go antap long ples na ol i singsing na *taim* ol i singsing pinis ol i go bek long solwara. Orait, ol i stap, na taim ol *manmeri* ronewe pinis ol i go antap long singsing.

[The ancestors told us that all the fish of the sea would come ashore and dance and when they had finished dancing they would go back into the sea. Well, they stayed, and after all the people had gone they would come ashore and dance.]

The items italicized in the text are of special interest:

1. *bin*: 'past tense'. In recent years tense has become a widespread feature of Tok Pisin, in addition to the long-established category of aspect.

Tense is one of the few innovations that can be ascribed to direct borrowing from English.
2. *olsem*: This adverb, meaning 'thus', is used as a complementizer. In other varieties the preposition *long* 'on, in, along' is found in the same function. Signaling of embedded sentences is the result of internal development.
3. *taim*: The noun 'time' is used as the conjunction 'when', allowing the embedding of time clauses.
4. *manmeri*: The Tok Pisin expression for 'people' illustrates the additive type of compound. Other compounds corresponding to this pattern are *papamama* 'parents', *susoks* 'footwear', *naiptamiok* 'cutting instruments', and many others. Apart from this very basic type of compounding, other types are also found.

No treatment of Tok Pisin's structural expansion can be complete without a mention of the stylistic diversification that has occurred in recent years, particularly in the urban context. The three most important registers are secret Tok Pisin (generally known as *tok bokis*), the taboo register, and language play (generally known as *tok pilai*). The latter register involves the liberal use of metaphors, often in an ad hoc way and over long stretches of speech.

The following example was recorded by Mühlhäusler on the campus of the University of Papua New Guinea. The tok pilai is triggered by a woman wearing a T-shirt with the letters PDF and her remark *mi bagarap* 'I'm buggered'. In the ensuing conversation, one of the male students (M1) attempts to build up a tok pilai around the workshop motif and another (M3) attempts to do the same with the medicine/hospital motif. Eventually the workshop motif takes over (M1, M2, M3 = male students, F = female student):

M1: Dispela meri i toktok, lukim em i lap.
M2: Pi Di Ef, Pi Di Ef!
F: A, mi bagarap.
M1: A, dispela kain bai fiksim long woksap.
M2: Bagarap long wanem ya?
M3: Ating marasin i stap.
M1: Gutpela long wokim long woksap.
M2: PDF woksap i gutpela.
M1: PDF woksap ya, man!
M2: Ol i fiksim gut.
M1: Ol i laik grisim gut.
M2: Ol i save holim gut.
M3: Wanem?
M1: Samting ya.

[*M1:* This girl that is talking, see how she is laughing.
M2: PDF, PDF!
F: I'm buggered.
M1: This sort of thing can be fixed in the workshop.
M2: How come buggered?
M3: Perhaps there is a medicine for it.
M1: It's OK to do it in the workshop.
M2: The PDF workshop is fine.
M1: The PDF workshop, yeah man!
M2: They fix it properly.
M1: They can grease it up well.
M2: They can get a grip on it.
M3: What?
M1: You know what.]

The Creolization Phase

As noted earlier, a creole is a pidgin that has become the native language of a speech community. Because creolization can take place at any stage in the life cycle of a pidgin language, different types of creolization have to be distinguished. One type occurs when an unstable jargon is adopted as a first language, as, for instance, in the plantation context in the West Indies, where large immigrant groups were forced to form new societies. Because there were no dominant indigenous languages on these plantations, the jargon had to become the first language of the second generation. This kind of creolization involves considerable restructuring and repairing on the part of the first-generation creole speakers. Another type of creolization occurs after stabilization and expansion. In this case the transition from second to first language is gradual, involving bilingualism and gradual rather than sudden replacement of local vernaculars.

Because of the contract labor system (as opposed to the slave labor system in the West Indies), the social context for the first type of creolization has always been rather restricted in the southwest Pacific. There are examples of intermarriages between New Guineans from various areas on the Samoan plantations, and children grew up in Samoa speaking as their first language a pidgin closely related to Tok Pisin. When I interviewed two of these creole speakers they had virtually forgotten the language, and they used English and Samoan as their principal means of communication. The main reason for such a language shift is the limited usefulness of Samoan Plantation Pidgin in Samoan society. No viable creole can develop in a social vacuum, no matter how natural or ingenious the linguistic innovations of first-language speakers. The types of creolization found in Tok Pisin are thus not representative of the whole phenomenon of creolization. Nevertheless, the study of gradual creolization can also tell us a great deal about universals of language development.

In Papua New Guinea, creolization of Tok Pisin is found in a number of social settings, the most important ones being creolization in urban areas, creolization in nontraditional rural settlements, and creolization in traditional villages.

In the towns of Papua New Guinea intertribal marriages are common and, according to the latest available statistics, there are tens of thousands of households where Tok Pisin is spoken as the principal language. Creolization in the urban context is rather rapid. However, the English-language school system also constitutes a major influence, and the norms of Tok Pisin in the towns are still influenced by the very large number of second-language Tok Pisin speakers.

After World War II, population movement from the interior to the coast and the introduction of new cash crops such as the oil palm resulted in the establishment of nontraditional settlements where Papua New Guineans of different origins would form a new community. One such community is Hoskins on New Britain; another is Malabang on Manus Island. When I studied Malabang Tok Pisin in 1974, the second generation of native speakers was growing up. As contacts with the ouside world are frequent, the linguistic developments are regulated and checked by the fact that communication with second-language Tok Pisin speakers remains one of the principal functions of the language. Thus, only young children were found to be significantly ahead in their language development; adults actively discourage children from using forms which they consider too progressive.

Creolization in traditional villages is often paired with the gradual disappearance of the traditional vernaculars, since the latter are felt to be useful in fewer and fewer functions and domains. As new technologies find their way to the villages and as communication with the outside world becomes more important, many vernaculars with few speakers experience structural and functional decline. The more useful Tok Pisin becomes, the earlier it is learned; the age of learning is a true continuum, and the distinction between first- and second-language learning is becoming blurred.

The structural consequences of creolization of Tok Pisin are less dramatic than in the case of creolization of an unstable jargon. Both Sankoff's and my own findings indicate that, instead of radical restructuring, the trends already present in expanded Tok Pisin are carried further in its creolized varieties:

1. The grammatical categories of tense, aspect, and number are becoming obligatory and redundant.
2. Reduction in unstressed syllables is becoming more common, resulting in increased stylistic potential.
3. Multiple embedding in syntax and cyclic application of word-formation rules is increasingly common.
4. Existing rules of word formation are exploited more fully.
5. Rules catering to the nonreferential functions of Tok Pisin (e.g., discourse structure rules, rules providing stylistic synonyms, etc.) are becoming common.

The following text represents Tok Pisin as spoken in the nontraditional rural settlement of Malabang. Its speaker is a first-generation native speaker of Tok Pisin:

> Tupela kilim pik na mipela karim i kam na i hevi tru, biiiikpela tru, orait, em mipela i karim i kam long bris. Na tupela ya na mipela i wokim wanrot, mipela wokim wanpela rot. Tupela i no laikim mipela long go tambulo na tupela i brukim long bris na i bruk, tupela bris i bruk, tupela i brukbruk, orait, na tupela i pundaun long wara, na tupela ya i go hait pinis hait pinis, na mipela painim mekim.
> Tupela winim tru, tupela ya winwinim wara na tupela kam antap.

[These two killed the pig and we (exclusive) carried it and it was very heavy, really huge, well, this one we carried toward the bridge. And these two and us were walking along the same path, we were walking along one path. The two did not want us to go down and the two broke a bridge so that it was broken, two bridges were broken, two were broken, well, and the two dived into the water, and the two hid, they were hidden, and we were busy looking for them.
The two conquered it, these two really conquered the river and the two appeared again.]

The grammatical complexity of the above passage can be seen in the following constructions:

1. *em mipela i karim* 'it we carried' illustrates change in basic word order for focalizing.
2. *wanrot/wanpela rot* 'same road' illustrates variable deletion of adjective suffix *-pela* for stylistic purposes.
3. Reduplication of the verb or repetition of verb phrase with dual subjects appears, as in *tupela i brukbruk, tupela i go hait pinis hait pinis*. (This type of concord has been observed many times in Malabang Tok Pisin.)
4. *laikim mipela long* 'wanted that we' illustrates the use of the preposition *long* as complementizer, a development also found in noncreolized varieties of Tok Pisin.

The Postpidgin/(Postcreole) Phase

When a pidgin or creole language comes into renewed contact with its original lexifier language after a period of independent development, the resulting language mixture tends to develop either relatively unstable new linguistic systems or a linguistic continuum intermediate between the pidgin or creole and its lexifier language. Such a continuum is found between Guyanese Creole and

Guyanese English (see Bickerton 1975*a*). The principal reason for a renewal of linguistic contact between a pidgin and its lexifier language is the changeover from a hierarchically structured colonial society to a socially mobile postcolonial society. While in the 1920s and 1930s Papua New Guineans had little access to English (in fact, they were often actively discouraged from learning English), the social changes after World War II provided contacts with a basic form of English to an ever-growing number of indigenes. At the same time, better jobs requiring a knowledge of English were made available to those Papua New Guineans who were able to fill them. In addition, English was regarded as the key to power and prosperity by many Papua New Guineans and thus enjoyed considerable prestige. In the recent past, there appears to have occurred a reassessment of the role of English, and Tok Pisin has regained much of its lost prestige.

There is still a sizable population of speakers who are Tok Pisin–English bilinguals. While in most rural areas the functional range of English tends to be restricted to the school context, in the urban areas English may occupy a considerable range of functions in private and public life, very often overlapping with Tok Pisin. It is in this context of urban bilingualism that language mixing occurs. No continuum intermediate between Tok Pisin and English has yet developed, but some experts forecast that one will soon emerge (e.g., Bickerton 1975*b*). Because the development of the postpidgin Tok Pisin is restricted to a certain social group, it is more commonly referred to as the sociolect of Urban Pidgin.

The structure of Urban Tok Pisin is largely the result of contact with the type of English that is spoken in Papua New Guinea. However, it would be an oversimplification to assume that borrowing from English will make Tok Pisin more like English. It is true that one of the tacit assumptions in many studies of postpidgin or postcreole continua has been that the eventual outcome of contact between an English-derived pidgin and English is English. Yet it is not obvious why the mixing of two linguistic systems should lead to the replacement of one system by another.

My own data suggest that the result of renewed contact between a pidgin or creole and its original lexifier language is a new third system. Thus, in spite of heavy borrowing, postpidgin Tok Pisin, or Urban Pidgin, does not appear to be more readily intelligible to a speaker of English than the standard rural form of Tok Pisin. At the same time, speakers of the standard rural form will find Urban Pidgin hard to follow. The following text illustrates postpidgin Tok Pisin; it is an extract from a spontaneous conversation recorded on the campus of the University of Papua New Guinea.

"Daru olsem wanem?"
"O, wanpela gutpela ples, liklik taun."
"Em nau, yumi kamap long Daru, nau, em nau, samting ya i stap."

"Mi ting Nambai i save lukautim yu."
"Man, Daru nau, yu ken tok, samting i stap."
"Nau dispela taim mi kam nupela ya, na mi no nap raun, na bikos mi laik traiim long painim ples bilong slip ya, bat laki, taim mi laik kam mi tokim brata bilong mi na em go toksave long brata long stesen ya na ring i kam long faders long hap hia long bukim sit bilong mi na ol i save olsem bai mi kam. So when I came, mi kam stret pundaun long epot, mi go lukim, I pay half the price, suppose to be fifty na mi peim twentifaiv. I brought fifty Kina just to pay for that plane bat ol i hapim prais na ol i given twentifaiv na mi lus with twentifaiv, o nau shit, mi amamas pinis."

["Why Daru?" (name of town and island)
"Oh, its a good place, a little town."
"That's right, we arrived in Daru, right, there were lots of attractive women."
"I was under the impression that Nambai was looking after you."
"Man, Daru at that time, you have to admit, there really were women."
"When I first arrived, I wasn't able to stroll around, because I wanted to try to find a place to sleep, but luckily, when I first thought of going there, I mentioned it to one of the (religious) brothers and he informed a brother on this station and he rang up the fathers over there to book a seat for me and so they knew that I was coming. So, when I went, I had just got off at the airport, I went to see them, I paid half price, it was supposed to be fifty and I paid twenty-five. I brought fifty Kina just to pay for that plane, but they halved the price and they returned twenty-five and there I was with twenty-five, oh shit, I was really happy."]

The above passage illustrates a number of characteristics of anglicized Tok Pisin, as well as code switching between English and Tok Pisin. That code switching can be pinpointed is an indication that one is not dealing with a postpidgin continuum. Note the following characteristics:

1. The use of *samting* 'something' for *women* (which illustrates the *tok bokis* 'hidden or secret register')
2. Use of borrowed subordinating conjunctions *bikos*, *when*, and the coordinating conjunction *bat*
3. Use of English plural -s in *faders*
4. A large proportion of recently borrowed lexical items, including *epot* 'airport' for *ples balus*, *brata* for *bruder* 'religious brother' and *bukim sit* 'to book a seat'. (In traditional Tok Pisin *sit* means 'leftovers, ashes, feces'.)
5. Use of English counting system rather than the traditional Melanesian one, that is, the use of *twentifaiv* instead of *tupela ten faiv*

Tok Pisin in Present-day Papua New Guinea

As the development of Tok Pisin did not proceed at the same pace in all areas and began at different times in different areas, almost the entire life cycle of this language is still found in present-day Papua New Guinea. The unstable jargon is found in remote areas and occasionally among expatriates, while stable and expanded Tok Pisin is found in the majority of rural communities. Here the length of contact with government and missions and the functions in which Tok Pisin is put to use determine its degree of sophistication. Anglicized Tok Pisin is found in the urban centers and among Papua New Guineans in nontraditional professions. Creolized Tok Pisin is found in both rural and urban settings.

Speakers of Tok Pisin are well aware of the ever-increasing social diversification of the language. In their folk classification one finds the names *Tok Pisin bilong bus* 'Bush Pidgin', *Tok Masta* 'Europeans' Pidgin', *Tok Pisin bilong ples* 'Rural Pidgin', and *Tok Pisin bilong taun* 'Urban Pidgin'. With regard to these four main sociolects the following generalizations can be made:

1. Bush Pidgin and Tok Masta are relatively marginal varieties, dependent on disappearing social contexts.
2. There is relatively low mutual intelligibility between the sociolects.
3. Because of increased social mobility, the gap between Rural and Urban Pidgin is widening.

Because Bush, Rural, and Urban Pidgin are identical in the developmental phases of jargon, stabilized or extended, and postpidgin Tok Pisin, no more needs to be said about their linguistic structure.

Tok Masta

Tok Masta represents the European side of the jargon stage. Functionally, it is restricted to the giving of orders and instructions, mainly in the domestic context. Its most outstanding structural property is instability, stemming from the assumption by its speakers that Tok Pisin is just a garbled and simplified type of English. In the colonial past of Papua New Guinea, friction between expatriates and indigenes was often triggered by the former using Tok Masta. Some of its characteristics can be seen from the following sentence from a radio talk show on the BBC (15 May 1970):

'Im fellow Matthew e got im three fellow egg.

[Matthew has three eggs.]

Even in this single sentence of alleged Tok Pisin, a number of typical European misconceptions can be pointed out: It is not the case, as claimed by many European writers, that each noun is preceded by *fellow*. Instead *-pela* (from *fellow*) is used as a suffix with monosyllabic adjectives; *em* (from *him*) serves as a third person singular pronoun and as an emphasizer when preceding nouns. *Im* (from *him*) marks transitivity and causativity with verbs. It is not sufficient to sprinkle a sentence liberally with *im*'s. The first *im* in the above text is ungrammatical as it is not followed by a noun; the second one is also ungrammatical because *gat* is one of the lexically marked verbs that do not take *im*; many words of Tok Pisin, particularly those referring to aspects of flora and fauna, are not of English origin. The word for egg in Tok Pisin is *kiau* (from Tolai). Thus, in ordinary Rural Pidgin the above sentence would read, "Matthew i gat tripela kiau."

Bell has observed that "a rough and hopeful guess is that one in fifty [expatriates] can understand Pidgin as spoken by the indigenes to each other" (1971, p. 38). Today the picture is changing, as a good mastery of Tok Pisin is a necessity for expatriates who want to get on in Papua New Guinea. Tok Pisin teaching facilities are available in both Papua New Guinea and Australia (see Dutton 1977), and there is also a growing collection of teaching materials. Tok Masta thus no longer poses a communication problem.

Present-day Communication Difficulties

The main function of Tok Pisin is to provide a means of intercommunication in a linguistically diversified country. In the past, the enormous pressure for communication helped to consolidate a relatively stable and uniform language in most parts of the country (the exception being Papua because of its different early history). This uniform Rural Pidgin has come to serve as a basis for standardized Tok Pisin as used in the New Testament translations and the newspaper *Wantok*. Some language planning in the areas of the lexicon and orthography provided additional stability to the core rural dialects. Finally, the stability of the language in the past was the result of rigid social structures in the colonial era, when all indigenes constituted a single and powerless class vis-à-vis the German and Australian colonizers. Thus, Tok Pisin was both born in and kept going by the colonial system.

The development of Tok Pisin after World War II illustrates the principle that languages tend to lag behind social and technical innovations in times of revolutionary changes. Thus, sudden access to English, the change to political and social equality, and the influx of new technologies and modes of life in the Papua New Guinea of the 1960s and 1970s created a situation with which the language could no longer cope. In the absence of planned language enrichment, heavy borrowing from English was resorted to, as illustrated by the political vocabulary introduced in the House of Assembly in 1968: *eleksen* 'election', *komisin* 'commission', *mosin* 'motion', *privilij* 'privilege', *spika* 'speaker'. The following discussion will show that some of this new vocabulary cannot be integrated into existing Tok Pisin grammar.

To make things worse, new expressions were introduced in an ad hoc way in different parts of the country or in different institutions. This lack of coordination has resulted in a very large number of synonyms and homophones in Urban Pidgin. Traditional rural Papua New Guineans tend to confuse new expressions with existing ones, particularly in cases such as *slek komiti* 'select committee'—which is often interpreted as *slek* 'slack, inefficient' and *komiti* 'second in the village hierarchy'—and *investim* 'to invest' which gets confused with *westim* 'to waste, squander'. It could be argued that misunderstanding arising out of new concepts and new names for them are an unavoidable transitional phenomenon in any culture change. However, borrowing of English grammar and lexicon is not restricted to additions, but often results in replacement and restructuring of already-established Tok Pisin terms. As a result, misunderstandings between rural and urban Papua New Guineans can arise even in simple conversations. For example, answers to negative questions in Rural and Urban Pidgin produce confusion. The function of *yes* in Rural Pidgin is to confirm that what was asked in a yes/no question is the case, whether the question is negative or not. *Nogat* 'no' refers to the opposite cases. The reinterpretation of *yes* and *nogat* in the light of English semantics, however, has led to a situation in which there is utter confusion about the meaning of answers to negative questions, as illustrated by the accompanying table.

Tok Pisin	Interpretation in Rural Pidgin	Interpretation in Urban Pidgin
Yu no kam asde? Yes.	Didn't you come yesterday? No, I didn't.	Didn't you come yesterday? Yes, I did.
Masta i no stap? Nogat.	Isn't your employer at home? Yes, he is.	Isn't your employer at home? No, he isn't.

More detailed studies about the implications of the development of a new urban sociolect have led to a general agreement that the developing language problem can only be solved by changes in Government language policy and by language planning.[3] Otherwise, the consequences will be those described in the following letter to *Wantok* of 3 May 1972:

Sapos yumi mekim dispela pasin nogut, bai bihain tok pisin bilong bus na tok pisin bilong taun tupela i kamap narakain tru. Olsem bai tok pisin i bruk nabaut nogut. Nogut yumi hambak nabaut na bagarapim tok ples bilong yumi olsem.

[If we indulge in this bad habit (i.e., mixing Tok Pisin and English) then Rural and Urban Pidgin will become quite different languages. Thus, Tok Pisin will really become fragmented. Let's not mess about and thus ruin our common language.]

Language Planning and the Future of Tok Pisin

Following Wurm (e.g., 1975), we can distinguish between external and internal language planning—the former being policies and official practices, the latter language engineering in the narrower sense. Language engineering can be further subdivided into graphization (provision of standard spelling), standardization (establishment of a superimposed standard variety), and modernization (adapting the language to meet the requirements of a modern society). As the problems of spelling systems and standardization are not specifically Papua New Guinean problems and have furthermore been dealt with in considerable detail by a number of writers (see the references in Wurm, Mühlhäusler, and Laycock 1977), the remainder of this section will deal with modernization only. Modernization has been characterized by Rosario as "the fitting of a language to recent or present times and conditions, which are characterized by the dominance of science and technology in all areas of human activity" (1968, p. 4).

It would be wrong to look at language modernization as merely a linguistic problem, since the aim is to fit a language to a changing society and not a society to a changing language. It would be equally wrong to equate modernization with westernization. In fact, many developments in postindependence Papua New Guinea proceed along entirely nonwestern lines.

From a structural point of view, languages are regarded as being modern for two reasons: first, because of their ability to meet the referential requirements of a modern society; and second, because of their internal consistency. Planning a political vocabulary for Tok Pisin involves both considerations.

When Tok Pisin was first used as a parliamentary language in the late 1960s, it was hopelessly inadequate from the referential point of view. When I visited the Parliament in 1976, most referential inadequacies had been repaired, but at a cost. Most new expressions were loans from English and thus hard to understand for the occasional visitors to the House and for the voters back in the villages. The following list of expressions were noted in the Parliament and subsequently discussed with a group of students of the University of Papua New Guinea on the occasion of a Tok Pisin workshop in September 1976: *konstitusen* 'constitution', *praim minista* 'prime minister', *amenmen* 'amendment', *ekspendisa* 'expenditure', *disait* 'to decide', *responsibel* 'responsible', *pis* 'peace', and *invesmen* 'investment'.

The participants in the workshop noted that all of these terms either run counter to the grammar of Tok Pisin or are infelicitous for other reasons. Some of the objections were:

> 1. The principle that no phonological word should consist of more than three syllables is violated by *konstitusen*, *ekspendisa*, and *responsibel*. New word bases such as *invesmen*, they said, are "bad" because no derivational affixes can be added.

2. Abstract nouns are typically derived from verbs in Tok Pisin, but this principle is violated by *amenmen* and *invesmen*.
3. Homophones are dysfunctional. *Pis* can already mean 'piece', 'fish', and 'piss'; the possible confusion of *westim* 'waste' and *investim* 'invest' has been mentioned earlier.
4. Semantically complex concepts are typically expressed by means of compounds in Tok Pisin. This principle is violated by *konstitusen* and *disait*.
5. Suppletive forms are uneconomical. Next to *praim minista* one finds *sif minista* 'chief minister', *asbisop* 'archbishop', and *nambawan kiap* 'chief patrol officer'.

In view of these deficiencies a number of proposals were made. Some of them are similar to proposals arising out of an earlier workshop held by Lynch (1975). Special attention was paid to the internal word-formation potential of the language. These proposals include:

1. *Konstitusen* should be replaced by *aslo* 'fundamental law'. The prefix *as-* 'foundation, origin' (from English *arse*) is used in many other expressions, including *asples* 'home village', *astingting* 'basic idea', and *asbuk* 'basic reference book'.
2. *Praim minista* should be replaced by *nambawan minista*. This expression would conform to similar ones such as *nambawan dokta* 'head doctor', *nambawan gavman* 'administrator', and *nambawan luluai* 'paramount chief'.
3. *Amenmen* expresses a verbal concept and should therefore be encoded as a verb base. The basic idea is already expressed in Tok Pisin *stretim* 'to straighten, correct'. The verbal compounds *tokstretim* and *wokstretim* would express the idea of 'to make a verbal amendment' and 'to improve by physical labor' respectively. Note that these proposals would also render superfluous the recent loans *impruvmen* 'improvement' and *koreksen* 'correction'.
4. *Ekspendisa* also expresses a verbal concept. Again, the existing verb *spenim* 'to spend' and the possibility of deriving the reduplicated form *spenspenim* 'to spend money in a number of areas' makes borrowing superfluous.
5. *Disait* in Tok Pisin as in English has two meanings: first, that someone is making decisions for others; and second, that a decision is arrived at jointly. Only the latter meaning is appropriate in the context of a democratic parliament. Because one is dealing with a complex concept, a verbal phrase was suggested: *bungim ting* 'to bring together thoughts, to be in the process of making a decision'. As the concept of completion is typically signaled by the completion marker *pinis*, 'to have arrived at a decision' would be *bungim ting pinis*.

6. *Responsible* expresses a nominal concept. As its semantic structure is complex, it is best rendered by a compound noun such as *asman* 'originator man'. This word is already documented for some varieties of Tok Pisin.
7. It was argued that *peace* is a simple and basic concept and should therefore be represented by a simple stem. The word *sana* was suggested, as this is the word for 'peace' in Prime Minister Somare's home language and the title of his biography which is widely read in Papua New Guinea.
8. *Invesmen* is a verbal concept. The existing verbal phrase *putim mani* 'to put money' was suggested as a good alternative.

The adoption of such proposals as these would mean that Tok Pisin could meet all referential requirements of parliamentary transaction. At the same time, parliamentary and political language would become more transparent to the average Papua New Guinea villager and thus enable a larger part of the population to get involved in national politics. The transparency of the planned forms is a result of the fact that they conform to the patterns of word formation already established in expanded Rural Pidgin (cf. Mühlhäusler 1976a). Thus, language planning is seen as a predictive process; that is, once Tok Pisin is seen as a dynamic and developing system, future natural developments can be predicted with fair accuracy. In contrast to borrowing, the character of the language remains intact.

It is not entirely clear at this stage to what degree the government will support language planning for Tok Pisin.[4] The establishment of a bureau for translation, together with the fact that the first Papua New Guineans are at present receiving training in language planning, indicate that this question will receive more attention in the near future.

The key to Tok Pisin's future appears to lie in sensible planning of its development so a smooth transition can be made from a functionally restricted language to one that can meet all the requirements of a modern independent nation. Unlike most developing countries, Papua New Guinea has a firmly established and widely spoken lingua franca, and it would be a pity if the potential of this means of communication were not fully used in developing the country.

As I was writing this article, the following piece of news reached me:

Shortly before he met the Japanese Prime Minister, Mr. Fukuda, a few days ago, Mr. Somare surprised Japanese officials by requesting a three-way interpretation. When the talks got underway Mr. Somare, whose English is excellent, spoke in pidgin. The secretary for Foreign Relations, Mr. Tony Siaguru, translated the pidgin into English and this in turn was translated for Mr. Fukuda by the Japanese Interpreter. A Papua New Guinea official said later Mr. Somare believed he should use pidgin because he could express his thoughts better. [*Papua New Guinea Post Courier*, Port Moresby, 14 December 1977]

It appears that Tok Pisin will continue to be a strong emotional link between Papua New Guineans of different social, regional, and ethnic backgrounds.

APPENDIX: *Tok Pisin, Solomon Islands Pidgin, and Bichelamar*

The following translations of Mark 5:1–5 represent a rather formal register of the respective languages, and none of them are entirely free from European influence. A comparison of rapid conversations would reveal even more far-reaching differences at all levels of grammar.

English

So they came to the other side of the lake, into the country of the Gerasenes. As he stepped ashore, a man possessed by an unclean spirit came up to him from among the tombs where he had his dwelling. He could no longer be controlled; even chains were useless; he had often been fettered and chained up, but he had snapped his chains and broken the fetters. No one was strong enough to master him. And so, unceasingly, he would cry aloud among the tombs and on the hill-sides and cut himself with stones. [The New English Bible, Oxford and Cambridge University Presses, 1961]

Tok Pisin

Ol i kamap long hapsait bilong raunwara, long graun bilong ol Gerasa. Em i lusim bot pinis, na kwiktaim wanpela man i gat spirit doti i stap long en, em i kam painim Jisas. Dispela man i stap nabaut long ples matmat na i kam. Em i save slip long ples matmat. Na i no gat wanpela man inap long pasim em. Sen tu i no inap. Planti taim ol i bin pasim em long hankap na sen. Tasol em i save brukim sen na hankap tu. Em i strongpela tumas, na i no gat man inap long holim pas em. Oltaim long san na long nait em i stap long matmat na long maunten. Na em i save singaut nogut na katim skin bilong em yet long ston. [*Tok Pisin Nupela Testamen*, Canberra and Port Moresby: The British and Foreign Bible Society, 1969]

Solomon Islands Pidgin English

Bihaen olketa i go long narasaet long big wata Galili. Desfala haf ia olketa i go soa long hem, i haf bulong olketa pipol long Gerasa. Steretwe taem Jisas i go soa, wanfala man wea i stap long berigiraon i kamaot fo mitim hem. Desfala man ia devol nogud i stap long hem. Ples bulong hem nao long berigiraon. Bikos hem i karangge tumas, no man i save taemapim. Plande taem olketa i hankapem han an lek bulong hem, bat hem i smasing olgeta nomoa. No man i storong fitim fo holem. De an naet hem i no save stap kwait. Hem i waka long go olabaot long melewan berigiraon an olketa hil. Hem i waka tu long singaot karangge an katem bodi bulong hem wetem ston. [From an unpublished translation by T. Faifu under the auspices of the Roman Catholic, Anglican, and United and South Seas Evangelical Church]

New Hebrides Bichelamar

Nao olgeta oli kam kasem narasaid long bigfala lugun ia, oli gosoa long ples bilong man Gerasa. Jisas i gosoa. Nao i gat wan man i kamaot long berigraon i kam bilong lukem em. Man ia i gat devel i stap long em, nao i stap mekem ples bilong em long berigraon. I no moa gat man nao i save fasem em. Olgeta oli fasem em long jen, oli no save mekem. Plante taem oli fasem em long jen mo hankaf, be jen, man ia i pulum i brok, hankaf tu em i brekem em. I no gat sam man oli strong i naf bilong mekem man ia i kwaet. Oltaem, long nait mo long de, em i stap long berigraon mo antap long hil. Em i stap singaot nogud, i stap tekem ston i katem bode bilong em long em. [Camden 1972]

A brief lexical comparison illustrates the heavy reliance of Solomon Pidgin and Bichelamar on borrowing from English. Tok Pisin, on the other hand, has a much more developed word formation component and borrows more heavily from local vernaculars. There are considerable differences in idiomatic usage. It takes a speaker of Solomon Pidgin or Bislama about three months to master Tok Pisin.

English	Tok Pisin	Solomon Islands Pidgin English	Bichelamar
lake	raunwara	big wata	lugun
unclean spirit	spirit doti	devol nogud	devel
cemetery	(ples) matmat	berigiraon	berigiraon
strong enough to master him	inap long holim pasem	storong fitim fo holem	save fasem
to cry	singaut nogut	singaot karangge	singaot nogud
body	skin	bodi	bode
but	tasol	bat	be

NOTES

1. For more details, see Mühlhäusler 1976a, pp. 18–27.
2. For preliminary results, see Mühlhäusler 1979b.

3. See Franklin 1975; Mühlhäusler, 1976a; Wurm 1978; and Wurm, Mühlhäusler, and Laycock 1977.
4. For a detailed discussion, see Mühlhäusler, Wurm, and Dutton 1979.

REFERENCES

Baker, Sidney J. *New Zealand Slang*. Christchurch: Whitecomb and Tombs, 1941.
Bell, H. L. "Language and the Army in Papua New Guinea." *Australian Army Journal* 264 (1971):31–42.
Bickerton, Derek. *Dynamics of a Creole System*. Cambridge: At the University Press, 1975a.
———. "Can English and Pidgin Be Kept Apart?" In *Tok Pisin i go we?*, edited by K. A. McElhanon, pp. 21–27. *Kivung* Special publication, no. 1. Port Moresby: Linguistic Society of Papua New Guinea, 1975b.
Brash, Elton. "Tok Pisin." *Meanjin Quarterly* 34, no. 3 (1975):320–27.
Camden, William, trans. *Gud Nyus Bilong Jisas Krais* (Translation of the New Testament into New Hebrides Bichelamar). Auckland: Bible Society in New Zealand, 1972.
Churchill, William. *Beach-La-Mar: The Jargon or Trade Speech of the Western Pacific*. Washington D.C.: Carnegie Institution of Washington, 1911.
Clark, Ross. *In Search of Beach-La-Mar*. Working Papers in Anthropology, Archeology, Linguistics, Maori Studies. Auckland: University of Auckland, 1977.
David, Caroline M. Edgeworth. *Funafuti; or, Three Months on a Remote Coral Island*. London: John Murray, 1899.
Dutton, Tom E. "The Teaching of New Guinea Pidgin to Europeans." In *New Guinea Area Languages and Language Study*, edited by Stephen A. Wurm, vol. 3, pp. 733–48. 3 vols. Pacific Linguistics, ser. C, no. 40. Canberra: Australian National University, 1977.
Franklin, Karl J. "Vernaculars as Bridges to Cross-cultural Understanding." In *Tok Pisin i go we?*, edited by K. A. McElhanon, pp. 138–49. *Kivung,* Special publication, no. 1. Port Moresby: Linguistic Society of Papua New Guinea, 1975.
Hall, Robert A. *Melanesian Pidgin English: Grammar, Texts, Vocabulary*. Baltimore: Linguistic Society of America, 1943.
———. "English Loan-Words in Micronesian Languages." *Language* 21 (1945):214–19.
———. "The Life-Cycle of Pidgin Languages." *Lingua* 11 (1962):151–56.
Hollyman, K. J. "Les Pidgins Européens de la Région Calédonienne." MS. Auckland, 1976.
Laycock, Donald C. "Melanesia has a Quarter of the World's Languages." *Pacific Islands Monthly* 40, no. 9 (September 1969):71–76.
London, Jack. "Beche-de-Mer English." *Contemporary Review* 96 (1909):359–64.
Lynch, John. *Pidgins and Tok Pisin*. Occasional Paper, no. 1. Port Moresby: University of Papua New Guinea, Department of Language, 1975.
Mead, Margaret. "Talk Boy." *Asia* 31 (1931):141–51, 191.
Mühlhäusler, Peter. "The Influence of the German Administration on New Guinea Pidgin." *Journal of Pacific History* 10, no. 4 (1975):94–111.

———. "Growth and Structure of the Lexicon of New Guinea Pidgin." Ph.D. dissertation, Australian National University, 1976a.

———. "Samoan Plantation Pidgin English and the Origin of New Guinea Pidgin: An Introduction." *Journal of Pacific History* 11 (1976b):122–25.

———. "The Category of Number in New Guinea Pidgin." *Linguistic Communications* 13 (1976c):21–37.

———. "Bemerkungen zum 'Pidgin Deutsch' von Neuguinea." In *Deutsch im Kontakt mit anderen Sprachen*, edited by Carol Molony, Helmut Zobl, and Wilfried Stölting, pp. 71–82. Kronberg: Scriptor Verlag, 1977.

———. "Samoan Plantation Pidgin English and the Origin of New Guinea Pidgin." In *Papers in Pidgin and Creole Linguistics*, vol. 1, pp. 67–119. 3 vols. Pacific Linguistics, ser. A, no. 54. Canberra: Australian National University, 1978.

———. "Papuan Pidgin English Rediscovered." In *Proceedings of the Second International Conference on Austronesian Linguistics,* edited by Stephen A. Wurm and Lois Carrington, vol. 2, pp. 1377–1446, 2 vols. Pacific Linguistics, ser. C, no. 61. Canberra: Australian National University, 1979a.

———. "Remarks on the Pidgin and Creole Situation in Australia." *Newsletter* (Australian Institute of Aboriginal Studies), September 1979b, pp. 44–53.

Mühlhäusler, Peter; Wurm, Stephen A.; and Dutton, Tom E. "Language Planning and New Guinea Pidgin." In *New Guinea and Neighboring Areas: A Sociolinguistic Laboratory,* edited by Stephen A. Wurm, pp. 263–76. The Hague: Mouton, 1979.

Noel, John. "Legitimacy of Pidgin in the Development of Papua New Guinea toward Nationhood." In *Tok Pisin i go we?*, edited by K. A. McElhanon, pp. 76–84. *Kivung,* Special publication, no. 1. Port Moresby: Linguistic Society of Papua New Guinea, 1975.

Ribbe, Carl. *Zwei Jahre unter den Kannibalen der Salomoninseln*. Dresden-Blasewitz: H. Beyer, 1903.

Rosario, G. del. "A Modernization-Standardization Plan for the Austronesian-derived Languages of South East Asia." *Asian Studies* 6 (1968):1–18.

Sankoff, Gillian. "Sampela nupela lo i kamap long Tok Pisin." In *Tok Pisin i go we?*, edited by K. A. McElhanon, pp. 235–40. *Kivung,* Special publication, no. 1. Port Moresby: Linguistic Society of Papua New Guinea, 1975.

Sankoff, Gillian, and Laberge, Suzanne. "On the Acquisition of Native Speakers by a Language." *Kivung* 6, no. 1 (1973):32–47.

Schuchardt, Hugo. "Beiträge zur Kenntnis des englischen Kreolisch: II, Melaneso-Englisches." *Englische Studien* 13 (1889):158–62.

———. "Kreolische Studien V: Über das Melaneso-Englische," pp. 151–61. Sitzungsberichte 105. Vienna: Akademie der Wissenschaften, 1881.

Whinnom, Keith. "Linguistic Hybridization and the Special Case of Pidgins and Creoles." *Pidginization and Creolization of Languages,* edited by Dell Hymes, pp. 91–116. Cambridge: At the University Press, 1971.

Wu, D. Y. H. "Intrusive Languages Other Than English: Chinese." *New Guinea Area Languages and Language Study,* edited by Stephen A. Wurm, vol. 3, pp. 1047–56. 3 vols. Pacific Linguistics, ser. C, no. 40. Canberra: Australian National University, 1977.

Wurm, Stephen A. "The Question of Language Standardisation and Pidgin." In *Tok Pisin i go we?*, edited by K. A. McElhanon, pp. 108–17. *Kivung,* Special publication, no. 1. Port Moresby: Linguistic Society of Papua New Guinea, 1975.

———. "Descriptive and Prescriptive Grammar in New Guinea Pidgin." In *Papers in Pidgin and Creole Linguistics,* vol. 1, pp. 175–85. 3 vols. Pacific Linguistics, ser. A, no. 54. Canberra: Australian National University, 1978.

Wurm, Stephen A., ed. *New Guinea Area Languages and Language Study*, vol. 3. 3 vols. Pacific Linguistics, ser. C, no. 40. Canberra: Australian National University, 1977.

Wurm, Stephen A.; Mühlhäusler, Peter; and Laycock, D. C. "Language Planning and Engineering in Papua New Guinea." *New Guinea Area Languages and Language Study*, edited by Stephen A. Wurm, vol. 3, pp. 1151–78. 3 vols. Pacific Linguistics, ser. C, no. 40. Canberra: Australian National University, 1977.

Young, Hugh. "A Directory of Solomon Pidgin Idioms." Mimeographed. Honiara, 1976.

Suggested Readings

Bibliographies

Aggarwal, Narindar K. *English in South Asia: A Bibliographical Survey of Resources*. New Delhi: Indian Documentation Service, 1982.

Allen, Harold B. *Linguistics and English Linguistics*. 2d ed. Arlington Heights, Ill.: AHM Publishing, 1977.

Avis, Walter S., and Kinloch, A. M. *Writings on Canadian English, 1792–1975: An Annotated Bibliography*. Toronto: Fitzhenry and Whiteside, 1978.

Blair, David. "An Australian English Bibliography." *Macquarie University Speech and Language Research Centre Working Papers* 2, no. 1 (1978):1–46.

Brasch, Ila Wales, and Brasch, Walter Milton. *A Comprehensive Annotated Bibliography of American Black English*. Baton Rouge: Louisiana State University Press, 1974.

Görlach, Manfred. "A Selective Bibliography of *English as a World Language 1965–1979*." *Arbeiten aus Anglistik und Amerikanistik* 4, no. 2 (1979):231–68.

McMillan, James B. *Annotated Bibliography of Southern American English*. Coral Gables, Fla.: University of Miami Press, 1971.

Preliminary Bibliography of American English Dialects, A. Washington, D.C.: Center for Applied Linguistics, 1969.

Reinecke, John E., and DeCamp, David. *A Bibliography of Pidgin and Creole Languages*. Honolulu: University Press of Hawaii, 1975.

Viereck, Wolfgang. "A Bibliography of English as Used in England, Wales, Scotland and Ireland." *English World-Wide* 2, no. 2 (1981):181–224.

Dictionaries

Several important dictionary projects are in various stages of planning, but no portions have been published of the following to date.

Concise Scots Dictionary, The, edited by A. J. Aitken and M. Robinson.
Dictionary of American Regional English [DARE], edited by Frederic G. Cassidy.
Dictionary of Australian English on Historical Principles, edited by Robert D. Eagleson.
Dictionary of Briticisms, edited by Allen Walker Read.
Dictionary of Caribbean English Usage, edited by S. R. R. Allsopp.
Dictionary of Newfoundland English, edited by G. M. Story.
Dictionary of South African English on Historical Principles, edited by William Branford.
Dictionary of West African English, edited by Ayo Banjo and Peter Young.

Many dictionaries appear in national editions in which local lexis and usage is integrated, often without or with insufficient marking; others append the local English lexicon in an appendix. Such dictionaries are not included here.

Avis, Walter S. *A Dictionary of Canadianisms on Historical Principles*. Toronto: Gage, 1967.
Beeton, D. R., and Dorner, Helen. *A Dictionary of English Usage in Southern Africa*. Cape Town: Oxford University Press, 1975.
Branford, Jean. *A Dictionary of South African English*. Cape Town: Oxford University Press, 1978. 2d ed. Cape Town: Oxford University Press, 1980.
Camden, William G. *A Descriptive Dictionary, Bislama to English*. Vila, New Hebrides: W. G. Camden for Maropa Bookshop, 1977.
Cassidy, F. G., and Le Page, Robert B. *Dictionary of Jamaican English*. 2d ed. Cambridge: At the University Press, 1980.
Craigie, W. A., and Aitken, A. J. *A Dictionary of the Older Scottish Tongue*. Chicago: University of Chicago Press, 1937– .
Craigie, William A., and Hulbert, James P. *A Dictionary of American English on Historical Principles*. Chicago: University of Chicago Press, 1940.
Fyle, Clifford H., and Jones, Eldred D. *A Krio-English Dictionary*. Oxford and New York: Oxford University Press, 1980.
Graham, John J. *The Shetland Dictionary*. Stornoway, Lewis: Thule, 1979.
Graham, William. *The Scots Word Book: English-Scots/Scots-English Vocabularies*. Edinburgh: Ramsey Head, 1977. 2d ed. Edinburgh: Ramsey Head, 1978.
Grant, William, and Murison, David D. *The Scottish National Dictionary*. 10 vols. Edinburgh: Scottish National Dictionary Association, 1931–76.
Holm, John A., and Watt Shilling, Alison. *Dictionary of Bahamian English*. Cold Spring, N.Y.: Lexik House, 1982.
Mathews, Mitford M. *A Dictionary of Americanisms on Historical Principles*. 2 vols. Chicago: University of Chicago Press, 1956.
———. *Americanisms: A Dictionary of Selected Americanisms on Historical Principles*. Chicago: University of Chicago Press, 1966.
Mihalic, Francis. *The Jacaranda Dictionary and Grammar of Melanesian Pidgin*. Milton, Queensland: Jacaranda Press, 1971.
Morris, Edward E. *Austral English: A Dictionary of Australasian Words, Phrases and Usages*. London: Macmillan and Co., 1898. Reprinted under the title *Dictionary of Austral English*. Sydney: Sydney University Press, 1972.
Nihalani, Parao; Tongue, R. K.; and Hosali, Priya. *Indian and British English: A Handbook of Usage and Pronunciation*. New Delhi: Oxford University Press, 1979.
Partridge, Eric. *A Dictionary of Slang and Unconventional English*. 5th ed. New York: Macmillan Co., 1961. Abridged. *A Dictionary of Historical Slang*. Harmondsworth: Penguin, 1972.
Sandefur, John R., and Sandefur, Joy L. *Beginnings of a Ngukurr-Bamyili Creole Dictionary*. Darwin: Summer Institute of Linguistics, 1979.
Wentworth, Howard. *American Dialect Dictionary*. New York: Crowell, 1944.
Wentworth, Howard, and Flexner, Stuart Berg. *Dictionary of American Slang*. New York: Crowell, 1960. Supp. ed. New York: Crowell, 1967.
Wilkes, Gerald A. *A Dictionary of Australian Colloquialisms*. Sydney: Sydney University Press; London: Routledge and Kegan Paul, 1978.
Wright, Joseph. *The English Dialect Dictionary*. 6 vols. London: Oxford University Press, 1898–1905. Reprint. New York: Hacker Art Books, 1963.

Suggested Readings 469

Yule, Henry, and Burnell, A. C. *Hobson-Jobson: A Glossary of Colloquial Anglo-Indian Words and Phrases*. London: J. Murray, 1886. 2d ed., edited by William Crooke. London: John Murray, 1903. Reprint. New York: Humanities Press, 1968.

Sociolinguistics and the Sociology of Language

Alatis, James E., ed. *International Dimensions of Bilingual Education*. Washington, D.C.: Georgetown University Press, 1979.
Ardener, Edwin, ed. *Social Anthropology and Language*. New York: Tavistock, 1971.
Bailey, Charles-James N., and Shuy, Roger W., eds. *New Ways of Analyzing Variation in English*. Washington, D.C.: Georgetown University Press, 1973.
Bell, Roger T. *Sociolinguistics: Goals, Approaches and Problems*. London: Batsford, 1976.
Bernstein, Basil B. *Class, Codes and Control*. 3 vols. London: Routledge and Kegan Paul, 1971–75.
Bright, William, ed. *Sociolinguistics*. The Hague: Mouton, 1968.
Brook, G. L. *Varieties of English*. London: Deutsch, 1973. 2d ed. London: Macmillan and Co., 1979.
Chambers, J. K., and Trudgill, Peter. *Dialectology*. Cambridge: At the University Press, 1980.
Crystal, David, and Davy, Derek. *Investigating English Style*. London: Longman, 1969.
Dittmar, Norbert. *Sociolinguistics*. Frankfurt: Athenäum Fischer, 1973. Translated by Peter Sand. London: Arnold, 1976.
Dubois, Betty Lou, and Crouch, Isabel, eds. *The Sociology of the Languages of American Women*. San Antonio, Texas: Trinity University, 1976.
Fasold, Ralph W., and Shuy, Roger W., eds. *Analyzing Variation in Language*. Washington, D.C.: Georgetown University Press, 1975.
Fishman, Joshua A. *Sociolinguistics: A Brief Introduction*. Rowley, Mass.: Newbury, 1970.
———. *The Sociology of Language: An Interdisciplinary Social Science Approach to Language in Society*. Rowley, Mass.: Newbury, 1972.
Fishman, Joshua A., ed. *Readings in the Sociology of Language*. The Hague: Mouton, 1968. 2d ed. The Hague: Mouton, 1970.
———. *Advances in the Sociology of Language*. 2 vols. The Hague: Mouton, 1971–72.
———. *Advances in the Study of Societal Multilingualism*. The Hague: Mouton, 1978.
Giglioli, Pier Paolo, ed. *Language and Social Context*. Harmondsworth: Penguin, 1972.
Giles, Howard, ed. *Language, Ethnicity and Intergroup Relations*. London: Academic Press, 1977.
Giles, Howard, and Powesland, Peter F. *Speech Style and Social Evaluation*. New York: Academic Press, 1975.
Giles, Howard, and St. Clair, Robert, eds. *Language and Social Psychology*. London: Blackwell, 1979.
Giles, Howard, and Saint-Jacques, Bernard, eds. *Language and Ethnic Relations*. Oxford: Pergamon Press, 1979.
Goossens, Jan. *Strukturelle Sprachgeographie: Eine Einführung in Methodik und Ergebnisse*. Heidelberg: Winter, 1969.
Greenbaum, Sidney, ed. *Acceptability in Language*. The Hague: Mouton, 1978.

Gumperz, John J., and Hymes, Dell, eds. *Directions in Sociolinguistics: The Ethnography of Communication.* New York: Holt, Rinehart and Winston, 1972.
Halliday, M. A. K. *Explorations in the Function of Language.* London: Arnold, 1973.
———. *Language as a Social Semiotic: The Social Interpretation of Language and Meaning.* London: Arnold, 1978.
Halliday, M. A. K.; McIntosh, Angus; and Strevens, Peter. *The Linguistic Sciences and Language Teaching.* London: Longman, 1964.
Hornby, Peter A., ed. *Bilingualism: Psychological, Social and Educational Implications.* New York: Academic Press, 1977.
Hudson, R. A. *Sociolinguistics.* Cambridge: At the University Press, 1980.
Kurath, Hans. *Studies in Area Linguistics.* Bloomington: Indiana University Press, 1972.
Labov, William. *Sociolinguistic Patterns.* Philadelphia: University of Pennsylvania Press, 1972.
Mazrui, Ali A. *The Political Sociology of the English Language: An African Perspective.* The Hague: Mouton, 1975.
O'Donnell, W. R., and Todd, Loreto. *Variety in Contemporary English.* London: Allen and Unwin, 1980.
Petyt, K. M. *The Study of Dialect: An Introduction to Dialectology.* London: Deutsch, 1980.
Pride, J. B. *The Social Meaning of Language.* London: Oxford University Press, 1971.
Pride, J. B., ed. *Sociolinguistic Aspects of Language Learning and Teaching.* Oxford: Oxford University Press, 1979.
Pride, J. B., and Holmes, Janet, eds. *Sociolinguistics: Selected Readings.* Harmondsworth: Penguin, 1972.
Rubin, Joan, and Shuy, Roger W., eds. *Language Planning: Current Issues and Research.* Washington, D.C.: Georgetown University Press, 1973.
Sankoff, David, ed. *Linguistic Variation: Models and Methods.* New York: Academic Press, 1978.
Scherer, Klaus R., and Giles, Howard, eds. *Social Markers in Speech.* Cambridge: At the University Press; Paris: Maison des Sciences de l'Homme, 1979.
Shores, David L., ed. *Contemporary English: Change and Variation.* Philadelphia: J. B. Lippincott, 1972.
Spolsky, Bernard, and Cooper, Robert L., eds. *Studies in Bilingual Education.* Rowley, Mass.: Newbury, 1978.
Thorne, Barrie, and Henley, Nancy, eds. *Language and Sex: Difference and Dominance.* Rowley, Mass.: Newbury House, 1975.
Trudgill, Peter. *Sociolinguistics: An Introduction.* Harmondsworth: Penguin, 1974.
———. *Sociolinguistics and Linguistic Change.* Oxford: Blackwell, forthcoming.

English as a World Language

Bailey, Richard W., and Robinson, Jay L., eds. *Varieties of Present-Day English.* New York: Macmillan Co., 1973.
English as an International Language. London: English Language Teaching Documents, 1978.
Fishman, Joshua A.; Cooper, Robert L.; and Conrad, Andrew W.; eds. *The Spread of*

English: The Sociology of English as an Additional Language. Rowley, Mass.: Newbury House, 1978.

Fishman, Joshua A.; Ferguson, Charles; and Das Gupta, Joyatirinda; eds. *Language Problems of Developing Nations*. New York: John Wiley and Sons, 1968.

Görlach, Manfred, ed. *English World-Wide: A Journal of Varieties of English*. Heidelberg: Groos, 1980– .

Kachru, Braj B., ed. *The Other Tongue: English across Cultures*. Champaign and Urbana: University of Illinois Press, 1982.

Kloss, Heinz. *Die Entwicklung neuer germanischer Kultursprachen seit 1800*. 2d ed. Düsseldorf: Schwann, 1978.

Le Page, Robert B. *The National Language Question: Linguistic Problems of Newly Independent States*. London: Oxford University Press, 1964.

Partridge, Eric, and Clark, John W. *British and American English Since 1900, With Contributions on English in Canada, South Africa, Australia, New Zealand and India*. London: Dakers, 1951.

Pride, J. B., ed. *New Englishes*. Rowley, Mass: Newbury House, 1982.

Quirk, Randolph. *The English Language and Images of Matter*. London: Oxford University Press, 1972.

Richards, Jack C., ed. *New Varieties of English: Issues and Approaches*. Singapore: Regional English Language Centre, 1979.

Sager, Juan C.; Dungworth, David; and McDonald, Peter F. *English Special Languages: Principles and Practice in Science and Technology*. Wiesbaden: Brandstetter, 1980.

Smith, Larry, ed. *English for Cross-Cultural Communication*. London: Macmillan and Co., 1981.

Wächtler, Kurt. *Geographie und Stratifikation der englischen Sprache*. Düsseldorf: Bagel; Munich: Francke, 1977.

Wells, J. C. *Accents of English*. 3 vols. Cambridge: Cambridge University Press, 1982.

Pidgin and Creole Linguistics

Bickerton, Derek. "Pidgin and Creole Studies." *Annual Review of Anthropology* 5 (1976):169–93.

Day, Richard R., ed. *Issues in English Creoles: Papers from the 1975 Hawaii Conference*. Heidelberg: J. Groos, 1980.

DeCamp, David, and Hancock, Ian F., ed., *Pidgins and Creoles: Current Trends and Prospects*. Washington, D.C.: Georgetown University Press, 1974.

Hall, Robert A., Jr. *Pidgin and Creole Languages*. Ithaca: Cornell University Press, 1966.

Hancock, Ian F., ed. *Readings in Creole Studies*. Ghent: Story-Scientia, 1979.

Hill, Kenneth C., ed. *The Genesis of Language*. Ann Arbor: Karoma, 1979.

Hymes, Dell, ed. *Pidginization and Creolization of Languages*. Cambridge: At the University Press, 1971.

Papers in Pidgin and Creole Linguistics. Pacific Linguistics, ser. A, nos. 54 and 57. Canberra: Australian National University, 1978–79.

Todd, Loreto. *Pidgins and Creoles*. London: Routledge and Kegan Paul, 1974.

Valdman, Albert, ed. *Pidgin and Creole Linguistics*. Bloomington: Indiana University Press, 1977.

England

These selections include historical studies and comparisons with American English.

Barber, Charles. *Early Modern English*. London: Deutsch, 1976.
Baugh, Albert C., and Cable, Thomas. *A History of the English Language*. 3d ed. Englewood Cliffs, N.J.: Prentice Hall; London: Routledge and Kegan Paul, 1979.
Brook, G. L. *English Dialects*. London: Deutsch, 1965.
Edwards, V. K. *The West Indian Language Issue in British Schools: Challenges and Responses*. London: Routledge and Kegan Paul, 1979.
Fischer, Andreas. *Dialects in the South-West of England: A Lexical Investigation*. Cooper Monographs, no. 25. Berne: Francke, 1976.
Görlach, Manfred. *Einführung ins Frühneuenglische*. Heidelberg: Quelle and Meyer, 1978.
Heath, Christopher D. *The Pronunciation of English in Cannock, Staffordshire: A Socio-Linguistic Survey of an Urban Speech Community*. Publications of the Philological Society, no. 29. Oxford: Basil Blackwell, 1980.
Holmberg, Borje. *On the Concept of Standard English and the History of Modern English Pronunciation*. Lunds Universitets Årsskrift, vol. 56, no. 3. Lund: Lunds Universitets, 1964.
Hughes, Arthur, and Trudgill, Peter. *English Accents and Dialects: An Introduction to Social and Regional Varieties of British English*. London: Edward Arnold, 1979.
Jones, Richard Foster. *The Triumph of the English Language*. Stanford: Stanford University Press, 1953.
Kirk, John M.; Sanderson, Stewart F.; and Widdowson, John D. A.; eds. *Studies in Linguistic Geography: The British Dialects of English*. London: Croom Helm, forthcoming.
Kolb, Eduard. *Linguistic Atlas of England: Phonological Atlas of the Northern Region*. Berne: Francke, 1966.
Kolb, Eduard; Glauser, Beat; Elmer, Willy; and Stamm, Renate. *Atlas of English Sounds*. Berne: Francke, 1979.
Kurath, Hans, and Lowman, Guy S., Jr. *The Dialectal Structure of Southern England: Phonological Evidence*. Publications of the American Dialect Society, no. 54. University, Ala.: University of Alabama Press, 1970.
Matthews, William. *Cockney Past and Present: A Short History of the Dialect of London*. London: G. Routledge and Sons, 1938. Reprint. London: Routledge and Kegan Paul, 1972.
Orton, Harold, and Dieth, Eugen. *Survey of English Dialects*. Introduction and 4 vols. Leeds: Edward Arnold, 1962–71.
Orton, Harold, and Wright, Nathalia. *A Word Geography of England*. London, New York, and San Francisco: Seminar Press, 1974.
Orton, Harold; Sanderson, Stewart; and Widdowson, John. *The Linguistic Atlas of England*. London: Croom Helm; New York: Humanities Press, 1978.
Parry, David. *The Survey of Anglo-Welsh Dialects*. 2 vols. Swansea: University College, 1977–80.
Pyles, Thomas. *The Origins and Development of the English Language*. 2d ed. New York: Harcourt Brace Jovanovich, 1971.

Sivertsen, Eva. *Cockney Phonology*. Oslo Studies in English, no. 8. Oslo: Publications of the British Institute in the University of Oslo, 1960.

Strevens, Peter. *British and American English*. London: Collier-Macmillan, 1972.

Švejčer, Aleksandr D. *Standard English in the United States and England*. Janua Linguarum, ser. min. 159. The Hague: Mouton, 1978.

Trudgill, Peter. *The Social Differentiation of English in Norwich*. Cambridge: At the University Press, 1974.

Trudgill, Peter, ed. *Sociolinguistic Patterns in British English*. London: Edward Arnold, 1978.

Viereck, Wolfgang. *Lexikalische und grammatische Ergebnisse des Lowman-Survey von Mittel- und Südengland*. 2 vols. Munich: Fink, 1975.

———. *Regionale und soziale Erscheinungsformen des britischen und amerikanischen Englisch*. Tübingen: Niemeyer, 1975.

Wakelin, Martyn F. *English Dialects: An Introduction*. London: Athlone, 1972. 2d ed. London: Athlone, 1977.

Wakelin, Martyn F., ed. *Patterns in the Folk Speech of the British Isles*. London: Athlone, 1972.

Wells, J. C. *Jamaican Pronunciation in London*. Publications of the Philological Society, no. 25. Oxford: Blackwell, 1973.

Wright, Joseph. *English Dialect Grammar*. Oxford: Oxford University Press, 1905.

Wyld, H. C. *A History of Modern Colloquial English*. Oxford: Blackwell, 1936.

Scotland

Aitken, A. J., ed. *Lowland Scots*. Association for Scottish Literary Studies, Occasional Papers, no. 2. Edinburgh: Association for Scottish Literary Studies, 1973.

Aitken, A. J., and McArthur, Tom, eds. *Languages of Scotland*. Association for Scottish Literary Studies, Occasional Papers, no. 4. Edinburgh: W. and R. Chambers, 1979.

Glauser, Beat. *The Scottish-English Linguistic Border. Lexical Aspects*. Cooper Monographs, no. 20. Berne: Francke, 1974.

Görlach, Manfred, ed. *Focus On: Scotland*. Heidelberg: Groos, 1982.

Grant, William, and Dixon, James Main. *Manual of Modern Scots*. Cambridge: At the University Press, 1921.

Macauley, R. K. S. *Language, Social Class, and Education: A Glasgow Study*. Edinburgh: University of Edinburgh Press, 1977.

McClure, J. Derrick, ed. *The Scots Language in Education*. Association for Scottish Literary Studies, Occasional Papers, no. 3. Aberdeen: College of Education, n.d. [1975].

McClure, J. Derrick; Aitken, A. J.; and Low, John Thomas. *The Scots Language: Planning for Modern Usage*. Edinburgh: Ramsey Head, 1980.

McIntosh, Angus. *An Introductory Survey of Scottish Dialects*. Edinburgh: Nelson, 1952.

Mather, J. Y., and Speitel, H. H. *The Linguistic Atlas of Scotland*. 2 vols. London: Croom Helm; Hamden, Conn.: Shoe String, 1975–77.

Murison, David. *The Guid Scots Tongue*. Edinburgh: William Blackwood, 1977.

Murray, James A. H. *The Dialect of the Southern Counties of Scotland*. London: Asher, 1873.

Ireland

Adams, G. Brendan, ed. *Ulster Dialects: An Introductory Symposium*. Holywood: Ulster Folk Museum, 1964.
Barry, Michael V., ed. *Aspects of English Dialects in Ireland*. Belfast: Institute of Irish Studies, The Queen's University, 1981.
Bliss, Alan. *Spoken English in Ireland 1600–1740: Twenty-seven Representative Texts Assembled and Analysed*. Dublin: Dolmen; Atlantic Highlands, N.J.: Humanities Press, 1979.
Henry, P. L. *An Anglo-Irish Dialect of North Roscommon*. Dublin: University College, Department of English, 1957.
———. "A Linguistic Survey of Ireland: Preliminary Report." *Lochlann: A Review of Celtic Studies* 1 (1958):49–208.
Joyce, P. W. *English as We Speak It in Ireland*. London: Longmans, Green, 1910. Reprint. London: Wolfhound Press, 1979.
Milroy, James. *Regional Accents of English: Belfast*. Belfast: Blackstaff, 1981.
Milroy, Leslie. *Language and Social Networks*. Oxford: Blackwell, 1980.
Ó'Muirithe, Diarmaid, ed. *The English Language in Ireland*. Dublin: Mercier Press, 1977.

The United States

Allen, Harold B. *The Linguistic Atlas of the Upper Midwest*. 3 vols. Minneapolis: University of Minnesota Press, 1973–76.
Allen, Harold B., and Underwood, Gary N., eds. *Readings in American Dialectology*. New York: Appleton-Century-Crofts, 1971.
Atwood, E. Bagby. *A Survey of Verb Forms in the Eastern United States*. Ann Arbor: University of Michigan Press, 1953.
———. *The Regional Vocabulary of Texas*. Austin: University of Texas Press, 1962.
———. "The Methods of American Dialectology." *Zeitschrift für Mundartforschung* 30 (1963):1–30. Reprint. *English Linguistics: An Introductory Reader*, edited by Harold Hungerford, Jay Robinson, and James Sledd, pp. 176–216. Glenview, Ill.: Scott-Foresman, 1970. Reprint. *Readings in American Dialectology*, edited by Harold B. Allen and Gary N. Underwood, pp. 5–25. New York: Appleton-Century-Crofts, 1971.
Bickerton, Derek, and Odo, Carol. *Change and Variation in Hawaiian English*. 2 vols. Honolulu: Social Sciences and Linguistics Institute, University of Hawaii, 1976–77.
Bright, Elizabeth S. *A Word Geography of California and Nevada*. Berkeley and Los Angeles: University of California Press, 1971.
Burling, Robbins. *English in Black and White*. New York: Holt, Rinehart and Winston, 1973.
Carr, Elizabeth Ball. *Da Kine Talk: From Pidgin to Standard English in Hawaii*. Honolulu: University Press of Hawaii, 1972.
Davis, A. L., ed. *Culture, Class, and Language Variety*. Urbana, Ill.: National Council of Teachers of English, 1972.
DeStefano, Johanna S. *Language, Society and Education: A Profile of Black English*. Worthington, Ohio: Jones, 1973.

Suggested Readings

Dil, Anwar S., ed. *Varieties of American English: Essays by Raven I. McDavid, Jr.* Stanford: Stanford University Press, 1980.
Dillard, J. L. *Black English: Its History and Usage in the United States.* New York: Random House, 1972.
―――. *All-American English.* New York: Random House, 1975.
―――. *Lexicon of Black English.* New York: Seabury, 1977.
Dillard, J. L., ed. *Perspectives on American English.* The Hague: Mouton, 1980.
Eliason, Norman E. *Tarheel Talk: An Historical Study of the English Language in North Carolina to 1860.* Chapel Hill: University of North Carolina Press, 1956.
Fasold, Ralph W. *Tense Marking in Black English: A Linguistic and Social Analysis.* Washington, D.C.: Center for Applied Linguistics, 1972.
Fasold, Ralph W., and Shuy, Roger W., eds. *Teaching Standard English in the Inner City.* Washington, D.C.: Center for Applied Linguistics, 1970.
Feagin, Crawford. *Variation and Change in Alabama English. A Sociolinguistic Study of the White Community.* Washington, D.C.: Georgetown University Press, 1979.
Ferguson, Charles A., and Heath, S. B., eds. *Language in the U.S.A.* Cambridge: At the University Press, 1981.
Fishman, Joshua A.; Cooper, Robert L.; and Ma, Roxana. *Bilingualism in the Barrio.* Language Science Monographs, no. 7. Bloomington: Indiana University, 1975.
Folb, Edith A. *Runnin' Down Some Lines: The Language and Culture of Black Teenagers.* Cambridge, Mass.: Harvard University Press, 1980.
Francis, W. Nelson. *The Structure of American English.* New York: Ronald Press, 1958.
Harrison, Deborah Sears, and Trabasso, Tom, eds. *Black English: A Seminar.* Hillsdale, N.J.: Erlbaum, 1976.
Krapp, George P. *The English Language in America.* 2 vols. New York: Century, 1925. Reprint. New York: Ungar, 1960.
Kretzschmar, William A., Jr., ed. *Dialects in Culture. Essays in General Dialectology by Raven I. McDavid, Jr.* University, Ala: University of Alabama Press, 1979.
Kurath, Hans. *A Word Geography of the Eastern United States.* Ann Arbor: University of Michigan Press, 1949.
Kurath, Hans; Hanley, Miles L; Bloch, Bernard; Lowman, Guy S., Jr.; and Hansen, Marcus L. *Linguistic Atlas of New England.* 3 vols. in 6 pts. Providence: Brown University Press, 1939–43. Reprint. New York: AMS Press, 1972.
Kurath, Hans; Hansen, Marcus L.; Bloch, Julia; and Bloch, Bernard. *Handbook of the Linguistic Geography of New England.* Providence: Brown University Press, 1939.
Kurath, Hans, and McDavid, Raven I., Jr. *The Pronunciation of English in the Atlantic States.* Ann Arbor: University of Michigan Press, 1961.
Kurath, Hans; McDavid, Raven I., Jr.; and O'Cain, R. K. *The Linguistic Atlas of the Middle and South Atlantic States.* Chicago: Chicago University Press, 1980– .
Labov, William. *The Social Stratification of English in New York City.* Washington, D.C.: Center for Applied Linguistics, 1966.
―――. *Language in the Inner City: Studies in the Black English Vernacular.* Philadelphia: University of Pennsylvania Press, 1972.
Labov, William; Yaeger, Malcah; and Steiner, Richard. *A Quantitative Study of Sound Change in Progress.* 2 vols. Philadelphia: U.S. Regional Survey, 1972.

Leap, William L., ed. *Studies in Southwestern Indian English*. San Antonio: Trinity University, 1977.
Lourie, Margaret A., and Conklin, Nancy Faires, eds. *A Pluralistic Nation: The Language Issue in the United States*. Rowley, Mass.: Newbury, 1978.
Marckwardt, Albert H. *American English*. New York: Oxford University Press, 1958.
Mencken, H. L. *The American Language*. 1 vol. abridged ed., by Raven I. McDavid, Jr. New York: Knopf, 1963.
Metcalf, Allan A. *Chicano English*. Arlington, Va.: Center for Applied Linguistics, 1979.
Reed, Carroll E. *Dialects of American English*. Amherst, Mass.: University of Massachusetts Press, 1967. Rev. ed. Amherst, Mass.: University of Massachusetts Press, 1977.
Sebeok, Thomas A., ed. *Current Trends in Linguistics*. 14 vols. Vol. 10, *Linguistics in North America*. The Hague: Mouton, 1973.
Smitherman, Geneva. *Talkin and Testifyin: The Language of Black America*. Boston: Houghton Mifflin, 1977.
Turner, Lorenzo D. *Africanisms in the Gullah Dialect*. Chicago: University of Chicago Press, 1949. Reprint. Ann Arbor: University of Michigan Press, 1974.
Turner, Paul R., ed. *Bilingualism in the Southwest*. Tuscon: University of Arizona Press, 1973.
Williamson, Juanita V., and Burke, Virginia M., eds. *A Various Language: Perspectives on American Dialects*. New York: Holt, Rinehart and Winston, 1971.
Wolfram, Walter A. *A Sociolinguistic Description of Detroit Negro Speech*. Washington, D.C.: Center for Applied Linguistics, 1969.
———. *Sociolinguistic Aspects of Assimilation. Puerto Rican English in New York City*. Washington, D.C.: Center for Applied Linguistics, 1974.
Wolfram, Walter A., and Christian, Donna. *Appalachian Speech*. Arlington, Va.: Center for Applied Linguistics, 1976.
Wolfram, Walter A., and Clarke, Nona H., eds. *Black-White Speech Relationships*. Washington, D.C.: Center for Applied Linguistics, 1971.
Wolfram, Walter A., and Fasold, Ralph W. *The Study of Social Dialects in American English*. Englewood Cliffs, N.J.: Prentice-Hall, 1974.
Wood, Gordon R. *Vocabulary Change: A Study of Variation in Regional Words in Eight of the Southern States*. Carbondale and Edwardsville: Southern Illinois University Press, 1971.

Canada

Avis, Walter S. "The English Language in Canada." In *Current Trends in Linguistics*, edited by Thomas A. Sebeok. 14 vols. Vol. 10, *Linguistics in North America*, pt. 1, pp. 40–74. The Hague: Mouton, 1973.
Chambers, J. K., ed. *Canadian English: Origins and Structures*. Toronto: Methuen, 1975.
Darnell, Regna, ed. *Linguistic Diversity in Canadian Society*. Edmonton: Linguistic Research, 1971.
Léon, Pierre R., and Martin, Phillipe J., eds. *Toronto English*. Studia Phonetica, no. 14. Montreal: Didier, 1979.
McConnell, R. E. *Our Own Voice: Canadian English and How It Is Studied*. Toronto: Gage Educational Publishing, 1979.

Orkin, Mark M. *Speaking Canadian English: An Informal Account of the English Language in Canada.* Toronto: General Publishing Co., 1970.

Scargill, M. H. *Modern Canadian English Usage: Linguistic Change and Reconstruction.* Toronto: McClelland and Stewart, 1974.

———. *A Short History of Canadian English.* Victoria, B.C.: Sono Nis, 1977.

Vincent, Thomas; Parker, George; and Bonnycastle, Stephen; eds. *Walter S. Avis: Essays and Articles.* Kingston: Royal Military College of Canada, 1978.

The Caribbean

Alleyne, Mervyn C. *Comparative Afro-American: An Historical-Comparative Study of English-Based Afro-American Dialects of the New World.* Ann Arbor: Karoma, 1980.

Bailey, Beryl Loftman. *Jamaican Creole Syntax: A Transformational Approach.* Cambridge: At the University Press, 1966.

Cassidy, Frederic G. *Jamaica Talk: Three Hundred Years of the English Language in Jamaica.* New York: St. Martins Press, 1961.

Görlach, Manfred, ed. *Focus On: The Caribbean.* Heidelberg: Groos, 1982.

Grimes, Joseph E., ed. *Languages of the Guianas.* Norman, Okla: Summer Institute of Linguistics, 1972.

Holm, John A., ed. *Central American English.* Heidelberg: Groos, 1982.

Rickford, John R., ed. *A Festival of Guyanese Words.* Georgetown: University of Guyana, 1977. 2d ed. Georgetown: University of Guyana, 1978.

Taylor, Douglas M. *Languages of the West Indies.* Baltimore: Johns Hopkins University Press, 1977.

Africa

de Villiers, André, ed. *English-Speaking South Africa Today.* Cape Town: Oxford University Press, 1976.

Hauptfleisch, T. *Language Loyalty in South Africa.* 3 vols. Pretoria: Human Sciences Research Council, 1977–79.

Hocking, B. D. W. *All What I Was Taught, and Other Mistakes.* Nairobi: Oxford University Press, 1974.

Killam, G. D., ed. *African Writers on African Writing.* London: Heinemann, 1973.

Lanham, L. W. *The Pronunciation of South African English: A Phonetic-Phonemic Introduction.* Capetown and Amsterdam: A. A. Balkema, 1967.

Lanham, L. W., and Macdonald, C. A. *The Standard in South African English and Its Social History.* Heidelberg: Groos, 1979.

Lanham, L. W., and Prinsloo, K. P., eds. *Language and Communication Studies in South Africa: Current Issues and Directions in Research and Inquiry.* Cape Town: Oxford University Press, 1978.

McGregor, G. P. *English in Africa: A Guide to the Teaching of English as a Second Language with Particular Reference to the Post-Primary School Stages.* London: Heinemann Educational, 1971.

Schuring, G. K. *A Multilingual Society: English and Afrikaans Amongst Blacks in the RSA.* Pretoria: Human Sciences Research Council, 1979.

Sey, Kofi A. *Ghanaian English: An Exploratory Survey.* London: Macmillan and Co., 1973.

Spencer, John, ed. *The English Language in West Africa.* London: Longman, 1971.

Todd, Loreto. *Some Day Been Dey: West African Pidgin Folktales.* London: Routledge and Kegan Paul, 1979.

———. *Cameroon.* Heidelberg: Groos, 1981.

Ubahakwe, Ebo, ed. *Varieties and Functions of English in Nigeria.* Ibadan: African Universities Press, 1979.

South Asia

Bansal, R. K. *The Intelligibility of Indian English.* Hyderabad: Central Institute of English, 1969.

Crewe, William, ed. *The English Language in Singapore.* Singapore: Eastern Universities Press, 1977.

Gokak, V. K. *English in India: Its Present and Its Future.* Bombay and New York: Asia Publishing House, 1964.

Kachru, Braj B. *The Indianization of English: The English Language in India.* New Delhi: Oxford University Press, 1982.

Mohan, Ramesh, ed. *Indian Writing in English.* New Delhi: Orient Longman, 1978.

Pascasio, Emy M., ed. *The Filipino Bilingual: Studies on Philippine Bilingualism and Bilingual Education.* Quezon City: Ateneo de Manila University Press, 1977.

Platt, J. T., and Weber, Heidi. *English in Singapore and Malaysia: Status—Features—Functions.* Kuala Lumpur: Oxford University Press, 1980.

Spitzbardt, Harry. *English in India.* Halle: Max Niemeyer Verlag, 1976.

Tongue, R. K. *The English of Singapore and Malaysia.* Singapore: Eastern Universities Press, 1974.

Australia and New Zealand

Baker, Sidney J. *The Australian Language.* 2d ed. Sydney: Currawong Press, 1966.

Clyne, Michael, ed. *Australia Talks: Essays on the Sociology of Australian Immigrant and Aboriginal Languages.* Canberra: Australian National University Press, 1976.

Dabke, Roswitha. *Morphology of Australian English.* Munich: W. Fink, 1976.

Hammarström, Göran. *Australian English.* Hamburg: Buske, 1979.

Mitchell, A. G., and Delbridge, Arthur. *The Pronunciation of English in Australia.* Sydney: Angus and Robertson, 1965.

———. *The Speech of Australian Adolescents.* Sydney: Angus and Robertson, 1965.

Ramson, W. S. *Australian English: An Historical Study of the Vocabulary, 1788–1898.* Canberra: Australian National University Press, 1966.

Ramson, W. S., ed. *English Transported: Essays on Australian English.* Canberra: Australian National University Press, 1970.

Sandefur, John R. *An Australian Creole in the Northern Territory: A Description of Ngukurr-Bamyili Dialects.* Darwin: Summer Institute of Linguistics, 1979.

Turner, G. W. *The English Language in Australia and New Zealand.* London: Longman, 1966. 2d ed. London: Longman, 1972.
Turner, G. W., ed. *Good Australian English and Good New Zealand English.* Sydney: Reed Education, 1972.

English and English-Based Pidgins in the Southwest Pacific

Charpentier, Jean-Michel. *Le Pidgin Bislama(n) et le multilinguisme aux Nouvelles-Hébrides.* Paris: Société d'Etudes Linguistiques et Anthropologiques de France, 1979.
Llamzon, T. A. *Standard Filipino English.* Manila: Ateneo University Press, 1969.
McElhanon, K. A., ed. *Tok Pisin i go we? Kivung,* Special publication, no. 1. Port Moresby: Linguistic Society of Papua, New Guinea, 1975.
Mühlhäusler, Peter. *Growth and Structure of the Lexicon of New Guinea Pidgin.* Pacific Linguistics, ser. C, no. 52. Canberra: Australian National University, 1979.
Ross, Alan S. C., and Moverley, A. W. *The Pitcairnese Language.* London: Deutsch, 1964.
Wurm, Stephen A., ed. *New Guinea and Neighboring Areas: A Sociolinguistic Laboratory.* The Hague: Mouton, 1979.

Subject and Author Index

Page numbers for bibliographic references appear in italics.

Abbreviation, 397
Abercrombie, David, 69–70, *81*, 131, *132*, 170, *171*
Aberdeen(shire), 65, 75
Abeysinghe, A., 379, *380*
Abeysinghe, I., 379, *380*
Aboriginal English, 433
Aboriginal languages, 432
Aborigines, 431
Acadia, 138–39, 144, 146, 182
Accent, 27, 74, 76, 128, 325, 328, 336, 338, 424, 435
Acceptability, 77, 122, 214, 268, 434
Acculturation, 273
Achebe, Chinua, 298f., *303*, 376–77, *380*
Acrolect, 394, 402
Act of Settlement, 87
Act of Union, 31, 89, 90
Adams, G. Brendan, 90, 95, 110–11, 114–15, 117, 119, 131, *132*
Additional language, 2
Aeneid, 17, 57
Æthelwold, 14
Afendras, E. A., 393, *412*
Affectation, 426
Africa, 2, 5, 281–383
African Black English, 326, 333, 342, 347, 349–50
African Inland Mission, 310, *323*
African languages, 225
Afrikaans, 312, 329, 333, 344
Afrikaans English, 324, 327, 329, 331–32, 337–38, 342, 349–50
Age, 1, 72–73, 152, 210, 211, 336, 340, 390
Aggarval, N. K., 377, *380*
Agnihotri, Rama K., 50, *53*
Ahidjo, Ahmadou, 303
Aig-Imoudkhuede, Frank, 293
Aitken, A. J., 59, 77–78, 79, *81*, 170, *171*
Albert, Miller O., 291, *303*
Alexander, William, 68
Alfred the Great, 14
Algarín, Miguel, 224, *248*
Ali, Ahmed, 372, *380*
Allen, Harold B., 160, 170, *171–72*, 196, *208*

Alleyne, Mervyn C., 277–78, *279*
Allophone, 102–3, 107, 123–24
Allsopp, Richard, 251, 258, 271, *279*
American Dialect Society, 196
American Dictionary, 5
American English, 9, 26, 27, 30, 148, 152, 154, 160, 177–250, 258, 284, 300, 308
Americanisms, 31, 76, 149, 186, 430
Americanized, 160, 256
American language, 204
American Revolution, 139–42, 183
Amerindian, 138, 146, 168, 216–18
Amish, 165
Amur, G. S., 379, *382*
Analogy, 107
Anancy story, 269
Anand, Mulk Raj, 368, 370–71, 375, *380*
Andrew, J. V., 167, 171, *172*
Angelcynn, 11
Angles, 14, 56
Anglican church, 128, 328, 336
Anglicisms, 58
Anglicists, 355
Anglicization, 56, 58, 60, 70, 76–77, 131, 317, 324, 346; and Spanish, 273; and Tok Pisin, 455
Anglikaans, 342
Anglo-English, 69, 90, 95, 110, 118
Anglo-Irish, 45; literary movement, 92
Anglo-Normans, 84, 94
Anglophiles, 62
Anglophones, 134
Anglo-Romani, 3
Anglos, 221
Anglo-Saxon, 14
Anglo-Scots, 58
Anglo-Welsh, 110
Angogo, Rachel, 10, 306–23, *323*
Ansre, Gilbert, *380*
Appalachian English, 239–45
Appalachians, 183, 201, 203
Arabic, 295, 354, 364
Aragonese, 57
Archaism, 35, 37, 69, 86–88, 102, 121, 124–25, 151–52, 159, 191, 215, 246, 306

481

Arden, John, 47, *53*
Aristophanes, 243
Armah, A. K., 298, *303*
Articles, 33, 44–45, 361, 374, 400, 402, 410
Articulation, 7
"Ascendency accent," 128
Ashley, M. J., 331–32, 343, 346, *352*
Asian, 312
Aspect, 234, 239, 398–400, 402, 449, 452
Assimilation, 50, 167, 182
Astor, John Jacob, 138
Atlas Linguistique de France, 207
Attitude, 50, 75–76, 214, 218, 268, 328, 332, 344–45, 347, 356, 369–70, 372–73, 376
Atwood, E. Bagby, 196, 207, *208*, 219, 242, 247, *248*
Aubrey, John, 20, *53*
Australia, 4, 161, 415–38
Australian English, 30, 339, 411
Australian Language, The, 5, 435
Aviation, 5
Avis, Walter S., 138, 145, 149, 153, 155, 161–62, 168, 169, 170–71, *172*
Awareness, linguistic, 73, 338–39
Awoonor, Kofi, 298, *303*
Ayenbyte of Inwit, 16
Ayrshire, 61

Baba Malay, 386
Babu English, 357
Baby talk, 439
Bacon, Sir Francis, 19
Baeyer, Cornelius von, 157–58, 161, *172*
Bahasa Malaysia, 5, 387, 389, 393, 405
Bailey, Nathaniel, 27
Bailey, Richard W., 1–10, 52, 78, 134–76, 168, *172*
Baker, Herschel, 52, *55*
Baker, Philip, 310, *323*
Baker, Sidney J., 5, 420, 435, *437*, 439, *464*
Bald, M. A., 78, *81*
Bamgboṣe, Ayọ, 286, *304*
Bangladesh, 353, 355, 377
Banim, John, 93
Banim, Michael, 93
Banks, Sir Joseph, 419
Bantu, 312–19, 347; Education Act, 332
Baptists, 284
Barbados, 207, 252, 278
Barber, Charles, 20, 22, 23, 28–29, 30, *53*
Barbot, Jean, 282
Barbour, John, 57
Barden, Thomas E., 247, *249*
Barnes, William, 87, 131
Barry, Michael V., *6*, 10, *53*, *54*, 84–133, 97, 131, *132*, 154

Basilect, 394, 402, 404, 405
Basque, 138
Bautista, M. L., *380*
Bazaar Malay, 128, 170, 384, 387–88, 391, 396
BBC. *See* British Broadcasting Corporation
Be, 15, 37, 43, 171, 218, 236, 277–78, 399
Bede, 14
Beeching, Jack, 281–82, *304*
Behan, Brendan, 93
Belfast, 75, 86, 95, 120–23, 127
Belize, 251–52, 255, 277
Bell, H. L., 457, *464*
Bender, Lionel, 310, *323*
Bengal, 367
Bengtsson, Elna, 168, *172*
Bennett, Louise, 272, *279*
Bentick, Lord William, 355
Bernard, J. R. L., 426, *437*
Bernstein, Basil, 378, *380*
Berry, Jack, 281, *304*
Bertz, Siegfried, 124–26, *132*
BEV. *See* Black English Vernacular
Bible, 96, 290, 447; Authorized (King James) Version of the, 19, 37; quotations from the, 3, 64, 239, 296, 462–63; translation, 19, 58
Bichelamar (Beach-la-Mar, Bislama), 439, 440, 463
Bickerton, Derek, 253, *279*, 394, 397, 399, *412*, 434, *464*
Bidialectal, 97
Bilingualism, 31, 77, 136, 164, 167, 171, 217, 221–22, 324, 326, 332–33, 353, 377, 389, 451, 454
"Bilingual style," 93
Bills, Garland D., 219, *249*
Bimorpheme, 70
Birmingham, 27, 47
Black English Vernacular (BEV), 147–48, 182, 224–39, 395, 399
Blacks, 146, 203, 329, 332, 337, 346
Blair, Hugh, 62
Blair, Peter Hunter, 14, *53*
Blake, Philip, 283, *323*
Bliss, Alan J., 86–87, 90, 101, 102, 107, 131, *132*
Blom, Jan-Petter, 274, *279*
Boarding schools, 12, 308
Boers, 312
Boethius, 14
Bokamba, Eyamba, 374, *380*
Bollée, Annegret, 310, *323*
Book of Common Prayer, 19, 37
Bootle, Stan, 46, *55*
Borrowing, 11, 25, 26, 31, 38, 57, 64, 109–10, 164, 166, 379, 443, 450, 457. *See also* Loanwords

Bose, Amalendu, 367, *380*
Boswell, James, 62, *81*
Botany Bay, 4, 415
Botswana, 350
Boyle, Francis, 96
Braidwood, John, 95, *132*
Branford, Jean, 341, *351*
Brash, Elton, 448, *464*
Brebner, John Bartlet, 139–41, 168, *172, 173*
Breconshire, 33
Breton, 137
Bristol-Severnside, 47
Britain, 2, 5, 150
British Broadcasting Corporation, 12, 27
British Columbia, 137, 163, 169, 170
British Empire, 150
British English: dialects of, 21, 23, 34–51; how other Englishes differ from, 9, 111–14, 116–18, 314, 318, 430; spread of, 148, 255, 285–86, 300, 312, 325, 345, 373, 390, 394
Britons, 56
Broadcasting, 11, 52, 127, 167, 205, 214, 256, 328, 345, 348, 390, 392–93
Broken English, 285, 356, 364, 432
Brontë, Emily, 44
Brooklyn r, 203
Brown, Jennifer, 263
Bryden, Bill, 79, *81*
Bughwan, D., 327, 334, 348, *351*, 378, *380*
Burchfield, R. W., 4, 6
Bureaucracy, 366, 421
Burnell, A. C., 379, *383*
Burns, Robert, 62, 77, 96
Bush Pidgin, 456
Butler, Frances Anne, 187–88, *208*
Butler English, 357

Cabot, John, 137, 140
Caithness, 56
Calabar, 283
Caldwell, Sarah J. G., 78, *81*
Calques, 166, 258, 269, 271, 278, 289, 317, 361–62
Camden, William, *464*
Cameroon, 295–97, 298, 301; Pidgin English of, 295–97
Canada, 4, 5, 134–76
Canadian English, 268
Canadianisms, 137–38, 150, 156, 160, 162, 169
Canmore, Malcolm, 56
Cantonese, 384, 387, 406–7, 411
Cape Colony, 4, 327
Cape English, 327, 331
Cape Town, 324–25, 330
Caplan, Gerald L., 150, *172*
Cardiff, 11, 32

Cardinal vowel, 7
Caribbean, 251–80
Carleton, William, 93
Carter, Hazel, 257, *279*
Cartier, Jacques, 138
Cassidy, Frederic G., 23, 177–209, 207, *208*, 210, 216
Castilian, 57
Castro, Fidel, 272
Catford, J. C., 7, *10*, 67, 78, 79, *81*
Catholic church, 86, 94, 127, 295
Cave, G., 253, *279*
Cawdrey, Robert, 20
Caxton, William, 12, 17–18
Cebollero, Pedro A., 273, *279*
Celtic, 11, 110
Census, 93, 163–64, 206, 219, 329–30, 337, 440
Central America, 277
Central Institute of English and Foreign Languages, *381*
Central Scots, 69
Chambers, J. K., 170, *172*
Champlain, Samuel de, 138
Chan, Mimi, 407, *413*
Chancery, 18
Charton, N. C. J., 331–32, 343, 346, *352*
Chaucer, Geoffrey, 16, 58, 87–88
Chaudhuri, N. C., 354, 358, *380*
Cherokee, 217
Chicago, 247
Chicano English, 219, 276
Child language acquisition, 211–12
Chinese, 2, 384–85, 389, 391, 441; Pidgin English, 150, 406, 441
Chinook Jargon, 168–69
Christian, Donna, 229, 239–45, *249*
Christie, Pauline, 266, *279*
Churchill, Awnsham, 282, *304*
Churchill, John, 282, *304*
Churchill, William, 439, *464*
Civil service, 12
Clark, Ross, 440, *464*
Clarkson, John, 283
Claxton, A. O. D., 40, *53*
Cline of bilingualism, 4, 357
Cockney, 27, 45, 49
Code-mixing, 376
Code-shifting, 260–61, 267–68, 271, 274
Code-switching, 219, 223, 296–97, 455
Cohen, Louis, 328, *351*
Cohen, Paul, 225, 231, *248*
Collocations, 361
Colloquial speech and style, 58, 60, 308, 337, 349, 361, 404
Colonial administration, 4, 386–87, 406
Colonialism, 369

Colonization, 18, 26, 178–79, 282, 309, 353
Coloured English, 326, 329, 333, 337, 343, 348, 350
Common core, 57
Commonwealth writing in English, 372
Communication, 214, 223, 284, 439, 452, 457
Comoro Islands, 310
Competence, 342, 390, 406
Completive aspect, 234
Complexity, 439, 443, 449, 453
Concord, 242, 245, 342, 398
Conditioning, 70, 155
Confederation, 134, 165
Connaught, 89
Conrad, Joseph, 403
Conservatism, 23, 38, 65, 124, 128, 177, 246
Conservative South African English, 328, 336
Consonant cluster reduction, 218, 228–30, 287–88, 394, 398, 409
Consonants, 7, 32, 37, 98, 100–101, 118, 126, 223, 256
Contact language, 137, 146, 168, 442
Context, 270, 356
Continuum, 80, 286, 390, 424, 453
Contrast, 24, 69, 70, 102, 107, 122–23, 124, 126, 152, 154–55, 287
Conurbation, 41, 43, 45
Cook, James, 137, 419
Copula, 236, 260, 399; deletion, 147–48, 234, 239, 399, 402, 409, 433
Corder, S. Pitt, *412*
Cork, 84, 103, 128, 129
Cornish, 38
Cornwall, 14
Correctness, 12, 26, 62, 186–87, 260, 289, 331, 360
Corruption, 1, 19, 150, 156
Costa Rica, 277
Court, 12, 16
Coverdale, Miles, 19
Covert value, 74, 337
Craddock, Jerry R., 219, *249*
Craig, David, 62, *81*
Craigie, Sir William A., 78–80, *81*
Creative writing, 347, 366, 368, 403–5
Creole, 5, 137, 251, 399, 432, 443
Creolization, 225, 273, 443, 446, 451
Cromwell, Oliver, 87, 89, 143
Cuba, 272
Cubano English, 219
Cultivated speech, 149, 426
Culture-bound, 361, 364–65
Cumberland, 14
Cumbro-Normans, 84
Cunningham, P. M., 426, 434, *437*
Cursor Mundi, 16

Daily Gleaner (Jamaica), 259, 272
Dalby, David, 287, *304*
Danelaw, 15, 17
Dante, 207
Das, Kamala, 370, 372, *381*
Dave, P. B., 378, *382*
David, C. M. E., 439, *464*
Day, Lal B., 368, *381*
Day, Richard R., 267–68, *279*
De Camp, David, 394, *412*
Decker, Thomas, 292, *304*
Decreolization, 268
Defoe, Daniel, 302
de Fréine, Séan, 92, *132*
Delbridge, Arthur, 423–25, *437*
Demography, 5, 11, 252–53, 334–35, 415–16
Deprivation, 76
de Quincey, Paul, 293, *304*
Desai, S. K., 379, *382*
Desani, G. V., 375
Detroit, 213, 225, 229
Developmental continua, 409, 412, 443
Deviation, 260, 360, 374
Devon, 20, 75
deVries, John, 167, 171, *172–73*
Dialect: areas, 35; boundaries, 94, 127, 144, 153; differences, 338–40; geography, 196, 210; interference, 58; literature, 127; maps, 65
Dialect Notes, 196, 207
Dictionaries, 20, 27, 271
Dictionary of American Regional English (DARE), 181–82, 199, 206–7, 210
Dictionary of Canadianisms, 138, 151, 162
Dictionary of Jamaican English, 256–57, 259, 266, *279*
Dieth, Eugen, 34, *54*, 79, *81*
Diglossia, 31, 76, 219, 223, 269
Dil, Anwar S., 377, *381*
Diphthongs, 29, 100, 125, 153, 160, 203
Diplomacy, 5, 285
Distribution, 70, 79, 359
Diversity, linguistic, 56, 148, 152, 164, 315, 439
Dixon, James Main, 68, *82*
Dixon, John, 434, *437*
Dobson, Eric. J., 20, 52, *53*, 101, *132*
Domain, 18, 51, 63, 76–77, 311, 324, 337, 348, 390–94, 406–8, 445, 447–48, 454
Dominica, 255
Donegal, 115, 119–20
Dorall, Edward, 404, *412*
Douala, 303
Douglas, Gavin, 57, 64
Douglas-Cowie, Ellen, 130
Doukhobors, 165
Dravidian, 353
Drummond, William Henry, 166

Index

Dryden, John, 19
Dublin, 84–85, 86, 90, 97, 124–26, 128
Duke, Antera, 283
Dunbar, William, 60
Duran, James J., 322, *323*
Durban, 330
Dustoor, P. E., 361, 366, 379, *381*
Dutch, 78, 145–46, 182, 251, 386
Dutton, Tom E., 440, 457, *464*
Dwight, Timothy, 187, *208*
Dynamic view, 267

Eagleson, Robert D., 415–38, 428, *437*
Early Modern English, 18–24
East Africa Company, 309
East African English, 10, 306–23, 314
East African Journal, 321–22
East Anglia, 14, 143
Easter Rising, 92
East India Company, 353–54
Ebonics, 225
Edelstein, M. L., 347, *351*
Edgeworth, Maria, 93
Edinburgh, 57, 65, 70, 72–74, 79, 97
Edmont, E., 207, *208*
Educated speech, 20, 90, 118, 124, 126, 128, 378, 390, 411, 437
Education, 2, 17, 27, 52, 204, 214–15, 268, 299, 301, 312, 319, 324–26, 332, 333–34, 336, 338, 345, 347–48, 350, 357, 378, 384, 387–88, 390–91, 394–95, 405–6, 434, 448
Edwards, Jay, 259, *279*
Edwards, V. K., 51, *53*
Edwards, Walter, 278
Ee, T. H., 389, *414*
Eh, 161, 320, 429
Elaborated style, 321
Elite, 319
Elizabeth I, 20
Ellis, A. J., 34, 39, 45, *53*, 87, 131, *132*
Elmet, 42
Elocution teachers, 328
Elyot, Sir Thomas, 12
Embedding, 449, 452
Emeneau, Murray B., *173*
Emigration, 92
Emphasis, 258, 303
Employment, 390, 392–93, 406–7, 408, 454
England, 9, 11–28, 179; Church of, 12, 19
English Dialect Dictionary, 196
English Dialect Society, 196
English literature, 58, 62
English-medium schools, 308, 384, 387–88, 407
Environment, 153–54, 229, 234, 242
Erickson, Donna, 212, *249*
Ervin-Tripp, Susan, 213, *248*

Escalante, A., 253, *279*
Escure, G. J., 251, *279*
Ethiopia, 310
Ethnicity, 1, 210, 214, 216, 218, 261, 330, 336, 343, 356, 367, 388–89
Etymological Dictionary of the Scottish Language, 64
Euphemism, 211
Evaluation, 27, 34, 62, 74–76, 97, 435
Eweka, Iro, 263
Exonormative, 390
Expansion of English, 1, 443, 446
Expatriates, 308, 456
Expletives, 213
Extinct language, 87
Extreme South African English, 336–37, 340, 345, 349
Eye dialect, 65

False cognates, 275–76
Fasold, Ralph W., 225, 227, 234, 236, 238–39, 247, *248*, *249*, 397, 399, *413*
Fawcett, Margot J., 157, *173*
Febles, María Esther M. de, 275, *279*
Fennell, C. A. M., *381*
Fergusson, Robert, 62
Fernando Po, 283, 300
Fetherling, Douglas, 161, *173*
Films, 300, 308, 332, 392
Fingal, 86
Finkenstaedt, Thomas, 18, *53*
First language, 443
Fischer, Andreas, 38, *53*
Fisher, John H., 18, *53*
Fishman, Joshua A., 2, 6, 269, *279*
Fitzgerald, Edward, 46
Flamboyance, 290, 375
Flash language, 434
Fluency, 94
Focal areas, 65, 157
Focalizing, 453
Folk etymology, 419
Folk speech, 150
Fonlon, Bernard, 290–91, *304*
Forde, C. D., 283, 300, *304*
Ford Foundation Survey, 310
Foreigner talk, 443
Foreign language, 5, 308
Formality, 60, 73, 74, 358, 434, 462
Forth and Bargy, 86–87, 99
Fortman, Clasina de Gaay, 316, *323*
Fowler, H. W., 360
Foxcroft, Tina, 48, *55*
Francophones, 138
Francophone West African English, 285
Franglais, 166

Franklin, Benjamin, 186
Franklin, Karl J., *464*
Freetown, 283
French, 2, 12, 16, 26, 56–57, 84, 134, 137–39, 146, 164–65, 166, 167, 171, 179, 251, 281, 285, 295, 303, 310
Frenchified English, 56
Fries, Charles C., 214, *248*
Frontier tradition, 344
Frye, Northrop, 156, *173*
Fudge, Erik, 30, 53
Fulton, Robin, 64, *81*
Functional load, 102
Fyle, Clifford H., 284, 302, *304*

Gaelic, 6, 56–57, 67, 86, 87, 94, 110, 115, 134
Gaelicized English, 89, 102, 119, 128
Gaelic League, 93
Gaeltacht, 110, 127
Gallagher, Christine, 110–11, 119, 127, *132*
Galloway, 57
Galt, John, 63, *81*
Gambia, 283
Garioch, Robert, 64
Garnett, Alf, 51
Geike, A. Constable, 150, 155–56, 169, *173*
General Canadian, 151
General Certificate of Education (GCE), 395
General South African English, 339
Generational differences, 29, 159, 162, 212. See also Age
Georgia, 191
Germanic, 11
Germans, 134, 139, 182, 309, 312, 444–45
Ghana, 282, 286, 298
Ghanaian English, 286, 288, 290
Ghosh, Kashiprasad, 367
Gibbon, Lewis Grassic, 63
Gilbert, Sir Humphrey, 137
Giles, Howard, 27, 34, 53
Gilliéron, Jules, 207, *208*
Gitlin, Todd, 244, *248*
Given, Thomas, 96
Gladstone, W. E., 25
Glamorgan, 11, 32
Glasgow, 57, 65, 70–72, 74, 75, 76, 78, 79, 120
Glauser, Beat, 43, 53, 68
Glen, Duncan, 65, *82*
Glissmeyer, Gloria, 146, *173*
Glottal stop, 48, 71, 73, 76, 80, 152, 228, 394, 409
Gneuss, Helmut, 14, 53
Godley, John Robert, 150, 156, *173*
Goffin, R. C., 361, 366, 380, *381*
Gokak, V. K., 369, 372, 375, *381*
Goonewardene, James, 379, *381*

Gordon, David C., 3, 6
Gorman, T. P., 319, *323*
Gower, John, 16
Görlach, Manfred, 1–6, 52, 78
Grahamstown, 324–25
Grammar, 59, 271, 341, 360, 374, 397, 409, 442
Grammatical change, 27
Grandeur, 343
Grant, Charles, 355
Grant, William, 68, *82*
Gray, Hugh, 165–66, *173*
Great Vowel Shift, 5, 21, 23, 24, 43, 153
Greek, 18, 26
Greenberg, Joseph H., 281, *304*
Gregg, Robert J., 95, 111, 114–15, 118, 120, 127, *132*, 153, 163, 169, *173*, 207
Gregory, Lady Augusta, 93
Gregory, Pope, 14
Grieve, D. W., 288, *304*
Griffin, Gerald, 93
Gujarati, 50–51
Gullah, 225
Gumperz, John J., 274, *279*
Gunn, J. S., 435, *437*
Gustafson, Ralph, 167, *173*
Guyana, 251, 268, 278
Guyanese Creole, 453–54
Gwei, Solomon Nfor, 284, 300, *304*

Habitual aspect, 236, 278, 401
Hakka, 387
Haliburton, Thomas Chandler, 145, *173*
Hall, Robert A., Jr., 168, *174*, 247–48, 439, *447*, *464*
Halliday, M. A. K., 211, *248*
Halliday, Wilfrid J., 131, *133*
Halverson, John, 378, *381*
Hamilton, Donald E., 155–56, 170, *173*
Hancock, Ian F., 10, 138, *173*, 284, 301, *304*, 306–23
Hansen, Marcus, 139–41, *173*, 178–79, *208*
Hartman, James, 207, *208*
Hastings, 16
Hattersley, Alan F., 325, *351*
Hauptfleisch, T., 331, 335, *351*
Hausa, 281, 287
Havelok, 16
Hawaiian Pidgin English, 146
Hawkins, P., 426, 436, *437*
Hawkins, R. A., 362
Hawkins, William, 281
Hebdige, Dick, 51, 53
Hebrides, 57
Hedge schools, 92
Henry, P. L., 86, 90, 94, 95, 97, 128, 131, *132*
Henry VIII, 19

Index

Herzfeld, Anita, 277, *279*
Hiberno-English, 84–133, 154, 171
Highland English, 67, 75
Highlands, Scottish, 2, 57, 75, 141
Hill, Trevor, 313, *323*
Hindi, 255, 371, 379
Hiri Motu, 440
Hispanic American English, 219–24
Hobson-Jobson, 362, 379
Hocking, B. D. W., 306, 317, *323*
Hodgins, J. George, 169, *174*
Hokkien, 387, 396
Hollander, Nanci, 244, *248*
Hollyman, K. J., 440, *464*
Homophone, 30, 48, 67, 103, 107, 121, 124, 152, 163, 170, 228, 231–32, 233, 288, 301, 460
Hong Kong, 405–14
Hopi, 217
Hore, Edmund, 87
Hore, M., 137
Horton, J. W., 327, *351*
Hosali, P., 362,, *383*
Howison, John, 149, *174*
Huber, B. J. 331–32, 343, 346, *352*
Hudson's Bay Company, 137–38
Hudson Valley, 140, 145, 182–83
Hughes, Arthur, 11, 47, *54*, 80, *82*
Hull, Alexander, 166, *174*
Hultín, Neil C., 150–51, 153, *174*
Human Sciences Research Council's (HSRC) *Language Survey*, 330, 341, 348, 350
Humber-Lune Belt, 41, 43
Hybridization, 273, 363
Hyde, Douglas, 93
Hymes, Dell, 253, *280*
Hyperbole, 146
Hypercorrection, 45, 48, 98, 232, 237, 289, 313, 339

Identity, 268, 324, 328, 331–32, 343, 345, 347–48, 389, 448
Idiom, 109, 289
Igbo, 287, 293, 298, 315
Ijaw, 291
Illiteracy, 268, 273
Immigrants, 50, 136, 138, 140, 221, 327, 429
Implicational scale, 394, 397–98, 399
Independence, 140, 204
India, 2, 4, 5, 50, 309, 312, 326, 330, 338, 353, 385–86, 407
Indian English, 4, 27, 51, 218, 327, 334, 343, 348, 356–57, 373, 377–78, 388
Indianism, 355, 374
Indianizing, 368, 375
Indigenization, 4
Indo-Aryan, 353

Industrialization, 31, 205, 216
Industrial Revolution, 12, 26, 420
Inflection, 11, 14, 17, 59
Informants, 35, 71–72, 124, 181, 210
Inglis, 57
Inherent variability, 234
Initial clusters, 257
Injun talk, 147
Inland Northern, 9, 197
Innovation, 38, 41, 57, 65, 178, 363, 449, 450
Instrumental function, 3, 357, 388–897, 406
Insular Scots, 67
Intelligibility, 3, 57, 187, 284, 306, 325, 327, 333, 342, 378, 456
Interethnic communication, 388–89, 391
Interference, 119, 164, 223, 267, 285, 312, 360, 378
Interlanguage, 406
International English, 4, 286, 332, 384, 390
Interrogative, 59
Interview style, 48, 80
Intonation, 110, 213, 223, 227, 274, 314, 409
Inuit, 161
Inventory, 69, 359
Ireland, 5, 6, 84–133, 134, 144
Irish, 84–85, 92, 94, 102, 106, 154, 416; English, 10, 27, 28, 84–133, 395; Gaelic, 126
Irving, Washington, 182, *208*
Isichei, Elizabeth, 284, 301, *304*
Isodemographic map, 157–58, endsheets
Isogloss, 36, 41, 43, 68, 210
Ivory Coast, 285–86
Iyengar, K. R. S., 367, *381*

Jackson, Andrew, 204
Jacobite risings, 57
Jacobson, Rodolfo, 274, *279*
Jamaica, 5, 146, 252, 255, 283, 302
Jamaican Creole, 51, 250–81
Jamaican English, 250–81
James, Geoffrey, 161, *174*
James IV, 57
James VI, 58
Jamieson, John 64
Jargon, 214, 439, 443
Jefferson, Thomas, 204
Jespersen, Otto, 360
Johannesburg, 327; *Sunday Times*, 346
Johnson, Samuel, 27
Jones, C. Stanley, 163, 171, *175*
Jones, Daniel, 7, *10*, 28, *54*
Jones, Eldred, 302, *304*
Jones, Val, 48, *54*
Jonson, Ben, 177, *208*
Joual, 162, 167, 171
Joy, Richard J., 167, *174*

Joyce, James, 93, 131
Jumbam, Kenjo, 298, *304*
Jutes, 14

Kachru, Braj B., 4, 353–83, 355–56, 362, 364, 374, 376–80, *381*
Kandiah, Thiru, 377, 379, *382*
Kannada, 370
Kansakar, T. K., 377, *382*
Kaplan, Irving, 310, *323*
Kashoki, Mubanga E., *323*, 350, *352*
Kelly, Stan. *See* Bootle, Stan
Kelvinside, 74
Kemble, Fannie. *See* Butler, Frances Anne
Kennedy, Robert, 204, 214
Kent, 14
Kenya, 315
Key, Mary Ritchie, *248*
Kildare, 124; poems, 86, 98
Kilkenny, 85
King Lear, 20
Kingsley, Mary H., 301, *304*
Kingsnorth, G. W., 309, *323*
Kingston, Jamaica, 266
Kirk-Green, Anthony, 380, *382*
kiSwahili, 309, 312–13
Knapp, Herbert, 247, *248*
Knapp, Mary, 247, *248*
Kobbah, E., 284, *304*
Kolb, Eduard, 41, 42, 53, *54*
Kökeritz, Helge, 40, *54*
Krio, 284, 286, 292, 300, 302
Kriol, 432–33
Krishnamurti, Bh., 358, *382*
Kuala Lumpur, 386, 404
Kuo, E. C. Y., 389, 392, *413*
Kurath, Hans, 40, *54*, 143–45, 153, 168, 170, *174*, 196, 207, *208*, *209*, 210
Kwok, Helen, 407, *413*

[l], 26, 36, 47, 107, 115, 123, 126, 228, 232–33, 241, 339
Labarthe, Pierre, 283, *304*
Laberge, Suzanne, 449, *465*
Labov, William, 6, 22–23, *54*, 70, *82*, 170, *174*, 207, *209*, 224, 225, 228, 231, 232, 234–38, 247, *248*, 328, 337, 347, *351*, 397, 399, *413*
Labrish, 271
Ladefoged, Peter, 7, 9, *10*
Lagos Weekend, 293
Lakoff, Robin, 213, *248*
Lal, P., 367, 372, 379, *382*
Lallans, 64
Landed gentry, 128
Lane, T. W., 192, *209*

Language: academy, 204; acquisition, 4, 211, 267, 356, 358, 373, 432, 443; attitude, 50; contact, 255, 273, 274; imposition, 1; learning, 267; loyalty, 51, 65, 77, 331–32, 335, 343; mixing, 166, 223, 443, 453–54; planning, 5, 355, 377, 458, 459–61; play, 450; shift, 31–32, 57, 451
Language in contact, 5
Lanham, L. W., 324–52, *351*, 378, *382*
Lankan English, 356, 359, 361–62
Larne, 120
Lass, Roger, 79, *82*
Late Modern English, 25–45
Latin, 11, 12, 18, 26, 388
Latinos, 221
Lauder, Afferbeck, 343, *437*
Lawrence, D. H., 43
Lawrence, Lars, 222, *248*
Lawton, David L., 250–81, 226, 274, 277, *280*
Laxer, James, 150, *172*
Laycock, D. C., 439, 459, *464*, *466*
Leacock, Stephen, 156, *174*
Leap, William, 218, 247, *248*
Learned style, 360
Learner's errors, 306
Learner's language, 409–10
Lect, 4
Lectal continua, 401, 412
Leechman, Douglas, 168, *174*, 247–48
Leeds, 50
Legal English, 17, 365
Legal system, 356–57, 408
Leinster, 90
le Muire, An tSiúr Annuntiata, 131, *133*
Lenisation, 99
Leonard, Tom, 64
Le Page, R. B., 251, *280*
Lescarbot, Marc, 137
Letters (correspondence), 19, 348, 365–66
Leveling of dialects, 426
Lewis, John, 225, 231, *248*
Lexicon, lexis, 362–63
Lexifier language, 443, 445, 453
Liberia, 284, 286
Liberian English, 284
Lieberman, Philip, 212, *249*
Life cycle (of a pidgin), 443, 456
Light, Francis, 386
Lim, Catherine, 404, *413*
Limerick, 84
Lincoln, 42
Lindsay, Maurice, 65, *82*
Lingua franca, 2, 168, 282, 295, 300, 306, 309, 319, 384, 387, 440, 447, 461
Linguistic area, 353

Index

Linguistic Atlas of England, 35, 171, 178
Linguistic Atlas of New England, 143, *174,* 196, 208, 210, *248*
Linguistic Atlas of the Gulf Coast States, 196
Linguistic Atlas of the United States and Canada, 196
Linguistic Atlas of the Upper Midwest, 196
Linguistic change, 19, 79, 159, 210, 212–13, 225, 376
Linguistic enclaves, 165
Linguistic insecurity, 77
Linguistic properties, 338–40
Linguistic Survey of England, 65
Link language, 357, 367
Literacy, 19, 205, 214, 388, 390
Literary dialect, 20, 62, 92, 95–96, 146, 188–95, 218, 222
Literature, 14, 268, 290–91, 297–99, 366, 369–72, 403–5
Little Oxford Dictionary, 362
Liturgy, 295
Liverpool, 45–47, 120, 126
Livingstone, David, 309
Loan translations, 217
Loanwords, 16, 26, 32, 50, 69, 139, 161–62, 169, 171, 179, 181, 204, 217, 219–20, 317, 340, 396, 427, 429, 431, 459. *See also* Borrowing
Local identity, 74
Localized English, 4, 289, 319, 328
Local standard, 5, 346, 390
London, Jack, 439, *464*
London, 12, 16, 18, 22, 62, 101, 143, 177, 426
Lord, Robert, 406, *413*
Lord's Prayer, 210
Lothian, 62, 79
Louisiana, 182
Loutfut, Adam, 57
Low, John Thomas, 75–76, *82*
Lower social class, 58, 80, 311, 343, 420
Lowland Scots, 3–4, 34, 43, 111
Lowman, Guy S., 40, *54,* 246
Loyalists, 140–43, 149, 160, 168
Loyalties, 50, 52
Lunenburg, Nova Scotia, 139, 143, 147, 157, 168
Lunny, A., 102–3, 128–29, 131, *133*
Lynch, John, 460, *464*

McAllister, Anne H., 76, *82*
Macaulay, Ronald K. S., 70–72, 76, 80, *82*
McAuley, James, 420, *437*
Macauley, T. B., *82,* 355
Maccoby, Eleanor E., 212, *248*
McClure, J. Derrick, 65, 79, *82*
McConnell, R. E., 164, 168, 169, *174*

McDavid, Raven I., Jr., 153, 168, 170, *174,* 196, 207, *209,* 247, *249*
MacDiarmid, Hugh, 64, *82*
Macdonald, C. A., 328, 331, 338, 345–46, *351*
Mackie, Alastair, 64
McKie, Ian, 428, *437*
McKnight, F., 259
McMillan, Roddy, 78, *82*
McNaught, Kenneth, 168, *174*
MacQueen, John, 61, *82*
Magniloguence, 188, 195
Maine, 144, 189
Major, Clarence, 227, *249*
Makars, 64
Malacca, 386
Malawi, 310
Malay, 384–85, 389
Malaysia, 5, 384–405
Malla, K. P., 377, *382*
Mandarin, 411
Manding, 281
Mann, J. W., *352*
Maori, 415, 427, 431–32
Maps, 13, 35, 66, 91, 104–5, 111, 135, 158, 180–81, 184–85, 202, 220, 226, 254, 307, 335, 354, 385, 416, 440
Marchand, Hans, 27, *54*
Marckwardt, Albert H., 182, *209*
Maritimes, 134, 140, 142–43, 146
Markers, 152
Marlowe, Christopher, 19
Maroons, 283
Marsh, Zoë, 309, *323*
Martha's Vineyard, 170, 246
Masica, Colin P., 353, 378, *382*
Massachusetts, 143, 179, 183, 210
Masters, Donald C., 168, *172*
Matched guise technique, 27, 34
Mather, J. Y., 67, *82*
Mathews, Mitford M., 179, *209*
Matrimonial advertisements, 364
Maugham, Somerset, 403
Mauritius, 310
Mazrui, Ali A., 3, 6
Mead, Margaret, 447, *464*
Meaning, expansion of, 396, 418
Mears, Robert, 50–51, *54*
Media, 332, 408, 448
Mehrotra, R. R., 364, 377, *382*
Meier, Hans H., 79, *82*
Melville, James, 59
Menner, Robert J., 187–88, *209*
Mercer, Elizabeth, 50–51, *54*
Mercer, Neil, 50–51, *54*
Mercian, 14

Merger, 38–39, 42–44, 46–49, 51, 67, 123, 152–53, 160, 169, 203, 215–16, 231, 313
Merriam-Webster dictionaries, 362
Merritt, Robert, 433, *437*
Mesolect, 394, 402
Metcalf, Allan A., 219, 223, *249*
Metís, 136
Mickson, E. K., 290, *304*
Micronesia, 439
Middle class, 20, 27, 74, 76, 123, 212, 261, 269, 271, 325
Middle English, 15–17, 78, 97
Midland dialects, 18, 110
Midlands, 14, 15
Mid-Ulster English, 90, 95, 115–19, 130
Miller, Jane, 51, *54*
Miller, Mary Rita, 218, *249*
Milroy, James, 80, 120–23, *133*
Milroy, Lesley, 80, *82*, 120–23
Milton, John, 2, *6*, 19
Minimal pair, 70, 102, 257
Minority language, 51, 165, 216, 286
Mintz, Sidney W., 273, *280*
Mirapuri, Mervin, 403, *413*
Missionaries, 4, 283, 309, 312, 326, 353, 447
Mitchell, A. G., 423–25, *437*
Mitford, Nancy, 31
Mobility, 52
Modes of speech, 212
Moira, Lord. *See* Rawdon, Francis
Mokashi-Punekar, S., 380, *382*
Mombasa, 309
Monoglot, 92, 93, 127
Montero, Gloria, 157, *174*
Montreal, 134, 170
Moore, Francis, 283, *304*
Moore, Gerald, 322, *323*
Moresby Treaty, 309
Morningside, 74, 80
Morphological changes, 24
Morphology, 37, 101, 115, 215, 233, 258
Morphophonology, 229
Mother country, 1, 148
Mphahlele, E., 333, 347
Mühlhäusler, Peter, 439–66, 440, 441, 445, 459, 463–64, *464*, *465*, *466*
Mukherjee, M., 379, *382*
Multilingualism, 163, 295, 299
Munonye, John, 290, *304*
Murison, David, 65, 67–68, 78, 90, *82*
Murray, Brian, 64, *83*
Murray, Sir James A. H., 60, 69, *83*
Mutation plural, 15

Naik, M. K., 379, *382*
Naipaul, Vidia, 225

Namibia, 350
Napoleonic Wars, 26
Narasimhaiah, C. D., 379, *383*
Narayan, R. K., 376, 380
Nasals, 188, 231, 313
Natal English, 326–27, 328–29, 331, 334, 338, 339, 346
National identity, 92
Nationalism, 57, 63, 78, 127, 160, 331, 367
National language, 152, 157, 310, 390, 392, 405
National Understanding, A, 167, *174*, 410
National unity, 134
Native Americans. *See* Amerindian
Nativization, 358, 364, 370, 374–75, 376
Nativized pidgins, 439
Navajo, 217
Navalkar, R. H., 354
Negation, 47, 49, 59, 61, 73, 115, 148, 150, 213, 216, 218, 223, 237, 239, 244
Nehru, Jawaharlal, 369
Neologism, 186
Neomelanesian, 441
Nepal, 353, 355, 357
Nesfield, J. C., 360
Network, 93
Nevada, 194–95
New Caledonia, 440
New England, 139–42, 179, 190, 196–97
Newfoundland, 137, 163
Newfoundland Dialect Dictionary, 171
New Guinea, 439, 444
New Hebrides, 439–40
Newport, 11
Newspaper, 302, 333, 347, 356–57, 362, 392–93, 408, 448
New Testament in Braid Scots, 63
New York, 70, 190, 203, 225, 231, 236, 275
New Zealand, 4, 415–38, 439
-ng [ŋ], 26, 41, 46, 73, 80, 213, 231, 247
Ngome, Manasseh, 303
Nichols, Thomas Low, 188, *209*
Nicholson, Brian, 170, *174*
Nigeria, 5, 298
Nigerian English, 288, 315
Nigerian Pidgin English, 293–95
Nihalani, P., 362, *383*
Noel, John, 448, *465*
Nonnative Englishes, 308, 373–75
Nonstandard, 22, 27, 115, 163, 216, 218, 237, 241, 243, 301, 420, 422, 429, 432–33
Norman Conquest, 11, 56
Normandy, 16
Norman French, 11
Norms, 72, 136, 285, 308, 373, 411, 444, 445
Norn, 56, 67
Norse, 84–85

Index

Northeast Scots, 67–68
Northern Hiberno-English, 94, 95, 110–11, 127, 130
Northumbrian burr, 44
Northwest passage, 138
Norwich, 48–49, 70, 399
Nouns, 14, 400
Nova Scotia, 140, 142, 145, 283
Nunberg, Geoffrey, 22–23, *54*
Nyuorican, 224

Obiechina, E. N., 301, *304*
Obsolete, 64, 68
O'Casey, Sean, 92, 93
Occupation, 1, 71, 210, 308, 338, 345, 356
O'Connell, Daniel, 92
O'Cuiv, Brian, 131, *133*
OED. See *Oxford English Dictionary*
Offa's Dike, 94
Official language, 252, 295, 324, 335, 392, 440
Official Languages Act, 167
Ohannessian, Sirarpi, *323*, 350, *352*
Ohio, 194
Ó'Huallacháin, An tAthair Colmán, 131, *133*
Okara, Gabriel, 291, 298, *305*
Oklahoma, 217
Old English, 14–15
Ó'Muirithe, Diarmaid, 87, 131, *133*
O'Neill, William, 87
Onitsha Market Literature, 291, 301
Ontario, 134, 153
Opie, Iona, 247, *249*
Opie, Peter, 247, *249*
O'Rahilly, Thomas F., 94, *133*
Orbeck, Anders, 143, *174*, 178, *209*
Orientalists, 355
Orkin, Mark M., 155, 169, *174*
Orkney, 56, 67
Ormulum, 16
Orr, James, 96
Orthography, 285, 302–3
Orton, Harold, 34, 40, 52, *54*, 107, 131, *133*, 171, *174*, 178, *209*, 247, *249*
Ottawa "twang," 163
Ottawa Valley, 134, 141, 154, 163, 170
Overt standards, 338, 348
Owl and the Nightingale, 16
"Oxbridge" accents, 128
Oxford English Dictionary (*OED*), 4, 362, 379

Pacifíco, Patricia, 276, *280*
Padolosky, Enoch, 163, 170, 171, *175*
Påhlsson, Christer, 44, *54*
Pakistan, 4, 353, 355, 367, 377
Pakistani English, 356

Palatalization, 106, 256
Pale, the, 86, 90, 95, 105, 128
Panama, 253, 255, 277
Pan-loaf, 74
Papiamentu, 268
Papua New Guinea, 4, 439–66
Papuan Pidgin English, 445
Park, Michael, 45, *54*
Parker, Douglass, 243, *249*
Parliament, 356, 448
Parthasarthy, R., 372, 379, *383*
Participant observers, 1, 6
Participle, 38, 226
Passé, H. A., 359, 361, 378, *383*
Patois, 150, 251, 271
Pattanayak, D. P., 357, 377–78, *383*
Paxton, John, 377, *383*
Peace Corps, 300
Pearl, 16
Pederson, Lee A., 207
Peenie Wallie, 261, *280*
Peer associations, 211
Pejorative terms, 211
Pellowe, John, 48, *54*
Pembroke, 84, 131
Penn, C., 345, *352*
Pennsylvania, 141; Dutch, 182
Pérez Sala, P., 276, *280*
Perfective, 239, 243, 265
Periphrastic constructions, 59
Persian, 364, 375
Pettman, Charles, 1, 6
Petty, William, 86–87, *133*
Petyt, Malcolm, 43, 47, *55*
Philadelphia, 143, 201
Philippines, 380
Phillips, Robert K., 247, *249*
Phiri, A. G., *323*
Phoneme, 102
Phonemic clash, 105
Phonetic alphabet, 7–10
Phonetics, 359, 409
Phonetic similarity, 102
Phonology, 25, 124, 215, 257, 266, 287–88, 312, 317, 359
Phrasal verbs, 289, 316
Picard, Marc, 170, *174*
Picton, Sir James A., 87, *133*
Picts, 56
Pidgin, 5, 217, 384, 387, 442
Pidgin-creole continuum, 291–97
Pidgin English, 282, 284, 297, 300, 432, 439
Pietermaritzburg, 325
Pitch, 270
Place names, 84, 432
Plantations, 89, 95, 439, 442, 451

Platt, John T., 384–414, 392–93, 397–98, 400, 410, 412, *413*
Playground, 77
Plural, 215, 230, 237, 264, 302, 316, 400, 433, 444, 446, 452, 455
Plurality, 302
Plymouth, 179
Plymouth Colony, 142
Poetic language, 27
Pollard, Velma, 257, *280*
Polson, James, 170, *175*
Poole, Jacob, 87, 131, *133*
Popkin, Henry, 48, *55*
Population, 157–58, 207
Port Elizabeth, 324–25, 330
Portuguese, 137, 251, 281, 309, 386, 396; -based creole, 385
Possession, 108
Possessive, 215, 230, 237, 260, 433
Post-creole continuum, 267, 271, 397, 443, 453–54
Power, 214, 327–28, 330, 348
Powesland, Peter F., 27, 34, *53*
Prairie Provinces, 136
Prator, Clifford, 372, *383*
Presbyterian church, 97, 127
Prescriptivism, 1, 214
Present tense (consuetudinal, punctual), 109, 119
Press, 300, 347, 402
Press, John, 377, *383*
Prestige dialect, 11, 12, 16, 24, 27, 52, 69, 72, 74, 80, 85, 90, 92, 97, 118, 156, 159, 166, 179, 206, 214, 263, 284, 286, 300, 306, 309, 318, 326, 331, 350, 358, 384, 390, 395, 410–11, 445, 454
Primary education, 28, 75
Pringle, Ian, 154, 163, 168, 170, 171, *175*
Prinsep, H. T., 355
Printer, 58
Printing, 12, 17
Private schools, 327, 336
Proctor, Leslie, 346, *352*
Progressive form, 243, 360
Pronouns, 216, 243, 445
Pronunciation, 7, 12, 18, 25, 32, 35–51, 59, 67, 152–53, 161, 163, 182, 187–88, 201, 206, 214, 223, 227, 232, 423
Prosodic features, 256, 257, 264, 267, 269, 359
Protestant, 89
Providence, 179
Provincial, 62
Publishing, 136, 356
Puerto Rico, 253, 255, 267, 273–77
Puertoriqueño English, 219
Punjabi, 371
Purdue, Charles, L., 247, *249*
Purists, 26

Puritans, 20, 143
Puttenham, George, 52
Pyles, Thomas, 16, *55*

Quakers, 146, 201
Quantifications, 71–72, 79–80, 163, 229–30, 394–95, 398
Quebec, 134, 138, 167
Queen's English, 5, 347
Queensland Plantation (Kanaka) Pidgin, 440–41
Question, 216, 238, 374, 444, 458
Questionnaire, 35, 67, 169, 199, 350
Quirk, Randolph, 80, *83*, 377

[r], 24, 25, 43, 67, 107, 115, 118, 123, 124, 126, 143–45, 201–3, 204, 206, 227–28, 232–33, 242, 245, 246, 338. *See also* Rhoticity
Rabaul, 445
Radio Telefís Éireann (RTE), 90, 97, 127–28
Raffles, Sir Stamford, 386
Railroad, 92, 137
Raj, 355, 362
Raleigh, Sir Walter, 20
Ramanuyan, A. K., 370, 372
Ramish, Lucille, 388, *414*
Ramsay, Allan, 61
Random House Dictionary, 362, 379
Random sample, 337, 350
Rao, G. S., 379, *383*
Rao, Raja, 361, 370, 380
Ras Tafari, 261–62
Rawdon, Francis (Earl of Moira), 355
Read, Allen Walker, 186–87, 207, *209*
Reading, 80
Realizations, 71
Recaptives, 284
Received Pronunciation. *See* RP
Recessive, 40
Reckord, Michael, 262
Reduplication, 361, 380, 453
Reformation, 86
Regional dialect variation, 11, 12, 16, 17, 27, 30, 31, 61, 65, 163, 177–209, 422, 425
Register, 58, 365, 450, 455, 462
Regularization, 18
Reid, Euan C., 72, 79, *83*
Relative clause formation, 60, 78, 109
Relexification, 291, 298, 303
Relic area, 40, 171
Religion, 165, 447
Remote time, 234
Renaissance, 62
Report of the Royal Commission, 165, *175*
Reservation, 218
Respectable South African English, 328, 331, 336, 340, 345

Index

Retentions, 41, 42
Retroflex, 50, 67, 102, 105, 313, 359
Rhetorical questions, 108
Rhetorical style, 19, 363–64, 365, 375
Rhoticity, 9, 24, 25, 36, 42, 69
Rhyming slang, 435
Ribbe, Carl, 444, *465*
Richards, Jack C., 374, *383*, 401, 412, *414*
Riches, Judith, 130
Rickford, John R., 225, *249*, 258, *280*
Riel, Louis, 136
Riley, William K., 213, *249*
Robins, Clarence, 225, 231, *248*
Robinson, Mairi, 63, *83*
Rodman, Lilita, 169, *175*
Rollins, Hyder E., 52, *55*
Rolph, Thomas, 148–49, 169, *175*
Romaine, Suzanne, 56–83, 60, 67, 72–74, 79, *83*
Romanticism, 63
Roosevelt, Theodore, 214
Roper River, 432
Rosario, G. del, 459, *465*
Rose, C., 325, *352*
Ross, A. S. C., 31, *55*
RP (accent), 9–12, 23, 27, 28, 30, 32, 39–40, 45, 49, 52, 69, 72, 119, 128, 201, 203, 287, 356, 373, 390, 395, 423, 426
Rudnyckyj, J. B., 171, *175*
Rural dialects, 12, 34–45, 52, 187
Rural Southern Hiberno-English, 124
Russ, Charles V. J., 10, 11–55
Ryerson, Egerton 149

Sachs, Jacqueline, 212, *249*
Salomon, Laurence, 327, *352*
Salt Lake City, 236
Samoa, 439–40, 441
Samoan Plantation Pidgin, 444, 451
San Antonio, 221–22
Sandefur, John, 433, *437*
Sanderson, Stewart, 34, 40, 52, *54*, 171, *174*, 178, *209*, 247, *249*
Sankoff, Gillian, 449, 452, *465*
Sanskrit, 354, 361, 364, 367, 375
Santín, Miguel A., 274, *280*
Sarma, G. P., 368, *383*
Sawyer, Janet B., 221, *249*
Saxons, 14
Sayers, Dorothy, 231, 247
Scalability, 71, 399
Scandinavian, 15, 17, 43, 44, 67, 69
Scargill, M. H., 145, 159, 161, 170, *175*
Schlemmer, Lawrence, 331, 344–45, 346, *352*
School inspectors, 75
School teachers, 169
Schuchardt, Hugo, 322, *323*, 378, *383*, 440, *465*

Schuring, G. K., 326, 333, 337–38, 351, *352*
Science, 5, 285, 299
Scotland, 23, 56–83, 134, 144
Scots dialects, 56–83, 152, 154, 178, 183, 201
Scott, S. Osborne, 168, *175*
Scott, Sir Walter, 62
Scott, Tom, 61, *82*
Scotticisms, 59, 68, 69, 77
Scotticized, 63
Scottish Education Department, 75
Scottish English, 28, 56–83, 90, 95, 155, 169
Scottish Gaelic, 94
Scottish National Dictionary, 61, 65
Scottish Reformation, 58
Scottish vowel-length rule, 70, 79
Scouse, 46
Sea Island Creole, 225
Second language, 5, 306, 326, 329, 353–54, 357–58, 367, 390, 410, 449
Select Society for Promoting the Reading and Speaking of the English Language in Scotland, 61
Self-labeling, 373
Senghor, Leopold S., 3, 6
Serjeantson, Mary S., 379, *383*
Settlement, 177–78, 186, 207, 210, 309, 322, 324, 344, 415
Sex, 1, 52, 71–72, 73, 159, 212–13, 246, 336, 340, 425
Sey, Kofi, 286, *305*, 375, 380, *383*
Seychelles, 310
Shakespeare, William, 19, 20, 22, 33, 96, 177, 292, 333
Sharp, Henry, 355, *383*
Sharpe, Margaret C., 433, *437*
Sharwood, J., 428, 437, *438*
Shaw, Frank, 46, *55*
Shaw, George Bernard, 49, *55*
Sheldon, E. S., 196, *209*
Shepherd, R. H. W., 326, *352*
Sheridan, Thomas, 61
Shetland, 56, 67
Shibboleth, 124, 210, 339
Shores, David L., *249*
Shuy, Roger, 213, *249*
Sierra Leone, 141, 277, 292, 315
Sikh, 50
Simms, William Gilmore, 193, *209*
Singapore, 384–405
Singapore-Malaysian English, 388–405, 407
Singh, B., *382*
Singh, Khushwant, 368–69, 370, 380
Sinhalese, 359
Situation, context of, 210, 270, 401, 442
Sivertsen, Eva, 50, *55*
Skelton, John, 19

Slang, 195, 318
Slave narratives, 247
Slaves, 182, 251, 273, 282, 292
Slave trade, 4, 309
Sledd, James, 52
Smith, Henry Lee, Jr., 207
Smith, J. B., 39, *55*
Smith, Maria, 419
Smith, Sydney Goodsir, 64
Smith, William Wye, 64, *83*
Smyth, Sydney, 64, *83*
Social aspirations, 272
Social class, 1, 70–73, 77, 232–34, 263, 210–50, 325, 336, 428
Social functions, 439
Social mobility, 308, 334, 388
Social roles, 212, 214
Sociolect, 456, 458
Sociology of language, 5, 210
Solidarity, 211, 218, 223, 348
Solomon Islands Pidgin English, 440, 445, 462–63
Somalia, 310
Somare, Michael Thomas, 461
Somerset, Lord Charles, 324
Somerset, 27
Souleymane, Kone, 285–86, *305*
Sound change, 246
South Africa, 1, 4, 5, 161, 309, 378
South African English, 312, 324–52
South Asian English, 4, 353–83
South Carolina, 193
Southern Hiberno-English, 101–10, 127, 129–30
Southern Scots, 68
Southern United States, 178, 186, 188, 194, 197, 227, 231, 233, 247
South Wales, 27
Soweto, 333
Soyinka, Wole, 296–97, 298, *305*
Spanish, 137, 179, 217, 219–24, 251, 257, 272–77, 300
Speech community, 72, 95, 97, 233
Speech continuum, 224, 245, 394
Speech therapy, 76
Speech training, 76
Speitel, H. H., 67, *82*
Spelling, 7, 12, 14, 19, 26, 59, 69, 150, 263, 459
Spelling pronunciation, 318, 358
Spencer, John, 286, *305*
Spiegl, Fritz, 46, *55*
Sprauve, Gilbert A., 253, *280*
Spread of English, 3, 354
Sridhar, K. K., 377, *383*
Sri Lanka, 157, 353, 355, 359, 367, 377–78
Stability, 19, 21, 39, 443, 444
Staccato rhythm, 395

Stafford, S., 345, *352*
Staffrider, 347
Standard, 12, 16, 168, 182, 213, 315
Standard English, 17, 32, 36, 52, 70, 77, 266, 293, 331, 335
Standardization, 4, 14, 24, 39, 205, 459
Stanihurst, Richard, 87, 131, *133*
Starkey, Marion L., 210, *249*
Status, 211, 215, 272, 335, 353
Statutes of Iona, 2
Steiner, Richard, 170, *174*
Stereotype, 43, 46, 49, 74, 86, 152, 159, 161, 163, 166, 177, 188–89, 218, 223, 233, 241, 243–44, 313, 331, 344–48
Stevenson, Roberta C., 170, *175*
Stevenson, Robert Louis, 63
Stewart, George R., 139, *175*
Stewart, William A., 224–25, *249*
Stigmatization, 26, 47, 77, 123, 124, 126, 150, 163, 212, 215–16, 244, 309, 329, 331, 333, 343, 345, 348, 362, 434
Stivens, Dallas, 421–22, *438*
Storey, G. M., 171
Straits Settlements, 386
Strang, Barbara M. H., 26, *55*
Stratification, 72
Stress, 85, 257, 313, 395, 409
Strevens, Peter, 31, *55*
Strine, 434–35
Structured homogeneity, 72
Style, 29, 61, 72, 152, 154, 163, 215, 396, 449
Style-shifting, 72, 308
Stylistic variation, 155
Subject, 212
Substitution, 359
Substratum, 257, 443
Superstratum, 443
Survey of Canadian English, 145, 151–52, 153, 157, 160–61, 162, 169, 170
Survey of English Dialects (*SED*), 34, 40, 41, 115
Survey of Race Relations in Africa, 332, *352*
Swahili. *See* kiSwahili
Swalengleza, 313
Swansea, 11, 32
Swift, Jonathan, 92
Syllable-timed rhythm, 277, 288, 359, 395
Symons, R. D., 169, *175*
Synge, J. M., 92–93
Syntactic diffusion, 60
Syntactic environments, 234
Syntactic meaning, 270
Syntax, 24, 25, 27, 31, 33, 107–9, 119–20, 186, 214, 216, 265, 269–70, 288–91, 316, 446

[t], 152, 155
Taboo, 450

Index 495

Tag question, 33, 213, 360, 401, 429
Tall talk, 204
Tamil, 4, 255, 359, 386–87, 388
Tanzania, 309, 320
Tape-recorded Survey of Hiberno-English Speech, 97, 105, 111, 114, 127–28
Tay, Mary W. J., 412, *414*
Taylor, Douglas, 253, *280*
Teaching English as a foreign language (TEFL), 11
Teaching materials, 239
Tees, 15
Television, 308, 328, 346, 390, 408
Templeton, Janet M., 59, 78, *83*
Tennyson, Alfred, 43
Tenses, 108, 215, 229, 233, 242, 245, 260, 264, 394, 397, 410, 433, 449, 452
Terminology, 427–28
Teschner, Richard V., 219, *249*
Test Act, 97
Texas, 219
Tex-Mex English, 219
Texts, 20, 33, 34, 39, 40, 45–48, 64–65, 68, 73–75, 78, 146–48, 166–67, 188–95, 224, 232–33, 259, 262–63, 283, 290–98, 320–24, 365–66, 446–47, 453–55
Third-person singular, 48, 215, 230, 233, 398–99, 402, 409
Thomas, A. R., 52
Thomson, Derick S., 57, *83*
Thomson, Samuel, 96–97
Three-language formula, 355
Thumboo, Edwin, 403, *414*
Tilling, Philip M., 43, *55*
Todd, Loreto, 4, 10, 281–305, 301, *305*, 322
Tok Masta, 456
Tok Pisin, 3–4, 439–66
Tolai, 445
Tonal contrast, 257, 266, 270
Tone language, 227, 302, 313
Tongue, R. K., 362, *383*, 400, *414*
Toon, Thomas E., 64, 210–50
Toonheid vernacular, 64
Topicalization, 33, 109, 278
Tourism, 5, 285
Trade, 5, 285, 299, 387, 442
Traill, A., 342, 351
Transcribed text, 129–31, 315, 349–50, 424
Transcriptions, 7
Transference, 358, 360, 378
Translators, 14
Transmission of English, 311, 353–54
Travellers, 3
Treaty of Utrecht, 139
Treffgarne, Carew, 281, *305*
Trek, 324

Trevelyan, G. D., *82*
Trevisa, John, 53
Trinidad, 253, 255
Trinidadian English, 277–78
Trudgill, Peter, 11, 40, 47, 48, 53, 55, 70, 75, 80, *82*, *83*, 399, *414*
Turner, G. W., 430, *438*
Turner, Lorenzo Dow, 225, 249
Tutuola, Amos, 303
Twain, Mark, 194–95, *209*
Twi, 257
Tyndale, William, 19
Tyneside, 47–48
Tyrone, 92, 95, 119–20

"U," upper class, 31, 58, 62
Uganda, 310
Ulster, 89, 92, 95, 128
Ulster Anglo-Irish, 110–19
Ulster Folk and Transport Museum, 90
Ulster Scots, 90, 95, 97, 110–19, 127, 130
Uniformity, 20, 52, 436
Union of Crowns, 61
Union of Parliaments, 61
United States, 4, 5, 134, 137–41, 177–250, 268
Universal grammar, 443, 451
Universities, 12, 355–56, 388, 407
Unstressed syllables, 32, 452
Upper Canada, 141, 148
Urban dialect, 1, 12, 45–50, 51, 72–74, 107, 120–26, 170, 225, 454
Urbanization, 57, 308, 318, 330, 416, 422
Urban Pidgin, 454
Urban Scots English, 64
Use of English (statistics), 335–37, 390–91, 392, 441

Vaiana, Mary Estelle, 79, *83*
Valdman, Albert, 3, 6
Vallancey, Charles, 87, *133*
Valle, Frank G., 167, *173*
Vancouver, George, 137
Vancouver Island, 161, 169, 170
Van der Merwe, H. W., 331–32, 343, 346, *352*
Van Jaarsveld, F. A., 330, *352*
Van Wyk, E. B., 335, 337, *352*
Variability, 145, 152–53, 394
Variables, 70, 72–74, 77, 79–80, 329, 336, 394, 412
Variation, major dimensions of, 29, 60, 71, 210, 214, 229
Velarization, 106, 125
Verb, 59, 60, 233
Verb morphology, 243
Vernacular, 124
Verstegan, Richard, 20
Viereck, Wolfgang, 55

Vikings, 15
Vinay, Jean-Paul, 166, *175*
Virginia, 170, 179
Vocabulary, 14, 18, 19, 26, 31, 38, 40, 59, 67, 87, 101, 109–10, 137, 143, 155, 161, 179, 186, 197, 225, 288–91, 301, 340–41, 395–96, 402, 426, 435, 445
Vogue language, 206
Voicing of fricatives, 16, 37–39, 100, 178
Vorster, Jan, 346, *352*
Vowel: harmony, 287; length, 103, 120–21, 123–24, 154, 287
Vowels, 25, 32, 36–51, 221, 231, 338, 395; diagrams of, 9, 28–30, 98–100, 102–3, 111–14, 116–18, 123, 125, 256, 287, 314, 424; raising of, 23, 339; rounding of, 103, 105; + [r], 36, 41, 42, 47, 105, 114–15, 118–19, 122–23, 125–26, 143, 146, 156, 160, 168, 191, 201, 206, 227, 237, 240, 246–47, 255, 338

Wakefield, E. G., 422, *438*
Wakelin, Martyn F., 34, 53, *55*
Wales, 14, 28, 31–35, 84
Wali, O., 298, *305*
Walker, Douglas C., 169, *175*
Wa-Njau, Mwangi, 319, *323*
Wanjohi, G. J., *323*
Wantok, 457–58
Wasson, George S., 189, *209*
Waterford, 84, 86
Watts, H. L., 329, 331, 334–38, 351, *352*
Waugh, Evelyn, 33–34, *55*
Weak stress, 215, 227
Weber, Heidi, 410, 412, *413*
Webster, Noah, 5, 204
Welch, Frederick, 306, *323*
Welland, 15
Wells, J. C., 30, 51, 53, *55*
Welsh, 11, 28, 32, 53, 56
Welsh English, 28, 31–35
Werferth, Bishop, 14
Wesker, Arnold, 48
West, the, 183, 195, 204
West African English, 4, 10, 269, 281–305, 314–15, 380
West African languages, 227, 255, 257
Westcott, E. N., 191, 209
West Indian Creole, 51
West Indies, 50, 51, 271, 451
West Midland, 101
West Saxon, 14
Wexford, 84–85, 86–87
Whinnom, Keith, 444, *465*
White, Edgar, 319, *323*
Whiteley, W., 319, *323*

Whitworth, George Clifford, 361, 374, 380, *383*
Widdowson, John D. A., 34, 40, 52, *54*, 170, 171, *174, 175*, 178, *209*, 247, *249*
Wilde, Hans-Oskar, 53, *55*
Willard, Abijah, 144
Williams, Colin H., 53, *55*
Williams, Eric, 255, *280*
Willis, Clodius, 170, *175*
Wilson, H. H., 379, *383*
Wilson, H. Rex, 139, 143, 168, *175*, 207
Winchester, 14
Windsor French, 166
Winkle, Rip van, 182
Winnipeg, 136
Withers, C. W. J., 2, 6
Withrington, Donald J., 75, *83*
Witwatersrand, 327, 329–30, 336
Wolff, Dieter, 18, *53*
Wolfram, Walter A., 213, 225, 227, 229, 234, 236, 238–45, 247, *248, 249*
Wong, Frances Hoy Kee, 389, *414*
Wood, Richard E., 267, 279
Woods, Howard, 154, 170, *176*
Word creation, 25
Word formation 26, 417, 449–50, 452, 460–61
Word Geography of England, 34
Word order, 14, 162, 258, 270, 274
Word-stress, 163
Work situation, 333
Wright, Elizabeth Mary, 247, *250*
Wright, Joseph, 34, 45, 47, 53, *55*, 131, 196
Wright, Nathalia, 34, *54*
Written medium, 20, 358
Wu, D. Y. H., 441, *465*
Wurm, Stephen A., 459, 464, *465–66*
Wycliffe, John, 19
Wyld, H. C., 26, *55*, 201, *209*

[x], 24, 32, 69, 115, 118
Xhosa, 325

Yaeger, Malcah, 170, *174*
Yankee, 142, 146, 149, 150, 153, 169, 178, 188, 190
Yeats, William Butler, 93
Yeo, Robert, 403, 405, *414*
Yorkshire, 16, 43, 46–47
Yorkshire Dialect Society, 45
Yoruba, 296–97, 298, 303
Young, Arthur, 86, *133*
Young, Hugh, 445, *466*
Yule, Henry, 379, *383*

Zambianized English, 306, 310, 316, 350
Zimbabwe, 350

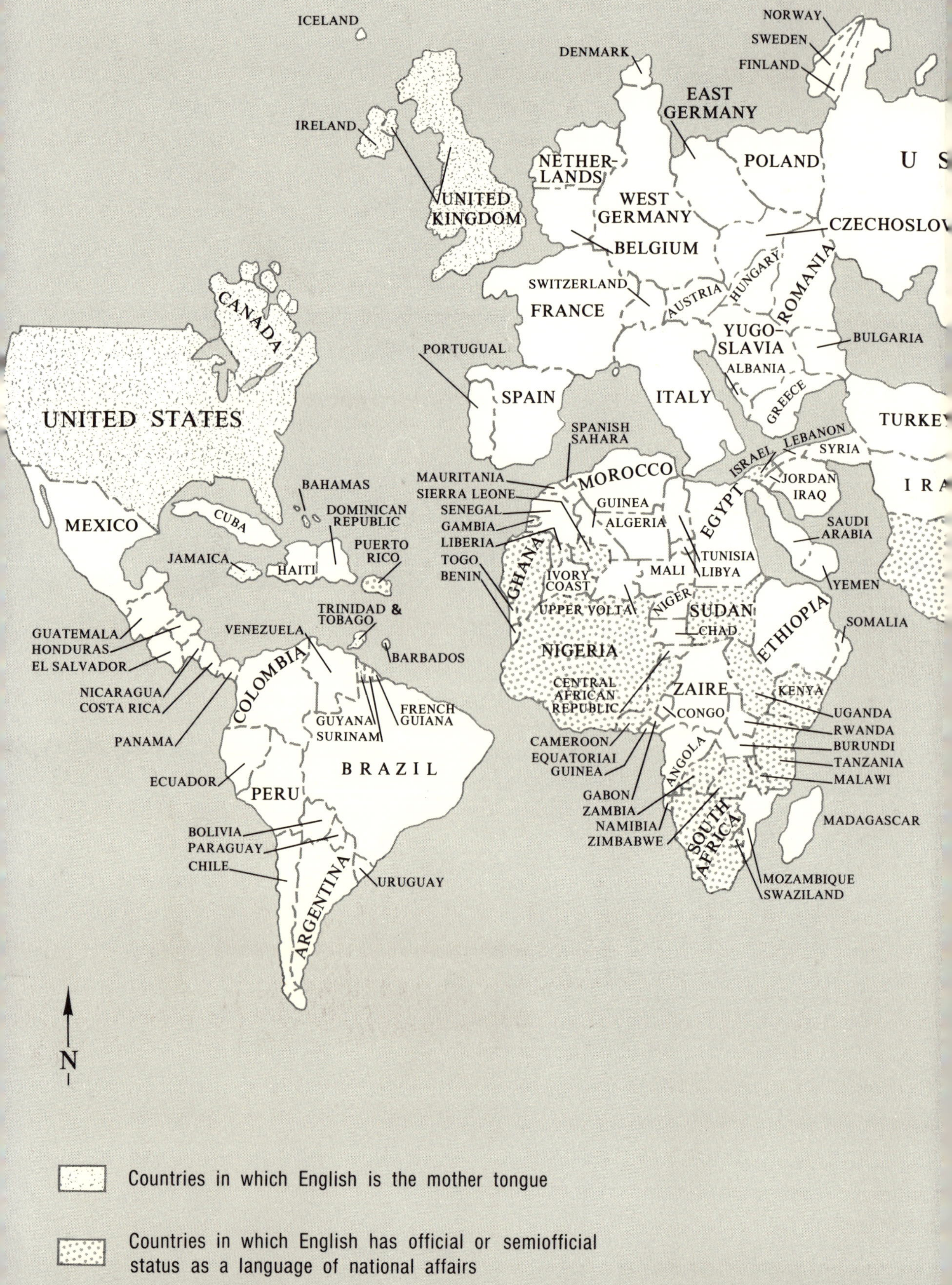
ICELAND
NORWAY
SWEDEN
FINLAND
DENMARK
EAST GERMANY
IRELAND
NETHERLANDS
POLAND
U S
UNITED KINGDOM
WEST GERMANY
CZECHOSLOV
BELGIUM
CANADA
SWITZERLAND
AUSTRIA
HUNGARY
ROMANIA
FRANCE
YUGOSLAVIA
BULGARIA
PORTUGAL
ALBANIA
SPAIN
ITALY
GREECE
UNITED STATES
TURKEY
SPANISH SAHARA
LEBANON
ISRAEL
SYRIA
MAURITANIA
MOROCCO
JORDAN
IRA
SIERRA LEONE
IRAQ
BAHAMAS
GUINEA
SENEGAL
DOMINICAN REPUBLIC
ALGERIA
EGYPT
MEXICO
CUBA
GAMBIA
SAUDI ARABIA
LIBERIA
PUERTO RICO
GHANA
JAMAICA
HAITI
TOGO
TUNISIA
BENIN
IVORY COAST
MALI
LIBYA
YEMEN
NIGER
TRINIDAD & TOBAGO
UPPER VOLTA
SUDAN
ETHIOPIA
GUATEMALA
VENEZUELA
SOMALIA
HONDURAS
CHAD
EL SALVADOR
BARBADOS
NIGERIA
COLOMBIA
CENTRAL AFRICAN REPUBLIC
ZAIRE
KENYA
NICARAGUA
FRENCH GUIANA
COSTA RICA
GUYANA
CONGO
UGANDA
SURINAM
RWANDA
PANAMA
CAMEROON
BURUNDI
EQUATORIAL GUINEA
ANGOLA
TANZANIA
BRAZIL
ECUADOR
MALAWI
PERU
GABON
ZAMBIA
SOUTH AFRICA
MADAGASCAR
BOLIVIA
NAMIBIA
PARAGUAY
ZIMBABWE
CHILE
URUGUAY
MOZAMBIQUE
SWAZILAND
ARGENTINA
N
Countries in which English is the mother tongue
Countries in which English has official or semiofficial status as a language of national affairs